THE BIRDWAT(

YEARBOOK :

Designed and published by
Hilary Cromack

Edited by
David Cromack

BUCKINGHAM PRESS LTD

In association with

SWAROVSKI
OPTIK

Published in 2010 by
Buckingham Press Ltd
55 Thorpe Park Road, Peterborough
Cambridgeshire PE3 6LJ
United Kingdom

(Tel/Fax) 01733 561 739
e-mail: admin@buckinghampress.com
www.buckinghampress.co.uk

© Buckingham Press Ltd 2010

ISBN 978-0-9550339-9-5
ISSN 0144-364 X

Cover image: Shelducks by Robert Greenhalf.
Robert is a fulltime painter and printmaker and a member of the Society of Wildlife Artists. He can be contacted by telephone on 01797 222 381 or by e-mail to robertgreenhalf@googlemail.com
www.robertgreenhalf.co.uk

Black and white illustrations: Dan Powell, who can be contacted at 01329 668 465 or dan.powell@care4free.net

Printed and bound in Great Britain by
Information Press, Oxford UK.

CONTENTS

CONTENTS

PREFACE

RECENT press speculation about the sale of National Nature Reserves to address shortfalls in the budget of the Dept for Environment and Rural Affairs (DEFRA) will have set alarm bells ringing for many birdwatchers.

Can the interests of commercial concerns such as Tesco, BP or Aviva be truly in step with the need to maintain and enhance habitats in some of the country's most vulnerable areas? Would visiting a rebranded McDonalds Cley Reserve enhance the quality of the experience for you?

England has 224 designated National Nature Reserves which are currently managed by Natural England, along with a network of 1,050 Local Nature Reserves which have recognised wildlife value. It is possible that vast tracts of forest managed by the Forestry Commission could also be sold or leased to reduce costs.

Of course many great wildlife sites are already in private ownership – take the impressive Anglian Water site of Rutland Water as an example – so could change actually lead to much-needed improvements to facilities as companies seek to attract more paying customers?

In view of this proposed development, I felt it was very timely that I'd invited RSPB staff member Andre Farrar to write the key article in this edition of the *Yearbook* on the topic of Nature Reserves for the 21st Century (see pages 15 to 20). I hope you will take the time to scrutinise it carefully and see how much thought goes into planning for the future.

I was interested to learn that more than two million day visits a year are made to RSPB reserves, which demonstrates what an important role they play in the lives of many people as well as the birds, animals and plants that exist within their boundaries. As a lobby group, birdwatchers need to make their feelings heard when the politicians come to take their decisions.

Of course, we need to be sure of our facts, so if you've not visited that many National or Local Nature Reserves, why not use the Birds Reserves Directory (pages 129 to 240) to plan some interesting new outings? We are indebted to the many dedicated staff members of Wildlife Trusts, RSPB, Countryside Rangers and council workers who help us compile the entries each year, making it the most up-to-date national guide there is.

As ever, Hilary and I would like to thank all our other contacts who provide the information for the Reserves, County, National and International sections of the *Yearbook*, plus our regular contributors Gordon Hamlett and Richard Facey and artists Robert Greenhalf (cover image) and Dan Powell (b/w illustrations).

David Cromack (EDITOR)

A MESSAGE FROM THE SPONSORS OF THIS BOOK

MAKING IMPROVEMENTS to a product that most people already rate as 'excellent' can be a challenge, but each new edition of *The Birdwatcher's Yearbook* manages to build on its past success by adding fresh features.

The Best Bird Books feature was introduced in the 2010 edition and, because it proved popular with readers, it has been retained for this year, along with the ever-popular round-ups of key birding websites and ornithological news stories.

New for this year is a list of collective nouns for birds, and regular buyers will notice a change in the Reserves Section (pages 129 to 240), with the English counties being grouped into regional areas rather than being listed alphabetically from Bedfordshire to Yorkshire. Now if you are planning a trip to Eastern England or another region, you'll have all the area's sites in one place.

These may only be small evolutionary steps, but it demonstrates the publishers' determination to make the *Yearbook* as relevant and indispensible as ever.

It is one of Swarovski Optik's concerns to enthuse as many people as possible to take up nature observation and birdwatching in order to encourage broader interest, understanding and support for environmental and animal protection. I feel that sponsoring the *Yearbook*, something we've done since the 2002 edition, helps to achieve that goal. Anyone picking up a copy of the book cannot fail to be amazed at the breadth of information contained within its pages and I'm sure it helps many people maximise the pleasure they get from the hobby.

Happy birding in 2011.

Peter Antoniou

(Manging Director, Swarovski Optik UK Ltd)

To discover more about Swarovski's extensive programme of nature conservation projects around the globe and the latest information about their award-winning binoculars and telescopes visit: www.swarovskioptik.com

SWAROVSKI
OPTIK

FEATURES

Maintaining reserves to ensure maximum benefit to wildlife can often be a costly affair — RSPB Titchwell has undergone major changes to prevent the sea inundating the freshwater marsh.

KEY ORNITHOLOGICAL NEWS

Undiscovered species, new breeding records and successful reintroductions act as a counter-balance to some of the year's gloomier bird-related stories. Words by Richard Facey, illustrations by Dan Powell.

BREEDING HERONS HIT A PURPLE PATCH

IN RECENT YEARS a number of species have bred for the first time on British soil, or at least returned after a lengthy absence – 2010 provided examples of both and surprisingly all were herons and their allies.

By far the biggest surprise was the UK's first ever breeding pair of Purple Herons, which chose one of the country's safest places to breed, settling as they did on the RSPB's Dungeness Nature Reserve in Kent. The nest of such a ground-breaking species must have been a tempting target for unscrupulous egg thieves, but the RSPB's round-the-clock surveillance ensured a happy outcome, with the first fledgling Purple Heron for the UK seen in July.

News of the UK's second confirmed breeding of Little Bittern was welcomed as its first success stretches back to 1984 in Yorkshire. This time the species chose a more southerly location, settling on the RSPB's Ham Wall reserve in Somerset.

In August 2010 Natural England announced the breeding of at least six pairs of Spoonbills at the Holkham National Nature Reserve in Norfolk. Although this is the fourth breeding record for the cutlery-faced bird, it has been a long wait since the last success. The previous time more than one pair bred within our shores was in the early 1700s.

As breeding behaviour has been noted from single pairs in 2004, 2006 and 2007, it is hoped that the UK will not have to wait another three centuries or so before the Spoonbill breeds again.

A Purple Heron carries more material to the nest site.

CRANE PROJECT OFF TO A NON-FLYING START

IN THE LAST EDITION of *The Birdwatcher's Yearbook* we reported on the first breeding success of Common Crane in 400 years. Anticipating that natural recolonisation might be a drawn-out affair, several organisations have collaborated in a reintroduction scheme called The Great Crane Project.

A wooden mock-up adult Crane was used to ensure the young chicks did not become imprinted on WWT staff.

A partnership between the Wildfowl & Wetlands Trust, RSPB and Pensthorpe Conservation Trust, with funding from Viridor Credits Environmental Company, aims to collect eggs from the wild and hatch them in the UK. The resulting chicks are then reared at the WWT's Crane School based at their Slimbridge Reserve before being released into the wild.

The eruption of Iceland's volcano nearly scuppered the scheme at the outset. WWT staff members Nigel Jarrett and Roland Digby picked up 18 eggs from Germany only to find their return flight had been grounded indefinitely. To ensure the eggs arrived at Crane School before they hatched, Jarrett and Digby had to embark on a 17-hour road trip.

Within hours of reaching their new home the eggs began to hatch and were later joined by other chicks from eggs collected with less drama. Eventually the class of 2010 numbered 21 chicks, which spent up to 14 weeks at the centre learning vital life skills such as how to forage for food, socialise and avoid predators in readiness for life in the wilds on the Somerset Levels and Moors.

In August they were moved to a top secret temporary release enclosure for acclimatisation before being set fee. To allow the birds to be monitored post-release they were fitted with a variety of tracking aids. Along with conventional colour rings, five birds were fitted with GPS backpacks and another five were given leg-mounted satellite PTTs, a device that stores data on an individual's movements before downloading it via satellite every few days.

Radio transmitters will allow the Crane team to keep track of their liberated charges in real time, while the more high tech devices will provide information on habitat use and movements. At the time of writing, the birds had settled in well to their temporary release enclosure and were already acting like wild cranes should.

One in 100 million

BIRDTRACK, the on-line data-gathering machine set up by the British Trust for Ornithology has made it easier than ever for ordinary citizens to contribute information about British birds… and they have responded with enthusiasm. In 2010 BirdTrack reached the memorable milestone of its 100 millionth record – of a Coal Tit in South Wales – not bad in six short years.

KEEP IT SECRET: BUSTARDS DOING WELL

ONE OF THE UK's established reintroduction projects goes from strength to strength. In 2009 wild Great Bustard chicks hatched in the UK for the first time since 1982 and there was repeated success in 2010 when four active nests were confirmed.

The locations of the nests were closely guarded secrets to deter over-eager birders from causing disturbance and more importantly to thwart egg thieves. As an added deterrent the eggs were marked with special DNA glue, which would have proved useful should a prosecution have been required.

However, at the time of writing, the nests have gone unnoticed and at least four young have hatched. As female Great Bustards are mistresses of disguise when incubating eggs it is hoped that more well-hidden females have successfully bred.

Filling the gap

A female Great Tit in Draycott, Gloucestershire, demonstrated in 2010 how with a little hard work and a lot of moss, even the largest of cavities can be turned in to an ideal nest. Deciding to nest in a revolving compost maker, substantially larger than the more traditional nest box or tree cavity, the female ended up building what could be the biggest nest made by this species, four and a half times bigger than the norm!

Great Bustards are slow-growing birds and take many years to mature so it will be some time before the newest additions to the UK's small, but establishing, bustard population will breed.

However, while one reintroduction project celebrates success in 2010, the controversial project to re-introduce White-tailed Eagles to Suffolk stalled as Natural England announced in June 2010 that it was stepping down as one of the project's lead partners. In the wake of the national austerity campaign, Natural England feels that its reduced budget is better spent on existing commitments to biodiversity.

JUNGLE BIRDS DECLARED AS NEW SPECIES

WHILE TAXONOMISTS have endless fun creating 'new species' by elevating sub-species to a higher designation, it is always more pleasing to discover birds that are completely unknown to science. George Fenwick of the American Bird Conservancy was honoured when a new species of Antpitta was named after him. Fenwick's Anptitta *Grallaria fenwickorum* was discovered in the Andes of Colombia in 2008 but it took two years to determine its status, because of the way it was sampled.

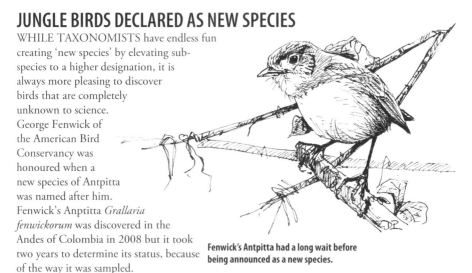

Fenwick's Antpitta had a long wait before being announced as a new species.

Traditionally, a specimen believed to be new to science was killed and preserved so that it and closely related species could be minutely examined to determine its uniqueness. Any unique 'type' specimen, (or more properly holotype), is used as a reference point to define the features of the new species.

In the case of Fenwick's Antpitta, the first bird was closely studied in the field, with DNA samples taken along with a host of measurements and images. This allowed its discoverers to release the bird while still having the information needed to determine whether it was new to science. This is one of the first times the official holotype has comprised of a selection of feathers and sound recordings.

Gull's home from home
RINGING RECORDS help show how site faithful birds can be. Take EH56982, the UK's oldest Black-headed Gull (*Chroicocephalus ridibundus*) for instance. Originally ringed in Regent's Park in November 1980, he was still going strong when re-sighted there 29 years later in December 2009.

Another new species whose turn in the spotlight took some time to arrive is the Limestone Leaf Wabler (*Phylloscopus calciatilis*) from the limestone karsts of Vietnam. First seen in 1994, the birds were initially thought to be members of a closely related species, but when they started to make different calls the expedition scientists changed their minds. After closer inspection — and 16 years after its initial discovery — the Limestone Leaf Warbler was declared.

GREBE'S DEMISE OFFICIALLY CONFIRMED

NEWS THAT a bird species has been officially declared extinct makes the 2010 update of the ICUN Red List particularly depressing to read and it is sad that the Alaotra Grebe (*Tachybaptus rufolavatus*) of Madagascar is probably better known now than when it was extant.

The demise of this flightless grebe is blamed on hybridisation with the similar Little Grebe, the introduction of carnivorous fish which competed for the available smaller fish in Lake Alaotra, habitat destruction and the increased use of nylon gill nets which drowned birds that become entangled.

The Alaotra Grebe was one of the 99 species whose category listing changed, either for better or worse, but only nine were the result of a genuine change in the species' status. The remaining 90 simply resulted from increased knowledge of the species or the relentless march of taxonomic changes.

When there is so much gloom attached to the health of the

Active habitat management is helping to boost numbers of Yellow-eared Parrot.

11

world's birds, it is worth celebrating those species whose fortunes are improving. For instance, the Azores Bullfinch (*Pyrrhula murina)*, has been downlisted from Critically Endangered to Endangered. The LIFE Priolo project (Priolo being the local name for the Azores Bullfinch) began in 2003 through the combined efforts of SPEA (Portugal) and the RSPB and is the reason for the species' improved status. Since the inception of the project the Azores Bullfinch has seen its population increase from 120 pairs to somewhere between 500 and 800 pairs. This spectacular rise has been accompanied by the restoration of some 230 hectares of the finch's habitat.

Across the water in Colombia, the Yellow-eared Parrot (*Ognorhynchus icterotis)* has also benefited from intensive conservation efforts. The species had been presumed extinct until a colony of a mere 81 individuals was discovered in the Colombian Andes. Over a decade later thanks to the work of Fundación ProAves and its partners, the American Bird Conservancy and Loro Paraque, the species has gone from strength to strength.

Initiatives such as a nestbox scheme set up in 2003 and a Parrot Conservation corridor have helped the species to recover. Set up in 2009, the Corridor saw the acquisition of more than 4,000 hectares of the parrot's habitat being re-forested. All this means the parrot can now boast a population of more than 1,000 individuals and a ICUN listing of Endangered, down from Critically Endangered.

MORE BAD MEDICINE FOR VULTURES

THE FUTURE for India's beleaguered vulture species, which have suffered dramatic declines because of the poisonous effects of veterinary drug diclofenac, now looks even more uncertain since scientists discovered a second anti-inflammatory drug is equally lethal to the birds. With the banning of diclofenac and the establishment of captive breeding centres, there was the prospect of Slender-billed (*Gyps tenuirostris*), Oriental White-backed (*G. bengalensis*) and Long-billed Vultures (*G. indicus*) making a comeback but now it has been established that ketoprofen is also lethal to the birds at the levels administered to livestock.

Testing has revealed a new drug threat to Asias's already troubled vulture populations.

Researchers found that ketoprofen was being used widely. One in every 200 carcasses sampled in Southern Asia contained the drug and 70% of these contained potentially lethal concentrations. As with diclofenac, ketoprofen causes acute kidney failure in the birds within days of exposure.

They are among a suite of non-steroidal anti-inflammatory drugs sold for veterinary purposes. So far only three have been tested, with just melioxicam being shown not to be lethal to the vultures. The drug is no longer under patent and is now manufactured by a number of companies.

Along with the RSPB, Bombay Natural History Society and Bird Conservation Nepal are calling for much tighter controls over the use of ketoprofen in Southern Asia and the promotion of vulture-friendly alternatives such as melioxicam.

Happily, some good news has come from the captive breeding centres where all three species have now bred successfully.

SEABIRDS FALL FOUL OF FISHING POLITICS

SEABIRD CAMPAIGERS have been appalled by the failure of the International Commission for the Conservation of Atlantic Tunas (ICCAT) to adopt simple and effective methods to prevent the unnecessary deaths of thousands of seabirds each year.

The populations of at least 37 seabird species are at risk from long-line fishing, with albatrosses and petrels in particular undergoing colossal declines. Without changes to fishing practices, 18 out of the world's 22 albatross species face extinction, so ICCAT's failure to act will undoubtedly speed up the level of decline.

Closer to home the situation is no better. An estimated two million birds have died in the last decade due to failures of some sectors of the European fishing industry. The impact is so great that some species, such as the Critically Endangered Balearic Shearwater (*Puffinus mauretanicus*), may soon be a species of the past.

Fishing politics lies at the root of the problem. Despite the results of their own organisation's three-year assessment which found long-line fishing has significant impacts on seabird populations, ICCAT members failed to reach a consensus to adopt BirdLife International's recommendations for setting lines for tuna and swordfish.

The major stumbling block was Japan's insistence on including mitigation measures not proven to protect seabirds. Other member countries that have already made huge efforts to reduce their seabird by-catch (some are so

Duck world record-breakers

THE BTOs online annual ringing summary always holds a wealth of information, especially on bird movements and longevity records. One remarkable old-timer was FA00041, a male Shoveler (*Anas clypeata*) which was shot in France in May 2009 at the ripe old age of at least 22.5 years. Originally ringed as an adult at Slimbridge, FA00041 had travelled 328km before he met his untimely end.

But that was nothing compared to the oldest British ringed Tufted Duck (*Aythya fuligula*). Ringed as a first year bird in 1985, 24-year-old FR84887 was shot in Russia, 3,211km away from his ringing site in Peterborough.

Fishing boats which have not adopted proven conservation practices are likely to damage the prospects of species such as Balearic Shearwaters.

successful that they reduce the seabird-by-catch from one per every 1,000 hooks to one in every 10,000), were unwilling to accept such unproven methods.

However, BirdLife International and the RSPB are calling on the European Union to introduce a robust EU Seabird Action Plan, following the UN's Food and Agricultural Organisation's best practice guidelines, so that most seabirds in our region will enjoy an extra degree of protection.

BLUE TITS DOMINATE THE RINGING CHARTS

The rapid decline in Turtle Dove numbers is reflected in the ringing records.

WHICH SPECIES topped the list for the number of ringing records in 2009? Numbers can vary hugely from as few as one or a brace, as in the case of Great Crested Grebes (*Podiceps cristatus*), to individuals numbering in their tens of thousands in the case of the most ringed bird.

As any ringer will tell you, catching Blue Tits (*Cyanistes caeruleus*) is an occupational hazard and more than 97,000 of the little blue biters were ringed in 2009 alone.

It was also interesting to note that the BTO's army of ringers collectively ringed three times more Golden Eagles (*Aquila chrysaetos*) than Turtle Doves (*Streptopelia turtur*) in Britain and Ireland – 45 compared to 15.

NATURE RESERVES FIT
FOR THE 21ˢᵗ CENTURY

Andre Farrar, the RSPB's protected areas campaigner explains how the Society is developing its network of nature reserves for the benefit of both birds and people.

FOR SOME PEOPLE nature reserves are a window on the natural world – an unrivalled opportunity to see nature for real, unedited and on terms set by the seasons; a precious life-affirming balance-restoring sanctuary for our souls. For others there is a risk that they are seen at best as 'a good thing' but remote to their daily experience; places for others, for specialists; part of the 'keep out' countryside.

There was a time, now thankfully well in the past, when that was a view encouraged because to open the gates to the hordes of visitors would put at risk the special features of the reserve. Quite what those special features were was open to debate – sensitive wildlife or a quiet life for the in-crowd?

That approach was wrong back then and today it is simply untenable. Nature reserves provide a gateway for developing knowledge, stimulating interest and building support for conservation. The bigger risk is growing disinterest.

Today's nature reserve managers need to meet both the complexities of habitat management and the needs of visitors. This is often characterised as 'balancing the needs' of people and wildlife – but it isn't the model we believe should be adopted in those special pieces, because there is quite enough 'balancing' going on across the rest of our land surface. Nature reserves, at least, should be the places where nature's needs are fully met.

So how are we doing juggling the demands of the 13,300 species we currently know call our reserves home as well as the two million day visits each year? In headline terms we see the RSPB's nature reserves contributing to a wildlife-rich future. To do this we aim to double the area of land we manage over the next 25 years, focussing on the protection, management and restoration of habitats that modern land use has passed by, such as heathland, blanket bog, reedbed and native pinewood.

Stronger protection measures

An obvious role that establishing a nature reserve plays is that the land is better protected – and this role remains undiminished. In addition much of our land receives formal legal protection. For instance, more than 100 of our nature reserves are part of the European network of the finest sites for wildlife known as Natura 2000.

One fifth of the UK's native pine is protected on RSPB reserves. (RSPB Images).

NATURE RESERVES FIT FOR THE 21ST CENTURY

This isn't a label that is well known in the UK, but it means that sites are either designated for their bird conservation importance as Special Protection Areas under the European Birds Directive – or as Special Areas of Conservation under the Habitats Directive.

Around three-quarters of RSPB reserves holdings are designated as Sites/Areas of Special Scientific Interest. Nature reserves have a fundamental role in

Richard Allen's artwork shows the Wallasea Island Wild Coast Project — on-going work to restore the Essex coastline.

underpinning the protection these important designations give. Campaigns to stop the airport development at Cliffe and adjacent to Dungeness are cases in point.

RSPB nature reserves now cover more than 143,000ha which is 0.6% of the UK's land surface. They encompass many important habitats including 20% of the UK's native pinewood and 18% of its area of reedbeds.

In winter our reserves host around 680,000 wildfowl and waders. Of the total species list on our reserves 2,100 are rare or scarce species and more than 300 have more than 20% of their population or distribution on our sites.

Increasingly we will be restoring and re-creating habitat to redress some of the past losses. Nature reserves, on their own, are only part of the answer to the question 'how do you stop and reverse the loss of wildlife?' This question has been brought into focus during 2010, dubbed by the UN as International Year of Biodiversity.

This was the year biodiversity loss was to have been halted – a commitment signed up to by governments including our own. There has been a lot of commentary on the failure to meet the 2010 target – and rightly so, but it's important to highlight successes within the overall missed target.

Birds of particular conservation importance across the European Union have done measurably better than the same species beyond the EU – and Special Protection Areas have performed better than the wider countryside. In England there has been a creditable attempt to bring the SSSI network up to a stage where 95% of them are in favourable condition, or at least heading in that direction. The RSPB has been in the forefront of delivering this encouraging outcome.

The role of land dedicated to nature conservation is hugely important in tackling the biodiversity crisis – reserves and protected areas are the places that are most important for nature now and will be the essential spring-boards for future conservation strategies. It's important not just to focus on future threats – making the most of our best places for wildlife tackles some of the current threats to the natural world.

NATURE RESERVES FIT FOR THE 21ST CENTURY

Key role in the future

So, in moving beyond 2010 – what needs to happen to stop the declines, reverse them and bring to life the idea of a countryside rich in wildlife? We're convinced that in the UK's countryside of 2050 nature reserves and protected areas will be playing an even more important role than now – but there will be important differences.

The reserves will generally be bigger – size matters as it offers greater economies of scale in managing land and makes sites more robust in the face of climate change. Bigger sites hold more wildlife. We don't subscribe to the view that nature reserves have had their day. However, seeing them become islands in a landscape made more hostile by other land uses would clearly fail to deliver either a countryside rich in wildlife or populations sustainable in the long term. In the future nature reserves must become the centre-pieces of efforts to restore wildlife across the broadest canvas.

It's highly likely our nature reserves will host a mix of species that is determined in part by the changing climate – there will be winners and losers. Southern species moving into our 'climate space' that require high quality habitat to thrive – wetland species such as Spoonbills and Purple Herons will depend upon land managed for nature conservation. The Purple Herons that set up home at the RSPB's Dungeness nature reserve in 2010 are potentially the vanguard of more in the future.

Dartford Warblers are already moving north – with the UK becoming progressively more important for their survival in Europe. Lowland heathland will certainly be required in sufficient amounts and across a wide enough area to ensure they have the space to move. The signs are that they may well move up hill in areas such as the Peak District.

Thinking big to benefit wildlife

Bigger sites, more integrated into the landscape will change the way we visit, interact with and enjoy nature reserves. There is likely to be greater scope for more informal access with honeypots attracting more intense use. This is the model we are adopting for the Wallasea Island Wild Coast project in Essex. Our plans for restoring 650ha of the coast build in extensive access opportunities (including by boat), as well as a more intensive visitor experience zoned at one end of the site.

The range of interests of our nature reserves will expand – already we have started enhancing the conservation of our cultural heritage (supported by English Heritage) reflecting the diversity of archaeological and historic remains from pre-historic burial mounds to defences dating from the Second World War.

RSPB is developing a new emphasis on cultural heritage at its sites — here Roman life is re-enacted at The Lodge in Sandy. (Charlotte Madge).

17

NATURE RESERVES FIT FOR THE 21ST CENTURY

The framework we will use to develop our approach to landscape-scale nature conservation is called Futurescapes – we've been very careful to be clear about what this programme is and even clearer about what it is not – it's been important not just to regard the areas in our Futurescapes programme as 'reserves on steroids'.

While they will usually have a nature reserve or two at their heart, what goes on between and around the reserves is just as important, both in determining how the wildlife of the area flourishes and how we engage the people with the greatest stake in each area.

A decade in development, our landscape scale approach was launched last year with 35 areas identified. We will add to this portfolio, ending up with 80 or 90 Futurescape areas around the UK. We've been working with an impressive role call of partners and funders to start to put together bigger projects across the UK.

The rationale behind selecting the areas works on two levels – firstly they are all important for wildlife (or could become more so), secondly they are areas where the RSPB has particular strengths and real opportunity to deliver. What is absolutely certain is that we won't succeed on our own – each project within the Futurescapes programme will involve the active support and co-operation of hundreds of individuals and a wide range of organisations from business and industry as well as from the environmental and conservation family.

RSPB is not claiming sole intellectual rights to the concept of 'landscape scale conservation'. It has been a direction of travel for many conservation organisations both in the voluntary and statutory

Special event progrmmes at RSPB reserves are designed to appeal to all age groups and interests. (RSPB Images).

sectors over recent years. Futurescapes is our contribution to the landscape scale revolution and will complement and be coordinated with other programmes such as the Wildlife Trusts' Living Landscapes. The conservation movement has a huge opportunity to ensure that landscape scale conservation is supported by new legislation promised by the coalition Government.

So have nature reserves had their day? Far from it. Whether as last refuge or powerhouse of recovery, their role is growing in significance. Where nature reserves will fail is when they become isolated islands in a landscape that is hostile to the wildlife that they support.

At-risk birds making a comeback
So much for how our nature reserves will develop in the future – how are they doing now? For any reserve network to succeed in being the foundation of future conservation strategies, it needs to be effective at supporting today's wildlife.

NATURE RESERVES FIT FOR THE 21ST CENTURY

We are rigorous at assessing our performance – in the end it's our members' and supporters' generosity that enables us successfully to convert cash to bums on nests. Our reserves are very effective at conserving bird species with small or localised populations breeding in specialised habitats.

Over the last 50 years, RSPB reserves have played an important part in preventing the extinction of several UK breeding birds (such as Marsh Harriers and Dartford Warblers) and in greatly aiding the impressive recovery of others (such as Bitterns, Avocets and Corn Crakes). Most of the bird species that breed on RSPB reserves in numbers that are important as a UK scale, have either increased or remained stable on our reserves since 1990.

Nature reserves are better suited for some conservation jobs than others – rare and threatened species or those concentrated in relatively localised areas benefit from the security a nature reserve can bring. So Bitterns in reedbeds or internationally important waterfowl are examples of high biodiversity value that lend themselves to protection through from focussed nature reserve management.

But for the common (even if declining) and the still widespread species, different conservation strategies are required. Nature reserves don't work for Sky Lark recovery even if some sites are bursting with them – for Sky Larks it's the wider countryside and the contribution that farmers can make that will turn the corner for their fortunes. That's not to say that the recovery of more widespread species isn't enhanced by nature reserves – wetland reserve management has benefited species such as Marsh Harriers, Avocets and Cetti's Warblers.

The RSPB's earliest nature reserves date from the 1930s, but the bulk date from the 1970s and it is only during the last 25 years that we have fully developed a strategic approach to the acquisition and management of our nature reserves that can sit alongside a range of other vital initiatives, including our work with landowners and farmers.

Our advice and policy advocacy is made stronger because of our practical experience of land management. The establishment of nature reserves is only truly effective when they are integrated with wider land use policies and the full tool kit of conservation.

Keeping the customers satisfied

The variety of wildlife that's found on our reserves is only matched by the myriad of ways in which our visitors want to enjoy them. The presence of a nature reserve can bring real economic benefit to an area through the generation of employment (both directly and indirectly) and the use of local goods and services.

That's all very well, but in the end our individual experience of a nature reserve is not based on its worthiness, its top flight international designations or its role in conservation strategy – our primary impression is 'have we had a good time'? The quality of that good time defines our likelihood of coming back again and taking the time to find out more, to dig deeper to turn our enjoyment into commitment.

Of all the threats and issues facing the natural world, one of the greatest, perhaps the greatest – is the degree of disconnection between people today, especially children, and nature. The reasons for this are many; time pressures, unfounded fear of accidents and competing interests.

NATURE RESERVES FIT FOR THE 21ST CENTURY

But the consequences will be grave if we are not able to sustain interest in, and love, for the natural world. We certainly won't increase support for conservation by shutting people out.

We know that for many visitors (especially birders) the full dawn and dusk experience of the natural world is vital. Most of our reserves are actually open 24/7 (it's the opening hours of the visitor centres that are publicised). Where currently there are restrictions we are looking at what can be done to improve access.

We want to increase the number of visits to RSPB reserves over the next two years to 2.2m a year – and to boost our field teaching schemes. Of our 200 nature reserves, 184 have public access. We want to make access available to all and at around 30 of our sites we provide surfaced paths, fully accessible hides and have people on hand who can help with access issues.

Of course the facilities provided vary from simple trails and basic information for communities local to the reserve to large sites with substantial visitor infrastructure. In its first year Saltholme on Teesside attracted more than 100,000 visits. These sites provide for a wide range of visitor expectations including catering, shops and, yes, toilets.

Are we content with what we have on offer? In places yes, and we are very proud of that, but generally we know there is more to do. We listen carefully to our visitors and though delighted that the vast majority of them would come again – we recognise that the needs of different types of visitor need to met. As the range of landscapes featured within the RSPB's reserve network is increasing, new opportunities for wildlife watchers and lovers of the countryside will develop and we will be sensitive to their needs.

To find out more about the RSPB's reserves visit: **http://www.rspb.org.uk/reserves**. We welcome feedback and you can contact individual reserves through these pages.

POSTSCRIPT: As this article goes to print, the outcome of the 2010 Comprehensive Spending Review is not known. The natural world, alongside so much else, faces serious and deep cuts. Whatever the outcome, the conservation landscape in 2011 will be different.

The RSPB has campaigned to frame the cuts in a way that does least harm – and more than 300,000 people signed up to our Letter to the Future campaign to back our call. It will remain the coalition Government's responsibility to ensure that there is a national network of well-managed protected areas. How that is achieved will be a key test of their ability to meet their commitments to halt the decline of biodiversity by 2020 and add credibility to their claim to be the greenest government ever.

What is abundantly clear is that the role of the RSPB and our reserves will increase. We will oppose any moves by the coalition Government to ditch its responsibilities for nature conservation to balance the books but, along with the rest of the conservation movement, we will need to rise to the big challenge; nature will need the big society to step in to fill the gap.

GOOD READS FOR BIRDWATCHERS

Experienced book reviewer Gordon Hamlett sifts through the releases from the past 12 months to bring you his selection of the top dozen titles.

WHEN YOU consider the avalanche of books about birds and birdwatching published in the last decade, you could be forgiven for thinking every topic has been covered. Certainly, it is hard to think of anything that is really missing. There will be a few advances in identification and a few taxonomic splits that will 'necessitate' a new edition of a fieldguide. And the publisher of this *Yearbook* has requested an updated version of my site guide for the Scottish Highlands, so there is hope for us all in that direction. But only one of the books in my shortlist of 12 titles this year can be described as ground breaking.

When I was writing this article for last year's edition, I had more than 50 books on my desk to consider. This year, the pile was down to the low 20s and several of those are new editions of previously released titles, albeit significant ones, and there is a reprint of an old classic. So where do we go from here? There are a few advanced photographic guides in the pipeline and one of the sites listed in the website article (see pages 29 to 34) illustrates a prototype photographic fieldguide that is radically different.

Books of the year

Choosing just one title from each of the three categories – Art & Literature, Practical Birdwatching, Reference Books – my favourite books this year were:-
Barley Bird, The Collins Bird Guide, Migration.

ART & LITERATURE

The Barley Bird **by Richard Mabey (Full Circle Editions), ISBN 978-0-9561869-1-1. 80pp hbk, £20.**
Take one of our best nature writers, throw in some prints from Derrick Greaves, an artist from the 1950 'Kitchen Sink' school and one of our best loved birds and you have a pretty heady mix.

Barley Bird is an old Suffolk name for the Nightingale and though Richard Mabey tops and tails his book with some of his own notes, this is largely a look at the Nightingale in literature and music from Greek myth to bawdy folk song. 'Come and hear the Nightingale sing,' was the 18th Century equivalent of the would-be seducer's chat-up line 'Come up and see my etchings'.

One fascinating section deals with the cellist Beatrice Harrison playing live on the BBC with a Nightingale accompanying her, though there is no mention of the fact that this might have been an accomplished mimic, the sound crew having scared off the real bird. (See article on websites for appropriate links). This beautifully produced, slim volume – it took me only an hour to read – is an absolute joy from start to finish and one I shall be returning to many times.

Natures Powers and Spells **by Carry Akroyd (Langford Press) ISBN 978-1-904078-35-7. 168pp hbk £38.**
I first came across Carry Akroyd's work at the Rutland Bird Fair a few years ago and,

like her huge legion of fans, I've drooled over her art ever since. So this book, superbly produced as ever by Langford Press, was

always going to catch the eye.

The relationship between wildlife and landscape plays a huge part in these screenprints, watercolours and lino cuts, whether it is the small, intimate fields and gently rolling hills to the west of Peterborough, or the vast agri-dominated fields and the fens to the east. But this book is not just about the pictures.

Carry found a kindred spirit in the works of John Clare, probably our foremost wildlife poet and the text quotes heavily from his poems. As Clare also lived and wrote about the birds and villages near Peterborough, the source of inspiration is obvious and it is fascinating to read about the relationship between artist and muse.

There is some sloppy editing in the text (sheerwaters, Cuillens…) and pedants will bemoan the lack of an apostrophe in the book's title (a direct quote from John Clare) but for a heady mix of top notch bird poetry and art, this is pretty hard to beat.

The Peregrine by JA Baker (Collins) ISBN 978-0-00-734862-6. 416pp hbk, £20.
At long last! One of the all-time classic pieces of nature writing is back in print, and with an added bonus too. Not only do

you get the original masterpiece, dating back to 1967, but also *Hill of Summer*, a study of the author's local patch one year from April to September, and extracts from his diaries.

So what makes this so special? It's a

combination of a brilliant bird coupled with an exquisite, poetic use of language. Try this example, quoted on nothing more than a random opening of the book; I could have selected a thousand extracts. 'Over orchards smelling of vinegary windfalls, busy with tits and bullfinches, a peregrine glides to a perch in a riverside alder. River shadows ripple on the spare, haunted face of the hawk in the water…' Now tell me that you can't see, hear, feel and smell the scene.

The only problems with this book are in its production. Paper quality feels very cheap and as it comes without a dust-jacket, the matt, cream-coloured cover marks as soon as you look at it. What a shame that such amazing writing is marred by some penny-pinching accountants.

PRACTICAL ADVICE BOOKS

Advanced Bird ID Guide: the Western Palearctic by Nils van Duivendijk (New Holland), ISBN 978-184773607-9. Pbk 308pp, £14.99.
You can imagine the conversation between author and publisher at the initial pitch for this book. 'I've got this great idea for a new fieldguide.' 'OK, what makes it different from all the other fieldguides on the market?' 'Well to start with, it hasn't got any pictures in it…'

Originally published in Holland, where it was an instant success, the *Advanced Bird Guide* is a series of bullet-

pointed lists for each species, highlighting key plumage details for every age and subspecies. While this is not going to be of much use for easily recognised species such as Magpie, it is an absolute boon when it comes to sorting out the different plumages of gulls, Yellow Wagtail variants or all those tricky wader details.

The detail for each entry is really quite astonishing, with more than 1,300 species covered. Of course, all this comes at a price, especially if your eyesight is failing. Even with the small print size, there is still considerable use of abbreviations which does little to improve readability.

This is not a book for a beginner and you wouldn't want to use it on its own. But couple it with, say; the *Collins Bird Guide* (see below) and you have a pretty much unbeatable combination. Easily the most innovative book of the year, I can't see a single serious birder not buying a copy.

Bird Songs and Calls by Geoff Sample (Collins), ISBN 978-0-00-733976-1 3 CDs +232 pb book, £30.

The ability to identify birds by song as well as by sight is one that everyone aspires to but few achieve. We all know a few songs, but what are you like on the mobbing calls of thrushes, or the flight calls of waders?

The great thing about these CDs is that they come complete with a running commentary as Geoff Sample explains what you are listening to and how to separate it from similar species. The first two discs cover different habitats, with the third taking a look at the more complex songs and calls.

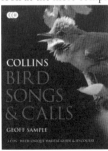

The book starts with a history of man's interaction with birdsong, before looking at how and why birds sing as well as various cultural connections – everything from Percy Edwards'

whistled bird impressions to Pink Floyd. A systematic description of songs from divers to buntings fills the second half of the book.

There isn't the space to get every species onto the CD, so there are no recordings of Marsh Harrier or Knot for example. These CDs are ideal for whiling away the car journey on your next birding trip. My one minor quibble is that you have to take the book with you to identify the track numbers for particular species – the listings aren't included on the CD packaging itself.

Collins Bird Guide (2nd edition) by Svensson et al (Collins) ISBN 978-0-00-726726-2. Hbk, 448pp, £25. (Also available in pbk).

A massive amount of hype, an even greater sense of anticipation. Could the world's best fieldguide possibly get any better? Of course it could. Many of the plates have been redrawn and reorganised on the page. Just compare the owls between old and new editions. What was 'merely' very good has now become drop dead gorgeous. The text and maps have been tweaked where necessary.

Among the 41 new species included, Caspian Gull is likely to be the main interest for British birders, though the whole of the large gull complex has been seriously expanded. Most of the new plates result from recent taxonomic splits, though the authors have taken a conservative approach to groups such as Redpolls where the taxonomists have yet to fully agree.

Just make sure that your copy has bird topography illustrations inside the front cover; the first printing didn't and had rather too many other printing errors.

If you haven't got a copy already, go online and find the best deal. Is it worth upgrading from the first edition? Absolutely. I know of several tour leaders who already own up to ten copies. This book is so good, people are buying it more than once!

***Where to Watch Birds in Britain* (2nd edition) by Simon Harrap and Nigel Redman (Helm) ISBN 978-1-4081-1059-1. Pbk 672pp, £19.99.**
My copy of the first edition has long since fallen to bits through over-use, so this was a timely arrival. Covering more than 450 sites, from Scilly pelagic trips to the northern tip of Shetland, there is a huge amount crammed in here.

As well as updating species and access details, most sites – including 30 new areas – now feature web addresses where appropriate. There are 300 maps, many covering more than one site. A few sites remain mapless though, a possible concern to some, though it is difficult to see where the extra space could come from – the print size is pretty small as it is. A new section targets the best places to go for 100 key species.

The book works best for designated reserves rather than general areas – there isn't the space to do justice to wide expanses of upland habitats. There is a coastal bias too, with, for example, the Northumberland coast included in some detail but inland sites such as Kielder not rating a mention.

A few decisions appear odd. There are a few lines on Skye, but nothing at all about Mull – probably the most popular birding destination in Scotland at the moment.

If you are looking for a single 'where to watch' volume, then this is the definitive book of choice. The first annotations have already appeared in my copy.

WORKS OF REFERENCE

***Bird Migration* by Ian Newton (Collins New Naturalist), ISBN 978-0-00-730732-6. Pbk 598pp, £30, (hbk available @£50)**
Barnacle Geese hatch from trees and Swallows hibernate at the bottom of ponds. Laughable now, but these ideas were still being taught 150 years ago. Considering how fundamental migration is to birds and birdwatching,  there is still an awful lot we don't know about the subject. Modern technology, satellite tracking and the like is giving us a better idea of where some of the larger birds go but we still don't know very much about the how and why.

This hugely readable book, packed full of fascinating snippets of information is as good an overview of the subject as you are going to find. It covers anything and everything to do with migration, including topics I had never even considered before; sex and age differences in migration patterns and the speed of migrants to name but a couple.

Profusely illustrated with photos, maps, graphs and tables, there isn't a birder reading this who won't find his or her understanding of the subject considerably enhanced after reading this. Highly recommended.

GOOD READS FOR BIRDWATCHERS

Essential Ornithology by Graham Scott (Oxford UP), ISBN 978-0-19-856997-8. Pbk 176pp, £27.50 (also in hbk @£60)

You know what a Jay or a Dunlin looks like on the outside, but have you ever stopped to consider what's going on underneath those surface plumage details?

Essential Ornithology is a modern textbook on bird biology. It is aimed at modular degree courses but anyone with a good scientific background shouldn't have too many problems, though a modern scientific dictionary might help – terminology has changed a lot since my day!

Starting with the theory that birds are descended from dinosaurs, subsequent chapters deal with feathers and flight, migration and navigation, eggs and chicks, reproduction, feeding methods and populations.

There are 75 black and white plus 30 colour illustrations. The text combines classic studies with modern research and there are plenty of suggestions for further reading. This relatively short book provides a good overview for anyone requiring information at an advanced level.

Helm Dictionary of Scientific Bird Names by James A Jobling (Helm) ISBN 978-1-4081-2501-4. Hbk 432pp, £40.

This is one of those books that comes complete with its own time machine. You go to research on item and find that you've lost an hour or so somewhere along the line.

Whereas birds might have several English names

such as Black-throated Diver/Arctic Loon, not to mention any numbers of names in other languages, they also have a definitive scientific universal name.

These names, usually based on Latin or Greek origins, adopt a binomial tag, based on an original idea from the Swedish scientist Linnaeus in 1751.

Unfortunately, few people receive a classical education these days, so exactly what do the names mean and where do they come from? This book explains all you need to know, with 20,000 entries covering every genus, species and subspecies in the world.

These names throw up some wonderful oddities. Thus the species name of Black-headed Gull (*ridibundus*) means 'laughing' whereas that of Laughing Gull (*atricilla*) means 'black-tailed' when it doesn't have one and Mediterranean Gull (*melanocephalus*) means 'black-headed'. A browser's joy.

Nightjars of the World by Nigel Cleere (Wild Guides), SBN 978-1-903657-07-2. Hbk 464pp, £45.

If you are anything like me, a typical view of a Nightjar will consist of a silhouette on branch, just before total darkness, or maybe a glimpse of the male's white wing patches as another moth meets its doom.

And to some extent, that's how it should be. There is something almost supernatural about these birds, known as goatsucker in days of old, and it doesn't seem proper somehow to get a good view.

Imagine my surprise then to see nearly 600 stunning photos of the world's 135 species of nightjars, potoos and frogmouths.

Admittedly some of the pictures are more impressive than others. All that is known of the Nechisar Nightjar of Ethiopia is a single wing from 1990, though there was a possible sighting last year.

After an introductory section, the latest taxonomic thoughts are discussed. For each species, there are brief identification notes, separation from confusion species and a large distribution map. The bulk of each species account though is devoted to the photos. And they are truly impressive.

Silent Summer edited by Norman Maclean, (Cambridge UP), ISBN 978-0-521-51966-3. Hbk 766pp, £27.99).

***The Status of Birds in Britain and Ireland* by David Parkin and Alan Knox (Helm) ISBN 978-1-4081-2500-7. Hbk 440pp, £50.**

Joni Mitchell wrote in *Big Yellow Taxi*, 'Don't it always seem to go/ That you don't know what you've got/ Till it's gone' a sentiment echoed by David Attenborough in his forward to *Silent Summer* '…how can you plan for the future if you do not know the state of the present?'

Both these books look at the current state of our knowledge, with one devoted entirely to birds and the other to wildlife in general. *Status of Birds* offers a systematic list, with entries for each species on taxonomy, distribution and status. The book is surprisingly up to date, with a photo, one of 86 included, of 2009's Eastern Crowned Warbler, even if a text account will have to wait for the next edition.

There are copious references in the text but these have the effect of breaking up the accounts which weren't particularly readable to begin with. And that's the main problem here. This book would make a superb website, easily updated as and when required. As someone who can spend days browsing reference books, this one just didn't grab me at all.

By way of contrast, I loved *Silent Summer* (the name is an homage to Rachel Carson's groundbreaking 1962 book *Silent Spring*). The book, a collection of essays and papers, is divided into three sections. Part one looks at factors driving changes in wildlife such as introduced species, recreation and pollution. Conservation in action is the theme of part two, including a look at Wildlife in British Overseas Territories and the UK's role in international conservation.

The case histories in part three cover the various groups of wildlife – bats, plants, dragonflies etc. Though there is only one chapter on birds per se, plus another case study on Grey Partridges, the nature of the papers is such

that they show how a change to one species or habitat impacts on something else. So, a quick check of the index turns up references to birds and heavy metal, industry and oil spills, as well as habitat changes such as afforestation.

Having discussed the state of play, two chapters consider 25 key questions in ecology and the likely future for our wildlife. If you want a good overall assessment of the current state of our natural heritage, then look no further. Wouldn't it be great if a few of our politicians read it too?

COLLECTIVE NOUNS
OF BIRDS

A
Auks (raft)

B
Birds (dissimulation, flight, flock, volery)
Bitterns (sedge or siege)
Bullfinches (bellowing)
Buzzards (wake)

C
Capercaillie (tok)
Chickens (peep)
Chicks (clutch)
Choughs (clattering)
Coots (commotion, covert, fleet, pod, raft)
Cormorants (flight)
Cranes (herd)

Crows (horde, hover, mob, murder, muster, parcel, parliament)
Curlews (head or herd)

D
Dotterel (trip)
Doves (cote, dole, flight, piteousness, pitying)
Ducks, diving (dopping)
Ducks, flying (plump)
Ducks (badling, flush, raft, sord, team)
Dunlin (fling)

E
Eagles (congress or convocation)
Emus (mob)

F
Falcons (cast)
Finches (charm, trembling, trimming)
Flamingoes (stand)

G
Goldfinches (charm, chirm, drum, troubling)
Geese (gaggle, nide, skein, wedge)
Goosanders (dopping)
Goshawks (flight)
Grouse (covey, lek, pack)
Guillemots (bazaar)
Guinea fowl (confusion)
Gulls (colony, screech)
Hawks (cast, lease, kettle)
Hens (brood)
Herons (siege)
Hummingbirds (charm or hover)

A group of flying geese is most likely to be called a skein, but a group on the ground is usually termed a gaggle.

COLLECTIVE NOUNS OF BIRDS

J
Jackdaws (clattering or train)
Jays (band, party, scold)

L
Lapwings (deceit or desert)
Larks (ascension, bevy, exaltation, exalting)
Linnets (parcel)

M
Magpies (congregation, conventicle, murder, tiding, tittering, tribe)
Mallards (sute or sord)
Martins (richness)

N
Nightingales (watch)

O
Owls (parliament or stare)

P
Parrots (company, prattle, pandemonium)
Partridges (covey)
Peacocks (muster, pride, ostentation)
Penguins (colony, creche, huddle, parcel, rookery)
Pheasants (bouquet, covey, nide, nye)
Pigeons (kit or loft)
Pintails (knob)
Plovers (congregation)
Pochard (rush)
Ptarmigan (covey)

Q
Quail (bevy or covey)

R
Ravens (unkindness)
Redwings (crowd)
Rooks (building, clamour, parliament)
Ruff (hill)

S
Sandpipers (fling)
Seaduck (cloud)
Sheldrakes (doading or dopping)
Skylarks (exultation)
Snipe (walk or wisp)
Sparrows (host, quarrel, scourge, ubiquity)
Starlings (chatter or murmuration)
Storks (muster or phalanx)
Swallows (flight or gulp)
Swans (bank, bevy, eyrar, gaggle, gargle, herd, lamentation, wedge, whiteness)

T
Teal (diving or spring)
Thrushes (mutation)
Turkeys (raffle or rafter)
Turtle Doves (dole or pitying)

V
Vultures (colony)

W
Waterfowl (knob or plump)
Wigeon (coil)
Wildfowl (plump or trip)
Woodcock (fall)
Woodpeckers (descent)
Wrens (herd)

50 CHOICE BIRDING WEBSITES WORTH VISITING

Internet enthusiast Gordon Hamlett presents his selection of the most interesting and innovative websites he's discovered in the past 12 months.

IN THE DARK OLD DAYS of the internet, about ten years ago, websites were little more than glorified fact sheets. As digital photography took off, so too did the appearance of websites. Suddenly, sites became colourful and we were amazed at the spectacular variety and quality of the images available. But still, the flow of information was largely one-way traffic, with little or no input from the user.

That has turned around totally. Websites are now actively seeking your input and this is particularly noticeable in the birding world, as you will see when you check out most of the sites in this year's survey.

Everybody wants details of your latest sightings, coloured-ringed birds, migration counts etc. Every time you read a blog or view a video, you are invited to leave your comments. Want to get something off your chest, or ask for information, then use one of the social networking sites or message boards. The flow of information has become a two-way affair.

The way information is presented is changing too, as we move from the photo age to the video age. You Tube had a reputation for featuring thousands of clips of skateboarding dogs and fat kids doing bad Star Wars impressions in their bedrooms, but now there is so much more to it than that.

Just as top quality photos were once the preserve of the professionals, now more and more people own video cameras and we are starting to see some very interesting footage of bird behaviour. To be sure, the quality isn't up to that of a BBC wildlife documentary, but people are witnessing – and filming – behaviour that would have been missed otherwise.

When a clip of something interesting is found, news of it spreads very rapidly – known colloquially as 'going viral'. Many of the clips featured here, I learned about through seeing a posting on some news group or other.

Someone posts a link saying 'watch this, it's amazing'. So we watch it and then pass the details on to all our friends as well. How else would get to find out about Spanish documentaries or American home videos?

By this time next year, I'm expecting to see many more video clips on websites. It's starting already. There is the usual website for the Rutland Water Birdfair (http://www.birdfair.org.uk/) but this year, another site (http://www.birdfair.tv/) featured video interviews and clips of the fair's events as well. Expect to see much more footage of birds being ringed, habitat shots and interviews as well as just photos. Everyman's video age has started.

INDEX OF WEBSITE SUBJECTS

ARTISTS

www.carryakroyd.co.uk/

http://www.hoopoeprints.co.uk
These are the websites of two of my current favourite artists, Lisa Hooper and Carry Akroyd. Lisa concentrates more on the species themselves while landscape plays a huge part in Carry's work. As well as showcasing various prints, there are pieces on the process of printmaking and details of forthcoming exhibitions etc.

Carry's work features in the article on Best Bird Books of the Year and you can see more of her work at http://www.langford-press.co.uk/ — a company publishing a wide range of beautifully produced wildlife art books.

BIOLOGY

www.michelklemann.nl/verensite/start/index.html
This Anglo-Dutch site is devoted to feathers. There are currently more than 250 European species illustrated. These are listed alphabetically but by scientific name with English names in parentheses. It is probably easier to click on the English site map button to bring up a complete list of species.

BLOGS AND MAGAZINES

www.bbcwildlifemagazine.com/
The site of the BBC's flagship wildlife magazine has had a major redesign, with plenty of background information on TV programmes, helpful hints, blogs, news, photos, fieldcraft tips and so on. There is a lot here to explore which may explain why I found the new design to be rather confusing.

http://fibowarden.blogspot.com/
All bird observatories are exciting places, especially in spring and autumn. Fair Isle is probably the best known observatory in Britain, with an unbelievable assortment of rarities to its name. This is the blog of the warden, Deryk Shaw, and you can't help but come away just a little bit green with envy of someone with one of the best jobs in the world.

http://nibirding.blogspot.com/
Northern Ireland doesn't often get a look in when it comes to birding so it is good see this blog, coupling recent sightings with just the right amount of irreverence and self mockery.

BOOKS

http://sites.google.com/site/avianreview/Home
Avian Review currently features and rates more than 2,100 bird books. The titles are arranged by geographical location or species as appropriate. What makes this site unique is that it includes sample scanned pages for each title so that you can get a feel for a book before investing in it.

http://www.birdsandpeople.org/
Anyone who loves Mark Cocker's monumental *Birds Britannica* will be delighted to know about his latest project - *Birds and People* - which deals with all aspects of man's relationship with birds. As with the previous title, you are invited to submit your own stories and memories and help contribute to what is certainly one of my most eagerly awaited titles.

www.crossleybirds.com
Is this the future of fieldguides? US-based Brit Richard Crossley thinks so. Take a look at the sample plates in the Gallery section

and you'll see species are illustrated by a montage of digital photos rather than a series of paintings. The effect feels decidedly strange and I'm not convinced that every plate works, but the concept is interesting and you can see the potential.

CONSERVATION

www.theeuropeannaturetrust.com/
The European Nature Trust is a brand new conservation body aimed at protecting the last great wildernesses. At the time of writing, the site was still being developed but projects supported in the UK include satellite tracking of Golden Eagles, plus wild cat and red squirrel conservation.

www.naturenet.net/index.php
For anyone interested in the practicalities of countryside management, there is wealth of information here including wildlife law, details of specially protected areas, planning applications, rights of way and finding a career in conservation to name but a few. With so many kids asking for help with their homework, there is a large section of links covering the current favourite essay topic 'What impact does tourism have on the environment?'

www.wingsoverwetlands.org/
Wings Over Wetlands looks at waterbird conservation in Europe and Africa with the aim of protecting important flyways across the borders of 118 countries. These flyways are used by a plethora of wildfowl, waders, storks, pelicans and the like. An introductory video introduces the rationale behind WOW and there are assorted case studies etc to read.

There is also access from here to the Critical Sites Network Tool, which promises to be a most useful graphical and mapping tool for relevant data, plotting either species or location. The website was still being tested at the time of writing and the web address is yet to be finalised, so access it from here. A PowerPoint presentation introduces the Tool. The two sites look very slick and offer much promise.

FOREIGN BIRDING

www.andaluciabirdsociety.org/
Southern Spain remains one of the most popular European holiday destinations and the website of the Andalucia Bird Society should provide you with much useful information. Guests can read posts on the forum and view the galleries etc. Joining the club brings access to the entire website as well as a copy of the annual report etc.

http://birdingcraft.com/wordpress/
Costa Rica has the enviable reputation of being one of the best birding destinations anywhere in the world. Reading this blog, it's not hard to see why — even the common garden birds look stunning. Written with all the enthusiasm of a convert — the author moved here about 15 years ago — anyone planning a visit will have their anticipation levels raised several notches.

www.birdingintas.net/
While there are many sites devoted to Australian birding, this is the first I have seen that deals exclusively with the birds of Tasmania. As well as 61 trip reports, there is a discussion forum, photo page and links to many other antipodean sites.

www.birdlifemalta.org/
Despite massive publicity campaigns, illegal hunting and trapping of migrants in Malta continues apace. This site, run by BirdLife International, highlights and explains the issues and campaigns actively. You can also volunteer for one of the Illegal Hunting Surveillance camps. It is not all doom and gloom though and there is plenty of practical advice for visiting birders.

www.lesvosbirding.com/
Lesvos (Lesbos) is easily the most popular Greek island for birding holidays and this site is a one-stop collection of all the information you will ever need. As well as up-to-date sightings, there are many trip reports, a systematic report for 2009 to download, checklists, photos and general tourist information.

heretowatchbirdsandotherwildlife
intheworld.co.uk/
Despite the less than catchy web address, this site offers all sorts of advice on the best places to go wildlife watching worldwide. Still under development at the time of writing, there are links to trip report sites, guides, accommodation and tour companies.

IDENTIFICATION

www.ispot.org.uk/
Run by the Open University, iSpot offers identification help, not just for birds, but any wildlife you might have trouble with. There is the old-fashioned way of identifying something i.e. ask a question on the forums and rely on someone else's expertise. Or you can try the artificial intelligence route, though at the moment, this is only available for earthworms, lichen and the like.

www.rspb.org.uk/wildlife/birdidentifier/
This is the RSPB's attempt at an artificial intelligence program. Feed in information on habitat, colour, bill shape etc and you are presented with a list of possibilities. I tried it with a garden Chiffchaff and the right answer came up — but only as one of 24 possibilities! Kids will love it but there is still some way to go, methinks.

MIGRATION

http://blx1.bto.org/euring/main/
To report sightings of any colour-ringed or dye-marked birds, this site is just what you need. Not only will you get sent full details of where and when your bird was ringed, the sightings automatically get passed to the BTO.

www.geese.org/Ganzen/index.jsp
Visit this site if you find a colour-ringed goose, or a bird with a neck collar. There is information on the different ringing schemes in operation and they will be able to give you more information on the individual you have logged.

http://medgull.free.fr/
Devoted to colour-ringed Mediterranean Gulls, as well as listing the various ringing schemes, you can also report your sightings. There are details of the best places to watch the gulls across Europe, as well as links to various

scientific papers and an excellent selection of photos.

http://pets.groups.yahoo.com/group/vismig/
For anyone interested in visible migration — vismiggers as they are colloquially known — then there is a Yahoo Group just for you. It is based largely in the Pennines, but covers everywhere north of a line from the Wash to the Severn. Message traffic is reasonably constant, with the expected huge peaks between September-November.

www.trektellen.nl/
This site logs migration counts across Europe. Most are from Holland (the site is Dutch) but there are currently records from more than 120 UK sites. You can sign up and add your own records too. There is comprehensive statistical analysis of the data, together with plenty of photos.

MULTIMEDIA

www.alip.co.uk/music_of_birds.htm

www.colander.org/gallimaufry/Birdsong.html
Composers have often been inspired by birdsong, from Beethoven including the songs of Quail, Cuckoo and Nightingale in his Pastoral Symphony, to fully inspired pieces such as Vaughan Williams' *The Lark Ascending* or *Scenes with Cranes* by Sibelius. These two pages offer a basic introduction to some of the pieces available, together with a few background notes and a suggested list of recordings. There is also an interesting coda to the Beatrice Harrison story (see next listing).

http://musicandnature.publicradio.org/features
Scroll down to the bottom of the page and you will find some background information on the famous BBC recordings of cellist Beatrice Harrison 'accompanied' by a local Nightingale (see also article on best bird books of the year). There are links to the recordings and on one (pulled by the BBC), you can hear the Nightingale with the drone of Lancaster bombers in the background, heading out for a raid over Germany.

www.neatorama.com/2010/06/12/bird-attacks-rc-airplane/
We've all seen members of the crow family

mobbing birds of prey that fly through their territory but do they recognise the raptor for what it is or will any flying object suffice? Watch this clip of a Hooded Crow attacking a model aeroplane and make up your own mind.

www.newforestgateway.org/TVFilmVideo/ FilmVideoSearch/tabid/260/Default.aspx
There are several films here taken in the New Forest including a Goshawk nest camera. The most interesting clip though is the one of a fox approaching a Nightjar nest. The wonderfully camouflaged adult bird flies at the fox at the last minute, allowing the chicks to run for safety a couple of moments later.

www.youtube.com/labofornithology
The Cornell Laboratory of Ornithology is an American educational institute. Here they have put many of their video clips online, offering a variety of mini tutorials. Some of the commentary is a bit twee and there is a massive North American bias to the subjects covered but the 50 or so clips offer some good practical advice.

www.youtube.com/watch?v=opPf1PMOYVg
This starts off as a home-made video with a group of American birders in a canoe, filming a Pileated Woodpecker but it quickly develops into a 'what happened next?' scenario. I won't spoil the surprise.

www.youtube.com/watch?v=VjE0Kdfos4Y
This is probably my favourite David Attenborough clip and features the amazing mimicry skills of the Superb Lyre Bird. Not only can it confuse the birds it is imitating, but it also includes man-made sounds in its repertoire; cameras with motor drives, car alarms and chain saws.

www.youtube.com/watch?v=Yz7FFlFy8eM&feature=player_embedded
This spectacular footage is taken from a Spanish wildlife documentary and shows Golden Eagles attacking young goats and dragging them off the mountain face in order to kill them. One wonders if all those Scottish crofters claiming that their lambs have been taken have a point after all.

RAPTORS

www.edinburghhawkwatch.org.uk/
If you have seen a Sparrowhawk within the city limits of Edinburgh, then this site would love to hear from you, as it is monitoring the status of the species. There is plenty of webcam footage to watch. The only problem is that you need a password more secure than that required by MI5 to access the forum.

http://europeanraptors.org/
Here are all sorts of news stories and articles about birds of prey in Europe, ranging from radio tagging Eastern Imperial Eagles in Bulgaria to an excellent interview about Golden Eagles in Britain. There are fact sheets and further links for every species.

www.globalraptors.org/grin/indexAlt.asp
The Global Raptors Information Network (GRIN) is a more academic site, devoted to raptor research across the world. Anyone involved in studying birds of prey is invited to contribute. There is plenty of information here too, as well as an impressive series of links to other raptor sites.

RESEARCH

www.aerc.eu/index.php
The site of the Association of European Records and Rarities Committees doesn't get off to the best of starts, with a large clickable map that didn't work. However, once you get past that, you will find all the various contact addresses, plus papers outlining their recommendations for taxonomic changes, be it something major such as a splitting or lumping of a particular species, or something relatively trivial such as a change to a scientific name.

www.amazing-journey.org/?utm_source=digitalspring
More satellite tracking, this time following the progress of nine Sociable Lapwings (Plovers) as they migrate from Kazakhstan to their wintering grounds in Africa. There are videos and news updates of the project too.

www.bouproc.net/
Here are various papers taken from conferences held by the British Ornithologists' Union. The latest additions look at non-native species and their impact on the environment, including Ruddy Ducks, parakeets, Eagle Owls and the effect of mammals in seabird colonies.

http://holarcticlisting.webs.com/
The Holarctic region covers the whole of the Palearctic and the Nearctic. An up-to-date checklist of every species, including subspecies, which has occurred in the area, is presented on a giant spreadsheet. Every conceivable split is covered, even though not every authority agrees with every decision. Several pages of notes explain the way the spreadsheet is set up.

http://radioactiverobins.com/
With a name that sounds like a third rate rock group, *Radioactive Robins* is a scientific study into the effects of the Chernobyl nuclear reactor disaster. At the time of writing, forest fires in Russia are threatening to move huge amounts of radioactive dust, so this could become a major story again. The website itself is poorly designed and an object lesson in how to make your pages unreadable but the content is important.

SOCIAL NETWORKING

http://www.collinsbirds.com/default.aspx
Set up with a great hullabaloo to coincide with the launch of the new edition of the *Collins Bird Guide*, this site is a perfect example of how to get a website completely wrong.

A clunky interface, too many blank pages, poor illustrations and text (ie not from the CBG), the site doesn't know what it wants to be. It aims at too many targets and misses them all by miles. Too few members mean that it won't improve either. Stick to Bird Forum instead (www.birdforum.net) which has the unbeatable edge of already having many tens of thousands of users.

SPECIES

www.pheasant.org.uk/
Despite its title, the World Pheasant Organisation is concerned with conserving all types of game birds. This site details projects around the world, though it really needs to be a lot more dynamic if it is to attract more members. Individual species accounts, maps, news, conservation threats and lots, lots more photos would be a start.

www.rspb.org.uk/ourwork/projects/details.aspx?id=198450
Was it or wasn't it? While the debate over the Druridge Bay Slender-billed Curlew continues to rage, this page has everything you need to know about this enigmatic bird. There are conservation projects, sound recordings and even a link to a video clip.

www.swift-conservation.org/
As every new building gets built, so the potential for Swift nesting sites decreases. This site looks at practical steps that can be taken by you, and developers, to remedy the situation for this most charismatic of our summer migrants. There is lots of information about the birds too.

www.worldwaders.org/index.php
This new site is still under development and records were scanty at the time of writing. Its aim is to invite members worldwide to submit their records for breeding and non-breeding waders so that a database of knowledge can be acquired and appropriate conservation action taken. There are recent news stories and a checklist of which birds you have seen.

WEATHER

http://magicseaweed.com/
Every devotee of the arcane art of seawatching knows the importance of getting ideal weather conditions. This site, which is primarily intended for surfers, plots the strength and direction of the wind around the coast for the next few days.

You can choose a graphic covering the whole of Britain (and many other places round the world), or choose a more specific location from a drop down menu. Tide times are also included. Hugely impressive.

DIARY 2011

Collared Doves are just one species that can be attracted to garden feeders — how many species will you record on Big Garden Birdwatch Day?

EVENTS DIARY 2011

JANUARY

24 to Feb 4: RSPB Big Schools Birdwatch 10th Anniversary
Continuing the initiative to get children interested in wild birds — see RSPB website for local area events.

29-30: RSPB Big Garden Birdwatch
Nationwide survey of garden birds.
Contact: RSPB on 01767 680 551.

FEBRUARY

2: World Wetlands Day
Various events at local level to raise awareness of 'wetlands and forests' to support the UN's decision to declare 2011 the International Year of Forests. www.wwd@ramsar.org

25-27: BTO bird identification course
Slapton Ley. South Devon.
Contact: steve.piotrowski@bto.org

MARCH

5-April 16: Society of Wildlife Artists prints exhibition
St Barbe Museum and Art Gallery, New Street, Lymington, Hants SO41 9BH. Contact: Steve Marshall at: office@stbarbe-museum.org.uk

20-27: Fifth Eilat migration festival
Bird tours, presentations and other bird-related events centred on Agamim Hotel in Eilat, southern Israel.
Contact: www.wix.com/lironziv/eilatspringfestival2011

23: Institute of Ecology & Environmental Management spring conference
Topic: Invasive species. Venue TBC.
Contact: www.ieem.net/conferences.asp

APRIL

5-7: BOU Annual Conference: Migratory Birds: Ecology and Conservation
University of Leicester. www.bou.org.uk

8-10: RSPB members weekend
York University.

8-10: BTO Bird Survey Techniques course
FSC Juniper Hall, Surrey.
Contact: su.gough@bto.org

16: African Bird Club AGM
Swedenborg Hall, 20-21 Bloomsbury Way, London WC1A 2TH.
Contact: contact@africanbirdclub.org

16: BTO/Lincs & Notts Regional Conference
Riseholme College, Campus, Riseholme, Lincoln.
Contact: www.bto.org

17: BTO Introduction to Ringing course
Retford, North Notts.
Contact: jez.blackburn@bto.org

17-19: BTO Bird Survey Techniques course
FSC Malham Tarn, Yorkshire.
Contact: su.gough@bto.org

MAY

2-5: Wind Energy and Wildlife Impacts Conference
Trondheim, Norway (Norwegian Institute for Nature Research)
Contact: www.cww2011.nina.no

4-6: BTO Bird Survey Techniques course
FSC Flatford Mill, Essex.
Contact: su.gough@bto.org

5: BTO Introduction to Ringing course
Flatford Mill, Essex.
Contact: enquiries.fm@field-studies-council.org

21-22: Birdwatcher's Spring Fair and Digital Photofair
Middleton Hall (near Drayton Manor Park), Tamworth, Staffs.
Contact: Organiser Alan Richards on 0152 785 2357; www.birdwatchers-springfair.co.uk

26: BTO Introduction to Ringing course
The Nunnery, Thetford, Norfolk.
Contact: jez.blackburn@bto.org

27-29: BTO bird identification course
FSC Rhyd-y-Creuau.
Contact: steve.piotrowski@bto.org

27-29: BTO Bird Survey Techniques course
FSC Dale Fort, Pembrokeshire.
Contact: su.gough@bto.org

29: Neotropical Bird Club general meeting
Talks, quizzes, book and audio sales at Cley Village Hall, Norfolk.
Contact: Secretary at g7ellis@googlemail.com

EVENTS DIARY 2011

JUNE

4-12: Make Your Nature Count
New RSPB scheme to survey garden wildlife in summer.
Contact: RSPB on 01767 680 551.

16: BTO Introduction to Ringing course
Flatford Mill, Essex.
Contact: enquiries.fm@field-studies-council.org

JULY

8-10: BTO Introduction to Ringing course
Flatford Mill, Essex.
Contact: enquiries.fm@field-studies-council.org

15 to 31: NEWA (National Exhibition of Wildlife Art)
Gordale Nursery, Burton, the Wirral. Preview evening July 14.
Contact: newa@mtuffrey.freeserve.co.uk or visit: www.newa-uk.com

16: Ornithological Society of Middle East, Caucasus & Central Asia (OSME) AGM and Summer Meeting
Doors open 10am. BTO HQ, The Nunnery, Thetford, Norfork.
Contact: Ian Harrison at: secretary@osme.org

AUGUST

12-14: BTO Introduction to Ringing course
Slapton Field Studies Centre, Devon.
Contact: enquiries.fm@field-studies-council.org

19-21: British Birdwatching Fair
Egleton Nature Reserve, Rutland Water, Rutland.
Contact: Call 01572 771 079 or e-mail: info@birdfair.org.uk

20: Neotropical Bird Club AGM
Plus lecture from guest speaker. Lecture Marquee at Birdfair.
Contact: Secretary at g7ellis@googlemail.com

27-30: European Ornithologists' Union Conference
Riga, Latvia.
Contact: http://eou.biology.lv/?id=13

SEPTEMBER

2-4: BTO Introduction to Ringing course
Flatford Mill, Essex.
Contact: enquiries.fm@field-studies-council.org

TBA: Scottish Ornithological Club annual weekend conference.
Contact: Date and venue details at mail@the-soc.org

26-30: World Conference on Marine Biodiversity
Aberdeen, Scotland.
Contact: For details visit Convention on Migratory Species website: www.cms.int/news/events/htm

27-30: Australasian Ornithological Conference
James Cook University, Cairns, Queenland.
Contact: Details at: www.birdsaustralia.org.au

OCTOBER

5-9 Raptor Research Foundation annual conference
University of Minnesota-Duluth.
Contact: Libby Mojica at: ekmojica@wm.edu

7-9: BTO Bird Survey Techniques course
FSC Kindrogan, Perth, Scotland.
Contact: james.bray@bto.org

8: RSPB AGM & members day
Queen Elizabeth II Conference Centre, Westminster, London.
Contact: wildlife@rspb.org.uk

26 to Nov 6: The Natural Eye
48th annual Society of Wildlife Artists exhibition The Mall Galleries, Pall Mall, London SW1.
Contact: Call gallery on 0207 930 6844 or visit: www.swla.co.uk

29: Feed The Birds Day
A programme of events across the UK — check local press and RSPB website for details in your area.

NOVEMBER

8-14: The IX Congress of Neotropical Ornithology
Cusco, Peru, organised by Neotropical Ornithological Society.

26-27: North-West Birdfair
WWT Martin Mere, Burscough, Lancs.
Contact: Tel: 01704 891 240 or e-mail: victoria.fellowes@wwt.org.uk

DECEMBER

2-4: BTO Annual Conference
The Hayes Conference Centre, Swanwick, Derbyshire.
Contact: ellen.walford@bto.org

1	Sat	
2	Sun	
3	Mon	New Year holiday
4	Tue	Holiday (Scotland)
5	Wed	
6	Thu	
7	Fri	
8	Sat	
9	Sun	
10	Mon	
11	Tue	
12	Wed	
13	Thu	
14	Fri	
15	Sat	
16	Sun	
17	Mon	
18	Tue	
19	Wed	
20	Thu	
21	Fri	
22	Sat	
23	Sun	
24	Mon	
25	Tue	
26	Wed	
27	Thu	
28	Fri	
29	Sat	
30	Sun	
31	Mon	

DIARY – FEBRUARY 2011

1	Tue	
2	Wed	
3	Thu	
4	Fri	
5	Sat	
6	Sun	
7	Mon	
8	Tue	
9	Wed	
10	Thu	
11	Fri	
12	Sat	
13	Sun	
14	Mon	
15	Tue	
16	Wed	
17	Thu	
18	Fri	
19	Sat	
20	Sun	
21	Mon	
22	Tue	
23	Wed	
24	Thu	
25	Fri	
26	Sat	
27	Sun	
28	Mon	

DIARY – MARCH 2011

1	Tue	
2	Wed	
3	Thu	
4	Fri	
5	Sat	
6	Sun	
7	Mon	
8	Tue	
9	Wed	
10	Thu	
11	Fri	
12	Sat	
13	Sun	
14	Mon	
15	Tue	
16	Wed	
17	Thu	St Patrick's Day (Bank Holiday N.Ireland)
18	Fri	
19	Sat	
20	Sun	
21	Mon	
22	Tue	
23	Wed	
24	Thu	
25	Fri	
26	Sat	
27	Sun	British Summertime begins
28	Mon	
29	Tue	
30	Wed	
31	Thu	

DIARY – APRIL 2011

1	Fri	
2	Sat	
3	Sun	Mothering Sunday
4	Mon	
5	Tue	
6	Wed	
7	Thu	
8	Fri	
9	Sat	
10	Sun	
11	Mon	
12	Tue	
13	Wed	
14	Thu	
15	Fri	
16	Sat	
17	Sun	
18	Mon	
19	Tue	
20	Wed	
21	Thu	
22	Fri	Good Friday
23	Sat	
24	Sun	Easter Day
25	Mon	Easter Monday
26	Tue	
27	Wed	
28	Thu	
29	Fri	
30	Sat	

DIARY – MAY 2011

1	Sun	
2	Mon	May Day
3	Tue	
4	Wed	
5	Thu	
6	Fri	
7	Sat	
8	Sun	
9	Mon	
10	Tue	
11	Wed	
12	Thu	
13	Fri	
14	Sat	
15	Sun	
16	Mon	
17	Tue	
18	Wed	
19	Thu	
20	Fri	
21	Sat	
22	Sun	
23	Mon	
24	Tue	
25	Wed	
26	Thu	
27	Fri	
28	Sat	
29	Sun	
30	Mon	Spring Bank Holiday
31	Tue	

DIARY – JUNE 2011

1	Wed	
2	Thu	
3	Fri	
4	Sat	
5	Sun	
6	Mon	
7	Tue	
8	Wed	
9	Thu	
10	Fri	
11	Sat	
12	Sun	
13	Mon	
14	Tue	
15	Wed	
16	Thu	
17	Fri	
18	Sat	
19	Sun	
20	Mon	
21	Tue	
22	Wed	
23	Thu	
24	Fri	
25	Sat	
26	Sun	
27	Mon	
28	Tue	
29	Wed	
30	Thu	

DIARY – JULY 2011

1	Fri	
2	Sat	
3	Sun	
4	Mon	
5	Tue	
6	Wed	
7	Thu	
8	Fri	
9	Sat	
10	Sun	
11	Mon	
12	Tue	Bank Holiday N.Ireland
13	Wed	
14	Thu	
15	Fri	
16	Sat	
17	Sun	
18	Mon	
19	Tue	
20	Wed	
21	Thu	
22	Fri	
23	Sat	
24	Sun	
25	Mon	
26	Tue	
27	Wed	
28	Thu	
29	Fri	
30	Sat	
31	Sun	

DIARY – AUGUST 2011

1	Mon	Bank Holiday Scotland
2	Tue	
3	Wed	
4	Thu	
5	Fri	
6	Sat	
7	Sun	
8	Mon	
9	Tue	
10	Wed	
11	Thu	
12	Fri	
13	Sat	
14	Sun	
15	Mon	
16	Tue	
17	Wed	
18	Thu	
19	Fri	
20	Sat	
21	Sun	
22	Mon	
23	Tue	
24	Wed	
25	Thu	
26	Fri	
27	Sat	
28	Sun	
29	Mon	Summer Bank Holiday
30	Tue	
31	Wed	

DIARY – SEPTEMBER 2011

1	Thu	
2	Fri	
3	Sat	
4	Sun	
5	Mon	
6	Tue	
7	Wed	
8	Thu	
9	Fri	
10	Sat	
11	Sun	
12	Mon	
13	Tue	
14	Wed	
15	Thu	
16	Fri	
17	Sat	
18	Sun	
19	Mon	
20	Tue	
21	Wed	
22	Thu	
23	Fri	
24	Sat	
25	Sun	
26	Mon	
27	Tue	
28	Wed	
29	Thu	
30	Fri	

DIARY 2011

DIARY – OCTOBER 2011

1	Sat	
2	Sun	
3	Mon	
4	Tue	
5	Wed	
6	Thu	
7	Fri	
8	Sat	
9	Sun	
10	Mon	
11	Tue	
12	Wed	
13	Thu	
14	Fri	
15	Sat	
16	Sun	
17	Mon	
18	Tue	
19	Wed	
20	Thu	
21	Fri	
22	Sat	
23	Sun	
24	Mon	
25	Tue	
26	Wed	
27	Thu	
28	Fri	
29	Sat	
30	Sun	British Summertime ends
31	Mon	

1	Tue	
2	Wed	
3	Thu	
4	Fri	
5	Sat	
6	Sun	
7	Mon	
8	Tue	
9	Wed	
10	Thu	
11	Fri	
12	Sat	
13	Sun	Remembrance Sunday
14	Mon	
15	Tue	
16	Wed	
17	Thu	
18	Fri	
19	Sat	
20	Sun	
21	Mon	
22	Tue	
23	Wed	
24	Thu	
25	Fri	
26	Sat	
27	Sun	
28	Mon	
29	Tue	
30	Wed	

DIARY – DECEMBER 2011

1	Thu	
2	Fri	
3	Sat	
4	Sun	
5	Mon	
6	Tue	
7	Wed	
8	Thu	
9	Fri	
10	Sat	
11	Sun	
12	Mon	
13	Tue	
14	Wed	
15	Thu	
16	Fri	
17	Sat	
18	Sun	
19	Mon	
20	Tue	
21	Wed	
22	Thu	
23	Fri	
24	Sat	
25	Sun	Christmas Day
26	Mon	Boxing Day
27	Tue	Bank holiday
28	Wed	
29	Thu	
30	Fri	
31	Sat	

YEAR PLANNER 2012

January

February

March

April

May

June

July

August

September

October

November

December

LOG CHARTS

Oliver Smart

Species such as the Red Kite, which has successfully re-established itself in former areas, has been recategorised as C3 on the BOU British List.

A CHECKLIST OF BIRDS

Based on the British List formulated by the British Ornithologists' Union

NEWCOMERS to birdwatching are sometimes baffled when they examine their first fieldguide as it is not immediately clear why the birds are arranged the way they are. The simple answer is that the order is meant to reflect the evolution of the included species. If one were to draw an evolutionary tree of birds, those families that branch off earliest (i.e are the most ancient) should be listed first.

Previously the British Ornithologists' Union British List was based on Voous Order (BOU 1977), the work of an eminent Dutch taxonomist and many of the popular fieldguides for British and European birds still follow this established order.

For more than 100 years, the British Ornithologists' Union Records Committee (BOURC) has maintained the official list of birds recorded in Britain — the British List. The BOURC periodically publishes up-to-date checklists incorporating changes the BOURC has announced in its reports and the Checklist published in *The Birdwatcher's Yearbook* reflects these changes.

In this edition, species in Category C (introduced species) have been sub-divided into six separate categories (see below).

SPECIES, CATEGORIES, CODES – YOUR GUIDE TO GET THE BEST USE FROM THE CHECKLIST

Species categories (column 1)

The following categories are those assigned by the British Ornithologists' Union.

A - Species that have been recorded in an apparently natural state at least once since January 1, 1950.

B - Species that were recorded in an apparently natural state at least once between January 1, 1800 and December 31,1949, but have not been recorded subsequently.

C - Species that, though introduced, now derive from the resulting self-sustaining populations.

C1 - *Naturalized introduced species* – Species that have occurred only as a result of introduction, e.g. Egyptian Goose (*Alopochen aegyptiacus*).

C2 - *Naturalized established species* - Species with established populations resulting from introduction by Man, but which also occur in an apparently natural state, e.g. Greylag Goose (*Anser anser*).

C3 - *Naturalized re-established species* - Species with populations successfully re-established by Man in areas of former occurrence, e.g. Red Kite (*Milvus milvus).*

C4 - *Naturalized feral species* - Domesticated species with populations established in the wild, e.g. Rock Pigeon (Dove)/Feral Pigeon (*Columba livia).*

C5 - *Vagrant naturalized species* - Species from established naturalized populations abroad,

e.g. Sacred Ibis (*Threskiornis aethiopicu)s* from the naturalized French populations. There are currently no species in category C5.

C6 - *Former naturalized species* – Species formerly placed in C1 whose naturalized populations are either no longer self-sustaining or are considered extinct, e.g. Lady Amherst's Pheasant (*Chrysolophus amherstiae).*

D - Species that would otherwise appear in Category A except that there is reasonable doubt that they have ever occurred in a natural state. Species placed solely in Category D form no part of the British List, and are not included in the species totals.

E - Species that have been recorded as introductions, human-assisted transportees or escapees from captivity, and whose breeding populations (if any) are thought not to be self-sustaining. Species in Category E that have bred in the wild in Britain are designated as E*. Category E species form no part of the British List (unless already included within Categories A, B or C).

A species is usually placed in only one category, but some are placed in multiple categories, for example, those species occurring in Category A which now have naturalised populations (e.g. Red Kite).

The British List comprises only those species in Categories A, B and C.

LOG CHARTS

Species list (column 2)

The charts include all species from categories A, B and C on the British List, based on the latest BOU listing. Selected species included in categories D and E are listed separately at the end of the log chart.

Vagrants which are not on the British List, but which may have occurred in other parts of the British Isles, are not included. Readers who wish to record such species may use the extra rows provided on the last page. In this connection it should be noted that separate lists exist for Northern Ireland (kept by the Northern Ireland Birdwatchers' Association) and the Isle of Man (kept by the Manx Ornithological Society), and that Irish records are assessed by the Irish Rare Birds Committee.

The commoner species in the log charts are indicated by the * symbol to help make record-keeping easier.

The species names are those most widely used in the current fieldguides and each is followed by its scientific name, printed in italics.

Life list (column 3)

Ticks made in the 'Life List' column suffice for keeping a running personal total of species. However, added benefit can be obtained by replacing ticks with a note of the year of first occurrence. To take an example: one's first-ever Marsh Sandpiper, seen on April 14, 2011, would be logged with '11' in the Life List and '14' in the April column (as well as a tick in the 2011 column). As Life List entries are carried forward annually, in years to come it would be a simple matter to relocate this record.

First and last dates of migrants

Arrivals of migrants can be recorded by inserting dates instead of ticks in the relevant month columns. For example, a Common Sandpiper on March 11 would be recorded by inserting '11' against Common Sandpiper in the March column. The same applies to departures, though dates of last sightings can only be entered at the end of the year after checking one's field notebook.

Unheaded columns

The three unheaded columns on the right of the December column of each chart are for special (personal) use. This may be, for example, to cater for a second holiday, a particular county or a 'local patch'. Another use could be to indicate species on, for example, the Northern Ireland List or the Isle of Man List.

BTO species codes (column 23)

British Trust for Ornithology two-letter species codes are shown in brackets in the fourth column from the right. They exist for many species, races and hybrids recorded in recent surveys. Readers should refer to the BTO if more codes are needed.

In addition to those given in the charts, the following are available for some well-marked races or forms - Whistling Swan (WZ), European White-fronted Goose (EW), Greenland White-fronted Goose (NW), dark-bellied Brent Goose (DB), pale-bellied Brent Goose (PB), Black Brant (BB), domestic goose (ZL), Green-winged Teal (TA), domestic duck (ZF), Yellow-legged Gull (YG),

Kumlien's Gull (KG), Feral Pigeon (FP), White Wagtail (WB), Black-bellied Dipper (DJ), Hooded Crow (HC), intermediate crow (HB).

Rare breeding birds (column 24)

Species monitored by the Rare Breeding Birds Panel (see National Directory) comprise all those on Schedule 1 of the Wildlife and Countryside Act 1981 (see Quick Reference) together with all escaped or introduced species breeding in small numbers. The following annotations in the charts (third column from the right) reflect the RBBP's categories:

A Rare species. All breeding details requested.

B Less scarce species. Totals requested from counties with more than 10 pairs or localities; elsewhere all details requested.

C Less scarce species (specifically Barn Owl, Kingfisher, Crossbill). County summaries only requested.

D Escaped or introduced species. County summaries only requested.

Rarities (column 25)

Rarities are indicated by a capital letter 'R' in the column headed BBRC (British Birds Rarities Committee).

EURING species numbers (column 26)

EURING databanks collects copies of recovery records from ringing schemes throughout Europe and the official species numbers are given in the last column. As they are taken from the full Holarctic bird list there are many apparent gaps. It is important that these are not filled arbitrarily by observers wishing to record species not listed in the charts, as this would compromise the integrity of the scheme.

Similarly, the addition of a further digit to indicate sub-species is to be avoided, since EURING has already assigned numbers for this purpose. The numbering follows the Voous order of species so some species are now out of sequence following the re-ordering of the British List. For full details, visit: www.euring.org

BOU	SWANS, GEESE, DUCKS		Life list	2011 list	24 hr	Garden	Holiday	Jan	Feb	Mar	Apr	May	Jun	Jul	Aug	Sep	Oct	Nov	Dec	BTO	RBBP	BBRC	EU No
*A/C2	Mute Swan	Cygnus olor																		MS			0152
*A	Bewick's Swan	C. columbianus																		BS	A		0153
*A	Whooper Swan	C. cygnus																		WS	A		0154
*A	Bean Goose	Anser fabalis																		BE			0157
*A	Pink-footed Goose	A. brachyrhynchus																		PG	D		0158
*A	White-fronted Goose	A. albifrons																		WG	D		0159
*A	Lesser White-fronted Goose	A. erythropus																		LC	D	R	0160
A/C2/C4/E	Greylag Goose	A. anser																		GJ			0161
*A	Snow Goose	A. aerulescens																		SJ	D		0163
C2/E	Canada Goose	Branta canadensis																		CG			0166
A/C2/E	Barnacle Goose	B. eucopsis																		BY	D		0167
*A	Brent Goose	B. bernicla																		BG			0168
A	Red-breasted Goose	B. ruficollis																		EB	D	R	0169
C1/E	Egyptian Goose	Alopochen aegyptiaca																		EG	D		0170
B/D/E	Ruddy Shelduck	Tadorna ferruginea																		UD	D		0171
*A	Shelduck	T. tadorna																		SU			0173
C1/E	Mandarin Duck	Aix galericulata																		MN	D		0178
*A	Wigeon	Anas penelope																		WN	A		0179
A	American Wigeon	A. americana																		AW			0180
*A/C2	Gadwall	A. strepera																		GA	B		0182
*A/E	Baikal Teal	A. formosa																					
*A	Teal	A. crecca																		T			0184
A	Green-winged Teal	A. carolinensis																			A		1842
A/C2/C4/E	Mallard	A. platyrhynchos																		MA			0186
	Sub total																						

BOU	DUCKS Cont		Life list	2011 list	24 hr	Garden	Holiday	Jan	Feb	Mar	Apr	May	Jun	Jul	Aug	Sep	Oct	Nov	Dec			BTO	RBBP	BBRC	EU No
A	Black Duck	A. rubripes																				BD	A	R	0187
*A	Pintail	A. acuta																				PT	A		0189
*A	Garganey	A. querquedula																				GY	A		0191
A	Blue-winged Teal	A. discors																				TB	D	R	0192
*A	Shoveler	A. clypeata																				SV	A		0194
A/C2/E	Red-crested Pochard	Netta rufina																				RQ	D		0196
A	Canvasback	Anas valisineria																						R	0197
*A	Pochard	A. ferina																				PO	B		0198
A	Redhead	A. americana																				AZ		R	0199
A	Ring-necked Duck	A. collaris																				NG	A		0200
A	Ferruginous Duck	A. nyroca																				FD			0202
*A	Tufted Duck	A. fuligula																				TU			0203
*A	Scaup	A. marila																				SP	A		0204
*A	Lesser Scaup	A. affinis																				AY		R	0205
*A	Eider	Somateria mollissima																				E			0206
*A	King Eider	S. spectabilis																				KE	A	R	0207
A	Steller's Eider	Polysticta stelleri																				ES		R	0209
A	Harlequin Duck	Histrionicus histrionicus																				HQ		R	0211
*A	Long-tailed Duck	Clangula hyemalis																				LN	A		0212
*A	Common Scoter	Melanitta nigra																				CX	A		0213
A	Black Scoter	M. americana																						R	2132
*A	Surf Scoter	M. perspicillata																				FS			0214
A	Velvet Scoter	M. fusca																				VS	A		0215
A	Bufflehead	Bucephala albeola																				VH		R	0216
	Sub total																								

67

BOU	DUCKS, GAMEBIRDS, DIVERS, ALBATROSS		Life list	2011 list	24 hr	Garden	Holiday	Jan	Feb	Mar	Apr	May	Jun	Jul	Aug	Sep	Oct	Nov	Dec	BTO	RBBP	BBRC	EU No
A	Barrow's Goldeneye	B. islandica																				R	0217
*A	Goldeneye	B. clangula																		GN	A		0218
*A	Smew	Mergellus albellus																		SY	A		0220
A	Hooded Merganser	Lophodytes cucullatus																				R	2190
*A	Red-breasted Merganser	Mergus serrator																		RM			0221
*A	Goosander	M. merganser																		GD			0223
C1/E	Ruddy Duck	Oxyura jamaicensis																		BY			0225
*A	Red Grouse	Lagopus lagopus																		RG			0329
*A	Ptarmigan	Lagopus muta																		PM			0330
*A	Black Grouse	Tetrao tetrix																		BK			0332
*B/C3	Capercaillie	T. urogallus																		CP	A		0335
C1/E	Red-legged Partridge	Alectoris rufa																		RL			0358
*A/C2/E	Grey Partridge	Perdix perdix																		P			0367
*A	Quail	Coturnix coturnix																		Q	B		0370
C1/E	(Common) Pheasant	Phasianus colchicus																		PH			0394
C1/E	Golden Pheasant	Chrysolophus pictus																		GF	D		0396
C6/E	Lady Amherst's Pheasant	C. amherstiae																		LM	D		0397
*A	Red-throated Diver	Gavia stellata																		RH	B		0002
*A	Black-throated Diver	G. arctica																		BV	A		0003
A	Pacific Diver	Gavia pacifica																				R	0033
*A	Great Northern Diver	G. immer																		ND	A		0004
A	White-billed Diver	G. adamsii																		IW	A		0005
A	Black-browed Albatross	Thalassarche melanophris																		AA	A	R	0014
A	Yellow-nosed Albatross	T. chlororhynchos																				R	0150
	Sub total																						

FULMAR, PETRELS, SHEARWATERS, CORMORANTS, FRIGATEBIRDS, BITTERNS

BOU	Species	Scientific	Life list	2011 list	24 hr	Garden	Holiday	Jan	Feb	Mar	Apr	May	Jun	Jul	Aug	Sep	Oct	Nov	Dec	BTO	RBBP	BBRC	EU No
*A	Fulmar	Fulmarus glacialis																		F			0020
A	Fea's Petrel	Pterodroma feae																				R	0026
A	Capped Petrel	Pt. hasitata																				R	0029
A	Cory's Shearwater	Calonectris diomedea																		CQ			0036
*A	Great Shearwater	Puffinus gravis																		GQ			0040
*A	Sooty Shearwater	P. griseus																		OT			0043
A	Manx Shearwater	P. puffinus																		MX			0046
A	Balearic Shearwater	P. mauretanicus																					0046
A	Macaronesian Shearwater	P. baroli																			A	R	0048
*A	Wilson's Petrel	Oceanites oceanicus																					0050
B	White-faced Petrel	Pelagodroma marina																				R	0051
*A	Storm Petrel	Hydrobates pelagicus																		TM			0052
*A	Leach's Petrel	Oceanodroma leucorhoa																		TL	A	R	0055
A	Swinhoe's Petrel	O. monorhis																				R	0056
A	Red-billed Tropicbird	Phaethon aethereus																				R	0064
*A	(Northern) Gannet	Morus bassanus																		GX			0071
*A	Cormorant	Phalacrocorax carbo																		CA			0072
A	Double-crested Cormorant	P. auritus																				R	0078
*A	Shag	P. aristotelis																		SA			0080
A	Magnificent Frigatebird	Fregata magnificens																				R	0093
A	Ascension Frigatebird	F. aquila																				R	
*A	Bittern	Botaurus stellaris																		BI	A		0095
A	American Bittern	B. lentiginosus																		AM		R	0096
A	Little Bittern	Ixobrychus minutus																		LL	A	R	0098
	Sub total																						

69

BITTERNS, HERONS, STORKS, SPOON-BILL, GREBES, RAPTORS

BOU	Species	Scientific name	Life list	2011 list	24 hr	Garden	Holiday	Jan	Feb	Mar	Apr	May	Jun	Jul	Aug	Sep	Oct	Nov	Dec	BTO	RBBP	BBRC	EU No
A	Night-heron	*Nycticorax nycticorax*																		NT	D		0104
A	Green Heron	*Butorides virescens*																		HR		R	0107
A	Squacco Heron	*Ardeola ralloides*																		QH		R	0108
A	Cattle Egret	*Bubulcus ibis*																		EC	A		0111
A	Snowy Egret	*Egretta thula*																				R	0115
*A	Little Egret	*E. garzetta*																		ET	A		0119
A	Great White Egret	*Ardea alba*																		HW			0121
A	Grey Heron	*A. cinerea*																		H			0122
A	Great Blue Heron	*A. herodias*																				R	1230
A	Purple Heron	*A. purpurea*																		UR	A		0124
A	Black Stork	*Ciconia nigra*																		OS		R	0131
A	White Stork	*C. ciconia*																		OR	A		0134
A	Glossy Ibis	*Plegadis falcinellus*																		IB		R	0136
*A	Spoonbill	*Platalea leucorodia*																		NB	A		0144
A	Pied-billed Grebe	*Podilymbus podiceps*																		PJ	A	R	0006
*A	Little Grebe	*Tachybaptus ruficollis*																		LG			0007
*A	Great Crested Grebe	*Podiceps cristatus*																		GG	A		0009
*A	Red-necked Grebe	*P. grisegena*																		RX	A		0010
*A	Slavonian Grebe	*P. auritus*																		SZ	A		0011
*A	Black-necked Grebe	*P. nigricollis*																		BN	A		0012
*A	Honey-buzzard	*Pernis apivorus*																		HZ	A		0231
A	Black Kite	*Milvus migrans*																		KB	A		0238
*A/C3	Red Kite	*M. milvus*																		KT	A		0239
*A/C3/E	White-tailed Eagle	*Haliaeetus albicilla*																		WE	A		0243
	Sub total																						

70

BOU	RAPTORS AND RAIL		Life list	2011 list	24 hr	Garden	Holiday	Jan	Feb	Mar	Apr	May	Jun	Jul	Aug	Sep	Oct	Nov	Dec				BTO	RBBP	BBRC	EU No
B	Egyptian Vulture	*Neophron percnopterus*																							R	0247
A	Short-toed Eagle	*Circaetus gallicus*																							R	0256
*A	Marsh Harrier	*Circus aeruginosus*																					MR	A		0260
*A	Hen Harrier	*C. cyaneus*																					HH	B		0261
A	Pallid Harrier	*C. macrourus*																						A	R	0262
*A	Montagu's Harrier	*C. pygargus*																					MO	A		0263
A/C3/E	Goshawk	*Accipiter gentilis*																					GI	B		0267
*A	Sparrowhawk	*A. nisus*																					SH			0269
*A	Buzzard	*Buteo buteo*																					BZ			0287
*A	Rough-legged Buzzard	*B. lagopus*																					RF	A		0290
B	Greater Spotted Eagle	*Aquila clanga*																							R	0293
*A	Golden Eagle	*A. chrysaetos*																					EA	B		0296
*A	Osprey	*Pandion haliaetus*																					OP	A		0301
A	Lesser Kestrel	*Falco naumanni*																							R	0303
*A	Kestrel	*F. tinnunculus*																					K			0304
A	American Kestrel	*F. sparverius*																							R	0305
*A	Red-footed Falcon	*F. vespertinus*																					FV			0307
A	Amur Falcon	*F. amurensis*																								
*A	Merlin	*F. columbarius*																					ML	B		0309
*A	Hobby	*F. subbuteo*																					HY	B		0310
A	Eleonora's Falcon	*F. eleonorae*																								0311
*A	Gyr Falcon	*F. rusticolus*																					YF	A	R	0318
*A	Peregrine	*F. peregrinus*																					PE	B		0320
*A	Water Rail	*Rallus aquaticus*																					WA	A	R	0407
	Sub total																									

71

CRAKES, GALLINULES, CRANES, BUSTARDS AND WADERS

BOU	Species	Scientific name	Life list	2011 list	24 hr	Garden	Holiday	Jan	Feb	Mar	Apr	May	Jun	Jul	Aug	Sep	Oct	Nov	Dec			BTO	RBBP	BBRC	EU No
*A	Spotted Crake	Porzana porzana																				AK	A		0408
A	Sora	P. carolina																						R	0409
A	Little Crake	P. parva																				JC		R	0410
A	Baillon's Crake	P. pusilla																				VC	A	R	0411
*A	Corncrake	Crex crex																				CE	A		0421
*A	Moorhen	Gallinula chloropus																				MH	A		0424
A	Allen's Gallinule	Porphyrio alleni																						R	0425
A	Purple Gallinule	P. martinica																						R	0426
*A	Coot	Fulica atra																				CO			0429
A	American Coot	F. americana																						R	0430
*A	Crane	Grus grus																				AN	A		0433
A	Sandhill Crane	G. canadensis																						R	0436
A	Little Bustard	Tetrax tetrax																						R	0442
A	Macqueen's Bustard	Chlamydotis macqueenii																						R	0444
A	Great Bustard	Otis tarda																				US	A	R	0446
*A	Oystercatcher	Haematopus ostralegus																				OC			0450
*A	Black-winged Stilt	Himantopus himantopus																				IT	A	R	0455
*A	Avocet	Recurvirostra avosetta																				AV	A		0456
*A	Stone-curlew	Burhinus oedicnemus																				TN	A		0459
A	Cream-coloured Courser	Cursorius cursor																						R	0464
A	Collared Pratincole	Glareola pratincola																						R	0465
A	Oriental Pratincole	G. maldivarum																				GM		R	0466
A	Black-winged Pratincole	G. nordmanni																				KW		R	0467
*A	Little Ringed Plover	Charadrius dubius																				LP	B		0469
	Sub total																								

BOU	WADERS Cont		Life list	2011 list	24 hr	Garden	Holiday	Jan	Feb	Mar	Apr	May	Jun	Jul	Aug	Sep	Oct	Nov	Dec				BTO	RBBP	BBRC	EU No
*A	Ringed Plover	C. hiaticula																					RP			0470
A	Semipalmated Plover	C. semipalmatus																					TV		R	0471
A	Killdeer	C. vociferus																					KL		R	0474
A	Kentish Plover	C. alexandrinus																					KP	A		0477
A	Lesser Sand Plover	C. mongolus																							R	0478
A	Greater Sand Plover	C. leschenaultii																							R	0479
A	Caspian Plover	C. asiaticus																							R	0480
*A	Dotterel	C. morinellus																					DO	B		0482
A	American Golden Plover	Pluvialis dominica																					ID			0484
A	Pacific Golden Plover	P. fulva																					IF		R	0484
*A	Golden Plover	P. apricaria																					GP			0485
*A	Grey Plover	P. squatarola																					GV			0486
A	Sociable Plover	Vanellus gregarius																					IP		R	0491
A	White-tailed Plover	V. leucurus																							R	0492
*A	Lapwing	V. vanellus																					L			0493
A	Great Knot	Calidris tenuirostris																					KO		R	0495
*A	Knot C. canutus	KN																								0496
*A	Sanderling	C. alba																					SS	A		0497
A	Semipalmated Sandpiper	C. pusilla																					PZ		R	0498
A	Western Sandpiper	C. mauri																					ER		R	0499
A	Red-necked Stint	C. ruficollis																							R	0500
*A	Little Stint	C. minuta																					LX			0501
*A	Temminck's Stint	C. temminckii																					TK	A		0502
A	Long-toed Stint	C. subminuta																							R	0503
	Sub total																									

73

BOU	WADERS Cont		Life list	2011 list	24 hr	Garden	Holiday	Jan	Feb	Mar	Apr	May	Jun	Jul	Aug	Sep	Oct	Nov	Dec	BTO	RBBP	BBRC	EU No
A	Least Sandpiper	C. minutilla																		EP		R	0504
A	White-rumped Sandpiper	C. fuscicollis																		WU			0505
A	Baird's Sandpiper	C. bairdii																		BP		R	0506
A	Pectoral Sandpiper	C. melanotos																		PP	A		0507
A	Sharp-tailed Sandpiper	C. acuminata																		VV		R	0508
*A	Curlew Sandpiper	C. ferruginea																		CV			0509
A	Stilt Sandpiper	C. himantopus																				R	5150
*A	Purple Sandpiper	C. maritima																		PS	A		0510
*A	Dunlin	C. alpina																		DN			0512
A	Broad-billed Sandpiper	Limicola falcinellus																		OA	A	R	0514
A	Buff-breasted Sandpiper	Tryngites subruficollis																		BQ			0516
*A	Ruff	Philomachus pugnax																		RU	A		0517
*A	Jack Snipe	Lymnocryptes minimus																		JS	A		0518
*A	Snipe	Gallinago gallinago																		SN			0519
A	Wilson's Snipe	G. delicata																				R	5192
A	Great Snipe	G. media																		DS		R	0520
A	Short-billed Dowitcher	Limnodromus griseus																				R	0526
A	Long-billed Cowitcher	Limnodromus scolopaceus																		LD		R	0527
*A	Woodcock	Scolopax rusticola																		WK			0529
*A	Black-tailed Godwit	Limosa limosa																		BW	A		0532
A	Hudsonian Godwit	L. haemastica																		HU		R	0533
*A	Bar-tailed Godwit	L. lapponica																		BA	A		0534
A	Little Whimbrel	Numenius minutus																				R	0536
B	Eskimo Curlew	N. borealis																				R	0537
	Sub total																						

LOG CHARTS

BOU	WADERS Cont, PHALAROPES AND SKUAS		Life list	2011 list	24 hr	Garden	Holiday	Jan	Feb	Mar	Apr	May	Jun	Jul	Aug	Sep	Oct	Nov	Dec	BTO	RBBP	BBRC	EU No
*A	Whimbrel	N. phaeopus																		WM	B		0538
A	Slender-billed Curlew	N. tenuirostris																				R	0540
*A	Curlew	N. arquata																		CU			0541
A	Upland Sandpiper	Bartramia longicauda																		UP		R	0544
A	Terek Sandpiper	Xenus cinereus																		TR		R	0555
*A	Common Sandpiper	Actitis hypoleucos																		CS			0556
A	Spotted Sandpiper	A. macularius																		PQ	A	R	0557
*A	Green Sandpiper	Tringa ochropus																		GE	A		0553
A	Solitary Sandpiper	T. solitaria																		I		R	0552
A	Grey-tailed Tattler	T. brevipes																		YT		R	0558
*A	Spotted Redshank	T. erythropus																		DR			0545
A	Greater Yellowlegs	T. melanoleuca																		LZ		R	0550
*A	Greenshank	T. nebularia																		GK	A		0548
A	Lesser Yellowlegs	T. flavipes																		LY		R	0551
*A	Marsh Sandpiper	T. stagnatilis																		MD		R	0547
*A	Wood Sandpiper	T. glareola																		OD	A		0554
*A	Redshank	T. totanus																		RK			0546
*A	Turnstone	Arenaria interpres																		TT	A		0561
A	Wilson's Phalarope	Phalaropus tricolor																		WF		R	0563
*A	Red-necked Phalarope	P. lobatus																		NK	A		0564
*A	Grey Phalarope	Phalaropus fulicarius																		PL			0565
*A	Pomarine Skua	Stercorarius pomarinus																		PK			0566
*A	Arctic Skua	S. parasiticus																		AC			0567
*A	Long-tailed Skua	S. longicaudus																		OG			0568
	Sub total																						

BOU	GULLS		Life list	2011 list	24 hr	Garden	Holiday	Jan	Feb	Mar	Apr	May	Jun	Jul	Aug	Sep	Oct	Nov	Dec				BTO	RBBP	BBRC	EU No
*A	Great Skua	S. skua																					NX			0569
A	Ivory Gull	Pagophila eburnea																					IV		R	0604
*A	Sabine's Gull	Larus sabini																					AB			0579
*A	Kittiwake	Rissa tridactyla																					KI			0602
A	Slender-billed Gull	Chroicocephalus genei																					EI	A	R	0585
A	Bonaparte's Gull	C. philadelphia																					ON		R	0581
*A	Black-headed Gull	C. ridibundus																					BH			0582
*A	Little Gull	Hydrocoloeus minutus																					LU	A		0578
A	Ross's Gull	Rhodostethia rosea																					QG		R	0601
*A	Laughing Gull	Larus atricilla																					LF		R	0576
A	Franklin's Gull	L. pipixcan																					FG		R	0577
*A	Mediterranean Gull	L. melanocephalus																					MU	A		0575
A	Audouin's Gull	L. audouinii																							R	0589
B	Great Black-headed Gull	L. ichthyaetus																							R	0573
*A	Common Gull	L. canus																					CM			0590
*A	Ring-billed Gull	L. delawarensis																					IN	A		0588
*A	Lesser Black-backed Gull	L. fuscus																					LB			0591
*A	Herring Gull	L. argentatus																					HG			0592
A	Yellow-legged Gull	L. michahellis																						A		5927
A	Caspian Gull	L. cachinnans																								5927
A	American Herring Gull	L. smithsonianus																							R	26632
*A	Iceland Gull	L. glaucoides																					IG	A		0598
A	Glaucous-winged Gull	L. glaucescens																							R	5960
*A	Glaucous Gull	L. hyperboreus																					GZ	A		0599
	Sub total																									

BOU	GULLS Cont, TERNS, AND AUKS		Life list	2011 list	24 hr	Garden	Holiday	Jan	Feb	Mar	Apr	May	Jun	Jul	Aug	Sep	Oct	Nov	Dec	BTO	RBBP	BBRC	EU No
*A	Great Black-backed Gull	L. marinus																		GB			0600
A	Aleutian Tern	Onychoprion aleutica																				R	0617
A	Sooty Tern	O. fuscata																				R	0623
A	Bridled Tern	O. anaethetus																				R	0622
*A	Little Tern	Sternula albifrons																		AF			0624
A	Gull-billed Tern	Gelochelidon nilotica																		TG	B	R	0605
A	Caspian Tern	Hydroprogne caspia																		CJ			0606
*A	Whiskered Tern	Chlidonias hybrida																		WD		R	0626
*A	Black Tern	C. niger																		BJ	A		0627
*A	White-winged Black Tern	C. leucopterus																		WJ			0628
*A	Sandwich Tern	Sterna sandvicensis																		TE			0611
A	Royal Tern	S. maxima																		QT		R	0607
A	Lesser Crested Tern	S. bengalensis																		TF	A	R	0609
A	Forster's Tern	S. forsteri																		FO		R	0618
*A	Common Tern	S. hirundo																		CN			0615
*A	Roseate Tern	S. dougallii																		RS	A		0614
*A	Arctic Tern	S. paradisaea																		AE			0616
*A	Guillemot	Uria aalge																		GU			0634
A	Brünnich's Guillemot	U. lomvia																		TZ		R	0635
*A	Razorbill	Alca torda																		RA			0636
B	Great Auk 1	Pinguinus impennis																					
*A	Black Guillemot	Cepphus grylle																		TY			0638
A	Long-billed Murrelet	Brachyramphus perdix																				R	6412
A	Ancient Murrelet	Synthliboramphus antiquus																				R	0645
	Sub total																						

77

AUKS, DOVES, CUCKOOS AND OWLS

BOU	Species	Scientific name	Life list	2011 list	24 hr	Garden	Holiday	Jan	Feb	Mar	Apr	May	Jun	Jul	Aug	Sep	Oct	Nov	Dec	BTO	RBBP	BBRC	EU No
*A	Little Auk	Alle alle																		LK			0647
*A	Puffin	Fratercula arctica																		PU			0654
A	Tufted Puffin	F. cirrhata																					
A	Pallas's Sandgrouse	Syrrhaptes paradoxus																				R	0663
A/C4/E	Rock Dove / Feral Pigeon	Columba livia																		DV			0665
*A	Stock Dove	C. oenas																		SD			0668
*A	Woodpigeon	C. palumbus																		WP			0670
*A	Collared Dove	Streptopelia decaocto																		CD			0684
*A	Turtle Dove	S. turtur																		TD			0687
A	Rufous Turtle Dove	S. orientalis																				R	0689
A	Mourning Dove	Zenaida macroura																				R	0695
C1/E	Ring-necked Parakeet	Psittacula krameri																		RI			0712
A	Great Spotted Cuckoo	Clamator glandarius																				R	0716
*A	Cuckoo	Cuculus canorus																		CK			0724
A	Black-billed Cuckoo	Coccyzus erythrophthalmus																				R	0727
A	Yellow-billed Cuckoo	C. americanus																				R	0728
*A	Barn Owl	Tyto alba																		BO			0735
A	Scops Owl	Otus scops																				R	0739
*A	Snowy Owl	Bubo scandiacus																		SO	A	R	0749
A	Hawk Owl	Surnia ulula																				R	0750
*C1	Little Owl	Athene noctua																		LO			0757
*A	Tawny Owl	Strix aluco																		TO			0761
*A	Long-eared Owl	Asio otus																		LE			0767
*A	Short-eared Owl	Asio flammeus																		SE			0768
	Sub total																						

NIGHTJARS, SWIFTS, KINGFISHERS, BEE-EATERS AND WOODPECKERS

BOU	Species	Scientific name	Life list	2011 list	24 hr	Garden	Holiday	Jan	Feb	Mar	Apr	May	Jun	Jul	Aug	Sep	Oct	Nov	Dec	BTO	RBBP	BBRC	EU No
A	Tengmalm's Owl	Aegolius funereus																				R	0770
*A	Nightjar	Caprimulgus europaeus																		NJ			0778
B	Red-necked Nightjar	C. ruficollis																				R	0779
A	Egyptian Nightjar	C. aegyptius																				R	0781
A	Common Nighthawk	Chordeiles minor																				R	0786
A	Chimney Swift	Chaetura pelagica																				R	0790
A	Needle-tailed Swift	Hirundapus caudacutus																		NI		R	0792
*A	Swift	Apus apus																		SI			0795
A	Pallid Swift	A. pallidus																				R	0796
A	Pacific Swift	A. pacificus																				R	0797
A	Alpine Swift	A. melba																		AI			0798
A	Little Swift	A. affinis																				R	0800
*A	Kingfisher	Alcedo atthis																		KF			0831
A	Belted Kingfisher	Megaceryle alcyon																				R	0834
A	Blue-cheeked Bee-eater	Merops persicus																				R	0839
*A	Bee-eater	M. apiaster																		MZ	A		0840
A	Roller	Coracias garrulus																				R	0841
*A	Hoopoe	Upupa epops																		HP	A		0846
*A	Wryneck	Jynx torquilla																		WY	A		0848
*A	Green Woodpecker	Picus viridis																		G			0856
A	Yellow-bellied Sapsucker	Sphyrapicus varius																				R	0872
*A	Great Spotted Woodpecker	Dendrocopos major																		GS			0876
*A	Lesser Spotted Woodpecker	D. minor																		LS			0887
A	Eastern Phoebe	Sayornis phoebe																				R	0909
	Sub total																						

BOU	VIREOS, SHRIKES, CORVIDS AND 'CRESTS		Life list	2011 list	24 hr	Garden	Holiday	Jan	Feb	Mar	Apr	May	Jun	Jul	Aug	Sep	Oct	Nov	Dec				BTO	RBBP	BBRC	EU No
A	Yellow-throated Vireo	Vireo flavifrons																							R	1628
A	Philadelphia Vireo	V. philadelphicus																							R	1631
A	Red-eyed Vireo	V. olivaceus																					EV		R	1633
*A	Golden Oriole	Oriolus oriolus																					OL	A		1508
A	Brown Shrike	Lanius cristatus																							R	1513
A	Isabelline Shrike	L. isabellinus																					IL		R	1514
*A	Red-backed Shrike	L. collurio																					ED	A		1515
A	Long-tailed Shrike	L. schach																							R	1517
*A	Lesser Grey Shrike	L. minor																							R	1519
*A	Great Grey Shrike	L. excubitor																					SR	A		1520
A	Southern Grey Shrike	L. meridionalis																							R	1520
A	Woodchat Shrike	L. senator																					OO			1523
A	Masked Shrike	L. nubicus																							R	1524
*A	Chough	Pyrrhocorax pyrrhocorax																					CF	B		1559
*A	Magpie	Pica pica																					MG			1549
*A	Jay	Garrulus glandarius																					J			1539
A	Nutcracker	Nucifraga caryocatactes																					NC		R	1557
*A	Jackdaw	Corvus monedula																					JD			1560
*A	Rook	C. frugilegus																					RO			1563
*A	Carrion Crow	C. corone																					C			1567
*A	Hooded Crow	C. cornix																					RN			1567
*A	Raven	C. corax																								1572
*A	Goldcrest	Regulus regulus																					GC			1314
*A	Firecrest	R. ignicapilla																					FC	A		1315
	Sub total																									

BOU	TITS, LARKS, MARTINS AND SWALLOWS		Life list	2011 list	24 hr	Garden	Holiday	Jan	Feb	Mar	Apr	May	Jun	Jul	Aug	Sep	Oct	Nov	Dec	BTO	RBBP	BBRC	EU No
A	Penduline Tit	*Remiz pendulinus*																		DT	A		1490
*A	Blue Tit	*Cyanistes caeruleus*																		BT			1462
*A	Great Tit	*Parus major*																		GT			1464
*A	Crested Tit	*Lophophanes cristatus*																		CI	B		1454
*A	Coal Tit	*Periparus ater*																		CT			1461
*A	Willow Tit	*Poecile montana*																		WT			1442
*A	Marsh Tit	*P. palustris*																		MT			1440
*A	Bearded Tit	*Panurus biarmicus*																		BR	B		1364
A	Calandra Lark	*Melanocorypha calandra*																				R	0961
A	Bimaculated Lark	*M. bimaculata*																				R	0962
A	White-winged Lark	*M. leucoptera*																				R	0965
A	Black Lark	*M. yeltoniensis*																				R	0966
A	Short-toed Lark	*Calandrella brachydactyla*																		VL			0968
A	Lesser Short-toed Lark	*C. rufescens*																				R	0970
A	Crested Lark	*Galerida cristata*																				R	0972
*A	Wood Lark	*Lullula arborea*																		WL	B		0974
*A	Skylark	*Alauda arvensis*																		S			0976
*A	Shore Lark	*Eremophila alpestris*																		SX	A		0978
*A	Sand Martin	*Riparia riparia*																		SM			0981
A	Tree Swallow	*Tachycineta bicolor*																				R	0983
A	Purple Martin	*Progne subis*																				R	0989
A	Crag Martin	*Ptyonoprogne rupestris*																				R	0991
*A	Swallow	*Hirundo rustica*																		SL			0992
*A	House Martin	*Delichon urbicum*																		HM			1001
	Sub total																						

BOU	SWALLOWS Cont, WARBLERS		Life list	2011 list	24 hr	Garden	Holiday	Jan	Feb	Mar	Apr	May	Jun	Jul	Aug	Sep	Oct	Nov	Dec	BTO	RBBP	BBRC	EU No
A	Red-rumped Swallow	Cecropis daurica																		VR			0995
A	Cliff Swallow	Petrochelidon pyrrhonota																				R	0998
*A	Cetti's Warbler	Cettia cetti																		CW	A		1220
*A	Long-tailed Tit	Aegithalos caudatus																		LT			1437
A	Eastern Crowned Warbler	Phylloscopus coronatus																				R	12910
A	Green Warbler	P. nitidus																		NP			1293
A	Greenish Warbler	P.D485 trochiloides																		AP		R	1295
A	Arctic Warbler	P. borealis																		PA			1298
A	Pallas's Warbler	P. proregulus																					
*A	Yellow-browed Warbler	P. inornatus																		YB			1300
A	Hume's Warbler	P. humei																				R	1300
A	Radde's Warbler	P. schwarzi																					1301
A	Dusky Warbler	P. fuscatus																		UY			1303
A	Western Bonelli's Warbler	P. bonelli																		IW		R	1307
A	Eastern Bonelli's Warbler	P. orientalis																				R	1307
*A	Wood Warbler	P. sibilatrix																		WO			1308
*A	Chiffchaff	P. collybita																		CC			1311
A	Iberian Chiffchaff	P. ibericus																				R	1311
*A	Willow Warbler	P. trochilus																		WW			1312
*A	Blackcap	Sylvia atricapilla																		BC			1277
*A	Garden Warbler	S. borin																		GW			1276
A	Barred Warbler	S. nisoria																		RR			1273
*A	Lesser Whitethroat	S. curruca																		LW			1274
A	Orphean Warbler	S. hortensis																				R	1272
	Sub total																						

LOG CHARTS

BOU	WARBLERS Cont		Life list	2011 list	24 hr	Garden	Holiday	Jan	Feb	Mar	Apr	May	Jun	Jul	Aug	Sep	Oct	Nov	Dec	BTO	RBBP	BBRC	EU No
A	Asian Desert Warbler	S. nana																			A	R	1270
*A	Whitethroat	S. communis																		WH			1275
A	Spectacled Warbler	S. conspicillata																				R	1264
*A	Dartford Warbler	S. undata																		DW	B		1262
A	Marmora's Warbler	S. sarda																		MM	A	R	1261
A	Rüppell's Warbler	S. rueppelli																				R	1269
A	Subalpine Warbler	S. cantillans																			A		1265
A	Sardinian Warbler	S. melanocephala																			A	R	1267
A	Pallas's Grasshopper Warbler	Locustella certhiola																					1233
A	Lanceolated Warbler	L. lanceolata																				R	1235
*A	Grasshopper Warbler	L. naevia																		GH			1236
A	River Warbler	L. fluviatilis																		VW	A	R	1237
A	Savi's Warbler	L. luscinioides																		VI	A	R	1238
A	Eastern Olivaceous Warbler	Hippolais pallida																				R	1255
A	Booted Warbler	H. caligata																			A	R	1256
A	Sykes's Warbler	H. rama																				R	2562
A	Olive-tree Warbler	H. olivetorum																				R	12580
*A	Icterine Warbler	H. icterina																		IC	A		1259
*A	Melodious Warbler	H. polyglotta																		ME			1260
A	Aquatic Warbler	Acrocephalus paludicola																		AQ			1242
*A	Sedge Warbler	A. schoenobaenus																		SW			1243
A	Paddyfield Warbler	A. agricola																		PY		R	1247
A	Blyth's Reed Warbler	A. dumetorum																			A	R	1248
*A	Marsh Warbler	A. palustris																		MW	A		1250
	Sub total																						

83

BOU	WARBLERS Cont, NUTHATCHES, TREECREEPERS, THRUSHES		Life list	2011 list	24 hr	Garden	Holiday	Jan	Feb	Mar	Apr	May	Jun	Jul	Aug	Sep	Oct	Nov	Dec	BTO	RBBP	BBRC	EU No
*A	Reed Warbler	A. scirpaceus																		RW			1251
A	Great Reed Warbler	A. arundinaceus																		QW	A	R	1253
A	Thick-billed Warbler	A. aedon																				R	1254
A	Fan-tailed Warbler	Cisticola juncidis																				R	1226
A	Cedar Waxwing	Bombycilla cedrorum																				R	1046
*A	Waxwing	B. garrulus																		WX	A		1048
A	Wallcreeper	Tichodroma muraria																				R	1482
A	Red-breasted Nuthatch	Sitta canadensis																				R	1472
*A	Nuthatch	S. europaea																		NH			1479
*A	Treecreeper	Certhia familiaris																		TC			1486
A	Short-toed Treecreeper	C. brachydactyla																		TH	A	R	1487
*A	Wren	Troglodytes troglodytes																		WR			1066
A	Northern Mockingbird	Mimus polyglottos																				R	1067
A	Brown Thrasher	Toxostoma rufum																				R	1069
A	Grey Catbird	Dumetella carolinensis																				R	1080
*A	Starling	Sturnus vulgaris																		SG			1582
A	Rose-coloured Starling	S. roseus																		OE		R	1594
*A	Dipper	Cinclus cinclus																		DI			1050
A	White's Thrush	Zoothera dauma																				R	1170
A	Siberian Thrush	Z. sibirica																				R	1171
A	Varied Thrush	Ixoreus naevius																		VT		R	1172
A	Wood Thrush	Hylocichla mustelina																				R	1175
A	Hermit Thrush	Catharus guttatus																				R	1176
A	Swainson's Thrush	C. ustulatus																				R	1177
	Sub total																						

BOU	THRUSHES Cont, CHATS		Life list	2011 list	24 hr	Garden	Holiday	Jan	Feb	Mar	Apr	May	Jun	Jul	Aug	Sep	Oct	Nov	Dec				BTO	RBBP	BBRC	EU No
A	Grey-cheeked Thrush	C. minimus																							R	1178
A	Veery	C. fuscescens																							R	1179
*A	Ring Ouzel	Turdus torquatus																					RZ			1186
*A	Blackbird	T. merula																					B			1187
A	Eyebrowed Thrush	T. obscurus																							R	1195
A	Dusky Thrush	T. naumanni																							R	1196
A	Naumann's Thrush	T. naumanni																							R	11960
A	Black-throated Thrush	T. atrogularis																								1197
A	Red-throated Thrush	T. ruficollis																							R	11970
*A	Fieldfare	T. pilaris																					FF	A		1198
*A	Song Thrush	T. philomelos																					ST			1200
*A	Redwing	T. iliacus																					RE	A		1201
*A	Mistle Thrush	T. viscivorus																					M			1202
A	American Robin	T. migratorius																					AR		R	1203
A	Asian Brown Flycatcher	Muscicapa dauurica																								
*A	Spotted Flycatcher	M.D581 striata																								1335
A	Rufous Bush Chat	Cercotrichas galactotes																							R	1095
*A	Robin	Erithacus rubecula																					R			1099
A	Rufous-tailed Robin	Luscinia sibilans																							R	1102
A	Thrush Nightingale	L. luscinia																					FN	A		1103
*A	Nightingale	L. megarhynchos																					N			1104
A	Siberian Rubythroat	L. calliope																							R	1105
A	Bluethroat	L. svecica																					BU	A		1106
A	Siberian Blue Robin	L. cyane																							R	1112
	Sub total																								

85

BOU	CHATS, WHEATEARS, FLYCATCHERS, SPARROWS		Life list	2011 list	24 hr	Garden	Holiday	Jan	Feb	Mar	Apr	May	Jun	Jul	Aug	Sep	Oct	Nov	Dec			BTO	RBBP	BBRC	EU No
A	Red-flanked Bluetail	Tarsiger cyanurus																						R	1113
A	White-throated Robin	Irania gutturalis																						R	1117
*A	Black Redstart	Phoenicurus ochruros																				BX	A		1121
*A	Redstart	P. phoenicurus																				RT			1122
A	Moussier's Redstart	P. moussieri																						R	1127
*A	Whinchat	Saxicola rubetra																				WC			1137
*A	Stonechat	S. torquatus																				SC			1139
A	Isabelline Wheatear	Oenanthe isabellina																						R	1144
*A	Wheatear	O. oenanthe																				W			1146
A	Pied Wheatear	O. pleschanka																				PI		R	1147
A	Black-eared Wheatear	O. hispanica																						R	1148
A	Desert Wheatear	O. deserti																						R	1149
A	White-crowned Black Wheatear	O. leucopyga																						R	1157
A	Rock Thrush	Monticola saxatilis																				OH		R	1162
A	Blue Rock Thrush	M. solitarius																						R	1166
*A	Red-breasted Flycatcher	Ficedula parva																				FY			1343
A	Taiga Flycatcher	F. albicilla																						R	1343
A	Collared Flycatcher	F. albicollis																						R	1348
*A	Pied Flycatcher	F. hypoleuca																				PF			1349
*A	Dunnock	Prunella modularis																				D			1084
A	Alpine Accentor	P. collaris																						R	1094
*A	House Sparrow	Passer domesticus																				HS			1591
A	Spanish Sparrow	P. hispaniolensis																						R	1592
*A	Tree Sparrow	P. montanus																				TS			1598
	Sub total																								

WAGTAILS, PIPITS AND FINCHES

BOU	Name	Scientific	Life list	2011 list	24 hr	Garden	Holiday	Jan	Feb	Mar	Apr	May	Jun	Jul	Aug	Sep	Oct	Nov	Dec	BTO	RBBP	BBRC	EU No
A	Rock Sparrow	Petronia petronia																				R	1604
*A	Yellow Wagtail	Motacilla flava																		YW			1017
A	Citrine Wagtail	M. citreola																			A	R	1018
*A	Grey Wagtail	M. cinerea																		GL			1019
*A	Pied Wagtail	M. alba																		PW			1020
A	Richard's Pipit	Anthus richardi																		PR			1002
A	Blyth's Pipit	A. godlewskii																				R	1004
A	Tawny Pipit	A. campestris																		TI			1005
A	Olive-backed Pipit	A. hodgsoni																		OV			1008
*A	Tree Pipit	A. trivialis																		TP			1009
A	Pechora Pipit	A. gustavi																				R	1010
*A	Meadow Pipit	A. pratensis																		MP			1011
A	Red-throated Pipit	A. cervinus																		VP			1012
*A	Rock Pipit	A. petrosus																		RC			1014
*A	Water Pipit	A. spinoletta																		WI			1014
A	Buff-bellied Pipit	A. rubescens																				R	1014
*A	Chaffinch	Fringilla coelebs																		CH			1636
*A	Brambling	F. montifringilla																		BL	A		1638
*A	Serin	Serinus serinus																		NS	A		1640
*A	Greenfinch	Carduelis chloris																		GR			1649
A	Citril Finch	C. citrinella																					
*A	Goldfinch	C. carduelis																		GO			1653
*A	Siskin	C. spinus																		SK			1654
*A	Linnet	C. cannabina																		LI			1660
	Sub total																						

87

BOU	FINCHES, NEW WORLD WARBLERS		Life list	2011 list	24 hr	Garden	Holiday	Jan	Feb	Mar	Apr	May	Jun	Jul	Aug	Sep	Oct	Nov	Dec	BTO	RBBP	BBRC	EU No
*A	Twite	C. flavirostris																	TW			1662
*A	Lesser Redpoll	C. cabaret																	LR			1663
*A	Mealy Redpoll	C. flammea																		A		1663
A	Arctic Redpoll	C. hornemanni																	AL			1664
*A	Two-barred Crossbill	Loxia leucoptera																	PD		R	1665
*A	Common Crossbill	L. curvirostra																	CR			1666
*A	Scottish Crossbill	L. scotica																	CY	A		1667
*A	Parrot Crossbill	L. pytyopsittacus																	PC	A		1668
A	Trumpeter Finch	Bucanetes githagineus																			R	1676
*A	Common Rosefinch	Carpodacus erythrinus																	SQ	A		1679
A	Pine Grosbeak	Pinicola enucleator																			R	1699
*A	Bullfinch	Pyrrhula pyrrhula																	BF			1710
*A	Hawfinch	Coccothraustes coccothraustes																	HF	A	R	1717
A	Evening Grosbeak	Hesperiphona vespertina																			R	1718
*A	Snow Bunting	Plectrophenax nivalis																	SB	A		1850
A	Lapland Bunting	Calcarius lapponicus																	LA	A		1847
A	Summer Tanager	Piranga rubra																			R	1786
A	Scarlet Tanager	P. olivacea																			R	1788
A	Rose-breasted Grosbeak	Pheucticus ludovicianus																			R	1887
A	Indigo Bunting	Passerina cyanea																			R	1892
A	Eastern Towhee	Pipilo erythrophthalmus																			R	1798
A	Lark Sparrow	Chondestes grammacus																			R	1824
A	Savannah Sparrow	Passerculus sandwichensis																			R	1826
A	Song Sparrow	Melospiza melodia																			R	1835
	Sub total																					

BOU	NEW WORLD WARBLERS, SPARROWS, BUNTINGS		Life list	2011 list	24 hr	Garden	Holiday	Jan	Feb	Mar	Apr	May	Jun	Jul	Aug	Sep	Oct	Nov	Dec					BTO	RBBP	BBRC	EU No
A	White-crowned Sparrow	Zonotrichia leucophrys																								R	1839
A	White-throated Sparrow	Z. albicollis																								R	1840
A	Dark-eyed Junco	Junco hyemalis																						JU		R	1842
A	Black-faced Bunting	Emberiza spodocephala																								R	1853
A	Pine Bunting	E. leucocephalos																						EL			1856
*A	Yellowhammer	E. citrinella																						Y			1857
*A	Cirl Bunting	E. cirlus																						CL	A		1958
A	Rock Bunting	E. cia																								R	1860
A	Ortolan Bunting	E. hortulana																						OB			1866
A	Cretzschmar's Bunting	E. caesia																								R	1868
A	Yellow-browed Bunting	E. chrysophrys																								R	1871
A	Rustic Bunting	E. rustica																									1873
A	Chestnut-eared Bunting	E. fucata																								R	1869
A	Little Bunting	E. pusilla																						LI			1874
A	Yellow-breasted Bunting	E. aureola																							A	R	1876
*A	Reed Bunting	E. schoeniclus																						RB			1877
A	Pallas's Reed Bunting	E. pallasi																								R	1878
A	Black-headed Bunting	E. melanocephala																								R	1881
*A	Corn Bunting	E. calandra																						CB			1882
A	Bobolink	Dolichonyx oryzivorus																								R	1897
A	Brown-headed Cowbird	Molothrus ater																								R	1899
A	Baltimore Oriole	Icterus galbula																								R	1918
A	Black-and-white Warbler	Mniotilta varia																								R	1720
A	Golden-winged Warbler	Vermivora chrysoptera																								R	1722
	Sub total																										

89

WARBLERS Cont

BOU		Scientific	Life list	2011 list	24 hr	Garden	Holiday	Jan	Feb	Mar	Apr	May	Jun	Jul	Aug	Sep	Oct	Nov	Dec	BTO	RBBP	BBRC	EU No
A	Tennessee Warbler	*V. peregrina*																				R	1724
A	Northern Parula	*Parula americana*																				R	1732
A	Yellow Warbler	*Dendroica petechia*																				R	1733
A	Chestnut-sided Warbler	*D. pensylvanica*																				R	1734
A	Blackburnian Warbler	*D. fusca*																				R	1747
A	Cape May Warbler	*D. tigrina*																				R	1749
A	Magnolia Warbler	*D. magnolia*																				R	1750
A	Yellow-rumped Warbler	*D. coronata*																				R	1751
A	Blackpoll Warbler	*D. striata*																				R	1753
A	Bay-breasted Warbler	*D. castanea*																				R	1754
A	American Redstart	*Setophaga ruticilla*																		AD		R	1755
A	Ovenbird	*Seiurus aurocapilla*																				R	1756
A	Northern Waterthrush	*S. noveboracensis*																				R	1757
A	Common Yellowthroat	*Geothlypis trichas*																				R	1762
A	Hooded Warbler	*Wilsonia citrina*																				R	1771
A	Wilson's Warbler	*W. pusilla*																				R	1772
	Sub total																						

BOU	CATEGORY D & E SPECIES, PLUS SELECTED EUROPEAN SPECIES		Life list	2011 list	24 hr	Garden	Holiday	Jan	Feb	Mar	Apr	May	Jun	Jul	Aug	Sep	Oct	Nov	Dec			BTO	RBBP	BBRC	EU No
D	Ross's Goose	Anas Vossii																							
D	Falcated Duck	A. falcata																				FT		R	0181
D	Baikal Teal	A. formosa																				IK		R	0183
D	Marbled Duck	Marmaronetta angustirostris																						R	0195
EU	White-headed Duck	O. Leucocephala																				WQ			0226
EU	Rock Partridge	Alectoris graeca																							0357
EU	Barbary Partridge	A. barbara																							0359
EU	Pygmy Cormorant	P. pygmeus																							0082
D	Great White Pelican	Pelecanus onocrotalus																				YP		R	0088
EU	Dalmatian Pelican	P. crispus																							0089
D	Greater Flamingo	Phoenicopterus roseus																				FL		R	0147
EU	Black-winged Kite	Elanus caeruleus																							0235
D	Bald Eagle	H. leucocephalus																						R	0244
EU	Lammergeier	Gypaetus barbatus																							0246
D	Black (Monk) Vulture	Aegypius monachus																						R	0255
EU	Levant Sparrowhawk	A. brevipes																							0273
EU	Long-legged Buzzard	B. rufinus																							0288
EU	Lesser Spotted Eagle	Aquila pomarina																							0292
EU	Imperial Eagle	A. heliaca																							0295
EU	Booted Eagle	Hieraaetus pennatus																							0298
EU	Bonelli's Eagle	H. fasciatus																							0299
EU	Lanner Falcon	Falco biarmicus																				FB			0314
D	Saker Falcon	F. cherrug																				JF		R	0316
EU	Andalusian Hemipode	Turnix sylvatica																							0400
	Sub total																								

BOU	CATEGORY D & E SPECIES, PLUS SELECTED EUROPEAN SPECIES	Life list	2011 list	24 hr	Garden	Holiday	Jan	Feb	Mar	Apr	May	Jun	Jul	Aug	Sep	Oct	Nov	Dec					BTO	RBBP	BBRC	EU No
EU	Purple (Swamp-hen) Gallinule *Porphyrio porphyrio*																									0427
EL	Crested Coot *F. cristata*																									0431
FA	Greater Sand Plover *C. leschenaultii*																						DP		R	0479
EU	Spur-winged Plover *Hoplopterus spinosus*																						UW			0487
EU	Black-bellied Sandgrouse *Pterocles orientalis*																									0661
EU	Pin-tailed Sandgrouse *P. alchata*																									0662
EU	(Eurasian) Eagle Owl *Bubo bubo*																						EO	bD		0744
EU	Pygmy Owl *Glaucidium passerinum*																									0751
EU	Ural Owl *S. uralensis*																									0765
EU	Great Grey Owl *S. nebulosa*																									0766
EL	White-rumped Swift *A. melba*																									0799
EU	Grey-headed Woodpecker *Picus canus*																									0855
EU	Black Woodpecker *Dryocopus martius*																									0863
EU	Syrian Woodpecker *D. syriacus*																									0878
EU	Middle Spotted Woodpecker *D. medius*																									0883
EU	White-backed Woodpecker *D. leucotos*																									0884
EU	Three-toed Woodpecker *Picoides tridactylus*																									0898
EU	Dupont's Lark *Chersophilus duponti*																									0959
EU	Thekla Lark *G. theklae*																									0973
EU	Black Wheatear *O. Leucura*																								R	1158
IA	Eyebrowed Thrush *T. obscurus*																								R	1195
EU	Olive-tree Warbler *H. olivetorum*																									1258
EU	Cyprus Warbler *S. melanothorax*																									1268
D	Mugimaki Flycatcher *F. mugimaki*																								R	1344
	Sub total																									

CATEGORY D & E SPECIES, PLUS SELECTED EUROPEAN SPECIES

BOU	Species	Scientific name	Life list	2011 list	24 hr	Garden	Holiday	Jan	Feb	Mar	Apr	May	Jun	Jul	Aug	Sep	Oct	Nov	Dec	BTO	RBBP	BBRC	EU No
EU	Semi-collared Flycatcher	F. semitorquata																					1347
EU	Sombre Tit	P. lugubris																					1441
EU	Siberian Tit	P. cinctus																					1448
EU	Krüper's Nuthatch	Sitta krueperi																					1469
EU	Corsican Nuthatch	S. whiteheadi																					1470
EU	Rock Nuthatch	S. neumayer																					1481
EU	Masked Shrike	L. nubicus																					1524
EU	Siberian Jay	Perisoreus infaustus																					1543
EU	Azure-winged Magpie	Cyanopica cyana																					1547
EU	Alpine Chough	Pyrrhocorax graculus																					1558
D	Daurian Starling	Sturnus sturninus																				R	1579
EU	Spotless Starling	S. unicolor																					1583
D	(White-winged) Snow Finch	Montifringilla nivalis																				R	1611
D	Palm Warbler	D. palmarum																				R	1752
D	Yellow-headed Blackbird	Xanthocephalus xanthocephalus																					1911
EU	Cinereous Bunting	E. cineracea																					1865
D	Chestnut Bunting	E. rutila																				R	1875
D	Red-headed Bunting	E. bruniceps																					1880
D	Blue Grosbeak	Guiraca caerulea																				R	1891
	Sub total																						

BRITISH DRAGONFLY LIST

SPECIES	2011 list	Life list
DAMSELFLIES		
Calopterygidae (Demoiselles)		
Beautiful Demoiselle		
Banded Demoiselle		
Lestidae (Emerald damselflies)		
Emerald Damselfly		
Scarce Emerald Damselfly		
Southern Emerald Damselfly		
Willow Emerald Damselfly		
Winter Damselfly		
Platycnemididae (White-legged damselflies)		
White-legged Damselfly		
Coenagrionidae (Blue, blue-tailed & red damselflies)		
Large Red Damselfly		
Red-eyed Damselfly		
Small Red Damselfly		
Southern Damselfly		
Northern Damselfly		
Irish Damselfly		
Azure Damselfly		
Variable Damselfly		
Common Blue Damselfly		
Scarce Blue-tailed Damselfly		
Blue-tailed Damselfly		
Small Red-eyed Damselfly		
DRAGONFLIES		
Aeshnidae (Hawkers and Emperors)		
Azure Hawker		
Common Hawker		
Migrant Hawker		
Southern Hawker		
Brown Hawker		
Southern Migrant Hawker		

SPECIES	2011 list	Life list
Norfolk Hawker		
Emperor		
Lesser Emperor		
Green Darner		
Vagrant Emperor		
Hairy Dragonfly		
Gomphidae (Club-tailed Dragonflies)		
Common Club-tail		
Cordulegastridae (Golden-ringed Dragonflies)		
Golden-ringed Dragonfly		
Corduliidae (Emerald dragonflies)		
Downy Emerald		
Brilliant Emerald		
Northern Emerald		
Libellulidae (Chasers, Skimmers and Darters)		
Four-spotted Chaser		
Scarce Chaser		
Broad-bodied Chaser		
Black-tailed Skimmer		
Keeled Skimmer		
Common Darter		
Highland Darter		
Red-veined Darter		
Yellow-winged Darter		
Ruddy Darter		
Black Darter		
Vagrant Darter		
Banded Darter		
Scarlet Darter		
Wandering Glider		
White-faced Darter		
TOTAL		

BRITISH BUTTERFLY LIST

SPECIES	2011 list	Life list
Hesperiidae - Skippers		
Chequered Skipper		
Dingy Skipper		
Grizzled Skipper		
Lulworth Skipper		
Essex Skipper		
Small Skipper		
Silver-spotted Skipper		
Large Skipper		
Papilionidae		
Swallowtail		
Pieridae - The Whites		
Wood White		
Clouded Yellow		
Brimstone		
Large White		
Small White		
Green-veined White		
Orange Tip		
Lycaenidae - Hairstreaks, Coppers and Blues		
Green Hairstreak		
Brown Hairstreak		
Purple Hairstreak		
White-letter Hairstreak		
Black Hairstreak		
Small Copper		
Small Blue		
Silver-studded Blue		
Northern Brown Argus		
Brown Argus		
Common Blue		
Chalkhill Blue		
Adonis Blue		
Holly Blue		

SPECIES	2011 list	Life list
Large Blue		
Duke of Burgundy		
Nymphalidae - The Nymphalids		
White Admiral		
Purple Emperor		
Painted Lady		
Small Tortoiseshell		
Red Admiral		
Peacock		
Comma		
Nymphalidae - The Fritillaries		
Small Pearl-bordered Fritillary		
Pearl-bordered Fritillary		
High Brown Fritillary		
Dark Green Fritillary		
Silver-washed Fritillary		
Marsh Fritillary		
Glanville Fritillary		
Heath Fritillary		
Nymphalidae - The Browns		
Speckled Wood		
Wall		
Mountain Ringlet		
Scotch Argus		
Marbled White		
Grayling		
Gate Keeper		
Meadow Brown		
Ringlet		
Small Heath		
Large Heath		
TOTAL		

LOG CHARTS

95

ID Insights Pocket Cards

Want practical identification help when you are in the field? Forget those heavyweight fieldguides — join the thousands of wildlife watchers who have discovered our postcard-size plates are perfect for solving those tricky ID problems. Lightweight and hard-wearing, each set provides the essential clues you need.

£5.95 per set or any three sets for just £15

SET 4

ID Insights Pocket Cards
Identify birds in your garden

■ Superb artwork for 65 species

■ Key ID tips for each species

■ All on 11 easy-to-carry cards

British Garden Birds

We are delighted to release our latest set covering 65 species most likely to be seen in and around gardens.

Beautifully illustrated by artists Dan and Rosie Powell, with useful ID tips on 11 cards. This set is perfect for children, 'armchair' birdwatchers and those new to birdwatching and is an exciting addition to our range.

Available from Buckingham Press, 55 Thorpe Park Road, Peterborough PE3 6LJ. 01733 561 739.
e-mail: admin@buckinghampress.com
Or order online at:
www.buckinghampress.co.uk

British Birds – 113 species of common but tricky bird species, illustrated by top artist Dave Nurney with ID advice from Dominic Couzens. Ten postcards printed on heavyweight coated card – slip them into your jacket pocket and you'll always have them when needed. **SET 1**

Butterflies of Great Britain – a set of 12 cards by Rosemary Powell, featuring 58 resident and commonly occurring migrant species. Features male and female, upper and lower wing patterns. Also information about habitats, distribution and main flight times. **SET 2**

British Dragonflies - Features 51 species of dragonflies and damselflies with artwork and ID advice from talented artist Dan Powell. £5.95 for a pack of 13 hard-wearing postcard-sized cards.

DIRECTORY OF ARTISTS, PHOTOGRAPHERS AND LECTURERS

Gehan da Silva Wijeyeratne

Sri Lanka, with its many colourful species such as the Black-hooded Oriole, is a great birding destination and is featured in lectures by David Cromack and Stephen Lovell.

DIRECTORY OF
WILDLIFE ART GALLERIES

BIRDSBIRDSBIRDS GALLERY

Paul and Sue Cumberland opened Birds Birds Birds in June 2001. Now it is becoming one of the nation's leading bird art galleries. A steady increase in sales has encouraged professional wildlife artists to join the roster. Prints are now being produced and published in-house, using the giclee system. The gallery exhibits at the British Birdfair and various game fairs and county shows.
Address: 4, Limes Place, Preston St, Faversham, Kent ME13 8PQ; 01795 532 370;
email: birdsbirdsbirds@birdsbirdsbirds.co.uk
www.birdsbirdsbirds.co.uk

BIRDSCAPES GALLERY

Offers top quality bird art all year round, plus landscapes and other wildlife originals, sculptures, prints, wildlife art books and cards. More than 30 regular artists, including SWLA members, are represented, with new exhibitions each month.
Located next to the Cley Spy optical dealership and offering the opportunity of exploring the Farmland Bird Project on the Bayfield Estate.
Opening times: Mon-Sat, (10am-5pm), Sunday, (10am-4pm). The gallery may be closed for part of the day before a new exhibition.
Address: The BIRDscapes Gallery, Manor Farm Barns, Glandford, Holt, Norfolk. NR25 7JP. 01263 741 742. (Follow the brown signs to Cley Spy from Blakeney Church).

NATURE IN ART

The world's first museum dedicated exclusively to art inspired by nature. The collection spans 1,500 years, covers 60 countries and includes work by Tunnicliffe, Harrison, Thorburn, Scott and other bird artists. See work being created by artists in residence (see website for dates), plus a vibrant exhibitions programme. Sculpture garden, coffee shop, gift shop and children's activity areas.
Opening times: 10am-5pm (Tuesday to Sunday and bank holidays).
Address: Wallsworth Hall, Twigworth, Gloucester GL2 9PA (two miles N of city on A38). 01452 731 422. e-mail: enquiries@nature-in-art.org.uk
www.nature-in-art.org.uk

THE WILDLIFE ART GALLERY

Opened in 1988 as a specialist in 20th Century and contemporary wildlife art. It exhibits work by many of the leading European wildlife artists, both painters and sculptors, and has published several wildlife books.
Opening times: Mon-Sat (10am-4.30pm) and Sun (2pm-4.30pm).
Address: 97 High Street, Lavenham, Suffolk CO10 9PZ; 01787 248 562; (Fax) 01787 247 356.
E-mail: wildlifeartgallery@btinternet.com
www.wildlifeartgallery.com

DIRECTORY OF
WILDLIFE ARTISTS

APLIN, Roy

Born in Swanage, Isle of Purbeck now part of the Jurassic coastline. Lives in Wareham with easy access to Arne RSPB nature reserve — Dartford Warbler habitat. Self-taught artist, carpenter/joiner by trade, also involved in aviculture since the age of 9.
Exhibitions for 2011: Purbeck art weeks - end of May to the first week of June, British Birdwatching Fair, Dorset Coppice Group country events.
Artwork for sale: Original watercolours plus goache paintings, limited edition prints, pencil sketches, cards.
Address: 11 Brixeys Lane, Wareham, Dorset, BH20 4HL; 01929 553 742; www.royaplin.com
e-mail: roy.aplin@ukonline.co.uk

DOODY, Dee

Dee is a South African born naturalist and wildlife artist. He is artist in residence at Gigrin Farm Kite feeding centre. Dee also personally looks after 90 pairs of Red Kites! He paints British and world birds of prey, (Red Kite a speciality), as well as powerful, large scale portraits on canvas of big cats — snow leopards, tigers, African wildlife.

Formats: Oils or acrylic on canvas plus original pencil sketches.

Artwork for sale: Dee's work can be seen in his marquee (mainly weekends), on his website or at various fine art galleries around Wales and the borders.

Address: The Studio, 2 Fan Terrace, Fan, Llanidloes, Powys, SY18 6NW. (Day) 01686 413 819; (eve) 01686 412 163; e-mail: dee.doody@virgin.net www.deedoodywildlife.co.uk

GALE, John

Bird illustrator and wildlife artist, concentrating on the Tropics and Antarctica.

Formats: Oil paintings and bird illustration work.

Exhibitions for 2011: 'Artists for Albatrosses', a major exhibition at the Air Gallery, London, October 2011, based on a recent expedition to South Georgia. Raising awareness and funds for albatross and petrel conservation.

Artwork for sale: Oil paintings and illustrations, as well as limited edition prints.

Address: 6 Underdown, Kennford, Exeter, Devon EX6 7YB; 01392 832 026. e-mail: johngale@birdart.fsnet.co.uk www.galleryofbirds.co.uk

GARNER (FRSA), Jackie

Professional wildlife artist specialising in original paintings based on field sketches. Current projects: illustrations for Snowy Owls monograph, illustrations for research projects on Egyptian wildlife. *Bird Art & Photography* contributor. See website for details.

Formats: Acrylics, watercolours, sketches, illustrations.

Exhibitions for 2011: Open Studio (June), Bird Fair, NEWA, SWLA, Nature in Art Residency, Art in Action.

Artwork for sale: Originals, limited edition prints, cards, puzzles. Commissions accepted.

Address: The Old Cider House Studio, Humphries End, Randwick, Stroud, Glos GL6 6EW; 01453 847 420; (M)07800 804 847. e-mail: artist@jackiegarner.co.uk www.jackiegarner.co.uk

GREENHALF, Robert

Fulltime painter and printmaker. Member of SWLA. Work features in many books including *Modern Wildlife Painting* (Pica Press 1998), Artists for Nature Foundation books on Poland and Extremadura and *Towards the Sea* (Pica Press 1999) — first solo book.

Formats: Watercolours, oils and woodcuts, sold mainly through galleries but some commissions undertaken.

Exhibitions for 2011: SWLA (Mall Galleries, Sept 2011).

Artwork for sale: Watercolours, oils and woodcuts, available through the website.

Address: Romney House, Saltbarn Lane, Playden, Rye, East Sussex, TN31 7PH; 01797 222 381. e-mail: robertgreenhalf@googlemail.com www.robertgreenhalf.co.uk

GRIFFITHS, Ian 'Griff'

Birds and their habitat is the main subject matter for Griff's paintings. Having lived in different parts of the UK and travelled widely, he has a wealth of field experience to draw upon. He also supports the World Parrot Trust by raising funds for conservation and education projects worldwide.

Formats: Acrylics, oils and watercolours.

Exhibitions for 2011: WWT Slimbridge Nov 2010-5th Jan 2011. See website for other exhibitions in 2011.

Artwork for sale: Commissions considered.

Address: Griff's wildlife studio, Creftow, 6 Church Street, Helston, Cornwall TR13 8TG; 07971 678 464; e-mail: mail@artbygriff.com www.artbygriff.com

LEAHY, Ernest

Original watercolours and drawings of Western Palearctic birds, wildlife and country scenes. Also paints British mammals and butterflies. Illustrations for many publications including Poysers. Wide range of framed and unframed originals available. Commissions accepted and enquiries welcome. See website for available artwork.

Formats: E-mail for details of current work available and for quotations on commissioned work.

Exhibitions for 2011: Email for details of pre-Christmas exhibitions.

Artwork for sale: See www.flickr.com/photos/ernsbirdart for latest work.

Address: 32 Ben Austins, Redbourn, Herts, AL3 7DR; 01582 793 144. e-mail: ernest.leahy@ntlworld.com www.flickr.com/photos/ernsbirdart

ART/PHOTOGRAPHY/LECTURERS

99

MILLER, David

David lives and works in the heart of west Wales in a wooded valley with the dramatic Pembrokeshire coastline on his doorstep. Well known for his underwater paintings of game, sea and coarse fish, David also specialises in sea-birds and waders and regularly exhibits at the British Birdfair.

Formats: Oils.

Exhibitions for 2011: Wildlife & Sporting Art Exhibitions at the Jerram Gallery (January) & the Wykeham Gallery, Stockbridge (26th Feb-12th March). One-man show at the BIRDscapes Gallery, Easter 2011, Birdfair 19th-21st August.

Artwork for sale: Original oils and prints of British wildlife, fish and birds.

Address: Nyth-Gwdi-Hw, New Mill, St Clears, Carmarthenshire SA33 4HY; 01994 453 545.

e-mail: david@davidmillerart.co.uk

www.davidmillerart.co.uk

POMROY, Jonathan

Works in watercolour and oils, always from sketches, made on trips across the British Isles, most recently to the Isles of Scilly, Anglesey and Snowdonia, North West Scotland, Yorkshire Dales and coast and Slimbridge as well as around home in by the North York Moors. Work always on show at BIRDscapes, Cley, Norfolk, Leverton Framers near Hungerford, Berkshire, The Wykeham Gallery, Stockbridge, Herriot Gallery, Hawes and at home in Ampleforth.

Exhibitions for 2011: Wildlife and Sporting Art, The Wykeham Gallery at Stockbridge, 27th Feb-12th Mar, Annual Summer Exhibition at The West Barn, Bradford on Avon, 23rd- 24th July, BIRDscapes Gallery Norfolk, August, Leverton Framers, Hungerford 7th- 9th October. See website for further details of these and other exhibitions. New website with blog in 2011.

Artwork for sale: Chiefly selling original watercolours and oils at one man exhibitions and from website.

Address: Swift House, Back Lane, Ampleforth, North Yorkshire YO62 4DE; 01439 788 014

e-mail: jonathan@pomroy.plus.com

www.jonathanpomroy.co.uk

ROSE, Chris

Originals in oils and acrylics of birds and animals in landscapes. Particular interest in painting water and its myriad effects. Limited edition reproductions available. Book; *In a*

Natural Light - the Wildlife Art of Chris Rose publised 2005. Illustrated many books including *Grebes of the World* (publ.2002) and *Handbook to the Birds of the World*.

Exhibitions for 2011: 'Artists for Albatrosses', first two weeks October 2011, The Air Gallery, Dover Street, London — a two-man show of drawings and paintings from South Georgia and the Southern Ocean with fellow artist John Gale, supporting the RSPB's 'Save the Albatross Campaign'.

Artwork for sale: Original drawings and paintings, linocuts, illustrations, limited edition reproductions, postcards.

Address: 6 Whitelee Cottages, Newtown St Boswells, Melrose, Scotland TD6 0SH; (Tel) 01835 822 547;

e-mail: chris@chrisrose-artist.co.uk

www.chrisrose-artist.co.uk

THRELFALL, John

Member of the Society of Wildlife Artists. Swarovski/*Birdwatch* Bird Artist of the Year 2007. Award winner at the NEWA 2001, 2004, 2006 exhibitions. BIRDscapes Gallery award 2007.

Formats: Paintings in acrylic or pastel.

Exhibitions for 2011: Slimbridge WWT March 6-May 8; Spring Fling Open Studios May 28-30 Rockcliffe, Dalbeattie; British Birdfair, Rutland August 19-21; BIRDscapes Gallery, Norfolk November 6.

Artwork for sale: Contact artist.

Address: Saltflats Cottage, Rockcliffe, Dalbeattie,Kirkcudbrightshire DG5 4QQ; 01556 630 262. www.johnthrelfall.co.uk

WARREN, Michael

Member of Society of Wildlife Artists (treasurer). President of Nottinghamshire Birdwatchers..

Exhibitions for 2011: WWT Slimbridge in May, Rutland Birdfair in August and Society of Wildlife Artists in October. See website for details.

Artwork for sale: Original watercolour paintings of birds, all based on field observations. Books, calendars and cards. Commissions welcomed.

Address: The Laurels, The Green, Winthorpe, Nottinghamshire, NG24 2NR; 01636 673 554.

e-mail: mike.warren@tiscali.co.uk

www.mikewarren.co.uk

WOOLF, Colin

Beautiful original watercolour paintings. The atmosphere of a landscape and the character of his subject are his hallmark, also the pure watercolour technique that imparts a softness to the natural subjects he paints. Owls, birds of prey and ducks are specialities. Wide range of limited edition prints and greetings cards, special commissions also accepted.

Formats: Original paintings, limited edition prints and greetings cards.

Exhibitions for 2011: Gardening Scotland, Scottish Game Fair, CLA Game Fair at Blenheim Palace, Ayr Flower Show.

Artwork for sale: Please ring for personal viewing or visit website.

Address: Ardbeg, 2 Blairhill View, Blackridge, West Lothian, EH48 3TR; 01501 751 796.

E-mail: colin@wildart.co.uk

www.wildart.co.uk

DIRECTORY OF WILDLIFE PHOTOGRAPHERS

BASTON, Bill

Photographer, lecturer.

Subjects: East Anglian rarities and common birds, Mediterranean birds and landscapes, UK wildlife and landscapes, Northern Greece, Spain, western Turkey, Goa. General wildlife photography, The Gambia, Northern India (birds and tigers).

Products and services: Prints, slides, digital, mounted/unmounted.

Address: 86 George Street, Hadleigh, Ipswich, IP7 5BU; 01473 827 062.

e-mail: billbaston@btinternet.com

www.billbaston.com

BATES, Tony

Photographer and lecturer.

Subjects: Mainly British wildlife, landscapes and astro landscapes.

Products and services: Prints (mounted or framed), original handmade photo greetings cards.

Address: 22 Fir Avenue, Bourne, Lincs, PE10 9RY; 01778 425137;

e-mail: tonybatesphotos@live.co.uk

www.tonybates-outside-in.co.uk

BEJARANO, Santiago

An Ecuadorean naturalist and wildlife photographer who worked in the Galapagos for almost two decades, with a great depth of knowledge and unique insight into these remarkable islands and their wildlife.

Subjects: Flora and fauna of Galapagos Islands and birds of Ecuador.

Products and services: Prints and posters of the wildlife of the Galapagos Islands and birds of Ecuador. Introductory classes to wildlife photography, including digital and basic Photoshop® techniques.

Address: 25 Trinity Lane, Beverley, East Yorkshire HU17 0DY; 01482 872 716.

e-mail: info@thinkgalapagos.com

www.thinkgalapagos.com

BELL, Graham

Professional ornithologist, photographer, author, cruise lecturer worldwide.

Subjects: Birds, animals, flowers and landscapes, all seven continents, from Arctic to Antarctic.

Products and services: Original slides for sale, £2 each. Lecture: 'Taking Better Photos'.

Address: Ros View, South Yearle, Wooler, Northumberland, NE71 6RB; 01668 281 310.

e-mail: seabirdsdgb@hotmail.com

BIRDS EYE VIEW PHOTOS

Company set up by James Bird, photographer, lecturer and former RSPB Local Group leader. Organiser of East African photo safari trips as well as South African trips into the Kruger for disabled travelers in adapted vehicles: for more info visit

www.epic-enabled.com or call.

Subjects: 14 plus slide talks and digital presentations on wildlife and worldwide travel, having spent 23 years living abroad.

Products for sale: Prints, postcards and mouse

ART/PHOTOGRAPHY/LECTURERS

mats plus free RSPB magazines and information leaflets given out.
Address: Six Valentine Gardens, Kimbolton, Huntingdon, Cambridgeshire PE28 0HX;Tel/fax: 01480 861 955; (M) 07914 633 355.
e-mail: jamesbird007@yahoo.co.uk or birdseyeviewphotos@yahoo.co.uk

BOULTON, David
Professional nature photographer and lecturer.
Subjects: All types of flora and fauna including wild flowers, dragonflies, butterflies, fungi, trees, birds and animals and landscape photography (Norfolk and the Broads, Peak District, Yorkshire Dales and Lake District).
Products and services:17 talks (audio/visual presentations with relaxing music and sounds of nature). Photographic workshops, greetings cards, bookmarks and prints also available.
Address:1 Mantle Close, Sprowston, Norwich, Norfolk NR7 8LD: 01603 415 610.
e-mail: dbp@ownersmail.co.uk
www.davidboulton.co.uk

BROADBENT, David
Professional photographer.
Subjects: UK birds and wild places.
Products and services: All new website features a fully searchable picture library of UK wildlife and landscapes to the editorial market, lectures and photo training days, print sales and gallery art prints.
Contact: 07771 664 973.
e-mail: info@davidbroadbent.com
www.davidbroadbent.com

BROOKS, Richard
Wildlife photographer, writer, lecturer.
Subjects: Owls (Barn especially), raptors, Kingfisher and a variety of European birds (Lesvos especially) and landscapes. Limited edition calendars available.
Products and services: Mounted and unmounted computer prints (6x4 - A3+ size), framed pictures, A5 greetings cards,surplus slides for sale.
Address: 24 Croxton Hamlet, Fulmodeston, Fakenham, Norfolk, NR21 0NP; 01328 878632.
e-mail: email@richard-brooks.co.uk
www.richard-brooks.co.uk

BUCKINGHAM, John
Worldwide bird and wildlife photographer
Subjects: Huge range of birds, botany and

wildlife in UK and Europe, plus great coverage from Africa, Americas, Australia and worldwide.
Products and services: Original slides for lectures and personal use.
Address: 3 Cardinal Close, Tonbridge, Kent, TN9 2EN; (Tel/fax) 01732 354 970.
e-mail: john@buckingham7836.freeserve.co.uk

COSTER, Bill
Professional wildlife photographer, writer and photographic tour leader, author of *Creative Bird Photography*.
Subjects: Wildlife and landscape images from around the world.
Products and services: Images for publication, prints for sale. See website for details. Stunning new digital shows (see Directory of Lecturers).
Address: 17 Elm Road, South Woodham Ferrers, Chelmsford, Essex CM3 5QB; 01245 320 066.
e-mail: billcoster@hotmail.com
www.billcoster.com

DENNING, Paul
Wildlife photographer, lecturer.
Subjects: Birds, mammals, reptiles, butterflies and plants from UK, Europe, Canaries, North and Central America.
Products and services: 35mm transparencies and digital images.
Address: 17 Maes Maelwg, Beddau, Pontypridd, CF38 2LD; (H) 01443 202 607; (W) 02920 6732 43; e-mail: pgdenning.naturepics@virgin.net

DUGGAN, Glenn
Specialist in tropical birding
Subjects: Tropical birds, Trogons, Tanagers, Birds of Paradise.
Address: 25 Hampton Grove, Fareham, Hampshire, PO15 5NL; 01329 845 976, (M) 07771 605 320; e-mail: glenn.m.duggan@ntlworld.com
www.birdlectures.com

LANE, Mike
Wildlife photographer and lecturer.
Subjects: Birds and wildlife from around the world, also landscapes and the environment.
Products and services: Website with instantly downloadable online pictures. Talks and workshops.
Address: 5 Paxford Close, Church Hill North, Redditch, Worcestershire B98 8RH;
07766 418 013;
e-mail: mikelane@nature-photography.co.uk
www.nature-photography.co.uk

DIRECTORY OF WILDLIFE PHOTOGRAPHERS

LANGLEY, John and Tracy
Wildlife photographers, workshop tutors and lecturers.
Subjects: Birds, mammals, butterflies and other wildlife. European plus India (especially tigers).
Products and services: Digital images for publication and commercial use. Mounted images, framed images, greeting cards, bookmarks and calendars.
Address: South Lodge, Berthlwyd Hall, Llechwedd, Conwy LL32 8DQ; 01492 572 109 ; e-mail: ourwildlife@btopenworld.com
www.ourwildlifephotography.com

LANGSBURY, Gordon FRPS
Professional wildlife photographer, author.
Subjects: Birds and mammals from UK, Europe, Scandinavia, N America, Gambia, Kenya, Tanzania, Morocco, Falklands and Spitzbergen.
Products and services: Digital images for publication plus prints on canvas and paper for sale.
Address: Sanderlings, 80 Shepherds Close, Hurley, Maidenhead, Berkshire, SL6 5LZ; 01628 824 252.
e-mail: gordonlangsbury@birdphoto.org.uk
www.birdphoto.org.uk

LENTON, Graham
PhD Ornithology/Ecology. Former lecturer at Oxford University and Oxford Brookes University. Lifetime photographer of wildlife — has published articles and photographs of birds and wildlife.
Subjects: Worldwide birds, mammals of Africa, wildlife, worldwide travel.
Products and services: Photos available for sale or reproduction.
Address: The Old School, 25A Standlake Road, Ducklington, Witney, Oxon OX29 7UR; 01993 899 033; www.gml-art.co.uk
e-mail: grahamlenton@btopenworld.com

LINGARD, David
Wildlife photographer, retired from RAF, now UK delegate to LIPU (BirdLife Partner in Italy).
Subjects: Birds and views of places visited around the world.
Products and services: 35mm transparencies but mainly digital images.
Address: Fernwood, Doddington Road, Whisby, Lincs LN6 9BX; 01522 689 030.
e-mail: mail@lipu-uk.org
www.lipu-uk.org

MOCKLER, Mike
Safari guide, tour leader, writer and photographer.
Subjects: Birds and wildlife of Britain, Europe, Central and South America, India, Japan and several African countries. Africa a speciality.
Products and services: Digital images and 35mm transparencies.
Address: Gulliver's Cottage, Chapel Rise, Avon Castle, Ringwood, Hampshire, BH24 2BL; 01425 478 103; e-mail: mike@mikemockler.co.uk
www.mikemockler.co.uk

NASON, Rebecca
East Anglia-based bird and wildlife photographer.
Subjects: Wildlife photography. Specializing in birds, common and rare from Suffolk to the Shetland Islands and beyond.
Products and services: Large image stock library. Professionally printed images available, various sizes, mounts and frames from 6 x 4 to A1+. Acrylics, aluminium and canvases, greetings card range.
Address: 8 Angel Lane, Woodbridge, Suffolk IP12 4NG; 01394 385 030; (M)07919 256 386.
e-mail: rebecca@rebeccanason.com
www.rebeccanason.com

OFFORD, Keith
Photographer, writer, tour leader, conservationist.
Subjects: Raptors, UK wildlife and scenery, birds and other wildlife of USA, Africa, Spain, Australia, India.
Products and services: Conventional prints, greetings cards, framed pictures.
Address: Yew Tree Farmhouse, Craignant, Selattyn, Nr Oswestry, Shropshire, SY10 7NP; 01691 718 740; e-mail: keith.offord@virgin.net
www.keithofford.co.uk

PARKER, Susan and Allan ARPS
Professional photographers (ASPphoto - Images of Nature) lecturers and tutors.
Subjects: Birds plus other flora and fauna from the UK, Spain, Lesvos, Cyprus, Florida and Texas.
Products and services: 35mm and digital images, mounted digital images, greetings cards and digital images on CD/DVD for reproduction (high quality scans up to A3+).
Address: Windhover Barn, 51b Kiveton Lane, Todwick, Sheffield, South Yorkshire, S26 1HJ; 01909 770 238; e-mail: aspphoto@tiscali.co.uk

DIRECTORY OF WILDLIFE PHOTOGRAPHERS

READ, Mike
Photographer (wildlife and landscapes), tour leader, writer.
Subjects: Birds, mammals, plants, landscapes, and some insects. UK, France, USA, Ecuador (including Galapagos) plus many more. Behaviour, action, portraits, artistic pictures available for publication. More than 100,000 images in stock.
Products and services: Canvas and ordinary prints, greetings cards, books. Extensive stock photo library.
Address: Claremont, Redwood Close, Ringwood, Hampshire, BH24 1PR; 01425 475 008.
e-mail: mike@mikeread.co.uk
www.mikeread.co.uk

SISSON, Mark
A professional nature photographer, journalist and photographic trip and workshop organiser.
Subjects: I have a large and constantly expanding library of wildlife images (principally European) available, either direct or through my representing agencies.
Products and services: High specification digital images, complete illustrated articles, talks and personalised as group photographic workshops and tours.
Address: 4 Deer Park Drive, Newport, Shropshire TF10 7HB; 01952 411 436.
e-mail: mark@marksissonphoto.co.uk
www.marksissonphoto.co.uk and
www.natures-images.co.uk

SMART, Oliver
Photographer and lecturer.
Subjects: All wildlife subjects, mainly UK based, also Canada, Cuba, various Europe, Madagascar and Seychelles.
Products and services: Bean bags, canvas prints, desk calendars, digital files, digital slideshow lectures, greeting cards, mounted prints (to A2 size) and photographic workshops.
Address: 78 Aspen Park Road, Weston-Super-Mare, Somerset BS22 8ER; 01934 628 888; (M)07802 417 810.
e-mail: oliver@smartimages.co.uk
www.smartimages.co.uk

SWASH, Andy and Gill
Professional wildlife photographers and authors.
Subjects: Birds, habitats, landscapes and general wildlife from all continents; photographic library currently more than 3,000 bird species.
Products and services: Images for publication and lectures. High resolution images on CD/DVD. Conventional and digital prints, unmounted, mounted or framed. Greetings cards.
Address: Stretton Lodge, 9 Birch Grove, West Hill, Ottery St Mary, Devon, EX11 1XP; 01404 815 383, (M)07760 188 594.
e-mail: swash@worldwildlifeimages.com
www.worldwildlifeimages.com

TYLER, John
Subjects: Plants, fungi, insects and other invertebrates.
Products and services: Images for sale.
Address: 5 Woodfield, Lacey Green, Buckinghamshire HP27 0QQ; 07814 392 335.
e-mail: johnclarketyler@gmail.com
www.johntyler.co.uk

WARD, Chris
Lecturer, N Bucks RSPB Local Group leader.
Subjects: Primarily birds (and some other wildlife) and landscapes from UK and worldwide (Spain, Mallorca, Cyprus, Americas, S. Africa, Goa, Australasia).
Products and services: Digital images and prints on request.
Address: 41 William Smith Close, Woolstone, Milton Keynes, MK15 0AN; 01908 669 448.
e-mail: cwphotography@hotmail.com
www.cwardphotography.co.uk

WILLIAMS, Nick
Photographer, lecturer, author.
Subjects: W.Palearctic also Cape Verde Islands and Falkland Islands.
Products and services: Glossy photographs and beautiful wildlife calendars for sale.
Address: Owl Cottage, Station Street, Rippingale, Lincs, PE10 0TA; (Tel/Fax)01778 440 500.
e-mail: birdmanandbird@hotmail.com
www.nickwilliams.eu

DIRECTORY OF LECTURERS

BASTON, Bill
Photographer, lecturer.
Subjects: East Anglian rarities and common birds, Mediterranean birds and landscapes, UK wildlife and landscapes, Northern Greece, Spain, western Turkey, Goa, General wildlife photography, The Gambia, Northern India (birds and tigers).
Fees: Negotiable. **Limits:** Preferably within East Anglia.
Address: 86 George Street, Hadleigh, Ipswich, IP7 5BU; 01473 827 062.
e-mail: billbaston@btinternet.com
www.billbaston.com

BATES, Tony
Photographer and lecturer.
Subjects: Nine disolve projection shows (all include some music), 'A Woodland Walk', 'Seasons and Sayings', 'From a Puddle to the Sea', 'Favourite Places', 'USA, East and West', 'Folklore of Woodland and Hedgerow', The Hare and the Owls', 'A Wildlife Garden', 'Folklore of Ponds, Rivers and Seashore'.
Fees: £80 plus travel. **Limits:** None.
Time limitations: To suit.
Address: 22 Fir Avenue, Bourne, Lincs PE10 9RY; 01778 425 137.
e-mail: tonybatesphotos@live.co.uk
www.tonybates-outside-in.co.uk

BEJARANO, Santiago
An Ecuadorean naturalist and wildlife photographer who worked in the Galapagos for over a decade, with a great depth of knowledge and unique insight into these remarkable islands and their wildlife.
Subjects: 'Galapagos Islands', 'Birds of Galapagos', 'Ecuador Land of Mega Diversity', 'Hummingbirds'.
Fees: £40. **Limits:** None.
Time limitations: None.
Address: 25 Trinity Lane, Beverley, East Yorkshire HU17 0DY; 01482 872 716.
e-mail: info@thinkgalapagos.com
www.thinkgalapagos.com

BELL, Graham
Cruise lecturer worldwide, photographer, author, former BBRC member.
Subjects: Arctic, Antarctic, Siberia, Australia, Iceland, Seychelles, UK - identification, behaviour, seabirds, garden birds, entertaining bird sound imitations, birds in myth and fact, bird names, taking better photos, etc.
Fees: £30 plus travel and B&B if required.
Limits: None. **Time limitations:** None.
Address: Ros View, South Yearle, Wooler, Northumberland, NE71 6RB; 01668 281 310.
e-mail: seabirdsdgb@hotmail.com

BIRD, James
Photographer, Lecturer and former RSPB Local Group leader. Organiser of African trips (see Birds Eye Photos in Photography Directory).
Subjects: 14 plus slide talks and digital presentations on wildlife and worldwide travel, having spent 23 years living abroad.
Fees: £60 within a 50 mile round trip from home, fuel inclusive. 50-100 miles is £75 inc fuel. Over 100 miles or overnight by arrangement. **Limits:** Nowhere too far. **Times:** Any time to suit.
Address: Six Valentine Gardens, Kimbolton, Huntingdon, Cambridgeshire PE28 0HX;Tel/fax: 01480 861 955; (M) 07914 633 355.
e-mail: jamesbird007@yahoo.co.uk or birdseyeviewphotos@yahoo.co.uk

BOND, Terry
Company Director, international consultant, ex-bank director, conference speaker worldwide, photographer, group field leader, lecturer on birds for more than 30 years.
Subjects: 6 talks - including Scilly Isles, Southern Europe, North America, Scandinavia, 'Birdwatching Identification - a New Approach' (an audience participation evening).
Fees: By arrangement (usually only expenses).
Limits: Most of UK. **Time limitations:** Evenings.
Address: 3 Lapwing Crescent, Chippenham, Wiltshire, SN14 6YF; 01249 462 674.
e-mail: terryebond@btopenworld.com

BOULTON, David
Professional nature photographer and lecturer.
Subjects: 17 talks (audio/visual presentations with relaxing music), including 'Images of Nature', 'Wild Flowers', 'Broadland', 'Gardens', 'Lakeland', 'Butterflies and Insects', 'Fungi', 'Norfolk', 'Garden Wildlife', 'The Seasons' (four talks), 'Images of Tranquility'.
Fees: £50 plus 30p per mile (negotiable depending on size of group). **Limits:** None.

Time limitations: None.
Address:1 Mantle Close, Sprowston, Norwich, Norfolk NR7 8LD:01603 415 610.
e-mail: dbp@ownersmail.co.uk
www.davidboulton.co.uk

BOWDEN, Paul

Birdwatcher and nature photographer (HD video and photos of birds and other wildlife) for 30+ years (serious amateur). Founder member of local Wildlife Photographic Club (website: http://www. glamorganwildlifephotoclub.org.uk/). Lectures to local bird clubs and RSPB Local Groups.
Subjects: Birds of UK, Europe, USA, Canada, Hong Kong, Japan, Oman, Libya or Australia (HD-video and/or Powerpoint). Butterflies and Dragonflies of UK.
Fees: £50 plus reasonable travelling expenses (also overnight accomodation where necessary for longer trips). **Limits:** None, but longer trips may require overnight stay.
Time limitations: Evenings and weekends only.
Address: 4 Patmore Close, Gwaelod-y-Garth, Cardiff, CF15 9SU; 029 2081 3044.
e-mail: bowden_pe@hotmail.com

BRIGGS, Kevin

Freelance ecologist.
Subjects: General wildlife in NW England; specialist topics - Raptors, Oystercatcher, Ringed Plover, Goosander, Yellow Wagtail, Ring Ouzel, Lune Valley, 'Confessions of a Lunatic'.
Fees: £60 + petrol. **Limits:** None.
Time limitations: None.
Address: The Bramblings, 1 Washington Drive, Warton, Carnforth, LA5 9RA; 01524 730 533.
e-mail: kbbriggs@yahoo.com

BROADBENT, David

Photographer.
Subjects: UK birds and wild places. In praise of natural places.
Fees: £50 plus travel. **Limits:** 50mls without o.n accom, anywhere otherwise.
Time limitations: None.
Contact: 07771 664 973.
e-mail: info@davidbroadbent.com
www.davidbroadbent.com

BROOKS, David

Freelance naturalist.
Subjects: Various talks on wildlife, principally birds, in UK and overseas.
Fees: £50 plus petrol. **Limits:** 50 mls without

o.n. accom. **Time limitations:** Any time.
Address: 2 Malthouse Court, Green Lane, Thornham, Norfolk, PE36 6NW; 01485 512548.
e-mail: brooks472@btinternet.com

BROOKS, Richard

Wildlife photographer, writer, lecturer.
Subjects: 12 talks (including Lesvos, Evros Delta, Israel, Canaries, E.Anglia, Scotland, Wales, Oman).
Fees: £75 plus petrol. **Limits:** None if accom provided. **Time limitations:** None.
Address: 24 Croxton Hamlet, Fulmodeston, Fakenham, Norfolk, NR21 0NP; 01328 878632.
e-mail: email@richard-brooks.co.uk
www.richard-brooks.co.uk

BUCKINGHAM, John

Lecturer, photographer, tour leader.
Subjects: 60+ titles covering birds, wildlife, botany, ecology and habitats in UK, Europe, Africa, Australia, Indian sub-continent, North-South and Central America incuding favourites such as 'How Birds Work', 'The Natural History of Birds' and 'Wonders of Bird Migration'.
Fees: £80 plus expenses. **Limits:** None.
Time limitations: None.
Address: 3 Cardinal Close, Tonbridge, Kent, TN9 2EN; (Tel/fax) 01732 354 970.
e-mail: john@buckingham7836.freeserve.co.uk

CARRIER, Michael

Lifelong interest in natural history.
Subjects: 1) 'Birds in Cumbria', 2) 'The Solway and its Birds' and 3)'The Isle of May', 4)'A look at Bird Migration', 5)'A Lifetime of Birds', 6)'Some Remarkable Islands.
Fees: £20. **Geographical Limits:** None but rail connection helpful. **Time limitations:** Sept-March inc., afternoons or evenings.
Address: Lismore Cottage, 1 Front Street, Armathwaite, Carlisle, Cumbria, CA4 9PB; 01697 472 218;
e-mail: m.carrier131@btinternet.com

CLEAVE, Andrew MBE

Wildlife photographer, author, lecturer and tour leader
Subjects: More than 30 talks (including India, Galapagos, Iceland, Mediterranean birds and wildlife, Lundy, Shetland, Ancient Woodlands, Dormice and Seashore). Full list available.
Fees: £65 plus petrol. **Limits:** Approx. 60 mls without o.n accom.

Time limitations: Afternoons and evenings, not school holidays.
Address: 31 Petersfield Close, Chineham, Basingstoke, Hampshire, RG24 8WP; 01256 320 050; e-mail: andrew@bramleyfrith.co.uk

COSTER, Bill
Professional wildlife photographer, writer and photographic tour leader, author of *Creative Bird Photography*.
Subjects: Stunning new digital shows provide a unique look at subjects around the world, including: Pacific Northwest USA, Antarctica, Shetland, Birds and Landscape of USA Deserts, Florida, Britain and more. See website for full details (www.billcoster.com). Even if you have seen lectures about the same location, my shows will be different.
Fees: £80, plus 30p per mile. **Limits:** None.
Time limitations: None.
Address: 17 Elm Road, South Woodham Ferrers, Chelmsford, Essex CM3 5QB; 01245 320 066.
e-mail: billcoster@hotmail.com
www.billcoster.com

COUZENS, Dominic
Full-time birdwatcher, tour leader (UK and overseas), writer and lecturer.
Subjects: The Secret Lives of Garden Birds'; 'Birds Behaving Badly — the trials and tribulations of birds through the year'; 'Have Wings Will Travel' — the marvel of bird migration; 'Vive la Difference' — a comparison of British birds with those across the Channel; 'My Family and 50 Other Animals' — a year spent trying to show 2 young children 50 species of mammals in Britain; 'Birding a Local Patch'.
Fees: £80 plus travel. **Limits:** London and south. **Time limitations:** None.
Address: 3 Clifton Gardens, Ferndown, Dorset, BH22 9BE; (Tel/fax) 01202 874 330.
e-mail: dominic.couzens@btinternet.com
www.birdwords.co.uk

CROMACK, David
Editor of *Bird Art & Photography* magazine, co-publisher of Buckingham Press Ltd, former chairman of Peterborough Bird Club.
Subjects: Subjects: 1) Bird Magazines and the Art of Bird Photography (the inside story of how publications choose and use images); 2) Wild West Birding (Arizona and California); 3) World Class Bird Images (Leading entries from International Wildbird Photographer competitions); 4) More World Class Bird Images (Outstanding entries from the 2007 IWP competition); 5) Asia's Teardrop - Birding in Sri Lanka (new talk); 6) Contemporary Bird Artists (new talk). All suitable for bird groups and photographic societies. Leaflet available on request.
Fees: £75 plus travel expenses (30p per mile). **Limits:** 150 miles from Peterborough. **Times:** All requests considered from January 2011.
Address: 55 Thorpe Park Road, Peterborough PE3 6LJ. 01733 566 815; (Fax) 01733 561 739; e-mail: editor@buckinghampress.com

CROUCHER, Roy
Tour leader, lecturer, former RSPB Staff Member, former local authority Ecologist and Countryside Ranger.
Subjects: The Wildlife of Northern France'; 'Managing the Countryside for Wildlife'.
Fees: £60 plus petrol from Leicester (return) at £15 per 100 miles. **Limits:** Anywhere in mainland Britain.
Time limitations: November and December.
Address: Place de L'Eglise, 53700, Averton, France; 0033 2430 069 69.
e-mail: nfwt@online.fr
www.northernfrancewildlifetours.com

DENNING, Paul
Wildlife photographer, lecturer.
Subjects: 15 talks, (birds, mammals, reptiles, butterflies etc, UK, western and eastern Europe, north and central America, Canaries).
Fees: £40 plus petrol. **Limits:** 100 mls.
Time limitations: Evenings, weekends.
Address: 17 Maes Maelwg, Beddau, Pontypridd, CF38 2LD; (H) 01443 202 607; (W) 02920 673 243; e-mail: pgdenning.naturepics@virgin.net

DOODY, Dee
Wildlife artist, television wildlife cameraman, presenter (radio and TV), bird of prey expert. Dee brings with him a good collection of wildlife art.
Subjects: Wild Wales' — birdlife from mountain to coasts; 'The Red Kite'; 'The Birds of Prey of Wales'.
Fees: £85 plus cost of petrol. **Limits:** None.
Time limitations: None.
Address: The Studio, 2 Fan Terrace, Fan, Llanidloes, Powys, SY18 6NW: (Day) 01686 413 819; (eve) 01686 412 163.
e-mail: dee.doody@virgin.net

ART/PHOTOGRAPHY/LECTURERS

DIRECTORY OF LECTURERS

DUGGAN, Glenn
Ex-Commander Royal Navy, tour leader, researcher.
Subjects: Ten talks: The rare and extinct birds of the world; Birds of paradise and bower birds; Trogons and Tanagers; History of bird art (caveman to present day); Modern day bird art; Famous Victorian bird artists (John Gould, the Birdman and John James Audubon); Scientific voyages of discovery.
Fees: £70 plus reasonable expenses. **Limits:** none with o.n accom.
Time limitations: None.
Address: 25 Hampton Grove, Fareham, Hampshire, PO15 5NL; 01329 845 976, (M) 07771 605 320; e-mail: glenn.m.duggan@ntlworld.com
www.birdlectures.com

EYRE, John
Author, photographer, conservationist and chairman Hampshire Ornithological Society.
Subjects: Many talks covering birding around the world (Europe, Africa, Asia, Australasia and the Americas), plus special Hampshire subjects. Examples include: 'New Zealand - Seabird Feast, Land Bird Famine'; California Birds - Sea; Sage and Spotted Owls'; 'Gilbert White's Birds' and 'The changing Fortunes of Hampshire Birds'. Please call to discuss options.
Fees: £70 plus travel. **Limits:** Any location negotiable. **Time limitations:** None.
Address: 3 Dunmow Hill, Fleet, Hampshire, GU51 3AN; 01252 677 850.
e-mail: John.Eyre@ntlworld.com

GALLOP, Brian
Speaker, photographer, tour leader.
Subjects: 35 talks covering UK, Africa, India, Galapagos, South America and Europe. All natural history subjects. Made-to-measure talks available on request. 24hr emergency service.
Fees: £50 plus 25p per ml. **Limits:** None - o.n acc. if over 100 mls. **Time limitations:** None.
Address: 13 Orchard Drive, Tonbridge, Kent, TN10 4LT; 01732 361 892.
e-mail: brian_gallop@hotmail.co.uk

GARNER, Jackie
Professional wildlife artist & illustrator.
Subjects: Birds/Wildlife in Art; Focus on the Falklands; Wildlife of Ancient Egypt.
Fees: £80 + expenses. **Distance limits:** None.
Time limits: None.
Address: The Old Cider House Studio, Humphries End, Randwick, Stroud, Glos GL6 6EW; 01453 847 420; (M)07800 804 847.
e-mail: artist@jackiegarner.co.uk
www.jackiegarner.co.uk

GARNER, David
Wildlife photographer.
Subjects: 20 live talks and audio-visual shows on all aspects of wildlife in UK and some parts of Europe — list available.
Fees: £40 plus 20p per ml. **Limits:** None.
Time limitations: None.
Address: 73 Needingworth Road, St Ives, Cambridgeshire, PE27 5JY; (H) 01480 463194; (W) 01480 463 194.
e-mail: david@hushwings.co.uk
www.hushwings.co.uk

GARTSHORE, Neil
23-years working in nature conservation (National Trust, South Africa, RSPB) now a freelance contractor, writer, lecturer, tour guide and natural history book seller.
Subjects: Various talks including South Africa; Sub-Antarctic Prince Edward Islands; Japan; Farne Islands; Heathlands; Poole Harbour.
Fees: Negotiable. **Limits:** Anything considered.
Time limitations: Flexible.
Address: Moor Edge, 2 Bere Road, Wareham, Dorset BH20 4DD; 01929 552 560.
e-mail: neil@onaga54.freeserve.co.uk

GLENN, Neil
Author of *Best Birdwatching Sites in Norfolk*; regular contributor to *Bird Art and Photography* and *Bird Watching* magazines; bird tour leader for Avian Adventures.
Subjects: Wildlife of the Lower Rio Grande Valley, Texas; Birding the Arctic Circle; Moroccan Spice: From The Sahara to The Atlas Mountains. More to follow!
Fees: Negotiable. **Limits:** None.
Time limitations: Any day.
Address: 13 Gladstone Avenue, Gotham, Nottingham NG11 0HN; 0115 983 0946.
e-mail: n.glenn@ntlworld.com

GRIFFITHS, Gerald (Gerry)
Founder of Avian Adventures; previously lectured in Field studies of Birds (Adult Evening Education) for University of Birmingham.
Subjects: Wild West Birding; Arctic Wonderland - Finland & Norway; Neotropical Paradise — Costa Rica; Birding The Tropics
Fees: (£55 to £100 + Expenses depending on Distance) but Negotiable.

DIRECTORY OF LECTURERS

Distance limits: England and Wales.
Contact details: Tel: 01384 372013   Email:
gerry@avianadventures.co.uk

GUNTON, Trevor
Ex.RSPB Staff, recruitment advisor, lecturer and
consultant.
Subjects: 15 different talks, featuring places
such as Shetland, other UK islands, Yorkshire
from dales to coast, Viking lands (four
different talks on Viking history). New talks
are 'A Norwegian coastal voyage' and 'Wild
goose chase (Holland and Romania)', 'Starting
Birdwatching', Great Gardens and Houses
of East Anglia', 'Garden Birds'. Other topics
include wildlife on National Trust properties
and gravel pits (Paxton Pits). Write/phone for
full list.
Fees: Variable (basic £60 plus expenses).
Limits: None. **Time limitations:** Anytime,
anywhere.
Address: 15 St James Road, Little Paxton,
St Neots, Cambs, PE19 6QW; (tel/fax)01480
473562.

HAMMOND, Nicholas
Lecturer, author, former RSPB and Wildlife
Trust staffer.
Subjects: More than 30 topics covering Art
and Wildlife, History and Wildlife, Wildlife and
Conservation. Popular topics include Modern
Wildlife Painting, Hippos and Hoopoes, The
Great Fen, Birds through Other People's Eyes.
E-mail for full list of subjects.
Fees: From £75, **Limits:** 150 miles from Sandy.
Address: 30 Ivel Road, Sandy, Beds SG19 1BA;
01767 680 504;
e-mail: n.hammond4@ntlworld.com

HASSELL, David
Birdwatcher and photographer.
Subjects: Six talks (including British Seabirds,
Shetland Birds, British Birds, USA Birds,
including Texas, California, Florida etc.).
Fees: £50 plus petrol. **Limits:** None.
Time limitations: None.
Address: 15 Grafton Road, Enfield, Middlesex,
EN2 7EY; 020 8367 0308; www.davehassell.com
e-mail: dave@davehassell.com

LANE, Mike
Wildlife photographer and lecturer.
Subjects: Three new digital talks from the UK
and abroad — see website for details.
Fees: Negotiable. **Limits:** None.
Time limitations: None.

Address: 5 Paxford Close, Church Hill North,
Redditch, Worcestershire B98 8RH;
07766 418 013;
e-mail: mikelane@nature-photography.co.uk
www.nature-photography.co.uk

LANGLEY, John and Tracy
Wildlife photographers, workshop tutors and
lecturers.
Subjects: Various talks on UK wildlife, wildlife
photography and Indian wildlife (with special
emphasis on tigers).
Fees: Variable. **Limits:** None.
Time limitations: None.
Address: South Lodge, Berthlwyd Hall,
Llechwedd, Conwy LL32 8DQ; 01492 572 109;
e-mail: ourwildlife@btopenworld.com
www.ourwildlifephotography.com

LENTON, Graham
PhD Ornithology/Ecology. Former lecturer
at Oxford University and Oxford Brookes
University. Lifetime photographer of wildlife —
has published articles and photographs of birds
and wildlife.
Subjects: Barn Owls of Malaysia and rat control;
Birds of the Seychelles; Wildlife and birds of
Antarctica; Birds of New Zealand; Birds of
Namibia; Two Islands (Handa & The Farnes); An
Arctic Journey.
Fees: £60. **Limits:** Preferably within 60mls.
Time limitations: One hour to 90 minute talks.
Address: The Old School, 25A Standlake Road,
Ducklington, Witney, Oxon OX29 7UR; 01993
899 033; www.gml-art.co.uk
e-mail: grahamlenton@btopenworld.com

LINGARD, David
Photographer, retired from RAF, now UK
delegate to LIPU (BirdLife Partner in Italy).
Subjects: Choice of talks on European birding
and the work of LIPU.
Fees: £75 donation to LIPU, plus petrol costs.
Limits: None. **Time limitations:** None.
Address: Fernwood, Doddington Road, Whisby,
Lincs LN6 9BX; 01522 689 030.
e-mail: mail@lipu-uk.org
www.lipu-uk.org

LINN, Hugh ARPS
Experienced lecturer, photographer.
Subjects: 12 talks, covering UK, Europe, Africa
and bird-related subjects.
Fees: £50 plus travel expenses. **Limits:** 100
miles without o.n. accom.
Time limitations: Flexible.

ART/PHOTOGRAPHY/LECTURERS

109

Address: 4 Stonewalls, Rosemary Lane, Burton, Rossett, Wrexham, LL12 0LG; 01244 571 942; e-mail: hugh.linn@btinternet.com

LOVELL, Stephen
Naturalist, RSPB lecturer, photographer.
Subjects: 18 topic including the natural history of several European destinations including Lesvos, Mallorca, Britain. Other talks available on New Zealand, Australia, St Lucia, Tanzania, Sri Lanka and Southern India.
Fees: According to distance — on request.
Limits: None. **Time limitations:** None.
Address: 6 Abingdon Close, Doddington Park, Lincoln LN6 3UH; 01522 689 456; (M) 07957 618 684; e-mail: stephenlovell58@btinternet.com

MOCKLER, Mike
Safari guide, tour leader, writer and photographer.
Subjects: Birds and other wildlife of: Botswana, Kenya, Tanzania, Zambia, Spain, Finland, Norway, Costa Rica, Antarctica and South Georgia, India and Brazil.
Fees: Negotiable. **Limits:** None.
Time limitations: Evenings.
Address: Gulliver's Cottage, Chapel Rise, Avon Castle, Ringwood, Hampshire, BH24 2BL; 01425 478 103; e-mail: mike@mikemockler.co.uk www.mikemockler.co.uk

NASON, Rebecca
UK, East Anglia-based bird and wildlife photographer.
Subjects: A Fair Isle Season — working, birding and photography at Britain's premier birding hotspot.
Fees: Please e-mail for fee details. There is a set fee plus travel expenses depending on location. **Limits:** Within 2 hours drive of Woodbridge, Suffolk.
Time limitations: Flexible. Slideshow talks last from 1-2 hours.
Address: 8 Angel Lane, Woodbridge, Suffolk IP12 4NG; 01394 385 030; (M)07919 256 386. e-mail: rebecca@rebeccanason.com www.rebeccanason.com

NOBBS, Brian
Amateur birdwatcher and photographer.
Subjects: Wildlife of the Wild West, Mediterranean, Florida, Wildlife Gardening, Reserves for Birds (RSPB); Trinidad and Tobago; The Way Birds Feed; Flight and Feathers.
Fees: £45 plus 25p per ml. **Limits:** Kent, Surrey, Sussex, Essex. **Time limitations:** None.

Address: The Grebes, 36 Main Road, Sundridge, Sevenoaks, Kent, TN14 6EP; 01959 563 530. e-mail: Brian.nobbs@tiscali.co.uk

OFFORD, Keith
Photographer, writer, tour leader, conservationist.
Subjects: 16 talks covering raptors, flight, uplands, gardens, migration, woodland wildlife, Australia, Iceland, Southern USA, Gambia, Spain, Costa Rica, Namibia, South Africa's Western Cape.
Fees: £100 plus travel. **Limits:** None.
Time limitations: Sept - April.
Address: Yew Tree Farmhouse, Craignant, Selattyn, Nr Oswestry, Shropshire, SY10 7NP; 01691 718 740; e-mail: keith.offord@virgin.net www.keithofford.co.uk

PARKER, Susan and Allan ARPS
Professional photographers, (ASPphoto – Images of Nature), lecturers and tutors.
Subjects: 16-plus slide and digital talks on birds and natural history, natural history photography — countries include UK, USA (Texas, Florida), Spain, Greece, Cyprus.
Fees: On application. **Limits:** Any distance with o.n accom or up to 120 mls without.
Time limitations: None.
Address: Windhover Barn, 51b Kiveton Lane, Todwick, Sheffield, South Yorkshire, S26 1HJ; 01909 770 238; e-mail: aspphoto@tiscali.co.uk

READ, Mike
Photographer, tour leader, writer.
Subjects: 12 talks featuring British and foreign subjects (list available on receipt of sae or see website).
Fees: £70 plus travel. **Limits:** 125 mls from Ringwood.
Time limitations: Talks available 1st Sept to 31st March each winter.
Address: Claremont, Redwood Close, Ringwood, Hampshire, BH24 1PR; 01425 475008. e-mail: mike@mikeread.co.uk www.mikeread.co.uk

REDMAN, Nigel
Tour leader, publisher and author.
Subjects: Mostly birds, including Morocco, Russia (and former Soviet Union), the Caucasus, Kenya, Ethiopia, and the Horn of Africa.
Fees: Negotiable. **Limits:** None (but overnight accommodation may be required).
Time limitations: None.
Address: Moons Hill Cottage, Moons Hill,

DIRECTORY OF LECTURERS

Ninfield, East Sussex TN33 9LH; 01424 893 023; 07734 886 515; e-mail: nredman@acblack.com

SISSON, Mark
A professional nature photographer, journalist and photographic trip and workshop organiser.
Subjects: All aspects of wildlife photography, along with specific or tailormade talks on countries such as Iceland or broader topics such as Northern European birdlife — all with a photographer's eye and style.
Fees: £95 + travel. **Limits:** Ideally 100ml radius, but willing to be persuaded to go further!
Time limitations: Need to fit into a busy schedule, so ideally plenty of notice.
Address: 4 Deer Park Drive, Newport,Shropshire,TF10 7HB; 01952 411 436.
e-mail: mark@marksissonphoto.co.uk
www.marksissonphoto.co.uk and
www.natures-images.co.uk

SMART, Oliver
Photographer and lecturer.
Subjects: 1)Birds of Lesvos; 2) Grizzly Bears of Alaska; 3) Wildlife on Handa Island, NW Scotland; 4) Cameras and Creatures, from Cumbria to Canada; 5) Cuba: A Flicker of Interest.
Fees: £75 plus 20p per mile. **Limits:** None but o.n. accom. may be required.
Time limitations: None.
Address: 78 Aspen Park Road, Weston-Super-Mare, Somerset BS22 8ER; 01934 628 888; (M)07802 417 810.
e-mail: oliver@smartimages.co.uk
www.smartimages.co.uk

SWASH, Andy
Professional wildlife photographer and author.
Subjects: Tales from travels in search of little-known birds around the world, including the Andamans, Australia, Brazil, Ethiopia, Galápagos, Peru, Southern Africa, Sri Lanka and various birding hotspots in the USA.
Fees: £90 plus travel. **Limits:** None.
Time limitations: Evenings preferred.
Address: Stretton Lodge, 9 Birch Grove, West Hill, Ottery St Mary, Devon, EX11 1XP; 01404 815 383, (M)07760 188 594.
e-mail: swash@worldwildlifeimages.com
www.worldwildlifeimages.com

TODD, Ralph
Lecturer & photographer, former tour leader and course tutor.
Subjects: 10 talks incl. 'Galapagos Wildlife',
'On the Trail of the Crane'; 'Polar Odyssey'; 'Operation Osprey'; 'Iceland & Pyrenees'; 'Man & Birds-Travels through time'; 'A summer in Northern Landscapes'; 'Where Yeehaa meets Ole'.
Fees: £70 plus expenses. **Limits:** None.
Time limitations: Anytime - also short notice.
Address: 9 Horsham Road, Bexleyheath, Kent, DA6 7HU; (Tel/fax)01322 528335.
e-mail: rbtodd@btinternet.com

TYLER, John
Wildlife walks and talks.
Subjects: Life in a Nutshell (The world of small things); The Island of Crabs; Volcanoes and Dragons; Changing Wildlife of the Chilterns; The Ridgeway; The Glow-worm; The World of Fungi; Making Space for Wildlife.
Fees: £60 plus 40p per mile. **Limits:** 25 mile radius from Princes Risborough, Bucks.
Time limitations: None.
Address: 5 Woodfield, Lacey Green, Buckinghamshire HP27 0QQ; 07814 392 335;
e-mail: johnclarketyler@gmail.com
www.johntyler.co.uk

WARD, Chris
Photographer, N Bucks RSPB Local Group leader.
Subjects: 20+ talks on UK and worldwide topics (Spain, Mallorca, Cyprus, Americas, Africa, Goa, Australasia) — primarily birds, some other wildlife.
Fees: £50 plus petrol @30p/mile. **Limits:** 120 miles.
Time limitations: Evenings.
Address: 41 William Smith Close, Woolstone, Milton Keynes, MK15 0AN; 01908 669 448.
e-mail: cwphotography@hotmail.com
www.cwardphotography.co.uk

WILLIAMS, Nick
Photographer, lecturer, author.
Subjects: Several audio visual shows (including Morocco, Mongolia, Spain, N.Germany, Camargue, Turkey, N.Norway, Cape Verde Islands, Falklands and Birds of Prey).
Fee: £110 - £140 depending on group size and distance. **Limits:** None.
Time limitations: None.
Address: Owl Cottage, Station Street, Rippingale, Lincs, PE10 0TA; (Tel/Fax) 01778 440 500.
e-mail: birdmanandbird@hotmail.com
www.nickwilliams.eu

ART/PHOTOGRAPHY/LECTURERS

BTO SPEAKERS

This directory has been compiled to help Bird Clubs and similar organisations in finding speakers for their indoor meetings. Each entry consists of an individual speaker, a list of talks/ lectures available, details of fees and expenses required and travel distance limitations. If you are interested in any of the speakers, please contact Ieuan Evans (e-mail: ieuan.evans@bto.org) or Ellen Walford (e-mail: ellen.walford@bto.org) directly. Alternatively, you can reach us at The British Trust For Ornithology, The Nunnery, Thetford, Norfolk IP24 2PU Telephone: 01842 750 050.If you are already a member of the Bird Club Partnership, please ask us about discounted rates.

* indicates that this is a non-BTO talk
** indicates that this is for private talks

APPLETON, Graham (Director of Communications)
Subjects: *Atlas 2007 - 11; The Work of the BTO; Flyway to Iceland; Time to Fly - Bird Migration.*
Fee: BTO fee £40. **Expenses:** Negotiable.
Distance: Dependant on expenses.

AUSTIN, Dr Graham (Senior Research Ecologist, Wetland & Marine Research)
Subjects: *Wetland Bird Survey.*
Fee: BTO fee £40. **Expenses:** Travel.
Distance: By agreement.

BAILLIE, Dr Stephen (Science Director, Modelling & Demography)
Subjects: *BirdTrack; Population Monitoring.*
Fee: BTO fee £40. **Expenses:** Travel.
Distance: By agreement.

BAKER, Jeff (Kevin) (Head of Marketing)
Subjects: *'Little brown jobs' — Warblers and how to identify them; The Work of the BTO; Garden birds and feeding.*
Fee: BTO fee £40. **Expenses:** Travel.
Distance: Dependent on expenses.

BALMER, Dawn (Atlas Coordinator)
Subjects: *Atlas 2007 - 11.*
Fee: BTO fee £40. **Expenses:** Travel.
Distance: 100 miles radius of Thetford.

BARIMORE, Carl (Nest Records Organiser)
Subjects: *Nest Record Scheme; Barn Owl Monitoring Programme.*
Fee: BTO fee £40. **Expenses:** Travel.
Distance: By agreement.

BLACKBURN, Jez (Licensing and Sales Manager, Demography Team)
Subjects: *Bird Moult (suitable for ringers); Ringing for Conservation; Sule Skerry.*
Fee: BTO fee £40 (£70 for private talks).
Expenses: Travel. **Distance:** East Anglia.

CLARK, Jacquie (Head of Demography Team and Head of Ringing Scheme)
Subjects: *Waders and Severe Weather; Ringing for Conservation; Why Ring Birds?*
Fee: BTO fee £40. **Expenses:** Travel.
Distance: 100 mile radius of Thetford.

CLARK, Dr Nigel (Head of Projects, Development Department)
Subjects: *Waders; Man and Estuaries; Horseshoe Crabs and Waders; Migration through Delaware Bay in Spring.*
Fee: BTO fee £40. **Expenses:** Travel.
Distance: 100 mile radius of Thetford.

CONWAY, Greg (Research Ecologist, Land-use Research)
Subjects: *Nightjars; Woodlarks & Dartford Warblers; Wintering Chiffchaffs & other Warblers in the UK; Firecrests in Britain.*
Fee: BTO fee £40. **Expenses:** Travel.
Distance: 100 miles radius of Thetford.

FULLER, Prof Rob (Director of Science)
Subjects: *Nightingales; Changing Times for Woodland Birds.*
Fee: BTO fee £40. **Expenses:** Travel.
Distance: Anywhere.

GILLINGS, Dr Simon (Senior Research Ecologist, Land-use Research)
Subjects: *Atlas 2007 - 11; Winter Golden Plovers and Lapwings; Waders; Knot Migration; Winter Farmland Birds.*
Fee: BTO fee £40. **Expenses:** Travel.
Distance: Negotiable.

GOUGH, Su (Editor, *BTO News* and Training Officer)
Subjects: *The Work of the BTO; Atlas 2007 - 11; Urban Birds ; Wildlife of Canada;* Wildlife of Southwestern USA;* Wildlife of European Mountains;* Wildlife of Texas.,**
Fee: BTO fee £40. **Expenses:** Travel.
Distance: Negotiable.

BTO SPEAKERS

HENDERSON, Dr Ian (Senior Research Ecologist, International Research)
Subjects: *Arable Farming and Birds.*
Fee: BTO fee £40. **Expenses:** Travel.
Distance: By agreement.

JOHNSTON, Dr Alison (Ecological Statistician, Population Ecology & Modelling)
Subjects: *Climate Change and Birds.*
Fee: BTO fee £40. **Expenses:** Travel. **Distance:** East Anglia.

LACK, Dr Peter (Information Services Manager)
Subjects: *Palearctic Migrants in Africa;* On Foot in Rwanda and Zambia;* Bird Ecology in East African Savannahs;* General Natural History of Eastern Africa.**
Fee: Negotiable. **Expenses:** Travel.
Distance: 60 miles from Bury St Edmunds.

MARCHANT, John (Projects Co-ordinator, Monitoring)
Subjects: *Heronries: Nine Decades of Monitoring; Waterways Bird & Breeding Bird Surveys.*
Fee: BTO fee £40. **Expenses:** Travel.
Distance: By agreement.

MORAN, Nick (BirdTrack Organiser)
Subjects: *BirdTrack; Birding Arabia - birds and birding in the UAE;* Migrant birds in Shanghai.**
Fee: BTO fee £40. **Expenses:** Travel.
Distance: By agreement.

MUSGROVE, Dr Andy (Head of Monitoring)
Subjects: *The Wetland Bird Survey; Little Egrets in the UK ; Out of Africa.*
Fee: BTO fee £40 . **Expenses:** Travel.
Distance: By agreement.

NEWSON, Dr Stuart (Senior Research Ecologist, Population Ecology & Modelling)
Subjects: *Tree Nesting Cormorants.*
Fee: BTO fee £40 . **Expenses:** Travel.
Distance: By agreement.

NOBLE, Dr David (Principal Ecologist, Monitoring)
Subjects: *Developing Bird Indicators; Population Trends.*
Fee: BTO fee £40. **Expenses:** Travel.
Distance: By agreement.

REHFISCH, Dr Mark (Director of Development)
Subjects: *Waterbird Alerts; Climate Change; Habitat Loss and Waterbirds; Monitoring Waterbirds; Introduced Species.*

Fee: BTO fee £40. **Expenses:** Travel.
Distance: By agreement.

RISLEY, Kate (Breeding Bird Survey National Organiser)
Subjects: *BTO/JNCC/RSPB Breeding Bird Survey.*
Fee: BTO fee £40. **Expenses:** Travel.
Distance: By agreement.

ROBINSON, Dr Rob (Principal Ecologist, Modelling & Demography)
Subjects: *Farming and Birds; Conservation Value of Ringing.*
Fee: BTO fee £40. **Expenses:** Travel.
Distance: By agreement.

SIRIWARDENA, Dr Gavin (Head of Land-use Research)
Subjects: *Farmland Birds (General); Marsh and Willow Tits; Quantifying Migratory Strategies; Winter Feeding of Farmland Birds.*
Fee: BTO fee £40. **Expenses:** Travel.
Distance: 50 mile radius of Thetford.

STANCLIFFE, Paul (Press Officer)
Subjects: *Atlas 2007 - 11; Homes to Let - Nestboxes; Birds, Birders and the Work of the BTO.*
Fee: £40. **Expenses:** Travel.
Distance: Negotiable.

TOMS, Mike (Head of Garden Ecology Team)
Subjects: *Are Gardens Good for Birds or Birdwatchers?*
Fee: £40.00. **Expenses:** Petrol.
Distance: 50 mile radius of Thetford.

WERNHAM, Dr Chris (Senior Research Ecologist, BTO Scotland)
Subjects: *The BTO's Migration Research; The work of BTO Scotland.*
Fee: £40. **Expenses:** Travel.
Distance: Scotland and NE England.

WRIGHT, Dr Lucy (Research Ecologist, Wetland and Marine Research)
Subjects: *Non-native Waterbirds in Eurasia & Africa.*
Fee: £40. **Expenses:** Travel.
Distance: By agreement.

Best Birdwatching Sites

The trusted name for accurate, accessible site information

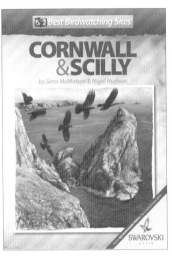

The newly-released **Best Birdwatching Sites in Cornwall & Scilly** features 52 mainland sites, plus seven routes around the key islands of Scilly. 208pp.

Price: £17.50

Extracts from the Birdguides website review, written by Cornishman Mark Golley on August 12.

"Buy this book. It's a simple as that. No fuss, no nonsense, this is a volume that anyone planning a trip to one of the very best birding areas in Britain would do well to pack in the rucksack, even if they've been to the far southwest of England on countless occasions before.

"The 208 pages that make up Best Birdwatching Sites: Cornwall & Scilly are a "must have" .... the book is jam-packed full of useful information without ever seeming cluttered..... Everything you need to know is listed.

"Authors Sara McMahon and Nigel Hudson have done a first-class job. The word 'essential' is often rather overblown and overused — but not here. As mentioned at the start of the review: buy this book. It's as simple as that." to read the full review please visit: http://www.birdguides.com/webzine/article.asp?a=1408

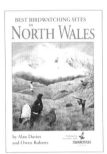

Best Birdwatching Sites in North Wales by Alan Davies and Owen Roberts. Features 58 major sites in Gwynedd and Clwyd, plus 11 smaller birding spots around Wrexham. 192pp. **Price: £15.95**

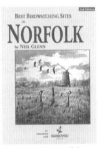

Best Birdwatching Sites in Norfolk (2nd Edition) by Neil Glenn. Contains 83 sites (ten more than 1st Edition) – all information updated. 256pp. **Price: £16.95.**

Best Birdwatching Sites in the Scottish Highlands by Gordon Hamlett. Features 22 birding routes from John O'Groats to Pitlochry. 164 maps, 240pp. **Price: £15.95**

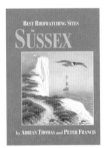

Best Birdwatching Sites in Sussex by Adrian Thomas and Peter Francis. Contains 57 sites, plus innovative migration charts. 192pp. **Price: £14.50**

For details of latest special offers on our books please contact Buckingham Press, 55 Thorpe Park Road, Peterborough PE3 6LJ. 01733 561 739. e-mail: admin@buckinghampress.com
www.buckinghampress.co.uk (see entry on page 117).

TRADE DIRECTORY

David Cromack

Bird tour companies offer trips to every part of the globe. Spain is a particularly popular destination — here a group checks wildfowl at Arrocampo in Extremadura.

TRADE DIRECTORY

BIRD GARDEN SUPPLIERS

ARK WILDLIFE LTD

Company ethos: Family-run garden wildlife mail order business offering a full range of high quality wild bird food produced on our premises in Hertfordshire.

Key product lines: Complete range of Ark® wild bird seed mixes with AdVit™ pro-biotics along with premium grade straights such as sunflower seeds, peanuts and niger, supported by a full range of accessories including bird feeders, wildlife habitats and more.

Other services: Mail order company, 24-hour shopping on-line, with free next day delivery. Phone for a catalogue.

Opening times: Mon - Fri (8.30am-6pm), Sat (9am-2pm). Out of hours answer phone service.

Address: Dog Kennel Farm, Charlton Road, Hitchin, Hertfordshire SG5 2AB. 0800 085 4865; (fax)01462 420 022; e-mail: office@arkwildlife.co.uk www.arkwildlife.co.uk

arkwildlife.co.uk

BAMFORDS TOP FLIGHT

Company ethos: Family-owned manufacturing company providing good quality bird foods via a network of UK stockists or mail order. RSPB Corporate Member, BTO Business Ally, Petcare Trust Member.

Key product lines: A range of wild bird mixtures containing the revolutionary new 'Pro-tec Health Aid', developed by Bamfords, to protect and promote the welfare of wild birds. Vast array of other foods and seeds for birds.

Other services: Trade suppliers of bulk and pre-packed bird and petfoods. Custom packing/own label if required.

New for 2011: Bird foods in a handy 12.75kg bag. No VAT and great value.

Opening times: Mon-Fri (8am-5.30pm); Sat (8am-12noon); Sunday (10am-12noon), Mill Shop only.

Address: Globe Mill, Midge Hall, Leyland, Lancashire PR26 6TN:01772 456 300; (Fax) 01772 456 302; e-mail: sales@bamfords.co.uk web: www.bamfords.co.uk

BIRD VENTURES

Company ethos: A comprehensive stock of wildlife products for everyone from garden bird enthusiasts to keen birdwatchers. The business operates as an online shop and retail outlet based in Holt, Norfolk. The business helps support Natural Surroundings, a wildlife centre with eight acres of gardens and education facilities for all ages, which won Environmental Small Business of the Year for north Norfolk from the district council.

Key product lines: Nest box cameras, moth traps, butterfly nets, wildbird food, bird feeders, nest boxes, hedgehog homes, insect habitats, bat boxes, squirrel-proof feeders, wildflower seeds, children's nature study equipment and much more.

Other services: On-line 24 hours.

Opening times: Mon-Sat (9am-5.30pm).

Contact: Bird Ventures, 9B Chapel Yard, Albert Street, Holt, Norfolk NR25 6HG; 01263 710 203; (fax) 01263 711 091. e-mail: paullaurie100@aol.com www.birdventures.co.uk

CJ WILDBIRD FOODS LTD

Company ethos: CJ WildBird Foods aims to make significant, recognisable contributions to the protection and welfare of wild birds and other wildlife. Our ornithologists and wildlife advisors undertake research projects to ensure we are continually producing not only high quality products, but products designed specifically for the wildlife they are intended for.

Key product lines: CJ Wildlife bird feeders, bird food, nest boxes, wildlife-friendly plants, bird tables and accessories, along with a broad range of wildlife care products, all available via our secure on-line web site or by mail order from our free catalogue.

Other services: Request a free *Handbook of Garden Wildlife* catalogue with advice, tips and products. CJ Wildlife brand products are stocked in selected supermarkets, garden centres and pet shops.

New for 2011: Continuously adding new products to the range, call for a brochure, visit the website, or sign up for our free monthly email updates.

Opening times: Call our friendly and knowledgeable team on free-phone 0800 731 2820 Monday to Friday (9am - 5pm), Saturday (9am - 12pm). Goods can be collected (10% discount excludes books and optics). Website 24 hours. Next working-day delivery on orders by 3pm & 2pm on Fridays. Delivery just £2.50 (UK only) and free on orders over £50.

Address: The Rea, Upton Magna, Shrewsbury, Shropshire SY4 4UR; 0800 731 2820; (Fax) 01743 709 504; e-mail: sales@birdfood.co.uk www.birdfood.co.uk

ERNEST CHARLES

Company ethos: Member of Birdcare Standards Assoc. ISO 9001 registered. Offering quality bird foods/wildlife products through a friendly mail-order service. Working in association with The British Trust for Ornithology.

Key product lines: Bird foods, feeders, nest boxes and other wildlife products.

Other services: Trade enquiries.

BOOK PUBLISHERS

New for 2011: A range of solutions to get tough on squirrels! Special incentive to join BTO's Garden BirdWatch.
Opening times: Mon to Fri (8am-5pm).
Address: Stuart Christophers, Copplestone Mills, Crediton, Devon EX17 5NF; 01363 84 842; (Fax) 01363 84 147; e-mail: stuart@ernest-charles.com www.ernest-charles.com

foodforbirds.co.uk
Company ethos: Specialist mail order company supplying high quality wild bird foods via a fast and friendly next day service. Supporter of RSPB and BTO through parent company.
Key product lines: A great range of tried and tested, freshly made wild bird mixtures, together with a whole host of straight foods – peanuts, sunflowers, nigerseed, fat foods etc.
Other services: Vast array of bird feeders for peanuts and seed, plus other wildlife foods, all of which can be ordered via a secure on-line website. Send for free catalogue.
New for 2011: Bird foods in a handy 12.75kg bag. No VAT and great value.
Opening times: Telesales (freephone) 8.00 - 5.30pm (order before midday for next day delivery). Answer phone outside these hours. On-line ordering and fax, 24 hours.
Address: Foodforbirds, Leyland, Lancs PR26 6TN; (Freephone) 0800 043 9022; (Fax) 01772 456 302.
e-mail: sales@foodforbirds.co.uk
www.foodforbirds.co.uk

BOOK PUBLISHERS

BUCKINGHAM PRESS LTD
Imprints: Single imprint company – publishers of *The Birdwatcher's Yearbook* since 1981, *Who's Who in Ornithology* (1997), *Best Birdwatching Sites* series covering Norfolk, Sussex, Highlands of Scotland, North Wales, Cornwall & Scilly. Plus sets of identification cards for British birds, dragonflies and butterflies.
New for 2011: *ID Insights*
Pocket Cards: Garden Birds, *Best Birdwatching Sites: The Solway* and *Best Birdwatching Sites: North East England.*
Address: 55 Thorpe Park Road, Peterborough, PE3 6LJ. Tel/Fax: 01733 561 739.
e-mail: admin@buckinghampress.com
www.buckinghampress.co.uk

CHRISTOPHER HELM PUBLISHERS
Imprints: *Christopher Helm*: the leading publisher of ornithology books in the world; includes many field guides, identification guides, family guides, county and country avifaunas, and a Where to Watch Birds series.

T & AD Poyser: an acclaimed series of respected ornithology monographs.
Birds of Africa – the standard series of handbooks on African birds.
A & C Black: publisher of definitive natural history books.
New for 2011: *Handbook of Western Palearctic Birds* by Hadoram Shirihai and Lars Svensson, *Surviving Extinction* by Clive Finlayson, *Butterflies of Europe* by Tari Haahtela et al, *Garden Pests of Britain and Europe* by Michael Chinery, *The Atlas of Birds* by Mike Unwin, *Watching Waterbirds with Kate Humble*, *Birds of Central Asia* by Raffale Ayé, Manuel Schweizer and Tobias Roth, *Birds of the Indian Subcontinent* (2nd edition) by Richard Grimmett, Carol and Tim Inskipp, *The Birds of the Malagasy Region* by Roger Safford and Frank Hawkins, and *Birds of Melanesia* by Guy Dutson. Also, e-books are now available for more than 100 titles and the entire Poyser monograph series is now back in print.
Address: 36 Soho Square, London, W1D 3QY; 020 7758 0200; (Fax) 020 7758 0222.
e-mail: nredman@acblack.com
www.acblack.com/naturalhistory

HARPER COLLINS PUBLISHERS
Collins Natural History — the leading publisher of fieldguides to the natural world.
Collins New Naturalist Series — the encyclopaedic reference for all areas of British natural history.
HarperCollins — publisher of the best illustrated books.
New for 2011: *Collins Fungi Guide*, *David Attenborough's First Life*, *New Naturalist Plant Pests*, *Field Guide Birds of North America*, *Collins Bird Guide*, 2nd Edition (large format), *Wonders of the Universe*.
Address: 77-85 Fulham Palace Rd, Hammersmith, London, W6 8JB; 020 8307 4998; (Fax)020 8307 4037;
e-mail: Myles.Archibald@harpercollins.co.uk
www.collins.co.uk
www.newnaturalists.co.uk

NEW HOLLAND PUBLISHERS (UK) LTD
Imprints; Imprints: New Holland: field guides, photographic guides, garden wildlife books and other illustrated titles on birds and general wildlife, plus personality-led natural history. Recent bestsellers include *New Holland Concise Bird Guide*, *Advanced Bird ID Guide*, *Tales of a Tabloid Twitcher*, *Atlas of Rare Birds*, *A Field Guide to the Birds of Borneo*, *A Field Guide to the Birds of South-East Asia* and *Creative Bird Photography*.

Struik: the world's leading natural history publisher on African wildlife.
New for 2011: *Barn Owl* and *Top Birding Sites of Europe.*
Address: Garfield House, 86-88 Edgware Road, London W2 2EA; 020 7724 7773; (Fax) 020 7258 1293; e-mail: simon.papps@nhpub.co.uk
www.newhollandpublishers.com

WILDGuides LTD
Imprints: *WILDGuides*: natural history fieldguides covering butterflies, dragonflies, orchids, arable plants.
OCEANGuides: identification guides to marine wildlife covering Antarctic, Atlantic and Pacific titles.
Destination Guides: lavishly illustrated visitor guides to Galapagos, Seychelles, South Georgia, Falklands.
Crossbill Guides: regional heritage guides for walkers covering Spain, France, Poland, Hungary.
Recently published: *Flowers of the New Forest, Natural History Guide to Finnish Lapland, Britain's Reptiles & Amphibians, Britain's Dragonflies 2nd Edition, Nightjars of the World, Britain's Butterflies 2nd edition, The Jewel Hunter.*
New for 2011: *Wildlife of Antarctica, Wildlife of South Georgia, Plants of South Georgia, Britain's Bees, Britain's Hoverflies, World's Rarest Birds, Natural History Guide to the Loire Valley.*
Address: PO Box 680, Maidenhead, Berkshire SL6 9ST; 01628 529 297; (Fax) 01628 525 314.
e-mail: info@wildguides.co.uk
www.wildguides.co.uk

BOOK SELLERS

CALLUNA BOOKS
Company ethos: We specialise in buying and selling out-of-print natural history titles, with an emphasis on quality stock at competitive prices.
Key subjects: Birds, mammals, flora, invertebrates in the UK and worldwide, including the Poyser and New Naturalist series, and general natural history, conservation and countryside titles including some reports and journals. Stock of 2000+ titles maintained.
Other services: Catalogues issued (usually 3 p.a). We exhibit at some bird fairs including Rutland Water. Wants lists welcomed – no obligation to buy.
Opening times: Mail order but viewing by appointment possible.
Address: Moor Edge, 2 Bere Road, Wareham, Dorset BH20 4DD; 01929 552 560.
e-mail: enquiries@callunabooks.co.uk
www.callunabooks.co.uk

NHBS - Everything for wildlife, science & environment

Everything for wildlife, science & environment

Company ethos: A unique natural history, conservation and environmental supplier offering the world's largest range of wildlife books and field equipment.
Key subjects: Natural history, birding, conservation, environmental science, zoology, habitats, botany, marine biology, bat detecting, entomology, GPS.
Other services: Search and browse our full online catalogue of more than 110,000 titles at www.nhbs.com
New for 2011: Rapidly growing range of field equipment and essential travel kit for safari and expeditions.
Opening times: Mon-Fri (9am-5pm), for mail-order service. Browse or order anytime at www.nhbs.com
Address: 2-3 Wills Road, Totnes, Devon TQ9 5XN; 01803 865 913; www.nhbs.com
e-mail: customer.services@nhbs.co.uk

PICTURE BOOK
Company ethos: Picture Book is a general bookshop specialising in bird books and local history.
Key subjects: Birdwatching, natural history, local history.
Other services: Mail order, new and secondhand books.
Opening times: The shop is open to the public Tuesday, Wednesday, Friday and Saturday (9am-4.30pm), (Mon-Sat in December).
Address: Picture Book, 6 Stanley Street, Leek, ST13 5HG; 01538 399 033 & 384 337; (Fax) 01538 399 696; e-mail: info@leekbooks.co.uk
www.birdbooksonline.co.uk
Churnet Valley publish local history and Arnold Bennett titles in paperback and hardback with introductions by the Arnold Bennett Society
View our website - click www.leekbooks.co.uk

SECOND NATURE
Company ethos: Buying and selling out-of-print/ secondhand/antiquarian books on natural history, topography and travel.
Key subjects: Birds, mammals, flowers and all other aspects of natural history.
Other services; Exhibits at bird/wildlife fairs.
New for 2011: A comprehensive website - www.secondnaturebooks.com
Opening times: Mail order only.
Address: Knapton Book Barn, Back Lane, Knapton, York YO26 6QJ; (Tel/fax) 01904 339 493.
e-mail: SecondnatureYork@aol.com
www.secondnaturebooks.com

CLOTHING AND EQUIPMENT SUPPLIERS

SUBBUTEO NATURAL HISTORY BOOKS

Company ethos: Specialisation and careful selection have allowed us to develop a fine reputation for supplying & publishing natural history books, DVDs, travel and field guides for those who enjoy bird watching and the natural world; while providing a fast, friendly and efficient service.

Key subjects: Natural history — ornithology; UK, Europe & worldwide, mammals, reptiles & amphibians; aquatic fauna; butterflies & moths; plants & fungi; ecology & environmental science; wildlife art & photography.

Other services: Comprehensive online bookstore, online book forum, gift wrap service, booklist service, worldwide book sourcing. On-line ordering, with free delivery on orders over £50 (in-print titles & UK titles only), free catalogue, updates & monthly e-newsletter. Sister company CJ WildBird Foods Ltd - www.birdfood.co.uk

New for 2011: Continuously adding new titles to the range, so call for a brochure, visit the website or alternatively visit us in Shropshire.

Opening times: Book shop: Monday to Friday (9am-5pm). Saturday (9am-12pm). Online ordering 24 hrs.

Address: The Rea, Upton Magna, Shrewsbury, Shropshire SY4 4UR; 01743 709 420; (Fax) 01743 709 504; e-mail: info@wildlifebooks.com www.wildlifebooks.com

CLOTHING SUPPLIERS

COUNTRY INNOVATION

Company ethos: Specialists in clothing, footwear and accessories specifically for the birdwatching market. Offering friendly advice by well trained staff.

Key product lines: Full range of outdoor wear: Jackets, fleeces, trousers, travel clothing, Ventile garments, Brasher footwear, Tilley hats, bags and accessories, Ladies fit available.

Other services: Mail order and website. Quality waterproof products for artists and birdwatchers.

New for 2011: Osprey Jacket - a fully featured Ventile jacket. Traveller Jacket - a unique multi-pocketed waterproof jacket. New range of ladies lightweight shirts and trousers.

Opening times; Mon-Fri (9am-5pm). Check website for appearances at birdfairs and other events.

Address: 1 Broad Street, Congresbury, North Somerset BS49 5DG; 01934 877 333. e-mail: sales@countryinnovation.com www.countryinnovation.com

PARÁMO DIRECTIONAL CLOTHING SYSTEMS

Company ethos: Innovators of technical mountain, birding and travel clothing using revolutionary Nikwax fabrics and functional design to provide performance and comfort for all outdoor enthusiasts and professionals, whatever their activity. Ethical manufacture.

Key product lines: Waterproof jackets and trousers, technical base layers, insulating overlayers and ultra cooling travel wear. Of especial note: Halcon and Pájaro birdwatching jackets and Pájaro waterproof trousers and Andy Rouse Limited Edition range of Aspira smock, Cascada trousers and Mountain Vent.

Other services: Repair and service of Páramo garments; online sales at www.naturallyparamo.co.uk

New for 2011: New colours and styles to be revealed.

Opening times; For independent retailers, consult our website or ring 01892 786 444 for stockist list and catalogue pack. See paramo.co.uk/londonstore for opening times of Covent Garden Store.

Address: Unit F, Durgates Industrial Estates, Wadhurst, East Sussex TN5 6DF, UK; 01892 786 444; e-mail: info@paramo.co.uk www.paramo.co.uk

EQUIPMENT SUPPLIERS

ALWYCH BOOKS

Company ethos: Quality waterproof products for artists and birdwatchers.

Key product lines: The Bird Watcher's All-Weather Flexible Pocket Note Book. Alwych Notebooks with their All-Weather Flexible Covers.

Address: Janette Scott, Wishaw Printing Company, 84 Stewarton Street, Wishaw, Lanarkshire ML2 8AG. Sales: 0845 270 2828; Admin: 01698 357 223. www.alwych.co.uk

BIRD IMAGES

Company ethos: High quality products at affordable prices.

Key product lines: Bird DVDs. A range of titles including identification guides and innovative guides to birdwatching places.

New for 2011: The Birds of North America.

Opening times: Telephone first.

Address: 28 Carousel Walk, Sherburn in Elmet, North Yorkshire LS25 6LP; 01977 684 666. e-mail: paul@birdvideodvd.com www.birdvideodvd.com

119

EQUIPMENT SUPPLIERS AND HOLIDAY COMPANIES

BIRDGUIDES LTD

BIRDGUIDES

Company ethos: Better birding through technology. The number one birder's website.
Key product lines: Software and video guides to British, European and American birds. Rare bird news services via e-mail, website and SMS. Books and an expanding range of natural history products for mobile phones.
New for 2011: New apps, search for BirdGuides on the iTunes store.
Address: BirdGuides Ltd, 3 Warple Mews, Warple Way, London W3 0RF; 020 8749 3354; order line (freephone) 0800 919 391;
e-mail: contact@birdguides.com
www.birdguides.com

BLUEBIRD TECHNOLOGY

Company ethos: Bluebird Technology focuses on creating quality wildlife recording software products for all birders to enjoy. All of our software is really easy to use; you don't have to be a computer or database geek to use it.
Key product lines: Bird Journal

New for 2011: Bird Journal Mobile.
Opening times: Lines are open 9am-5pm (UK time), Monday to Friday, except national holidays. Calls charged at local rate.
Address: Bluebird Technology, 28 Grebe Court, Cambridge, CB5 8FR; 0845 094 6012.
e-mail: mail@bluebirdtechnology.com
www.bluebirdtechnology.com
Follow us on Twitter:
http://twitter.com/Bluebird_Tech/
FaceBook: http://www.facebook.com/
BluebirdTechnology/

NEWART

Company ethos: Our company introduces its innovative products in specialised fields.
Key product lines: Clipmate was invented to prevent the swing and bounce of binoculars or other equipment when hung on a strap. The device is fitted to the binoculars which are then clipped to the user's coat, sweater or shirt. This gives the freedom of both hands, invaluable when walking with a dog lead, stick or nordic poles. The package retails at £10 + £2 p&p.
Address: Payment by cheque to 12 Verwood Drive, Barnet, Herts EN4 9TP; 020 8275 0018;
e-mail: Neil.newart@btinternet.com

WILDLIFE WATCHING SUPPLIES

Company ethos: To bring together a comprehensive range of materials, clothing and equipment to make it easier and more comfortable for you to blend in with the environment. Quick and friendly service.
Key product lines: Hides, camouflage, bean bags, lens and camera covers, clothing etc.etc.
Opening times: Mon to Fri (9am-5pm), Mail order. Visitors by appointment.
Address: Wildlife Watching Supplies, Tiverton Way, Tiverton Business Park, Tiverton, Devon EX16 6TG; +44 (0)1884 254 191; Fax: +44 (0)1884 250 460.
www.wildlifewatchingsupplies.co.uk

WILDSOUNDS

Company ethos: Donates a significant portion of profit to bird conservation, committed to sound environmental practices, official bookseller to African Bird Club and Oriental Bird Club.
Key product lines: Mail order, post-free books, multi-media guides and eGuides for PDAs — mobile versions of popular fieldguides complete with bird sounds and listing software e.g. *Collins Bird eGuide* and *Sasol eBirds of Southern Africa*. Publisher and distributor of *Birding in Eastern Europe* by Gerard Gorman. Field recording equipment stockist.
Opening times: Weekdays (9.30am-5pm).
Address: Cross Street, Salthouse, Norfolk NR25 7XH; +44(UK) (0)1263 741 100; (Fax) +44 (0)1263 741 838.
e-mail: isales@wildsounds.com
www.wildsounds.com

HOLIDAY COMPANIES

AIGAS FIELD CENTRE

Company ethos: Scotland's longest running nature holiday provider delivers outstanding wildlife watching holidays for groups and individuals. From birdwatching to pine martin, badger or beaver viewing — we've got the lot!
Types of tours: Birdwatching and wildlifewatching for all levels.
Destinations: Highlands and Islands of Scotland.
Office opening times: Mon-Fri (8.30am-5pm). Operating season April to mid-October.
Brochure from: Aigas Field Centre, Aigas, Beauly, Inverness-shire IV4 7AD; 01463 782 443; (Fax)01463 782 097. e-mail: info@aigas.co.uk www.aigas.co.uk

AVIAN ADVENTURES

Company ethos: Top quality, value for money tours, escorted by friendly, experienced leaders at a fairly relaxed pace. ATOL 3367.
Types of tours: Birdwatching, birds and wildlife photography and wildlife safaris, all suitable for both the first-time and the more experienced traveller.

Destinations: More than 50 tours worldwide.
New for 2011: Belarus, Ethiopia, Nile cruise, Ohio (Magee Marsh), Brazil – Pantanal Photographic.
Brochure from: 49 Sandy Road, Norton, Stourbridge, DY8 3AJ; 01384 372 013; (Fax)01384 441 340;
e-mail: info@avianadventures.co.uk
www.avianadventures.co.uk

BIRDFINDERS

Company ethos: Top-value birding tours to see all specialities/endemics of a country/area, using leading UK and local guides. ATOL 5406.
Types of tours: Birdwatching holidays for all abilities.
Destinations: Nearly 80 tours in UK, Europe, Africa, Asia, Australasia, North and South America and Antarctica.
New for 2011: Australia southeast and Tasmania, Bhutan, Estonia, Guyana, Kuwait and New England (USA).
Brochure from: Vaughan Ashby, Westbank, Cheselbourne, Dorset DT2 7NW. 01258 839 066.
e-mail: info@birdfinders.co.uk
www.birdfinders.co.uk
Our office is open seven days a week (8am-8pm).

BIRD WATCHING & WILDLIFE CLUB

Company ethos: To provide birdwatchers with high quality, reasonably priced accommodation, enabling them to experience the abundance of wildlife in the area.
Types of tours: Based at the 3-star, 50-bedroom Grant Arms Hotel, BWWC provides guides, maps and advice on wildlife-watching sites nearby, helping guests to make the most of their holiday whilst remaining free to create their own itinerary.

Destinations: Cairngorms, Speyside and North East Scotland.
New for 2011: Great rates for clubs and groups!
Opening times: (7am-10:30pm) seven days a week.
Brochure from: Grant Arms Hotel, 25 The Square, Grantown-on-Spey, Highlands PH26 3HF; 01479 872 526; e-mail: bookings@bwwc.co.uk
www.bwwc.co.uk

BRITISH-BULGARIAN FRIENDSHIP SOCIETY

Company ethos: To introduce people to the beauty of Bulgarian wildlife at exceptional value prices with expert leaders. ATOL 4465.
Types of tours: Birdwatching tours in winter, spring and autumn, also early summer and midsummer butterfly tours. Group size 12-14 persons.
Destinations: Specialists to Bulgaria, over 35 years experience.
New for 2011: Birds and Bears; Bulgaria and Romania's Danube Delta in Spring; Autumn Migration

on Bulgaria's Black Sea Coast and Turkey's Bosphorus.
Brochure from: Balkania Travel Ltd, 3.40, Morley House, 320 Regent Street, London W1B 3BE; (Tel) 020 7536 9400 or e-mail: ognian@balkaniatravel.com
www.balkaniatravel.com
or Dr Annie Kay (Tel) 020 7237 7616 or
e-mail: annie.kay@btinternet.com www.bbfs.org.uk

CLASSIC JOURNEYS

Company ethos: Professional and friendly company, providing well organised and enjoyable wildlife holidays.
Types of tours: General wildlife and photography holidays on the Indian sub-continent and beyond.
Destinations: Nepal, India, Bhutan, Sri Lanka, Tibet, Indonesia, Ecuador, Galapagos, Peru, Brazil, Tanzania, Spitsbergen, Antarctica.
New for 2011: Indonesia for Orangutans and Komodo Dragons, Brazil for Jaguars, Antarctica for amazing wildlife.
Opening times: Mon-Fri (9:30am-4pm).
Further Information: www.classicjourneys.co.uk
Tel: 01773 873 497;
e-mail: info@classicjourneys.co.uk

DORSET BIRDING

Company ethos: To provide a local knowledge and an expertise of Dorset's birds and wildlife catering for all levels of experience and tailor-made to your requirements.
Types of tours: A guiding service for individuals and small groups aimed at providing an experience of Dorset's birds, wildlife and landscapes. Although there is a particular emphasis on birds, all species groups are covered. Half-day, full day, weekends or longer breaks are available. Local accommodation can be arranged.
Destinations: Dorset, New Forest.
Brochure from: Moor Edge, 2 Bere Road, Wareham, Dorset BH20 4DD;01929 552 560.
e-mail: enquiries@dorsetbirdingandwildlife.co.uk
www.dorsetbirdingandwildlife.co.uk

GLENLOY WILDLIFE

Company ethos: We offer guided exploration of the stunning West Coast of Scotland, based from beautiful Glen Loy near Fort William in a former hunting lodge with views over the Nevis Range. The glen contains red deer, eagles, otter and chequered skippers with pine martens visiting the Lodge each evening.
Types of tours: We visit a variety of habitats by minibus and by foot. Suitable for anyone who can walk 3-4 miles.
Destinations: We explore the region of Lochaber, including the Great Glen, Ardnamurchan peninsula and the Small Isles.

HOLIDAY COMPANIES

Further information from: Jon Mercer, Glenloy Lodge Guest House, Banavie, Nr Fort William PH33 7PD; 01397 712 700 or 07817 443 370. e-mail: info@glenloylodge.co.uk www.glenloylodge.co.uk

HEATHERLEA

Company ethos: Exciting holidays to see all the birds of Scotland and selected overseas destinations. Experienced guides and comfortable award-winning hotel offering great customer service.
Types of tours: Birdwatching and other wildlife watching tours.
Destinations: Scottish Highlands, including holidays from our base in Nethybridge, plus Outer Hebrides, Orkney, Shetlands and more. Selected overseas destinations include the Pyrenees, Lesvos, Kenya and Trinidad.
New for 2011: Scotland - Heatherlea now have five stars from Visit *Scotland*, rating our Wildlife Experience as 'Exceptional'. We are the only operator in the Scottish Highlands with this, the highest possible grading. New holidays include Highlands and Orkney, Highlands and remotest Aberdeenshire, Natural History of Western Scotland. Overseas - new destinations include Nepal, Japan, Uganda, Croatia, mammals in Finland and Yellowstone in Winter.
Brochure from: The Mountview Hotel, Nethybridge, Inverness-shire PH25 3EB; 01479 821 248; (Fax) 01479 821 515; e-mail: info@heatherlea.co.uk www.heatherlea.co.uk

NATURETREK

Company ethos: Friendly, gentle-paced, birdwatching holidays with broad-brush approach. Sympathetic to other wildlife interests, history and local culture. Also operate faster-paced bargain birdwatching selection. ATOL no 2692
Types of tours: Escorted birdwatching, botanical and natural history holidays worldwide.

Destinations: Worldwide - see brochure.
New for 2011: 30+ exciting new European tours, plus several new long-haul destinations.
Brochure from: Cheriton Mill, Cheriton, Alresford, Hampshire SO24 0NG; 01962 733 051; (Fax) 01962 736 426; e-mail: info@naturetrek.co.uk www.naturetrek.co.uk

NORFOLK BIRDING

Company ethos: To provide an inspiring and educational experience watching & photographing birds and wildlife.
Types of tours: Birdwatching Tours & Wildlife Photography workshops. One-to-one tutorials.
Destinations: Norfolk, Scotland and Europe.
New for 2011: Andalucia — Autumn Amazing Migrants, Wales — Red kite photography, Outer

Hebrides — Birdwatching Tour.
Brochure from: Norfolk Birding, Lilac Cottage, Foxley Road, Themelthorpe, Norfolk NR20 5PU. 01362 683 520 or 07876 357 677; e-mail: chrismills@norfolkbirding.com www.norfolkbirding.com

NORTH WEST BIRDS

Company ethos: Friendly, relaxed and unhurried but targetted to scarce local birds.
Types of tours: Very small groups (up to four) based on large family home in South Lakes with good home cooking. Short breaks with birding in local area. Butterflies in season.
Destinations: Local to Northwest England. Lancashire, Morecambe Bay and Lake District.
Brochure from: Mike Robinson, Barn Close, Beetham, Cumbria LA7 7AL; (Tel/fax) 01539 563 191; e-mail: mike@nwbirds.co.uk www.nwbirds.co.uk

NORTHERN FRANCE WILDLIFE TOURS

Company ethos: Friendly personal attention. Normally a maximum of five in a group. Totally flexible.
Types of tours: Beginners to experienced birders. Local birds include Black Woodpecker, Bluethroat, Melodious Warbler.
Destinations: Brittany, Normandy and Pays de la Loire.
Brochure from: Roy and Shirley Croucher, Place de L'Eglise, 53700, Averton, France; 0033 243 006 969. e-mail: nfwt@online.fr www.northernfrancewildlifetours.com

ORIOLE BIRDING

Company ethos: Enhancing your ID skills and enjoyment of birding with small group tours.
Types of tours: Norfolk and South Wales birding tours year-round, covering all the best sites and species, plus a selection of Britain's best destinations. Also a comprehensive range of international holidays and pelagics. ATOL protected 6839.
Destinations: Norfolk, South Wales, Solway, Speyside, Cornwall, Isles of Scilly, pelagics, North-east England, Fair Isle, County Wexford, Mull and Iona, Extremadura, Romania, South Africa, The Gambia, Israel, Finland, Madeira, India, Lesvos, Turkey, Morocco, Poland, Holland.
New for 2011: Peru,

HOLIDAY COMPANIES

Panama, Iran, Botswana, Donana, Croatia, Sri Lanka.
Brochure from: Oriole Birding, 84 Coity Road,
Bridgend CF31 1LT; 01656 645 709.
e-mail: info@oriolebirding.com
www.oriolebirding.com

ORNITHOLIDAYS
Company ethos: Oldest bird tour company in the
world (established 1965). Friendly and fun holidays
led by full-time tour leaders. ATOL no 0743.
Types of tours: Escorted birdwatching and natural
history tours.
Destinations: Worldwide including Trinidad and
Tobago, Costa Rica, Kenya, Bhutan, Australia, South
Africa, Galapagos Islands and Antarctica.
New for 2011: Colombia, USA — Cape May, Italy
(Birds & Wine), Spain (Tarifa and also Barcelona),
South Africa — Eastern Cape and Karoo, India
(Photographic), Australia — Tasmania, Chile (Puma
tour), Iceland (Winter tours)
Brochure from: 29 Straight Mile, Romsey, Hampshire
SO51 9BB; 01794 519 445; (Fax) 01794 523 544.
e-mail: info@ornitholidays.co.uk
www.ornitholidays.co.uk

ROMNEY MARSH BIRDWATCHING BREAKS
Company ethos: To pass on an appreciation of the
wildlife of Romney Marsh in a family friendly
atmosphere.
Types of tours: Fully inclusive 3 or 5 day
Birdwatching Breaks based at our cottage in Lydd-on-
Sea. Also, one day birdwatching and historical tours
around Romney Marsh.
Destinations: Romney Marsh, including Dungeness and
Rye Harbour, and elsewhere across Kent and Sussex.
New for 2011: Day trips to northern France.
Brochure from: Paul Trodd, Plovers, 1 Toby Road,
Lydd-on-Sea, Romney Marsh, Kent TN29 9PG; 01797
366 935 & 07920 197 535; www. plovers.co.uk
e-mail: troddy@plovers.co.uk

SPEYSIDE WILDLIFE

Company ethos: Fun-filled wildlife experiences
with expert guides, where
you are always treated as an
individual, not one of a crowd.
Types of tours: Fully inclusive
bird and mammal watching
holidays in Scotland and
overseas (ATOL no 4259). Also
tailor-made trips, day guiding
and hides.
Destinations: Speyside in
the Cairngorms National Park
and around Scotland, Europe;
Scandinavia and the Arctic; North, Central and South
America; Africa.
New for 2011: Wildlife for Beginners; Wildlife
and Walking; Grampian Coast and Speyside; Morocco;
Turkey; Estonia Mammals; Hungary Mammals; Holland
in Summer.

Brochure from: Garden Office, Inverdruie House,
Inverdruie, Aviemore, Inverness-shire PH22 1QH;
01479 812 498 (tel/fax);
e-mail: enquiries@speysidewildlife.co.uk
www.speysidewildlife.co.uk, www.facebook.com/
speysidewildlife

SUNBIRD
Company ethos: Enjoyable birdwatching tours lead
by full-time professional leaders. ATOL no 3003.
Types of tours: Birdwatching, Birds and Music, Birds
and History, Birds and Butterflies.
Destinations: Worldwide.
Brochure from: 26B The Market Square, Potton,
Sandy, Bedfordshire SG19 2NP; 01767 262 522; (Fax)
01767 262 916.
e-mail: sunbird@sunbirdtours.co.uk
www.sunbirdtours.co.uk check new destinations

THE TRAVELLING NATURALIST
Company ethos: Friendly, easy-going, expertly-led
birdwatching and wildlife tours. ATOL no.3435. AITO
1124.
Types of tours: Tours include Birds and Butterflies,
Butterflies and Flowers, Tigers, Arctic Cruises, Whale-
watching.
Destinations: Worldwide.
New for 2011: Our new holiday brand: Wild
Ambitions — wildlife holidays for independent
travellers. www.wildambitions.co.uk
Brochure from: PO Box 3141, Dorchester, Dorset DT1
2XD; 01305 267994; (Fax) 01305 265 506.
e-mail: info@naturalist.co.uk
www.naturalist.co.uk

THE WILDLIFE GOURMET
Company ethos: To pass on our knowledge of wildlife
for future generations, through watching great birds
and wildlife that can be found around us, and to
enjoy good food and good wine in each area.
Types of tours: Birdwatching and general wildlife
trips including butterflies, wild flowers and mammals.
Destinations: Day trips to the Everglades, longer trips
to Texas, Alaska, Yellowstone, Rocky Mountain NP,
Florida and Europe.
Details from: Brett Hogan, P.O.Box 4, Islamorada,
Florida, U.S.A 33036. www.thewildlifegourmet.com
e-mail: thewildlifegourmet@yahoo.com

THINKGALAPAGOS
Company ethos: Specialists in the Galapagos Islands,
great value, expert guides and personal attention to
ensure a once-in-a-
lifetime adventure
travel experience.
Types of tours:
Friendly and relaxed
holidays that are
educationally
orientated for people
with a keen interest

in wildlife and photography. Suitable for both the first-time and more experienced traveller.
Destinations: Galapagos and mainland Ecuador.
New for 2011: Birding Special Trip to Ecuador and Galapagos in May, led by top birding guides.
Brochure from: Rachel Dex, 25 Trinity Lane, Beverley, East Yorkshire HU17 0DY; 01482 872 716. e-mail: info@thinkgalapagos.com
www.thinkgalapagos.com

WILD INSIGHTS
Company ethos: Friendly, no-rush tours designed to savour, understand and enjoy birds and wildlife fully, rather than simply build large tick lists. Emphasis on quality. ATOL no 5429 (in association with Wildwings).
Types of tours: Relaxed UK workshops, skills-building UK courses, plus selected overseas tours.
Destinations: Various UK locations, plus selected destinations throughout USA, Africa, Northern India and Europe.
Calendar brochure from: Yew Tree Farmhouse, Craignant, Selattyn, Oswestry, Salop SY10 7NP; (Tel/fax) 01691 718 740; e-mail: keith.offord@virgin.net
www.wildinsights.co.uk

WILDWINGS
Company ethos: Superb value holidays led by expert guides.
Types of tours: Birdwatching holidays, Whale and Dolphin Watching Holidays, Mammal Tours and Wildlife Cruises worldwide.
Destinations: Europe, Arctic, Asia, The Americas, Antarctica, Africa, Australasia and the Pacific.
Brochure from: 577-579 Fishponds Road, Fishponds, Bristol, BS16 3AF; e-mail: wildinfo@wildwings.co.uk
www.wildwings.co.uk

OPTICAL DEALERS

To assist readers in locating optics dealers in their own area more easily, this section is devoted into five regions, listed alphabetically as follows: Eastern England, Northern England, South East England, South West England and Western England.

EASTERN ENGLAND

BIRDNET OPTICS LTD
Company ethos: To provide the birdwatcher with the best value for money on optics, books and outdoor clothing.
Viewing facilities: Clear views to distant hills for comparison of optics at long range and wide variety of textures and edges for clarity and resolution comparison.
Optical stock: Most leading binocular and telescope ranges stocked. If we do not have it, we will endeavour to get it for you.
Non-optical stock: Books incl. New Naturalist series

and Poysers, videos, CDs, audio tapes, tripods, hide clamps, accessories and clothing.
Opening times: Mon-Sat (9:30am-5:30pm). Sundays, see website for details.
Address: 5 London Road, Buxton, Derbyshire SK17 9PA; 01298 71 844. e-mail: paulflint@birdnet.co.uk
www.birdnet.co.uk

IN-FOCUS
Company ethos: The binocular and telescope specialists, offering customers informed advice at birdwatching venues throughout the country. Leading sponsor of the British Birdwatchng Fair.
Viewing facilities: Available at all shops (contact your local outlet), or at field events (10am-4pm) at bird reserves (see *Bird Watching* magazine or website www.at-infocus.co.uk for calendar)
Optical stock: Many leading makes of binoculars and telescopes, plus own-brand Delta range of binoculars and tripods.
Non-optical stock: Wide range of tripods, clamps and other accessories. Repair service available.
Opening times: These can vary, so please contact local shop or website before travelling.

NORFOLK
Address: Main Street, Titchwell, Nr King's Lynn, Norfolk, PE31 8BB; 01485 210 101.

RUTLAND
Address: Anglian Water Birdwatching Centre, Egleton Reserve, Rutland Water, Rutland, LE15 8BT; 01572 770 656.

LONDON CAMERA EXCHANGE
Company ethos: To supply good quality optical equipment at a competitive price, helped by knowlegeable staff.
Viewing facilities: In shop and at local shows. Contact local branch for details of local events.
Optical stock: All leading makes of binoculars and scopes.
Non-optical stock: All main brands of photo, digital and video equipment.
Opening times: Most branches open 9am to 5.30pm.

CHESTERFIELD
Address: 1A South Street, Chesterfield, Derbyshire, S40 1QZ; 01246 211 891; (Fax) 01246 211 563; e-mail: chesterfield@lcegroup.co.uk

COLCHESTER
Address: 12 Led Lane, Colchester, Essex CO1 1LS; 01206 573 444.

DERBY
Address: 17 Sadler Gate, Derby, Derbyshire, DE1 3NH; 01332 348 644; (Fax) 01332 369 136; e-mail: derby@lcegroup.co.uk

LINCOLN
Address: 6 Silver Street, Lincoln, LN2 1DY; 01522 514 131; (Fax) 01522 537 480; e-mail: lincoln@lcegroup.co.uk

OPTICAL DEALERS

NORWICH
Address: 12 Timber Hill, Norwich, Norfolk NR1 3LB;
01603 612 537.

NOTTINGHAM
Address: 7 Pelham Street, Nottingham, NG1 2EH;
0115 941 7486; (Fax) 0115 952 0547;
e-mail: nottingham@lcegroup.co.uk

NORTHERN ENGLAND

FOCALPOINT
Company ethos: Friendly advice by well-trained
staff, competitive prices, no 'grey imports'.
Viewing facilities: Fantastic open countryside for
superb viewing from the shop, plenty of wildlife.
Parking for up to 20 cars.
Optical stock: All leading brands of binoculars
and telescopes from stock, plus many pre-owned
binoculars and telescopes available.
Non-optical stock: Bird books, outdoor clothing,
boots, tripods plus full range of Skua products etc.
available from stock.
Opening times: Mon-Fri (9:30am-5pm); Sat (10am-
4pm)
Address: Marbury House Farm, Bentleys Farm Lane,
Higher Whitley, Warrington, Cheshire WA4 4QW;
01925 730 399; (Fax) 01925 730 368.
e-mail: focalpoint@dial.pipex.com
www.fpoint.co.uk

IN-FOCUS
LANCASHIRE
Address: WWT Martin Mere, Burscough, Ormskirk,
Lancs, L40 0TA: 01704 897 020.

WEST YORKSHIRE
Address: Westleigh House Office Est. Wakefield Road,
Denby Dale, West Yorks, HD8 8QJ: 01484 864 729.

LONDON CAMERA EXCHANGE
CHESTER
Address: 9 Bridge Street Row, CH1 1NW; 01244 326
531.

MANCHESTER
Address: 37 Parker Street, Picadilly, M1 4AJ; 0161
236 5819.

WILKINSON CAMERAS
Company ethos: The widest range of photographic
and birdwatching equipment available at competitive
prices at all times.
Viewing facilities: Optical field days at selected
nature reserves in northern England. See website for
details of photographic courses and other events.
Optical stock: Binoculars from Bushnell, Canon,
Hawke, Leica, Nikon, RSPB, Steiner, Swarovski,
Vanguard and Viking. Spotting scopes from Bushnell,
Hawke, Leica, Nikon, Summit, Swarovski and
Vanguard. Wide range of bags, digital cameras, lenses
and video equipment.
Opening times: Branches open 9am to 5:30pm
Monday to Saturday. Sunday 11am to 4pm (Preston
only). e-mail: sales@wilkinson.co.uk
www.wilkinson.co.uk

BLACKBURN
42 Northgate, Blackburn, Lancs BB2 1JL: 01254 581
272; (Fax) 01254 695 867.

BURNLEY
95 James Street, Burnley, Lancs BB11 1PY; 01282 424
524; (Fax) 01282 831 722.

BURY
61 The Rock, Bury, Greater Manchester BL9 0NB;
01617 643 402; (Fax) 01617 615 086.

CARLISLE
13 Grapes Lane, Carlisle, Cumbria CA3 8NQ; 01228
538 583; (Fax) 01228 514 699.

KENDAL
19A The Westmorland Centre, Kendal, Cumbria LA9
4AB; 01539 735 055; (Fax) 01539 734 929.

LANCASTER
6 James Street, Lancaster, Lancs LA1 1UP; 01524 380
510; (Fax) 01524 380 512.

PRESTON
27 Friargate, Preston, Lancs PR1 2NQ; 01772 556 250;
(Fax) 01772 259 435.

SOUTHPORT
38 Eastbank Street, Southport, Merseyside, PR8 1ET.
01704 534 534; (Fax) 01704 501 546;
e-mail: southport@wilkinson.co.uk

SOUTH EAST ENGLAND

GREEN WITCH
Company ethos: World-renowned Binocular and
Telescope Specialists, Friendly expert advice,
Competitive prices, Support and aftercare,
Top range products, No grey imports.
Viewing facilities: Showroom and outside area with
feeding stations and pond, Tuition available.
Optical stock: Wide range from leading brand names
of binoculars and telescopes.
Non-optical stock: Tripods and clamps, camera
adaptors, scope covers, nest boxes and feeders, bat
detectors, night vision, microscopes, books, DVDs
Opening times: Monday to Saturday (10am-5pm).
Address: Green Witch, 2 Bakers Court, Great
Gransden, Sandy, Beds SG19 3PF; 01767 677 025.
E-mail: lee@green-witch.com
www.green-witch.com

OPTICAL DEALERS

IN-FOCUS
(see introductory text in Eastern England).

ST ALBANS
Address: Bowmans Farm, London Colney, St Albans, Herts, AL2 1BB: 01727 827 799: (Fax) 01727 827 766.

SOUTH WEST LONDON
Address: WWT The Wetland Centre, Queen Elizabeth Walk, Barnes, London, SW13 9WT: 020 8409 4433.

LONDON CAMERA EXCHANGE
(see introductory text in Eastern England).

FAREHAM
Address: 135 West Street, Fareham, Hampshire, PO16 0DU; 01329 236 441; (Fax) 01329 823 294; e-mail: fareham@lcegroup.co.uk

GUILDFORD
Address: 8/9 Tunsgate, Guildford, Surrey, GU1 2DH; 01483 504 040; (Fax) 01483 538 216; e-mail: guildford@lcegroup.co.uk

PORTSMOUTH
Address: 40 Kingswell Path, Cascados, Portsmouth, PO1 4RR; 023 9283 9933; (Fax) 023 9283 9955; e-mail: portsmouth@lcegroup.co.uk

READING
Address: 7 Station Road, Reading, Berkshire, RG1 1LG; 0118 959 2149; (Fax) 0118 959 2197; e-mail: reading@lcegroup.co.uk

SOUTHAMPTON
Address: 10 High Street, Southampton, Hampshire, SO14 2DH; 023 8022 1597; (Fax) 023 8023 3838; e-mail: southampton@lcegroup.co.uk

STRAND, LONDON
Address: 98 The Strand, London, WC2R 0AG; 020 7379 0200; (Fax) 020 7379 6991; e-mail: strand@lcegroup.co.uk

WINCHESTER
Address: 15 The Square, Winchester, Hampshire, SO23 9ES; 01962 866 203; (Fax)01962 840 978; e-mail: winchester@lcegroup.co.uk

SOUTH WEST ENGLAND

LONDON CAMERA EXCHANGE
(see introductory text in Eastern England).

BATH
Address: 13 Cheap Street, Bath, Avon, BA1 1NB; 01225 462 234; (Fax) 01225 480 334. e-mail: bath@lcegroup,co.uk

BOURNEMOUTH
Address: 95 Old Christchurch Road, Bournemouth, Dorset, BH1 1EP; 01202 556 549; (Fax) 01202 293 288; e-mail: bournemouth@lcegroup.co.uk

BRISTOL
Address: 53 The Horsefair, Bristol, BS1 3JP; 0117 927 6185; (Fax) 0117 925 8716; e-mail: bristol.horsefair@lcegroup.co.uk

EXETER
Address: 174 Fore Street, Exeter, Devon, EX4 3AX; 01392 279 024/438 167; (Fax) 01392 426 988. e-mail: exeter@lcegroup.co.uk

PAIGNTON
Address: 71 Hyde Road, Paington, Devon, TQ4 5BP;01803 553 077; (Fax) 01803 664 081. e-mail: paignton@lcegroup.co.uk

PLYMOUTH
Address: 10 Frankfort Gate, Plymouth, Devon, PL1 1QD; 01752 668 894; (Fax) 01752 604248. e-mail: plymouth@lcegroup.co.uk

SALISBURY
Address: 6 Queen Street, Salisbury, Wiltshire, SP1 1EY; 01722 335 436; (Fax) 01722 411 670; e-mail: salisbury@lcegroup.co.uk

TAUNTON
Address: 6 North Street, Taunton, Somerset, TA1 1LH; 01823 259955; (Fax) 01823 338 001. e-mail: taunton@lcegroup.co.uk

WESTERN ENGLAND

CLIFTON CAMERAS
Company ethos: Specialists for binoculars and spotting scopes based near Slimbridge Wetland Centre in Gloucestershire. We sponsor the Dursley birdwatching society.
Optical stock: All top brands stocked. Nikon Premier Dealer, Swarovski Premier Dealer, Zeiss Centre Partner and Leica Premier Dealer.
Non-optical stock: Professional camera supplier, Nikon, Pentax, Sigma and Gitzo Tripods to name a few.

cliftoncameras.co.uk

New products to try: Zeiss Victory Diascopes, Swarovski SLC HD and Nikon EDG Binocular.
Opening times: Mon-Sat (9am-5.30pm).
Address: 28 Parsonage Street, Dursley, Gloucestershire GL11 4AA; 01453 548 128.
e-mail: sales@cliftoncameras.co.uk
www.cliftoncameras.co.uk

FOCUS OPTICS
Company ethos: Friendly, expert service. Top quality instruments. No 'grey imports'.
Viewing facilities: Our own pool and nature reserve with feeding stations.
Optical stock: Full range of leading makes of binoculars and telescopes.
Non-optical stock: Waterproof clothing, fleeces,

walking boots and shoes, bird food and feeders. Books, videos, walking poles.

Opening times: Mon-Sat (9am-5pm). Some Bank-holidays.

Address: Church Lane, Corley, Coventry, CV7 8BA; 01676 540 501/542 476; (Fax) 01676 540 930.

e mail: enquiries@focusoptics.eu

www.focusoptics.eu

IN-FOCUS

GLOUCESTERSHIRE

Address: WWT Slimbridge, Gloucestershire, GL2 7BT: 01453 890 978. 22314; (Fax) 01905 724 585; e-mail: worcester@lcegroup.co.uk

LONDON CAMERA EXCHANGE

(see introductory text in Eastern England).

CHELTENHAM

Address: 10-12 The Promenade, Cheltenham, Gloucestershire, GL50 1LR; 01242 519 851; (Fax) 01242 576 771; e-mail: cheltenham@lcegroup.co.uk

GLOUCESTER

Address: 12 Southgate Street, Gloucester, GL1 2DH; 01452 304 513; (Fax) 01452 387 309; e-mail: gloucester@lcegroup.co.uk

LEAMINGTON

Address: Clarendon Avenue, Leamington, Warwickshire, CV32 5PP; 01926 886 166; (Fax)01926 887 611; e-mail: leamington@lcegroup.co.uk

WORCESTER

Address: 8 Pump Street, Worcester, WR1 2QT; 01905 22314; (Fax) 01905 724 585; e-mail: worcester@lcegroup.co.uk

OPTICAL IMPORTERS AND MANUFACTURERS

CARL ZEISS LTD

Company ethos: World renowned, high quality performance and innovative optical products.

Product lines: Victory FL, Conquest, Stabilised, Victory and Classic compacts and Diascope FL telescopes.

New for 2011: Photoscope 85T + FL.

Address: PO Box 78, Woodfield Road, Welwyn Garden City, Hertfordshire AL7 1LU; 01707 871 350; (Fax) 01707 871 426; e-mail: binos@zeiss.co.uk

www.zeiss.co.uk

INTRO 2020 LTD

Company ethos: Experienced importer of photo and optical products.

Product lines: Steiner Binoculars, Tamron Lenses, Crumpler Bags, Tamrac Bags, Velbon Tripods, Slik Tripods, Kenko Scopes, Summit Binoculars, Hoya and Cokin filters. Plus many other.

Address: Unit 1, Priors Way, Maidenhead, Berkshire SL6 2HP; 01628 674 411; (Fax)01628 771 055.

e-mail: sales@intro2020.co.uk

www.intro2020.co.uk, www.cokin.co.uk, www. metzflash.co.uk, www.sliktripod.co.uk, www.velbon. co.uk, www.tamrac.co.uk, www.steiner-binoculars. co.uk, www.sliktripod.co.uk

LEICA CAMERA LTD

Company ethos: A passion for developing innovative products of the highest quality which expand the natural limits of the human eye — bringing people closer to the outdoor world.

Product lines: Ultravid HD (High Definition) Binoculars — for the definitive full size viewing experience. Ultravid and Trinovid Compact Binoculars — small in size, big in performance. Duovid — the world's first dual magnification binocular. APO-Televid 82 and 65 Spotting Scopes with the world's first 25:50x wide angle zoom eyepiece. Monovid — convenient and versatile monocular with macro lens and outstanding close-focus length of only 10inches. Premium range of compact digital cameras.

New for 2011: Leica V-LUX 20 — the high performance compact digital camera with super-zoom and GPS tagging — allowing birders to record the exact geographical coordinates, as well as the local time, for any photograph taken.

Office address: Leica Camera Limited, 34 Bruton Place, London W1J 6NR; www.leica-camera.com e-mail: enquiries@leica-camera.co.uk

NEWPRO UK LTD

Company ethos: Some very well-established and even old brand names with new company technology and attitude.

Product lines: Op/Tech straps, pouches and harnesses, Cullman tripods and monopods. ROR optics cleaner.

Hoodman 3" LCD Screen Loupes and accessory fittings.

Opening times: Mon-Fri (8.30am-5pm) plus many outdoor events.

Address: Old Sawmills Road, Faringdon, Oxon SN7 7DS. 01367 242 411; (Fax) 01367 241 124; e-mail: sales@newprouk.co.uk

www.newprouk.co.uk

TRADE DIRECTORY

OPTICAL REPAIRS AND SERVICING

OPTICRON

Company ethos: To continuously develop high quality binoculars, telescopes and accessories that are useful, ergonomically sound and exceptional value for money.

Product lines: Opticron binoculars, monoculars, telescopes, tripods, telephotography/digi-scoping equipment and accessories.
Address: Unit 21, Titan Court, Laporte Way, Luton LU4 8EF; (Tel) 01582 726 522, (fax) 01582 273 559; e-mail: sales@opticron.co.uk
www.opticron.co.uk

SWAROVSKI OPTIK

Company ethos: Constantly improving on what is good in terms of products and committed to conservation world-wide.
Product lines: ATS 65 spotting scope and EL 8x32 and 10x32 binoculars, the latest additions to a market-leading range of telescopes and binoculars. Swarovski tripods also available.
Address:
Perrywood Business Park, Salfords, Surrey RH1 5JQ; 01737 856 812: (Fax)01737 856 885.
e-mail: christine.percy@swarovski.com

VICKERS SPORTS OPTICS

Company ethos: o supply world-leading optical products to UK and Ireland birdwatchers, exclusively distributing brands Bushnell®, Tasco® and Premierlight® to retailers.

Product lines: The extensive Bushnell range offers cutting-edge binoculars, spotting scopes, nightvision equipment and more. Binoculars and spotting scopes by Tasco offer similarly high quality at entry-level. Premierlight LED lighting instruments perform exceptionally.
Other services: UK and Eire returns service.
New for 2011: Innovative new products arriving frequently.
Opening times: Mon-Thu (8.30am-5pm), Fri (8.30am-4pm).
Address: Unit 9, 35 Revenge Road, Lordswood, Chatham, Kent ME5 8DW; 01634 201 284.
e-mail: info@jjvickers.co.uk
www.jjvickers.co.uk

OPTICAL REPAIRS AND SERVICING

OPTREP Optical Repairs

Company ethos: To give a speedy, economical and effective repair service.
Key services: Servicing and repair of binoculars, telescopes etc. Conversant with the special needs of birdwatchers.
Opening times: Mon-Thu (9am-5pm), Fri (9am-3pm)
Address: 16 Wheatfield Road, Selsey, West Sussex PO20 0NY; 01243 601 365.
e-mail: info@opticalrepairs.com
www.opticalrepairs.com

While the publishers strive to make the Trade Directory as comprehensive as possible, we are aware that some companies slip through the net.

To ensure your company is included in the next edition, please contact us by e-mail to editor@buckinghampress.com or by telephone to 01733 561 739, before May 2011, to obtain full details.

BIRD RESERVES AND OBSERVATORIES

David Cromack

The Sands of Forvie National Nature Reserve in NE Scotland is a great place to connect with a wide range of waders at passage times.

THIS YEAR the publishers have taken the decision to standardise the presentation of entries in the Reserves Directory on a regional basis. This has been the standard practice for Scotland and Wales in recent editions, whereas the English counties have been listed alphabetically, but it is felt that grouping counties into regions will be more helpful to our readers.

In this edition you will find sections for Central England, Eastern England, Northern England, South-Eastern England and South-Western England. We hope this proves helpful but welcome reader feedback on any way we can improve this section of the *Yearbook*. Please e-mail your comments to the Editor David Cromack at: editor@buckinghampress.com

Central England

Derbyshire

1. CARR VALE NATURE RESERVE

Derbyshire Wildlife Trust.
Location: SK 45 70. 1km W of Bolsover on A632 to Chesterfield. Turn L at roundabout (follow brown tourist signs) into Riverside Way. Car park at end of road. Follow footpath (waymarked) around Peter Fidler reserve.
Access: Open all year.
Facilities: Car park, coach parking on approach road, good disabled access, paths, viewing platforms.
Public transport: Various Stagecoach services from Chesterfield (Stephenson Place) all pass close to the reserve: Mon to Sat: 83 serves Villas Road, 81, 82, 82A and 83 serve the roundabout on the A632. Sun: 81A, 82A serve the roundabout on the A632.
Habitat: Lakes, wader flashes, reed bed, sewage farm, scrub, arable fields.
Key birds: Up to 150 species seen annually at this productive site. *Winter*: Large numbers of wildfowl including flocks of Wigeon and Teal, also wintering flocks of finches and buntings, Water Rail. Large skeins of geese fly over in early and late winter. *Spring/autumn*: Birds on migration including swallows, pipits and thrushes. In September Swallows gather in the marsh, in a gigantic roost of between 10-12,000 birds. They usually attract Hobbies. *Early summer*: Breeding birds, including Reed and Sedge Warblers, Whitethroat, Yellowhammer, Moorhen and Gadwall, plus Sky Lark. Long list of rarities.
Other notable flora and fauna: Dragonflies, mammals (hare, water vole, harvest mouse, water shrew).
Contact: Derbyshire Wildlife Trust, East Mill, Bridgefoot, Belper, Derbyshire, DE56 1XH. 01773 881 188. e-mail: enquiries@derbyshirewt.co.uk www.derbyshirewildlifetrust.org.uk

2. CARSINGTON WATER

Severn Trent Water.
Location: SK 24 51 (for visitor centre and main facilities). Off B5035 Ashbourne to Cromford road.
Access: Open all year except Christmas Day. The car parks are open from 7am to sunset (Apr - end Oct) and 7.30am to sunset (winter). There are various access points. New lower track opened in spring 09 to improve access.
Facilities: Visitor centre with exhibition, restaurant, four shops (inc RSPB), play area and toilets. RSPB 'Aren't Birds Brilliant' project operates here twice a week. Four bird hides and three car parks (two chargeable, one free).
Public transport: TM Travel operates service 411

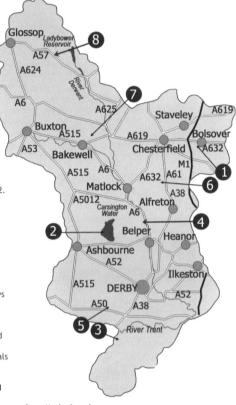

from Matlock and Ashbourne. The nearest train station is at Cromford. Call TM on 01142 633 890.
Habitat: Open water, islands, mixed woodland, scrub and grasslands, small reedbed.
Key birds: *Winter*: Wildfowl and a large gull roost plus possibility of divers and rare grebes. *Spring*: Good spring passage including Yellow and White Wagtails, Whimbrel, Black and Arctic Terns. *Summer*: Warblers and breeding waders. *All year*: Tree Sparrows and Willow Tits.
Other notable flora and fauna: Species-rich hay meadows, ancient woodlands with bluebells, three species of orchid, five species of bat, 21 species of butterfly and water vole.
Contact: Carsington Water, The Visitor Centre, Ashbourne, Derbyshire DE6 1ST. 01629 540 696.

e-mail: customer.relations@severntrent.co.uk
www.moretoexperience.co.uk and
www.carsingtonbirdclub.co.uk

3. DRAKELOW NATURE RESERVE

E-ON, leased to Derbyshire Wildlife Trust.
Location: SK 223 204 (Landranger 128). Drakelow
Power Station, one mile NE of Walton-on-Trent, off
A38.
Access: Dawn to dusk for permit-holders only (plus
up to two guests). Annual permit can be obtained
from Derbyshire Wildlife Trust.
Facilities: Seven hides, no other facilities.
Public transport: None.
Habitat: Disused flooded gravel pits with wooded
islands and reedbeds.
Key birds: *Summer:* Breeding Reed and Sedge
Warblers. Water Rail, Hobby. *Winter:* Wildfowl
(Goldeneye, Gadwall, Smew), Merlin, Peregrine.
Recent rarities include Great White and Little Egrets,
Bittern and Spotted Crake, Ring-necked Duck and
American Wigeon.
Other notable flora and fauna: Good for common
species of dragonflies and butterflies.
Contact: Contact: Trust HQ, 01773 881 188,
e-mail: enquiries@derbyshirewt.co.uk
www.derbyshirewildlifetrust.org.uk

4. EREWASH MEADOWS

Derbyshire & Notts Wildlife Trusts
Location: SK 441 517. In three parts: Aldercar Flash,
Brinsley Meadows and part of Cromford Canal. Ripley
is nearest large town.
Access: Open all year — please keep to paths.
Facilities: None.
Public transport: Local bus services.
Habitat: The sites are now part of the largest
floodplain grassland and wetlands in Erewash Valley.
Key birds: *Spring/summer:* Breeding Lapwing, Snipe,
Reed Bunting and warblers. Raptors, waders and
wildfowl seen on passage. *Winter:* Wildfowl species.
Other notable flora and fauna: Grass snake,
amphibians, dragonflies, butterflies.
Contact: Contact: Trust HQ, 01773 881 188,
e-mail: enquiries@derbyshirewt.co.uk
www.derbyshirewildlifetrust.org.uk

5. HILTON GRAVEL PITS

Derbyshire Wildlife Trust.
Location: SK 249 315 (OS Langranger 128). From
Derby, take A516 from Mickleover W past Etwall onto
A50 junction at Hilton. Turn R at first island onto
Willow Pit Lane. Turn L next to a large white house
and park next to the gate. Follow track along S side
of the pools.
Access: Open all year.
Facilities: Tracks and boardwalks, viewing screens.
Public transport: Local bus services from Derby.
Habitat: Ponds, scrub, wood, fen.
Key birds: *Spring/summer:* Great Crested Grebe,
Common Tern, warblers. *Winter:* Wildfowl, Siskin,
Goldcrest. *All year:* All three woodpeckers,

Kingfisher, tits inc possible Willow Tit, Tawny Owl,
Bullfinch.
Other notable flora and fauna: Dragonflies (15
species inc emperor, ruddy darter and red-eyed
damselfly), great crested newt, orchids, black poplar,
fungi.
Contact: Trust HQ, 01773 881 188,
e-mail: enquiries@derbyshirewt.co.uk
www.derbyshirewildlifetrust.org.uk

6. OGSTON RESERVOIR

Severn Trent Water Plc.
Location: SK 37 60 (Landranger map 119). From
Matlock, take A615 E to B6014, just after Tansley.
From Chesterfield take A61 S of Clay Cross onto
B6014, towards Tansley. Cross railway, the reservoir
is on L after the hill.
Access: View from roads, car parks or hides. Suitable
for coaches. Heronry in nearby Ogston Carr Wood
(Derbyshire Wildlife Trust) viewable from road, W of
reservoir.
Facilities: Three car parks (no charges), with toilets
at N and W locations. Ogston BC members-only
hide and public hide both wheelchair-accessible.
Information pack on request.
Public transport: Hulleys 63 bus service (Chesterfield
to Clay Cross) and 64 service (Clay Cross to Matlock)
both serves N end of reservoir (not Sundays).
Habitat: Open water, pasture, mixed woodland.
Key birds: All three woodpeckers, Little and Tawny
Owls, Kingfisher, Grey Wagtail, warblers. Passage
raptors (inc. Osprey), terns and waders. *Winter:* Gull
roost attracts thousands of birds, inc regular Glaucous
and Iceland Gulls. Top inland site for Bonaparte's
Gull and also attracts Caspian/ Herring Gull complex.
Good numbers of wildfowl, tit and finch flocks.
Contact: Malcolm Hill, Treasurer, Ogston Bird Club,
c/o 2 Sycamore Avenue, Glapwell, Chesterfield, S44
5LH. 01623 812 159. www.ogstonbirdclub.co.uk

7. PADLEY GORGE

The National Trust (East Midlands).
Location: From Sheffield, take A625. After eight
miles, turn L on B6521 to Nether Padley. Grindleford
Station is just off B6521 (NW of Nether Padley) and
one mile NE of Grindleford village.
Access: All year. Not suitable for disabled people or
those unused to steep climbs. Some of the paths are
rocky. No dogs allowed.
Facilities: Café and toilets at Longshaw lodge.
Public transport: Bus: from Sheffield to Bakewell
stops at Grindleford/Nether Padley. Tel: 01709 566
000. Train: from Sheffield to Manchester Piccadilly
stops at Grindleford Station. Tel: 0161 228 2141.
Habitat: Steep-sided valley containing largest area of
sessile oak woodland in south Pennines.
Key birds: *Summer:* Pied Flycatcher, Spotted
Flycatcher, Redstart, Wheatear, Whinchat, Wood
Warbler, Tree Pipit.
Contact: National Trust, High Peak Estate Office,
Edale End, Edale Road, Hope S33 2RF. 01433 670 368.
www.nationaltrust.org.uk

8. WILLINGTON GRAVEL PITS

Derbyshire Wildlife Trust.
Location: SK 285 274. From A50 'Toyota Island' turn onto Repton Road towards Willington and Repton. Go through village towards Repton. Just before bridge over River Trent, turn R onto un-made track (Meadow Lane). Park on track and walk along lane.
Access: Access along Meadow Lane to viewing platforms all year. No access on site.
Facilities: Viewing platforms. Limited parking in lane.
Public transport: Local trains stop at Willington, local bus service from Derby.

Habitat: Open water, reedbed, shingle island, grassland.
Key birds: *Summer:* Breeding Lapwing, other waders, Common Tern, raptors, including Peregrine, Kestrel, Hobby and Sparrowhawk, Sand Martin, wildfowl. *Winter:* Waders and large flocks of wildfowl including Wigeon, Teal, Pochard and Shoveler. *Passage:* Large numbers of Curlew in spring, up to 20 species of waders in spring/autumn.
Other notable flora and fauna: Short-leaved water starwort. Several species of dragonfly, plus occasional otter signs, fox and other mammals.
Contact: Contact: Trust HQ, 01773 881 188, e-mail: enquiries@derbyshirewt.co.uk

Gloucestershire

1. ASHLEWORTH HAM NATURE RESERVE

Gloucestershire Wildlife Trust.
Location: SO 830 265. Leave Gloucester N on A417; R at Hartpury and follow minor road through Ashleworth towards Hasfield.
Access: Access prohibited at all times but birds may be viewed from new hide in Meerend Thicket.
Facilities: Bird viewing hide and screen, interpretation panels.
Habitat: Low-lying grassland flood plain.
Key birds: *Winter:* Wildfowl (inc. 4,000 Wigeon, 1,500 Teal, Pintail, Goldeneye, Bewick's Swan), passage waders, Peregrine. *Summer:* Hobby.
Contact: Trust HQ, 01452 383 333.
e-mail: info@gloucestershirewildlifetrust.co.uk
www.gloucestershirewildlifetrust.co.uk

2. COTSWOLD WATER PARK

Cotswold Water Park Society.
Location: The CWP comprises 163 lakes in the Upper Thames Valley, between Cirencester and Swindon. Many lakes are accessible by public rights of way. Start from Cotswold Water Park Gateway Visitor Centre (SU 072 971), immediately on L after A419. For Millenium Visitor Centre at Keynes Country Park (SU 026 957) from A419, take B4696 towards Ashton Keynes. At staggered crossroads, go straight over, heading towards Somerford Keynes. Take next R turn to Cirencester. Entrance to Keynes Country Park is second entrance on R.
Access: Cotswold Water Park is open all year round. The visitor centres are open every day except Christmas Day.
Facilities: Paths are flat but with stiles and footbridges. Many are wheelchair accessible. Toilets, refreshments, car parking and information available from the visitor centres. Hides available at Cleveland Lakes/Waterhay (lakes 68a and 68c), Shorncote Reed Bed (lakes 84/85), Cokes Pit (Lake 34) and Whelford Pools (Lake 111). Free copies of the CWP Leisure Guide are available from the visitor centres, also the guidebook *Wildlife in the Cotswold Water Park: Where to go and what to see.*

Public transport: Bus: from Kemble, Cheltenham, Cirencester and Swindon. 08457 090 899. Train: nearest station is four miles away at Kemble. 08457 484 950.
Habitat: Gravel extraction has created more than 1,000ha of standing open water, plus other associated wetland habitats, creating one of the largest man-made wetlands in Europe.
Key birds: *Winter:* Common wildfowl, Smew, Red-crested Pochard, Merlin, Peregrine. *Summer:* Breeding ducks, warblers, Nightingale, Hobby, Common Tern, Black-headed Gull colony, Reed Bunting, hirundines.
Contact: Cotswold Water Park Society, Cotswold House, Down Ampney Estate, Cirencester, Glos GL7 5QF. 01793 752 413. e-mail: info@waterpark.org www.waterpark.org

3. HIGHNAM WOODS

RSPB (South West England Office).
Location: SO 778 190. Signed on A40 three miles W of Gloucester.
Access: Open at all times, no permit required. The nature trails can be very muddy. Some limited wheelchair access. Dogs allowed on leads.
Facilities: One nature trail (approx 1.5 miles).
Public transport: Contact Traveline (public transport information) on 0871 2002 233 between 7am-10pm each day.
Habitat: Ancient woodland in the Severn Vale with areas of coppice and scrub.
Key birds: *Spring/summer:* The reserve has about 12 pairs of breeding Nightingales. Resident birds include all three woodpeckers, Buzzard and Sparrowhawk. Ravens are frequently seen. *Winter:* Feeding site near car park good for woodland birds.
Other notable flora and fauna: Tintern spurge in late June-early July. White-letter hairstreak and white admiral butterflies seen annually.
Contact: Barry Embling, Site Manager, The Puffins, Parkend, Lydney, Glos, GL15 4JA. 01594 562 852. e-mail: barry.embling@rspb.org.uk www.rspb.org.uk

4. LOWER WOODS NATURE RESERVE

Gloucestershire Wildlife Trust.
Location: ST 749 885. Reserve is about one mile E

NATURE RESERVES - CENTRAL ENGLAND

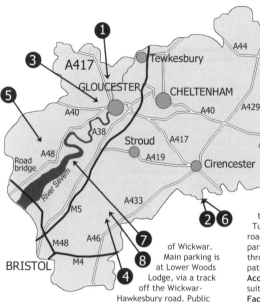

Key birds: *Spring*: Pied Flycatcher, Wood Warbler, Redstart, warblers. *Summer*: Nightjar. *Winter*: Siskin, Crossbill in some years. *All year*: Buzzard, Raven, Hawfinch, all three woodpeckers.
Other notable flora and fauna: Golden-ringed dragonfly seen annually. Silver-washed and small pearl-bordered fritillaries and white admiral butterflies present.
Contact: Barry Embling, Site Manager, 01594 562 852.
e-mail: barry.embling@rspb.org.uk www.rspb.org.uk

6. SHORNCOTE REEDBED (LAKES 84/85)

Cotswold Water Park Society.
Location: Lakes 84 and 85, Cotswold Water Park. From A419 Cirencester to Swindon road, take B4696 towards Cotswold Water Park West. Turn R at crossroads towards South Cerney. Follow road through village and park in playing fields car park after sharp R bend (SU 044 970). Take footpath through playing fields, cross road and continue on path through reedbeds to small lakes and hides.
Access: Open at all times, most paths firm and flat so suitable for wheelchairs.
Facilities: Toilets, refreshments, car parking and information available from nearby Keynes Country Park adjacent. Two hides.
Public transport: Bus: from Kemble, Cheltenham, Cirencester and Swindon. Tel: 08457 090 899. Train: nearest station is four miles away at Kemble. Tel: 08457 484 950.
Habitat: Lakes with reedbed, marsh, ditches, islands and loafing areas.
Key birds: *Winter*: Common wildfowl, Smew, Peregrine, Merlin, Bittern, Stonechat. *Summer*: Breeding ducks, warblers, Hobby, Sand Martin, Reed Bunting.
Other notable flora and fauna: Several species of dragonfly.
Contact: Cotswold Water Park Society, 01793 752 413.

7. SLIMBRIDGE

The Wildfowl & Wetlands Trust.
Location: SO 723 048. S of Gloucester. Signposted from M5 (exit 13 or 14).
Access: Open daily (9am-5.30pm or 5pm in winter) except Dec 25. Last entry 30 mins before closing. Wheelchair hire (book beforehand) – all paths wheelchair accessible. Free parking for cars and coaches.
Facilities: Restaurant, gift shop, gallery, cinema, discovery centre. Outdoor facilities inc 15 hides, tropical house, worldwide collection of wildfowl species, observatory and observation tower. Plenty of family attactions including a pond zone, wader aviary, commentated swan feeds in the winter, Land Rover safaris and a canoe safari trail.
Public transport: Request bus service – contact www.

of Wickwar. Main parking is at Lower Woods Lodge, via a track off the Wickwar-Hawkesbury road. Public footpaths and bridleways cross the reserve.
Access: Open all year.
Facilities: Well-marked footpaths and bridleways. Walk leaflet available.
Habitat: Mixed woodland, mildly acidic or slightly calcareous clay, grassland, river, springs.
Key birds: *Spring/summer*: Nightingale. *All year*: Usual woodland species including Tawny Owl, Jay, Nuthatch and Sparrowhawk. Kingfisher on river.
Other notable flora and fauna: 71 species of ancient woodland plants.
Contact: Trust HQ. 01452 383 333,
e-mail: info@gloucestershirewildlifetrust.co.uk
www.gloucestershirewildlifetrust.co.uk

5. NAGSHEAD

RSPB (South West England Office).
Location: SO 097 085. In Forest of Dean, N of Lydney. Signed immediately W of Parkend village on the road to Coleford.
Access: Open at all times, no permit required. The reserve is hilly but there is limited wheelchair access. Dogs must be kept on leads during bird nesting season and under close control at all other times.
Facilities: There are two nature trails (one mile and 2.25 miles). Information centre, with toilet facilities (including disabled), open at weekends mid-Apr to end Aug. Schools education programme available.
Public transport: Contact Traveline (public transport information) on 0871 2002 233 (7am to 10pm each day).
Habitat: Much of the reserve is 200-year-old oak plantations, grazed in some areas by sheep. The rest of the reserve is a mixture of open areas and conifer/mixed woodland.

stroud.gov.uk. Nearest train station at Cam and Dursley (4 miles).
Habitat: Reedbed, saltmarsh, freshwater pools, mudflats and wet grassland.
Key birds: *Winter:* Between 30,000 to 40,000 wildfowl esp. Bewick's Swan, White-fronted Goose, Wigeon, Teal, Pintail. Waders inc Lapwing, Golden Plover, Spotted Redshank and Little Stint. Often there are large roosts of Starlings and gulls. *Breeding:* Kingfisher, Lapwing, Redshank, Oystercatcher, Common Tern, Reed Bunting and a good range of warblers. *Passage:* Waders, terns and gulls, inc Mediterranean and Yellow-legged Gulls. Yellow Wagtail and large passerine movements. Hobbies now reach double figures and there is an impressive list of rarities.
Other notable flora and fauna: Brown hare, otter, polecat and water vole. Scarce chaser and hairy dragonfly among 22 recorded species.
Contact: Marketing Manager, WWT, Slimbridge, Gloucester, GL2 7BT. 01453 891 900; e-mail: info.slimbridge@wwt.org.uk

8. SYMOND'S YAT

RSPB/Forestry Commission England.
Location: SO 563 160. Hill-top site on the edge of Forest of Dean, three miles N of Coleford on B4432, signposted from Forest Enterprise car park. Also signposted from A40, S of Ross-on-Wye.
Access: Open at all times. RSPB Information Officer on site daily, April to August.
Facilities: Car park, toilets with adapted facilities for disabled visitors, picnic area, drinks and light snacks. Environmental education programmes available.
Public transport: Very limited.
Habitat: Cliff above the River Wye and woodland.
Key birds: *Summer:* Peregrine, Buzzard, Goshawk, Raven and woodland species. Telescope is set up daily to watch the Peregrines on the nest.
Contact: RSPB, 01594 562 852.

Leicestershire and Rutland

1. BEACON HILL COUNTRY PARK

Leicestershire County Council.
Location: SK 522 149. From Loughborough, take A512 SW for 2.5 miles. Turn L onto Woodhouse Lane and follow it for 2.5 miles through Nanpantan. The Lower car park is on the right. For the Upper car park, continue past the Lower car park, turn right onto Beacon Road, car park is on right at top of the hill.
Access: Open all year from 7am. Closing times are clearly displayed at the park. A permissive path from Deans Lane to Woodhouse Lane is occasionally closed during the year. Please check first.
Facilities: Two pay-on-entry car parks, easy-to-follow, waymarked tracks and woodland paths. Several climbs to hill tops. Rocky outcrops slippery after rain. Information boards. Toilets at lower & upper car parks. Wheelchair access along park paths but no access to summit. Refreshments at Bull's Head, Woodhouse Eaves.
Public transport: Bus: Nos 54, 121 and 123 from Loughborough call at Woodhouse Eaves. Tel: 0870 608 2608.
Habitat: Forest, one of the oldest geological outcrops in England and the second highest point in Leicestershire.
Key birds: *All year:* Treecreeper, Nuthatch, Lesser Spotted, Greater Spotted and Green Woodpeckers, Great and Coal Tits, Little Owl, wagtails. *Summer:* Pied Flycatcher, Whitethroat, Blackcap, Whinchat, Garden Warbler, Stonechat, Tree Pipit.
Contact: Beacon Hill Estate Office, Broombriggs Farm, Beacon Road, Woodhouse Eaves, Loughborough LE12 8SR. 0116 305 8790.

2. EYEBROOK RESERVOIR

Corby & District Water Co.
Location: SP 853 964. Reservoir built 1940. S of Uppingham, from unclassified road W of A6003 at Stoke Dry.
Access: Access to 150 acres private grounds granted to members of Leics and Rutland OS and Rutland NHS. All visitors should sign in at fishing lodge. Organised groups should contact Andy Miller on 01536 772 930.
Facilities: SSSI since 1956. Three bird hides. Fishing season March - Nov. Toilets and visitor centre at fishing lodge.
Habitat: Open water, plantations and pasture.
Key birds: *Summer:* Good populations of breeding birds, sightings of Ospreys and Red Kite. Passage waders and Black Tern. *Winter:* Wildfowl (inc. Goldeneye, Goosander, Smew) and waders. Tree Sparrow and Yellowhammer at feeding station. During winter months, Barn and Short-eared Owl can be seen hunting at dusk near Great Easton village (close to recycling centre).
Other notable flora and fauna: Otter, muntjac deer, red darter, demoiselles and blue damselfly.
Contact: Andy Miller, Fishery Estate Manager, 01536 772 930. www.eyebrook.com

3. NARBOROUGH BOG

Leics and Rutland Wildlife Trust.
Location: SP 549 979. Reserve lies between River Soar and M1, 8km S of Leicester. From city, turn L off B4114 just before going under motorway, follow track to sports club. Park near club house and walk across recreation ground to reserve entrance.
Access: Open at all times, please keep to paths. Not suitable for wheelchairs. Dogs on short leads only.
Facilities: None. Small bus/coach could park in sports field car park
Public transport: Narborough train station. Buses X5, 140 to Narborough then 1km walk.
Habitat: Peat bog SSSI (the only substantial deposit in Leicestershire), wet woodland, reedbed, dense scrub and fen meadow.
Key birds: More than 130 species of birds have been

recorded including all three species of woodpeckers, six species of tit, Tawny Owl, Sparrowhawk and Kingfisher.
Other notable flora and fauna: Good variety of butterflies including large and small skippers, small heath and gatekeeper. Banded demoiselles, also good for moths and beetles. Harvest mice and water voles recorded, also breeding grass snakes. Meadow saxifrage, common meadow-rue and marsh thistle.
Contact: Trust HQ. 0116 272 0444.

4. RUTLAND WATER

Leics and Rutland Wildlife Trust.
Location: Two nature reserves 1. Egleton Reserve SK 878 075: from Egleton village off A6003 or A606 S of Oakham. Hosts British Birdwatching Fair every August. 2. Lyndon Reserve SK 894 058: south shore E of Manton village off A6003 S of Oakham. Follow 'nature reserve' signs to car park.
Access: 1. Open daily 9am-5pm, (4pm Nov to Jan). 2. Open winter (Sat, Sun 10am-4pm), Summer daily (9am-5pm). Day permits available for both. Reduced admission for disabled and carers. Closed Dec 25 and 26. Badger-watching hide can be booked from mid-April to July.
Facilities: 1: Anglian Water Birdwatching Centre has toilets and disabled access, mobility scooter to hire, conference facilities. Disabled access possible to 20 hides, incl three new hides on newly-created lagoon 4. Over three years it is planned to create nine new lagoons. 2: Interpretive centre now upgraded with new toilets, including disabled, new paths, use of a mobility scooter. New interpretive material covers climate change and the impact to UK wildlife. Marked nature trail leaflet.
Habitat: Ramsar designated reservoir, lagoons, scrapes, woods, meadows, plantations, reedbeds.
Key birds: *Spring/autumn*: Outstanding wader passage, with up to 28 species recorded. Also wide range of harriers, owls, passerine flocks, terns (Black, Arctic, breeding Common, occasional Little

and Sandwich). *Winter*: Up to 28 species of wildfowl (inc international important numbers of Gadwall and Shoveler). Also Goldeneye, Smew, Goosander, rare grebes, all divers, Ruff. *Summer*: Ospreys among 70 breeding species.
Other notable flora and fauna: Otter, badger, fox, weasel, stoat. Up to 20 species of dragon and damselflies and 24 butterfly species.
Contact: Tim Appleton, 01572 770 651; e-mail awbc@rutlandwater.org.uk; www.rutlandwater.org.uk www.ospreys.org.uk

5. SENCE VALLEY FOREST PARK

Forestry Commission
Location: SK 400 115. Within The National Forest. Ten miles NW of Leicester and two miles SW of Coalville, between Ibstock and Ravenstone. The car park is signed from A447 N of Ibstock.
Access: Open all year. Car park open 8.30am-dusk (precise times on noticeboard). Lower car park (2.2m height barrier) gives easy access to wheelchair-friendly surfaced paths. Week's notice required for coach or minibus visits.
Facilities: Two car parks, toilets (including disabled and baby-changing facilities), information and recent sightings boards, hide, surfaced trails.
Public transport: None.
Habitat: New forest (native broadleaf, mixed and pine), rough grassland, wildflower meadow, pools, wader scrape, river.
Key birds: *Spring/summer*: Artificial Sand Martin nesting wall, Wheatear, Whinchat, Redstart, Common and Green Sandpiper, Ringed and Little Ringed Plovers, Redshank. Dunlin and Greenshank frequent, possible Wood Sandpiper. Reed Bunting, Meadow Pipit, Sky Lark, Linnet, Yellow Wagtail. Possible Quail. Kestrel and Barn Owl seen occasionally. *Winter*: Stonechat, Redpoll, Short-eared Owl, Goosander and Wigeon possible.
Contact: Forestry Commission, 01889 586 593. www.forestry.gov.uk

Lincolnshire

1. DONNA NOOK

Lincolnshire Wildlife Trust.
Location: TF 422 998. Near North Somercotes, off A1031 coast road, S of Grimsby.
Access: Donna Nook beach is closed on weekdays as this is an active bombing range, but dunes remain open. Dogs on leads. Some disabled access.
Facilities: No toilets or visitor centre.
Habitat: Dunes, slacks and intertidal areas, seashore, mudflats, sandflats.
Key birds: *Summer*: Little Tern, Ringed Plover, Oystercatcher. *Winter*: Brent Goose, Shelduck, Twite, Lapland Bunting, Shore Lark, Linnet.
Other notable flora and fauna: The reserve has one of the largest and most accessible breeding colonies

of grey seals in the UK. Other mammals include fox, badger, stoat and weasel and three species of shrew have been identified. Common lizard.
Contact: Lincolnshire Wildlife Trust, Banavallum House, Manor House Street, Horncastle, Lincs, LN9 5HF. 01507 526 667. e-mail: lincstrust@cix.co.uk www.lincstrust.co.uk

2. EPWORTH TURBERY

Lincolnshire Wildlife Trust.
Location: SE 758 036. SW of Scunthorpe. Take A18 W from Scunthorpe then A161 S to Epworth. Turn R on High Street, continue onto Tottermire Lane then bear left onto Battle Green. Turn L onto Fieldside, R onto Carrside then L onto Turbary Road. The entrance is near bridge over Skyer's Drain. Parking available through gate, which should be kept closed, or on verge adjoining reserve. Park well away from corner.
Access: Open at all times. Keep to waymarked paths

and use hides when viewing open area. In order to avoid disturbing birds on the ponds, please do not climb on the banks.

Facilities: Car park, way-marked trail, two hides.
Public transport: None.
Habitat: One of the few relicts of raised bog in Lincolnshire. Although extensively dug for peat in the past, areas of active sphagnum bog still exist. Areas of reed swamp and mixed fen vegetation, also fen and wet heath conditions and a considerable area of birch woodland of varying ages.
Key birds: Breeding birds include Tree Pipit, warblers, finches, Green and Great Spotted Woodpeckers and Woodcock. Greenshank, Green Sandpiper and Little Grebe on wet area. Around Steve's Pond, occasional Hobby and Marsh Harrier, plus Teal, Little Grebe, Tree Pipit, Sparrowhawk and Buzzard. Willow Tit, Long-tailed Tit, Reed Bunting and Willow Warbler in the woodland areas. Occasionally Corn Buntings on adjoining farmland. In the autumn and winter large flocks of Rooks, Carrion Crows and Jackdaws fly into reserve to roost. At Pantry's Pond in winter occasional Hen Harrier. Other birds include Yellowhammer and Linnet. Sometimes in winter Long-eared Owls can be observed roosting close to the path.
Other notable flora and fauna: Eleven species of breeding dragonflies and damselflies have been recorded. Wood tiger moth is well established. Plants include sneezewort, yellow and purple-loosestrife, meadow-rue, and devil's-bit scabious.
Contact: Trust HQ, 01507 526 667,
e-mail: lincstrust@cix.co.uk www.lincstrust.co.uk

3. FRAMPTON MARSH

RSPB (Eastern England Office).
Location: TR 364 385. Four miles SE of Boston. From A16 follow signs to Frampton then Frampton Marsh.
Access: Visitor Centre open 10am-4pm each day except Dec 25. Footpaths are open at all times, free. Visitor Centre (including toilets), footpaths and hides all suitable for wheelchairs.
Facilities: Visitor Centre with hot drinks and snacks, three hides, footpaths, benches, viewpoints, 50-space car park (three for disabled visitors), bicycle rack, free information leaflets and events programmes. Childrens activities.
Public transport: None.
Habitat: Saltmarsh, wet grassland, freshwater scrapes and developing reedbed.
Key birds: *Summer*: Breeding Redshank, Avocet, Lapwing, Sky Lark, Little Ringed Plover, Ringed Plover, Sand Martin and several species of ducks plus passage waders (inc Greenshank, Curlew Sandpiper, Wood Sandpiper, Little and Temminck's Stints, Ruff and Black-tailed Godwit), Marsh Harrier and Hobby. *Winter*: Hen Harrier, Short-eared Owl, Merlin, dark-bellied Brent Goose, Twite, Golden Plover, Lapland Bunting.
Other notable flora and fauna: Water vole, muntjac and roe deer, stoat. Dragonflies inc emperor, hawkers, chasers and darters. Common butterflies

plus wall brown, painted lady and speckled wood. Scarce pug, star wort and crescent striped moths on saltmarsh. Important brackish water flora and fauna includes nationally scarce spiral tassleweed and several rare beetles.
Contact: John Badley, Site Manager, Roads Farmhouse, Frampton Roads, Frampton, Boston, Lincs PE20 1AY. 01205 724 678. www.rspb.org.uk
e-mail: johnbadley@rspb.org.uk

4. FREISTON SHORE

RSPB (Eastern England Office).
Location: TF 397 424. Four miles E of Boston. From A52 at Haltoft End follow signs to Freiston Shore.
Access: Open at all times, free.
Facilities: Footpaths, two car parks, bird hide. Free information leaflets on site, guided walks programme. Bicycle rack, benches, viewpoints, seawatching shelter, reservoir viewing screen, wet grassland viewing platform.
Public transport: None.
Habitat: Saltmarsh, saline lagoon, mudflats, wet grassland.
Key birds: *Summer*: Breeding waders including Avocet, Ringed Plover and Oystercatcher, Common Tern, Corn Bunting and Tree Sparrow. *Winter*: Twite, dark-bellied Brent Goose, wildfowl, waders, Short-eared Owl and Hen Harrier. *Passage*: Waders, including Greenshank, Curlew Sandpiper and Little Stint. *Autumn*: Occasional seabirds including Arctic and Great Skuas.
Other notable flora and fauna: Water vole, muntjac and roe deer, stoat. Dragonflies inc emperor, hawkers, chasers and darters. Common butterflies plus wall brown, painted lady and speckled wood. Scarce pug, star wort and crescent striped moths on saltmarsh. Important lagoon invertebrates and plants.
Contact: John Badley, Site Manager, 01205 724 678, e-mail: john.badley@rspb.org.uk www.rspb.org.uk

5. GIBRALTAR POINT NNR & BIRD OBSERVATORY

Lincolnshire Wildlife Trust.
Location: TF 556 580. Three miles S of Skegness on the N edge of The Wash. Signposted from Skegness town centre.
Access: Reserve open dawn-dusk all year. Charges for car parking. Free admission to reserve, visitor centre and toilets. Some access restrictions to sensitive sites at S end, open access to N. Dogs on leads at all times — no dogs on beach during summer. Visitor centre and toilets suitable for wheelchairs, as well as network of surfaced foot paths. Bird observatory and four hides suitable for wheelchairs. Day visit groups must be booked in advance. Access for coaches. Contact The Wash Study Centre for residential or day visits.
Facilities: Site also location of Wash Study Centre and Bird Observatory. Field centre is an ideal base for birdwatching/natural history groups in spring, summer and autumn. Visitor centre, gift shop and cafe. Toilets open daily. Network of footpaths bisect all major habitats. Public hides overlook freshwater and brackish lagoons. Wash viewpoint overlooks

saltmarsh and mudflats.

Public transport: Bus service from Skegness runs occasionally but summer service only. Otherwise taxi/car from Skegness. Cycle route from Skegness.

Habitat: Sand dune grassland and scrub, saltmarshes and mudflats, freshwater marsh and lagoons.

Key birds: Large scale visible migration during spring and autumn passage. Internationally important populations of non-breeding waders Jul-Mar (peak Sep/Oct). Winter flocks of Brent Geese, Shelduck and Wigeon on flats and marshes with Hen Harrier, Merlin and Short-eared Owl often present. Red-throated Divers offshore, peak Feb. A colony of Little Tern and Ringed Plover in summer. More than 100 species can be seen in a day during May and Sept. Good passage of autumn seabirds in northerly winds.

Other notable flora and fauna: Pyramidal orchids occur in patches. Grey and common seal colonies, with porpoises offshore in most months. Butterflies include brown argus and green hairstreak.

Contact: Reserve and wildlife: Kev Wilson. Visit bookings: Jill Hardy, Sykes Farm, Gibraltar Point Nature Reserve, Gibraltar Road, Skegness, Lincs PE24 4SU. 01754 898 057. www.lincstrust.org.uk e-mail: kwilson@linwtrust.co.uk or gibpoint@btconnect.com

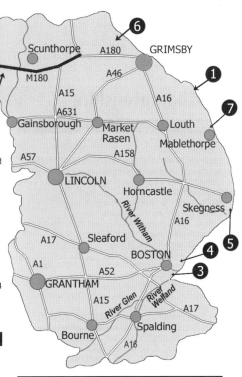

6. KILLINGHOLME HAVEN PITS

Lincolnshire Wildlife Trust.

Location: TA 165199 NW of Grimsby. Take A180 W, turn R on A1173 towards Immingham. Turn L at roundabout and continue to A160. Turn L then R onto Eastfield road. Turn R onto Chase Hill road then L onto Haven road. The reserve is situated to the S of Haven Road on the approach to North Killingholme Haven. Park carefully on the road.

Access: No general access to the reserve, but adequate viewing points are available from the public road and bank-top footpath.

Facilities: None.

Habitat: Marsh/wetland.

Key birds: A good site for water birds. Diving ducks, such as Pochard, Tufted Duck and, occasionally, Scaup. Breeding species include Little Grebe, and Reed, Sedge, Willow and Grasshopper Warblers. Ruddy Duck has also been known to breed here. The two large shallow pits, are of the greatest importance for birds, particularly for migrant waders in spring and autumn. Spotted Redshank, Dunlin, Greenshank, Common Sandpiper, Little Ringed Plover, Ruff and Black-tailed Godwit, the latter often in large numbers, are regular visitors.

The list of scarce and rare species is long and includes Spoonbill, Avocet, Little Egret, Little and Temminck's Stints, Red-necked Phalarope, and Curlew, Pectoral, Baird's And White-rumped Sandpipers.

Contact: Trust HQ, 01507 526 667, e-mail: lincstrust@cix.co.uk www.lincstrust.co.uk

7. SALTFLEETBY-THEDDLETHORPE DUNES NNR

Natural England.

Location: TF 465 924 - TF 490 883. Approx two miles N of Mablethorpe. All the following car parks may be accessed from the A1031: Crook Bank, Brickyard Lane, Churchill Lane, Rimac, Sea View.

Access: Open all year at all times. Keep dogs under close control. Easy access half mile trail suitable for wheelchair users starts adjacent to Rimac car park. Includes pond and saltmarsh viewing platforms.

Facilities: Toilets, including wheelchair suitability at Rimac car park. May-to-end-of-Sept events programme. Easy access trail at Rimac with viewing platforms.

Public transport: Grayscroft coaches (01507 473 236) and Lincolnshire Roadcar (01522 532 424) run services past Rimac entrance (Louth to Mablethorpe service). Lincs Roadcar can connect with trains at Lincoln. Applebys Coaches (01507 357 900) Grimsby to Saltfleet bus connects with Grimsby train service.

Habitat: 13th Century dunes, freshwater marsh, new dune ridge with large areas of sea buckthorn, saltmarsh, shingle ridge and foreshore.

Key birds: *Summer:* Breeding birds in scrub include Nightingale, Grasshopper Warbler, Whitethroat, Lesser Whitethroat, Redpoll. *Winter:* Large flocks of Brent Goose, Shelduck, Teal and Wigeon. Wintering

Short-eared Owl, Hen Harrier. Migrant birds in scrub and waders on Paradise

Other notable flora and fauna: Impressive show of sea lavendar in late summer, orchids in marsh and dunes including pyramidal, marsh and bee. Fourteen

species of dragonfly including emperor. Water vole, roe and muntjac deer, badgers are common.

Contact: Reserve Manager, Natural England Workshops, Seaview, Saltfleetby St Clements, Louth LN11 7TR. 01507 338 611. www.naturalengland.org.uk

Northamptonshire

1. DITCHFORD LAKES

Beds, Cambs, Northants and Peterborough Wildlife Trust.

Location: SP 931 678. From Wellingborough, take A45 towards Rushden and Higham Ferrers. Take exit marked A5001 to Rushden. Turn L at roundabout onto Ditchford Road towards Irthlingborough/Ditchford. 500 m on right is small car park with height restriction. Entrance is off car park.

Access: Rough grass paths, flat overall. Some areas soft and muddy especially in winter. Grazing animals at certain times of the year.

Facilities: None.

Public transport: Northampton/Wellingborough-Irthlingborough bus, then walk 1.5 miles.

Habitat: Part of the upper Nene valley floodplain — a complex of old gravel pits, grassland, lakes surrounded by mature scrub.

Key birds: *Winter:* Common Sandpiper, Snipe, Teal, Wigeon, Gadwall, Tufted Duck. *Spring:* Redshank, Oystercatcher, Cetti's Warbler, Little Grebe, Grey Heron. *Summer:* Reed Warbler, Sedge Warbler, Swift, House Martin. *Autumn:* Snipe, Great Crested Grebe, Moorhen, Coot, Grey Heron.

Other notable flora and fauna: Hairy dragonfly, grass snake. Otter. Plants include marsh woundwort, dropwort, great burnet.

Contact: Trust HQ, 01954 713 500, e-mail: cambridgeshire@wildlifebcnp.org

2. OLD SULEHAY

Beds, Cambs, Northants and Peterborough Wildlife Trust.

Location: TL 060 985 Stamford seven miles. From A1 take exit to Wansford. In Wansford take minor road past church towards Fotheringhay, Nassington and Yarwell. After one mile turn right at crossroads in Yarwell onto Sulehay Road. From here access can be gained to nature reserve by various public rights of way. Limited parking in lay-bys along Sulehay Road.

Access: Main ride is surfaced in woodland although other paths can get muddy. Quarry has uneven paths and steep slopes. Grazing animals at certain times of the year

Facilities: Ring Haw section has surfaced track and grassed paths.

Public transport: Bus Oundle to Peterborough stops at Yarwell (Stagecoach).

Habitat: Mosaic of limestone quarries, grassland, woodland and wetland.

Key birds: *Winter:* Snipe, Woodcock. *Spring:* Nuthatch, migrant warblers. *Summer:* Buzzard, Red

Kite. *Autumn:* Fieldfare, Redwing. *All year:* Green Woodpecker, Jay, Bullfinch.

Other notable flora and fauna: Butterflies, green tiger beetle, long horn beetle. Common lizard, grass snake. Badger, fox. Plants include stinking hellebore, spurge laurel, toothwort, ramsons, nettle-leaved bellflower, ploughman's spikenard, yellow-wort, clustered bellflower, common spotted-orchid, woodland and limestone grassland fungi.

Contact: Trust HQ, 01954 713 500, e-mail: cambridgeshire@wildlifebcnp.org www.wildlifebcnp.org

3. PITSFORD RESERVOIR

Beds, Cambs, Northants and Peterborough Wildlife Trust.

Location: SP 787 702. Five miles N of Northampton. On A43 take turn to Holcot and Brixworth. On A508 take turn to Brixworth and Holcot.

Access: Lodge open mid-Mar to mid-Nov from 8am-dusk. Winter opening times variable, check in advance. Permits for reserve available from Lodge on daily or annual basis. Reserve open to permit holders 365 days a year. No dogs. Disabled access from Lodge to first hide.

Facilities: Toilets available in Lodge, 15 miles of paths, nine bird hides, car parking.

Public transport: None.

Habitat: Open water (up to 120 ha), marginal vegetation and reed grasses, wet woodland, grassland and mixed woodland (40 ha).

Key birds: Typically 165-170 species per year with a total list of 250 species. *Summer:* Breeding warblers, terns, grebes, herons. *Autumn:* Waders if water levels suitable. *Winter:* Up to 10,000 wildfowl, feeding station with Tree Sparrow and occasional Corn Bunting.

Other notable flora and fauna: 31 butterfly species, 384 macro moths, 20 dragonfly species (including damselflies), 377 species of flora and 105 bryophytes, 404 fungi species.

Contact: Dave Francis, Pitsford Water Lodge, Brixworth Road, Holcot, Northampton, NN6 9SJ. 01604 780 148. e-mail: dave.francis@wildlifebcnp.org

4. STORTON'S PITS LNR

Beds, Cambs, Northants and Peterborough Wildlife Trust.

Location: SP 732 600. Next to Sixfields football ground. Follow signs for Sixfields - at mini-roundabout by stadium turn down to river. Small car park on L. The two lakes are either side of the track.

Access: Flat overall. Section of surfaced path to viewing platform, other paths soft and uneven in places with many steps on peninsula. The two reserves are adjoining.

Facilities: Viewing platform, paths, some surfaced.

Public transport: Train to Northampton then walk 1 mile or bus to St Giles and get off at Sixfields roundabout.

Habitat: One of a number of old gravel pits along the Nene valley.

Key birds: *Winter*: Water Rail, Snipe, Teal, Tufted Duck, Starling. *Spring*: Cuckoo, Green Woodpecker, Reed Bunting, Bullfinch, tits, Whitethroat, Blackcap. *Summer*: Reed Warbler, Sedge Warbler, Common Tern, Swift, House Martin. *Autumn*: Snipe, Great Crested Grebe, Moorhen, Coot, Grey Heron.

Other notable flora and fauna: Holly blue and green-veined white butterflies, water beetles. Grass snake. Bats. Cuckooflower, reed sweet-grass, marsh woundwort, purple loosestrife, water mint.

Contact: Trust HQ, 01954 713 500, e-mail: cambridgeshire@ wildlifebcnp.org

L. Take footpath to reserve.

Access: As well as the Aldwincle access point, there is a public footpath from layby on A605 N of Thrapston.

Facilities: Six hides.

Public transport: Bus service to Thrapston. Site can be muddy in winter. Wheelchair access limited.

Habitat: Alder/birch/willow wood; old duck decoy, series of water-filled gravel pits.

Key birds: *Summer*: Breeding Grey Heron (no access to heronry), Common Tern, Little Ringed Plover; warblers. Hobby now frequent and Kingfisher all year round. *Winter*: Good range of wildfowl inc Goosander and gulls.

Contact: Northants Wildlife Trust, 01604 405 285, e-mail: northamptonshire@wildlifebcnp.org

5. SUMMER LEYS LNR

Northamptonshire CC.

Location: SP 886 634. Three miles from Wellingborough, accessible from A45 and A509, situated on Great Doddington to Wollaston Road.

Access: Open 24 hours a day, 365 days a year, no permits required. Dogs welcome but must be kept on leads at all times. 40 space car park, small tarmaced circular route suitable for wheelchairs.

Facilities: Three hides, one feeding station. No toilets, nearest are at Irchester Country Park on A509 towards Wellingborough.

Public transport: Nearest main station is Wellingborough. No direct bus service, though buses run regularly to Great Doddington and Wollaston, both about a mile away. Tel: 01604 670 060 (24 hrs) for copies of timetables.

Habitat: Scrape, two ponds, lake, scrub, grassland, hedgerow.

Key birds: Hobby, Lapwing, Golden Plover, Ruff, Gadwall, Garganey, Pintail, Shelduck, Shoveler, Little Ringed Plover, Tree Sparrow, Redshank, Green Sandpiper, Oystercatcher, Black-headed Gull colony, terns.

Contact: Chris Haines, Countryside Service, Northamptonshire Council, PO Box 163, County Hall, Northampton, NN1 1AX. 01604 237 227. e-mail: countryside@northamptonshire.gov.uk

6. THRAPSTON GRAVEL PITS & TITCHMARSH LNR

Beds, Cambs, Northants and Peterborough Wildlife Trust/Natural England.

Location: TL 008 804. Seven miles E of Kettering. From A14 take A605 N. For Titchmarsh turn L at Thorpe Waterville, continue towards Aldwincle. Take first L after church and continue to small car park on

7. TOP LODGE FINESHADE WOOD

Forestry Commission

Location: SP 978 983. Off the A43 between Stamford and Corby. Follow brown tourist signs to Top Lodge Fineshade Woods.

Access: Visitor Centre (10am – 5pm), Car parking (7am – 7pm) always open except Christmas Day. Caravan Club site open Mar–Nov – please see CC website for details. Visitor centre is fully accessible – Smelter's Walk is an all-ability trail leading to hide.

Facilities: Visitor centre, toilets, Top Lodge Café, RSPB shop, with live footage of Red Kite nests in season. Guided walks and events throughout the year. Wildlife hide in wood. Three waymarked walking trails (one is for all abilities, two are surfaced), 1 horse trail, 1 family cycle trail, dedicated coach and horse box parking.

Public transport: None.

Habitat: Ancient woodland, coniferous woodland, beech woodland, open areas, small pond.

Key birds: Centre of Northants' Red Kite reintroduction scheme. A wide range of birds of

mixed woodlands. *All year*: Red Kite, Great Spotted Woodpecker, Goshawk, Nuthatch, Crossbill, Marsh Tit, Willow Tit. *Summer*: Turtle Dove, warblers. *Winter*: Hawfinch.
Other notable flora and fauna: Adder, grass snake, slow worm, common lizard. Fallow deer, badger. Orchids including greater butterfly, early purple and

common spotted, other flora of ancient woodland.
Contact: Sarah Walker, Visitor and Community Services Manager, Forestry Commission Northants, Top Lodge, Fineshade, Nr. Corby NN17 3BB. 01780 444 920, e-mail: sarah.walker@forestry.gsi.gov.uk
www.forestry.gov.uk/toplodge

Nottinghamshire

1. ATTENBOROUGH NATURE RESERVE

Nottinghamshire Wildlife Trust.
Location: SK 523 343. On A6005, seven miles SW of Nottingham alongside River Trent. Signposted from main road.
Access: Open at all times. Dogs on leads (guide dogs only in visitor centre). Paths suitable for disabled access. Coaches welcome by prior appointment.
Facilities: Education and visitor centre with café and shop, all accessible to wheelchair users. Nature trail (leaflet from Notts WT), one hide.
Public transport: Railway station at Attenborough - reserve is five mins walk away, visitor centre a further 10 minutes. Rainbow 5 bus service between Nottingham Broadmarsh and Derby bus station runs regularly throughout day. Alight at Chilwell Retail Park and walk 500m along Barton Lane.
Habitat: Disused, flooded gravel workings with associated marginal and wetland vegetation.
Key birds: *Spring/summer*: Breeding Common Tern (40-plus pairs), Reed Warbler, Black Tern regular (bred once). *Winter*: Wildfowl (including Bittern), Grey Heron colony, adjacent Cormorant roost.
Other notable flora and fauna: Smooth newt, dragonflies including four-spotted chaser and migrant hawker.
Contact: Attenborough Nature Centre, Barton Lane, Attenborough, Nottingham, NG9 6DY. 01159 721 777. e-mail: enquiries@attenboroughnaturecentre.co.uk
www.attenboroughnaturecentre.co.uk

2. BESTHORPE NATURE RESERVE

Nottinghamshire Wildlife Trust.
Location: SK 817 640 and SK813 646 (access points). Take A1133 N of Newark. Turn into Trent Lane S of Besthorpe village, reserve entrances second turn on L and R turn at end of lane (at River Trent).
Access: Open access to two hides (one with disabled access from car park at present). No access to SSSI meadows. Limited access to areas grazed with sheep. Dogs on leads.
Facilities: No toilets (pubs etc in Besthorpe village), two hides, paths, nature trail (northern part).
Public transport: Buses (numbers 22, 67, 68, 6, S7L) run by Marshalls, Lincs, Road Car and Travel Wright along A1133 to Besthorpe village (0.75 mile away). Tel: 0115 924 0000 or 01777 710 550 for information.
Habitat: Gravel pit with islands, SSSI neutral grasslands, hedges, reedbed, etc.
Key birds: *Spring/summer*: Breeding Grey Heron,

Cormorant, Little Ringed Plover, Kingfisher, Grasshopper Warbler. *Winter*: Large numbers of ducks (Pochard, Tufted Duck, Pintail, Wigeon) and Peregrine.
Contact: Trust HQ, 01159 588 242; e-mail: info@nottswt.co.uk
www.wildlifetrust.org.uk/nottinghamshire

3. BUNNY OLD WOOD WEST

Nottinghamshire Wildlife Trust.
Location: Limited parking off the A60 at Bunny Hill (SK 579 283). Please do not obstruct access. Further footpath access is at SK 584 293 off Wysall Lane.
Access: Open all year. No coach parking available.
Facilities: None. **Public transport:** None.
Habitat: Ancient coppiced woodland.
Key birds: *All year*: Usual woodland species, all three woodpeckers, Tawny and Little Owls. *Spring/summer*: Usual visitors, including Blackcap, Spotted Flycatcher and Tree Pipit.

Other notable flora and fauna: Bluebells, plus good selection of common woodland plants. Butterflies including white-letter hairstreak.
Contact: Trust HQ, 01159 588 242;
e-mail: info@nottswt.co.uk
www.wildlifetrust.org.uk/nottinghamshire

4. COLWICK COUNTRY PARK

Nottingham City Council.
Location: SK 610 395. Off A612 between Sneinton and Colwick, three miles E of Nottingham city centre.
Access: Open at all times, but no vehicle access after dusk or before 7am. Park in Colwick Hall access road from racecourse entrance.
Facilities: Nature trails. Sightings log book in Fishing Lodge.
Habitat: Lakes, pools, woodlands, grasslands, new plantations, River Trent.
Key birds: *Summer*: Warblers, Hobby, Common Tern (15+ pairs). *Winter*: Wildfowl and gulls. Passage migrants.
Other notable flora and fauna: Purple and white letter hairstreak butterflies, 16 species of dragonfly.
Contact: Head Ranger, The Fishing Lodge, Colwick, Country Park, River Road, Colwick, Nottingham NG4 2DW. 01159 870 785. www.nottinghamcity.gov.uk

5. IDLE VALLEY

Tarmac Ltd/ Hanson/ Nottinghamshire Wildlife Trust.
Location: SK 690 856. Formerly listed as Lound Gravel Pits. Two miles N of Retford off A638 adjacent to Sutton and Lound villages.
Access: Open at all times. Use public rights of way only (use OS Map Sheet No 120 Landranger Series).
Facilities: Two public viewing screens off Chainbridge Lane (overlooking Chainbridge NR Scrape) and two more overlooking Neatholme Scrape.
Public transport: Buses from Bawtry (Church Street), Retford bus station and Worksop (Hardy Street) on services 27/27A/83/83A/84 to Lound Village crossroads (Chainbridge Lane).

Habitat: Working sand and gravel quarries, restored gravel workings, woodland, reedbeds, fishing ponds, river valley, in-filled and disused fly ash tanks, farmland, scrub, willow plantations, open water. Wildlife Trust has received a large lottery grant to transform site into a wetland reserve.
Key birds: 250 bird species recorded. *Summer*: Gulls, terns, wildfowl and waders. Passage waders, terns, passerines and raptors. *Winter*: Wildfowl, gulls, raptors. Rarities have inc. Ring-billed Gull, Caspian, White-winged Black, Gull-billed and Whiskered Terns, Richard's Pipit, Baird's, Pectoral and Buff-breasted Sandpipers.
Contact: Lound Bird Club, Gary Hobson (Secretary), 18 Barnes Avenue, Wrenthorpe, Wakefield WF1 2BH. 01924 384 419; e-mail: gary.lbc1@tiscali.co.uk
www.loundbirdclub.piczo.com

6. WOLLATON PARK

Wollaton Hall.
Location: 500 acre deer park situated approx 3 miles W of Nottingham City Centre. Follow brown signs from A52 or A6514.
Access: Open all year from 8am-dusk.
Facilities: Pay/display car parks. Some restricted access (deer), leaflets.
Public transport: Trent Buses: no 22 and Nottingham City Transport: no's 31, and 28 running at about every 15 mins.
Habitat: Lake, small reedbed, woodland.
Key birds: *All year*: Main woodland species present, with good numbers of Nuthatch, Treecreeper and all three woodpeckers. *Summer*: Commoner warblers, incl Reed Warbler, all four hirundine species, Spotted Flycatcher. *Winter*: Pochard, Gadwall, Wigeon, Goosander, occasional Smew and Goldeneye. Flocks of Siskin and Redpoll, often feeding by the lake.
Contact: Wollaton Hall & Park, Wollaton, Nottingham, NG8 2AE. 01159 153 900.
e-mail: wollaton@ncmg.org.uk
www.wollatonhall.org.uk

Oxfordshire

1. ASTON ROWANT NNR

Natural England.
Location: SU 731 966. From the M40 Lewknor interchange at J6, travel NE for a short distance and turn R onto A40. After 1.5 miles at the top of the hill, turn R and R again into a narrow, metalled lane. Drive to car park, which is signposted from the A40.
Access: Open all year. Some wheelchair access, please contact site manager for more information.
Facilities: On-site parking, easy access path to viewpoint, seats, interpretation panels.
Public transport: Regular bus services to Stokenchurch, 2km S of reserve. Red Rose Travel bus goes to Aston Rowant village (call 01296 747 926).

Habitat: Chalk grassland, chalk scrub, beech woodland.
Key birds: *Spring/summer*: Blackcap, other warblers, Turtle Dove. Passage birds inc Ring Ouzel, Wheatear and Stonechat. *Winter*: Brambling, Siskin, winter thrushes. *All year*: Red Kite, Buzzard, Sparrowhawk, Woodcock, Tawny Owl, Green and Great Spotted Woodpeckers, Sky Lark, Meadow Pipit, Marsh Tit.
Other notable flora and fauna: Rich chalk grassland flora, including Chiltern gentian clustered bellflower, frog, bee, pyramidal and fragrant orchids. Good range of less common butterflies, inc silver-spotted, dingy and grizzled skippers, chalkhill blue, green hairstreak and green fritillary.
Contact: Natural England, 01844 351 833.
email: thames.chilterns@naturalengland.org.uk
www.naturalengland.org.uk

NATURE RESERVES - CENTRAL ENGLAND

2. FOXHOLES RESERVE

Berks, Bucks & Oxon Wildlife Trust.

Location: SP 254 206. Head N out of Burford on the A424 towards Stow-on-the-Wold. Take third turning on R. Head NE on unclassified road to Bruern for 3.5km. Just before reaching Bruern, turn L along track following Cocksmoor Copse. After 750m, park in car park on R just before some farm buildings.

Access: Open all year. Please keep to the paths.

Facilities: Car park, footpaths. Can be very muddy in winter.

Habitat: River, woodland, wet meadow.

Key birds: *Spring/summer*: Nightingale, Yellow Wagtail, possible Redstart, Wood Warbler, Spotted Flycatcher. *Winter*: Redwing, Fieldfare, Woodcock. *All year*: Little Owl, all three woodpeckers, possible Hawfinch.

Other notable flora and fauna: Fantastic show of bluebells in May. Autumn fungi.

Contact: Trust HQ, 01865 77 5476. www.bbowt.org.uk

3. OTMOOR NATURE RESERVE

RSPB (Central England Office).

Location: SP 570 126. Car park seven miles NE of Oxford city centre. Take B4027, to Islip and on to Horton-cum-Studley, then first L to Beckley. After 0.67 miles at the bottom of a short hill turn R (before the Abingdon Arms public house). After 200 yards, turn L into Otmoor Lane. Reserve car park is at the end of the lane (approx one mile).

Access: Open dawn-dusk. No permits or fees. No dogs allowed except on public rights of way. In wet conditions, the visitor route can be muddy and wellingtons are essential.

Facilities: Limited. Small car park with cycle racks, visitor trail (3 mile round trip) and two screened viewpoints. The reserve is not accessible by coach and is unsuitable for large groups.

Public transport: None.

Habitat: Wet grassland, reedbed and open water.

Key birds: *Summer*: Breeding birds include Cetti's and Grasshopper Warblers, Lapwing, Redshank, Curlew, Snipe, Yellow Wagtail, Shoveler, Gadwall, Pochard, Tufted Duck, Little and Great Crested Grebes. Hobby breeds locally. *Winter*: Wigeon, Teal, Shoveler, Pintail, Gadwall, Pochard, Tufted Duck, Lapwing, Golden Plover, Hen Harrier, Peregrine, Merlin. *Autumn and spring passage*: Marsh Harrier, Short-eared Owl, Greenshank, Green Sandpiper, Common Sandpiper, Spotted Redshank and occasional Black Tern.

Contact: RSPB, c/o Folly Farm, Common Road, Bexley, OX3 9YR. 01865 351 163. www.rspb.org.uk

4. SHOTOVER COUNTRY PARK

Oxford City Council.

Location: SP 565 055. Lies E of Oxford. From A420 in Headington, turn onto B4495 (Windmill Road) and Old Road.

Access: Open all year, best early morning or late in the evening.

Facilities: Car park, toilets, nature trails, booklets.

Public transport: None.

Habitat: Woodland, farmland, heathland, grassland, scrub.

Key birds: *Spring/summer*: Willow Warbler, Blackcap, Garden Warbler, Spotted Flycatcher, Whitethroat, Lesser Whitethroat, Pied Flycatcher, Redstart, Tree Pipit. *Autumn*: Crossbill, Redpoll, Siskin, thrushes. *All year*: Sparrowhawk, Jay, tits, finches, woodpeckers, Corn Bunting.

Contact: Oxford City Council, 01865 249 811. www.oxford.gov.uk
e-mail: countryside@oxford.gov.uk

5. SYDLINGS COPSE

Berks, Bucks & Oxon Wildlife Trust.

Location: SP 559 096. 3.5 miles north-east of Oxford. From Headington roundabout, take Bayswater Road N through Barton; turn L on B4027; after 500 m, park opposite Royal Oak Farm and tea room; take bridleway for 600m, passing two small woods; reserve on R 100m from bridleway. Parking on soft verge.

Access: Open daily.

Facilities: Public footpath. Public hide.

Habitat: Reedbed, fen, a stream, ancient woodland, heath, limestone grassland in steep valley.

Key birds: Summer warblers, woodpeckers and occasional Stonechat.

Other notable flora and fauna: Mammals such as badgers, deer, foxes and bats.

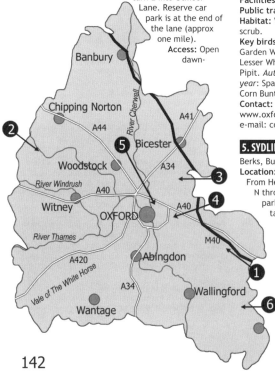

142

More than 400 species of chalk grassland, woodland and heath plants. Common lizard, grass snake, slow worm.
Contact: Trust HQ, 01865 77 5476.
www.bbowt.org.uk

6. WARBURG RESERVE

Berks, Bucks & Oxon Wildlife Trust.
Location: SU 720 879. Leave Henley-on-Thames NW on A4130. Turn R at the end of the Fair Mile onto B480. L fork in Middle Assendon. After 1 mile, follow road round to R at grassy triangle, then on for 1 mile. Car park is on R.
Access: Open all year – visitor centre opens 9am-5pm. Please keep dogs on a lead. In some areas, only guide dogs allowed.

Facilities: Visitor centre, toilets, car park, two hides, one with disabled access, nature trail, leaflets. Visitors with disabilities and groups should contact the warden before visits. Car park not suitable for coaches, only mini-buses.
Public transport: None.
Habitat: Scrub, mixed woodland, grassland, ponds.
Key birds: *Spring/summer*: Whitethroat, Lesser Whitethroat. *All year*: Sparrowhawk, Red Kite, Treecreeper, Nuthatch, Tawny Owl. *Winter*: Redpoll, Siskin, sometimes Crossbill, Woodcock.
Other notable flora and fauna: Good for orchids, butterflies, roe, fallow and muntjac deer.
Contact: Warburg Reserve, 01491 642 001.
e-mail: bbowtwarburg@cix.co.uk

Shropshire

1. BUSHMOOR COPPICE

Location: SO 430 880. Head S from Church Stretton and take first R off A49 signed Bushmoor.
Access: Park in Bushmoor village and follow track leading from right-angled bend. Follow green lane to gate and carry onto wood along field margin. Appox half mile from road.
Facilities: None.
Public transport: Buses stop at Bushmoor village.
Habitat: Small mixed woodland and scrub.
Key birds: *Spring/summer*: Migrant warblers and flycatchers, plus common woodland species.
Other notable flora and fauna: Golden saxifrage, bluebells and yellow archangel. Dormouse.
Contact: Trust HQ, 01743 284 280.
www.shropshirewildlifetrust.org.uk

2. CLUNTON COPPICE

Shropshire Wildlife Trust.
Location: SO 343 806. From Craven Arms, take B4368 to Clunton village, go straight over bridge and up hill to small car park just before reserve sign.
Access: Open at all times. Access along road and public rights of way only.
Facilities: Limited parking in small quarry entrance on R, or opposite The Crown pub.
Public transport: Buses between Craven Arms and Clun stop at Clunton. One mile walk to reserve is steep.
Habitat: Sessile oak coppice. Good for ferns, mosses and fungi.
Key birds: Buzzard and Raven regular. *Spring/summer*: Wide range of woodland birds, inc. Redstart, Wood Warbler and Pied Flycatcher, Woodcock.
Other notable flora and fauna: Dormouse, sessile oak woodland plants, bluebell, bilberry.
Contact: Trust HQ, 01743 284 280;
www.shropshirewildlifetrust.org.uk

3. EARL'S HILL

Shropshire Wildlife Trust
Location: SJ 409 048. Near Minsterley, SW of Shrewsbury. Turn off A488 at Pontesford along lane by Rea Valley Tractors. Car park 700 yards further on.
Access: Follow green route for easier walking. Purple route leads to summit. Car park at entrance.
Facilities: None.
Public transport: Buses to Bishops Castle and Minsterley stop at Pontesford.
Habitat: Steep-sided volcanic hill, scree slopes and crags, topped by Iron Age fort. Ancient woodland on eastern slopes.
Key birds: *Spring*: Migrant species such as Redstart, Pied Flycatcher and warblers. Dipper and Grey

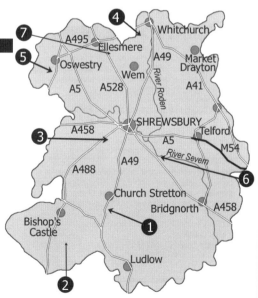

Wagtail on stream. Green Woodpecker common on open grassland.
Other notable flora and fauna: Dormouse. More than 30 species of butterfly recorded, plus bluebells and ash woodland plants. Yellow meadow ant.
Contact: Trust HQ, 01743 284 280; www.shropshirewildlifetrust.org.uk

4. FENN'S WHIXALL AND BETTISFIELD MOSSES NNR

Natural England (North Mercia Team).
Location: Located four miles SE of Whitchurch, ten miles SW of Wrexham, lying S of the A495 between Fenn's bank, Whixall and Bettisfield. There is roadside parking at entrances, car parks at Morris's Bridge, Roundthorn Bridge, World's End and a large car park at Manor House. Disabled access by prior arrangement along the railway line.
Access: Permit required except on Mosses Trail routes.
Facilities: There are panels at all of the main entrances to the site, and leaflets when applying for permits. Three interlinking Mosses Trails explore the NNR and canal from Morris's and Roundthorn bridges.
Public transport: Bus passes nearby. Railway two miles away.
Habitat: 2,000 acres of raised peatland meres and mosses.
Key birds: *Spring/summer*: Nightjar, Hobby, Curlew, Tree Sparrow. *All year*: Sky Lark, Linnet. *Winter*: Short-eared Owl.
Other notable flora and fauna: Water vole, brown hare, polecat, adder, 2,000 species of moth, 27 species of butterfly, nationally important for dragonflies, inc white-faced darter.
Contact: Natural England, Attingham Park, Shrewsbury, Shropshire SY4 4TW. 01743 282 000; e-mail: north.mercia@natural-england.org.uk

5. LLYNCLYS COMMON

Shropshire Wildlife Trust.
Location: SJ 273 237. Five miles SW of Oswestry. Park in layby on A495 at SJ 277 242, opposite Dolgoch and walk up Turner's Lane or follow footpaths.
Access: Open at all times.
Facilities: None.
Public transport: Buses stop at Pont and Dolgoch.
Habitat: Old mixed limestone sward with some woodland and scrub, small pond.
Key birds: Sparrowhawk, Green Woodpecker, Goldcrest, large warbler population. Occasional Peregrine, Buzzard.
Other notable flora and fauna: Great crested, common and palmated newts in Oliver's Pond. More than 300 species of plant, including 12 species of orchid and limestone flowers. Bluebells and ramsons in woods. Good site for skippers and pearl-bordered fritillary butterflies, horned dung beetle and hairy-footed flower bee.
Contact: Trust HQ, 01743 284 280; www.shropshirewildlifetrust.org.uk

6. VENUS POOL

Shropshire Ornithological Society.
Location: SJ 5478 0607. Site located 6 miles SE of Shrewsbury in angle formed by A458 Shrewsbury to Much Wenlock road and minor road leading S to Pitchford. Entrance is half a mile along minor road which leaves A458 half a mile (0.8 km) SE of Cross Houses.
Access: Public access to much of site, including four hides. Please keep to footpaths shown on notice boards at both entrances. Wheelchair-friendly paths to two public hides and Lena's Hide overlooking feeding station. Dogs not allowed anywhere.
Facilities: Car park with height restricting barrier. Five hides (one for SOS members only). Information boards.
Public transport: Shrewsbury-Bridgnorth buses stop at Cross Houses, which is one mile walk from Venus Pool, partly along busy main road.
Habitat: Site extends to almost 27 hectares (66 acres) and incorporates the pool itself, several islands and areas of open shoreline, fringing tall vegetation, marshy grassland, hedgerows, and areas of scrub and woodland. Species-rich meadows surround the pool, with an arable field growing bird-friendly crops.
Key birds: Venus Pool is noted for wintering wildfowl and passage waders, plus a sprinkling of county rarities, which have included Black-necked Grebe, Purple Heron, Spoonbill, Red Kite, Hen Harrier, Pectoral Sandpiper, Long-eared Owl, Black Redstart, and Wood Lark. *All year*: Common ducks and waterfowl, many resident passerines, including Tree Sparrow. *April-June*: Passage waders include Curlew, Ringed Plover, Dunlin, Redshank, Green and Common Sandpipers, and both godwits. Passage Black Tern. Breeding Oystercatcher, Little Ringed Plover, Lapwing, warblers, hirundines. *July-September*: Return wader passage from late July can include Little Stint, Greenshank, Green, Wood, Curlew and Common Sandpipers, and possible unusual species such as Pectoral Sandpiper. *October-March*: Occasional wintering Bittern, Tundra and Whooper Swans (both scarce). Geese include occasional White-fronted. Ducks include Wigeon, Teal, Pintail, Shoveler, Pochard, Goosander (up to 50 in evening roosts) and occasional Goldeneye. Water Rail, vagrant raptors and owls, winter thrushes and large passerine flocks including Lesser Redpoll, Linnet, Tree Sparrow, Reed Bunting and Yellowhammer.
Contact: For full details about Venus Pool, visit www.shropshirebirds.com

7. WOOD LANE

Shropshire Wildlife Trust.
Location: SJ 421 331. Turn off A528 at Spurnhill, 1 mile SE of Ellesmere. Car park is three quarter miles down on R.
Access: Open at all times. Apply to Trust for permit to use hides. Reserve accessible to people of all abilities.

Facilities: Car parks clearly signed. Hides (access by permit).
Public transport: None.
Habitat: Gravel pit restored by Tudor Griffiths.
Key birds: *Summer*: 168 species recorded since 1999. Breeding Sand Martin, Lapwing, Little Ringed Plover and Tree Sparrow. Osprey platforms erected to tempt

over-flying birds. Popular staging post for waders (inc. Redshank, Greenshank, Ruff, Dunlin, Little Stint, Green and Wood Sandpiper). *Winter*: Large flocks of Lapwing, plus Curlew and common wildfowl.
Other notable flora and fauna: Hay meadow plants.
Contact: Trust HQ, 01743 284 280; www.shropshirewildlifetrust.org.uk

Staffordshire

1. BELVIDE RESERVOIR

British Waterways Board and West Midland Bird Club.
Location: SJ865102. Near Brewood, 7 miles NW of Wolverhampton.
Access: Access only by permit from the West Midland Bird Club.
Facilities: Hides.
Public transport: Bus to Kiddermore Green (eight minute walk to reserve). Traveline - 0870 608 2608.
Habitat: Canal feeder reservoir with marshy margins and gravel islands.
Key birds: Important breeding, moulting and wintering ground for wildfowl, including Ruddy Duck, Goldeneye and Goosander, passage terns and waders. Night roost for gulls.
Contact: Miss M Surman, 6 Lloyd Square, 12 Niall Close, Edgbaston, Birmingham B15 3LX.
www.westmidlandbirdclub.com/belvide

2. BLITHFIELD RESERVOIR

South Staffs Waterworks Co.
Location: SK 058 237. View from causeway on B5013 (Rugeley/Uttoxeter).
Access: Access to reservoir and hides by permit from West Midland Bird Club.
Facilities: None. **Public transport:** None.
Habitat: Large reservoir.
Key birds: *Winter*: Good populations of wildfowl (inc. Bewick's Swan, Goosander, Goldeneye, Ruddy Duck), large gull roost (can inc. Glaucous, Iceland). Passage terns (Common, Arctic, Black) and waders, esp. in autumn (Little Stint, Curlew Sandpiper, Spotted Redshank regular).
Contact: Miss M Surman, 6 Lloyd Square, 12 Niall Close, Edgbaston, Birmingham B15 3LX.

3. BRANSTON WATER PARK

East Staffordshire Borough Council.
Location: SK 217 207. Follow brown tourist sign from A38 N. No access from A38 S — head to the Barton-under-Needwood exit and return N. The park is 0.5 miles S of A5121 Burton-upon-Trent exit.
Access: Open all year, flat, wheelchair-accessible stone path all round the lake.
Facilities: Green Flag Award-winning park. Parking, public toilets including a radar key operated disabled toilet, picnic area (some wheelchair accessible tables), modern children's play area.

Public transport: Contact Arriva bus services or any of the rail links.
Habitat: Reedbed, willow carr woodland, scrub, meadow area.
Key birds: *Spring/summer*: Reed Warbler, Cuckoo, Reed Bunting. Important roost for Swallow and Sand Martin. *Winter*: Waders, Little Ringed Plover occasionally, Pied Wagtail roost.
Other notable flora and fauna: Wide range of butterflies and dragonflies.
Contact: East Staffordshire Borough Council, Town Hall, Burton-on-Trent, Staffordshire DE14 2EB. 01283 508 000;
e-mail: greenspaces@eaststaffsbc.gov.uk
www.eaststaffsbc.gov.uk/Services/GreenSpaces/Pages/GreenSpacesBranstonWaterpark.aspx

4. CASTERN WOOD

Staffordshire Wildlife Trust.
Location: SK 119 537. E of Leek. Unclassified road SE of Wetton, seven miles NW of Ashbourne.
Access: Use parking area at end of minor road running due

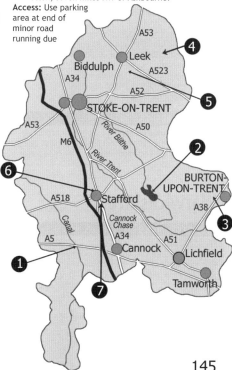

SE from Wetton.
Facilities: None.
Public transport: None.
Habitat: Limestone grassland and woodland, spoil heaps from former lead mines.
Key birds: All three woodpeckers, warblers, Pied Flycatcher, Redstart, Sparrowhawk, Tawny Owl.
Other notable flora and fauna: More than 240 species of plants have been recorded, including cowslips and violets, several species of orchids, small scabious, ladies mantle and salad burnet, plus good numbers of woodland flowers and ferns. Five species of bats have been known to over-winter.
Contact: Staffordshire Wildlife Trust, The Wolseley Centre, Wolseley Bridge, Stafford, ST17 0WT. 01889 880 100. e-mail: staffswt@cix.co.uk www.staffs-wildlife.org.uk

5. COOMBES VALLEY

RSPB (Midlands Regional Office).
Location: SK 005 530. Four miles from Leek along A523 between Leek and Ashbourne and 0.5 miles down unclassified road — signposted.
Access: Open daily — no charge. Free parking. Coach groups welcome by prior arrangement. No dogs allowed. Most of the trails are unsuitable for disabled visitors.
Facilities: Visitor centre, toilets, two miles of nature trail, one hide.
Public transport: Contact local bus company First Potteries on 01782 207 999.
Habitat: Sessile oak woodland, unimproved pasture and meadow.
Key birds: *Spring:* Pied Flycatcher, Redstart, Wood Warbler. Jan-Mar: Displaying birds of prey.
Other notable flora and fauna: Bluebells, various butterflies.
Contact: Jarrod Sneyd, Six Oaks Farm, Bradnop, Leek, Staffs, ST13 7EU. 01538 384 017. www.rspb.org.uk

6. DOXEY MARSHES

Staffordshire Wildlife Trust.
Location: SJ 903 250. In Stafford. Parking 0.25 miles off M6 J14/A513 Eccleshall Road or walk from town centre.

Access: Open at all times. Dogs on leads. Disabled access being improved. Coach and car parking off Wooton Drive.
Facilities: One hide, three viewing platforms, two are accessible to wheelchairs.
Public transport: Walk from town centre via Sainsbury's.
Habitat: Designated SSSI for wet meadow habitats. Marsh, pools, reedbeds, hedgerows, reed sweet-grass swamp.
Key birds: *Spring/summer:* Breeding Snipe, Lapwing, Redshank, Little Ringed Plover, Oystercatcher, warblers, buntings, Sky Lark, Water Rail. *Winter:* Snipe, wildfowl, thrushes, Short-eared Owl. Passage waders, vagrants.
Other notable flora and fauna: Otter, noctule bat, musk beetle.
Contact: Trust HQ, 01889 880 100; e-mail: info@staffs-wildlife.org.uk www.staffs-wildlife.org.uk

7. RADFORD MEADOWS

Staffordshire Wildlife Trust.
Location: SJ 938 216. South of Radford Bridge on A34, Stafford and alongside Staffs & Worcs Canal.
Access: View reserve from canal towpath only (access to path from A34 between bridge and BMW garage or via Hazelstrine Lane (over canal bridge). On-site visits restricted to special events only. No formal carpark.
Facilities: Trust intends to erect information boards along towpath.
Public transport: Site is close to National Cycle Network routes (www.sustrans.co.uk).
Habitat: 104 acres of lowland wet grassland, forming part of River Penk floodplain.
Key birds: Largest heronry in county (more than 20 pairs of Grey Heron). Breeding Sky Lark, Lapwing, Snipe and Reed Bunting. *Winter:* Wildfowl, Kingfisher, Buzzard.
Other notable flora and fauna: Several veteran black poplar trees.
Contact: Trust HQ, 01889 880 100; e-mail: info@staffs-wildlife.org.uk www.staffs-wildlife.org.uk; Leaflet about birding the Trent Valley available on request.

Warwickshire

1. ALVECOTE POOLS

Warwickshire Wildlife Trust.
Location: SK 253 034. Located alongside River Anker E of Tamworth. Access via Robey's Lane (off B5000) just past Alvecote Priory car park. Also along towpath via Pooley Hall visitor centre, also number of points along towpath.
Access: Some parts of extensive path system are accessible to wheelchair-users. Park in Alvecote Priory car park.

Facilities: Nature trail.
Public transport: Within walking distance of the Alvecote village bus stop.
Habitat: Marsh, open pools and reedbeds plus woodland.
Key birds: *Spring/summer:* Breeding Oystercatcher, Common Tern and Little Ringed Plover. Common species include Great Crested Grebe, Tufted Duck and Snipe. Important for wintering, passage and breeding wetland birds.
Other notable flora and fauna: *Spring:* Dingy skipper, frog, toad, great crested newt, grass snake. *Summer:* Southern marsh orchid, hairy dragonfly, damselflies,

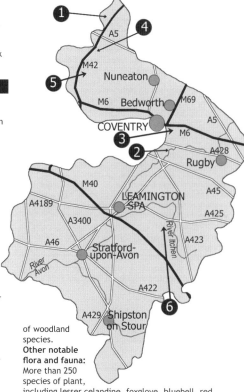

purple hairstreak butterfly and elephant hawkmoth.
Contact: Reserves Team, Brandon Marsh Nature
Centre, Brandon Lane, Brandon, Coventry, CV3
3GW. 02476 302 912. e-mail: enquiries@wrwt.org.uk
www.warwickshire-wildlife-trust.org.uk

2. BRANDON MARSH

Warwickshire Wildlife Trust.
Location: SP 386 762. Three miles SE of Coventry,
200 yards SE of A45/A46 junction (Tollbar End). Turn
E off A45 into Brandon Lane. Reserve entrance 1.25
miles on R.
Access: Open weekdays (9am-4.30pm), weekends
(10am-4pm). Entrance charge currently £2.50 (free
to Wildlife Trust members). Wheelchair access to
nature trail and Wright hide. No dogs. Parking for 2
coaches.
Facilities: Visitor centre, toilets, tea-room (open
daily 10am-3pm weekdays, 10am-4pm weekends),
nature trail, seven hides.
Public transport: Bus service from Coventry to
Tollbar End then 1.25 mile walk. Tel Travel West
Midlands 02476 817 032 for bus times.
Habitat: Ten pools, together with marsh, reedbeds,
willow carr, scrub and small mixed woodland in 260
acres, designated SSSI in 1972.
Key birds: *Spring/summer:* Garden and Grasshopper
Warblers, Whitethroat, Lesser Whitethroat, Hobby,
Little Ringed Plover, Whinchat, Wheatear. *Autumn/
winter:* Bittern (last two winters), Dunlin, Ruff,
Snipe, Greenshank, Green and Common Sandpipers,
Wigeon, Shoveler, Pochard, Goldeneye, Siskin,
Redpoll. *All year:* Cetti's Warbler, Kingfisher, Water
Rail, Gadwall, Little Grebe, Buzzard.
Other notable flora and fauna: More than 20
species of butterfly and 18 species of dragonfly
recorded. Almost 500 plants species listed on www.
brandonbirding.co.uk
Contact: Ken Bond, Hon. Sec. Brandon Marsh
Voluntary Conservation Team, 54 Wiclif Way,
Stockingford, Nuneaton CV10 8NF. 02476 328 785.

3. COOMBE COUNTRY PARK

Coventry City Council
Location: CV3 2AB. SP 402 795. Five miles East of
Coventry city centre, on B4027 Coventry to Brinklow
road.
Access: Park opens everyday, 7.30am to dusk. Entry
by foot is free with pay and display parking for
vehicles. Paths mainly hard surfaces accessible for
wheelchairs. Manual wheelchairs can be hired for a £5
returnable deposit.
Facilities: Information centre, toilets, including
disabled, café, bird hide, gift shop, picnic benches
and wildflower meadow (March to September).
Public transport: By rail: To Coventry City Centre,
20 minute bus journey to park. By bus: No-585 Mike
de Courcey Travel (for timetable please ring 024 7630
2656).
Habitat: Parkland, lake, woodland, formal gardens.
Key birds: Large heronry, plus many Cormorants.
Lesser Spotted Woodpecker and Marsh Tit top the list

of woodland
species.
**Other notable
flora and fauna:**
More than 250
species of plant,
including lesser celandine, foxglove, bluebell, red
campion and herb robert. Mammals include wood
mouse and muntjac deer.
Contact: Coombe Country Park, Brinklow Road,
Binley, Nr Coventry, CV3 2AB. 024 7645 3720.
e-mail: Coombe.countrypark@coventry.gov.uk

4. KINGSBURY WATER PARK

Warwickshire County Council.
Location: SP 203 960. Signposted `Water Park' from
J9 M42, A4097 NE of Birmingham.
Access: Open all year except Christmas Day.
Facilities: Four hides, two with wheelchair access.
Miles of flat surfaced footpaths, free loan scheme
for mobility scooters. Cafes, Information Centre with
gift shop.
 Habitat: Open water; many small pools, some with
gravel islands; gravel pits; silt beds with reedmace,
reed, willow and alder; rough areas and grassland.
Key birds: *Summer:* Breeding warblers (nine species),
Little Ringed Plover, Great Crested and Little
Grebes. Shoveler, Shelduck and a thriving Common
Tern colony. Passage waders (esp. spring). *Winter:*
Wildfowl, Short-eared Owl.
Contact: Paula Cheesman, Kingsbury Water Park,
01827 872 660. e-mail: parks@warwickshire.gov.uk
www.warwickshire.gov.uk/countryside

5. MARSH LANE NATURE RESERVE

Packington Estate Enterprises Limited.
Location: SP 217 804. Equidistant between Birmingham and Coventry, both approx 7-8 miles away. Off A452 between A45 and Balsall Common, S of B4102/A452 junction. Turn R into Marsh Lane and immediately R onto Old Kenilworth Road (now a public footpath), to locked gate. Two other entrances; gateway off B4102 east of Hampton in Arden (SP 212 814) and the other off Marsh Lane, Hampton in Arden, via bridge under railway (SP 211 805).
Access: Only guide dogs allowed. Site suitable for disabled on east side of river only. Access by day or year permit. Contact reserve for membership rates. Day permits: adult £4, OAP £3.50, children (under 16) £3 obtained from the Somers Fishery (top end of car park to Stonebridge Golf Centre), Somers Road, Meriden, CV7 7PL.
Facilities: No toilets or visitor centre. Six hides and hard tracks between hides. Three car parks behind locked gates.
Public transport: Hampton-in-Arden railway station within walking distance on footpath loop. Bus no 194 stops at N end of Old Kenilworth Road, one mile from reserve gate.
Habitat: Two large pools with islands, three small and one large (Siden Hill) areas of woodland and crop field for finches and buntings as winter feed.
Key birds: 190 species. *Summer:* Breeding birds include Little Ringed Plover, Common Tern, most species of warbler including Grasshopper. Good passage of waders in Apr, May, Aug and Sept. Hobby and Buzzard breed locally.
Other notable flora and fauna: Attractive display in spring/summer of wild flowers in woodlands, including lesser celandine, foxglove, bluebell, red campion, herb robert and many more.
Contact: Nicholas P Barlow or Kay Gleeson, Packington Hall, Packington Park, Meriden, Nr Coventry CV7 7HF. 01676 522 020.
e-mail: kay@packingtonestate.co.uk
www.packingtonestate.net

6. UFTON FIELDS

Warwickshire Wildlife Trust.
Location: SP 378 615. Located SE of Leamington Spa off A425. At South Ufton village, take B4452.
Access: Open at all times. Access via Ufton Fields Lane, South Ufton village.
Facilities: Two hides, nature trail.
Public transport: Within walking distance of Ufton village bus stop.
Habitat: Grassland, woodland, pools with limestone quarry.
Key birds: Usual species for pools/woodland/grassland including Willow Tit, Goldcrest, Green Woodpecker, Little Grebe and up to nine warbler species.
Contact: Trust HQ, 02476 302 912;
e-mail: reserves@warkswt.cix.co.uk
www.warwickshire-wildlife-trust.org.uk

West Midlands

1. LICKEY HILLS COUNTRY PARK

Birmingham County Council.
Location: Eleven miles SW of Birmingham City Centre.
Access: Open all year, (10am-7pm in summer; 10am-4.30pm in winter). Land-Rover tours can be arranged for less able visitors.
Facilities: Car park, visitor centre with wheelchair pathway with viewing gallery, picnic site, toilets, café, shop.
Public transport: Bus: West Midlands 62 Rednal (20 mins walk to visitor centre. Rail: Barnt Green (25 mins walk through woods to the centre).
Habitat: Hills covered with mixed deciduous woodland, conifer plantations and heathland.
Key birds: *Spring/summer:* Warblers, Tree Pipit, Redstart. *Winter:* Redwing, Fieldfare. *All year:* Common woodland species.
Contact: The Visitor Centre, Lickey Hills CP, Warren Lane, Rednal, Birmingham, B45 8ER. 01214 477 106.
e-mail: lickey.hills@birmingham.gov.uk

2. ROUGH WOOD CHASE LNR

Walsall Metropolitan Borough Council
Location: SJ 987 012. From M6 (Jt 10) head for Willenhall and A462. Turn R into Bloxwich Road North and R again into Hunts Lane. Car park on bend.
Access: Open all year.
Facilities: Circular nature trail.
Public transport: WMT bus 341 from Walsall.
Habitat: 70 acres of oakwood, significant for West Midlands. Also meadows, ponds, pools, marsh and scrubland.
Key birds: Great Crested and Little Grebes on pools in the north end of Chase. Breeding Jay and Sparrowhawk. Common woodland species all year and warblers in summer.
Other notable flora and fauna: Great crested and smooth newts, water vole, various dragonfly species, purple hairstreak, brimstone and small heath butterflies.
Contact: Walsall Countryside Services, Walsall Metropolitan Borough Council, Top Hangar, Bosty Lane, Aldridge, Walsall WS9 0QQ. 01922 458 328, e-mail: countrysideservices@walsall.gov.uk
www.walsall.gov.uk

NATURE RESERVES - CENTRAL ENGLAND

3. SANDWELL VALLEY COUNTRY PARK

Sandwell Metropolitan Borough Council.
Location: Entrances at SP 012 918 & SP 028 992. Located approx. 1 mile NE of West Bromwich town centre. Main entrance off Salters Lane or Forge Lane.
Access: Car parks open 8am to sunset. Wheelchair access to Priory Woods LNR, Forge Mill Lake LNR and other parts of the country park.
Facilities: 1,700 acre site. Visitor centre, toilets, café at Sandwell Park Farm (10am-4.30pm). Good footpaths around LNRs and much of the country park. Coach parking by appointment. Also 20 acre RSPB reserve (see below).
Public transport: West Bromwich bus station West Bromwich central metro stop. (Traveline 0871 200 2233).
Habitat: Pools, woodlands, grasslands, including three local nature reserves.
Key birds: Wintering wildfowl including regular flock of Goosander, small heronry. *All year*: Grey Heron, Great Crested Grebe, Lapwing, Reed Bunting, Great Spotted and Green Woodpecker, Sparrowhawk, Kestrel. *Spring*: Little Ringed Plover, Oystercatcher, up to 8 species of warber breeding, passage migrants. *Autumn*: Passage migrants. *Winter*: Goosander, Shoveler, Teal, Wigeon, Snipe.
Other notable flora and fauna: Common spotted and southern marsh orchid. Ringlet butterfly. Water vole, weasel.
Contact: Senior Countryside Ranger, Sandwell Park Farm, Salters Lane, West Bromwich, W Midlands B71 4BG. 01215 530 220 or 2147.

4. SANDWELL VALLEY

RSPB (Midlands Regional Office).
Location: SP 035 928. Great Barr, Birmingham. Follow signs S from M6 J7 via A34. Take R at 1st junction onto A4041. Take 4th L onto Hamstead Road (B4167), then R at 1st mini roundabout onto Tanhouse Avenue.
Access: 800 metres of paths accessible to assisted and powered wheelchairs with some gradients (please ring centre for further information), centre fully accessible.
Facilities: Visitor centre and car park (open Tue-Fri 9am-5pm, Sat-Sun 10am-5pm. Closes at dusk in winter), with viewing area, small shop and hot drinks, four viewing screens, one hide. Phone centre for details on coach parking.
Public transport: Bus: 16 from Corporation Street (Stand CJ), Birmingham City Centre (ask for Tanhouse Avenue). Train: Hamstead Station, then 16 bus for one mile towards West Bromwich from Hamstead (ask for Tanhouse Avenue).
Habitat: Open water, wet grassland, reedbed, dry grassland and scrub.
Key birds: *Summer*: Lapwing, Little Ringed Plover, Reed Warbler, Whitethroat, Sedge Warbler, Willow Tit. *Passage*: Sandpipers, Yellow Wagtail, chats, Common Tern. *Winter*: Water Rail, Snipe, Jack Snipe, Goosander, Bullfinch, woodpeckers and wildfowl.
Contact: Lee Copplestone, 20 Tanhouse Avenue, Great Barr, Birmingham, B43 5AG. 0121 3577 395.

Worcestershire

1. BEACONWOOD/THE WINSEL

Worcestershire Wildlife Trust.
Location: SO 974 759. N of Bromsgrove. Entrance near Lydiate Ash, three miles north of Bromsgrove, at end of cul-de-sac of Old Birmingham Road. Take public footpath along metalled track going N and enter reserve through a metal gate on L after about 20 yards.
Access: The reserve is open throughout the year but please keep to the footpaths.
Facilities: None.
Public transport: Nearest station – Longbridge (three miles). Nearest bus stops in Rubery (1 mile).
Habitat: Mixed woodlands.
Key birds: Buzzard, Kestrel, Sparrowhawk, Tawny Owl, Little Owl, Great Spotted Woodpecker, Spotted Flycatcher, Nuthatch, Treecreeper and many other woodland birds are resident. *Summer*: Pied and Spotted Flycatcher, warblers.
Other notable flora and fauna: In May there is an unbroken sea of bluebells over 5 acres. Good variety of trees including the Great Oak, probably 250 years old.
Contact: Worcestershire Wildlife Trust, Lower Smite

Farm, Smite Hill, Hindlip WR3 8SZ. 01905 754 919.
e-mail: enquiries@worcestershirewildlifetrust.org
www.worcswildlifetrust.co.uk

2. BROADWAY GRAVEL PIT

Worcestershire Wildlife Trust.
Location: SP 087 379. Approx. half mile NW of Broadway on the N side of Broadway to Childswickham road and E of old disused railway line.
Access: Open access at all times. Disabled access to hide only. Parts of circular path sometimes flooded but hide is usually clear.
Facilities: 1 hide. Cafes and toilets in Broadway. Very limited car parking (2-3 cars), no room for a coach. Large car park within half mile in Broadway.
Public transport: No rail connection. Buses to Broadway from Evesham etc. Check the timetable.
Habitat: Open water, wet woodland, dry scrub.
Key birds: As this is a very small site (1.6ha), it does not hold great numbers of bird species. Wintering Chiffchaff with tit and crest flocks, finches and buntings. Whitethroat, Blackcap, Chiffchaff, Cuckoo in spring/summer.
Other notable flora and fauna: A good dragonfly site for commoner species. Butterflies in dryer, grassy areas. Mare's tail (unusual in Worcestershire wetland sites) found in abundance in June and August.

NATURE RESERVES - CENTRAL ENGLAND

Contact: Trust HQ, 01905 754 919;
e-mail: enquiries@worcestershirewildlifetrust.org
www.worcswildlifetrust.co.uk

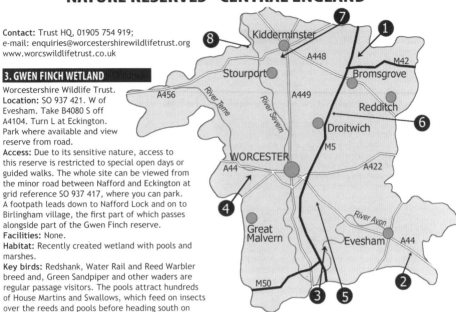

3. GWEN FINCH WETLAND

Worcestershire Wildlife Trust.
Location: SO 937 421. W of
Evesham. Take B4080 S off
A4104. Turn L at Eckington.
Park where available and view
reserve from road.
Access: Due to its sensitive nature, access to
this reserve is restricted to special open days or
guided walks. The whole site can be viewed from
the minor road between Nafford and Eckington at
grid reference SO 937 417, where you can park.
A footpath leads down to Nafford Lock and on to
Birlingham village, the first part of which passes
alongside part of the Gwen Finch reserve.
Facilities: None.
Habitat: Recently created wetland with pools and
marshes.
Key birds: Redshank, Water Rail and Reed Warbler
breed and, Green Sandpiper and other waders are
regular passage visitors. The pools attract hundreds
of House Martins and Swallows, which feed on insects
over the reeds and pools before heading south on
migration.
Other notable flora and fauna: Dragonflies and
damselflies are abundant along the margins of the
river and the pools. Regular haunt for otters.
Contact: Trust HQ, 01905 754 919;
e-mail: enquiries@worcestershirewildlifetrust.org
www.worcswildlifetrust.co.uk

4. KNAPP AND PAPERMILL

Worcestershire Wildlife Trust.
Location: SO 749 522. Take A4103 SW from
Worcester; R at Bransford roundabout then L towards
Suckley and reserve is approx three miles (do not turn
off for Alfrick). Park at Bridges Stone layby (SO 751
522), cross road and follow path to the Knapp House.
Access: Open daily. Large parties should contact
Warden
Facilities: Nature trail, small information centre,
wildlife garden, Kingfisher viewing screen.
Public transport: None.
Habitat: Broadleaved woodland, unimproved
grassland, fast stream, old orchard in Leigh Brook
Valley.
Key birds: *Summer:* Breeding Grey Wagtail,
Kingfisher, Spotted Flycatcher nests in warden's
garden, all three woodpeckers. Buzzard,
Sparrowhawk and Redstart also occur.
Other notable flora and fauna: Otters have returned
recently. Good numbers of dragonflies and butterflies
on all three meadows include holly blue, purple
hairstreak and white admiral. Bluebells, green-winged
and spotted orchids.
Contact: The Warden, Knapp and Papermill reserve,
The Knapp, Alfrick WR6 5HR. 01886 832 065.

5. TIDDESLEY WOOD NATURE RESERVE

Worcestershire Wildlife Trust.
Location: SO 929 462. Take B4084 from Pershore to
Worcester. Turn L towards Besford and Croome near
town boundary just before the summit of the hill.
Entrance is on L after about 0.75 miles.
Access: Open all year except Christmas Day. Cycles
and horses only allowed on the bridleway. Please
keep dogs fully under control. Military firing range
at the SW corner of wood, so do not enter the area
marked by red flags. The NE plot is private property
and visitors should not enter the area. Main ride
contains some potholes. Small pathways difficult if
wet. Coach parking by appointment.
Facilities: Information board. Circular trail around
small pathways.
Public transport: First Midland Red services (see
above).
Habitat: Ancient woodland, conifers.
Key birds: *All year:* Crossbill, Coal Tit, Goldcrest,
Sparrowhawk, Willow Tit, Marsh Tit. *Spring:*
Chiffchaff, Blackcap, Cuckoo. *Winter:* Redwing,
Fieldfare.
Other notable flora and fauna: Dragonflies including
club-tailed and white-legged damselflies. Good
for butterflies, including white admiral, peacock
and gatekeeper. Important invertebrates include
nationally rare noble chafer beetle which has
been recorded here for many years. Plants include
uncommon violet helleborine and herb paris, greater
butterfly orchid and twayblade.
Contact: Trust HQ, 01905 754 919;
e-mail: enquiries@worcestershirewildlifetrust.org

6. UPTON WARREN

Worcestershire Wildlife Trust.
Location: SO 936 675. Two miles S of Bromsgrove on A38. Leave M5 at junction 5.
Access: Christopher Cadbury Wetland Reserve divided into two parts — Moors Pools and Flashes Pools. Always open except Christmas Day. Trust membership gives access, or day permit from sailing centre. Disabled access to hides at Moors Pools only. No dogs.
Facilities: Seven hides, maps at entrances, paths can be very muddy. Coach parking at sailing centre by previous booking.
Public transport: Birmingham/Worcester bus passes reserve entrance.
Habitat: Fresh and saline pools with muddy islands, some woodland and scrub.
Key birds: *Winter:* Wildfowl. *Spring/autumn:* Passage waders. *Summer:* Breeding Avocet, Redshank, Little Ringed Plover, Oystercatcher, Common Tern, Sedge, Reed, Grasshopper and Cetti's Warblers. Hobby nearby.
Other notable flora and fauna: Saltmarsh plants, dragonflies.
Contact: A F Jacobs, 3 The Beeches, Upton Warren, Bromsgrove, Worcs B61 7EL. 01527 861 370.

7. WILDEN MARSH

Worcestershire Wildlife Trust.
Location: SO 825 730 and SO 829 735. S of Kidderminster. Take A449 S from Kidderminster. At junction with A442 go straight across roundabout into Wilden Lane. This is a very busy road with few parking spaces so park carefully. There are gated entrances off Wilden Lane.
Access: Parts of reserve accessed by gated entrances are open at all times. Visitors to the more northerly part of the reserve should obtain a permit from the Trust's office. This reserve is complex and new visitors should consult a map. Cattle will be on the reserve at all times so ensure that all gates are secured after use. Parts of this reserve are dangerous with boggy areas, steep banks by the River Stour and deep ditches.
Public transport: Nearest bus stop at Wilden, half mile from reserve.
Habitat: Dry and marshy fields with small alder and willow woods, reed beds and many drainage ditches.
Key birds: 192 bird species have been recorded since 1968 and about 70 breed, including Yellow Wagtail, nine species of warblers and Redshank. It is one of the few wintering places for Water Pipits in county, though numbers have declined recently.
Other notable flora and fauna: Plants include southern marsh orchids, marsh cinquefoil, marsh arrow-grass, marsh pennywort and lesser water parsnip.
Contact: Trust HQ, 01905 754 919; e-mail: enquiries@worcestershirewildlifetrust.org

8. WYRE FOREST

Natural England/Worcs Wildlife Trust.
Location: SO 750 760. Half a mile NW of Bewdley (on the A456) and four and a half miles W of Kidderminster.
Access: Observe reserve signs and keep to paths. Forestry Commission visitor centre at Callow Hill. Fred Dale Reserve is reached by footpath W of B4194 (parking at SO 776 763).
Facilities: Toilet and refreshment facilities at Wyre Forest Visitor Centre (near the Discovery Centre) at Callow Hill. Several waymarked trails in the Forest (some suitable for wheelchair users) as well as regular guided walks, also family cycle routes through the reserve. The Visitor Centre and Discovery Centre provide facilities for disabled visitors.
Public transport: The nearest train station is in Bewdley, served by the Severn Valley Railway (01299 403 816) although service is seasonal and sometimes infrequent. Also Central Trains to Kidderminster (0121 634 2040) and local bus services between Bewdley and Kidderminster.
Habitat: Oak forest, conifer areas, birch heath, lowland grassland, stream.
Key birds: Breeding birds include Redstart, Pied Flycatcher, Wood Warbler, Buzzard and Raven, with Dipper, Grey Wagtail and Kingfisher found on the larger streams.
Other notable flora and fauna: Mammals include, fallow, roe and muntjac deer, polecat, otter and mink, yellow neck mouse, dormouse, voles and water shrew. Several bat species including pipistrelle and Daubenton's. Important site for invertebrates including England's largest colony of pearl-bordered fritillary butterflies.
Contact: Tim Dixon, Natural England, Block B, Government Buildings, Whittington Road, Worcester WR5 2LQ. 01905 763 355; (Fax)01905 764 973 e-mail: herefordshire.worcestershire@ www.naturalengland.org.uk

Eastern England

Bedfordshire, Cambridgeshire, Essex, Hertfordshire, Norfolk, Suffolk

Bedfordshire

1. BEGWARY BROOK

Beds, Cambs, Northants and Peterborough Wildlife Trust.
Location: TL 169 564. 2 miles S of St Neots. From A1 S take A428 E and continue to Wyboston Lakes complex. Pass through complex and follow nature reserve signs to car park.
Access: Open all year. Partially suitable for wheelchairs.
Facilities: None.
Public transport: Bus, St Neots to Sandy, some stop in Wyboston (Saffords Coaches - 01767 677 395).
Habitat: Former gravel pit. Marsh and open pools next to Great Ouse.
Key birds: Wildfowl and wader species. *Spring*: Sedge, Reed and Willow Warblers, Blackcap. *All year*: Reed Bunting, Kingfisher, Goldcrest.
Other notable flora and fauna: Orange-tip and speckled wood butterflies, dragonflies and grass snakes. Plants include great burnet, common fleabane and marsh woundwort.
Contact: Beds, Cambs, Northants & Peterborough Wildlife Trust, The Manor House, Broad Street, Great Cambourne, Cambridgeshire CB23 6DH. 01954 713 500; e-mail: cambridgeshire@wildlifebcnp.org www.wildlifebcnp.org

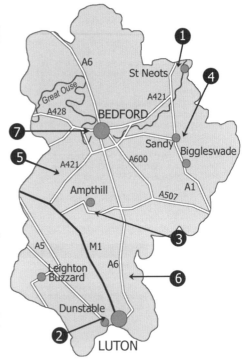

2. BLOW'S DOWNS

Beds, Cambs, Northants and Peterborough Wildlife Trust.
Location: TL 033 216. On the outskirts of Dunstable. Take A5065 from W of Luton, cross M1, take first exit at roundabout, park with care on verge. Alternatively, walk half mile from Dunstable centre to W entrance at Half Moon Lane off A5.
Access: Open all year, not suitable for wheelchairs.
Facilities: None.
Public transport: None.
Habitat: SSSI, chalk downland, scrub and grassland, that is a traditional resting place for incoming spring migrants.
Key birds: *Winter*: Lapwing, Meadow Pipit, Sky Lark, Stonechat. *Spring/autumn*: Ring Ouzel, Wheatear, Whinchat, Black Redstart, Willow Warbler.
Other notable flora and fauna: Chalkhill blue, brown argus and marbled white butterflies. Plants include small scabious, burnet-saxifrage, squinancywort, great pignut, common spotted and bee orchids.
Contact: Trust HQ, 01954 713 500;
e-mail: bedfordshire@wildlifebcnp.org www.wildlifebcnp.org

3. FLITWICK MOOR

Beds, Cambs, Northants and Peterborough Wildlife Trust.

Location: TL 046 354. E of Flitwick. From Flitwick town centre (Tesco roundabout) on A5120, cross railway bridge, R at roundabout, immediately L into King's Road. After 500m, L into Moulden Road towards A507. After quarter mile R at Folly Farm, follow track to small car park. Also footpath to reserve from Moor Lane.
Access: Open all year.
Facilities: Car park. Please stick to public paths.
Public transport: Frequent buses (United Counties) from Bedford and Luton to Flitwick, or take train to Flitwick and then three quarter mile walk.
Habitat: SSSI. Important wetland for the area, blend of fen, meadow, wet woodland and fragile peaty soil. Supports mosses ferns and flowers.
Key birds: *Winter*: Siskin, Water Rail, Great Spotted Woodpecker. *Spring*: Lesser Spotted Woodpecker, Willow Warbler, Blackcap. *Summer*: Water Rail, Grasshopper and Garden Warblers, Cuckoo. *Autumn*: Brambling.
Other notable flora and fauna: Good variety of butterflies and dragonflies, plus chimney sweeper moth and conehead bush cricket. Plants include nine species of sphagnum moss, marsh pennywort, black

knapweed, water figwort plus fly agaric and yellow brain fungus in autumn.
Contact: Trust HQ, 01954 713 500;
e-mail: bedfordshire@wildlifebcnp.org
www.wildlifebcnp.org

4. LODGE (THE)

RSPB (Central England Office).
Location: TL 191 485. Reserve lies 1 mile/1.6km E of Sandy on the B1042 to Potton.
Access: Reserve is open daily 9am-9pm (or sunset when earlier); shop 9am-5pm weekdays, 10am-5pm weekends. Non-members: £4 per motor vehicle. Dogs only allowed on bridleway.
Facilities: Nature trails being extended to 5 miles. One bridleway (half mile) and gardens are wheelchair/pushchair accessible. One hide (wheelchair accessible), 50 yards from car park. Coach parking at weekends by arrangement. Refreshments at shop.
Public transport: Buses to Sandy Market Square from Bedford, infrequent service. One mile walk or cycle from centre of Sandy or half mile from Sandy railway station, in part along trail through heathland restoration.
Habitat: This 180-hectare reserve is a mixture of woodland, heathland and acid grassland and includes the formal gardens of the RSPB's UK headquarters. New land being restored to heathland.
Key birds: *Spring/summer*: Hobby, Spotted Flycatcher. *All year*: Woodpeckers, woodland birds. *Winter*: Winter thrushes, woodland birds.
Other notable flora and fauna: Natterjack toads, common lizard, grass snake, rare heathland insects, dragonflies and butterflies. Particularly good site for fungi, and lichens. Garden pools are good for dragonflies.
Contact: RSPB, The Lodge Shop, Sandy, Beds SG19 2DL. 01767 680 541. www.rspb.org.uk/reserves/
e-mail: thelodgereserve@rspb.org.uk

5. MARSTON VALE MILLENNIUM COUNTRY PARK

Marston Vale Trust (Regd Charity No 1069229).
Location: SW of Bedford off A421 at Marston Moreteine. Only five mins from J13 of M1.
Access: Park and forest centre open seven days a week. Summer 10am-6pm, winter 10am-4pm. No dogs in wetlands reserve, rest of site OK for dogs and horses. Entry charge for wetland reserve (£2.50 for adults and £1.75 for Concessions). Main 8km trail surfaced for wheelchair and pushchair access. All-terrain wheelchair available for free loan. Coach parking available.
Facilities: Cafe bar, gift shop, art gallery, exhibition. Free parking.
Public transport: Bedford to Bletchley line – trains to Millbrook and Stewartby station, 20 minute walk to Forest Centre.
Habitat: Lake - 610 acres/freshwater marsh (man-made), reedbed, woodland, hawthorn scrub and grassland.

Key birds: *Winter*: Iceland and Glaucous Gulls (regular), gull roost, wildfowl, Great Crested Grebe. *Spring*: Passage waders and terns (Black Tern, Arctic Tern), Garganey. *Summer*: Nine species of breeding warblers, Hobby, Turtle Dove, Nightingale, Bearded Tit. *Autumn*: Passage waders and terns. *Rarities*: White-winged Black Tern, Laughing Gull, divers, Manx Shearwater, Bittern.
Other notable flora and fauna: Dingy and grizzled skipper butterflies, excellent for dragonflies, red-veined darter in 2008. Also otter and brown hare, plus bee and pyramidal orchids and stoneworts.
Contact: Forest Centre, Station Road, Marston Moreteine, Beds, MK43 0PR. 01234 767 037.
e-mail: info@marstonvale.org
www.marstonvale.org

6. PEGSDON HILL RESERVE

Beds, Cambs, Northants and Peterborough Wildlife Trust.
Location: TL 120 295. 5 miles W of Hitchin. Take B655 from Hitchin towards Barton-le-Clay. Turn R at Pegsdon then immediately L and park in lay-by. Reserve entrance across B655 via footpath.
Access: Open all year. Dropping off point for coaches only.
Facilities: None.
Public transport: Luton to Henlow buses (United Counties) stop at Pegsdon.
Habitat: Chalk grassland, scrub and woodland.
Key birds: *Winter*: Brambling, Stonechat, winter thrushes, raptors including Buzzard. *Spring*: Wheatear, Ring Ouzel, Tree Pipit, Yellowhammer. *Summer*: Turtle Dove, Grey Partridge, Lapwing, Sky Lark.
Other notable flora and fauna: Dragonflies, dark green fritillary, dingy and grizzled skippers, chalkhill blue, brown argus and small heath butterflies. Glow worms. Plants include pasqueflower in spring, fly, spotted and pyramidal orchids.
Contact Trust HQ, 01954 713 500;
e-mail: bedfordshire@wildlifebcnp.org
www.wildlifebcnp.org

7. PRIORY COUNTRY PARK AND MARINA

Bedford Borough Council.
Location: TL 071 495. 1.5 miles SE from Bedford town centre. Signposted from A428 & A421. Entry point to new 'River Valley Park'
Access: Park and hides open at all times. No access to fenced/gated plantations.
Facilities: Toilets and visitor centre open daytime, all-year-round disabled access on new path around lake. Hides, nature trails, labyrinth, cycle hire, Premier Inn for meals, accomodation.
Public transport: Stagecoach (01604 676 060) 'Blue Solo 4' every 20 mins. Mon-Sat. Alight 1st stop Riverfield Drive (200 m). Rail station at Bedford (approx 2.5 miles)
Habitat: Lakes, reedbeds, scrub and woodland, meadows adjoining Great Ouse.

153

Key birds: Good numbers/variety of winter wildfowl, varied mix of spring passage species, with breeding warblers and woodpeckers, augmented by feeding terns, hirundines and raptors. *Winter*: Grebes, Pochard, Shoveler, Gadwall, Merlin, Water Rail, gulls, thrushes, Chiffchaff, corvids, buntings. *Passage*: Raptors, waders, terns, pipits. *Summer*: Hobby, Turtle Dove, Swift, hirundines, *acrocephalus* and *sylvia* warblers. *All year*: Cormorant, Little Egret,

Heron, Stock Dove, woodpeckers, Kingfisher, Grey Wagtail, Treecreeper, Goldfinch, Bullfinch.
Other notable flora and fauna: 23 species of dragonfly, incl small red-eyed damsel & hairy hawker. 20 species of butterfly. Large plant list. Fox, muntjac and otter.
Contact: Jon Bishop, Wardens Office, Visitor Centre, Priory CP, Barkers Lane, Bedford, MK41 9SH. 01234 211 182.

Cambridgeshire

1. BRAMPTON WOOD

Beds, Cambs, Northants and Peterborough Wildlife Trust.
Location: TL 184 698. 4 miles W of Huntingdon. From A1 take A14 exit towards Huntingdon. Take first exit off A14 to Brampton (B1514). Go straight at first roundabout then R at second. Turn R at T-junction onto Grafham road, go through village, over A1, reserve is on N side of road 1.5 miles out of Brampton. Park in small car park.
Access: Open daily. Coaches able to drop passengers off but not enough space to park.
Facilities: Car park, interpretative shelter.
Public transport: Bus from Huntingdon to Brampton (H&D) then 2 mile walk.
Habitat: Ancient woodland, primarily oak, ash and field maple with hazel coppice.
Key birds: *Autumn/winter*: Marsh Tit, Woodcock, winter thrushes. *Spring/summer*: Common woodland birds, Green Woodpecker, Spotted Flycatcher.
Other notable flora and fauna: Brown argus, white admiral and black hairstreak butterflies, pine beauty and pine hawk moths. Dormouse, glow worms, smooth and great crested newts, plus various dragonfly species. Plants include meadow grasses, cowslip, yellow rattle, devil's-bit scabious, primrose, hairy and trailing St John's wort.
Contact: Beds, Cambs, Northants & Peterborough Wildlife Trust, The Manor House, Broad Street, Great Cambourne, Cambridgeshire CB3 6DH. 01954 713 500; e-mail: cambridgeshire@wildlifebcnp.org www.wildlifebcnp.org

2. FEN DRAYTON

RSPB (Eastern England Office).
Location: TL 352 680. NW of Cambridge. Leave A14 at Junction 28; follow signs to Swavesey. Turn L in Boxworth End (signed to Fen Drayton). Turn R onto minor road (signed to Swavesey), then L into entrance to Fen Drayton Lakes. Follow signs to car park.
Access: Open at all times. Dogs are only allowed on public footpaths and bridleways. Disabled birders can get car access to one viewing screen.
Facilities: There are a number of public and permissive rights of way around the lakes and two open access fields. Information boards give access details. Free trail guides and events leaflets are available from the Elney car park.

Public transport: Huntingdon: Stagecoach service 553 (with change to service 15 at St Ives), alight at Fen Drayton High Street. Cambridge: Stagecoach service 15 to Swavesey Middle Watch or Whippet No 15 to Fenstanton, alight in Fen Drayton High Street. Walk north (600 m) from Fen Drayton High Street onto Holywell Ferry Road, past recreation ground on left. Cambridgeshire guided bus service will have a request stop in reserve.
Habitat: A complex of lakes and traditional riverside meadows next to the River Great Ouse that used to be gravel workings.
Key birds: At least 213 species have been recorded in the area with some 65 species being regular breeders including Common Tern. Hobby, waders on passage. Rarities include Great White Egret, Purple Heron, Glossy Ibis, Common Crane, Red-Footed Falcon, Honey Buzzard and Whiskered Tern. Bitterns are now a regular sight, with Holywell Lake and Elney Lake being the favoured sites. *Winter*: Nationally important numbers of Gadwall and Coot.
Other notable flora and fauna: Good site for butterflies, dragonflies and mammals.
Contact: The Warden, RSPB Fens area office, The Grange, Market Street, Swavesey, Cambridge, Cambs CB24 4QG. 01603 661 662. www.rspb.org.uk/reserves/

3. FERRY MEADOWS COUNTRY PARK

Nene Park Trust.
Location: TL 145 975. Three miles W of Peterborough town centre, signposted off A605.
Access: Open all year, 7am to dusk (summer), 8am until sunset (winter). Electric scooters and wheelchair available for loan — call to book in advance. Coach parking free at all times. Car parking charges apply at weekends and Bank Holidays between April - Oct.
Facilities: Car park, visitor centre, toilets (inc disabled), café, two wheelchair-accessible hides in nature reserve area. Hard surface paths in park's central areas, but steep slopes in Bluebell Wood.
Public transport: Stagecoach X14 stops on A605 by Notcutts Nursey. Half mile walk to park entrance. Tel. Traveline 0870 6082 608 or www.traveline.org.uk
Habitat: Lakes, meadows, scrub, broadleaved woodland and small wetland nature reserve.
Key birds: *Spring*: Terns, waders, Yellow Wagtail. *Winter*: Grebes, Siskin, Redpoll, Water Rail, occasional Hawfinch. *All year*: Good selection of woodland and water birds, Kingfisher.
Other notable flora and fauna: Bluebell, wood

anenome, wild garlic in woodland.
Contact: Visitor Services Officer, Nene Park Trust, Ham Farm House, Orton, Peterborough, PE2 5UU. 01733 234 443. e-mail: visitor.services@nene-park-trust. org.uk
www.nene-park-trust.org.uk

4. FOWLMERE

RSPB (Eastern England Office).
Location: TL 407 461. 7 miles S of Cambridge. Turn off A10 Cambridge to Royston road by Shepreth and follow sign.
Access: Access at all times along marked trail.
Facilities: One and a half miles of trails. Three hides, toilets. Space for one coach, prior booking essential. Wheelchair access to one hide, toilet and some of the trails.
Public transport: Shepreth railway station 2 miles.
Habitat: Reedbeds, meres, woodland, scrub.
Key birds: *Summer*: Nine breeding warblers. *All year*: Water Rail, Kingfisher. *Winter*: Snipe, raptors.
Other notable flora and fauna: Healthy population of water shrews. 18 species of dragonfly recorded.
Contact: The Warden, RSPB, Manor Farm, High Street, Fowlmere, Royston, Herts SG8 7SH. Tel/Fax 01763 208 978.

5. GRAFHAM WATER

Beds, Cambs, Northants and Peterborough Wildlife Trust.
Location: TL 143 671. Follow signs for Grafham Water from A1 at Buckden or A14 at Ellington. Nature Reserve entrance is from Mander car park, W of Perry village.
Access: Open all year. Dogs barred in wildlife garden only, on leads elsewhere. Car parking £2 for day ticket.
Facilities: Five bird hides in nature reserve, two in the bird sanctuary area. Two hides in wildlife garden accessible to wheelchairs. Cycle track through reserve also accessible to wheelchairs. Visitor centre with restaurant, shop and toilets. Disabled parking. Use Plummer car park for lagoons and Marlow car park for dam area (good for waders and vagrants).
Public transport: Bus, St Neots to Bedford. Get off at Great Staughton then 2 mile walk.
Habitat: Open water, settlement lagoons ranging from reedbeds, open water, wet mud and willow carr, ancient and plantation woodland, scrub, species rich grassland.
Key birds: *Resident*: Common woodland birds, wildfowl. *Winter*: Waders including Common Sandpiper and Dunlin, Great Crested Grebe, Wildfowl including large flocks of Tufted Duck and Coot, Pochard, Shoveler, Shelduck, Goldeneye, Goosander and Smew, gulls (can be up to 30,000 roosting in mid-winter). *Spring/summer*: Breeding Nightingale, Reed, Willow and Sedge Warblers, Common and Black Terns.

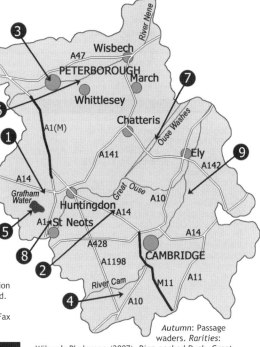

Autumn: Passage waders. *Rarities*: Wilson's Phalarope (2007), Ring-necked Duck, Great Northern Diver, Glaucous, Iceland and Mediterranean Gulls.
Other notable flora and fauna: Bee and common spotted orchids, early purple orchid, common twayblade (in woods), cowslip. Common blue and marbled white butterflies, dragonflies including broad-bodied chaser, voles, grass snakes.
Contact: The Warden, Grafham Water Nature Reserve, c/o The Lodge, West Perry, Huntingdon, Cambs, PE28 0BX. 01480 811 075. e-mail: matt.hamilton@wildlifebcnp.org
www.wildlifetrust.org.uk/bcnp

6. NENE WASHES

RSPB (Eastern England Office).
Location: TL 317 992. N of Whittlesey and six miles E of Peterborough.
Access: Open at all times along South Barrier Bank, accessed at Eldernell, one mile NE of Coates, off A605. Group visits by arrangement. No access to fields. No access for wheelchairs along bank.
Facilities: Small car park - one coach max. Information board. No toilets or hide.
Public transport: Bus and trains to Whittlesey, bus to Coates -Stagecoach 01733 554 575.
Habitat: Wet grassland with ditches. Frequently flooded.
Key birds: *Spring/early summer*: Corn Crake release scheme. Breeding waders (inc Black-tailed Godwit), duck (inc Garganey), Marsh Harrier and Hobby.

Winter: Waterfowl in large numbers (inc Bewick's Swan, Pintail, Shoveler), Barn and Short-eared Owls, Hen Harrier.
Other notable flora and fauna: Water vole, otter, water violet, flowering rush and fringe water lily.
Contact: Charlie Kitchin, RSPB Nene Washes, 21a East Delph, Whittlesey, Cambs PE7 1RH. 01733 205 140.

7. OUSE WASHES

RSPB (Eastern England Office).
Location: TL 471 860. Between Chatteris and March on A141, take B1093 to Manea. Reserve signposted from Manea. Reserve office and visitor centre located off Welches Dam. Approximately ten miles from March or Chatteris.
Access: Access at all times from visitor centre (open 9am - 5pm every day except Dec 25/26). Welches Dam to public hides approached by marked paths behind boundary bank. No charge. Dogs to be kept on leads at all times. Disabled access to Welches Dam hide, 350 yards from car park. Track between Kingfisher and Stevens Hides very muddy following maintenance work. Groups welcome, but note that large coaches (36+ seats) cannot traverse final bend to reserve.
Facilities: Car park (inc 2 disabled bays) and toilets. Space for up to two small coaches. Visitor centre – unmanned but next to reserve office. Ten hides overlooking the reserve: nearest 350 yards from visitor centre (with disabled access) up to 1.8 miles from visitor centre. Boardwalk over pond – good for dragonflies in summer.
Public transport: No public transport to reserve entrance. Buses and trains stop at Manea – three miles from reserve.
Habitat: Lowland wet grassland – seasonally flooded. Open pool systems in front of some hides, particularly Stockdale's hide.
Key birds: *Summer:* Around 70 species breed including Black-tailed Godwit, Lapwing, Redshank, Snipe, Shoveler, Gadwall, Garganey and Spotted Crake. Also Hobby and Marsh Harrier. *Autumn:* Passage waders including Wood and Green Sandpipers, Spotted Redshank, Greenshank, Little Stint, plus terns and Marsh and Hen Harriers. *Winter:* Large number of wildfowl (up to 100,000 birds) including Bewick's and Whooper Swans, Wigeon, Teal, Shoveler, Pintail, Pochard.
Other notable flora and fauna: Good range of dragonflies, butterflies and fenland flora.
Contact: Jon Reeves, (Site Manager), Ouse Washes Reserve, Welches Dam, Manea, March, Cambs, PE15 0NF. 01354 680 212. e-mail: jon.reeves@rspb.org.uk

8. PAXTON PITS NATURE RESERVE

Huntingdonshire District Council.
Location: TL 197 629. Access from A1 at Little Paxton, two miles N of St Neots.
Access: Free entry. Open 24 hours. Visitor centre open 7 days a week. Dogs allowed under control. Heron trail suitable for wheelchairs during summer.

Extensive programme of guided walks to see Nightingales in spring.
Facilities: Visitors centre provides information about the surrounding area and light refreshments are available. Toilets available most days 9am-5pm (including disabled), two bird hides (always open), marked nature trails.
Public transport: Buses run from St Neots and Huntingdon to Little Paxton (enquiries 0845 045 5200). The nearest trans station is St Neots (enquiries 08457 484 950).
Habitat: Grassland, scrub, lakes. Site being expanded over the next 10 years, to include extensive reedbed.
Key birds: *Spring/summer:* Nightingale, Kingfisher, Common Tern, Sparrowhawk, Hobby, Grasshopper, Sedge and Reed Warblers, Lesser Whitethroat, Cetti's Warbler. *Winter:* Smew, Goldeneye, Goosander, Gadwall, Pochard.
Other notable flora and fauna: Wildflowers, butterflies and dragonflies are in abundance. Along the meadow trail there are common spotted and pyramidal orchids. Bee orchids are found around the car park. Otters are known to use the reserve.
Contact: The Rangers, The Visitor Centre, High Street, Little Paxton, St Neots, Cambs, PE19 6ET. 01480 406 795; e-mail: paxtonpits@btconnect.com www.paxton-pits.org.uk

9. WICKEN FEN

The National Trust.
Location: TL 563 705. Lies 17 miles NE of Cambridge and ten miles S of Ely. From A10 drive E along A1123.
Access: Reserve is open daily except Christmas Day. Visitor centre is open daily all year round. Cafe open daily March - Oct, Weds - Sun Nov - Feb. Boardwalk suitable for wheelchairs, with 2 hides.
Facilities: Toilets (inc disabled), visitor centre, café, hides, boardwalk, footpaths, cycle route (NCN Route 11 passes through the reserve), coach and disabled parking. Dragonfly Centre open weekends during the summer months.
Public transport: Nearest rail link either Cambridge or Ely. Buses only on Thu and Sun. No buses to Wicken.
Habitat: Open fen, cut hay fields, sedge beds, grazing marsh, partially flooded wet grassland, reedbed, scrub, woodland.
Key birds: *Spring:* Passage waders and passerines. *Summer:* Marsh Harriers, waders and warblers. *Winter:* Wildfowl, Hen Harrier, Bittern.
Other notable flora and fauna: More than 8,000 species recorded: 22 species of dragonfly/damselfly, 27 species of butterfly and 1,000-plus species of moth. Water vole, otter.
Contact: Isobel Sedgewick, Wicken Fen, Lode Lane, Wicken, Cambs, CB7 5XP. 01353 720 274. e-mail: isabel.sedgwick@nationaltrust.org.uk or wickenfen@nationaltrust.org.uk www.wicken.org.uk

Essex

1. ABBERTON RESERVOIR

Essex Wildlife Trust.
Location: TL 963 185. Five miles SW of Colchester on B1026. Follow signs from Layer-de-la-Haye.
Access: Open Tue-Sun and Bank Holiday Mondays (9am-5pm). Closed Christmas Day and Boxing Day.
Facilities: Reserve is undergoing re-development as part of Essex & Suffolk Water's reservoir enhancement scheme. Visitor centre, toilets, nature trails with panoramic views, gift shop and light refreshments. Ample parking, including coaches. Also good viewing where roads cross reservoir.
Public transport: Phone Trust for advice.
Habitat: 100 acres on edge of 1,200-acre reservoir.
Key birds: *Winter*: Nationally important for Mallard, Teal, Wigeon, Shoveler, Gadwall, Pochard, Tufted Duck, Goldeneye (most important inland site in Britain). Smew, Bittern and Goosander regular. Passage waders, terns, birds of prey. Tree-nesting Cormorant colony; raft-nesting Common Tern. *Summer*: Hobby, Yellow Wagtail, warblers, Nightingale, Corn Bunting; *Autumn*: Red-crested Pochard, Water Rail.
Other notable flora and fauna: Dragonflies including broad-bodied chaser, small red-eyed damselfly, butterflies including green and purple hairstreak, roesel's bush-cricket. Brown hare.
Contact: Abberton Reservoir Visitor Centre, 01206 738 172. e-mail: abberton@essexwt.org.uk

2. ABBOTTS HALL FARM

Essex Wildlife Trust.
Location: TL 963 145. Seven miles SW from Colchester. Turn E off B1026 (Colchester-Maldon road) towards Peldon. Entrance is 0.5 mile on R.
Access: Weekdays (9am-5pm). Two hides with wheelchair ramps. No dogs please. Working farm so please take care.
Facilities: Toilets, hides, guided walks, fact-sheets, information boards.
Public transport: None.
Habitat: Saltmarsh, saline lagoons, grazing marsh, farmland, woodland, freshwater lakes and ponds.
Key birds: *Winter*: Waders and wildfowl. Passage migrants and summer warblers.
Other notable flora and fauna: Range of butterflies, reptiles, newts and water vole.
Contact: Trust HQ, 01621 862 960; e-mail: admin@essexwt.org.uk

3. BRADWELL BIRD OBSERVATORY

Essex Birdwatching Society
Location: 100 yards S of St Peter's Chapel, Bradwell-on-Sea. Mouth of Blackwater estuary, between Maldon and Foulness.
Access: Open all year.
Facilities: Accommodation for eight in hut; two rooms each with four bunks; blankets, cutlery, etc. supplied.
Habitat: Mudflats, saltmarsh.
Key birds: *Winter*: Wildfowl (inc. Brent Geese, Red-throated Diver, Red-breasted Merganser), large numbers of waders; small numbers of Twite, Snow Bunting and occasional Shore Lark on beaches, also Hen Harrier, Merlin and Peregrine. Good passage of migrants usual in spring and autumn. *Summer*: Small breeding population of terns and other estuarine species.
Other notable flora and fauna: A variety of dragonflies inc hairy dragonfly and scarce emerald damselfly.
Contact: Graham Smith, 48 The Meads, Ingatestone, Essex CM4 0AE. 01277 354 034.

4. FINGRINGHOE WICK

Essex Wildlife Trust.
Location: TM 046 197. Colchester five miles. The reserve is signposted from B1025 to Mersea Island, S of Colchester.
Access: Open 7 days a week. Winter Opening: 1st November – 31st March 9am – 4pm Tuesday to Sunday (Closed Christmas Day & Boxing Day) Summer Opening: 1st April – 31st October 9am – 5pm. Entry by donation: Adult £2, Child £1 and Family £5. Dogs limited to Dog Trail only and must be kept on a lead.
Facilities: Visitor centre: toilets Inc: baby changing facilities, easy access toilet and one wheelchair is available, Gift shop, light refreshments, optics, observation room with displays, sea and sky observatory, car park, Reserve: seven bird hides, nature trails.
Habitat: Old gravel pit, large lake, many ponds, sallow/birch thickets, young scrub, reedbeds, saltmarsh, gorse heathland.

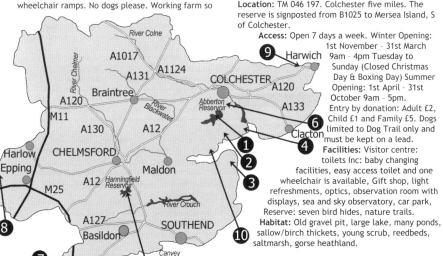

Key birds: *Autumn/winter*: Brent Goose, waders, Hen Harrier, Little Egret. *Spring*: 30 male Nightingales. Good variety of warblers in scrub, thickets, reedbeds and Turtle Dove, Green/Great Spotted Woodpeckers. *Winter*: Little Grebe, Mute Swan, Teal, Wigeon, Shoveler, Gadwall on lake.
Contact: Louise Dowrick, Fingringhoe Wick Visitor Centre, South Green Road, Fingringhoe, Colchester, Essex, CO5 7DN. 01206 729 678.
e-mail: louised@essexwt.org.uk - Follow us on Facebook: www.facebook.com/EWTFingringhoe

5. HANNINGFIELD RESERVOIR

Essex Wildlife Trust.
Location: TQ 725 972. Three miles N of Wickford. Exit off Southend Road (Old A130) at Rettendon onto South Hanningfield Road. Follow this for two miles until reaching the T-junction with Hawkswood Road. Turn R and the entrance to the visitor centre and reserve is one mile on the R.
Access: Open daily (9am-5pm) all year. Closed Christmas Day and Boxing Day. Disabled parking, toilets, and adapted birdwatching hide. No dogs. No cycling.
Facilities: Visitor centre, gift shop, optics, refreshments, toilets, four bird hides, nature trails, picnic area, coach parking, education room.
Public transport: Chelmsford to Wickford bus no 14 to Downham village and walk half mile down Crowsheath Lane.
Habitat: Mixed woodland (110 acres) with grassy glades and rides, adjoining 870-acre Hanningfield Reservoir, designated an SSSI due to its high numbers of wildfowl.
Key birds: *Spring*: Good numbers and mix of woodland warblers. *Summer*: Vast numbers of Swifts, Swallows and martins feeding over the water. Hobby and Osprey. *Winter*: Good numbers and mix of waterfowl. Large gull roost.
Other notable flora and fauna: Spectacular displays of bluebells in spring. Damselflies and dragonflies around the ponds. Grass snakes and common lizards sometimes bask in rides.
Contact: Hanningfield Reservoir Visitor Centre, Hawkswood Road, Downham, Billericay, CM11 1WT. 01268 711 001; www.essexwt.org.uk

6. OLD HALL MARSHES

RSPB (Eastern England Office).
Location: TL 975 125. Approx 10 miles S of Colchester. From A12 take B1023, via Tiptree, to Tolleshunt D'Arcy. Then take Chapel Road (back road to Tollesbury), after one mile turn L into Old Hall Lane. Continue up Old Hall Lane, over speed ramps and through iron gates, over cattle grid and straight ahead to car park.
Access: By permit only (free in advance from Warden. Write to address below). Open 9am-9pm or dusk. No wheelchair access or facilities. No coaches.
Facilities: Two trails — one of three miles and one of 6.5 miles. Viewing screens overlooking saline lagoon

area at E end of reserve. No visitor centre or toilets.
Public transport: Limited bus service to Tollesbury (one mile from reserve).
Habitat: Coastal grazing marsh, reedbed, open water saline lagoon, saltmarsh and mudflat.
Key birds: *Summer*: Breeding Avocet, Redshank, Lapwing, Pochard, Shoveler, Gadwall, Marsh Harrier and Barn Owl. *Winter*: Large assemblies of wintering wildfowl: Brent Goose, Wigeon, Teal, Shoveler, Goldeneye, Red-breasted Merganser, all the expected waders, Hen Harrier, Merlin, Short-eared Owl and Twite. *Passage*: All expected waders inc Spotted Redshank, Green Sandpiper and Whimbrel. Yellow Wagtail, Whinchat and Wheatear.
Other notable flora and fauna: Brown hare, water vole, hairy dragonfly, scarce emerald damselfly, ground lackey and cream spot tiger moths, white letter hairstreak.
Contact: Paul Charlton, Site Manager, c/o 1 Old Hall Lane, Tolleshunt D'Arcy, Maldon, Essex CM9 8TP. 01621 869 015. e-mail: paul.charlton@rspb.org.uk

7. RAINHAM MARSHES

RSPB (South Eastern Regional Office).
Location: On N bank of River Thames, SE of Dagenham. From London take A13 to A1306 turn-off and head towards Purfleet for half a mile. At traffic lights, turn right, signposted A1090 and reserve entrance is 300 metres along this road.
Access: Open all year. Extensive programme of guided walks — check RSPB website for details. Approx 2.5 miles of boardwalks suitable for wheelchairs and pushchairs.
Facilities: Visitor centre, disabled toilets, car park on site, picnic area, shop, refreshments available. Two bird hides and another on the way.
Public transport: Route 44 (Ensignbus - 01708 865 656) runs daily between Grays and Lakeside via Purfleet. Arriva service (0870 120 1088) hourly Sundays and most public holidays.
Habitat: A former MoD shooting range, the site is the largest remaining expanse of lowland wetland along the upper reaches of the Thames.
Key birds: *Spring*: Marsh Harrier, Hobby, Wheatear, hirundines and other migrants. *Summer/autumn*: Many waders, including Black-tailed Godwit, Whimbrel, Greenshank, Snipe, Lapwing, Avocet. Yellow-legged Gull. Merlin and Peregrine hunt among the gathering flocks. *Winter*: Waders, wildfowl, Water Pipit, Short-eared Owl, Little Egret and Penduline Tit most winters.
Other notable flora and fauna: 21 species of dragonfly, including hairy hawker, scarce emerald and small red-eyed damselfly. Marsh frogs, water vole, water shrew, fox, stoat, weasel, 30 species of butterfly, and 13 species of grasshoppers and crickets. Deadly nightshade.
Contact: The Warden, The Visitor Centre, Rainham Marsh Nature Reserve, New Tankhill Road, Purfleet, Essex RM19 1SZ. 01708 899 840.
www.rspb.org.uk/rainham

8. RIVER LEE COUNTRY PARK

Lee Valley Regional Park
Location: The Country Park spreads from Waltham Abbey in Essex to Broxbourne in Hertfordshire. Car parks at Waltham Abbey Gardens (EN9 1XD), Fishers Green (EN9 2EF), Cheshunt (EN9 1XQ) and Broxbourne (EN10 6LX).
Access: All hides open to public daily (excepting Christmas Day). Hides and paths are suitable for wheelchair users.
Facilities: There is a café, toilet and shop at Lee Valley Park Farms and toilet facilities are also available at Fishers Green, Cheshunt and Broxbourne car parks.
Public transport: All sites served by buses – call Arriva on 0871 200 2233.
Habitat: Former gravel pits now flooded, with wooded islands, reedbeds and marshy corners.
Key birds: *Winter:* Bittern at Fishers Green. Wide variety of wildfowl incl. Smew, Goosander, Shoveler and Gadwall. *Summer:* Breeding Warblers, Nightingale, Little Ringed Plover, Turtle Dove and various birds of prey. Wide variety of species on spring/autumn passage.
Other notable flora and fauna: Two orchid meadows within the Country Park, and a dragonfly sanctuary in the south of the Country Park.
Contact: Lee Valley Regional Park Authority, 08546 770 600; e-mail: info@leevalleypark.org.uk www.leevalleypark.org.uk

9. STOUR ESTUARY

RSPB (Eastern England Office).
Location: Between Manningtree and Harwich. From Manningtree, stay on B1352 past Strangers Home pub in Bradfield, then look for brown sign to reserve just past Wrabness village.
Access: Open all year. Stour wood walk (1 mile) OK for wheelchairs in dry conditions. Walks to estuary and furthest hide not suitable, due to terrain and kissing gates. Dogs only allowed in Stour Wood and on public footpaths.
Facilities: Two hides, one viewing screen. Two picnic tables.
Public transport: Nearest train station (One Railway) at Wrabness is 1 mile away. Hourly buses (Mon - Sat) running between Colchester and Harwich will stop at entrance to woods on request or at new bus stop at SW corner of Stour Wood.

Habitat: Extensive woodland leading down to the River Stour estuary, saltmarsh at Deep Fleet and mudflats at Copperas Bay.
Key birds: *Spring/autumn:* Black-tailed Godwit, Dunlin, Pintail. *Summer:* Nightingale and warblers. *Winter:* Brent Goose, plus nationally important numbers of wildfowl and waders.
Other notable flora and fauna: Woodland wildflowers in spring.
Contact: RSPB Eastern England Office, 01473 328 006. www.rspb.org.uk/reserves/

10. TOLLESBURY WICK MARSHES

Essex Wildlife Trust.
Location: TL 969 104. On Blackwater Estuary eight miles E of Maldon. Follow B1023 to Tollesbury via Tiptree, leaving A12 at Kelvedon. Then follow Woodrolfe Road S towards the marina. Use small public car park at Woodrolfe Green (TL 964 107), 500m before reserve entrance on sea wall. Car park suitable for mini-buses and small coaches.
Access: Open all times along public footpath on top of sea wall. The route is exposed to the elements so be prepared with adequate clothing. Motorised wheelchair access possible to Block House Bay.
Facilities: Public toilets at Woodrolfe Green car park.
Public transport: Hedingham bus services run to Tollesbury from Maldon, Colchester and Witham – call 01621 869 214 for information.
Habitat: Estuary with fringing saltmarsh and mudflats with some shingle. Extensive freshwater grazing marsh, brackish borrowdyke and small reedbeds.
Key birds: Winter: Large numbers of wintering wildfowl and waders, particularly Brent Geese and Wigeon, Lapwing and Golden Plover. Short-eared Owl, Hen Harrier and, increasingly, Marsh Harrier. Summer: Breeding Avocet, Redshank, Lapwing, Little Tern, Reed and Sedge Warblers, Reed Bunting, Barn Owl. Passage: Whimbrel, Spotted Redshank, Green Sandpiper.
Other notable flora and fauna: Plants include spiny restharrow, grass vetchling, yellow horned-poppy, slender hare's-ear. Hairy dragonfly, Roesel's and great green bush-crickets. Hares and occasional common seals can be seen from the footpath on top of the sea wall.
Contact: Jonathan Smith, Tollesbury, Maldon, Essex, CM9 8RJ. 01621 868 628.
e-mail: jonathans@essexwt.org.uk

Hertfordshire

1. AMWELL NATURE RESERVE

Herts Wildlife Trust.
Location: TL 375 128. SE of Ware, on the back road to Stanstead Abbotts near Great Amwell village. Park in Amwell Lane, St Margarets.
Access: Open all year. Dragonfly trail open May to September.

Facilities: Public hide and viewing area.
Public transport: Nearest station is St Margarets.
Habitat: Disused gravel pit with reedbeds and woodland.
Key birds: *Spring/summer:* Ringed Plover, Little Ringed Plover. *Winter:* Smew, other ducks, Bittern. Of international importance for wintering Gadwall and Shoveler.
Other notable flora and fauna: Otter, 17 species of dragonfly, marsh dock.

Contact: Trust HQ, 01727 858 901;
e-mail: info@hmwt.org
www.hertswildlifetrust.org.uk

2. CASSIOBURY PARK

Welwyn & Hatfield Council.
Location: TL 090 970. 190 acres of green space close to Watford town centre.
Access: Open all year.
Facilities: Car park, footpaths.
Public transport: Watford Metropolitan Underground station.
Habitat: Municipal park, wetland, river, alder/willow wood.
Key birds: *Spring/summer*: Hobby, Kingfisher, Grey Wagtail. *Winter*: Wildfowl, Snipe, Water Rail, occasional Bearded Tit.
Contact: Welwyn & Hatfield Council, 01707 357 000.
e-mail: council.services@welhat.gov.uk

3. KINGS MEADS

Herts & Middlesex Wildlife Trust on behalf of various owners.
Location: Between Hertford and Ware, lying alongside A119 Ware Road. Park in Priory Street and Broadmeads (Ware) and streets in Hertford.
Access: Open all year.
Facilities: None.
Public transport: Bus stops on Hertford Road (A119). Trains to Ware (5 mins walk) station and Hertford East Station (10 mins walk).
Habitat: Largest remaining area of grazed riverside flood meadow in Hertfordshire.
Key birds: *Summer*: Sky Lark, Reed Warbler, Reed Bunting, Sedge Warbler, Yellow Wagtail. *Winter/spring*: Gadwall, Shoveler, Wigeon, Teal, Snipe, gulls, Stonechat, waders.
Other notable flora and fauna: 265 species of wildflower, 18 species of dragonfly.
Contact: Herts & Middlesex Wildlife Trust, 01727 858 901. e-mail: info@hmwt.org
www.hertswildlifetrust.org.uk

4. LEMSFORD SPRINGS NATURE RESERVE

Herts & Middlesex Wildlife Trust.
Location: TL 223 123. Lies 1.5 miles W of Welwyn Garden City town centre, off roundabout leading to Lemsford village on B197, W of A1(M).
Access: Access, via key, by arrangement with warden. Open at all times, unless work parties or group visits in progress. Keep to paths. Dogs on leads. 150m earth path to hide. Wheelchair access ramp to hide. Coaches welcome and room to park on road, but limit of 30 persons.
Facilities: Two hides, classroom, chemical toilet, paths and bridges. Circular walk.

Public transport: Bus service to Valley Road, WGC & Lemsford Village No 366 (Arriva, Traveline 0871 200 2233). Nearest railway station Welwyn Garden City.
Habitat: Former water-cress beds, open shallow lagoons. Stretch of the River Lea, marsh, hedgerows. Nine acres.
Key birds: *Spring/summer*: Breeding warblers, Grey Wagtail, Kestrel, Green Woodpecker. *Autumn/winter*: Green Sandpiper, Water Rail, Snipe, Siskin, Little Egret, occasional Jack Snipe. *All year*: Mandarin Duck, Kingfisher, Grey Heron, Sparrowhawk.
Other notable flora and fauna: Muntjac, fox and stoat. Common butterflies and damselflies in summer.
Contact: Barry Trevis, Warden, 11 Lemsford Village, Welwyn Garden City, Herts, AL8 7TN. 01707 335 517.
e-mail: info@hmwt.org www.hertswildlifetrust.org.uk

5. MAPLE LODGE NATURE RESERVE

Thames Water/Maple Lodge Conservation Society
Location: TQ 036 925. South of Ricksmanworth, close to village of Maple Cross. From M25 (Jt 17) turn left at traffic lights by The Cross pub. Drive down Maple Lodge Close and park in social club car park.
Access: Restricted to members of MLCS. Visits by non-members and groups can be arranged in advance. Site can be boggy — please keep to designated paths.
Facilities: Information centre, toilets. Eight bird hides — two wheelchair-friendly. Winter feeding station.
Habitat: A man-made wetland habitat formed from two gravel pits and a sludge settlement area. Mixed broadleaf plantation on eastern side.
Key birds: Wildfowl throughout year, numbers building in winter. All three woodpeckers, plus variety of finches, thrushes and woodland species. Nesting species include

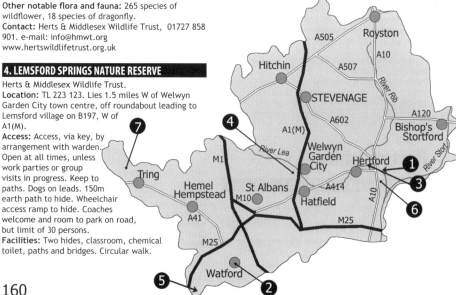

Kingfisher, Tawny Owl, migrant warblers.
Green, Common and Wood Sandpipers on passage.
Other notable flora and fauna: 170 species of moth recorded, plus many butterflies and aquatic insects. 125 species of wildflower recorded.
Contact: For membership of MLCS or to arrange visits, contact chairman Miss Gwyneth Bellis on 01923 230 277. www.maplelodge.org

6. RYE MEADS

RSPB/Hertfordshire & Middlesex Wildlife Trust.
Location: TL 387 099. Take Hoddesdon turn off A10 and follow brown duck signs. Near Rye House railway station.
Access: Open every day 10am-5pm (or dusk if earlier), except Christmas Day and Boxing Day.
Facilities: Disabled access and toilets. Drinks machine, staffed reception, classrooms, picnic area, car park, bird feeding area. Nature trails, hides. RSPB reserve has close-circuit TV on Kingfisher and Common Tern nests in summer.
Public transport: Rail (Rye House) 55 metres, bus (310) stops 600 metres from entrance.
Habitat: Marsh, willow scrub, pools, scrapes, lagoons and reedbed.
Key birds: *Summer*: Breeding Tufted Duck, Gadwall, Common Tern, Kestrel, Kingfisher, nine species of warblers. *Winter*: Bittern, Shoveler, Water Rail, Teal, Snipe, Jack Snipe, Redpoll and Siskin.
Other notable flora and fauna: Fen vegetation, invertebrates and reptiles.
Contact: RSPB Rye Meads Visitor Centre, Rye Road, Stanstead Abbotts, Herts, SG12 8JS. 01992 708 383;

7. TRING RESERVOIRS

All four reservoirs – British Waterways / Herts & Middlesex Wildlife Trust / Friends of Tring Res. WTW lagoon – Thames Water/FOTR.
Location: Wilstone Res. SP 905 134. Other reservoirs SP 920 135. WTW Lagoon SP 923 134 adjacent to Marsworth Res. Reservoirs 1.5 miles due N of

Tring, all accessible from B489 which crosses A41 Aston Clinton by-pass. NB: exit from by-pass only Southbound
Access: Reservoirs – open at all times. Events need to be cleared with British Waterways. WTW Lagoon & Hide – open at all times by permit from FoTR. Coaches can only drop off and pick up, for advice contact FoTR. Wilstone Res. has restricted height access of 2.1 metres Disabled access available for Startops & Marsworth Reservoirs from Car park, as well as FoTR Lagoon Hide.
Facilities: Café and Pubs adjacent to Startops Res. car park, safe parking for cycles. Wilstone Res.: Pub 0.5 mile away in village. Cafe and farm shop 0.25 mile from car park. Hides on all reservoirs.
Public Transport: Buses from Aylesbury & Tring including a weekend service, tel. 0871 200 2233. Tring Station is 2.5 miles away via canal towpath.
Habitat: Four reservoirs with surrounding woodland, scrub and meadows. Two of the reservoirs have extensive reedbeds. WTW Lagoon with islands and dragonfly scrape, surrounding hedgerows and scrub.
Key birds: *Spring/summer*: Breeding water birds Common Terns and heronry. Regular Hobby, Black Terns and Red Kite, Warblers including Cetti's. Occasional Marsh Harrier, Osprey. *Autumn/winter passage*: Waders, occasional White-winged Black Tern. *Winter*: Gull roost, large wildfowl flocks, bunting roosts, Bittern.
Other notable flora and fauna: Black poplar trees seen from banks, some locally rare plants in damp areas. 18 species of dragonfly include black-tailed skimmer, ruddy darter and emerald damselfly. Holly blue and specked wood butterflies. Chinese water deer, Daubenton's, Natterer's and both pipistrelle bats.
Contact: Herts & Middsx Wildlife Trust: see Directory entry, FoTR: see Directory entry, www.fotr.org.uk, British Waterways, 510-524 Elder House, Eldergate, Milton Keynes MK9 1BW. 01908 302500, e-mail: enquiries.southeast@britishwaterways.co.uk www.waterscape.com

Norfolk

1. CLEY MARSHES NNR

Norfolk Wildlife Trust.
Location: TG 054 441. NWT Cley Marshes is situated four miles N of Holt on A149 coast road, half a mile E of Cley-next-the-Sea. Visitor centre and car park on inland side of road.
Access: Open all year round, except Christmas Day. Visitor centre open Apr-Oct (10am-5pm daily), Nov-early Dec (10am-4pm Wed-Sun). Cost: adults £3.75, children under 16 free. NWT members free. Out of season, obtain permit from Watcher's Cottage, 400m along coast road towards Cley village. No dogs.
Facilities: Environmentally-friendly visitor centre incorporates an observation area, interactive

interpretation including a remote controllable wildlife camera, a café, and sales area. Five hides (with excellent wheelchair access) provide birdwatching within metres of the pools where the birds congregate. Audio trail. Wildlife Detective Bumbags for children are free to hire. Boardwalk and information boards. Reserve leaflet.
Public transport: Coasthopper bus service stops outside, every two hours. Connections for train and bus services at Sheringham. Special discounts to visitors arriving by bus. Call Norfolk County Bus Information Line on 01603 223 800 for info.
Habitat: Reedbeds, salt and freshwater marshes, scrapes and shingle ridge with international reputation as one of the finest birdwatching sites in Britain.
Key birds: Bittern, Avocet, Marsh Harrier, Spoonbill, Bearded Tit and large numbers of wildfowl, including

NATURE RESERVES - EASTERN ENGLAND

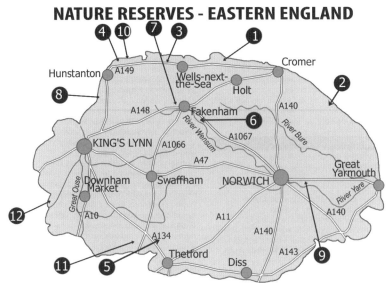

Wigeon, Teal, Pintail and Brent Goose. Migrating waders such as Ruff and Temminck's Stint. Many rarities.
Contact: NWT, Bewick House, 22 Thorpe Road, Norwich, Norfolk NR1 1RY. 01263 740 008.
e-mail: admin@norfolkwildlifetrust.org.uk
www.wildlifetrust.org.uk.Norfolk

2. HICKLING BROAD NNR

Norfolk Wildlife Trust.
Location: TG 428 222. Approx four miles SE of Stalham, just off A149 Yarmouth Road. From Hickling village, follow the brown badger tourist signs into Stubb Road at the Greyhound Inn. Take first turning L to follow Stubb Road for another mile. Turn R at the end for the nature reserve. Car park is ahead of you.
Access: Open all year. Visitor centre open Apr-Sep (10am-5pm daily). Cost: adults £3.50, children under 16 and NWT members free. No dogs.
Facilities: Visitor centre, boardwalk trail through reedbeds to open water, birdwatching hides, wildlife gift shop, refreshments, picnic site, toilets, coach parking, car parking, disabled access to broad, boardwalk and toilets.
Groups welcome. Water trail mid-May to mid-Sept (additional charge – booking essential).
Public transport: Morning bus service only Mon-Fri from Norwich (Neaves Coaches) Cromer to North Walsham (Sanders). Buses stop in Hickling village, a 25 minute walk away.
Habitat: Hickling is the largest and wildest of the Norfolk Broads with reedbeds, grazing marshes and wide open skies.
Key birds: Marsh Harriers, Bittern, warblers. From October to March Stubb Mill provides excellent views of raptors flying in to roost. Likely birds include Marsh Harriers, Hen Harriers, Merlins, Cranes and Pink-footed Geese.
Other notable flora and fauna: Swallowtail butterfly,

Norfolk hawker (rare dragonfly)
Contact: John Blackburn, Hickling Broad Visitor Centre, Stubb Road, Hickling, NR12 0BW.
e-mail: johnb@norfolkwildlifetrust.co.uk
www.norfolkwildlifetrust.org.uk

3. HOLKHAM NNR

Natural England (Norfolk and Suffolk Team).
Location: TF 890 450. From Holkham village turn N off A149 down Lady Anne's Drive to park.
Access: Access unrestricted, but keep to paths and off grazing marshes and farmland. Car parks at Burnham Overy (free), Lady Anne's Drive and Wells Beach Road.
Facilities: Two hides. Disabled access.
Public transport: Bus Norbic Norfolk bus information line 0845 3006 116.
Habitat: Sandflats, dunes, marshes, pinewoods.
Key birds: *Passage:* Migrants. *Winter:* Wildfowl, inc. Brent, Pink-footed and White-fronted Geese. *Summer:* Breeding Little Tern.
Other notable flora and fauna: Seablite bushes, attractive to incoming migrant birds, sea aster and sea lavender.
Contact: M. Rooney, Hill Farm Offices, Main Road, Holkham, Wells-next-the-Sea, Norfolk NR23 1AB. 01328 711 183; Fax 01328 711 893.

4. HOLME BIRD OBSERVATORY

Norfolk Ornithologists' Association (NOA).
Location: TF 717 450. E of Hunstanton, signposted from A149. Access from Broadwater Road, Holme. The reserve and visitors centre are beyond the White House at the end of the track.
Access: Reserve open daily to members dawn to dusk; non-members (9am-5pm) by permit from the Observatory. Please keep dogs on leads in the reserve. Parties by prior arrangement.

162

NATURE RESERVES - EASTERN ENGLAND

Facilities: Accredited Bird Observatory operating all year for bird ringing (new Heligoland trap), MV moth trapping and other scientific monitoring. Visitor centre, car park and five hides (seawatch hide reserved for NOA members), together with access to beach and coastal path.
Public transport: Coastal bus service runs from Hunstanton to Sheringham roughly every 30 mins but is seasonal and times may vary. Phone Norfolk Green Bus, 01553 776 980.
Habitat: In ten acres of diverse habitat: sand dunes, Corsican pines, scrub and reed-fringed lagoon make this a migration hotspot.
Key birds: Species list over 320. Ringed species over 150. Recent rarities have included Red Kite, Common Crane, Red-backed Shrike, Osprey, Yellow-browed, Pallas's, Greenish and Barred Warblers.
Contact: Jed Andrews, Holme Bird Observatory, Broadwater Road, Holme, Hunstanton, Norfolk PE36 6LQ. 01485 525 406. e-mail: info@noa.org.uk www.noa.org.uk

5. LYNFORD ARBORETUM AND LYNFORD WATER

Forestry Commission.
Location: TL 821 953, 818 953 and 821 946. SatNav: IP26 5HW. On the Downham Market – Thetford road on A134(T). At Mundford roundabout, follow signs to Swaffham (A1065). Take the first R to Lynford Hall. Follow road past the Hall to car park on the L. Disabled drivers have very limited car parking to the R.
Access: Open all year.
Facilities: Car park, tracks and surfaced paths. Suitable for wheelchairs. Seating at 100 metre intervals in arboretum. No dogs in arboretum. Bird hide.
Public transport: None.
Habitat: Plantations, arboretum and lakes.
Key birds: *Spring/summer*:Tree Pipit, possible Firecrest, Goldcrest. Kingfisher, waterfowl. *Autumn/winter*: Crossbills, possible Hawfinch. *All year*: Usual woodland species, woodpeckers, owls.
Other notable flora and fauna: More than 200 species of trees. 270 species of moth,140 species of fungi.
Contact: Forestry Commission, Santon Downham. Brandon, Suffolk, IP27 0TJ. 01842 816 030.

6. PENSTHORPE NATURE RESERVE AND GARDENS

Private ownership /Pensthorpe Conservation Trust.
Location: TG 950 295. Take A1067 Norwich road E from Fakenham. After 1 mile look for signs for Pensthorpe Nature Reserve & Gardens. Reserve is well signposted off all major roads, look for Brown Tourist signs.
Access: Designated route for wheelchair users allowing access to both hides overlooking wader scrape. Paths are firm, but those S of River Wensum can be muddy in wet conditions. Toilets for disabled at cafe and main toilet block. Designated parking for those displaying Blue Badges. Admission - £9 adults, £7.50 seniors, £25 family tickets.

Facilities: Ample parking. Cafe serves freshly prepared meals. Shop sells bird food, nest boxes, natural history books and optical equipment.
Public transport: Bus stops at top of drive; Norfolk Green's X29 is an hourly service between Norwich and Fakenham. The X10 connects to King's Lynn; the 'Coast Hopper' service links Fakenham to the north Norfolk coast.
Habitat: Woodland, farmland, the River Wensum, eight large lakes, gardens and wildflower meadows. The diversity of habitats and the species they attract was why the BBC *Springwatch* series was based on the reserve for the last three years.
Key birds: *Spring/summer*: At wader scrape - Little Ringed Plover, Lapwing, Oystercatcher and Redshank breed, with Green Sandpipers and other waders on migration. Reed and Sedge Warblers breed in the reed beds, while Blackcap, Chiffchaff and Willow Warbler occur in the woods. Whitethroat and smaller numbers of Garden Warbler occur in areas of scrub while Linnets nest in the gorse. Cuckoo heard on the wildflower meadows and in the surrounding area. Hobbies are over wader scrape and wildflower Meadow, while Buzzards regularly breed on the reserve as do Kestrels, Sparrowhawks and Barn Owls. Marsh Harriers breed nearby. *Winter*: large flocks of Wigeon and Teal occur and Shoveler and Gadwall. Birds of prey inc. Buzzard, Marsh Harrier and Peregrine may be seen patrolling the wide valley below the hides at the wader scrape. Bittern is regularly seen here in winter too. The woodland and its feeders attract finches in winter including Brambling, with Nuthatch and Treecreeper also noted, while Marsh Tit are regular in the old alder carr nearby.
Other notable flora and fauna: 21 species of butterfly and 19 species of dragonfly. Southern marsh and common spotted orchid, many other plant species including yellow rattle. Regular sightings updates on website www.pensthorpe.com/wildlife/sightings-board.htm
Contact: Pensthorpe Nature Reserve and Gardens, Fakenham Norfolk NR21 0LN. 01328 851 465. e-mail: info@pensthorpe.com www.pensthorpe.com

7. SCULTHORPE MOOR COMMUNITY NATURE RESERVE

Hawk and Owl Trust.
Location: TF 900 305. In Wensum Valley, just W of Fakenham, on a148 to King's Lynn, brown sign signposted 'Nature Reserve' opposite village of Sculthorpe. Follow Turf Moor Road to the Visitor and Education Centre.
Access: Open Tue-Sun plus Bank Holiday Mondays (except Christmas Day). April to September: Tues-Wed (8am-6pm), Thur-Sun (8am-dusk). October to March: Tues-Sun (8am-4pm). £3 suggested donation for adult visitors. A car park at visitor and education centre. Guide dogs only.
Facilities: Visitor and education centre open 9am-5pm Tuesday - Sunday, with adapted toilets, hot

drinks dispenser, interpretive displays and live CCTV coverage from around the reserve. Base for specialist courses, school visits and other events. Reserve and 2 hides accessible to wheelchairs and buggies via 1 mile of boardwalk. Additional hide accessed by bark chipping path. Coach parking available.

Public transport: Norfolk Green (tel: 01553 776 980 website: www.norfolkgreen.co.uk) bus X8 Fakenham to King's Lynn stops at the end of Turf Moor Road. Sustrans no.1 cycle route from Harwich to Hull runs within 200 metres of the end of Turf Moor Road.

Habitat: Wetland reserve, with fen containing saw sedge (a European priority habitat), reedbed, wet woodland, pools, ditches and riverbank.

Key birds: More than 80 species recorded, including breeding Marsh Harrier, Barn Owl and Tawny Owl, visiting Buzzard, Goshawk, Hobby, Kestrel, Osprey, Sparrowhawk, also Water Rail, Kingfisher, Marsh Tit, Willow Tit and Golden Pheasant.

Other notable flora and fauna: Mammals include otter, water vole and roe deer, 19 species of dragonfly/damselfly, butterflies including white admiral, glow-worms, fungi including scarlet elf cup and a host of plants including marsh fern and saw sedge.

Contact: The Hawk and Owl Trust, Sculthorpe Moor Community Nature Reserve, Turf Moor Road, Sculthorpe, Fakenham, Norfolk NR21 9GN. 01328 856 788. e-mail: leanne.thomas@hawkandowl.org

8. SNETTISHAM

RSPB (Eastern England Office).

Location: TF 651 330. Car park two miles along Beach Road, signposted off A149 King's Lynn to Hunstanton, opposite Snettisham village.

Access: Open at all times. Dogs to be kept on leads. Two hides are suitable for wheelchairs. Disabled access is across a private road. Please phone office number for permit and directions. Coaches welcome, but please book in advance as a height barrier needs to be removed.

Facilities: Four birdwatching hides, connected by 3.5 mile reserve footpath. No toilets on site. Furthest hide c1.5 miles from car park.

Public transport: Nearest over two miles away.

Habitat: Intertidal mudflats, saltmarsh, shingle beach, brackish lagoons, and unimproved grassland/scrub. Highest tides best for good views of waders.

Key birds: *Autumn/winter/spring:* Waders (particularly Knot, Bar and Black-tailed Godwits, Dunlin, Grey Plover), wildfowl (particularly Pink-footed and Brent Geese, Wigeon, Gadwall, Goldeneye), Peregrine, Hen Harrier, Merlin, owls. Migrants in season. *Summer:* Breeding Mediterranean Gull, Ringed Plover, Redshank, Avocet, Common Tern. Marsh Harrier regular.

Other notable flora and fauna: Yellow horned poppies and other shingle flora along the beach.

Contact: Jim Scott, RSPB, Barn A, Home Farm Barns, Common Road, Snettisham, King's Lynn, Norfolk PE31 7PD. 01485 542 689. e-mail: snettisham@rspb.org.uk www.rspb.org.uk

9. STRUMPSHAW FEN

RSPB (Eastern England Office).

Location: TG 33 06. Seven miles ESE of Norwich. Follow signposts. Entrance across level-crossing from car park, reached by turning sharp R and R again into Low Road from Brundall, off A47 to Great Yarmouth.

Access: Open dawn-dusk. RSPB members free, adults £2.50, children 50p, family £5. Guide dogs only. Limited wheelchair access — please phone for advice.

Facilities: Toilets, reception hide and two other hides, five miles of trails.

Public transport: Brundall train station about one mile from reserve. Bus stops half a mile from reserve - contact NORBIC (0845 300 6116).

Habitat: Reedbed and reedfen, wet grassland and woodland.

Key birds: *Summer:* Bittern, Little Egret, Bearded Tit, Marsh Harrier, Hobby, Kingfisher, Cetti's Warbler and other reedbed birds. *Winter:* Bittern, wildfowl, Marsh and Hen Harrier.

Other notable flora and fauna: Rich fen flora inc marsh pea, milk parsley, marsh sowthistle, six species of orchid, inc marsh helleborine and narrow-leaved marsh orchid. Otter, Chinese water deer and water vole. Norfolk hawker, scarce chaser and variable damselfly among 20 dragonfly species. Swallowtail, white admiral and small heath butterflies.

Contact: Tim Strudwick, Staithe Cottage, Low Road, Strumpshaw, Norwich NR13 4HS. 01603 715 191. e-mail: strumpshaw@rspb.org.uk www.rspb.org.uk

10. TITCHWELL MARSH

RSPB (Eastern England Office).

Location: TF 749 436. E of Hunstanton, off A149.

Access: Wheelchairs available free of charge. All paths and trails suitable for wheelchairs. Reserve and hides open at all times. Coach parking — pre-booking essential. Coastal project work has caused restrictions to visitors - for latest info, call 01485 210 779 before visiting.

Facilities: Visitor centre, shop with large selection of binoculars, telescopes and books, open every day 9.30am to 5pm (Nov 5 - Feb 10, 9.30 to 4pm). Tearoom open from 9.30am to 4.30pm every day (Nov 5 - Feb 10, 9.30 to 4pm). Visitor centre and tearoom closed on Christmas Day and Boxing Day.

Public transport: Phone Traveline East Anglia on 0871 200 22 33.

Habitat: Freshwater reedbed, brackish and fresh water lagoons, extensive salt marsh, dunes, sandy beach with associated exposed peat beds.

Key birds: Diverse range of breeding reedbed and wetland birds with good numbers of passage waders during late summer/autumn. *Spring/summer:* Breeding Avocet, Bearded Tit, Bittern, Marsh Harrier, Reed Sedge and Cetti's Warbler, Redshank, Ringed Plover and Common Tern. *Summer/autumn:* Passage waders including Knot, Wood and Green Sandpiper, Little Stint, Spotted Redshank, Curlew Sandpiper and many more. *Winter:* Brent Goose, Hen/Marsh Harrier roost, Snow Bunting. Offshore Common and Velvet Scoter, Long-tailed Duck, Great Northern and Red-throated Divers.

Other notable flora and fauna: 25 species of butterfly, including all the common species plus Essex skipper and annual clouded yellow. 21 species of dragonfly, including small red-eyed damselfly. Good diversity of salt marsh plants including shrubby sea-blite *(suaeda vera)* and three species of sea lavender.

Contact: Centre Manager, Titchwell Marsh Reserve, King's Lynn PE31 8BB. Tel/Fax 01485 210 779. e-mail: titchwell@rspb.org.uk www.rspb.org.uk

11. WEETING HEATH

Norfolk Wildlife Trust.

Location: TL 756 881. Weeting Heath is signposted from the Weeting-Hockwold road, two miles W of Weeting near to Brandon in Suffolk. Nature reserve can be reached via B1112 at Hockwold or B1106 at Weeting.

Access: Open daily from Apr-Sep. Cost: adults £2.50, children free. NWT members free. Disabled access to visitor centre and hides.

Facilities: Visitor centre open daily Apr-Aug, birdwatching hides, wildlife gift shop, refreshments, toilets, coach parking, car park, groups welcome (book first).

Public transport: Train services to Brandon and bus connections (limited) from Brandon High Street.

Habitat: Breckland, grass heath.

Key birds: Stone Curlew, migrant passerines, Wood Lark.

Contact: Bev Nichols, Norfolk Wildlife Trust, Bewick house, 22 Thorpe Road, Norwich NR1 1RY. 01603 625 540. e-mail: BevN@norfolkwildlifetrust.org.uk www.wildlifetrust.org.uk/Norfolk

12. WELNEY

The Wildfowl & Wetlands Trust.

Location: TL 546 944. Ten miles N of Ely, signposted from A10 and A1101.

Access: Open daily (9.30am-5pm) except Christmas Day. Free admission to WWT members, otherwise £6.70 (Adult), £5.05 (Concession), £3.30 (Child), £17.90 (Family). Wheelchair accessible. During wet winter, paths to remote hides may be flooded.

Facilities: Visitor centre (wheelchair-friendly), café open 9.30am-4.30pm) daily. Large, heated observatory, additional 6 hides. Free parking and coach parking. Provision for disabled visitors.

Public transport: Poor. Train to Littleport (6 miles away), but from there, taxi is only option. Welney is on the National Cycle route.

Habitat: 1,000 acres of washland reserve, spring damp meadows, winter wildfowl marsh (SPA, Ramsar site, SSSI, SAC).

Key birds: Large numbers of wintering wildfowl are replaced by breeding waders, gulls, terns and warblers. *Winter*: Bewick's and Whooper Swans, wintering wildfowl e.g. Wigeon. *Spring/summer*: Common Tern, Avocet, Lapwing, Black-tailed Godwit, House Martin, occasional rarities.

Other notable flora and fauna: Key flora includes: purple loosestrife, meadow rue, mixed grasses. Dragonflies include emperor, scarce chaser, banded damselfly, small red-eyed damselfly. Approx. 400 species of moth including goat moth. Butterflies include brown argus.

Contact: Sarah Graves, Marketing and Learning Manager, WWT, Hundred Foot Bank, Welney, Nr Wisbech, PE14 9TN. 01353 860 711. e-mail: info.welney@wwt.org.uk www.wwt.org.uk

Suffolk

1. BOYTON MARSHES

RSPB (Eastern England Office).

Location: TM 387 475. Approx. seven miles E of Woodbridge. Follow B1084 to village of Butley. Turn R and follow road through to Capel St. Andrew. Turn L and follow road towards Boyton village. Approximately 0.25 mile (400 m) before village, bear L down concrete track on sharp right-hand turn.

Access: Open at all times. Entrance free but donations welcome. Public footpath on site not suited to wheelchair use.

Facilities: Car park too small for coaches. No toilets or hides.

Public transport: None.

Habitat: 57 ha of coastal grazing marsh. Also saltmarsh.

Key birds: *Spring*: Breeding waders and wildfowl, such as Lapwing, Redshank, Shoveler and Gadwall. Spring migrants inc Yellow Wagtail and Whitethroat.

Barn and Little Owls. *Autumn*: Wintering wildfowl such as Teal and Wigeon. Migrating waders inc Whimbrel, Black-tailed Godwit and Greenshank. *Winter*: Wintering wildfowl and wading birds, including Pintail, Curlew, Dunlin and Redshank. Fieldfare, Redwing and Mistle Thrush.

Other notable flora and fauna: Grassland butterflies such as skippers, wall and meadow browns and dragonflies.

Contact: RSPB Havergate, Unit 3, Richmond Old Dairy, Gedgrave, Woodbridge, Suffolk IP12 2BU. 01394 450 732. www.rspb.org.uk/reserves/

2. BRADFIELD WOODS NNR

Suffolk Wildlife Trust.

Location: TL 935 581. W of Stowmarket. From J46 on A14 take road through Beyton and Hessett towards Felsham. Turn R on Felsham road towards Cargate. Wood and parking is on L.

Access: Often wet and muddy, Wheelchair/pushchair accessible in parts, please phone 01449 737 996 for advice. Dogs on leads only.

Facilities: Visitor centre (open at weekends, no toilets), local pubs. Three coloured trails of different lengths, trail guide available.
Habitat: Broadleaved woodland.
Key birds: Good range of woodland birds and migrant warblers.
Contact: Suffolk Wildlife Trust, Brooke House, The Green, Ashbocking, Ipswich, IP6 9JY. 01473 890 089.
e-mail: info@suffolkwildlife.cix.co.uk
www.wildlifetrust.org.uk/suffolk

3. CASTLE MARSHES

Suffolk Wildlife Trust.
Location: TM 471 904. Head E on the A146 from Beccles to Lowestoft. Take the first L turn after Three Horseshoes pub. Continue on the minor road which bends round to the R. Carry straight on — the road bends to the R again. The car park is on the L just after White Gables house.
Access: Public right of way. Unsuitable for wheelchairs. Stiles where path leaves the reserve. Unmanned level crossing is gated.
Facilities: None.
Public transport: Bus: nearest bus route is on the A146 Lowestoft to Beccles road. Tel: 0845 958 3358. Train: Beccles and Oulton Broad South on the Ipswich to Lowestoft line.
Habitat: Grazing marshes, riverbank.
Key birds: *Spring/summer:* Marsh Harrier, Cetti's Warbler, occasional Grasshopper Warbler. *Winter:* Hen Harrier, wildfowl, Snipe.
Contact: Trust HQ, 01473 890 089.
e-mail: info@suffolkwildlifetrust.org
www.suffolkwildlifetrust.org

4. DINGLE MARSHES NNR

Suffolk Wildlife Trust/RSPB.
Location: TM 48 07 20. Eight miles from Saxmundham. Follow brown signs from A12 to Minsmere and continue to Dunwich. Forest car park (hide) TM 467 710. Beach car park TM 479 707. The reserve forms part of the Suffolk Coast NNR.
Access: Open at all times. Access via public rights of way and permissive path along beach. Dogs on lead please. Coaches can park on beach car park.
Facilities: Toilets at beach car park, Dunwich. Hide in Dunwich Forest overlooking reedbed, accessed via Forest car park. Circular trail waymarked from car park.
Public transport: Via Coastlink, Dial-a-

ride service to Dingle (01728 833 546) links to buses and trains.
Habitat: Grazing marsh, reedbed, shingle beach and saline lagoons
Key birds: *All year:* In reedbed, Bittern, Marsh Harrier, Bearded Tit. *Winter:* Hen Harrier, White-fronted Goose, Wigeon, Snipe, Teal on grazing marsh. *Summer:* Lapwing, Avocet, Snipe, Black-tailed Godwit, Hobby. Good for passage waders.
Other notable flora and fauna: Internationally important site for starlet sea anemone — the rarest sea anemone in Britain. Otter and water vole.
Contact: Alan Miller, Suffolk Wildlife Trust, Moonrakers, Back Road, Wenhaston, Halesworth Suffolk IP16 4AP. www.suffolkwildlife.co.uk
e-mail: alan.miller@suffolkwildlifetrust.org

5. HAVERGATE ISLAND

RSPB (Eastern England Office).
Location: TM 425 496. Part of the Orfordness-Havergate Island NNR on the Alde/Ore estuary. Orford is 17km NE of Woodbridge, signposted off the A12.
Access: Open Apr-Aug (1st & 3rd weekends and every Thu), Sep-Mar (1st Sat every month). Book in advance through Minsmere RSPB visitor centre, tel 01728 648 281. Park in Orford at the large pay and display car park next to the quay.
Facilities: Toilets, picnic area, five birdwatching hides, viewing platform, visitor trail (approx 2km).
Public transport: Orford served by local buses (route 160). For timetable info, 0870 608 2608. Bus stop is 0.25 miles from quay. Boat trips from Orford (one mile)
Habitat: Shallow brackish water, lagoons with islands, saltmarsh, shingle beaches.
Key birds: *Summer:* Breeding gulls, terns, Avocet, Redshank and Oystercatcher. *Winter:* Wildfowl and waders.
Contact: RSPB Havergate Reserves, Unit 3, Richmond Old Dairy, Cedgrave, Woodbridge Suffolk IP12 2BU. 01394 450 732.

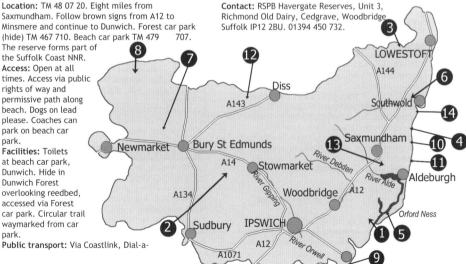

6. HEN REEDBED NNR

Suffolk Wildlife Trust.
Location: TM 470 770. Three miles from Southwold. Turn off A12 at Blythburgh and follow along A1095 for two miles where brown signs guide you to the car park. Not suitable for coaches. The reserve forms part of the Suffolk Coast NNR.
Access: Open at all times.
Facilities: Two hides and two viewing platforms on waymarked trails.
Public transport: Bus service between Halesworth and Southwold.
Habitat: Reedbed, grazing marsh, scrape and estuary.
Key birds: *Spring/summer:* Marsh Harrier, Bittern, Bearded Tit, Hobby, Lapwing, Snipe, Avocet, Black-tailed and Bar-tailed Godwits. *Passage:* Wood and Green Sandpipers. *Winter:* Large flocks of waders on estuary, inc Golden and Grey Plovers, Bar and Black-tailed Godwits, Avocet and Dunlin.
Other notable flora and fauna: Otters and water voles frequently seen. Hairy dragonfly, occasional Norfolk hawker. Brown argus butterfly colony close to car park.
Contact: Alan Miller, www.suffolkwildlife.co.uk e-mail: alan.miller@suffolkwildlifetrust.org

7. LACKFORD LAKES NATURE RESERVE

Suffolk Wildlife Trust.
Location: TL 803 708. Via track off N side of A1101 (Bury St Edmunds to Mildenhall road), between Lackford and Flempton. Five miles from Bury.
Access: Visitor centre open winter (10am-4pm), summer (10am-5pm) Wed to Sun (closed Mon and Tues). Tea and coffee facilities, toilets. Visitor centre and 4 hides with wheelchair access.
Facilities: Visitor centre with viewing area upstairs. Tea and coffee facilities, toilets. Eight hides. Coaches should pre-book.
Public transport: Bus to Lackford village (Bury St Edmunds to Mildenhall service) — walk from church.
Habitat: Restored gravel pit with open water, lagoons, islands, willow scrub, reedbeds.
Key birds: *Winter:* Bittern, Water Rail, Bearded Tit. Large gull roost. Wide range of waders and wildfowl (inc. Goosander, Pochard, Tufted Duck, Shoveler). *Spring/autumn:* Migrants, inc. raptors. Breeding Shelduck, Little Ringed Plover and reedbed warblers.
Other notable flora and fauna: 17 species of dragonfly including hairy dragonfly and emperor. Early marsh and southern orchid.
Contact: Lackford Lakes Visitor Centre, Lackford, Bury St Edmunds IP28 6HX. 01284 728 706. www.suffolkwildlifetrust.org e-mail: lackford@suffolkwildlifetrust.org

8. LAKENHEATH FEN

RSPB (Eastern England Office).
Location: TL722 864. W of Thetford, straddling the Norfolk/Suffolk border. From A11, head N on B1112 to Lakenheath and then two miles further. Entrance is 200 metres after level crossing.
Access: Dawn to dusk, year round. Group bookings welcome. Visitor centre accessible to wheelchair users and a few points on the reserve.
Facilities: Visitor centre, toilets (inc disabled). Coach parking (must book). Hard and grass paths. Viewpoints. Picnic area with tables. Events programme.
Public transport: Limited weekend stops at Lakenheath train station.
Habitat: Reedbed, riverside pools, poplar woods.
Key birds: Principally a site for nesting migrants but ducks and some wild swans in winter. *Spring:* Marsh Harrier, Crane. *Summer:* Bittern, Golden Oriole, Hobby, Reed and Sedge Warblers. *Autumn:* Harriers, Bearded Tit. *Winter:* Ducks, swans, Peregrine.
Other notable flora and fauna: More than 15 species of dragonflies and damselflies, inc hairy dragonfly and scarce chaser. Range of fenland plants e.g. water violet, common meadow rue and fen ragwort. Roe deer, otter and water vole.
Contact: Becky Pitman (Information Officer), Visitor Centre, RSPB Lakenheath Fen, Lakenheath, Norfolk IP27 9AD. 01842 863 400. www.rspb.org.uk/reserves/ e-mail: lakenheath@rspb.org.uk

9. LANDGUARD BIRD OBSERVATORY

Landguard Conservation Trust
Location: TM 283 317. Road S of Felixstowe to Landguard Nature Reserve and Fort.
Access: Visiting by appointment.
Facilities: Migration watch point and ringing station.
Public transport: Call for advice.
Habitat: Close grazed turf, raised banks with holm oak, tamarisk, etc.
Key birds: Unusual species and common migrants.
Other notable flora and fauna: 18 species of dragonfly and 29 species of butterfly have been recorded on the site. Several small mammal species plus sightings of cetaceans and seals off-shore.
Contact: Landguard Bird Observatory, View Point Road, Felixstowe, Suffolk IP11 3TW. 01394 673 782. e.mail: landguardbo@yahoo.co.uk www.lbo.co.uk

10. MINSMERE

RSPB (Eastern England Regional Office)
Location: TM 452 680. Six miles NE of Saxmundham. From A12 at Yoxford or Blythburgh. Follow brown tourist signs via Westleton village. Car park is two miles from the village.
Access: Open every day except Dec 25/26. Visitor centre open 9am-5pm (9am-4pm Nov-Jan). Shop and tea-room open from 10am. Free entry to visitor centre. Nature trails free to RSPB/Wildlife Explorer members, otherwise £5 adults, £1.50 children, £3 concession, family £10. Site partially accessible to wheelchairs.
Facilities: Car park, hides, toilets (inc disabled and nappy changing), visitor centre with RSPB shop and tearoom. Family activity packs. Volunteer guides. Guided walks and family events (see website for details). Educational programme. Coaches by

appointment only (max two per day, not bank holidays).

Public transport: Train to Saxmundham or Darsham (6 miles) then Coastlink (book in advance on 01728 833 526).

Habitat: Coastal lagoons, 'the scrape', freshwater reedbed, grazing marsh, vegetated dunes, heathland, arable reversion and woodland.

Key birds: *All year:* Marsh Harrier, Bearded Tit, Bittern, Cetti's and Dartford Warblers, Little Egret, Green and Great Spotted Woodpeckers. *Summer:* Breeding Hobby, Avocet, Lapwing, Redshank, Common, Sandwich and Little Terns, Mediterranean Gull, Sand Martin, warblers, Nightingale, Nightjar, Wood Lark, Redstart (scarce). *Winter:* Wildfowl inc White-fronted Goose, Bewick's Swan, Smew, Hen Harrier (scarce), Water Pipit, Siskin. *Autumn/spring:* Passage waders inc Black-tailed Godwit, Spotted Redshank, Ruff. Regular Wryneck, Red-backed Shrike, Yellow-browed Warbler.

Other notable flora and fauna: Red and muntjac deer, otter, water vole, badger. Dragonflies inc emperor, Norfolk hawker and small red-eyed damselfly. Butterflies inc purple and green hairstreaks, brown argus, silver-studded blue. Adder. Antlion. Marsh mallow, southern marsh orchid. Shingle flora.

Contact: RSPB Minsmere, Westleton, Saxmundham, Suffolk, IP17 3BY. 01728 648 281.
e-mail: minsmere@rspb.org.uk
www.rspb.org.uk/minsmere

11. NORTH WARREN & ALDRINGHAM WALKS

RSPB (Eastern England Office).

Location: TM 468 575. Directly N of Aldeburgh on Suffolk coast. Use signposted main car park on beach.

Access: Open at all times. Please keep dogs under close control. Beach area suitable for disabled.

Facilities: Three nature trails, leaflet available from Minsmere RSPB. Toilets in Aldeburgh and Thorpeness. Three spaces for coaches at Thorpeness beach car park.

Public transport: Bus service to Aldeburgh. First Eastern Counties (08456 020 121). Nearest train station is Saxmundham.

Habitat: Grazing marsh, lowland heath, reedbed, woodland.

Key birds: *Winter:* White-fronted Goose, Tundra Bean Goose, Wigeon, Shoveler, Teal, Gadwall, Pintail, Snow Bunting. *Spring/summer:* Breeding Bittern, Marsh Harrier, Hobby, Nightjar, Wood Lark, Nightingale, Dartford Warbler.

Other notable flora and fauna: Hairy dragonfly, Norfolk hawker and red-eyed damselfly, green and purple hairstreak butterflies and southern marsh orchid.

Contact: Dave Thurlow, RSPB Minsmere, Westleton, Saxmundham, Suffolk IP17 3BY. 01728 648 082; (M)07980 278 586. e-mail: dave.thurlow@rspb.org.uk

12. REDGRAVE AND LOPHAM FENS

Suffolk Wildlife Trust.

Location: TM 05 07 97. Five miles from Diss, signposted and easily accessed from A1066 and A143 roads.

Access: Open all year (10am - 5pm summer, 10am - 4pm winter), dogs strictly on short leads only. Visitor centre open all year at weekends and bank holidays: call for details on 01379 688 333. Circular trails can be muddy after rain (not wheelchair accessible).

Facilities: Visitor centre with café, gift shop, toilets, including disabled toilet, car park with coach space. Bike parking area, wheelchair access to visitor centre and viewing platform/short boardwalk. Regular events and activities — call for details or look on website.

Public transport: Buses and trains to Diss — Coaches to local villages of Redgrave and South Lopham from Diss. Simonds Coaches 01379 647 300 and Galloway Coaches 01449 766 323.

Habitat: Calcareous fen, wet acid heath, river corridor, scrub and woodland

Key birds: *All year:* Water Rail, Snipe, Teal, Shelduck, Gadwall, Woodcock, Sparrowhawk, Kestrel, Great Spotted and Green Woodpeckers, Tawny, Little and Barn Owls, Kingfisher, Reed Bunting, Bearded Tit, Willow and Marsh Tits, Linnet. *Summer:* Reed, Sedge, Grasshopper and Willow Warblers, Whitethroat, Hobby plus large Swallow and Starling roosts. *Winter/occasionals on passage:* Marsh Harrier, Greenshank, Green Sandpiper, Shoveler, Pintail, Garganey, Jack Snipe, Bittern, Little Ringed Plover, Oystercatcher, Wheatear, Stonechat.

Other notable flora and fauna: Otter, water vole, roe, muntjac and Chinese water deer, stoat, pipistrelle and natterer's bats. Great crested newts, grass snake, adder, slow worm, common lizard. More than 270 flowering plants inc water violet, saw sedge, black bog-rush and bladderwort. 19 species of dragonfly inc emperor, hairy dragonfly, black-tailed skimmer and emerald damselfly. Visit website for more species information.

Contact: Bev Blackburn (visitor centre co-ordinator), Redgrave and Lopham Fens, Low Common Road, South Lopham, Diss, Norfolk IP22 2HX. 01379 688 333. e-mail: redgrave.centre@suffolkwildlifetrust.org
www.suffolkwildlife.co.uk

13. RSPB SNAPE

RSPB (Eastern England Regional Office)

Location: TM393574. Five miles S of Saxmundham. From A12 take A1094 towards Aldeburgh. At Snape crossroads, turn right on B1069. Car park is at Snape Maltings, half a mile after passing through Snape village.

Access: Snape Warren and riverside walks open at all times. No access to Snape Wetlands. RSPB Information Centre open Thursday to Tuesday 10am to 4pm. (Check website for winter opening times). Free entry to Information centre and Snape Warren. Shops and cafes at Snape Maltings open daily 10am to

5.30pm (to 6pm in August or 5pm in winter)
Facilities: Car park, toilets, shops, cafes, pub, art galleries and concert hall at Snape Maltings. RSPB Information Centre at Snape Maltings. Guided walks and family activities.
Public transport: Train to Saxmundham (5 miles distant), then taxi or bus. Anglia Buses 165 from Aldeburgh and Leiston to Woodbridge and Ipswich. Some routes via Saxmundham.
Habitat: Estuary, heathland, grazing marsh, tidal reedbed, freshwater reedbed creation.
Key birds: *All year*: Little Egret, Shelduck, Marsh Harrier, Avocet, Barn Owl, Kingfisher, Wood Lark, Cetti's and Dartford Warblers. *Breeding*: Hobby, Cuckoo, Hirundines, Warblers, including Grasshopper Warbler and Lesser Whitethroat. *Winter*: Wigeon, Hen Harrier (rare), Water Rail, Black-tailed Godwit, Curlew, Bearded Tit, Starling Roost. *Autumn/spring*: Waders, especially Black-tailed Godwit, Whimbrel, Common Sandpiper.
Other notable flora and fauna: Otter, common seal, adder, slow worm. Dragonflies, including banded demoiselle, emperor. Butterflies. Saltmarsh flora.

Contact: RSPB Snape nature reserve, c/o RSPB Minsmere, Westleton, Saxmundham, Suffolk, IP17 3BY. 01728 687 192. e-mail: snape@rspb.org.uk www.rspb.org.uk/snape

14. WALBERSWICK

Natural England (Suffolk Team).
Location: TM 475 733. Good views from B1387 and from lane running W from Walberswick towards Westwood Lodge; elsewhere keep to public footpaths or shingle beach.
Access: Parties and coach parking by prior arrangement.
Facilities: Hide on S side of Blyth estuary, E of A12.
Public transport: Call for advice.
Habitat: Tidal estuary, fen, freshwater marsh and reedbeds, heath, mixed woodland, carr.
Key birds: Spring/summer: Marsh Harrier, Bearded Tit, Water Rail, Bittern, Nightjar. Passage/winter: Wildfowl, waders and raptors.
Contact: The Warden, Natural England, Regent House, 110 Northgate Street, Bury St Edmunds IP33 1HP. 01502 676 171.

Northern England

Cheshire, Cleveland, Cumbria, Durham, Lancashire, Manchester (Greater), Merseyside, Northumberland, Tyne & Wear, East Yorkshire, North Yorkshire, South Yorkshire, West Yorkshire

Cheshire

1. ALDERLEY EDGE

National Trust.
Location: SJ 860 773. The woods are on the B5087 Alderley Edge-Macclesfield road, 2km from Alderley.
Access: Open all year (8am-5pm Sept-May; 8am-6pm rest of year). Please keep to the paths.
Facilities: Car parks, paths. Tearoom (10am to 5pm). Guided walks from Easter to Sept.
Public transport: Alderley Edge train station 1.5 miles away.
Habitat: Dramatic red sandstone escarpment, woodland, mainly oak.
Key birds: *Spring/summer*: Woodcock, warblers. *Winter*: Finches, woodpeckers, Redpoll, Siskin, Brambling.
Contact: National Trust, The Cheshire Countryside Office, 01625 584 412.
e-mail: alderleyedge@nationaltrust.org.uk
www.nationaltrust.org.uk/main/w-alderleyedge2

2. DEE ESTUARY (INNER MARSH FARM)

RSPB Dee Estuary Office.
Location: SJ 305 742. Located on the Wirral. From Chester High Road (A540) follow signs for Ness Botanical Gardens. At Burton turn into Station Road until it reaches Burton Point Farm.
Access: Open between 9am and 9pm (or dusk if earlier) each day except Tuesdays. £3 admission for non-RSPB members. Guide dogs only.
Facilities: 12-berth car park. Single hide overlooks three pools and wetland area. Guided walks.
Public transport: Trains stop at Neston. Buses between Neston and Hooton stop at Burton post office, from where it is a 1.5km walk to reserve. Contact Traveline on 0871 200 2233.
Habitat: Former farm now converted to wetland and meadow habitats.
Key birds: *All year*: Little Egret. *Spring/summer*: Avocet and Black-headed Gull colonies, Grasshopper and other commoner warblers, passage Black-tailed Godwit and regular Mediterranean Gulls. Hobby, Marsh Harrier. *Autumn*: Passage waders (inc Little Stint, Ruff, Spotted Redshank, Green, Curlew and

Wood Sandpipers). *Winter*: Linnet, Brambling, Fieldfare, Redwing, Whooper and Bewick's Swans, Teal, Water Rail, Hen Harrier.
Other notable flora and fauna: Extensive butterfly list. Pipistrelle and noctule bats, water vole, wide array of orchids. Red-eyed damselfly.
Contact: Colin E Wells, 151 3367 681.
e-mail: colin.wells@rspb.org.uk

2. DEE ESTUARY (PARKGATE)

RSPB Dee Estuary Office.
Location: SJ 275 785. On W side of Wirral, S of Birkenhead. View high tide activity from Old Baths car park near Boathouse pub, Parkgate off B5135.
Access: Open at all times. Viewing from public footpaths and car parks. Please do not walk on the saltmarsh, the tides are dangerous.
Facilities: Car park, picnic area, group bookings, guided walks, special events, wheelchair access. Toilets at Parkgate village opposite the Square.
Public transport: Bus to Parkgate every hour. Rail station at Neston, two miles from reserve.
Habitat: Estuary, saltmarsh, pools, mud, sand.
Key birds: *Spring/summer/autumn*: Little Egret, Greenshank, Spotted Redshank, Curlew Sandpiper, Sky Lark, Reed Bunting. *Winter*: Shelduck, Teal, Wigeon, Pintail, Oystercatcher, Black-tailed Godwit, Curlew, Redshank, Merlin, Peregrine, Water Rail, Short-eared Owl, Hen Harrier.
Other notable flora and fauna: On very high tides, the incoming water displaces several mammal species inc pygmy shrew, water shrew, harvest mouse, weasel and stoat.
Contact: Colin E Wells, Burton Point Farm, Station Road, Burton, Nr Neston, Cheshire, CH64 5SB. 0151 3367 681. e-mail: colin.wells@rspb.org.uk

4. GOWY MEADOWS

Shell UK/Cheshire Wildlife Trust.
Location: SJ 435 740. Lies alongside River Gowy at Thornton-le-Moors, N of Chester, between

A5117 and M56.
Access: Park next to church in Thornton-le-Moors and take footpath opposite into reserve. Open all year.
Facilities: None.
Public transport: The Arriva bus service stops on the Thornton Green Lane opposite the church.
Habitat: 410 acres of lowland grazing marsh, rich in flora.
Key birds: Approx 100 species recorded, inc Barn Owl, Buzzard, Peregrine, Merlin, Hobby. *Spring/summer*: Wildfowl, warblers, Whinchat, Green Sandpiper, Lapwing, Jack Snipe, Snipe. *Winter*: Pintail, Shoveler, Reed Bunting. *Passage*: Stonechat, Wheatear.
Other notable flora and fauna: Stronghold of endangered silver water beetle. 14 species of dragonfly; 17 species of butterfly.
Contact: Trust HQ, 01948 820 728;
e-mail: info@cheshirewt.org.uk
www.cheshirewildlifetrust.co.uk

5. MOORE NATURE RESERVE

Waste Recycling Group.
Location: SJ 577 854. SW of Warrington, via A56 Warrington-to-Chester road. At traffic lights at Higher Walton, follow signs for Moore. Take Moore Lane over swing bridge to reserve. Sat Nav users follow WA4 6XE.
Access: Open all year. One hide suitable for wheelchairs, other parts of site unsurfaced or gravel paths.
Facilities: Car park, coaches by prior arrangement. Paths, ten bird hides, bird feeding area. Guided walks available on request. See website for wildlife events throughout the year.
Public transport: 62 and 66 buses from Warrington and Runcorn stop in Moore village, less than 1km from reserve. Call 0870 608 2608 for times.
Habitat: Wetland, woodland, grasslands, five pools.
Key birds: More than 130 species every year, inc. occasional rarities. *Spring/summer*: Breeding wildfowl and waders, warblers. *Autumn/winter*: Wide variety of wildfowl, Bittern. Also good for gulls, woodpeckers, owls and raptors. See website for list and latest sightings.
Other notable flora and fauna: Wildfowers including some rarities. Great crested newts.
Contact: Paul Cassidy/Brian Webber, c/o Waste Recycling Centre, Arpley Landfill Site, Forest Way, Sankey Bridge, Warrington, Cheshire WA4 6YZ. 01925 444 689.
e-mail: paul.cassidy@wrg.co.uk
www.wrg.co.uk/moorenaturereserve

6. SANDBACH FLASHES

Management Committee.
Location: SJ 720 590. Leave M6 at junction 17 for Sandbach.

NATURE RESERVES - NORTHERN ENGLAND

Access: Elton Hall Flash from new road at SJ 716 595; Foden's Flash from road at SJ 730 614; Watch Lane Flash from car park at SJ 728 608.
Facilities: None.
Public transport: None.
Habitat: Fresh and brackish water, reedbed, carr woodland, inland saltmarsh.
Key birds: Wildfowl including Mallard, Teal, Shoveler, Wigeon, Gadwall, Barnacle Goose, Shelduck, occasional Garganey, Mandarin Duck. Waders including Black-tailed Godwit, Lapwing, Common Sandpiper, Dunlin, Green Sandpiper, Curlew, Snipe, Redshank, Little Ringed Plover, Little Stint, Ruff, Oystercatcher, Ringed Plover, Greenshank, Spotted Redshank. Raptors including Sparrowhawk, Kestrel, Buzzard, Hobby. Warblers including Lesser Whitethroat, Blackcap, Garden Warbler. Ravens, Water Rail, Kingfisher, Wheatear, Stonechat, Turtle Dove, Swift, Yellow Wagtail also seen. Many rarities occur.

7. WOOLSTON EYES

Woolston Eyes Conservation Group.
Location: SJ 654 888. E of Warrington between the River Mersey and Manchester Ship Canal. Off Manchester Road down Weir Lane or from Latchford to end of Thelwall Lane. Do not park at the bottom end of weir lane.

Access: Open all year. Permits required from Chairman, £8 each, £16 per family (see address below).
Facilities: Toilets are available on No 3 bed.
Public transport: Buses along A57 nearest stop to Weir Lane, or Thelwell Lane, Latchford. Take No.3 bus to Weir Lane, Martinscroft (access reserve from the N) along A57 from Central Station and Terminus. To access reserve from S take either No1 or No2 bust to Westy, Whitley Avenue and walk to the E end of Thelwall Lane. For further info go to www.warrington borough transport.co.uk
Habitat: Wetland, marsh, scrubland, wildflower meadow areas.
Key birds: Breeding Black-necked Grebe, warblers (including Grasshopper Warbler), raptors (inc. Merlin, Peregrine, Marsh Harrier). SSSI for wintering wildfowl, many duck species breed.
Other notable flora and fauna: 19 mammal species recorded, plus 241 species of lepidoptera, four species of bat. Wide variety of butterflies and 22 species of dragonfly. Notable plants include marsh and bee orchids, helleborine, snakeshead fritillary and cowslip.
Contact: BR Ankers, Chairman, 9 Lynton Gardens, Appleton, Cheshire, WA4 5ED. 01925 267 355. Please enclose A5 S.A.E. for reply
www.woolstoneyes.co.uk

Cumbria

1. CAMPFIELD MARSH

RSPB (Northern England).
Location: NY 197 615. At North Plain Farm, on S shore of Solway estuary, W of Bowness-on-Solway. Signposted on unclassified coast road from B5307 from Carlisle.
Access: Open at all times, no charge. Disabled visitors can drive to wheelchair-friendly hide to view high-tide roosts.
Facilities: Hide overlooking wetland areas, along nature trail (1.5 miles). No toilets or visitor centre.
Public transport: Bus No 93 from Carlisle terminates at reserve's eastern end — 1.5 mile walk to North Plain Farm.
Habitat: Saltmarsh/intertidal areas, open water, peat bog, wet grassland.
Key birds: *Winter:* Waders and wildfowl include Barnacle and Pinkfooted Geese, Shoveler, Scaup, Grey Plover. *Spring/summer:* Breeding Lapwing, Curlew, Redshank, Snipe, Tree Sparrow and warblers. *Spring/autumn:* Passage waders such as Black-tailed Godwit, Whimbrel. Look for Pomarine, Arctic, Great and Long-tailed Skuas over the Solway. *Autumn/ winter:* Up to 10,000 Oystercatchers among large roosting wader flocks. Hen Harrier.
Other notable flora and fauna: Roe deer, brown hare. Bog rosemary, bog asphodel, sundews and

cotton grass. Large numbers of dragonflies (inc azure and emerald damselflies and four-spotted chaser).
Contact: RSPB Office, North Plain Farm, Bowness-on-Solway, Wigton, Cumbria, CA7 5AG.
e-mail: dave.blackledge@rspb.org.uk

2. DRUMBURGH MOSS NNR

Cumbria Wildlife Trust.
Location: NY 255 586 (OS Landranger 85). From Carlisle city centre, head W on B5307 to Kirkbride. After about one mile, turn R to Burgh by Sands. Follow road for 7.5 miles to Drumburgh village. Turn L by post office, continue down track and park on R past Moss Cottage.
Access: Open all year. Difficult terrain, so it is best to walk on bunds built to re-wet the site.
Facilities: None.
Public transport: Bus service between Carlisle and Bowness-on-Solway stops in Drumburgh.
Habitat: Raised bog, woodland, grassland.
Key birds: *Summer:* Red Grouse, Curlew, Grasshopper Warbler. *Autumn:* Short-eared Owl. *Winter:* Geese from the Solway.
Other notable flora and fauna: Large heath butterfly, emperor moth, adder and lizards, roe deer, brown hare. Specialist plants include 13 species of sphagnum moss, sundews, cotton grass and bog rosemary.
Contact: Trust HQ, 01539 816 300;
e-mail: mail@cumbriawildlifetrust.org.uk
www.cumbriawildlifetrust.org.uk

NATURE RESERVES - NORTHERN ENGLAND

3. FOULNEY ISLAND

Cumbria Wildlife Trust.
Location: SD 246 640. Three miles SE of Barrow town centre on the A5087 from Barrow or Ulverston. At a roundabout 2.5 miles S of Barrow take a minor road through Rampside to Roa Island. Turn L into reserve car park. Walk to main island along stone causeway.
Access: Open all year. Access restricted to designated paths during bird breeding season. Slitch Ridge is closed at this time. No dogs allowed during bird breeding season. The island may be cut off for several hours around high-tide, so please consult tide tables.
Facilities: None.
Public transport: Bus: regular service from Barrow to Roa Island.
Habitat: Shingle, sand, grassland.
Key birds: *Summer*: Arctic and Little Terns, Oystercatcher, Ringed Plover, Eider Duck. *Winter*: Brent Goose, Redshank, Dunlin, Sanderling.
Other notable flora and fauna: Sea campion, yellow horned poppy. Six spot burnet and common blue butterfly.
Contact: Trust HQ, 01539 816 300;
e-mail: mail@cumbriawildlifetrust.org.uk
www.cumbriawildlifetrust.org.uk

4. HAWESWATER

RSPB and United Utilities.
Location: NY 470 108. Golden Eagle viewpoint, near Bampton, 5 miles NW of Shap, off A6. Turn L in Bampton to car park at S of reservoir.
Access: The viewpoint is always open but only manned as below. Visitors are asked not to go beyond the viewpoint. There is no wheelchair access.
Facilities: Golden Eagle viewpoint, open Saturday and Sunday, plus bank holidays, Apr to end Aug (11am-4pm), telescopes available. No coach parking.
Public transport: None.
Habitat: Fells with rocky streams, steep oak and birch woodlands.
Key birds: *Upland breeders*: Golden Eagle, Peregrine, Raven, Ring Ouzel, Curlew, Redshank, Snipe. *Woodlands*: Pied Flycatcher, Wood Warbler, Tree Pipit, Redstart, Buzzard, Sparrowhawk.
Contact: RSPB Office, 01931 713 376;
e-mail: haweswater@rspb.org.uk

5. SMARDALE GILL NNR

Cumbria Wildlife Trust.
Location: NY 727 070. NNR occupies a 6km stretch of the disused railway between Tebay and Darlington. Approx 2.5 miles NE of Ravenstonedale on A685 or 0.5 miles S of Kirkby Stephen station, take turning signed to Smardale. Cross over railway and turn L to junction, ignoring turn to Waitby. Cross over railway and turn L at junction ignoring sign for Smardale. Cross disused railway, turn L immediately and L again to car park.
Access: Railway line is open to members and non-members but non-members should obtain a permit before visiting other parts of the reserve.

Facilities: None.
Public transport: Train: nearest station Kirkby Stephen. Buses from here to Kendal, Brough and Sedburgh.
Habitat: Limestone grassland, river, ancient semi-natural woodland, quarry.
Key birds: *Summer:* Redstart, Pied Flycatcher, Wood Warbler and commoner woodland species. *All year:* Usual woodland birds, Buzzard, Sparrowhawk.
Other notable flora and fauna: Scotch argus, northern brown argus, common blue and dark green fritillary butterflies. Fragrant orchid, common rockrose, bluebell and bloody cranesbill. Red squirrel.
Contact: Trust HQ, 01539 816 300;
e-mail: mail@cumbriawildlifetrust.org.uk

6. ST BEES HEAD

RSPB (Northern England).
Location: NX 962 118. S of Whitehaven via the B5345 road to St Bees village.
Access: Open at all times, no charge. Access via coast-to-coast footpath. The walk to the viewpoints is long and steep in parts.
Facilities: Three viewpoints overlooking seabird colony. Public toilets in St Bees beach car park at entrance to reserve.
Public transport: Nearest trains at St Bees (0.5 mile).
Habitat: Three miles of sandstone cliffs up to 300 ft high.
Key birds: *Summer:* Largest seabird colony on W coast of England: Guillemot, Razorbill, Puffin, Kittiwake, Fulmar and England's only breeding pairs of Black Guillemot.

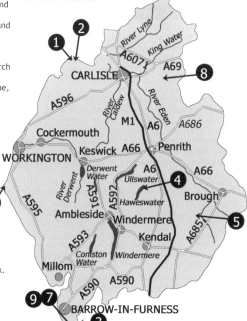

172

Contact: North Plain Farm, 01697 351 330; e-mail: dave.blackledge@rspb.org.uk
www.rspb.org.uk

7. SOUTH WALNEY

Cumbria Wildlife Trust.
Location: SD 215 620. Six miles S of Barrow-in-Furness. From Barrow, cross Jubilee Bridge onto Walney Island, turn L at lights. Continue through Biggar village to South End Caravan Park. Follow road for 1 mile to reserve.
Access: Open daily (10am-5pm) plus Bank Holidays. No dogs except assistance dogs. Day permits: £2 adults, 50p children. Cumbria Wildlife Trust members free.
Facilities: Toilets, nature trails, eight hides (two are wheelchair accessible), 200m boardwalk, cottage available to rent – sleeps 10. Electric wheelchair for hire. Coach parking available.
Public transport: Bus service as far as Biggar.
Habitat: Shingle, lagoon, sand dune, saltmarsh.
Key birds: *Spring/autumn*: Passage migrants. *Summer*: 14,000 breeding pairs of Herring, Greater and Lesser Black-backed Gulls, Shelduck, Eider. *Winter*: Teal, Wigeon, Goldeneye, Redshank, Greenshank, Curlew, Oystercatcher, Knot, Dunlin, Merlin, Short-eared Owl, Twite.
Other notable flora and fauna: 450 species of flowering plants. Natterjack toad at North Walney.
Contact: The Warden, No 1 Coastguard Cottages, South Walney Nature Reserve, Walney Island, Barrow-in-Furness, Cumbria LA14 3YQ. 01229 471 066. e-mail: mail@cumbriawildlifetrust.org.uk
www.cumbriawildlifetrust.org.uk

8. TALKIN TARN COUNTRY PARK

Carlisle City Council
Location: NY544 591. Twelve miles E of Carlisle. From A69 E at Brampton, head S on B6413 for two miles. Talkin Tarn is on E just after level crossing.
Access: All year. Wheelchair access around tarn, two kissing gates accessible. Tearoom has lift. Coaches welcome. Three trails into surrounding countryside.
Facilities: Tearoom open all year (10.30am-4pm), Takeaway service on Mondays and Tuesdays only during winter and weekends throughout year. Dogs allowed around Tarn. Rowing boat hire at weekends and school holidays.

Public transport: Bus: infrequent. Tel: 0870 608 2608. Train: nearest station is Brampton Junction. Tel: 0845 748 4950. One mile away by footpath.
Habitat: Natural glacial 65-acre tarn, mature oak/beech woodland, orchid meadow (traditionally managed), wet mire and farmland.
Key birds: *Spring/summer*: Pied Flycatcher, Spotted Flycatcher, Redstart, Chiffchaff, Wood Warbler. *Winter*: Grebes, Smew, Long-tailed Duck, Goosander, Gadwall, Wigeon, Brambling, swans.
Other notable flora and fauna: Common blue damselfly, common darter, small copper butterfly, otter, red squirrel.
Contact: Countryside Ranger, Talking Tarn Country Park, Tarn Road, Brampton, Cumbria CA8 1HN. 01697 73129. e-mail: fionash@carlisle.gov.uk

9. WALNEY BIRD OBSERVATORY

Location: Walney Island, Barrow-in-Furness, Cumbria.
Access: Several areas, notably the golf course and airfield, are restricted but the island's narrow width means most sites are viewable from the road or footpaths. Access to South Walney Nature Reserve (10am-5pm) is along permitted trails.
Facilities: Monitoring and ringing of breeding and migrant birds occurs across the island, with ringing opportunities for qualified ringers. For availability write to Walney Bird Observatory (address below).
Public transport: Barrow-in-Furness connects to the rail network and local bus routes serve Walney Island. Routes 1 and 1A cover the central area while 6 and 6A cover the north end of the island. No bus route is available for the southern end.
Habitat: Estuarine, maritime, dunes, freshwater and brackish pools, scrub and farmland.
Key birds: Renowned Eider and gull colonies at south end. The winter months provide a wildfowl and wader spectacular across the island. Migrants aplenty appear during both passage periods — the island has a proven pedigree for attracting rare and unusual species.
Other notable flora and fauna: Famed for Walney geranium, but also important for coastal shingle species such as sea holly, sea rocket and sea kale. Almost 500 species of moth recorded, inc sand dune specialities such as coast dart and sand dart.
Contact: Walney Bird Observatory, Coastguard Cottages, Walney Island, Barrow-in-Furness, Cumbria LA14 3YQ.

Durham

1. BEACON HILL AND HAWTHORN DENE MEADOW

Durham Wildlife Trust and National Trust
Location: NZ 427 458. Hawthorn Dene and Meadow located between Easington and Seaham on Durham Coast. Leave A19 at Easington or Seaham and join B1432, turn into Hawthorn village. From N end of village, follow minor road E, signposted 'Quarry Traffic'. After quarter mile, road ends at two metal

gates, with a cottage and farmhouse on the right. Park on grass verge on opposite side to cottage, taking care not to obstruct gateways. Access is by foot taking the right-hand path. Access to Beacon Hill (NZ 440 455) is along coastal footpath or through southern end of Hawthorn Dene.
Access: Open all year, dogs on leads in spring.
Facilities: Information point. Footpaths.
Public transport: Regular bus services from Durham to Hawthorn.
Habitat: Extensive area of semi-natural habitat situated on magnesian limestone escarpment.

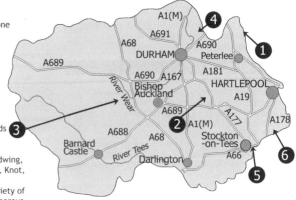

Steep- sided ravine woodland and limestone grassland.

Key birds: *Summer*: Sky Lark (important conservation site), Twite, Linnet, Yellowhammer, Goldfinch, Whitethroat, Blackcap, Wren, Long-tailed Tit, Grasshopper Warbler, Reed Bunting, Green Woodpecker, Kestrel, Sparrowhawk. *Winter*: Wide variety of waders inc Turnstone, Purple Sandpiper, Redshank, Curlew, Oystercatcher. Seabirds inc Red-throated Diver, Common Scoter, Guillemot, Cormorant and Great Crested Grebe. *Passage*: Wheatear, Fieldfare, Redwing, Waxwing, Buzzard, Ringed Plover, Dunlin, Knot, Lapwing.

Other notable flora and fauna: Good variety of butterflies. Snowdrops, bluebells and numerous species of orchid grow here, including early purple, bird's nest, lesser butterfly and bee orchids. Grassland plants include field scabious, greater knapweed, wild carrot, cowslip and bee, fragrant, common spotted and northern marsh orchids. Roe deer, badger and brown hare.

Contact: Durham Wildlife Trust, 0191 584 3112. e-mail: mail@durhamwt.co.uk www.durhamwt.co.uk

2. BISHOP MIDDLEHAM QUARRY

Durham Wildlife Trust.

Location: NZ 331 326. Half mile N of Bishop Middleham Village, to W of A177. Car parking restricted to two lay-bys on the west side of the road adjacent to the reserve entrances.

Access: Open all year. Limited car parking restricted to two lay-by's. Keep to footpaths, dogs on leads in spring.

Public transport: Regular bus service from Durham and Darlington to Coxhoe and Sedgefield.

Habitat: A large magnesian limestone quarry.

Key birds: Good range of farmland birds inc. Corn Bunting, Tree Sparrow, Willow Tit and Yellow Wagtail. Rare breeding record of Bee-eater.

Other notable flora and fauna: Butterflies including northern brown argus, dingy skipper, common blue, small heath, ringlet and small and large skippers. Internationally rare habitat, rich in orchid species such as pyramidal, common spotted, fragrant and bee plus large numbers of dark red helleborines. Other plants include blue moor grass, moonwort, autumn gentian and fairy flax.

Contact: Trust HQ, 0191 584 3112. e-mail: mail@durhamwt.co.uk www.durhamwt.co.uk

3. HAMSTERLEY FOREST

Forestry Commission

Location: NZ 091 312. Eight miles W of Bishop Auckland. Main entrance is five miles from A68, S of Witton-le-Wear and signposted through Hamsterley village and Bedburn.

Access: Open all year. Toll charge (£3). Forest drive and car park close 8pm (dusk in winter). Visitor centre open weekdays (10am-4pm) and weekends (11am-5pm).

Facilities: Visitor Centre, tearoom, toilets, shop, access for disabled. Visitors should not enter fenced farmland.

Public transport: None.

Habitat: Commercial woodland, mixed and broadleaved trees.

Key birds: *Spring/summer*: Nightjar, Willow Warbler, Chiffchaff, Wood Warbler, Redstart, Pied Flycatcher. *Winter*: Redwing, Fieldfare. *All year*: Crossbill, Jay, Dipper, Green Woodpecker, Goshawk, Peregrine.

Other notable flora and fauna: Hay meadows have wide variety of plants including globe flower.

Contact: Forestry Commission, Eals Burn, Bellingham, Hexham, Northumberland, NE48 2HP. 01434 220 242. e-mail: richard.gilchrist@forestry.gsi.gov.uk

4. MAZE PARK AND PORTRACK MARSH

Tees Valley Wildlife Trust.

Location: Maze Park: NZ 467 191, Portrack Marsh: NZ 465 194. Located midway between Middlesbrough and Stockton. Access from A66 at Tees Barrage. Sites are located on opposite banks of the River Tees, E of the barrage.

Access: No permits required. National cycle route passes through Maze Park. Surfaced paths at both sites. Hide suitable for disabled users at Portrack Marsh. Please keep to the permissive paths and public rights of way.

Facilities: Hide at Portrack Marsh. No toilets or visitor centre.

Public transport: Regular buses between Middlesbrough and Stockton stop at the Tees Barrage (Arriva, tel 0870 608 2608). Thornaby Station one mile. Frequent trains from Darlington and Middlesbrough.

Habitat: Freshwater marsh, scrub, post-industrial grassland, riverside.

Key birds: *Winter*: Ducks, passage waders, Redshank, Snipe and Jack Snipe, Lapwing, Grey Heron, Sky Lark, Grey Partridge, Sand Martin, occasional Kingfisher and Grasshopper Warbler.

Contact: Steve Ashton, Tees Valley Wildlife Trust, 01287 636 382; e-mail: teesvalleywt@cix.co.uk www.wildlifetrust.org.uk/teesvalley

NATURE RESERVES - NORTHERN ENGLAND

5. SALTHOLME, THE WILDLIFE RESERVE AND DISCOVERY PARK

RSPB.

Location: NZ 506 231. From A19, take A689 north of Stockton and then A1185. After four miles join A178 at mini roundabout. Take third exit and reserve is 250 yards on right.

Access: Open April 1 to Sept 30 (10am-5pm), Oct 1 to March 31 (10am-4pm). £3 per car, RSPB members, users of public transport and cyclists free. Open every day except Christmas Day.

Facilities: Award-winning visitor centre with cafe and shop, large car park, including wheelchair-friendly and coach parking, toilets (inc disabled), picnic area. Crushed stone paths ¬ wheelchair users may need assistance to reach bird hides. Walled garden designed by TV gardener Chris Beardshaw

Public transport: Stagecoach No1 bus from Hartlepool stops at reserve entrance. Cycle track across reserve from Port Clarence; cycle storage in car park.

Habitat: Wet grasslands, reedbeds, pools with tern islands, wader scrapes.

Key birds: *All year:* Lapwing, Peregrine, Water Rail. *Spring/summer:* Snipe, Common Tern, Yellow Wagtail. *Autumn:* Varied waders inc Black-tailed Godwit and Green Sandpiper, occasional rarer species. *Winter:* Large numbers of wildfowl and waders.

Other notable flora and fauna: Hares, orchids, butterflies and dragonflies.

Contact: The Warden, Saltholme, Seaton Carew Road, Port Clarence, Middlesbrough TS2 1TU. 01642 546 625; e-mail: saltholme@rspb.org.uk www.rspb.org.uk/reserves

6. TEESMOUTH NNR

Natural England (North East Region).

Location: Two components, centred on NZ 535 276 and NZ 530 260, three and five miles S of Hartlepool, E of A178. Access to northern component from car park at North Gate (NZ 534 282), 0.5 miles E of A178. Access to southern part from A178 bridge over Greatham Creek at Cowper Marsh (NZ 510 254). Car park adjacent to A178 at NZ 508 251. Both car parks can accommodate coaches.

Access: Open at all times. In northern component, no restrictions over most of dunes and North Gare Sands (avoid golf course, dogs must be kept under close control). In southern component, disabled access path to public hides at NZ 516 255 and NZ 516 252 (no other access).

Fa ilities: Nearest toilets at Seaton Carew, one mile to the N. Disabled access path and hides (see above), interpretive panels and leaflet. Teesmouth Field Centre (Tel: 01429 264 912).

Public transport: Half-hourly bus service (service 1) operates Mon-Sat between Middlesbrough and Hartlepool (hourly on Sundays), along A178, Stagecoach Hartlepool, Tel: 01429 267 082.

Habitat: Grazing marsh, dunes, intertidal flats.

Key birds: Passage and winter wildfowl and waders. Passage terns and skuas in late summer. Scarce passerine migrants and rarities. *Winter:* Merlin, Peregrine, Snow Bunting, Twite, divers, grebes.

Other notable flora and fauna: Northern component has large marsh orchid populations in damp dune grassland. Seal Sands supports a colony of 70 common seals.

Contact: Mike Leakey, Natural England, c/o British Energy, Tees Road, Hartlepool, TS25 2BZ. 01429 853 325; e-mail: northumbria@naturalengland.org.uk www.naturalengland.org.uk

Lancashire

1. CUERDEN VALLEY PARK

Cuerden Valley Park Trust.

Location: SD 565 238. S of Preston on A49. Easy access from J28 and J29 of the M6, J8 and J9 on M61 and the end of M65.

Access: Open all year.

Facilities: Visitor centre at Berkeley Drie, Bamber Bridge with toilets available between 9am and 5pm on weekdays. Track from Town Brow to lake is wheelchair friendly.

Public transport: None.

Habitat: 650 acres of mixed woodland, river, pond, lake, wildflower meadow, agricultural grassland.

Key birds: *All year:* Great Crested Grebe, Little Grebe, Kingfisher, Dipper, Great Spotted Woodpecker, Goldcrest, Little Owl and usual woodland and river birds.

Other notable flora and fauna: Dragonflies including emperor, emerald, black darter and migrant hawker.

Butterflies including large and small skipper, holly blue, small copper, comma and gatekeeper. Roe deer and seven species of bat. Common spotted and marsh orchid, moschatel.

Contact: Cuerden Valley Park Trust, 01772 324 436. e-mail: rangers@cuerdenvalleypark.org

2. HEYSHAM NATURE RESERVE AND BIRD OBSERVATORY

The Wildlife Trust for Lancashire, Manchester and North Merseyside in conjunction with British Energy Estates.

Location: Main reserve is at SD 404 596 W of Lancaster. Take A683 to Heysham port. Turn L at traffic lights by Duke of Rothesay pub, then first R after 300m.

Access: Gate to reserve car park usually open 9.30am-6pm (longer in summer and shorter in winter). Pedestrian access at all times. Dogs on lead. Limited disabled access.

Facilities: Hide overlooking Power Station outfalls. Map giving access details at the reserve car park. No

175

manned visitor centre or toilet access, but someone usually in reserve office, next to the main car park, in the morning. Latest sightings board can be viewed through the window if office is closed.

Public transport: Train services connect with nearby Isle of Man ferry. Plenty of buses to Lancaster from various Heysham sites within walking distance (ask for nearest stop to the harbour).

Habitat: Varied: wetland, acid grassland, alkaline grassland, foreshore.

Key birds: Passerine migrants in the correct conditions. Good passage of seabirds in spring, especially Arctic Tern. Storm Petrel and Leach's Petrel during strong onshore (SW-WNW) winds in midsummer and autumn respectively. Good variety of breeding birds (e.g. eight species of warbler on the reserve itself). Two-three scarce land-birds each year, most frequent being Yellow-browed Warbler.

Other notable flora and fauna: Notable area for dragonflies, red-veined darter breeds at nearby Middleton Community Woodland main pond (SD 418 592) between mid June - mid July. Bee orchid.

Contact: Reuben Neville, Reserve Warden, 01524 855 030; 07979 652 138. www.lancswt.org.uk http://heyshamobservatory.blogspot.com; Annual report from Leighton Moss RSPB reserve shop.

3. LEIGHTON MOSS

RSPB (Northern England).

Location: SD 478 750. Four miles NW of Carnforth. Signposted from A6 N of Carnforth.

Access: Reserve open daily 9am-dusk. Visitor centre open daily 9.30am-5pm (9.30am-4.30pm Nov-Jan inclusive), except Christmas Day. No charge to RSPB members or those who arrive by public transport or bike. Dogs allowed on causeway only. Groups and coaches welcome — please book in advance.

Facilities: Visitor centre, shop, tea-room and toilets. Nature trails and five hides (four have wheelchair access), plus two hides at saltmarsh pools.

Public transport: Silverdale train station 150 metres from reserve. Tel: 08457 484 950.

Habitat: Reedbed, shallow meres and woodland. Saltmarsh pool approx 1 mile.

Key birds: All year: Bittern, Bearded Tit, Water Rail, Pochard and Shoveler. Summer: Marsh Harrier, Reed and Sedge Warblers. Avocet at saltmarsh pools.

Other notable flora and fauna: Common reed, otter, red deer.

Contact: RSPB Leighton Moss Nature Reserve, Myers Farm, Silverdale, Carnforth, Lancashire, LA5 0SW. 01524 701 601. e-mail: leighton.moss@rspb.org.uk

4. MARTIN MERE

The Wildfowl & Wetlands Trust.

Location: SD 428 145. Six miles N of Ormskirk via Burscough Bridge (A59), 20 miles from Liverpool and Preston.

Access: Opening times: 9.30am-5.00pm (Nov-Feb), 9.30am-5.30pm (rest of year). Special dawn and evening events. Guide dogs allowed. Admission charge except for WWT members. Fully accessible to disabled, all hides suitable for wheelchairs. Coach park available. Special rates for coach parties.

Facilities: Visitor centre with toilets, gift shop, restaurant, education centre, play area, nature reserve and nature trails, hides, waterfowl collection and sustainable garden. Provision for disabled visitors.

Public transport: Bus service to WWT Martin Mere from Ormskirk. Train to Burscough Bridge or New Lane Stations (both 1.5 miles from reserve). For bus times contact Traveline 0870 608 2608.

Habitat: Open water, wet grassland, moss, copses, reedbed, parkland.

Key birds: Winter: Whooper and Bewick's Swans, Pink-footed Goose, various ducks, Ruff, Black-tailed Godwit, Peregrine, Hen Harrier, Tree Sparrow. Spring: Ruff, Shelduck, Little Ringed and Ringed Plover, Lapwing, Redshank. Summer: Marsh Harrier, Garganey, hirundines, Tree Sparrow. Breeding Avocets, Lapwing, Redshank, Shelduck. Autumn: Pink-footed Goose, waders on passage.

Other notable flora and fauna: Whorled caraway, golden dock, tubular dropwort, 300 species of moth.

Contact: WWT Martin Mere Wetland Centre, 01704 895 181; e-mail: info.martinmere@wwt.org.uk

5. MERE SANDS WOOD

The Wildlife Trust for Lancashire, Manchester and North Merseyside.

Location: SD 44 71 57. 12 miles by road from Southport, 0.5 miles off A59 Preston – Liverpool road,

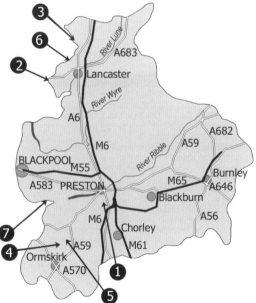

in Rufford along B5246 (Holmeswood Road).
Access: Visitor centre open 9.30am-4.30pm — closed Fridays and Christmas Day. Car park open until 8pm in summer. Three miles of wheelchair-accessible footpaths. All hides accessible to wheelchairs.
Facilities: Visitor centre with toilets (disabled), six viewing hides, three trails, exhibition room, latest sightings board. Feeding stations. Booking essential for two motorised buggies.
Public transport: Bus: Southport-Chorley 347 and Preston-Ormskirk 2B stop in Rufford, 0.5 mile walk. Train: Preston-Ormskirk train stops at Rufford station, one mile walk.
Habitat: 40h inc freshwater lakes, mixed woodland, sandy grassland/heath.
Key birds: *Winter:* Regionally important for Teal and Gadwall, good range of waterfowl, Kingfisher. Feeding stations attract Tree Sparrow, Bullfinch, Reed Bunting, Water Rail. *Woodland:* Treecreeper, Nuthatch. *Summer:* Kingfisher. *Passage:* Most years, Osprey, Crossbill, Green Sandpiper, Greenshank.
Other notable flora and fauna: 18 species of dragonfly recorded annually.
Contact: Lindsay Beaton, Reserve Manager, Mere Sands Wood Nature Reserve, 01704 821 809.
e-mail: meresandswood@lancswt.org.uk
www.lancswt.org.uk

6. MORECAMBE BAY (HEST BANK)

RSPB (Northern England).
Location: SD 468 667. Two miles N of Morecambe at Hest Bank off A5105.
Access: Open at all times. Do not venture onto saltmarsh or intertidal area, as there are dangerous channels and quicksands.

Facilities: Viewpoint at local council car park best for disabled visitors. Coast paths too rough for wheelchairs.
Public transport: No 5 bus runs between Carnforth and Morecambe. Tel: 0870 608 2608.
Habitat: Saltmarsh, coastal pools, estuary.
Key birds: *Winter:* Wildfowl (Pintail, Shelduck, Wigeon) and waders. This is an important high tide roost for Oystercatcher, Curlew, Redshank, Dunlin and Bar-tailed Godwit.
Contact: RSPB Leighton Moss & Morecambe Bay Nature Reserves, 01524 701 601.
e-mail: leighton.moss@rspb.org.uk

7. RIBBLE ESTUARY

Natural England (Cheshire to Lancashire team).
Location: SD 380 240. W of Preston.
Access: Open at all times.
Facilities: No formal visiting facilities.
Public transport: None.
Habitat: Saltmarsh, mudflats.
Key birds: High water wader roosts (of Knot, Dunlin, Black-tailed Godwit, Oystercatcher and Grey Plover) are best viewed from Southport, Marshside, Lytham St Annes. Pink-footed Geese and wintering swans are present in large numbers from Oct-Feb on Banks Marsh and along River Douglas respectively. The large flocks of Wigeon, for which the site is renowned, can be seen on high tides from Marshside but feed on saltmarsh areas at night. Good numbers of raptors also present in winter.
Contact: Site Manager, English Nature, Ribble Estuary NNR, Old Hollow, Marsh Road, Banks, Southport PR9 8DU. 01704 225 624.

Manchester, Greater

1. ASTLEY MOSS

The Wildlife Trust for Lancashire, Manchester and North Merseyside.
Location: Lies 7km S of Leigh at SJ 692 975. S of A580 at Astley; follow Higher Green Lane to Rindle Farm.
Access: Permit required — apply to Trust office.
Facilities: None.
Habitat: Remnant peat bog, scrub, oak/birch woodland.
Key birds: *Spring/summer:* Breeding Tree Pipit, Willow Tit, Whinchat and Curlew. *Winter:* Raptors (inc. Merlin, Hen Harrier), finch flocks, thrush flocks; Long- and Short-eared Owls.
Other notable flora and fauna: Sphagnum mosses, 10 species of dragonfly recorded.
Contact: Trust HQ, 01772 324 129.
e-mail: info@lancswt.org.uk www.lancswt.org.uk

2. ETHEROW COUNTRY PARK

Stockport Metropolitan Borough Council.
Location: SJ 965 908. In Compstall on the B6104 between Romiley and marple Bridge. Site is well

signposted.
Access: Open at all times; permit required for conservation area. Keep to paths.
Facilities: Reserve area has SSSI status. Hide, nature trail, visitor centre, motorised scooters for disabled, (best to book at weekends).
Public transport: None.
Habitat: River Etherow, woodlands, marshy area (240 acres in total) .
Key birds: Sparrowhawk, Buzzard, Dipper, all three woodpeckers, Pied Flycatcher, warblers. *Winter:* Brambling, Siskin, Water Rail. Frequent sightings of Merlin and Raven over hills.
Other notable flora and fauna: 200 species of plant.
Contact: John Rowland, Etherow Country Park, Compstall, Stockport, Cheshire SK6 5JD. 01614 276 937; e-mail: parks@stockport.gov.uk

3. HOLLINGWORTH LAKE

Rochdale MBC.
Location: SD 939 153 (visitor centre). Four miles NE of Rochdale, signed from A58 Halifax Road and J21 of M62. Take B6225 to Littleborough.
Access: Access open to lake and surroundings at all times.

NATURE RESERVES - NORTHERN ENGLAND

Facilities: Cafes, hide, trails and education service, pay-and-display car parks, coach park by prior arrangement. Free wheelchair hire, disabled toilets and baby changing facilities. Visitor centre open 10.30am-6pm in summer, 11am-4pm (Mon-Fri), 10.30am-5pm (Sat & Sun) in winter.
Public transport: Bus Nos 452, 450. Train to Littleborough or Smithy Bridge.
Habitat: Lake (116 acres, includes 20 acre nature reserve), woodland, streams, marsh, willow scrub.
Key birds: *All year*: Great Crested Grebe, Kingfisher, Lapwing, Little Owl, Bullfinch, Cormorant. Occasional Peregrine, Sedge Warbler, Water Rail, Snipe. *Spring/ autumn*: Passage waders, wildfowl, Kittiwake. *Summer*: Reed Bunting, Dipper, Common Sandpiper, Curlew, Oystercatcher, Black Tern, 'Commic' Tern, Grey Partridge, Blackcap. *Winter*: Goosander, Goldeneye, Siskin, Redpoll, Golden Plover.
Contact: The Ranger, Hollingworth Lake Visitor Centre, Rakewood Road, Littleborough, OL15 0AQ. 01706 373 421. www.rochdale.gov.uk

4. PENNINGTON FLASH COUNTRY PARK
Wigan Leisure and Culture Trust
Location: SJ 640 990. One mile from Leigh town centre. Main entrance on A572 (St Helens Road).
Access: Park is signposted from A580 (East Lancs Road) and is permanently open. Five largest hides, toilets and information point open 9am-dusk (except Christmas Day). Main paths flat and suitable for disabled. Main car park pay & display with coach parking available if booked in advance.
Facilities: Toilets (including disabled) and information point. Total of eight bird hides. Site leaflet available and Rangers based on site. Group visits welcome but please book your visit in advance.
Public transport: Only 1 mile from Leigh bus station. Several services stop on St Helens Road near entrance to park. Contact GMPTE on 0161 228 7811.
Habitat: Lowland lake, ponds and scrapes, fringed with reeds, rough grassland, scrub and young woodland.
Key birds: Waterfowl all year, waders (14-plus

species) and terns (4-plus species) mainly on passage in both spring and autumn. Breeding birds include 9 species of warbler. Feeding station attracts Willow Tit, Stock Dove and up to 40 Bullfinch all year. Large gull roost in winter. Over 240 species recorded including 7 county firsts in the last decade alone.
Other notable flora and fauna: Several species of orchid including bee orchid. Wide variety of butterflies and dragonflies.
Contact: Peter Alker, WLCT, Pennington Flash Country Park, St Helens Road, Leigh, WN7 3PA. 01942 605 253 (Also Fax number); e-mail: pfcp@wlct.org

5. WIGAN FLASHES LNR
Lancashire Wildlife Trust/Wigan Council.
Location: SD 580 035. Leave M6 at J25 head N on A49, turn R on to Poolstock Lane (B5238). There are several entrances to the site; at end of Carr Lane near Hawkley Hall School, one off Poolstock Lane, two on Warington Road (A573). Also accessible from banks of Leeds and Liverpool Canal.
Access: Free access, open at all times. Areas suitable for wheelchairs but there are some motorcycle barriers (gates can be opened by reserve manager for large groups). Paths being upgraded. Access for coaches - contact reserve manager for details.
Facilities: Six hide screens.
Public transport: 610 bus (Hawkley Hall Circular). Local timetable info - call 0161 228 7811.
Habitat: Wetland with reedbed.
Key birds: Black Tern on migration. *Summer*: Nationally important for Reed Warbler and breeding Common Tern. Willow Tit, Cetti's and Grasshopper Warblers, Kingfisher. *Winter*: Wildfowl, especially diving duck and Gadwall. Bittern (especially winter).
Other notable flora and fauna: Interesting orchids, with the eight species including marsh and dune helleborine. One of the UK's largest feeding assemblage of noctule bats. Eighteen species of dragonfly which has included red-veined darter.
Contact: Mark Champion, Lancashire Wildlife Trust, Highfield Grange, Wigan, Lancs WN3 6SU. 01942 233 976. e-mail: wiganflashes@lancswt.org.uk

Merseyside

1. AINSDALE & BIRKDALE SANDHILLS LNR
Sefton Council.
Location: SD 300 115. SD 310 138. Leave the A565 just N of Formby and car parking areas are off the un-numbered coastal road.
Access: Track from Ainsdale or Southport along the shore. Wheelchair access across boardwalks at Ainsdale Sands Lake Nature Trail and the Queen's Jubilee Nature Trail, opposite Weld Road.
Facilities: Ainsdale Discovery Centre open summer. Shore Road toilets open Easter-Oct.
Public transport: Ainsdale and Southport stations 20 minute walk. Hillside Station is a 30 minute walk across the Birkdale Sandhills to beach.
Habitat: Foreshore, dune scrub and pine woodland.

Key birds: *Spring/summer*: Grasshopper Warbler, Chiffchaff, waders. *Winter*: Blackcap, Stonechat, Redwing, Fieldfare, waders and wildfowl. *All year*: Sky Lark, Grey Partridge.
Other notable flora and fauna: Red squirrel, natterjack toad, early marsh orchid and marsh helleborine.
Contact: Sefton Council Leisure Services, 0151 934 2967; e-mail: coast-countryside@leisure.sefton.gov.uk www.visitsouthport.com/sefton/nature-and-wildlife

2. DEE ESTUARY
Metropolitan Borough of Wirral.
Location: SJ 255 815. Leave A540 Chester to Hoylake road at Heswall and head downhill (one mile) to the free car park at the shore end of Banks Road. Heswall is 30 mins from South Liverpool and Chester by car.

178

Access: Open at all times. Best viewpoint 600 yards along shore N of Banks Road. No disabled access along shore, but good birdwatching from bottom of Banks Road. Arrive 2.5 hours before high tide. Coach parking available.

Facilities: Information board. No toilets in car park. Wirral Country Park Centre three miles N off A540 has toilets, hide, café, kiosk (all accessible to wheelchairs). Birdwatching events programme on RSPB website.

Public transport: Bus service to Banks Road car park from Heswall bus station, or bus to Irby village then walk one mile. Mersey Travel (0151 236 7676).

Habitat: Saltmarsh and mudflats.

Key birds: *Autumn/winter*: Large passage and winter wader roosts — Redshank, Curlew, Black-tailed Godwit, Oystercatcher, Golden Plover, Knot, Shelduck, Teal, Red-breasted Merganser, Peregrine, Merlin, Hen Harrier, Short-eared Owl. Smaller numbers of Pintail, Wigeon, Bar-tailed Godwit, Greenshank, Spotted Redshank, Grey and Ringed Plovers, Whimbrel, Curlew Sandpiper, Little Stint, occasional Scaup and Little Egret.

Contact: The Senior Ranger, Wirral Country Park Centre, 01516 484 371/3884; www.wirral.gov.uk/er e-mail: wirralcountrypark@wirral.gov.uk

3. HILBRE ISLAND LNR

Wirral Country Park Centre (Metropolitan Borough of Wirral).

Location: SJ 184 880. Three tidal islands in the mouth of the Dee Estuary. Park in West Kirby which is on the A540 Chester-to-Hoylake road – 30 minutes from Liverpool, 45 minutes from Chester. Follow the brown Marine Lake signs to Dee Lane pay and display car park. Coach parking available at West Kirby but

please apply for permit to visit island well in advance as numbers limited.

Access: Two mile walk across the sands from Dee Lane slipway. No disabled access. Do not cross either way within 3.5 hours of high water – tide times and suggested safe route on noticeboard at slipway. Prior booking and permit needed for parties of five or more – maximum of 50. Book early.

Facilities: Hilbre Bird Observatory. Toilets at Hilbre (primitive!) and Marine Lake. Permits, leaflets and tide times from Wirral Country Park Centre.

Public transport: Bus and train station (from Liverpool) within 0.5 mile of Dee Lane slipway. Contact Mersey Travel, tel 0151 236 7676.

Habitat: Sandflats, rocky shore and open sea.

Key birds: *Late summer/autumn*: Seabird passage Gannets, terns, skuas, shearwaters and after NW gales good numbers of Leach's Petrel. *Winter*: Wader roosts at high tide, Purple Sandpiper, Turnstone, sea ducks, divers, grebes. Passage migrants.

Other notable flora and fauna: Nationally scarce rock sea lavender.

Contact: The Senior Ranger, Wirral Country Park Centre, 01516 484 371/3884; www.wirral.gov.uk/er e-mail: wirralcountrypark@wirral.gov.uk

4. MARSHSIDE

RSPB (Northern England).

Location: SD 355 202. On south shore of Ribble Estuary, one mile north of Southport centre on Marine Drive.

Access: Open 8.30am-5pm all year. Toilets. No dogs please. Coach parties please book in advance. No charges but donations welcomed. Park in Sefton Council car park along Marine Drive.

Facilities: Information centre, toilets (inc disabled), two hides and trails accessible to wheelchairs. Two viewing screens and a viewing platform.

Public transport: Bus service to Elswick Road/Marshside Road half-hourly, bus No 44, from Lord Street. Contact Traveline (0870 608 2608).

Habitat: Coastal grazing marsh and lagoons.

Key birds: *Winter*: Pink-footed Goose, wildfowl, waders, raptors. *Spring*: Breeding waders, inc. Avocet and wildfowl, Garganey, migrants inc Black-tailed Godwit, Ruff and Wheatear. *Autumn*: Migrants. **Other notable flora and fauna:** Hares, various plants including marsh orchid, migrant hawker dragonfly.

Contact: Graham Clarkson, Warden, RSPB, 24 Hoghton Street, Southport, PR9 0PA. 01704 536 378. e-mail: graham.clarkson@rspb.org.uk

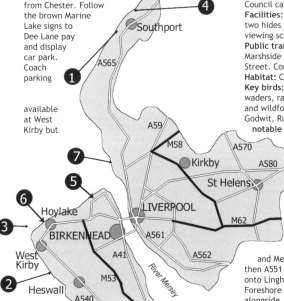

5. N. WIRRAL COASTAL PARK

Metropolitan Borough of Wirral.
Location: SJ 241 909. Located SW of new Brighton, between the outer Dee and Mersey Estuaries. From Moreton take A553 E then A551 N. Turn left onto Tarran Way South then R onto Lingham Lane. Parking available by lighthouse. Foreshore can be viewed from footpath which runs alongside.

Access: Open at all times.
Facilities: Visitor centre, several car parks, 3 toilet blocks (one summer-only), extensive footpath network and public bridleways, 4 picnic areas.
Public transport: The area being served by Grove Road (Wallasey), Leasowe, Moreton, and Meols Merseyrail Stations, and with bus routes along Leasowe Road, Pasture Road and Harrison Drive.
Habitat: Saltmarsh.
Key birds: Important as a feeding and roosting site for passage and wintering flocks of waders, wildfowl, terns and gulls. Wintering populations of Knot (20,000+), Bar-tailed Godwit (2,000+) and Dunlin (10,000). Redshank (1,000+) and Turnstone (500+) feed on the rocky shore at Perch Rock and on the rocky sea walls. Oystercatcher (500+), Curlew, Grey Plover and Black-tailed Godwit also regularly roost here in relatively high numbers. Small populations of wildfowl, including Common Scoter, Scaup and Goldeneye, Red-throated Divers and Great Crested Grebes also frequently winter on this site.
Other notable flora and fauna: Sea holly, marram grass, storksbill, burnet rose and rarities like the Isle of Man cabbage can be found. This area is one of only two known sites in the world for the very rare British sub-species of the belted beauty moth.
Contact: Ranger Service, North Wirral Coastal Park, Leasowe Lighthouse, Moreton Common, Wirral CH46 4TA. 0151 678 5488. www.wirral.gov.uk
e-mail: coastalpark@wirral.gov.uk

6. RED ROCKS MARSH

Cheshire Wildlife Trust.
Location: SJ 206 880. 9 km west of Birkenhead immediately W of Hoylake and adjacent to the Dee estuary.
Access: Open all year.

Facilities: Car park, hide.
Habitat: Sand dune, reedbed.
Key birds: *Spring/summer:* Wildfowl, warblers. *Passage:* Finches, Snow Bunting, thrushes.
Other notable flora and fauna: The only breeding colony of natterjack toads on the Wirral Peninsula. More than 50 species of flowering plant recorded, including parsley, quaking grass, Danish scurvy grass, wild asparagus and various orchid species.
Contact: Trust HQ, 01948 820 728;
e-mail: info@cheshirewt.cix.co.uk
www.cheshirewildlifetrust.co.uk

7. SEAFORTH NATURE RESERVE

The Wildlife Trust for Lancashire, Manchester and North Merseyside.
Location: SJ 315 970. Five miles from Liverpool city centre. From M57/M58 take A5036 to docks.
Access: Only organised groups which pre-book are now allowed access. Groups should contact the reserve office (see below) at least seven days in advance of their planned trip. Coaches welcome.
Facilities: Toilets at visitor centre when open, three hides.
Public transport: Train to Waterloo or Seaforth stations from Liverpool. Buses to dock gates from Liverpool.
Habitat: Saltwater and freshwater lagoons, scrub grassland.
Key birds: Noted site for Little Gull on passage (Apr), plus Roseate, Little and Black Terns. Breeding and passage Common Tern (Apr-Sept). Passage and winter waders and gulls. Passage passerines, especially White Wagtail, pipits and Wheatear.
Contact: Steve White, Seaforth Nature Reserve, Port of Liverpool, L21 1JD. 0151 9203 769.
e-mail: swhite@lancswt.org.uk

Northumberland

1. ARNOLD MEMORIAL, CRASTER

Northumberland Wildlife Trust.
Location: NU255197. Lies NE of Alnwick on Sw edge of Craster village. Take minor road to coast off B1339.
Access: Public footpath from car park in disused quarry.
Facilities: Information centre (not NWT) open in summer. Interpretation boards.Toilets (incl disabled) and picnic site in quarry car park. Easy going access along path through site. Coach parking in adjacent public car park.
Public transport: Arriva Northumberland nos. 500, 505. Travelsure No 401
Habitat: Semi-natural woodland and scrub near coast.
Key birds: Good site for migrant passerines to rest and feed. Interesting visitors can inc. Bluethroat, Red-breasted Flycatcher, Barred and Icterine Warblers, Wryneck; moulting site for Lesser Redpoll.

Breeding warblers in summer.
Other notable flora and fauna: Spring flora including primrose and non-native periwinkle.
Contact: Trust HQ, 01912 846 884;
e-mail: mail@northwt.org.uk www.nwt.org.uk

2. DRURIDGE POOLS - CRESSWELL POND

Northumberland Wildlife Trust.
Location: Two sites lying on coast between Newbiggin and Amble, off A1068. 1. Druridge Pools NZ 272 965. 2. Cresswell Pond NZ 283 945. Half mile N of Cresswell.
Access: Wheelchair users can view northern part of Cresswell Pond from public footpath or roadside.
Facilities: 1. Three hides. 2. Hide.
Public transport: Arriva No 420 (to within 2 miles).
Habitat: 1. Deep lake and wet meadows with pools behind dunes. 2. Shallow brackish lagoon behind dunes fringed by saltmarsh and reedbed, some mudflats.
Key birds: 1. Especially good in spring. Winter and breeding wildfowl; passage and breeding waders. 2.

Good for waders, esp. on passage.
Other notable flora and fauna: The sheltered sunny banks are good for a range of butterflies and dragonflies in summer at Druridge Pools. Otters are often seen on the lakes.
Contact: Trust HQ, 01912 846 884;
e-mail: mail@northwt.org.uk www.nwt.org.uk

3. EAST CHEVINGTON

Northumberland Wildlife Trust.
Location: NZ 265 985. Overlooking Druridge Bay, off A 1068 between Hauxley and Cresswell.
Access: Main access from overflow car park at Druridge Bay Country Park (signed from main road).
Facilities: Four public hides, café, toilets and information at Country Park (County Council). ID boards for coastal plants.
Public transport: Arriva 420 and 423 bus services.
Habitat: Ponds and reedbeds created from former open cast coal mine. Areas of scrub and grassland.
Key birds: Large numbers of wildfowl, including Greylag and Pinkfooted Geese in winter. Breeding Sky Lark, Stonechat, Reed Bunting, plus Reed, Sedge and Grasshopper Warblers. Capable of attracting rarities at any time of year. Marsh Harriers around the reedbeds.
Other notable flora and fauna: Coastal wildflowers.
Contact: Trust HQ, 01912 846 884;
e-mail: mail@northwt.org.uk www.nwt.org.uk

4. FARNE ISLANDS

The National Trust.
Location: NU 230 370. Access by boat from Seahouses Harbour. Access from A1.
Access: Inner Farne and Staple 10.30am-6pm (majority of boats land at Inner Farne when conditions are calm). In April and between Aug 1 and Oct 31: Staple Island 10.30am-1.30pm, Inner Farne: 1.30pm-5pm between May 1 and July 31. Disabled access possible on Inner Farne, telephone Property Manager for details. Dogs allowed on boats but not on islands.
Facilities: Toilets on Inner Farne.
Public transport: Nearest rail stations at Alnmouth and Berwick. Hourly Travelsure buses between Budle and Beadnell Bays (Mon-Sat). Call 01665 720 955.
Habitat: Maritime islands — between 15-28 depending on state of tide.
Key birds: 18 species of seabirds/waders, four species of tern (including Roseate), 55,000-plus pairs of Puffin, 1,200 Eider, Rock Pipit, Pied Wagtail etc.
Other notable flora and fauna: Grey seals.
Contact: John Walton, 8 St Aidans, Seahouses, Northumberland NE68 7SR. 01665 720 651.

5. HAUXLEY

Northumberland Wildlife Trust
Location: NU 285 023. South of Amble.
Access: Day permit required available from Reception hide. Access through High Hauxley village.

Site is signposted off A1068.
Facilities: Reception hide open daily from 10am-5pm (summer) or 10am-3pm (winter) and six public hides. Toilets and information.
Public transport: Arriva 420 and 423 bus services.
Habitat: Ponds created from former opencast coal mine. Areas of woodland and grassland.
Key birds: Waders use the site at high tide. Roseate Terns sometimes join commoner species in late summer. Waders and migrants on passage. *Winter*: Bewick's Swan, Shoveler, plus larg number of other wildfowl species, Lapwing and Purple Sandpiper.
Other notable flora and fauna: A variety of invertebrates, including butterflies, dragonflies and amphibians such as great crested newt.
Contact: Trust HQ, 01912 846 884;
e-mail: mail@northwt.org.uk www.nwt.org.uk

6. KIELDER FOREST PARK

Forestry Commission
Location: NY 632 934. Kielder Castle is situated at N end of Kielder Water, NW of Bellingham.
Access: Forest open all year. Toll charge on 12 mile forest drive and car park charge applies. Visitor centre has limited opening in winter.
Facilities: Three visitor centres (Castle, Tower Knowe and Leapish Waterside Park), exhibition, toilets, shop, access for disabled, licensed café. Local facilities include youth hostel, camp site, pub and garage.

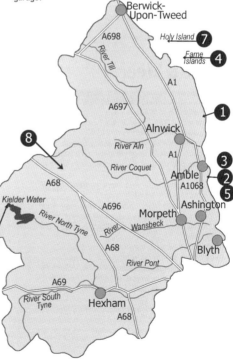

Public transport: Bus: 814, 815, 816 from Hexham and seasonal service 714 from Newcastle.
Habitat: Commercial woodland, mixed and broadleaved trees.
Key birds: *Spring/summer*: Goshawk, Chiffchaff, Willow Warbler, Redstart, Siskin. *Winter*: Crossbill. *Resident*: Jay, Dipper, Great Spotted Woodpecker, Tawny Owl, Song Thrush, Goldcrest.
Other notable flora and fauna: Impressive display of northern marsh orchids at entrance to Kielder Castle. Red Squirrel hide at Lepish WP.
Contact: Forestry Commission, 01434 220 242. e-mail: richard.gilchrist@forestry.gsi.gov.uk

7. LINDISFARNE NNR

Natural England (Northumbria Team).
Location: NU 090 430. Island access lies two miles E of A1 at Beal, eight miles S of Berwick-on-Tweed.
Access: Causeway floods at high tide, so check when it is safe to cross. Some restricted access (bird refuges). Coach parking available on Holy Island.
Facilities: Toilets, visitor centre in village. Hide on island (new hide with disabled access at Fenham-le-Moor). Self-guided trail on island.
Public transport: Irregular bus service to Holy Island, mainly in summer. Main bus route follows mainland boundary of site north-south.
Habitat: Dunes, sand, mudflats and saltmarsh.
Key birds: *Passage and winter*: Wildfowl and waders, including pale-bellied Brent Goose, Long-tailed Duck and Whooper Swan. Rare migrants.
Other notable flora and fauna: Butterflies include dark green fritillary (July) and grayling (August). Guided walks advertised for 9 species of orchid

including coralroot and Lindisfarne helleborine.
Contact: Phil Davey, Senior Reserve Manager, Beal Station, Berwick-on-Tweed, TD15 2PB. 01289 381 470.

8. WHITELEE MOOR

Northumberland Wildlife Trust
Location: NT 700 040. Reserve located at head of Redesdale, south of A68 Newcastle to Jedburgh road where it crosses Scottish Border at Carter Bar.
Access: There is parking at tourist car park at Carter Bar and on laybys on forest track at reservoir end. A public footpath leads along old track to Whitelee Limeworks and then southwards. This footpath extends to southern boundary of site and eastwards along it to link up with a bridleway from White Kielder Burn via Girdle Fell to Chattlehope Burn. Additionally there is access on foot via Forest Enterprise road near eastern corner of reserve. reserve is remote and wild, and weather can change quickly. Visitors should have hill-walking experience if attempting long walks.
Facilities: Car park and laybys.
Habitat: Active blanket bog and heather heath.
Key birds: The River Rede and its tributaries add to the habitat diversity. Notable breeding birds include Merlin and Stonechat. Black Grouse, Sky Lark, Meadow Pipit, Dunlin, Curlew, Golden Plover, Grey Wagtail, Dipper and Ring Ouzel regularly visit the reserve.
Other notable flora and fauna: Otters often hunt along the Rede and a herd of feral goats may be seen.
Contact: Trust HQ, 01912 846 884; e-mail: mail@northwt.org.uk www.nwt.org.uk

Tyne & Wear

1. BIG WATERS

Northumberland Wildlife Trust.
Location: NZ 227 734 N of Newcastle upon Tyne. Drive under A1 flyover, W of B1318 in Wideopen and through Brunswick Village, turning R after last house. Reserve is entered from car park via a path that meets public right of way from access road just S of the car park.
Access: Hides are locked, keys available to NWT members. Public viewing areas.
Facilities: Two hides, viewing areas, easy going footpath access.
Public transport: Arriva Northumberland nos 45, 45a, 45b.
Habitat: Pond with surrounding reedbed.
Key birds: Wintering wildfowl including Teal, Tufted Duck and Shoveler. Breeding species include Great Crested and Little Grebe and Coot. Tree Sparrow, Yellowhammer and Great Spotted Woodpecker use feeding station all year.
Other notable flora and fauna: Otters are frequently seen from the hide. The small pond on site is used by dragonflies, while woodland edges and fields are used

by a variety of butterflies, including large skipper and small copper.
Contact: Trust HQ, 01912 846 884; www.nwt.org.uk e-mail: mail@northwt.org.uk

2. BOLDON FLATS

South Tyneside Council.
Location: NZ 377 614. Turn west along Moor Lane at Cleadon on A1018 (Sunderland to South Shields Road).
Access: View from limited lay-by parking along Moor Lane.
Facilities: None.
Public transport: East Boldon Metro Station approx. 800 metres from site. www.nexus.org.uk
Habitat: Managed winter flood, ponds, ditches, summer meadow.
Key birds: *Winter*: Large numbers of wildfowl, inc Wigeon, Teal, occasional Whooper Swan and Bean Goose. Waders include Golden Plover. *Spring*: Little Ringed Plover, Lapwing, Tree Sparrow. *Summer*: Farmland species.
Other notable flora and fauna: Good range of dragonflies, inc occasional vagrants in late summer.
Contact: Countryside Officer, South Tyneside Metropolitan Council, 01914 271 717. www.southtyneside.info

NATURE RESERVES - NORTHERN ENGLAND

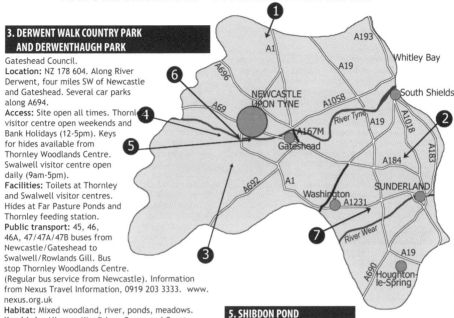

3. DERWENT WALK COUNTRY PARK AND DERWENTHAUGH PARK

Gateshead Council.
Location: NZ 178 604. Along River Derwent, four miles SW of Newcastle and Gateshead. Several car parks along A694.
Access: Site open all times. Thornley visitor centre open weekends and Bank Holidays (12-5pm). Keys for hides available from Thornley Woodlands Centre. Swalwell visitor centre open daily (9am-5pm).
Facilities: Toilets at Thornley and Swalwell visitor centres. Hides at Far Pasture Ponds and Thornley feeding station.
Public transport: 45, 46, 46A, 47/47A/47B buses from Newcastle/Gateshead to Swalwell/Rowlands Gill. Bus stop Thornley Woodlands Centre. (Regular bus service from Newcastle). Information from Nexus Travel Information, 0919 203 3333. www.nexus.org.uk
Habitat: Mixed woodland, river, ponds, meadows.
Key birds: *All year*: Kingfisher, Green and Great Spotted Woodpecker, Nuthatch. *Summer*: Red Kite, Grasshopper Warbler, Lesser Whitethroat, Dipper, Blackcap, Garden Warbler. *Winter*: Teal, Tufted Duck, Brambling, Marsh Tit, Bullfinch, Great Spotted Woodpecker, Nuthatch, Goosander, Kingfisher.
Contact: Trevor Weston, Thornley Woodlands Centre, 01207 545 212. e-mail: countryside@gateshead.gov.uk
www.gatesheadbirders.co.uk
www.gateshead.gov.uk

4. RYTON WILLOWS

Gateshead Council.
Location: NZ 155 650. Five miles W of Newcastle. Access along several tracks running N from Ryton.
Access: Open at all times.
Facilities: Nature trail and free leaflet.
Public transport: Regular service to Ryton from Newcastle/Gateshead. Information from Nexus Traveline on 0191 232 5325.
Habitat: Deciduous woodland, scrub, riverside, tidal river.
Key birds: *Winter*: Goldeneye (now rare), Goosander, Green Woodpecker, Nuthatch, Treecreeper. *Autumn*: Greenshank. *Summer*: Lesser Whitethroat, Sedge Warbler, Yellowhammer, Linnet, Reed Bunting, Common Sandpiper.
Other notable flora and fauna: Invertebrate species associated with acid grassland.
Contact: Brian Pollinger, Thornley Woodlands Centre, 1208 545 212. e-mail: countryside@gateshead.gov.uk
www.gatesheadbirders.co.uk

5. SHIBDON POND

Gateshead Council.
Location: NZ 192 628. E of Blaydon, S of Scotswood Bridge, close to A1. Car park at Blaydon swimming baths. Open access from B6317 (Shibdon Road).
Access: Open at all times. Disabled access to hide.
Facilities: Hide in SW corner of pond. Free leaflet available.
Public transport: At least six buses per hour from Newcastle/Gateshead to Blaydon (bus stop Shibdon Road). Information from Nexus Travel Line (0191 232 5325).
Habitat: Pond, marsh, scrub and damp grassland.
Key birds: *Winter*: Wildfowl, Water Rail, occasional white-winged gulls. *Summer*: Reed Warbler, Sedge Warbler, Lesser Whitethroat, Grasshopper Warbler, Water Rail. *Autumn*: Passage waders and wildfowl, Kingfisher.
Other notable flora and fauna: 18 species of butterfly, inc dingy skipper. Dragonflies inc ruddy darter, migrant hawker, occasional emperor and vagrants.
Contact: Brian Pollinger, Thornley Woodlands Centre, 1208 545 212. e-mail: countryside@gateshead.gov.uk
www.gatesheadbirders.co.uk

6. TYNE RIVERSIDE COUNTRY PARK

Newcastle City Council
Location: NZ 158 658 in Newburn on W edge of Newcastle. From the Newcastle to Carlisle by-pass on the A69(T) take the A6085 into Newburn. The park is signposted along the road to Blaydon. 0.25 miles after this junction, turn due W (the Newburn Hotel is on the corner) and after 0.5 miles the parking and

information area is signed just beyond the Newburn Leisure Centre.
Access: Open all year.
Facilities: Visitor centre (open weekend afternoons and other times when staff available. Toilets open 9am-5pm in summer and most winter days. Car park. Leaflets and walk details available.
Habitat: River, pond with reed and willow stands, mixed woodland, open grassland.
Key birds: *Spring/summer*: Swift, Swallow, Whitethroat, Lesser Whitethroat. *Winter*: Sparrowhawk, Kingfisher, Little Grebe, finches, Siskin, Fieldfare, Redwing, Goosander. *All year*: Grey Partridge, Green and Great Spotted Woodpecker, Bullfinch, Yellowhammer.
Contact: Newcastle City Council, The Riverside Country Park, Newburn, Newcastle upon Tyne, NE15 8BW. 0191 264 8501; www.newcastle.gov.uk
e-mail: newburn.countrypark@newcastle.gov.uk

7. WASHINGTON

The Wildfowl & Wetlands Trust.
Location: NZ 331 566. In Washington. On N bank of River Wear, W of Sunderland. Signposted from A195, A19, A1231 and A182.

Access: Open 9.30am-5pm (summer), 9.30am-4pm (winter). Free to WWT members. Admission charge for non-members. No dogs except guide dogs. Good access for people with disabilities.
Facilities: Visitor centre, toilets, parent and baby room, range of hides. Shop and café.
Public transport: Buses to Waterview Park (250 yards walk) from Washington, from Sunderland, Newcastle-upon-Tyne, Durham and South Shields. Tel: 0845 6060 260 for details.
Habitat: Wetlands, woodland and meadows.
Key birds: *Spring/summer*: Nesting colony of Grey Heron, other breeders include Common Tern, Oystercatcher, Lapwing. *Winter*: Bird-feeding station visited by Great Spotted Woodpecker, Bullfinch, Jay and Sparrowhawk. Goldeneye and other ducks.
Other notable flora and fauna: Wildflower meadows - cuckoo flower, bee orchid and yellow rattle. Dragonfly and amphibian ponds.
Contact: Dean Heward, (Conservation Manager),, Wildfowl & Wetlands Trust, Pottinson, Washington, NE38 8LE. 01914 165 454 ext 231.
e-mail: dean.heward@wwt.org.uk
www.wwt.org.uk

Yorkshire, East Riding

1. BEMPTON CLIFFS

RSPB (Northern England).
Location: TA 197 738. On coast N ofBridlington. Take Cliff Lane N from Bempton Village off B1229 to car park and visitor centre.
Access: Visitor centre open year round (phone for opening times). Public footpath along cliff top with observation points. Limited access for wheelchairs to some observation points.
Facilities: Visitor centre, toilets, light refreshments, observation points, picnic area, limited coach parking. Four miles of chalk cliffs, highest in the county.
Public transport: Bempton railway station (limited service) 1.5 miles — irregular bus service to village 1.25 miles.
Habitat: Seabird nesting cliffs, farmland, coastal scrub.
Key birds: Breeding seabirds from March to October, peak in May to July. Largest mainland Gannet colony in the UK. Also Kittiwakes, Puffins, Guillemots, Razorbill s and Fulmars. Nesting Tree Sparrows and Corn Buntings. Passage skuas, shearwaters, terns and passerine migrants.
Other notable flora and fauna: Harbour porpoises regularly offshore. Also bees and northern marsh orchids occur.
Contact: Site Manager, RSPB, Bempton Cliffs Nature Reserve, 11 Cliff Lane, Bempton, Bridlington, E Yorks, YO15 1JF. 01262 851 179.

2. BLACKTOFT SANDS

RSPB (Northern England).
Location: SE 843 232. Eight miles E of Goole on minor road between Ousefleet and Adlingfleet.
Access: Open 9am-9pm or dusk if earlier. RSPB members free, £3 permit for non-members, £2 concessionary, £1 children, £6 family.
Facilities: Car park, toilets, visitor centre (open 9am to 5pm April to Oct and weekends between Nov and March), six hides, footpaths suitable for wheelchairs.
Public transport: Goole/Scunthorpe bus (Sweynes' Coaches stops outside reserve entrance. Bus timetable on main RSPB website (see Blacktoft Reserve details).
Habitat: Reedbed, saline lagoons, lowland wet grassland, willow scrub.
Key birds: *Summer*: Breeding Avocet, Marsh Harrier, Bittern, Bearded Tit, passage waders (exceptional list inc many rarities). *Winter*: Hen Harrier, Merlin, Peregrine, wildfowl.
Other notable flora and fauna: Good place to see water vole. Small number of dragonflies and damselflies including black-tailed skimmer, four-spotted chaser, large red damselfly. Marsh sow thistle easily seen from footpaths in summer.
Contact: Mike Andrews, Visitor Development Officer, Blacktoft Sands RSPB reserve, Hillcrest, Whitgift, Nr Goole, E Yorks DN14 8HL. 01405 704 665.
e-mail: michael.andrews@rspb.org.uk

3. FLAMBOROUGH CLIFFS NATURE RESERVE

Yorkshire Wildlife Trust
Location: TA 240 722. The reserve is part of

the Flamborough headland, approx 4 miles NE of Bridlington. From Bridlington take B1255 to Flamborough and follow the signs for the North Landing.

Access: Open all year. Public pay and display car park at North Landing gives access to both parts of the reserve. Paths not suitable for wheelchairs.

Facilities: Car park (pay and display), trails, refreshments available at café at North Landing (open Apr-Oct 10am-5pm), toilets.

Public transport: Flamborough is served by buses from Bridlington and Bempton. Phone 01482 222 222 for details.

Habitat: Coastal cliffs, rough grassland and scrub, farmland.

Key birds: *Summer*: Puffin, Guillemot, Razorbill, Kittiwake, Shag, Fulmar, Sky Lark, Meadow Pipit, Linnet, Whitethroat, Yellowhammer, Tree Sparrow, occasional Corn Bunting. *Passage migrants*: Fieldfare, Redwing and occasional rarities such as Wryneck and Red-backed Shrike.

Contact: Yorkshire Wildlife Trust, 1 St George's Place, York, YO24 1GN. 01904 659 570. www.ywt.org.uk e-mail: info@ywt.org.uk

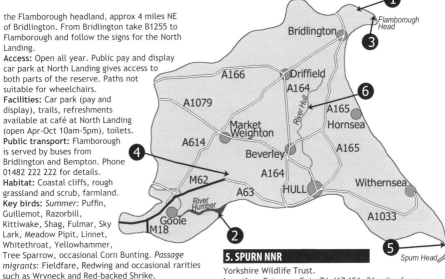

4. NORTH CAVE WETLANDS

Yorkshire Wildlife Trust.

Location: SE 887 328. At NW of North Cave village, approx 10 miles W of Hull. From junction 28 of M62, follow signs to North Cave on B1230. In village, turn L and follow road to next crossroads where you go L, then take next L onto Dryham Lane. Alternatively, from N, follow minor road direct from Market Weighton. After the turning for Hotham, take the next R (Dryham Lane), which is one mile further down the road.

Access: Open all year with car parking on Dryham Lane. Some of the footpaths are suitable for all abilities.

Facilities: Three bird-viewing hides, two accessible to wheelchair users. Nearest toilet and refreshment facilities in North Cave, one mile away,

Public transport: Buses serve North Cave from Hull and Goole: telephone 01482 222 222 for details.

Habitat: Six former gravel pits have been converted into various lagoons for wetland birds, including one reedbed. There are also grasslands, scrub and hedgerows.

Key birds: More than 150 different species have been recorded including Great Crested Grebe, Gadwall, Pochard, Sparrowhawk, Avocet, Ringed Plover, Golden Plover, Dunlin, Ruff, Redshank, Green Sandpiper, Common Sandpiper and Tree Sparrow.

Contact: Trust HQ, 01904 659 570; www.ywt.org.uk e-mail: info@ywt.org.uk

5. SPURN NNR

Yorkshire Wildlife Trust.

Location: Entrance Gate TA 417 151. 26 miles from Hull. Take A1033 from Hull to Patrington then B1445 from Patrington to Easington and unclassed roads on to Kilnsea and Spurn Head.

Access: Normally open at all times. Vehicle admission fee (at present £3). No charge for pedestrians. No dogs allowed under any circumstances, not even in cars. Coaches by permit only (must be booked in advance).

Facilities: Centre open weekends, Bank Holidays, school holidays. Four hides. Cafe at point open weekends Apr to Oct 10am to 5pm. Public toilets in Blue Bell car park Blue Bell café, Kilnsea open seven days a week 10am till 5pm.

Public transport: Nearest bus service is at Easington (3.5 miles away). 2010 Sunday service to the Point, hail and ride, Easter to last weekend of October.

Habitat: Sand dunes with marram and sea buckthorn scrub. Mudflats around Humber Estuary.

Key birds: *Spring*: Many migrants on passage and often rare birds such as Red-backed Shrike, Bluethroat etc. *Autumn*: Passage migrants and rarities such as Wryneck, Pallas's Warbler. *Winter*: Waders and Brent Goose.

Other notable flora and fauna: Unique habitats and geographical position make Spurn the most important site in Yorkshire for butterflies (25 species recorded) and moths.

Contact: Outer Humber Officer, Spurn NNR, Blue Bell, Kilnsea, Hull HU12 0UB. e-mail: andrew.gibson@ywt.org.uk

6. TOPHILL LOW NATURE RESERVE

Yorkshire Water.

Location: TA 071 482. Nine miles SE of Driffield and ten miles NE of Beverley. Signposted from village of Watton on A164.

Access: Open daily (9am-6pm). Charges: £2.50 per person. £1 concessions. No dogs allowed. Provision for disabled visitors (paths, ramps, hides, toilet etc). Coaches welcome.
Facilities: Visitor Centre with toilets open every weekend and most week days. Disabled toilet open at all times, 12 hides (five with access for wheelchairs), good paths and sightings board.
Public transport: None.
Habitat: Open water (two reservoirs), marshes, wader scrapes, woodland and thorn scrub.
Key birds: 160 to 170 species each year. *Winter:* SSSI for wildfowl numbers, plus one of the UK's largest Black-head and Common Gull roosts. Regular wintering Bittern. Active feeding station with Brambling. Woodcock. *Spring/early summer:* Passage waders, Black Tern and Black-necked Grebe. Breeding Little Ringed Plover, Common Tern, Kingfisher and Barn Owl with a diverse variety of warblers. *Late summer/autumn:* Up to 20 species of passage wader.
Other notable flora and fauna: Specialist grassland and wetland flora including orchids. Fauna includes red-eyed damselfly, marbled white and brown argus butterflies, grass snake, otter, water vole and roe deer.
Contact: Richard Hampshire, Tophill Low Nature Reserve, 01377 270 690.
e-mail: richard.hampshire@yorkshirewater.co.uk

Yorkshire, North

1. BOWESFIELD

Tees Valley Wildlife Trust.
Location: NZ 440 160. SE of Stockton on Tees. From A66 take A135 to Yarm. At first roundabout turn L along Concord Way. At next roundabout go straight onto the new Bowesfield Industrial Estate, the reserve is on the floodplain below the development.
Access: Public footpaths around the site open at all times.
Facilities: None. **Public transport:** None.
Habitat: New wetland reserve on the edge of the River Tees.
Key birds: The reserve is home to a growing number of birds including Reed Bunting, Stonechat, Water Rail, Lapwing and Curlew which roost and feed in the rich, wet grassland and lakes found on the site.
Other notable flora and fauna: The reserve offers opportunities to see otter, harvest mouse and roe deer.
Contact: Trust HQ, 01287 636 382;
e-mail: info@teeswildlife.org www.teeswildlife.org

2. COATHAM MARSH

Tees Valley Wildlife Trust.
Location: NZ 585 250. Located on W edge of Redcar. Access from minor road to Warrenby from A1085/A1042.
Access: Reserve is open throughout daylight hours. Please keep to permissive footpaths only.
Facilities: Good footpaths around site. Facilities available in Redcar close by.
Public transport: Very frequent bus service between Middlesbrough and Redcar. Nearest stops are in Coatham 0.25 mile from reserve (Arriva tel 0871 200 2233). Redcar Central Station one mile from site. Frequent trains from Middlesbrough and Darlington.
Habitat: Freshwater wetlands, lakes, reedbeds.
Key birds: *Spring/autumn:* Wader passage (including Wood Sandpiper and Greenshank). *Summer:* Passerines (including Sedge Warbler, Yellow Wagtail). *Winter:* Ducks (including Smew). *Occasional rarities:* Water Rail, Great White Egret, Avocet, Bearded Tit and Bittern.

Other notable flora and fauna: The lime-rich soil allows wildflower meadows to grow around the site, including northern marsh orchid. Also good for insects incuding migrant hawker dragonfly.
Contact: Tees Valley Wildlife Trust, 01287 636 382; e-mail: info@teeswildlife.org

3. FILEY BRIGG ORNITHOLOGICAL GROUP BIRD OBSERVATORY

FBOG and Yorkshire Wildlife Trust (The Dams).
Location: TA 10 68 07. Two access roads into Filey from A165 (Scarborough to Bridlington road). Filey is ten miles N of Bridlington and eight miles S of Scarborough.
Access: Open at all times. Dogs only in Parish Wood and The Old Tip (on lead). Coaches welcome. Park in the North Cliff Country Park.
Facilities: No provisions for disabled at present. Two hides at The Dams, one on The Brigg (open most weekends from late Jul-Oct, key can be hired from Country Park café). Toilets in Country Park (Apr-Nov 1) and town centre. Nature trails at The Dams, Parish Wood/Old Tip. Cliff top walk for seabirds along Cleveland Way.
Public transport: All areas within a mile of Filey railway station. Trains into Filey tel. 08457 484 950; buses into Filey tel. 01723 503 020
Habitat: The Dams — two freshwater lakes, fringed with some tree cover and small reedbeds. Parish Wood — a newly planted wood which leads to the Old Tip, the latter has been fenced (for stock and crop strips) though there is a public trail. Carr Naze has a pond and can produce newly arrived migrants.
Key birds: The Dams: Breeding and wintering water birds, breeding Sedge Warbler, Reed Warbler and Tree Sparrow. The Tip: Important for breeding Sky Lark, Meadow Pipit, common warblers and Grey Partridge. *Winter:* Buntings, including Lapland. Seawatch Hide: *Jul-Oct.* All four skuas, shearwaters, terns. *Winter:* Divers and grebes. Totem Pole Field: A new project should encourage breeding species and wintering larks, buntings etc. Many sub-rare/rare migrants possible at all sites.
Contact: e-mail: secretary-at-fbog.co.uk
www.fbog.co.uk

4. FYLINGDALES MOOR CONSERVATION AREA

Hawk and Owl Trust /Strickland Estate/Fylingdales Moor ESS Co Ltd.
Location: NZ 947 003.
Off A171 S of Whitby. On eastern side of North York Moors National Park, stretching between Sneaton High Moor (Newton House Plantation) and the coast at Ravenscar. Crossed by A171 Scarborough to Whitby road.
Access: Open access. Parking (inc for coaches) available at Jugger Howe Layby (OS NZ 947 003) on A171 Scarborough to Whitby road.
Facilities: Numerous footpaths including the Jugger Howe Nature Trail, Lyke Wake Walk and Robin Hood's Bay Road.
Public transport: Half-hourly bus service (No. 93 and X93) between Scarborough and Whitby, nearest stop at Flask Inn (approx. 1 mile N of Jugger Howe Layby). Services run by Arriva (0191 281 1313) www.arrivabus.co.uk
Habitat: About 6,800 acres (2,750 hectares) of heather moorland (former grouse moor), with scattered trees and wooded valleys and gulleys. Managed exclusively for wildlife and archaeological remains, the moor is an SSSI and SPA (Merlin and Golden Plover) and a special area of conservation.
Key birds: As well as more than 80 more common bird species, rare and endangered breeding birds include harriers, Merlin, Golden Plover, Red Grouse, Curlew, Wheatear, Stonechat, Whinchat, Sky Lark, Marsh Tit, Willow Tit, Linnet, Bullfinch, Reed Bunting and Yellowhammer. The moor is also home to Kestrel, Lapwing, Snipe, Cuckoo, Meadow Pipit, Grey Wagtail and Wood Warbler and visited by Peregrine.
Other notable flora and fauna: Mammals include otter, roe deer, brown hare, stoat, weasel and badger. Important for water vole. Three species of heather, plus cranberry, cowberry, moonwort and, in wetter parts, bog myrtle, lesser twayblade, bog asphodel, butterwort, marsh helleborine, and sundews can be found. Also rare orchids and sedges. Insect species include large heath and small pearl-bordered fritillary butterflies and emperor moth.
Contact: Professor John Edwards, The Hawk and Owl Trust, 01751 417 398. www.hawkandowl.org
e-mail: john.edwards@wildfylingdales.co.uk

5. GOUTHWAITE RESERVOIR

Yorkshire Water.
Location: SE 12 69. 2.5miles NW of Pately Bridge on the B6265.
Access: Open all hours, all year.
Facilities: Three viewing areas on edge of reservoir.

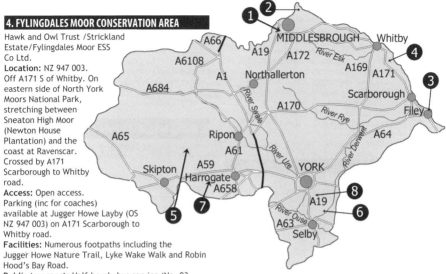

Public transport: Nidderdale Rambler route 24/25 (summer Sundays and bank holidays). Harrogate and District Travel 01423 566 061.
Habitat: Reservoir, deciduous woodland shoreline, moors.
Key birds: Green Woodpecker, Nuthatch, Merlin and Buzzard all year. Summer warblers with passage Osprey. *Winter:* Surrounding morland good for raptors such as Red Kite, Buzzard Hen Harrier, Merlin and Kestrel as well as Red Grouse and Lapwing. Goosander, Goldeneye and Whooper Swan.
Contact: Geoff Lomas, Catchment & Recreation Officer, PO Box 52, Bradford, BD6 2LZ www.yorkshirewater.co.uk (turn to recreation page).

6. LOWER DERWENT VALLEY

Natural England (Yorkshire and Humber Region), Yorkshire Wildlife Trust and Countryside Trust.
Location: Six miles SE of York, stretching 12 miles S along the River Derwent from Newton-on-Derwent to Wressle and along the Pocklington Canal. Visitor facilities at Bank Island (SE 691 448), Wheldrake Ings YWT (SE 691 444 see separate entry), Thorganby (SE 692 418) and North Duffield Carrs (SE 697 367).
Access: Open all year. No dogs. Disabled access at North Duffield Carrs.
Facilities: Bank Island — two hides, viewing tower. Wheldrake Ings — four hides. Thorganby — viewing platform. North Duffield Carrs — two hides and wheelchair access. Car parks at all sites, height restriction of 2.1m at Bank Island and North Duffield Carrs. Bicycle stands in car parks at Bank Island and North Duffield Carrs.
Public transport: Bus from York/Selby — contact First (01904 622 992).
Habitat: Hay meadow and pasture, swamp, open water and alder/willow woodland.

Key birds: *Spring/summer*: Breeding wildfowl and waders, incl. Garganey, Snipe and Ruff. Barn Owl and warblers. *Winter/spring*: 20,000-plus waterfowl including Whooper Swan, wild geese, Teal and Wigeon. Large gull roost, incl. white-winged gulls. Also passage waders, incl. Whimbrel.
Other notable flora and fauna: A walk alongside the Pocklington Canal is particularly good for a wide range of aquatic plants and animals.
Contact: Peter Roworth, Senior Reserve Manager, 01904 435 500; email: york@naturalengland.org.uk
www.naturalengland.org.uk
Pocklington Canal: www.pocklington.gov.uk/pcas

7. TIMBLE INGS

Yorkshire Water.
Location: SE 15 53. West of Harrogate, north of Otley. Off the A59 south of Blubberhouses, near Timble village.
Access: Open at all times, all year.
Facilities: Toilets, cafes, pubs, coach parking all nearby. Hard forest tracks.
Habitat: Woodland and nearby reservoir.
Key birds: Bradford OG species list stands at 134. Habitat management work by Yorkshire Water makes site attractive to Long-eared and Tawny Owls, Nightjars and Tree Pipits. Buzzards now nest and Red Kites seen regularly. Goshawk numbers in decline. *Summer*: Breeding species inc Redpoll, Siskin, Crossbill, Woodcock, Redstart and Grasshopper Warbler. Short-eared Owls hunt adjacent moorland. *Winter*: Fieldfare, Redwing, Brambling, occasional Waxwings and Hawfinches.

Yorkshire South & West

1. BOLTON INGS (DEARNE VALLEY)

RSPB North West Office
Location: SE 425 020. Lies SE of Barnsley. From M1 take A61 in direction of Barnsley and continue on A6195 for four miles. After Morrisons superstore, follow A6195 and brown signs for RSPB Old Moor.
Access: Dearne Way footpath and Trans-Pennine Trail open at all times, but not suitable for wheelchair users.
Facilities: None. Old Moor site close by.
Public transport: Nearest train stations at Wombwell and Swinton both 3m from reserve. Buses run to Old Moor reserve from Barnsley, Doncaster and Meadowhall — call Traveline on 01709 515 151 for details. Trans-Pennine Way runs along southern edge of reserve.
Habitat: 43 hectares of reedbed.
Key birds: *All year*: Kingfisher, Little Egret, Stonechat, Reed Bunting. *Spring/summer*: Breeding waders and warblers, Cuckoo, Garganey. *Autumn*: Passage waders including Greenshank, Green Sandpiper, Golden Plover. *Winter*: Wildfowl, including Goosander, Wigeon and Teal. Rarer species include Spoonbill and Avocet.

Other notable flora and fauna: Roe deer, badger, brown hare, shrew, vole and mouse species (all detected from owl pellets). New ponds attractive to amphibians and dragonflies, inc broad-bodied chaser, emperor and black darter.
Contact: Geoff Lomas, Catchment & Recreation Officer, Yorkshire Water, Western House, Halifax Road, Bradford BD6 2LZ.
www.yorkshirewater.co.uk (turn to recreation page).

8. WHELDRAKE INGS LOWER DERWENT VALLEY NNR

Yorkshire Wildlife Trust.
Location: From York ring-road head S onto A19 Selby road. After one mile turn L, signed Wheldrake and Thorganby. Continue through Wheldrake towards Thorganby. After a sharp R bend, turn L after 0.5 miles onto an unsigned tarmac track. Look for two stone gateposts with pointed tops. Car park is about 0.25 miles down the track. To reach the reserve, cross the bridge over river and turn R over a stile.
Access: Open all year. Please keep to the riverside path. From Apr-Sep.
Facilities: Car park, four hides.
Habitat: Water meadows, river, scrub, open water.
Key birds: *Spring/summer*: Duck species, Grey Partridge, Turtle Dove, some waders, Spotted Flycatcher, warblers. *Winter*: Occasional divers and scarce grebes. wildfowl inc. Pintail, Pochard, Goshawk, Hen Harrier, Water Rail, Short-eared Owl, thrushes, good mix of other birds.
Contact: Trust HQ, 01904 659 570; www.ywt.org.uk
e-mail: info@ywt.org.uk

Other notable flora and fauna: Dragonflies inc banded demoiselle, roe deer.
Contact: 01226 751 593;
e-mail: old.moor@rspb.org.uk

2. CARLTON MARSH

Barnsley MBC Parks Services.
Location: SE 379 103. Small car park off Shaw Lane, Cudworth, Barnsley.
Access: Access only along public rights of way and disused railway.
Facilities: Single hide.
Public transport: None.
Habitat: Marsh with reed and sedge, some open water, plus grassland and woodland strips.
Key birds: *Summer*: Breeding Water Rail, Little Ringed Plover, Sedge, Reed and Grasshopper Warblers. *Autumn*: Swallow roost; Barn Owl, Jack Snipe, visiting Bitterns.
Contact: Trevor Mayne, Parks Officer — Countryside, Barnsley MBC, 01226 772 646.
e-mail: trevormayne@barnsley.gov.uk

3. DENABY INGS NATURE RESERVE

Yorkshire Wildlife Trust.
Location: Reserve on A6023 from Mexborough. Look for L fork, signed Denaby Ings Nature Reserve.

Proceed along Pastures Road for 0.5 miles and watch for a 2nd sign on R marking entrance to car park. From car park, walk back to the road to a set of concrete steps on R leading to a small visitor centre and a hide.
Access: Open all year.
Facilities: Car park, visitor centre, hide, nature trail.
Public transport: None.
Habitat: Water, deciduous woodland, marsh, willows.
Key birds: *Spring/summer:* Waterfowl, Little Ringed Plover, Turtle Dove, Cuckoo, Little Owl, Tawny Owl, Sand Martin, Swallow, Whinchat, possible Grasshopper Warbler, Lesser Whitethroat, Whitethroat, other warblers, Spotted Flycatcher, Red-legged and Grey Partridges, Kingfisher. *Passage:* Waders, Common, Arctic and Black Terns, Redstart, Wheatear. *Winter:* Whooper Swan, wildfowl, Jack Snipe, waders, Grey Wagtail, Short-eared Owl, Stonchat, Fieldfare, Redwing, Brambling, Siskin. *All year:* Corn Bunting, Yellowhammer, all three woodpeckers, common woodland birds, possible, Willow Tit.
Contact: Trust HQ, 01904 659 570.
e-mail: info@ywt.org.uk www.ywt.org.uk

4. FAIRBURN INGS

RSPB (Northern England).
Location: SE 452 277. 12 miles from Leeds, six miles from Pontefract, three miles from Castleford, situated next to A1246 from J42 of A1.
Access: Reserve and hides open every day except Dec 25/26. Centre and shop open each day (9am-5pm). Dogs on leads welcome. Boardwalks leading to Pickup Pool, feeding station and Kingfisher viewpoint are all wheelchair-friendly.
Facilities: Five hides open at all times. Toilets open 9am-5pm. Disabled toilets and baby-changing facilities. Hot and cold drinks, snacks available.

Wildlife garden, pond-dipping and mini beast areas, plus duck feeding platform. Coach parking for club visits.
Public transport: Nearest train stations are Castleford, Micklefield and Garforth. No bus service.
Habitat: Open water, wet grassland, marsh and fen scrub, reedbed, reclaimed colliery spoil heaps.
Key birds: *All year:* Tree Sparrow, Willow Tit, Green Woodpecker, Bullfinch. *Winter:* Smew. Goldeneye, Goosander, Wigeon, Peregrine. *Spring:* Osprey, Little Gull, Wheatear, five species of tern inc annual Black Tern. *Summer:* Nine species of breeding warbler, Grey Heron, Gadwall, Little Ringed Plover.
Other notable flora and fauna: Brown hare, harvest mouse, roe deer, Leisler's and Daubenton's bats, 28 species of butterfly and 20 species of dragonfly.
Contact: Laura Bentley, Visitor Services Manager, Fairburn Ings Visitor Centre, 01977 628 191.

5. HARDCASTLE CRAGS

National Trust.
Location: From Halifax, follow A646 W for five miles to Hebden Bridge and pick up National Trust signs in town centre to the A6033 Keighley Road. Follow this for 0.75 miles. Turn L at the National Trust sign to the car parks. Alternate pay-and-display car park at Clough Hole on Widdop Road, Heptonstall.
Access: Open all year. NT car park charges: £3.50 all day weekdays and for up to 3 hours at weekends, £5 at weekends and bank holidays. No charge for NT members and disabled badge holders.
Facilities: 2 small pay car parks, cycle racks and several way-marked trails. Gibson Mill visitor centre (not NT property) has toilets, café, exhibitions. Not connected to any mains services, in extreme conditions the mill may be closed for health and safety reasons.
Public transport: Good public transport links. Trains to Hebden Bridge from Manchester or Leeds every 30 minutes. Call 08457 484 950. Weekday buses every 30 minutes to Keighley Road, then 1 mile walk to Midghole. Summer weekend bus 906 Widdop-Hardcastle Crags leaves Hebden Bridge rail station every 90 minutes 9.20am-6.05pm. Tel: 0113 245 7676.
Habitat: 400 acres of unspoilt wooded valleys, ravines, streams, hay meadows and moorland edge.
Key birds: *Spring/summer:* Cuckoo, Redstart, Lesser Whitethroat, Garden Warbler, Blackcap, Wood Warbler, Chiffchaff, Spotted Flycatcher, Pied Flycatcher, Curlew, Lapwing, Meadow Pipit. *All year:* Sparrowhawk, Kestrel, Green and Greater Spotted Woodpeckers, Lesser Spotted Woodpecker, Tawny Owl, Barn Owl, Little Owl, Jay, Coal Tit, Dipper, Grey Wagtail and other woodland species. Goshawk in Crimsworth Dean.
Other notable flora and fauna: Northern hairy wood ant, moss carder bee, tree bumble bee, killarney fern (*gametophyte stage*), brittle bladder fern.
Contact: National Trust, Hardcastle Crags, 01422 844 518. www.nationaltrust.org.uk

6. INGBIRCHWORTH RESERVOIR

Yorkshire Water.
Location: Leave the M1 at J37 and take the A628 towards Manchester and Penistone. After five miles you reach a roundabout. Turn R onto the A629 Huddersfield road. After 2.5 miles you reach Ingbirchworth. At a sign for The Fountain Inn, turn L. Pass a pub. The road bears L to cross the dam, proceed straight forward onto the track leading to the car park.
Access: Open all year. One of the few reservoirs in the area with footpath access.
Facilities: Car park, picnic tables.
Habitat: Reservoir, small strip of deciduous woodland.
Key birds: *Spring/summer*: Whinchat, warblers, woodland birds, House Martin. *Spring/autumn passage*: Little Ringed Plover, Ringed Plover, Dotterel, other waders, Common Tern, Arctic Tern, Black Tern, Yellow Wagtail, Wheatear. *Winter*: Wildfowl, Golden Plover, waders, occasional rare gull such as Iceland or Glaucous, Grey Wagtail, Fieldfare, Redwing, Brambling, Redpoll.
Other notable flora and fauna: Woodland wildflowers, inc bluebells.
Contact: Yorkshire Water, PO Box 52, Bradford, BD6 2LZ. www.yorkshirewater.co.uk (recreation page).

7. OLD MOOR (DEARNE VALLEY)

RSPB (Northern England).
Location: SE 422 022. From M1 J36, take A61 towards Barnsley, then A6195 towards Doncaster. From A1 J37, then A635 and A6195 - follow brown signs.
Access: Open daily except Christmas day and Boxing day. April 1st-Sept 30th (9.30am-8.00pm) Oct 1st March 31st (9.30am 4.00pm). Members free. Non-members £3. Concessions £2. Electric scooters available on request.
Facilities: Toilets (including disabled), large visitor centre, tearoom and shop, five superb hides fully accessible for disabled. Two trails suitable for wheelchairs.
Public transport: Buses from Barnsley, Doncaster, Meadowhall, Wombwell and Swinton stop near reserve — for information Traveline 01709 515 151.
Habitat: Lakes and flood meadows, wader scrape and reedbeds.
Key birds: *All year*: Kingfisher, Little Owl. *Winter*: Large numbers of wildfowl, spectacular flocks of Lapwing and Golden Plover, Peregrine, Tree Sparrow in garden feeding area. *Summer*: Breeding waders, inc drumming Snipe, and wildfowl. Rare vagrants recorded annually.
Contact: The Warden, RSPB Old Moor, Old Moor Lane, Wombwell, Barnsley, South Yorkshire, S73 0YF. 01226 751 593 Fax: 01226 341 078. www.rspb.org.uk

8. POTTERIC CARR

Yorkshire Wildlife Trust.
Location: SE 589 007. From M18 junction 3 take A6182 (Doncaster) and at first roundabout take third

exit; entrance and car park are on R after 50m.
Access: Open daily 9am-5pm. Obtain ticket on arrival, YWT members free; Single £3; family £6.50 (two adults and up to three children); concession £2.50; child £1.50. Groups of ten or more should book in advance.
Facilities: Around 8 km of paths (5 km accessible to wheelchairs, unassisted, 14 viewing hides (10 suitable for the disabled) and a Field Centre with café, open daily (10am-4pm) with hot and cold drinks, snacks and meals. Toilets at entrance reception, in Field Centre (during café opening times), and outside Field Centre.
Public transport: Nearest railway station is Doncaster. From the Frenchgate Interchange, take bus number 72 or 75, and alight at B&Q on Woodfield Way. Cross White Rose Way, walk down Mallard Way. Cross the car park to the reserve entrance in Sedum House.
Habitat: Reed fen, subsidence ponds, artificial pools, grassland, woodland.
Key birds: 96 species have bred. Nesting waterfowl (inc. Shoveler, Gadwall, Pochard), Water Rail, Kingfisher, all three woodpeckers, Lesser Whitethroat, Reed and Sedge Warblers, Willow Tit. *Passage/winter*: Bittern, Marsh Harrier, Black Tern, waders, wildfowl.
Other notable flora and fauna: 20 species of dragonfly recorded, 28 species of butterfly including purple hairstreak and dingy skipper. Palmate and great crested newt.
Contact: Trust HQ, 01904 659 570.
e-mail: potteric.carr@ywt.org.uk
www.potteric-carr.org.uk

9. SPROTBOROUGH FLASH RESERVE AND THE DON GORGE

Yorkshire Wildlife Trust.
Location: From A1, follow A630 to Rotherham 4.8km W of Doncaster. After 0.8km, turn R at traffic lights to Sprotborough. After approx 1.6km the road drops down the slopes of the Gorse. Cross a bridge over river, then another over a canal, turn immediately L. Park in a small roadside parking area 45m on L beside canal. Walk along canal bank, past The Boat Inn to reserve entrance approx 90m further on.
Access: Open all year.
Facilities: Three hides, footpaths.
Public transport: River bus from Doncaster in summer months.
Habitat: River, reed, gorge, woodland.
Key birds: *Summer*: Turtle Dove, Cuckoo, hirundines, Lesser Whitethroat, Whitethroat, Garden Warbler, Blackcap, Chiffchaff, Willow Warbler, Spotted Flycatcher. *Spring/autumn passage*: Little Ringed Plover, Dunlin, Greenshank, Green Sandpiper, waders, Yellow Wagtail. *Winter/all year*: Wildfowl, Water Rail, Snipe, Little Owl, Tawny Owl, all three woodpeckers, thrushes, Siskin, possible Corn Bunting.
Contact: Trust HQ, 01904 659 570; www.ywt.org.uk
e-mail: info@ywt.org.uk

South East England

Berkshire

1. DINTON PASTURES

Wokingham District Council.
Location: SU 784 718. Country Park, E of Reading off B3030 between Hurst and Winnersh.
Access: Open all year, dawn to dusk. Car parking charges apply 8am to 6pm each day. Dogs allowed.
Facilities: Three hides (one adapted for wheelchairs), information centre, car park, café, toilets (suitable for wheelchairs). Electric buggies for hire. Various trails between one and three miles in length.
Public transport: Not known.
Habitat: Mature gravel pits and banks of River Loddon. Sandford Lake managed for wildfowl, Lavell's Lake best for waders and scrub species.
Key birds: *All year*: Kingfisher, Water Rail. *Spring/summer*: Hobby, Little Ringed Plover, Common Tern, Nightingale, common warblers. *Winter*: Bittern, wildfowl (inc. Goldeneye, Wigeon, Teal, Gadwall), thrushes. Waders include Green and Common Sandpipers, Snipe, Redshank.
Other notable flora and fauna: Water vole, harvest mouse, great crested newt, Loddon pondweed and Loddon lily. Good range of dragonflies inc emperor, black-tailed skimmer, white-legged and banded agrion damselfies and migrant hawker.
Contact: The Ranger, Dinton Pastures Country Park, Davis Street, Hurst, Berks. 0118 934 2 016.
e-mail: countryside@wokingham.gov.uk

2. HUNGERFORD MARSH

Berks, Bucks & Oxon Wildlife Trust.
Location: SU 333 687. On W side of Hungerford, beside the Kennet and Avon Canal. From town centre, go along Church Street past the town hall. Turn R under the railway. Follow public footpath over swing bridge on the canal near the church. The reserve is separated from Freeman's Marsh by a line of willows and bushes.
Access: Open all year. Please keep to the footpath. Dogs on leads please.
Facilities: Car park.
Public transport: Hungerford railway station half mile from reserve.
Habitat: An idyllic waterside site with unimproved rough grazing and reedbed.
Key birds: 120 species recorded. *Spring/summer*: Reed and Grasshopper Warblers. *Winter*: Siskin. *All year*: Mute Swan, Mallard, Little Grebe. Birds seen in the last ten years include Kingfisher, Yellow Wagtail, Water Rail.
Other notable fauna: Water vole, grass snake.
Contact: BBOWT, The Lodge, 1 Armstrong Road, Littlemore, Oxford OX4 4XT. 01865 775 476.
e-mail: info@bbowt.org.uk www.bbowt.org.uk

3. LAVELL'S LAKE

Wokingham District Council.
Location: SU 785 727. Via Sandford Lane off B3030 between Hurst and Winnersh E of Reading.
Access: Dawn to dusk. No permit required. Dogs on leads all year.
Facilities: Car park, two public hides, one with disabled access, one members-only hide (see below), viewing screen.
Public transport: Thames Travel bus services 128/129 run between Reading and Wokingham, stopping outside Dinton Pastures main entrance. Nearest train services are at either Winnersh, or Winnersh Triangle.
Habitat: Gravel pits, two wader scrapes, reed beds, rough grassland, marshy area, Sand Martin banks, between River Loddon and Emm Brook. To N of Lavell's Lake gravel pits are being restored to attract birds. The lake at Lea Farm is viewable walking N along the River Loddon from Lavell's Lake over small

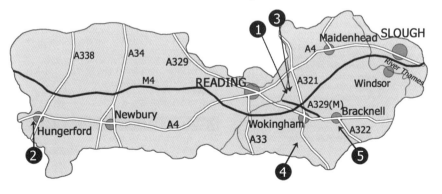

191

green bridge. It is on R and can be seen through a viewing screen and a members-only hide for Friends of Lavell's Lake (see www.foll.org.uk). No access is permitted.
Key birds: *All year*: Great Crested Grebe, Gadwall, Sparrowhawk, Kingfisher, Red Kite, Buzzard, Cetti's Warbler. *Summer*: Common Tern, Redshank, Lapwing, Hobby, warblers include Reed, Sedge, Whitethroat. *Passage*: Garganey, Little Ringed Plover, Common and Green Sandpiper and Greenshank. *Winter*: Water Rail, Bittern, Little Egret, Teal, Shoveler, Pochard, Goldeneye, occasional Smew and Goosander along River Loddon. -Siskin, Lesser Redpoll, Fieldfare and Redwing.
Contact: As for Dinton Pastures or via www.foll.org.uk

4. MOOR GREEN LAKES

Blackwater Valley Countryside Partnership.
Location: SU 805 628. Main access and parking off Lower Sandhurst Road, Finchampstead. Alternatively, Rambler's car park, Mill Lane, Sandhurst (SU 820 619).
Access: Car parks open dawn-dusk. Two bird hides open to members of the Moor Green Lakes Group (contact BVCP for details). Dogs on leads. Site can be used by people in wheelchairs, though surface not particularly suitable.
Facilities: Two bird hides, footpaths around site, Blackwater Valley Long Distance Path passes through site.
Public transport: Nearest bus stop, Finchampstead (approx 1.5 miles from main entrance). Local bus companies - Stagecoach Hants & Surrey, tel 01256 464 501, First Beeline and Londonlink, tel 01344 424 938.
Habitat: Thirty-six hectares (90 acres) in total. Three lakes with gravel islands, beaches and scrapes. River

Blackwater, grassland, surrounded by willow, ash, hazel and thorn hedgerows.
Key birds: *Spring/summer*: Redshank, Little Ringed Plover, Sand Martin, Willow Warbler, and of particular interest, a flock of Goosander. Also Whitethroat, Sedge Warbler, Common Sandpiper, Common Tern. Dunlin and Black Tern on passage. Lapwings breed on site and several sightings of Red Kite. *Winter*: Ruddy Duck, Wigeon, Teal, Gadwall.
Contact: Blackwater VCP, Ash Lock Cottage, Government Road, Aldershot, Hants, GU11 2PS. 01252 331 353. e-mail: blackwater.valley@hants.gov.uk www.blackwater-valley.org.uk

5. WILDMOOR HEATH

Berks, Bucks & Oxon Wildlife Trust.
Location: SU 842 627. Between Bracknell and Sandhurst. From Sandhurst shopping area, take the A321 NW towards Wokingham. Turn E at the mini-roundabout on to Crowthorne Road. Continue for about one mile through one set of traffic lights. Car park is on the R at the bottom of the hill.
Access: Open all year. No access to woodland N of Rackstraw Road at Broadmoor Bottom. Please keep dogs on a lead.
Facilities: Car park.
Habitat: Wet and dry lowland heath, bog, mixed woodland and mature Scots pine plantation.
Key birds: *Spring/summer*: Wood Lark, Nightjar, Dartford Warbler, Tree Pipit, Stonechat.
Other notable flora and fauna: Good range of dragonflies including keeled skimmer and ruddy darter, slow worm, adder, grass snake, lizard. Bog plants inc sundews.
Contact: Trust HQ. 01865 775 476. e-mail: info@bbowt.org.uk www.bbowt.org.uk

Buckinghamshire

1. BURNHAM BEECHES NNR

City of London.
Location: SU 950 850. N of Slough and on W side of A355, running between J2 of the M40 and J6 of M4. Entry from A355 via Beeches Road. Also smaller parking areas in Hawthorn Lane and Pumpkin Hill to the S and Park Lane to the W.
Access: Open all year, except Dec 25. Main Lord Mayor's Drive open from 8am-dusk. Beeches Café, public toilets and information point open 10am to 5pm. Motorised buggy available for hire. Network of wheelchair accessible roads and paths.
Facilities: Car parks, toilets, café, visitor information centre. Easy access path network, suitable for wheelchairs, most start at Victory Cross. Coach parking possible, additional coach parking on request.
Public transport: Train: nearest station Slough on the main line from Paddington. Arriva, First and Jason Tours buses 40 and 74 stop at reserve. Call Traveline

on 0870 608 2608.
Habitat: Ancient woodland, streams, pools, heathland, grassland, scrub.
Key birds: *Spring/summer*: Cuckoo, possible Turtle Dove. *Winter*: Siskin, Crossbill, regular large flocks c100 Brambling. Possible Woodcock. *All year*: Mandarin (good population), all three woodpeckers, Sparrowhawk, Marsh Tit, possible Willow Tit, Red Kite and Buzzard.
Other notable flora and fauna: Ancient beech and oak pollards with associated wildlife. Rich array of fungi.
Contact: City of London Corporation, Burnham Beeches Office, Hawthorn Lane, Farnham Common, SL2 3TE . 01753 647 358.
e-mail: burnham.beeches@cityoflondon.gov.uk www.cityoflondon.gov.uk

2. CALVERT JUBILEE

Berks, Bucks & Oxon Wildlife Trust.
Location: SP 849 425. Near Steeple Claydon, NW of Aylesbury, Bucks.

Access: Access by permit (free) only. Apply to Trust who provide map and information with permit. Please keep to network of paths.
Facilities: Two hides, small car park.
Public transport: None.
Habitat: Ex-clay pit, railway and landfill site. Now with deep lake, marginal reedbed and scrub habitat.
Key birds: *Summer*: Nesting Common Tern, Kingfisher, warblers, occasional Nightingale, Lapwing. Passage migrants include Black-tailed Godwit, Greenshank. *Winter*: Bittern, Water Rail, Lesser Black-backed Gull roost. Wigeon. Rarer birds turn up regularly.
Other notable flora and fauna: Rare butterflies, including dingy and grizzled skippers.
Contact: Trust HQ. 01865 775 476.
e-mail: info@bbowt.org.uk www.bbowt.org.uk

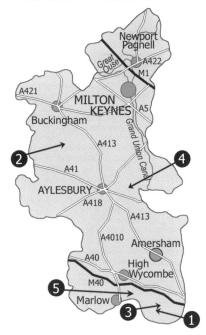

3. CHURCH WOOD RESERVE

RSPB (Midlands Regional Office).
Location: SU 971 872. Reserve lies three miles from J2 of M40 in Hedgerley. Park in village, walk down small track beside pond for approx 200m. Reserve entrance is on L.
Access: Open all year. Not suitable for wheelchair users.
Facilities: Two marked paths with some inclines.
Public transport: None.
Habitat: Mixed woodland.
Key birds: *Spring/summer*: Red Kite, Buzzard, Blackcap, Garden Warbler, Swallow. *Winter*: Redpoll, Siskin. *All year*: Marsh Tit, Willow Tit, Nuthatch, Treecreeper, Great Spotted and Green Woodpeckers.
Other notable flora and fauna: Wood anenome, wood sorrel, bluebell and other woodland plants. Brimstone, comma, white admiral and peacock butterflies. Good range of fungi species.
Contact: RSPB central England Office, 01865 351 163. www.rspb.org.uk/wildlife/reserves

4. COLLEGE LAKE

Berks, Bucks & Oxon Wildlife Trust.
Location: SU 934 140. 2 miles N of Tring on B488, quarter mile N of canal bridge at Bulbourne turn L into gated entrance.
Access: Open Apr-Oct (10am-5pm); Nov-Mar (10am-4pm), closed Mondays. Wheelchair access to hides and disabled toilets.
Facilities: Large car park, coach park, many hides, interpretive buildings. Network of wheelchair-friendly paths, visitor centre, toilets.
Public transport: Tring railway station, 2 miles walk.
Habitat: Deep lake in former chalk pit, shallow pools, wet, chalk and rough grasslands, scrub.
Key birds: *Spring/summer*: Lapwing, Redshank, Little Ringed Plover, Sand Martin, Hobby, Common Tern, Sky Lark. *Winter*: Wildfowl (Wigeon, Shoveler, Teal, Gadwall), waders, inc. Snipe, Peregrine Falcon.
Other notable flora and fauna: Orchids including white helleborines, bee and fragrant orchids. Chalk grassland flowers. Butterflies include small blue and skippers. Good numbers of dragonflies (16 species). Hares.
Contact: The Warden, College Lake, Upper Icknield Way, Bulbourne, Tring, Herts HP23 5QG. 01442 826 774; (M)07711 821 303.
e-mail: info@bbowt.org.uk www.bbowt.org.uk

5. LITTLE MARLOW GRAVEL PITS

Lefarge Redland Aggregates.
Location: SU 880 880. NE of Marlow from J4 of M40. Use permissive path from Coldmoorholm Lane to Little Marlow village. Follow path over a wooden bridge to N end of lake. Permissive path ends just past the cottages where it joins a concrete road to sewage treatment works.
Access: Open all year. Please do not enter the gravel works.
Facilities: Paths.
Public transport: None.
Habitat: Gravel pit, lake, scrub.
Key birds: *Spring*: Passage migrants, Sand Martin, Garganey, Hobby. *Summer*: Reedbed warblers, Kingfisher, wildfowl. Autumn: Passage migrants. *Winter*: Wildfowl, possible Smew, Goldeneye, Yellow-legged Gull, Lapwing, Snipe.
Contact: Ranger Service, Wycombe District Council, Queen Victoria Road, High Wycombe, Buckinghamshire HP11 1BB.

Hampshire

1. BLASHFORD LAKES

Hampshire & Isle of Wight Wildlife Trust in partnership with Wessex Water, Bournemouth and West Hampshire Water and New Forest District Council.

Location: SU 153 080. From Ringwood take A338 for two miles towards Fordingbridge/Salisbury, pass Ivy Lane R and take next R to Moyles Court / Linwood at Ellingham Cross, into Ellingham Drove. The main car park for hides is first L (entrance shared with Hanson works) after 400 yards. For Education Centre turn R opposite (entrance shared with Wessex Water and water-ski club) and straight on through gate and bear R between wooden pillars. Parking is just inside pillars or in front of centre.

Access: A network of permissive paths in the reserve link to New Forest and Avon Valley Long Distance footpaths. These paths and a number of wildlife viewing screens are always open. The six hides and Centre are open daily (9am-4.30pm). The Centre is also used for school and other organised visits, please phone for further details. No dogs allowed. The paths are fully wheelchair accessible and kissing gates are RADAR key-operated to allow passage of disability buggies.

Facilities: Parking, footpaths, six hides, viewing screens, toilets and information including recent sightings board. Coach parking by arrangement. Picnic tables available beside the centre when not being used by booked groups.

Public transport: Bus service on the A338 Ringwood to Salisbury/Fordingbridge road stops just north of Ivy Lane, Ellingham Cross and Ibsley Church.

Habitat: Flooded gravel pits, areas of wet woodland, some of it ancient also dry grassland and lichen heath.

Key birds: *Winter*: Large number of over-wintering wildfowl, inc. Tufted Duck, Pochard, Wigeon, Shoveler, Goosander and internationally important numbers of Gadwall. Also a large gull roost. *Spring/summer*: Breeding birds include Common Tern, Lapwing, Redshank, Oystercatcher, Kingfisher, Garden Warblers are especially common. *Autumn*: Waders on migration including Green and Common Sandpipers and Greenshank, also Hobby, Black Tern and passerines.

Other notable flora and fauna: Dragonflies (23 species recorded) including brown hawker, scarce chaser and large and small red-eyed damselfly. Roe deer are regular, also present badgers, otters, foxes, reptiles include adders and grass snakes.

Contact: Blashford Lakes Centre, Ellingham Drove, Ringwood, Hampshire BH24 3PJ. 01425 472 760. e mail: feedback@hwt.org.uk www.hwt.org.uk

2. FARLINGTON MARSHES

Hampshire & Isle of Wight Wildlife Trust.

Location: SU 685 045. North of Langstone Harbour. Main entrance off roundabout junction A2030/A27.

Access: Open at all times, no charge or permits, but donations welcome. Dogs on leads only. Wheelchair access via RADAR gates. Short slopes up to sea wall. Paths around site are mostly level but the main path running along the sea wall can be uneven in places and muddy in wet weather. Groups — please book to avoid clash of dates.

Facilities: 2.5 mile trail. Information at entrance and shelter. No toilets.

Public transport: By bus: Several bus routes pass along the A2030 (Easter Road), close to the western entrance to the marsh. Contact First bus service on 023 8058 4321. By train: Hilsea station is one mile from reserve. Contact South West Trains on 0845 6000 650.

Habitat: Coastal grazing marsh with pools and reedbed within reserve. Views over intertidal mudflats/saltmarshes of Langstone Harbour.

Key birds: *Summer*: Breeding waders and wildfowl (including Lapwing, Redshank and Shelduck) also breeding Cetti's, Sedge and Reed Warbler, Bearded Tit. *Autumn to spring*: Waders and wildfowl, good numbers of migrating Yellow Wagtail among the cattle. *Winter*: Brent Goose, Wigeon, Pintail etc and waders (Dunlin, Grey Plover etc). On migration wide range of waders including rarities. Reedbeds with Bearded Tit, Water Rail etc, scrub areas attract small migrants (Redstart, Wryneck, warblers etc).

Contact: Mike Allen, Hampshire and Isle of Wight Wildlife Trust, Beechcroft House, Vicarage Lane, Curdridge, Hants SO32 2DP. 01489 774 439. www.hwt.org.uk — go to 'Reserves' and then 'news' for sightings, etc

3. FLEET POND LNR

Hart District Council Service/Fleet Pond Society.

Location: SY 85. Located in Fleet, W of Farnborough. From the B3013, head to Fleet Station. Park in the long-stay car park at Fleet Station. Parking also available in Chestnut Grove and Westover Road. Pond car park off B3013.

Access: Open all year.

Facilities: Some surfaced paths, boardwalks in wet areas.

Public transport: Fleet railway station lies N of site.

Habitat: Lake, marshes, reedbeds, heathland, wet and dry woodland.

Key birds: *Spring/autumn*: Migrant waders incl. Little Ringed Plover, Dunlin, Greenshank, Little Gull, Lesser Spotted Woodpecker, occasional Kittiwake, terns, Wood Lark, Sky Lark, occasional Ring Ouzel, Firecrest, Pied Flycatcher. *Summer*: Hobby, Common Tern, Tree Pipit, occasional Red Kite and Osprey. *Winter*: Bittern, wildfowl, occasional Smew, Snipe, occasional Jack Snipe, Siskin, Redpoll.

194

Other notable flora and fauna: Dragonflies and damselflies in wet areas of marshes and heathlands. Butterflies, roe deer. Plants include ling and bell heather, phragmites reeds.
Contact: Hart District Council, Civic Office,, Harlington Way, Fleet, Hampshire, GU51 4AE. 01252 622 122, e-mail: countryside@hart.gov.uk

4. LANGSTONE HARBOUR

RSPB (South East Region Office).
Location: SU 695 035. Harbour lies E of Portsmouth, one mile S of Havant. Car parks at Broadmarsh (SE of A27/A3(M) junction) and West Hayling LNR (first R on A2030 after Esso garage).
Access: Restricted access to ensure birds not disturbed. Good views from West Hayling LNR, Broadmarsh and Farlington Marshes LNR (qv).
Facilities: Mainline trains all stop at Havant. Local bus service to W Hayling LNR.
Public transport: See Farlington Marshes.
Habitat: Intertidal mud, saltmarsh, shingle islands.
Key birds: *Summer:* Breeding waders and seabirds inc. Mediterranean Gull and Little Tern. *Passage/winter:* Waterfowl, inc. Black-necked Grebes, c5,000 dark-bellied Brent Geese, Shelduck, Shoveler, Goldeneye and Red-breasted Merganser. Waders inc. Oystercatcher, Ringed and Grey Plover, Dunlin, Black and Bar-tailed Godwits and Greenshank. Peregrine, Merlin and Short-eared Owl.
Contact: Chris Cockburn (Warden), RSPB Langstone Harbour, Unit B3, Wren Centre, Emsworth, Hants PO10 7SU. 01243 378 784.
e-mail: chris.cockburn@rspb.org.uk

5. LOWER TEST

Hampshire & Isle of Wight Wildlife Trust.
Location: SU 364 150. From M271 N of Southampton take A36 (Commercial Road) W to Totton. Viewing screens accessed from Compton Road.
Access: Open at all times, guide dogs only. No coach parking facilities. Disabled access limited. Park on Testwood Lane near Salmon Leap pub.
Facilities: One hide and two screens. Hide open 9.30-4.30pm every day, screens open at all times.
Public transport: Totton train station and bus stops within easy walking distance. Tel 01983 827 005 for bus details.
Habitat: Saltmarsh, brackish grassland, wet meadows, reedbed, scrapes, meres, estuary.
Key birds: *Summer:* Breeding Little, Sandwich and Common Terns, Black-headed and Mediterranean Gulls, waders. *Passage/winter:* Waders. *Autumn/winter:* Waders (inc. Black-tailed and Bar-tailed Godwits, Oystercatcher, Ringed and Grey Plover, Dunlin). Wildfowl (inc. Shelduck, Shoveler, Goldeneye, Red-breasted Merganser and c7000 dark-bellied Brent Geese). Black-necked Grebe, Short-eared Owl, Peregrine.

Other notable flora and fauna: Good range of common butterflies. Dragonflies including scarce chaser, emperor and migrant hawker. Plants include early marsh, green winged, southern marsh orchids and green flowered helleborine. Otter, water vole.
Contact: Clare Bishop, Trust HQ, 02380 424 206.
e-mail: clareb@hwt.org.uk www.hwt.org.uk

6. LYMINGTON REEDBEDS

Hampshire & Isle of Wight Wildlife Trust.
Location: SZ 324 965. From Lyndhurst in New Forest take A337 to Lymington. Turn L after railway bridge into Marsh Lane. Park in the lay-by next to allotments. The reserve entrance is on opposite side, to R of the house and over railway crossing. The footpath exits the reserve near the Old Ampress Works, leading to a minor road between the A337 and Boldre.
Access: Open all year. The best viewpoint over the reedbeds is from Bridge Road or from the Undershore leading from the B3054.
Facilities: None.
Public transport: Bus: at either end of the footpath through site, Marsh Lane and on the A337 (route 112). Five minutes walk from train station.
Habitat: One of largest reedbeds on S coast, fringed by alder and willow woodland.
Key birds: One of highest concentrations of Water Rail in the country; resident but most evident in winter. *Spring/summer:* Cetti's Warbler, Bearded Tit, Yellow Wagtail, Swallow, martins, Reed Warbler.

195

Passage: Snipe, ducks. Otters are in the area.
Contact: Michael Boxall, Hampshire and Isle of Wight Wildlife Trust, 01489 774 400.
e-mail: feedback@hwt.org.uk www.hwt.org.uk

7. LYMINGTON-KEYHAVEN NNR

Hampshire County Council.
Location: SZ 315 920. S of Lymington along seawall footpath; car parks at Bath Road, Lymington and at Keyhaven Harbour.
Access: Open all year.
Facilities: None.
Habitat: Coastal marshland and lagoons.
Key birds: *Spring*: Passage waders (inc. Knot, Sanderling, Bar-tailed and Black-tailed Godwits, Whimbrel, Spotted Redshank), Pomarine and Great Skuas. Breeding Oystercatcher, Ringed Plover, Sandwich, Common and Little Terns. *Autumn*: Passage raptors, waders and passerines. *Winter*: Wildfowl (inc. Brent Goose, Wigeon, Pintail, Red-breasted Merganser), waders (inc. Golden Plover), Little Egret, gulls.
Contact: Hampshire County Council, Mottisfont Court, High Street, Winchester, Hants SO23 8ZF.
www3.hants.gov.uk/countryside/lymington-keyhaven

8. MARTIN DOWN

Natural England (Wiltshire Team).
Location: SU 05 19. Nine miles SW of Salisbury. Car park on A354.
Access: Open access, organised groups of 10+ should book in advance. Car park height barrier of 7ft 6 ins. Coaches only by prior arrangement. Hard flat track from A354 car park suitable for wheelchairs.
Facilities: Two car parks, interpretative boards.
Public transport: One bus Salisbury/Blandford. Call 01722 336 855 or visit www.wdbus.co.uk
Habitat: Chalk downland and scub.
Key birds: *Spring/summer*: Grey Partridge, Turtle Dove, warblers, Nightingale. *Winter*: Occasional Merlin, Hen Harrier.
Other notable flora and fauna: Species-rich chalk downland with a variety of orchids. *The Times online* rates Martin Down in its Britain's Best 50 Days Out list.
Contact: South Wiltshire NNR Office, Parsonage Down NNR, Cherry Lodge, Shrewton, Nr Salisbury, Wilts, SP3 4ET 01980 620 485, www.naturalengland.org.uk
e-mail: wiltshire@naturalengland.org.uk

9. TESTWOOD LAKES

Hampshire & Isle of Wight Wildlife Trust
Location: SU 347 155. M271 West J2 towards Totton.

Left at first roundabout, then left onto A36. Left at next roundabout onto Brunel Rd. Entrance on left after ¼ mile.
Access: Car parks open 8am until 4pm in winter and from 8am until 6pm in summer. Surfaced paths around lakes and to hides are relatively flat. Dogs under control allowed in some parts of the reserve but not the conservation and education areas.
Facilities: Two hides and two screens. Hides open 10am-4pm daily. Disabled toilet in the Education Centre.
Public Transport: Totton rail station is 1.5 miles from the reserve. Bluestar and Wilts & Dorset buses stop ¼ mile from entrance. Tel 01983 827 005.
Habitat: Flooded gravel pits, scrapes, wet and dry grasslands, woodland and hedgerows.
Key Birds: *Winter*: Various wildfowl (inc. Tufted Duck, Wigeon, Pochard, Teal, Gadwall, Goosander), Siskin, Hawfinch, Meadow Pipit, Common Sandpiper, Green Sandpiper, Pochard, Redwing, Fieldfare. *Spring*: Shelduck, Sand Martin, Little Ringed Plover, Willow Warbler. *Summer*: Swift, Swallow, Blackcap, Whitethroat. *Autumn*: Wheatear, Yellow Wagtail, Goldfinch.
Other notable flora and fauna: Good range of butterflies. Dragonflies including emperor, scarce chaser, southern and migrant hawker and golden ring.
Contact: Clare Bishop, Trust HQ, 02380 424 206.
e-mail: clareb@hwt.org.uk www.hwt.org.uk

10. TITCHFIELD HAVEN

Hampshire County Council.
Location: SU 535 025. From A27 W of Fareham; public footpath follows derelict canal along W of reserve and road skirts S edge.
Access: Open Wed-Sun all year, plus Bank Hols, except Christmas and Boxing Days.
Facilities: Centre has information desk, toilets, tea room and shop. Guided tours (book in advance). Hides.
Public transport: None.
Habitat: Reedbeds, freshwater scrapes, wet grazing meadows.
Key birds: *Spring/summer*: Bearded Tit, waders (inc. Black-tailed Godwit), wildfowl, Common Tern, breeding Cetti's Warbler, Water Rail. Offshore seabirds include Gannet, Common Scoter, Yellow-legged Gull, Kittiwake and Little Tern. *Winter*: Bittern.
Contact: Barry Duffin, Titchfield Haven Visitor Centre, Cliff Road, Hill Head, Fareham, Hants PO14 3JT. 01329 662 145; Fax 01329 667 113.

Kent

1. BLEAN WOODS NNR

RSPB (South East Region Office).
Location: TR 126 592 (CT2 9DD). From Rough
Common (off A290, 1.5 miles NW of Canterbury).
Access: Open 8am-9pm for cars, open at all times for
visitors on foot. No parking for coaches — please drop
passengers off in Rough Common village. Green Trail
suitable for wheelchair users.
Facilities: Public footpaths and five waymarked trails.
Public transport: No 27 from Canterbury hourly,
stops at entrance (ask for Lovell Road). No 4/4A
every 20 minutes from Canterbury to Whitstable
(ask for Rough Common Road), 500m walk from site.
Stagecoach 0870 243 3711.
Habitat: Mature oak woodland, plus birch, sweet
chestnut, hazel and hornbeam coppice. Grazed and
ungrazed heathland.
Key birds: Good for woodpeckers, warblers and
Nightingale in spring, fairly quiet the rest of the
year. *All year:* Woodpecker (3 species), Nuthatch,
Treecreeper, tits (5 species). *Spring:* Nightingale,
Blackcap, Garden Warbler, Hobby, Nightjar.
Other notable flora and fauna: Badger, dormouse.
Heath fritillary, white admiral, silver-washed
fritillary. Common spotted orchid, wild service.
Contact: Michael Walter, Site Manager, 01227 455
972.

2. BOUGH BEECH RESERVOIR

Kent Wildlife Trust.
Location: TQ 49 64 89. Bough Beech is situated 3.5
miles S of Ide Hill. From Sevenoaks, site is signposted
off B2042.
Access: Confined to holders of permits granted for
recording and study purposes only on application to
the warden. The whole of the reserve may be viewed
from the public road just S of Winkhurst Green (TQ
496 494). Park on roadside (one side only).
Facilities: Toilets and visitor centre open between
Apr-Oct, Wed, Sat, Sun & Bank Holiday Mon (11am-
4.30pm).
Public transport: Rail service to Penshurst Station
(two miles south)
Habitat: Reservoir and adjacent woodland and
farmland.
Key birds: Approx 60 species of birds breed in and
around the reserve annually, with Mallard, Tufted
Duck, Mandarin, Canada Goose, Coot and Great
Crested Grebe notable among the waterfowl. Little
Ringed Plover nest most years. *Autumn:* Especially
good for numbers of waders like Green and Common
Sandpipers and Greenshank. Many rarities have been
recorded. Ospreys recorded most years. *Winter:*
wildfowl numbers are much higher than summer and
include Goldeneye and Goosander.
Other notable flora and fauna: Great crested newt,
toad, dragonflies (black-tailed skimmer, ruddy darter,
emperor, southern aeshna, migrant hawker, red-eyed
damselfly), common lizard, Roesel's bush cricket,
long-winged conehead, dormouse, water shrew,
white admiral butterfly, glow-worm, bats (pipistrelle,
Daubenton, noctule, brown long-eared).
Contact: Dave Hutton, Bough Beech Visitor Centre,
01732 453 880. e-mail: info@kentwildlife.org.uk
www.kentwildlifetrust.org.uk

3. CLIFFE POOLS

RSPB (South East Region Office).
Location: TQ 722 757. On S bank of River Thames,
N of Rochester. Take A289 off the A2 at Strood and
follow B2000 to reserve. See RSPB website for more
detailed directions.
Access: Free admission at all times, but donations
welcome. Group bookings welcome. Monthly guided
walks available. Dogs only on public footpaths.
Facilities: Six viewing points. Public rights of
way encircle reserve and bisect it.
Public transport:
Nearest bus stop
at Six Bells pub in
Cliffe.
Habitat: RAMSAR
site with a mix
of saline lagoons,
freshwater
pools, grassland,
saltmarsh and scrub.
Key birds: Massed
flocks of waders in
winter, plus a wide
range of wildfowl. A
great variety of passage birds
in spring and autumn. Breeding
species include Lapwing, Redshank,
Avocet, Ringed Plover, Shelduck. Also
look out for Nightingale, Hobby and
Turtle Dove.

NATURE RESERVES - SOUTH EAST ENGLAND

Other notable flora and fauna: Good range of insects (rare bumblebees include shrill carder bee, brown-banded carder bee). Butterflies, including marbled white, common blue, Essex skipper and the migrant clouded yellow, plus large range of grasshoppers and bush crickets, including Roesel's bush cricket. Dragonflies include ruddy darters and migrant hawkers.
Contact: Jason Mitchell, RSPB Nature Reserve, Northwood Hill, Bromhey Farm, Eastborough, Cooling, Rochester, Kent ME3 8DS. 01634 222 480.

4. DUNGENESS NATURE RESERVE

RSPB (South East Region Office).
Location: TR 063 196. SE of Lydd.
Access: Open daily (9am-9pm) or sunset when earlier. Visitor centre open (10am-5pm, or 4pm Nov-Feb). Parties over 12 by prior arrangement. Closed Dec 25 & 26.
Facilities: Visitor centre, toilets (including disabled access), seven hides, viewing screen, two nature trails, wheelchair access to visitor centre and six hides. Fully equipped classroom/meeting room. Coach parking available.
Public transport: Limited service. Bus 11 from Ashford stops at reserve entrance on request – one mile walk to visitor centre. Contact reserve for details.
Habitat: Shingle, flooded gravel pits, sallow scrub, reedbed, wet grassland.
Key birds: All year: Bittern, Marsh Harrier, Bearded Tit. Spring: Little Ringed Plover, Wheatear, Yellow Wagtail, Lesser Whitethroat. Autumn: Migrant waders and passerines. Winter: Smew, Goldeneye, Slavonian Grebe, Wigeon, Goosander and Bewick's Swan.
Other notable flora and fauna: Jersey cudweed, Nottingham catchfly, brown hare.
Contact: Christine Hawkins/Bob Gomes, Boulderwall Farm, Dungeness Road, Lydd, Romney Marsh, Kent, TN29 9PN. 01797 320 588,www.rspb.org.uk e-mail: dungeness@rspb.org.uk

5. DUNGENESS BIRD OBSERVATORY

Dungeness Bird Observatory Trust.
Location: TR 085 173. Three miles SE of Lydd. Turn south off Dungeness Road at TR 087 185 and continue to end of road.
Access: Observatory open throughout the year. No wheelchair access.
Facilities: Accommodation available. Bring own sleeping bag/sheets and toiletries. Shared facilities including fully-equipped kitchen. Coach parking available at railway station.
Public transport: Bus service between Rye and Folkestone, numbers 11, 12, 711, 712. Alight at the Pilot Inn, Lydd-on-Sea. Tel: 01227 472 082.
Habitat: Shingle promontory with scrub and gravel pits. RSPB reserve nearby.
Key birds: Breeding birds include Wheatear and Black Redstart and seabirds on RSPB Reserve. Important migration site. Excellent seawatching when weather

conditions are suitable. Power station outfall, 'The Patch' good for gulls and terns.
Other notable flora and fauna: Long Pits are excellent for dragonflies, including small red-eyed damselfly. Moth trapping throughout the year.
Contact: David Walker, Dungeness Bird Observatory, 11 RNSSS, Dungeness, Kent, TN29 9NA. 01797 321 309, e-mail: dungeness.obs@tinyonline.co.uk www.dungenessbirdobs.org.uk

6. ELMLEY MARSHES

RSPB (South East Region Office).
Location: TQ 93 86 80. Isle of Sheppey signposted from A249, one mile beyond old Kingsferry Bridge. Reserve car park is two miles from the main road.
Access: Use old bridge road – access road is one mile from bridge. Open every day (9am-9pm or dusk if earlier) except Tues, Christmas and Boxing days. No charge to RSPB members. Dogs are not allowed on the reserve. Less able may drive closer to the hides.
Facilities: Five hides. Disabled access to Wellmarsh hide. No visitor centre. Toilets located in car park 1.25 miles from hides.
Public transport: Swale Halt nearest railway station on Sittingbourne to Sheerness line. From there it is a three mile walk to reserve.
Habitat: Coastal grazing marsh, ditches and pools alongside the Swale Estuary with extensive intertidal mudflats and saltmarsh.
Key birds: Spring/summer: Breeding waders – Redshank, Lapwing, Avocet, Yellow Wagtail, passage waders, Hobby. Autumn: Passage waders. Winter: Spectacular numbers of wildfowl, especially Wigeon and White-fronted Goose. Waders. Hunting raptors – Peregrine, Merlin, Hen Harrier and Short-eared Owl.
Contact: Gordon Allison, Warden (RSPB North Kent Marshes), Elmley RSPB Reserve, Kingshill Farm, Elmley, Sheerness, Kent ME12 3RW. 01795 665 969.

7. NOR MARSH

RSPB (South East Region Office).
Location: TQ 810 700. One mile NE of Gillingham in the Medway Estuary.
Access: No access as it is an island. It is viewable from Riverside Country Park (B2004) at the Horrid Hill Peninsula, giving overviews of the Medway Estuary saltmarsh and mudflats.
Facilities: None.
Public transport: Buses can be caught to Riverside Country Park. Phone Medway Council for the bus numbers, 01634 727 777.
Habitat: Saltmarsh and mudflats.
Key birds: Winter: Large numbers of wildfowl, including Brent Goose, Pintail, Dunlin and Avocet. Spring and autumn: Look out for Black-tailed Godwits, Whimbrel and Greenshank.
Contact: RSPB North Kent Marshes, 01634 222 480.

8. NORTHWARD HILL

RSPB (South East Region Office).
Location: TQ 781 757. Adjacent to High Halstow, off

198

A228, approx four miles NE of Rochester.

Access: Open all year, free access, trails in public area of wood joining Saxon Shoreway link to grazing marsh. Dogs allowed in public area on leads. Trails often steep and not suitable for wheelchair users.

Facilities: Four trails vary in length from 0.5 to 4km. The Toddler trail is surfaced and suitable for push-chairs. Woodland trail is entirely within the public area of the wood. Heron trail takes in Woodland and Heronry viewpoints. Marshland trail is accessed from new car park at Bromhey Farm and incorporates Marshland and Ernie Hemsley viewpoints. Both car parks signposted from High Halstow village. Toilets at Bromhey Farm or at High Halstow village hall. Information and leaflets in car parks.

Public transport: Buses to village of High Halstow. Contact Arriva buses (01634 283 600) for timetable.

Habitat: Ancient and scrub woodland (approximately 130 acres), grazing marsh (approximately 350 acres).

Key birds: *Spring/summer*: Wood holds UK's largest heronry, with c.130 pairs of Grey Heron and c.120 pairs of Little Egret in 2009, breeding Nightingale, Turtle Dove, scrub warblers and woodpeckers. Marshes — breeding Lapwing, Redshank, Avocet, Marsh Harrier, Shoveler, Pochard. *Winter*: Wigeon, Teal, Shoveler. Passage waders (ie Black-tailed Godwit), raptors, Corn Bunting. Long-eared Owl.

Other notable flora and fauna: Good range of dragonflies over the marsh, white-letter hairstreak butterfly in the woods.

Contact: Jason Mitchell, RSPB North Kent Marshes, 01634 222 480.

9. OARE MARSHES LNR

Kent Wildlife Trust.

Location: TR 01 36 48 (car park). Two miles N of Faversham. From A2 follow signs to Oare and Harty Ferry.

Access: Open at all times. Access along marked paths only. Dogs under strict control to avoid disturbance to birds and livestock.

Facilities: Three hides. Roadside viewpoint of East Hide accessible to wheelchair users. Those with pneumatic tyres can reach seawall path and hide. Small car park, restricted turning space, not suitable for coaches.

Public transport: Bus to Oare Village one mile from reserve. Arriva service (Mon-Sat), Jaycrest (Sun) — call Traveline on 0870 608 2608. Train: Faversham (two miles distance).

Habitat: Grazing marsh, mudflats/estuary.

Key birds: *All year*: Waders and wildfowl. *Winter*: Merlin, Peregrine. Divers, grebes and sea ducks on Swale. *Spring/summer*: Avocet, Garganey, Green, Wood and Curlew Sandpipers, Little Stint, Black-

tailed Godwit, Little Tern, Marsh Harrier.

Contact: Tony Swandale, Kent Wildlife Trust, 01622 662 012. e-mail: info@kentwildlife.org.uk www.kentwildlifetrust.org.uk

10. SANDWICH BAY BIRD OBSERVATORY

Sandwich Bay Bird Observatory Trust.

Location: TR 355 575. 2.5 miles from Sandwich, five miles from Deal. A256 to Sandwich from Dover or Ramsgate. Follow signs to Sandwich Station and then Sandwich Bay.

Access: Open daily. Disabled access.

Facilities: New Field Study Centre. Visitor centre, toilets, refreshments, hostel-type accommodation, plus self-contained flat.

Public transport: Sandwich train station two miles from Observatory.

Habitat: Coastal, dune land, farmland, marsh, two small scrapes.

Key birds: *Spring/autumn passage*: Good variety of migrants and waders, specially Corn Bunting. Annual Golden Oriole. *Winter*: Golden Plover.

Other notable flora and fauna: Sand dune plants such as lady's bedstraw and sand sedge.

Contact: The Secretary, Sandwich Bay Bird Observatory, Guildford Road, Sandwich Bay, Sandwich, Kent, CT13 9PF. 01304 617 341. e-mail: sbbot@talk21.com www.sbbo.co.uk

11. STODMARSH NNR

Natural England (Kent Team).

Location: TR 222 618. Lies alongside River Stour and A28, five miles NE of Canterbury.

Access: Open at all times. Keep to paths. No dogs.

Facilities: Fully accessible toilets are available at the Stodmarsh entrance car park. Five hides (one fully accessible), easy access nature trail, footpaths and information panels. Car park, picnic area and toilets adjoining the Grove Ferry entrance with easily accessible path, viewing mound and two hides.

Public transport: There is a regular Stagecoach bus service from Canterbury to Margate/Ramsgate. Alight at Upstreet for Grove Ferry. Hourly on Sun.

Habitat: Open water, reedbeds, wet meadows, dry meadows, woodland.

Key birds: *Spring/summer*: Breeding Bearded Tit, Cetti's Warbler, Garganey, Reed, Sedge and Willow Warblers, Nightingale. Migrant Black Tern, Hobby, Osprey, Little Egret. *Winter*: Wildfowl, Hen Harrier, Bittern.

Other notable flora and fauna: Nationally rare plants and invertebrates, including shining ram's horn snail.

Contact: David Feast, Natural England, 07767 321 058 (mobile).

London, Greater

1. BEDFONT LAKES COUNTRY PARK

Continental Landscapes Ltd.
Location: TQ 080 728. OS map sheet 176 (west London). 0.5 miles from Ashford, Middx, 0.5 miles S of A30, Clockhouse Roundabout, on B3003 (Clockhouse Lane).
Access: Park open (7.30am-9pm or dusk, whichever is earlier), all days except Christmas Day. Disabled friendly. Dogs on leads. Main nature reserve only open Sun (2pm-4pm). Keyholder membership available.
Facilities: Toilets, information centre, several hides, nature trail, free parking, up-to-date information.
Public transport: Train to Feltham and Ashford. Bus — H26 and 116 from Hounslow.
Habitat: Lakes, reedbed, wildflower meadows, wet woodland, scrub.
Key birds: *Winter:* Water Rail, Bittern, Smew and other wildfowl, Meadow Pipit. *Summer:* Common Tern, Willow, Garden, Reed and Sedge Warblers, Whitethroat, Lesser Whitethroat, hirundines, Hobby, Blackcap, Chiffchaff, Sky Lark. *Passage:* Wheatear, Wood Warbler, Spotted Flycatcher, Ring Ouzel, Redstart, Yellow Wagtail.
Other notable flora and fauna: 140 plant species inc bee and pyramidal orchid. Nathusius pipistrelle bat, emperor dragonfly plus other butterflies and dragonflies.
Contact: James Herd, Ranger, BLCP, Clockhouse Lane, Bedfont, Middx, TW14 8QA. 0845 456 2796. e-mail: bedfont.lakes@continental-landscapes.co.uk

2. CHASE (THE) LNR

London Wildlife Trust.
Location: TQ 515 860. Lies in the Dagenham Corridor, an area of green belt between the London Boroughs of Barking & Dagenham and Havering.
Access: Open throughout the year and at all times. Reserve not suitable for wheelchair access. Eastbrookend Country Park which borders The Chase LNR has surfaced footpaths for wheelchair use.
Facilities: Millennium visitor centre, toilets, ample car parking, Timberland Trail walk.
Public transport: Rail: Dagenham East (District Line) 15 minute walk. Bus: 174 from Romford five minute walk.
Habitat: Shallow wetlands, reedbeds, horse-grazed pasture, scrub and wetland. These harbour an impressive range of animals and plants including the nationally rare black poplar tree. A haven for birds, with approx 190 different species recorded.
Key birds: *Summer:* Breeding Reed Warbler, Lapwing, Water Rail, Lesser Whitethroat and Little Ringed Plover, Kingfisher, Reed Bunting. *Winter:* Significant numbers of Teal, Shoveler, Redwing, Fieldfare and Snipe dominate the scene. *Spring/autumn migration:* Yellow Wagtail, Wheatear, Ruff, Wood Sandpiper, Sand Martin, Ring Ouzel, Black Redstart and Hobby regularly seen.

Other notable flora and fauna: 140 plant species, wasp spider, butterflies and dragonflies.
Contact: Gareth Winn/Tom Clarke, Project Manager/Project Officer, The Millennium Centre, 02085 938 096, e-mail: lwtchase@cix.co.uk
www.wildlifetrust.org.uk/london/

3. WWT LONDON WETLAND CENTRE

The Wildfowl & Wetlands Trust.
Location: TQ 228 770. Less than 1 mile from South Circular (A205) at Roehampton. In London, Zone 2/3, one mile from Hammersmith.
Access: Winter (9.30am-5pm: last admission 4pm), summer (9.30am-6pm: last admission 5pm). Charge for admission. Coach parking by arrangement.
Facilities: Visitor centre, hides, nature trails, discovery centre and children's adventure area, restaurant (hot and cold food), cinema, shop, observatory centre, seven hides (all wheelchair accessible), three interpretative buildings.
Public transport: Train: Barnes. Tube: Hammersmith then bus 283 (comes into centre). Other buses from Hammersmith are 33, 72, 209; from Richmond, 33.
Habitat: Main lake, reedbeds, wader scrape, mudflats, open water lakes, grazing marsh.
Key birds: *Winter:* Nationally important numbers of wintering waterfowl, including Gadwall and Shoveler. Important numbers of wetland breeding birds, including grebes, swans, a range of duck species such as Pochard, plus Lapwing, Little Ringed Plover, Redshank, warblers, Reed Bunting and Bittern.
Other notable flora and fauna: Large population of water voles. Slow worm, grass snake, common lizard. Seven species of bat inc soprano pipistrelle, noctule, Daubenton's and serotine. 17 species of dragonfly and 25 species of butterfly. Notable plants inc cowslip, pyramidal and bee orchids.
Contact: The Receptionist, London Wetland Centre, 020 8409 4400. e-mail: info.london@wwt.org.uk
www.wwt.org.uk

4. SYDENHAM HILL WOOD

London Wildlife Trust.
Location: TQ 335 722. Forest Hill, SE London, SE26, between Forest Hill and Crystal Palace, just off South Circular (A205). Entrances as Crescent Wood Road and Coxs Walk.
Access: Open at all times, no permits required. Some steep slopes, so wheelchair access is difficult.
Facilities: Nature trail, information boards. No toilets.
Public transport: Train stations: Forest Hill (from London Bridge) or Sydenham Hill (from Victoria). Buses 363, 202, 356, 185, 312, 176, P4. Call Transport for London 0207 5657 299 for details.
Habitat: Ancient woodland, reclaimed Victorian gardens, meadow and small pond.
Key birds: Woodland and gardens species all year round. *All year:* All three woodpeckers, Tawny Owl, Kestrel, Sparrowhawk, Goldcrest, Nuthatch, Treecreeper, Stock Dove. *Summer:* Blackcap,

Chiffchaff, Willow Warbler. *Winter*: Fieldfare, Redwing.
Other notable flora and fauna: Five species of bat, including noctule and brown long-eared. Bluebell, wood anemone, dog violet and primrose. Oak and hornbeam. Speckled wood, comma, painted lady and orange-tip butterflies.
Contact: Chantal Brown, London Wildlife Trust, Centre for Wildlife Gardening, 28 Marsden Road, London SE15 4EE. 0207 252 9186.
e-mail: cbrown@wildlondon.org.uk
www.wildlondon.org.uk

Surrey

1. BRENTMOOR HEATH LNR

Surrey Wildlife Trust.
Location: SU 936 612. The reserve runs along the A322 Guildford to Bagshot road, at the intersection with the A319/B311 between Chobham and Camberley. Best access is by Brentmoor Road, which runs W from West End past Donkey Town.
Access: Open all year.
Facilities: Local buses, nos 34, 590 and 591 stop less than half a miles away.
Public transport: None.
Habitat: Heathland, woodland, grassland, ponds.
Key birds: *Spring/summer*: Stonechat, Nightjar, Hobby. *All year*: Usual woodland birds.
Contact: Surrey Wildlife Trust, 01483 795 440.
e-mail: surreywt@cix.co.uk
www.surreywildlifetrust.org.uk

2. FARNHAM HEATH

RSPB (South East Region Office).
Location: SU 859 433. S of Farnham. Take the B3001 south from Farnham. Take the right hand fork, signposted Tilford, immediately past level crossing. Keep to that road. Just outside Tilford village it is signed to the Rural Life Centre. Follow those signs. Entrance is on the right after 0.5 mile.
Access: Reserve open at all times. Car park opens 9.30 am weekdays and 10.30 am weekends. Parking lay-bys on adjacent roads outside those hours.

Rural Life Centre open Wed-Fri and Sundays all year. Open on Saturdays April-September. Tea room opens at 11 am.
Facilities: Large grass car park, shared with Rural Life Centre. No height barrier, but gates may be locked outside opening hours. No bike racks. Toilets (including disabled), picnic area, refreshments. Group bookings accepted, guided walks available. Good for walking, pushchair friendly.
Public transport: Bus route is number 19 (Farnham to Hindhead service). Nearest stop is in Millbridge village, outside entrance to Pierrepont House. Reserve is a mile away, along Reeds Road (follow signs to the Rural Life Centre).
Habitat: Heathland and pine woodland.
Key birds: *Spring*: Blackcap, Tree Pipit, Woodcock, Wood Lark. *Summer*: Woodcock and Nightjar, woodland birds, including Stock Dove and Green and Great Spotted Woodpeckers. *Winter*: Crossbills in the pine woods, winter finches, including Brambling around the feeders, winter thrushes.
Other notable flora and fauna: Fungi — more than 150 species. Bats in summer.
Contact: Mike Coates, c/o The Rural Life Centre, Reeds Road, Tilford, Surrey GU10 2DL. 01252 795 632.

3. FRENSHAM COMMON AND COUNTRY PARK

Waverley BC and National Trust .
Location: SU 855 405. Common lies on either side of A287 between Farnham and Hindhead.
Access: Open at all times. Car park (locked 9pm-9am). Keep to paths.
Facilities: Information rooms, toilets and refreshment kiosk at Great Pond.
Public transport: Call Trust for advice.
Habitat: Dry and humid heath, woodland, two large ponds, reedbeds.
Key birds: *Summer*: Dartford Warbler, Wood Lark, Hobby, Nightjar, Stonechat. *Winter*: Wildfowl (inc. occasional Smew), Bittern, Great Grey Shrike.
Other notable flora and fauna: Tiger beetle, purple hairstreak and silver-studded blue butterflies, sand lizard, smooth snake.
Contact: Steve Webster, Rangers Office, Bacon Lane, Churt, Surrey, GU10 2QB. 01252 792 416.

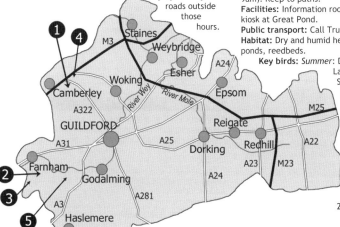

4. LIGHTWATER COUNTRY PARK

Surreyheath Council
Location: SU 921 622. From J3 of M3, take the A322 and follow brown Country Park signs. From the Guildford Road in Lightwater, turn into The Avenue. Entrance to the park is at the bottom of the road.
Access: Open all year, dawn-dusk.
Facilities: Car park, toilets, waymarked trails with leaflets available.
Public transport: Train: Bagshot two miles. SW Trains 0845 6000 650. Arriva Bus: No 34. 01483 306 397.
Habitat: Heathland, woodland, three ponds and meadows.
Key birds: *All year*: All three woodpeckers, Goldcrest in woods, Coot, Moorhen, Grey Heron and Kingfisher on ponds. *Summer*: Nightjar, Willow Warbler, Chiffchaff, Blackcap, Whitethroat. *Winter*: Fieldfare, Redwing, Siskin.
Other notable flora and fauna: Flora includes ox-eye daisies, knapweed and common spotted orchid in meadow, three heathers and two gorse species on heath. Wood ant nests in woodlands. Good range of dragonflies and butterflies.
Contact: Surreyheath Ranger Service, Lightwater Country Park, The Avenue, Lightwater, Surrey, GU18 5RG. 01276 479 582. www.surreyheath.gov.uk
e-mail: rangers@surreyheath.gov.uk

5. THURSLEY COMMON

Natural England (Sussex and Surrey Team).
Location: SU 900 417. From Guildford, take A3 SW to B3001 (Elstead/Churt road). Use the Moat car park, S of Elstead village.
Access: Open access. Parties must obtain prior permission.
Facilities: Boardwalk in wetter areas.
Public transport: None.
Habitat: Wet and dry heathland, woodland, bog.
Key birds: *Winter*: Hen Harrier and Great Grey Shrike. *Summer*: Hobby, Wood Lark, Dartford Warbler, Stonechat, Curlew, Snipe, Nightjar.
Other notable flora and fauna: Large populations of silver-studded blue, grayling and purple emperor butterflies can be seen here, alongside 26 recorded dragonfly species. Sandier sites on the reserve provide homes for many species of solitary bees and wasps. Damp areas support carnivorous plants such as sundew and bladderwort. Bog asphodel and marsh orchid may also be seen.
Contact: Simon Nobes, Natural England, The Barn, Heathhall Farm, Bowlhead Green, Godalming, Surrey GU8 6NW. 01483 307 703.
e-mail: enquiries.southeast@naturalengland.org.uk
www.naturalengland.org.uk

Sussex, East

1. CASTLE WATER, RYE HARBOUR

Sussex Wildlife Trust.
Location: TQ 942 189. Reserve is one mile SE of Rye along Harbour Road.
Access: Open at all times, entry is free. Information centre at Limekiln Cottage open every day 10am-4pm. The site is quite flat with some wheelchair access to all four hides, although there are stiles where the sheep are grazing the fields.
Facilities: Information centre, large car park at Rye Harbour with nearby toilets.
Habitat: Intertidal, saltmarsh, marsh, drainage ditches, shingle ridges, pits, sand, scrub, woodland.
Key birds: Many birds occur here in nationally important numbers, such as Shoveler and Sanderling in the winter and breeding Little Tern and Mediterranean Gull. Nesting Black-headed Gull colony, Common and Sandwich Terns and a good range of waders and ducks. Barn and Short-eared Owls.
Other notable flora and fauna: The saltmarsh supports such unusual plants as sea-heath and marsh mallow, and even highly specialised insects including the star-wort moth and saltmarsh bee.
Contact: Sussex Wildlife Trust, Woods Mill, Henfield, West Sussex, BN5 9SD. 01273 492 630.
e-mail: enquiries@sussexwt.org.uk
www.sussexwt.org.uk

2. ERIDGE ROCKS RESERVE

Sussex Wildlife Trust.
Location: Located at Eridge Green 4 miles S of Tunbridge Wells. Car park at TQ 555 355. From A26, turn into Warren Farm Lane, next to a church and small printing works.
Access: Open all year.
Facilities: Car park.
Public transport: Bus stop on A26. Call Traveline on 0871 200 2223. Nearest railway station at Eridge (one mile).
Habitat: Sandstone rock outcrop, mixed woodland.
Key birds: *All year*: Range of common woodland birds. *Spring/summer*: Warblers.
Other notable flora and fauna: Mosses and liverworts on the rocks. Good for general woodland butterflies, inc white admiral.
Contact: Trust HQ, 01273 492 630.
e-mail: enquiries@sussexwt.org.uk

3. FORE WOOD

RSPB (South East Region Office).
Location: TQ 758 123. From the A2100 (Battle/Hastings) take lane to Crowhurst at Crowhurst Park Caravan Park. Park at Crowhurst village hall and walk up Forewood Lane for 500 yards. Look for the finger post on L and follow the public footpath across farmland to reserve entrance.
Access: Open all year. No disabled facilities. No dogs. No coaches.
Facilities: Two nature trails.

NATURE RESERVES - SOUTH EAST ENGLAND

Public transport: Station at Crowhurst, about 0.5 mile walk. Charing Cross/Hastings line. No buses within one mile.

Habitat: Semi-natural ancient woodland.

Key birds: A wide range of woodland birds. *Spring*: Chiffchaff, Greater Spotted Woodpecker, Nuthatch, Treecreeper. *Summer*: Blackcap, Bullfinch, Mistle Thrush, Green Woodpecker. *Autumn*: Goldcrest, Jay, Marsh Tit. *Winter*: Fieldfare, Rook, Redwing.

Other notable flora and fauna: Rare ferns, bluebells, wood anemonies, purple orchid. Butterflies including silver-washed fritillary and white admiral.

Contact: Martin Allison, RSPB Broadwater Warren, Unit 10, Sham Farm Business Units, Eridge Green, Tunbridge Wells, Kent TN3 9JA.

4. LULLINGTON HEATH

Natural England (Sussex and Surrey Team).

Location: TQ 525 026. W of Eastbourne, between Jevington and Litlington, on northern edge of Friston Forest.

Access: Via footpaths and bridleways. Site open for access on foot as defined by CROW Act 2000.

Facilities: None. Nearest toilets/refreshments at pubs in Jevington, Litlington or Seven Sisters CP, 2km to S.

Public transport: Nearest bus stop is Seven Sisters Country Park. Phone Brighton and Hove services on 01273 886 200 or visit: www.buses.co.uk/bustimes/

Habitat: Grazed chalk downland and heath, with mixed scrub and gorse.

Key birds: *Summer*: Breeding Nightingale, Turtle Dove, Nightjar and diverse range of grassland/scrub-nesting species.Passage migrants include Wheatear, Redstart, Ring Ouzel. *Winter*: Raptors (inc. Hen Harrier), Woodcock.

Other notable flora and fauna: Bell heather, ling and gorse on chalk heath; orchid species in grassland.

Contact: Senior Reserve Manager, East Sussex NNRs, Natural England, 01273 476 595; e-mail sussex.surrey@natural-england.org.uk; www.natural-england.org.uk

5. PEVENSEY LEVELS

Natural England (Sussex and Surrey Team).

Location: TQ 665 054. A small reserve of 12 fields, within the 3,500 ha SSSI/Ramsar site of Pevensey Levels. NE of Eastbourne. S of A259, one mile along minor road from Pevensey E towards Norman's Bay.

Access: Please view from road to avoid disturbance to summer nesting birds and sheltering flocks in winter. Access

on foot allowed at Rockhouse Bank (TQ 675 057) — panoramic view of whole reserve.

Facilities: None. Nearest toilets at Star Inn (TQ 687 062) or petrol station (TQ 652 052).

Public transport: Nearest railway stations: Pevensey Bay or Cooden Beach. Eastbourne buses to Pevensey Bay — call 01323 416416.

Habitat: Freshwater grazing marsh with extensive ditch system, subject to flooding.

Key birds: *Summer*: Breeding Reed and Sedge Warblers, Yellow Wagtail, Snipe, Redshank, Lapwing. Raptors include Peregrine and Hobby. Passage migrants include Whimbrel, Curlew, Brent Geese. *Winter*: Flocks of wildfowl and waders, Short-eared Owl, Merlin and other raptors.

Other notable flora and fauna: Variable damselfly, many rare snails and other molluscs, the most important site in the UK for fen raft spider. Unusual wetland plants.

Contact: Site Manager, East Sussex NNRs, Natural England, 01273 476 595; e-mail sussex.surrey@natural-england.org.uk; www.natural-england.org.uk

6. RYE HARBOUR

Rye Harbour LNR Management Committee.

Location: TQ 941 188. One mile from Rye off A259 signed Rye Harbour. From J10 of M20 take A2070 until it joins A259.

Access: Open at all times by footpaths. Organised groups please book.

Facilities: Car park in Rye Harbour village. Information kiosk in car park. Shop, two pubs, toilets and disabled facilities near car park, four hides (wheelchair access), information centre open most days (10am-4pm) by volunteers.

Public transport: Train (08457 484 950), bus (0870 608 2608), tourist information (tel: 01797 226 696).

Habitat: Sea, sand, shingle, pits and grassland.

Key birds: *Spring*: Passage waders, especially roosting Whimbrel. *Summer*: Turtle Dove, terns (3 species), waders (7 species), gulls (6 species), Garganey, Shoveler, Cetti's Warbler, Bearded Tit. *Winter*: Wildfowl, Water Rail, Bittern, Smew.

Other notable flora and fauna: Good shingle flora including sea kale, sea pea, least lettuce and stinging hawksbeard. Excellent range of dragonflies including breeding red-veined

203

darter and scarce emerald damselfly.
Contact: Barry Yates, (Manager), 2 Watch Cottages, Winchelsea, East Sussex, TN36 4LU. 01797 223 862.
e-mail: rhnr.office@eastsussex.gov.uk

www.wildrye.info
See also www.rxwildlife.org.uk for latest sightings in area.

Sussex, West

1. ARUNDEL

The Wildfowl and Wetlands Trust.
Location: TQ 020 081. Clearly signposted from Arundel, just N of A27.
Access: Summer (9.30am-5.30pm) winter (9.30am-4.30pm). Closed Christmas Day. Approx 1.5 miles of level footpaths, suitable for wheelchairs. No dogs except guide dogs. Admission charges for non-WWT members.
Facilities: Visitor centre, restaurant, shop, hides, picnic area, seasonal nature trails. Corporate hire facilities.
Public transport: Arundel station, 15-20 minute walk. Tel: 01903 882 131.
Habitat: Lakes, wader scrapes, reedbed.
Key birds: *Summer*: Nesting Redshank, Lapwing, Oystercatcher, Common Tern, Sedge, Reed and Cetti's Warblers, Peregrine, Hobby. *Winter*: Teal, Wigeon, Reed Bunting, Water Rail, Cetti's Warbler and occasionally roosting Bewick's Swan.
Contact: James Sharpe, Mill Road, Arundel, West Sussex, BN18 9PB. 01903 883 355, www.wwt.org.uk
e-mail: info.arundel@wwt.org.uk

2. PAGHAM HARBOUR

West Sussex County Council.
Location: SZ 857 966. Five miles S of Chichester on B2145 towards Selsey.
Access: Open at all times, dogs must be on leads, disabled trail with accessible hide. All groups and coach parties must book in advance.
Facilities: Visitor centre open at weekends (10am-4pm), toilets (including disabled), three hides, one nature trail.
Public transport: Bus stop by visitor centre.
Habitat: Intertidal saltmarsh, shingle beaches, lagoons and farmland.
Key birds: *Spring*: Passage migrants. *Autumn*: Passage waders, other migrants. *Winter*: Brent Goose, Slavonian Grebe, wildfowl. *All year*: Little Egret.
Other notable flora and fauna: Wide range of grasses, butterflies and dragonflies.
Contact: Kathryn Hampson, Pagham Harbour LNR, Selsey Road, Sidlesham, Chichester, West Sussex, PO20 7NE. 01243 641 508.
e-mail: pagham.nr@westsussex.gov.uk

3. PULBOROUGH BROOKS

RSPB (South East Region Office).
Location: TQ 054 170. Signposted on A283 between Pulborough (via A29) and Storrington (via A24). Two miles SE of Pulborough.

Access: Open daily. Visitor centre open 9.30am-5pm (tea-room 4.30pm), closed Christmas Day and Boxing Day. Nature trail and hides (9am-9pm or sunset), closed Christmas Day. Admission fee for nature trail (free to RSPB members). No dogs. All four hides accessible to wheelchair users, though strong helper is needed.
Facilities: Visitor centre (incl RSPB shop, tea room with terrace, displays, toilets). Nature trail, four hides and additional viewpoints. Large car park including coach area. Play and picnic areas. An electric buggy is available for free hire, for use on trail.
Public transport: Two miles from Pulborough train station. Connecting bus service regularly passes reserve entrance (not Sun). Compass Travel (01903 690 025). Cycle stands.
Habitat: Lowland wet grassland (wet meadows and ditches). Hedgerows and woodland.
Key birds: *Winter*: Wintering waterbirds, Bewick's Swan. *Spring*: Breeding wading birds and songbirds (incl Lapwing and Nightingale). *Autumn*: Passage wading birds, Redstart, Whinchat.
Other notable flora and fauna: Good range of butterflies and dragonflies.
Contact: The Administrator, Pulborough Brooks Nature Reserve, Upperton's Barn, Wiggonholt, Pulborough RH20 2EL. 01798 875 851.
e-mail: pulborough.brooks@rspb.org.uk

4. THORNEY/PILSEY

RSPB (South East Region Office).
Location: SW of Chichester. Park in Emsworth and walk over sea walls to view both Thorney and Pilsey islands.
Access: No vehicle access to Thorney Island, viewing from footpaths only. Pilsey Island can also be viewed from coastal path (the Sussex Border Path) that runs around the Thorney Island MoD base. Long, exposed walk.
Facilities: Footpath.
Public transport: None.
Habitat: Intertidal sandflats and mudflats, fore dunes and yellow dunes, bare and vegetated shingle and saltmarsh.
Key birds: The reserve, together with the adjacent area of Pilsey Sand, forms one of the most important pre-roost and roost site for passage and wintering waders in the area.
Contact: Tim callaway, RSPB Pulborough Brooks, Wiggonholt, Pulborough, West Sussex RH20 2EL. 01798 875 851.

5. WARNHAM LNR

Horsham District Council.
Location: TQ 167 324. One mile from Horsham town

NATURE RESERVES - SOUTH EAST ENGLAND

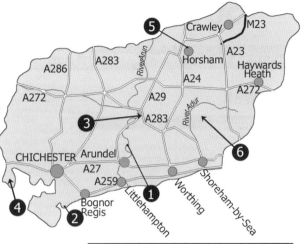

centre, just off A24 'Robin Hood' roundabout on B2237.

Access: Open every day, all year, including bank holidays (10am-6pm or dusk if earlier). Day permits: Adults £1, children under 16 free. Annual permits also available. No dogs or cycling allowed. Good wheelchair access over most of the Reserve.

Facilities: Visitor centre and café open every day except Christmas Day and Boxing Day (10am-5.30pm). Also new stag beetle loggery. Ample car park – coaches by request. Toilets (including disabled), two hides, reserve leaflets, millpond nature trail, bird feeding station, boardwalks, benches and hardstanding paths.

Public transport: From Horsham Railway Station it is a mile walk along Hurst Road, with a R turn onto Warnham Road. Buses from 'CarFax' in Horsham Centre stop within 150 yards of the reserve. Travel line, 0870 608 2608.

Habitat: 17 acre millpond, reedbeds, marsh, meadow and woodland (deciduous and coniferous).

Key birds: *Summer:* Common Tern, Kingfisher, woodpeckers, Mandarin Duck, Marsh Tit, Goldcrest, hirundines, Hobby, warblers. *Winter:* Cormorant, gulls, Little Grebe, Water Rail, Brambling, Siskin, Lesser Redpoll, thrushes and wildfowl. *Passage:* Waders, pipits, terns and hirundines.

Other notable flora and fauna: Extensive invertebrate interest, including 33 species of butterfly and 25 species of dragonfly. Mammals including harvest mouse, water vole and badger. More than 450 species of plant, including broad-leaved helleborine and common spotted orchid.

Contact: Sam Bayley, Countryside Warden, Leisure Services, Park House Lodge, North Street, Horsham, W Sussex, RH12 1RL. 01403 256 890.
e-mail: sam.bayley@horsham.gov.uk
www.visithorsham.co.uk www.market-towns.info

6. WOODS MILL

Sussex Wildlife Trust.

Location: TQ 218 138. Located NW of Brighton, one mile S of Henfield on A2037.

Access: Open every day except Christmas week. All-weather surface nature trail suitable for wheelchairs. HQ of Sussex Wildlife Trust.

Facilities: Toilets (including disabled), nature trail, car parking and parking for two coaches.

Public transport: Bus route 100 stops outside. Compass Travel 01903 690 025.

Habitat: Wetland, woodland and meadow habitats.

Key birds: General woodland birds and Kingfisher all year. *Summer:* Warblers (Reed and Garden Warblers, Blackcap, Whitethroat, Lesser Whitethroat) and Nightingales.

Other notable flora and fauna: Dragon and damselflies including beautiful demoiselle, red and ruddy darter and the rare scarce chaser. Wide range of water, woodland and meadow plants. Spring flowers include bluebells, wood anemones and common spotted orchids.

Contact: Woods Mill, 01273 492 630.
e-mail: enquiries@sussexwt.co.uk

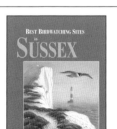

South West England

Cornwall, Devon, Dorset, Somerset, Wiltshire

Cornwall

1. BRENEY COMMON

Cornwall Wildlife Trust.
Location: SX 054 610. 2.5 miles S of Bodmin. Take minor road off A390 one mile W of Lostwithiel to Lowertown. For Breney Common entrance, turn R at Reperry Cross, then L fork to Trebell Green and on towards Gurtla. The entrance track is on the left in Gurtla, after the Methodist church, opposite The Barn.
Access: Open at all times but please keep to paths. Disabled access from small car park at Breney.
Facilities: Wilderness trail. Boardwalk sections the only suitable surface for wheelchairs.
Public transport: None.
Habitat: Huge site (536 acres) includes wetland, grassland, heath and scrub.
Key birds: Willow Tit, Nightjar, Tree Pipit, Sparrowhawk, Lesser Whitethroat, Curlew.
Other notable flora and fauna: Royal fern, sundews and other bog plants. Butterflies (inc marsh and small pearl-bordered fritillaries, silver-studded blue).
Contact: Sean O'Hea, Cornwall Wildlife Trust, 01872 273 939. e-mail: info@cornwt.demon.co.uk www.cornwallwildlifetrust.org.uk

2. CROWDY RESERVOIR

South West Lakes Trust.
Location: Follow signs from A39 at Camelford to Davidstow Airfield and pick up signs to reservoir. On edge of forestry plantation, park in pull-in spot near cattle grid. A track leads to a hide via stiles. Main car park located a little further down the lane.
Access: Open all year.
Facilities: Hide. **Public transport:** None.
Habitat: Reservoir, bog, moorland, forestry.
Key birds: *Spring*: Passage migrants, inc Wheatear, Whimbrel, Ruff. *Summer*: Black-headed Gull, Reed and Sedge Warblers, returning waders. *Autumn*: Waders, raptors possible inc Peregrine, Goshawk, Merlin. *Winter*: Wild swans, wildfowl, possible Smew. Golden Plover, Woodcock, Fieldfare, Redwing.
Other notable flora: Mire floral communities.
Contact: South West Lakes Trust, 01566 771 930. www.swlakestrust.org.uk

3. HAYLE ESTUARY

RSPB (South West England Office).
Location: SW 550 370. In town of Hayle. Follow signs to Hayle from A30. Take B3301 through Hayle past the Tempest factory, turn L into Chenells Rd and R into Ryans Field.
Access: Open at all times. No permits required. No admission charges. Not suitable for wheelchair users. Dogs on leads please. Sorry – no coaches.
Facilities: Eric Grace Memorial Hide at Ryan's Field has parking and viewing, but birds here only at high tide. Nearest toilets in town of Hayle. No visitor centre but information board at hide.
Public transport: Buses and trains at Hayle. Call 0871 200 2233 for details.
Habitat: Intertidal mudflats, saltmarsh, lagoon and islands, sandy beaches and sand dunes.
Key birds: *Winter*: Wildfowl, gulls, Kingfisher, Great Northern Diver and waders. *Spring/summer*: Migrant waders, breeding Shelduck. *Autumn*: Rare waders, often from N America. Terns, gulls.
Contact: RSPB South West Regional Office, 01392 432 691; www.rspb.org.uk

4. MARAZION MARSH

RSPB (South West England Office).
Location: SW 510 315. Reserve is one mile E of Penzance, 500 yards W of Marazion. Entrance off seafront road near Marazion.
Access: Open at all times. No permits required. No admission charges. Not suitable for wheelchair users. Dogs on leads please. Sorry – no coaches.
Facilities: No toilets or visitor centre. Nearest toilets in Marazion and seafront car park.
Public transport: First Group Nos 2, 7 and 8, plus Sunset Bay2Bay service 340 from

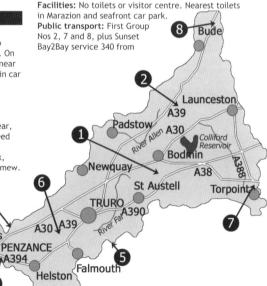

Penzance. Call 0871 200 2233 for details.
Habitat: Wet reedbed, willow carr.
Key birds: *Winter*: Wildfowl, Snipe, occasional
Bittern. *Spring/summer*: Breeding Reed, Sedge and
Cetti's Warblers, herons, swans. *Autumn*: Large
roost of swallows and martins in reedbeds, migrant
warblers and Water Rail.
Other notable flora and fauna: Up to 22 species of
dragonfly, plus 500 species of vascular plants, inc
lawn camomile and yellow flag.
Contact: RSPB South West Regional Office, 01392 432
691; www.rspb.org.uk

5. NARE HEAD

National Trust.
Location: Approx ten miles SE of Truro. from A390
head S on A307 to two miles S of Tregony just past
the garage. Follow signs to Veryan then L signposted
to Carne. Go straight over at crossroad, following
Carne and Pendower. Turn L on a bend following NT
signs for Nare Head. Bearing R, cross over a cattle
grid to the car park. From the garage, Nare Head is
about four miles.
Access: Open all year.
Facilities: Car park.
Public transport: None.
Habitat: Headland.
Key birds: *Spring/summer*: Razorbill, Guillemot,
Sandwich, Common and Arctic Terns, possible
Whimbrel, Fulmar. *Winter*: Black-throated and
Great Northern Divers. Red-throated Diver possible.
Common Scoter, Velvet Scoter, Slavonian, Black-
necked and Red-necked Grebes.
Contact: National Trust, Lanhydrock House,
Lanhydrock, Cornwall, PL30 4DE. 01208 432 691.

6. STITHIANS RESERVOIR

South West Lakes Trust.
Location: SS 715 365. From B3297 S of Redruth.
Access: Good viewing from causeway.
Facilities: New hide near main centre open to all.
Public transport: None.
Habitat: Open water, marshland.
Key birds: Country's best open water site for winter
wildfowl. Good for waders such as Common, Green
and Wood Sandpipers, plus rarities, eg. Pectoral and
Semipalmated Sandpipers, Lesser Yellowlegs.
Contact: South West Lakes Trust, Centre Manager,
01209 860 301. www.swlakestrust.org.uk

7. TAMAR ESTUARY

Cornwall Wildlife Trust.
Location: SX 434 631 (Northern Boundary). SX 421 604
(Southern Boundary). From Plymouth head W on A38.
Access parking at Cargreen and Landulph from minor
roads off A388.
Access: Open at all times. Access bird hides from
China Fleet Club car park, Saltash. Follow path
alongside golf course — do not walk on course itself.
Combination number for hide locks available at club
reception.
Facilities: Two hides on foreshore, first (0.25 miles
from car park) overlooks estuary, second (0.5 miles)
has excellent views across Kingsmill Lake.
Public transport: None.
Habitat: Tidal mudflat with some saltmarsh.
Key birds: *Winter*: Avocet, Snipe, Black-tailed
Godwit, Redshank, Dunlin, Curlew, Whimbrel,
Spotted Redshank, Green Sandpiper, Golden Plover,
Kingfisher.
Contact: Cornwall Wildlife Trust, St Dominick,
Cornwall PL12 6TA. 01579 351 155.
e-mail: peter@cornwt.demon.co.uk
www.cornwallwildlifetrust.org.uk

8.TAMAR LAKES

South West Lakes Trust
Location: SS 295 115. Follow brown tourist signs from
Holsworthy or Kilkhampton.
Access: Open all year. Limited wheelchair access.
Facilities: Bird hides on Upper and Lower lakes. Café
(limited opening) at Upper Tamar. Toilets at Upper
open all year, those at Lower only open in summer.
Public transport: None.
Habitat: Two lfreshwater lakes, plus swamp, scrub
and grassland.
Key birds: *All year*: Great Crested Grebe, Black-
headed Gull, Kingfisher, Willow Tit, Reed Bunting.
Spring: Black Tern. *Summer*: Breeding Sedge, Reed
and Willow Warblers and House Martin.*Winter*:
Moderate numbers of wildfowl, inc Wigeon and Teal
and gulls.
Other notable flora and fauna: Badger, roe deer,
otter, southern marsh orchid, wood white butterfly,
grass snake.
Contact: Mark Green, Conservation Officer, Upper
Tamar Lakes Visitor Centre, Kilkhampton, Bude,
Cornwall EX23 9SA. 01288 321 262.

For a comprehensive survey of bird reserves in the county
and The Isles of Scilly, see the latest, highly acclaimed *Best
Birdwatching Sites in Cornwall and Scilly* book from Buckingham
Press. See page 114 for more details.

Devon

1. AYLESBEARE COMMON

RSPB (South West England Office).
Location: SY 058 897. Five miles E of J30 of M5 at Exeter, 0.5 miles past Halfway Inn on B3052. Turn R to Hawkerland, car park is on L. The reserve is on the opposite side of the main road.
Access: Open all year. One track suitable for wheelchairs and pushchairs.
Facilities: Car park, picnic area, group bookings, guided walks and special events. Disabled access via metalled track to private farm.
Public transport: Buses (Exeter to Sidmouth, 52a, 52b). Request stop at Joneys Cross (reserve entrance). Tel: 01392 427 711.
Habitat: Heathland, wood fringes, streams and ponds.
Key birds: *Spring/summer*: Hobby, Nightjar, Tree Pipit, Stonechat. *All year*: Dartford Warbler, Buzzard, Yellowhammer. *Winter*: Possible Hen Harrier.
Other notable flora and fauna: Good range of dragonflies and butterflies.
Contact: Toby Taylor, Hawkerland Brake Barn, Exmouth Road, Aylesbeare, Nr Exeter, Devon, Nr Exeter, Devon, EX5 2JS. 01395 233 655. www.rspb.org.uk/reserves/guide/a/ aylesbearecommon/

2. BOVEY HEATHFIELD

Devon Wildlife Trust.
Location: SX 824 765. On the outskirts of Bovey Tracey on SE edge of Dartmoor. From A382 Bovey Straight take Battle Road into Heathfield Industrial estate. Turn L into Cavalier Road, then Dragoon Close - the reserve is along a gravel path.
Access: Open all year. Dogs allowed on leads. Please keep to paths. Rough paths not suitable for wheelchairs. No coach access.
Facilities: Information hut open when warden is on site.
Public transport: Buses to Battle Road, Heathfield.
Habitat: Heathland.
Key birds: Breeding Nightjar, Tree Pipit, Stonechat and Dartford Warbler, plus commoner species.
Other notable flora and fauna: Heathers, wet and dry heathland plants, more than 60 endangered insect species, plus grayling and green hairstreak butterflies, slow worm, adder.
Contact: Devon Wildlife Trust, Cricklepit Mill, Commercial Road, Exeter, EX1 4AB. 01392 279 244. e-mail: devonwt@cix.co.uk

3. BOWLING GREEN MARSH

RSPB (South West England Office).
Location: SX 972 876. On the E side of River Exe, four miles SE of Exeter, 0.5 miles SE of Topsham.
Access: Open at all times. Please park at the public car parks in Topsham, not in the lane by the reserve.
Facilities: RSPB shop at Darts Farm, 1.5km from reserve, east of Topsham across River Clyst.

Public transport: Exeter to Exmouth railway has regular (every 30 mins) service to Topsham station (half a mile from reserve). Stagecoach Devon 57 bus has frequent service (Mon-Sat every 12 mins, Sun every half-hour) from Exeter to Topsham. Traveline 0871 200 2233.
Habitat: Coastal grassland, open water/marsh.
Key birds: *Winter*: Wigeon, Shoveler, Teal, Black-tailed Godwit, Curlew, Golden Plover. *Spring*: Shelduck, passage waders, Whimbrel, passage Garganey and Yellow Wagtail. *Summer*: Gull/tern roosts, high tide wader roosts contain many passage birds. *Autumn*: Wildfowl, Peregrine, wader roosts.
Other notable flora and fauna: Hairy dragonfly, wasp spider.
Contact: RSPB, Darts Farm Shopping Village, Clyst St. George, Exeter EX3 0QH. 01392 879 438 or the reserve on 01392 824 614, www.rspb.org.uk

4. BURRATOR RESERVOIR

South West Lakes Trust.
Location: SX 551 681. Lies 10 miles NE of Plymouth, off A386 (Tavistock road). At Yelverton take B3212 towards Princeton. Turn R at Burrator Inn and follow signs to reservoir.
Access: Open all year. Numerous free parking areas around reservoir. Main route is suitable for disabled but is also used by motorists and cyclists. There are about 25 stiles around the reservoir but not on main route.
Facilities: Toilets (including disabled at Burrator Lodge). Snacks and ice-creams available during summer.
Public transport: Bus: daily from Plymouth to Dousland (a short walk from the reservoir). No 82 Western National or No 48 (Sun). Tel: 01752 402 060. Train: nearest station is Plymouth. Tel: 08457 484 950.
Habitat: Pine forests, wooded streams, open moorland scrub.
Key birds: *Winter*: Goosander, Dipper, Grey Wagtail, Green Sandpiper, Brambling, Crossbill, Siskin, Redpoll. *All year*: All three woodpeckers, Buzzard, Sparrowhawk, Kestrel, Barn Owl, Tree Sparrow.
Other notable flora and fauna: Marsh fritillary butterfly, dragonflies and damselflies, particularly in the arboretum, bats (various species), otter.
Contact: South West Lakes Trust, Lidn Park, Quarry Crescent, Pennygillam Industrial Estate, Launceston, Cornwall PL15 7PF. 01566 771 930. www.swlakestrust.org.uk

5. DART VALLEY

Devon Wildlife Trust.
Location: SX 680 727. On Dartmoor nine miles NW from Ashburton. From A38 'Peartree Cross' near Ashburton, follow signs towards Princetown. Access from National Park car parks at New Bridge (S) or Dartmeet (N).
Access: Designated 'access land' but terrain is rough with few paths. It is possible to walk the

NATURE RESERVES - SOUTH WEST ENGLAND

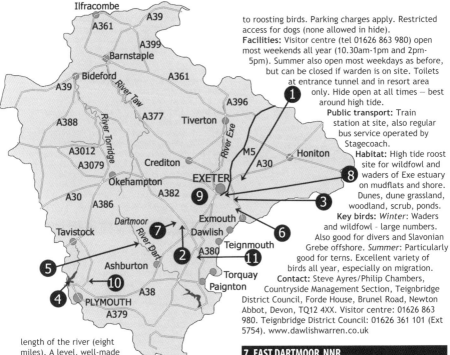

to roosting birds. Parking charges apply. Restricted access for dogs (none allowed in hide).
Facilities: Visitor centre (tel 01626 863 980) open most weekends all year (10.30am-1pm and 2pm-5pm). Summer also open most weekdays as before, but can be closed if warden is on site. Toilets at entrance tunnel and in resort area only. Hide open at all times – best around high tide.
Public transport: Train station at site, also regular bus service operated by Stagecoach.
Habitat: High tide roost site for wildfowl and waders of Exe estuary on mudflats and shore. Dunes, dune grassland, woodland, scrub, ponds.
Key birds: *Winter*: Waders and wildfowl - large numbers. Also good for divers and Slavonian Grebe offshore. *Summer*: Particularly good for terns. Excellent variety of birds all year, especially on migration.
Contact: Steve Ayres/Philip Chambers, Countryside Management Section, Teignbridge District Council, Forde House, Brunel Road, Newton Abbot, Devon, TQ12 4XX. Visitor centre: 01626 863 980. Teignbridge District Council: 01626 361 101 (Ext 5754). www.dawlishwarren.co.uk

length of the river (eight miles). A level, well-made track runs for a mile from Newbridge to give easy access to some interesting areas. Not suitable for large coaches (narrow bridges). Probably too rough for wheelchairs.
Facilities: Dartmoor National Park toilets in car parks at New Bridge and Dartmeet.
Public transport: Enquiry line 01392 382 800. Summer service only from Newton Abbot/Totnes to Dartmeet.
Habitat: Upland moor, wooded valley and river.
Key birds: *All year*: Raven, Buzzard. *Spring/summer*: Wood Warbler, Pied Flycatcher, Redstart in woodland, Stonechat and Whinchat on moorland, Dipper, Grey Wagtail, Goosander on river.
Contact: Devon Wildlife Trust, Cricklepit Mill, Commercial Road, Exeter, EX1 4AB. 01392 279 244. www.devonwildlifetrust.org

6. DAWLISH WARREN NNR

Teignbridge District Council.
Location: SX 983 788. At Dawlish Warren on S side of Exe estuary mouth. Turn off A379 at sign to Warren Golf Club, between Cockwood and Dawlish. Turn into car park adjacent to Lea Cliff Holiday Park. Pass under tunnel and turn L away from amusements. Park at far end of car park and pass through two pedestrian gates.
Access: Open public access, but avoid mudflats. Also avoid beach beyond groyne nine around high tide due

7. EAST DARTMOOR NNR

Natural England.
Location: SX 778 787. The NNR is two miles from Bovey Tracey on road to Becky Falls and Manaton. Road continues across Trendlebere Down, where there are roadside car parks and adjacent paths.
Access: Yarner Wood car park open from 8.30am-7pm or dusk if earlier. Outside these hours, access on foot from Trendlebere Down. Dogs welcome but must be kept under close control.
Facilities: Information/interpretation display and self-guided trails available in Yarner Wood car park also hide with feeding station (Nov-Mar).
Public transport: Nearest bus stops are in Bovey Tracey. Buses from here to Exeter and Newton Abbot (hourly).
Habitat: The reserve consists of three connected sites (Yarner Wood, Trendlebere Down and Bovey Valley Woodlands) totalling 365 hectares of upland oakwood and heathland.
Key birds: *All year*: Raven, Buzzard, Goshawk, Sparrowhawk, Lesser Spotted, Great Spotted and Green Woodpeckers, Grey Wagtail and Dartford Warbler (on Trendlebere Down). *Spring/summer*: Pied Flycatcher, Wood Warbler, Redstart, Tree Pipit, Linnet, Stonechat, Cuckoo, Whitethroat, Sky Lark. *Autumn/winter*: Good range of birds with feeding at hide, inc Siskin, Redpoll, plus Hen Harrier on Trendlebere Down.
Contact: Site Manager, Natural England, Yarner

Wood, Bovey Tracey, Devon, TQ13 9LJ. 01626 832 330. www.natural-england.org.uk

8. EXMINSTER MARSHES

RSPB (South West England Office).
Location: SX 954 872. Five miles S of Exeter on W bank of River Exe. Marshes lie between Exminster and the estuary.
Access: Open at all times.
Facilities: No toilets or visitor centre. Information in RSPB car park and marked footpaths across reserve.
Public transport: Exeter to Newton Abbot/Torquay buses — stops are 400 yds from car park. Traveline 0871 200 2233. No 2 buses Mon-Sat every 15 mins, Sun 1/2 hourly.
Habitat: Coastal grazing marsh with freshwater ditches and pools, reeds, scrub-covered canal banks, winter stubbles and crops managed for farmland birds.
Key birds: *Winter*: Brent Goose, Wigeon, Water Rail, Short-eared Owl. *Spring*: Lapwing, Redshank and wildfowl breed, Cetti's Warbler on canal banks. *Summer*: Gull roosts, passage waders. *Autumn*: Peregrine, winter wildfowl, finch flocks. There are also records of Cirl Bunting and Wood Lark.
Other notable flora and fauna: 23 species of dragonfly, including hairy and scarce chaser.
Contact: RSPB, Unit 3, Lions Rest Estate, Station Road, Exminster, Exeter, Devon, EX6 8DZ. 01392 824 614. www.rspb.org.uk

9. HALDON FOREST RAPTOR VIEWPOINT

Forestry Commission.
Location: Five miles W of Exeter.Turn off A38 at Haldon Racecourse junction, then follow signs for Dunchideock and Forest Walks. After just over 1 mile, turn L into Haldon Forest Park car park.Follow all-ability trail to the viewpoint.
Access: Open all year.
Facilities: Toilets in car park. Viewing point with benches. Path suitable for wheelchairs.
Habitat: Plantations, clearings.
Key birds: *Summer*: Hobby, Nightjar, Turtle Dove, Tree Pipit. *All year*: Goshawk, Sparrowhawk, Buzzard, all woodpeckers, Crossbill, Siskin.
Contact: Forestry Commission, Bullers Hill, Kennford, Exeter, Devon, EX6 7XR. 01392 832 262..
www.forestry.gov.uk/england

10. PLYMBRIDGE WOOD

National Trust/Forest Enterprise.
Location: At the Estover roundabout, Plymouth (near

the Wrigley company factory), take the narrow, steep Plymbridge Road. Park at the bridge area at the bottom of the hill. Coming from Plympton, pick up Plymbridge Road from either Plymouth Road or Glen Road.
Access: Open all year.
Facilities: Car park, woodland paths, picnic area.
Public transport: None.
Habitat: Mixed woodland, river, conifers.
Key birds: *Spring/summer*: Cuckoo, Wood Warbler, Redstart, Blackcap, possible Nightjar, Crossbill. *Winter*: Woodcock, Snipe, Fieldfare, Redwing, Brambling, Siskin, Redpoll, possible Crossbill. *All year*: Mandarin Duck, Sparrowhawk, Buzzard, Kestrel, Tawny Owl, all three woodpeckers, Kingfisher, Grey Wagtail, Dipper, Goldcrest, common woodland passerines, Marsh Tit, Raven.
Contact: National Trust, Lanhydrock House, Lanhydrock, Cornwall, PL30 4DE. 01208 432 691.

11. STOVER LAKE COUNTRY PARK

Devon County Council.
Location: Two miles N of Newton Abbot off A38 Exeter-Plymouth road. Follow the A382 L at Drumbridges roundabout, signed to Newton Abbot. After 0.25 miles follow the brown tourist sign L into the car park (fee payable).
Access: Open all year. Wheelchairs available for visitor use.
Facilities: Car park, information centre, notice board display, site leaflets, maps, feeding station, 90 metre aerial walkway.
Public transport: From Newton Abbot, Exeter or Plymouth. Info from Traveline 0871 200 2233.
Habitat: Mixed woodland, lake and lowland heath. SSSI.
Key birds: *Spring/summer*: Sand Martin, Chiffchaff, Willow Warbler, Spotted Flycatcher, Nightjar, Great Crested Grebe. *Winter*: Water Rail, Marsh Tit, Snipe. *All year*: Woodpeckers, Jay, Siskin, Kingfisher.
Other notable flora and fauna: More than 20 species of dragonfly and damselfly, including hairy dragonfly, downy, emerald and red-eyed damselflies. 34 species of butterfly have been recorded including white admiral, pearl-bordered and silver-washed fritillaries. A good site for bat watching with 10 species identified.
Contact: Rangers Office, Devon County Council, Stover Country Park, Stover, Newton Abbot, Devon, TQ12 6QG. 01626 835 236.
www.devon.gov.uk/stover_country_park

Dorset

1. ARNE

RSPB (South West England Office).
Location: SY 973 882. Four miles SE of Wareham, turn off A351 at Stoborough.
Access: Shipstal Point and Coombe Birdwatchers' trails open all year. Coombe birdwatchers' screen on Middlebere Channel and overlooking estuary open all year. Visitor centre open all year except Christmas. Bird hides available on both trails. Accessed from car park. Coaches and escorted parties by prior arrangement.
Facilities: Toilets in car park. Car park charge applies to non-members. Various footpaths. Visitor centre.
Public transport: None to reserve. Nearest station is Wareham.
Habitat: Lowland heath, woodland reedbed and saltmarsh, extensive mudflats of Poole Harbour.
Key birds: *All year*: Dartford Warbler, Little Egret, Stonechat. *Winter*: Hen Harrier, Red-breasted Merganser, Black-tailed Godwit. *Summer*: Nightjar, warblers. *Passage*: Spotted Redshank, Whimbrel, Greenshank, Osprey.
Other notable flora and fauna: Sika deer, all six species of UK reptile, silver-studded blue and 32 other butterflies, 23 dragonflies, 850 moths and 500 flowering plants.
Contact: Alaxia Hollinshead, Arne Nature Reserve, RSPB Work Centre, Arne, Wareham, Dorset, BH20 5BJ. 01929 553 360, e-mail: arne@rspb.org.uk www.rspb.org.uk/reserves/guide/a/arne/

2. BROWNSEA ISLAND

Dorset Wildlife Trust.
Location: SZ 026 883. Half hour boat rides from Poole Quay with Greenslade Pleasure Boats (01202 631 828) and Brownsea Island Ferries (01929 462 383). Ten minutes from Sandbanks Quay (next to Studland chain-ferry).
Access: Apr, May, Jun, Sept and Oct. Access by self-guided nature trail. Costs £2 adults, £1 children. Jul, Aug access by afternoon guided tour (2pm daily, duration 105 minutes). Costs £2 adults, £1 children.
Facilities: Toilets, information centre and shop, six hides, nature trail.
Public transport: Poole rail/bus station for access to Poole Quay and boats. Tel: 01202 673 555.
Habitat: Saline lagoon, reedbed, lakes, coniferous and mixed woodland.
Key birds: *Spring*: Avocet, Black-tailed Godwit, waders, gulls and wildfowl. *Summer*: Common and Sandwich Terns, Yellow-legged Gull, Little Egret, Little Grebe, Golden Pheasant. *Autumn*: Curlew Sandpiper, Little Stint.
Other notable flora and fauna: Red squirrel, water vole, Bechstein's bat found 2007.
Contact: Dorset Wildlife Trust, 01202 709 445. e-mail: brownseaisland@dorsetwildlife.co.uk www.wildlifetrust.org.uk/dorset

3. DURLSTON NNR AND COUNTRY PARK

Dorset County Council.
Location: SZ 032 774. One mile S of Swanage (signposted).
Access: Open between sunrise and sunset. Visitor centre open weekends and holidays during winter and daily in other seasons.
Facilities: Guided walks, visitor centre, café, toilets, hide, waymarked trails.
Habitat: Grassland, hedges, cliff, meadows.
Key birds: Cliff-nesting seabird colonies; good variety of scrub and woodland breeding species; spring and autumn migrants; seawatching esp. Apr/May and Aug/Nov.
Other notable flora and fauna: 34 species of butterfly and 500-plus species of flowering plants, inc nine species of orchid.
Contact: The Ranger, Durlston Country Park, 01929 424 443, e-mail: info@durlston.co.uk www.durlston.co.uk

4. GARSTON WOOD

RSPB (South West England Office).
Location: SU 004 194. SW from Salisbury. From A354 take turn to Sixpenny Handley then take Bowerchalke road (Dean Lane). Keeping R, proceed for approximately 1.5 miles. Garston Wood car park on L of road indicated by a finger post on R side of road.
Access: Pushchairs can be negotiated around all of the rides, though the terrain is best in dry weather. Dogs are only allowed on public footpaths and bridleways must be kept on a lead.
Facilities: Car park, reserve leaflet, picnic area, group bookings accepted, guided walks available, remote location, good for walking, pushchair friendly.
Public transport: The nearest train station is in Salisbury: from the bus station, take Wilts and Dorset 184 service to Sixpenny Handley (Roebuck Inn).
Habitat: Ancient woodland includes large area of coppiced hazel and maple. Other habitats include oak woodland, scrub and mixed plantation, with important features such as glades, rides and dead wood.
Key birds: Common woodland birds plus Turtle Dove and migrant warblers including Blackcap, Willow Warbler, Garden Warbler and Nightingale. Spotted Flycatcher. Raptors include Buzzard, Sparrowhawk and Goshawk. Winter thrushes.
Other notable flora and fauna: Butterflies, including silver-washed fritillary and elusive white admiral. Adders can be seen on the ride side. Good range of fungi. Fallow deer.
Contact: Alexia Hollinshead, Arne Nature Reserve, RSPB Work Centre, Arne, Wareham, Dorset BH20 5BJ. www.rspb.org.uk/reserves/guide/g/garstonwood//

5. HAM COMMON LNR

Poole Borough Council.
Location: SY 99. W of Poole. In Hamworthy, take the Blandford Road S along Lake Road, W along Lake Drive and Napier Road, leading to Rockley Park. Park

211

NATURE RESERVES - SOUTH WEST ENGLAND

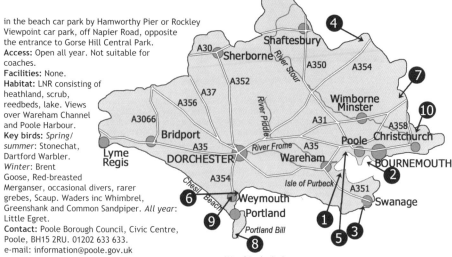

in the beach car park by Hamworthy Pier or Rockley Viewpoint car park, off Napier Road, opposite the entrance to Gorse Hill Central Park.
Access: Open all year. Not suitable for coaches.
Facilities: None.
Habitat: LNR consisting of heathland, scrub, reedbeds, lake. Views over Wareham Channel and Poole Harbour.
Key birds: *Spring/summer*: Stonechat, Dartford Warbler. *Winter*: Brent Goose, Red-breasted Merganser, occasional divers, rarer grebes, Scaup. Waders inc Whimbrel, Greenshank and Common Sandpiper. *All year*: Little Egret.
Contact: Poole Borough Council, Civic Centre, Poole, BH15 2RU. 01202 633 633.
e-mail: information@poole.gov.uk

6. LODMOOR

RSPB (South West England Office).
Location: SY 686 807. Adjacent Lodmoor Country Park, in Weymouth, off A353 to Wareham.
Access: Open all times.
Facilities: One viewing shelter, network of paths.
Public transport: Local bus service.
Habitat: Marsh, shallow pools, reeds and scrub, remnant saltmarsh.
Key birds: *Spring/summer*: Breeding Common Tern, warblers (including Reed, Sedge, Grasshopper and Cetti's), Bearded Tit. *Winter*: Wildfowl, waders. *Passage*: Waders and other migrants.
Contact: Nick Tomlinson, RSPB Visitor Centre, Swannery Car Park, Weymouth, DT4 7TZ. 01305 778 313. www.rspb.org.uk

7. MOORS VALLEY COUNTRY PARK AND RINGWOOD FOREST

East Dorset District Council/Forestry Commission
Location: Two miles W of Ringwood, well-signposted from A31 between Ringwood and Three Legged Cross.
Access: Open every day (except Christmas Day) 8am-dusk. Visitor centre open 9am to 4.30pm daily. Many trails wheelchair friendly.
Facilities: Visitor centre, toilets, tea-room, country shop. Coach parking. Way-marked trails in good condition.
Public transport: Accessible by Wilts and Dorset No 36 service. Call 01988 827 005 or visit: www.wdbus.co.uk
Habitat: River, wet meadow, lakes, scrub, broad-leaved woodland, extensive coniferous forest, golf course.
Key birds: *Spring/summer*: Cuckoo, Nightjar, Sand Martin, Tree Pipit, Whitethroat. Occasional

Wood Lark, Sedge Warbler. *Winter*: Teal, Pochard, Gadwall, Snipe, Redpoll. Occasional Brambling, Goosander. *Passage*: Whimbrel, Common Sandpiper, waders. *All year*: Buzzard, Lapwing, Woodcock, Little Owl, Grey Wagtail, Kingfisher, Dartford Warbler, Crossbill, usual woodland species.
Other notable flora and fauna: 27 species of dragonfly. Good numbers of butterflies and other invertebrates. Roe deer, muntjac, badger, fox, rabbit, grey squirrel.
Contact: Moors Valley Country Park, Horton Road, Ashley Heath, Nr Ringwood, Dorset, BH24 2ET. 01425 470 721, e-mail: moorsvalley@eastdorset.gov.uk www.moors-valley.co.uk

8. PORTLAND BIRD OBSERVATORY

Portland Bird Observatory (registered charity).
Location: SY 681 690. Six miles S of Weymouth beside the road to Portland Bill.
Access: Open at all times. Parking only for members of Portland Bird Observatory. Self-catering accommodation for up to 20. Take own towels, sheets, sleeping bags.
Facilities: Displays and information, toilets, natural history bookshop, equipped kitchen.
Public transport: Bus service from Weymouth (First Dorset Transit Route 1).
Habitat: World famous migration watchpoint. Scrub and ponds.
Key birds: *Spring/autumn*: Migrants including many rarities. *Summer*: Breeding auks, Fulmar, Kittiwake. A total of 355 species recorded.
Contact: Martin Cade, Old Lower Light, Portland Bill, Dorset, DT5 2JT. 01305 820 553.
e-mail: obs@btinternet.com
www.portlandbirdobs.org.uk

9. RADIPOLE LAKE

RSPB (South West England Office).
Location: SY 677 796. In Weymouth. Enter from Swannery car park on footpaths.
Access: Visitor centre and nature trail open every day, summer (9am-5pm), winter (9am-4pm). Hide open (8.30am-4.30pm). Permit (available from visitor centre) required by non-RSPB members.
Facilities: Network of paths, one hide, one viewing shelter.
Public transport: Close to train station serving London and Bristol.
Habitat: Lake, reedbeds.
Key birds: *Winter*: Wildfowl. *Summer*: Breeding reedbed warblers (including Cetti's), Bearded Tit, passage waders and other migrants. Garganey regular in spring. Good for rarer gulls.
Contact: Nick Tomlinson, RSPB Visitor Centre, Swannery Car Park, Weymouth, DT4 7TZ. 01305 778 313. www.rspb.org.uk

10. SOPLEY COMMON

Dorset Wildlife Trust.
Location: SZ 132 975. Four miles NW of Christchurch near Hurn village.
Access: Open at all times. Permits required for surveying and group visits. Dogs under close control and on leads Apr to Aug. Limited disabled access.
Facilities: None.
Public transport: None.
Habitat: Lowland heath (dry and wet) and deciduous woodland.
Key birds: *Summer*: Breeding Dartford Warbler, Nightjar, Wood Lark, Stonechat. Also Hobby. *Winter*: Snipe.
Other notable flora and fauna: Rare fauna includes sand lizard, smooth snake, green and wood tiger beetles, silver-studded blue butterfly. Wide range of dragonflies on many ponds.
Contact: Rob Brunt, Dorset Wildlife Trust, 01305 264 620, e-mail: rbrunt@dorsetwildlife.co.uk www.wildlifetrust.org.uk/dorset

Somerset

1. BREAN DOWN

National Trust (North Somerset).
Location: ST 290 590. 182 map. Juts into Bristol Channel five miles N of Burnham on Sea. J22 of M5, head for Weston-super-Mare on A370 and then head for Brean at Lympsham.
Access: Open all year. Dogs on lead. Steep slope — not suitable for wheelchair-users.
Facilities: Toilets one mile before property, not NT.
Public transport: Call Tourist Information Centre for details 01934 888 800 (bus services differ in winter/summer).
Habitat: Limestone and neutral grassland, scrub and steep cliffs.
Key birds: *All year*: Peregrine, Raven. *Summer*: Blackcap, Garden Warbler, Whitethroat, Stonechat. *Winter*: Curlew, Shelduck, Dunlin on mudflat. Migrants.
Other notable flora and fauna: Chalkhill blue, marbled white and commoner butterflies. Extremely rare white rock rose in June. Somerset hair grass, dwarf sedge.
Contact: The National Trust, Barton Rocks, 01934 844 518.

2. BRIDGWATER BAY NNR

Natural England (Dorset and Somerset Team)
Location: ST 270 470. Five kilometres N of Bridgwater and extends to Burnham-on-Sea. Take J23 or 24 off M5. Turn N off A39 at Cannington.
Access: Hides open every day except Christmas Day. Permits needed for Steart Island (by boat only). Dogs on leads to protect grazing animals/nesting birds. Disabled access to hides by arrangement, other areas accessible.
Facilities: Car park, interpretive panels and leaflet dispenser at Steart. Footpath approx 0.5 miles to tower and hides.
Public transport: Train and bus stations in Bridgwater. First Group buses on A39 stop at Stockland Bristol, 2km SW of Steart. www.firstgroup.com
Habitat: Estuary, intertidal mudflats, saltmarsh.
Key birds: *All year*: Approx 190 species recorded on this Ramsar and SPA site. Wildfowl includes large population of Shelduck and nationally important numbers of Wigeon. Internationally important numbers of Whimbrel and Black-tailed Godwit. Resident Curlews and Oystercatchers joined by many other waders on passage. Good for birds of prey. *Spring/autumn*: Passage migrants, including occasional vagrants.
Other notable flora and fauna: Saltmarsh flora. Rare invertebrates include great silver water beetle, aquatic snail and hairy dragonfly.
Contact: Senior Reserves Manager, Natural England, 0300 060 2570, www.naturalengland.org.uk

3. CATCOTT LOWS

Somerset Wildlife Trust.
Location: ST 400 415. Approx one mile N of Catcott village (off A39 from J23 of M5).
Access: Open at all times.
Facilities: River Parrett Trail passes through reserve.
Public transport: None.
Habitat: Wet meadows with winter flooding and summer grazing.
Key birds: *Winter*: Wigeon, Teal, Pintail, Shoveler, Gadwall, Bewick's Swan, Peregrine. *Spring*: Little Egret, passage waders, breeding Lapwing, Snipe, Redshank, Yellow Wagtail.
Contact: David Reid, SWT, Fyne Court, Broomfield, Bridgwater, Somerset, TA5 2EQ. 01823 451 587. e-mail: mail@avonwildlifetrust.org.uk

213

4. CHEW VALLEY LAKE

Avon Wildlife Trust, Bristol Water Plc.

Location: ST 570 600. Nine miles S of Bristol. Take B3114 south from Chew Stoke, bear L for West Harptree and head NE on A368. View reserve from causeway at Herriott's Bridge where there is car parking.

Access: Permit needed for access to hides (five at Chew, two at Blagdon). Best roadside viewing from causeways at Herriott's Bridge (nature reserve) and Herons Green Bay. Day, half-year and year permits from Bristol Water, Recreation Department, Woodford Lodge, Chew Stoke, Bristol BS18 8SH. Tel/ Fax 01275 332 339. Parking for coaches available.

Facilities: Hides.

Public transport: Traveline, 0870 6082 608.

Habitat: Largest artificial lake in SW England with important reedbed.

Key birds: Often attracts rarities. *Winter and passage:* Wildfowl include important numbers of Shoveler, Gadwall, Teal and Tufted Duck. Large numbers Of Goosander, Great Crested Grebe and Cormorant, with the grebe numbers often the highest in Britain in autumn. Plus Bewick's Swan, Goldeneye, Smew, Ruddy Duck. Huge winter gull roost (up to 50,000+), mostly Black-headed, Common and Mediterranean Gull. *Summer:* Breeding birds include Great Crested and Little Grebe, Gadwall, Tufted Duck, Shoveler, Pochard, Reed Warbler. Hobbies hunt in late summer. When the water level low, mud can attract waders such as Dunlin, Ringed Plover and Green Sandpiper.

Other notable flora and fauna: Ruddy darter and migrant hawker dragonflies.

Contact: Avon Wildlife Trust HQ or Bristol Water Recreation Dept, Woodford Lodge, Chew Stoke, Bristol, BS40 8XH. 01275 332 339.
e-mail: mail@avonwildlifetrust.org.uk
www.avonwildlifetrust.org.uk

5. GREYLAKE

RSPB (South West England Office).

Location: ST 399 346. Off A361 Taunton to Glastonbury road between Othery and Greinton.

Access: Open all year, dawn to dusk, free admission. No dogs, apart from guide-dogs. Wheelchair users can access a 700 metre-long boardwalk and viewing hide.

Facilities: Surfaced nature trail, interpretive signs. No toilets on site.

Public transport: Bus No 29 (First Group). Nearest stop is one mile along main road at Greinton phone box, but drivers may stop at reserve on request.

Habitat: A large wet grassland reserve bought by RSPB in 2003. Formerly arable farmland.

Key birds: *Spring/summer:* Kingfisher, Grey Heron, Little Egret and breeding Snipe, Lapwing, Redshank, Skylark, Meadow Pipit, Yellow Wagtail. *Autumn:* Green Sandpiper, waders on passage. *Winter:* Waders, wildfowl (including Lapwing, Golden Plover, Shoveler, Pintail, Teal and Wigeon). Peregrine, Hen Harrier.

Other notable flora and fauna: Roe deer, water vole, stoat, otter, dragonflies including four-spotted chaser.

Contact: Site Manager, Dewlands Farm, Redhill, Curry Rivel, Langport, TA10 0PH. 01458 252 805.
e-mail: west.sedgemoor@rspb.org.uk
www.rspb.org.uk/reserves/guide/g/greylake/

6. HAM WALL

RSPB (South West England Office).

Location: ST 449 397. W of Glastonbury. From A39 turn N in Ashcott and follow road onto the moor. After three miles pass Church Farm Horticultural building. Shortly after, at metal bridge, reserve is opposite side of road to Shapwick Heath NNR.

Access: Open all year. 2m height restriction on car park. Coach parking available at Peat Moors Centre, Shapwick Road. Dogs only on public footpaths and disused railway line. Wheelchair users can access viewing areas from main track. Other rougher tracks cover 3.8 miles.

Facilities: Two open-air viewing platforms, four roofed viewing screens. Part-time education officer available for school visits.

Public transport: By bus: Service 668 to Peat Moors Centre at Westhay village, approx I mile or St Mary's Road, Meare (approx 1.2 miles from reserve entrance).

Habitat: Recently-created 200-plus hectare wetland, including region's largest reedbed.

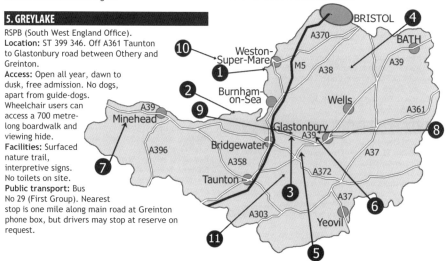

Key birds: *Spring/summer*: Cetti's Warbler, Water Rail. Bittern, warblers, Hobby, Barn Owl. *Autumn*: Migrant thrushes, Lesser Redpoll, Siskin, Kingfisher, Bearded Tit. *Winter*: Millions of Starlings roost, plus large flocks of ducks, Bittern, Little Egret, Peregrine, Merlin, Short-eared Owl.
Other notable flora and fauna: Otter, water vole, dragonflies, butterflies.
Contact: RSPB South West Regional Office, 01392 432 691.

7. HORNER WOOD NATURE RESERVE

National Trust
Location: SS 897 454. From Minehead, take A39 W to a minor road 0.8km E of Porlock signed to Horner. Park in village car park.
Access: Open all year. Car parking in Horner village, extensive footpath system.
Facilities: Tea-room and toilets. Walks leaflets available from Holnicote Estate office and Porlock visitor centre. Interpretation boards in car parks.
Public transport: Bus: Porlock.
Habitat: Oak woodland, moorland.
Key birds: *Spring/summer*: Wood Warbler, Pied Flycatcher, Redstart, Stonechat, Whinchat, Tree Pipit, Dartford Warbler possible. *All year*: Dipper, Grey Wagtail, woodpeckers, Buzzard, Sparrowhawk.
Other notable flora and fauna: Silver-washed fritillary in July.
Contact: National Trust, Holnicote Estate, Selworthy, Minehead, Somerset TA24 8TJ. 01643 862 452.
e-mail: holnicote@nationaltrust.org.uk
www.nationaltrust.org.uk

8. SHAPWICK HEATH NNR

Natural England (Dorset and Somerset Team)
Location: ST 426 415. Situated between Shapwick and Westhay, near Glastonbury. The nearest car park is 400 metres away at the Peat Moors Centre, south of Westhay.
Access: Open all year. Disabled access to displays, hides. No dogs.
Facilities: Network of paths, hides, elevated boardwalk. Toilets, leaflets and refreshments available at the Peat Moors Centre.
Public transport: None.
Habitat: Traditionally managed herb-rich grassland, ferny wet woodland, fen, scrub, ditches, open water, reedswamp and reedbed.
Key birds: *All year*: Ducks and waders. *Summer*: Bittern, Hobby, Cuckoo, Cetti's Warbler. *Winter*: Starling roost, large flocks of wildfowl.
Other notable flora and fauna: Wetland plants, otter and roe deer.
Contact: Senior Reserves manager, Natural England, 0300 060 2570, www.naturalengland.org.uk

9. SHAPWICK MOOR RESERVE

Hawk and Owl Trust
Location: ST417 398. On the Somerset Levels. Take A39 between Bridgwater and Glastonbury and turn N, signposted Shapwick, on to minor road, straight over crossroads and through Shapwick village, turn L at T- junction following signs for Westhay. The reserve is about a mile north of Shapwick village.
Access: Open all year. Access only along public foot-paths and permissive path (closed on Christmas Day). Dogs must be kept on leads.
Facilities: Information panels. No toilets on site but public toilets at nearby Avalon Marshes Centre (ST425 414).
Public Transport: Train to Bridgwater, then First Bus (01278 434 574) No 375 Bridgwater-Glastonbury, to Shapwick village. Sustrans National Route 3 passes through Shapwick village.
Habitat: A wet grassland reserve being created from arable farmland as part of the Avalon Marshes project. Grazing pasture with rough grass edges, fen, open ditches (known as rhynes), pollard willows and hedges.
Key birds: *Spring/summer*: Hobby, Barn Owl, Reed Bunting, and Cetti's Warbler. Whimbrel and other waders on passage. Sky Lark. Passerines such as Bullfinch and Yellowhammer. *Autumn/winter*: Flocks of finches, Snipe, Shoveler, Gadwall, Stonechat, Brambling. Peregrine and harriers may fly over. *All the year*: Buzzard, Kestrel, Sparrowhawk, Kingfisher, Lapwing, Grey Heron, Mute Swan.
Other notable flora and fauna: Roe deer, brown hare, badger, otter and water vole.
Contact: Hawk and Owl Trust, PO Box 400, Bishops Lydeard, Taunton, Somerset TA4 3WH 0844 984 2824.
e-mail: enquiries@hawkandowl.org
www.hawkandowl.org

10. STEEP HOLM ISLAND

Kenneth Allsop Memorial Trust.
Location: ST 229 607. Small island in Severn River, five miles from Weston-super-Mare harbour.
Access: Scheduled service depending on tides, via Knightstone Pier ferry. Advance booking necessary to ensure a place, contact Mrs Joy Wilson (01934 522 125). No animals allowed. Not suitable for disabled.
Facilities: Visitor centre, toilets, trails, basic refreshments and sales counter, postal service. Guidebook available, indoor exhibition area.
Public transport: None.
Habitat: Limestone grassland, scrub, rare flora, small sycamore wood.
Key birds: Important breeding station for Greater and Lesser Black-backed and Herring Gulls, largest colony of Cormorants in England. On migration routes.
Other notable flora and fauna: Rare plants include Steep Holm peony, henbane and many herbal/medicinal species. Butterflies are often abundant, dragonflies in migratory season and moths, particularly lackey and brown-tail larva/caterpillars. Muntjac deer roam wild.
Contact: For direct bookings: Mrs Joy Wilson, 01934 522 125, www.steepholm.org.uk

Scottish Border Counties

Borders, Dumfries and Galloway

Borders

1. DUNS CASTLE

Scottish Wildlife Trust.
Location: NT 778 550. Located N of the centre of Duns (W of Berwick upon Tweed).
Access: Access from Castle Street or at N end of reserve from B6365.
Facilities: None. **Public transport:** None.
Habitat: Loch and woodland.
Key birds: Woodland birds, waterfowl.
Other notable flora and fauna: Occasional otter.
Contact: SWT headquarters132 312 7765.

2. GUNKNOWE LOCH AND PARK

Scottish Borders Council.
Location: NT 518 345. 3.2km from Galashiels on the A6091. Park at Gunknowe Loch.
Access: Open all year. Surfaced paths suitable for wheelchair use.
Facilities: Car park, paths.
Public transport: Tweedbank is on the Melrose to Peebles bus route.
Habitat: River, parkland, scrub, woodland.
Key birds: *Spring/summer*: Grey Wagtail, Kingfisher, Sand Martin, Blackcap, Sedge and Grasshopper Warblers. *Passage*: Yellow Wagtail, Whinchat, Wheatear. *Winter*: Thrushes, Brambling, Wigeon, Tufted Duck, Pochard, Goldeneye. *All year*: Great Spotted and Green Woodpeckers, Redpoll, Goosander, possible Marsh Tit.
Contact: Scottish Borders Council Ranger Service, 01835 825 060. www.scotborders.gov.uk

3. ST ABB'S HEAD

National Trust for Scotland.
Location: NT 914 693. Lies five miles N of Eyemouth. Follow A1107 from A1.
Access: Reserve open all year. Keep dogs under control. Viewpoint at Starney accessible for disabled visitors. Coach parking at Northfield Farm by prior arrangement.
Facilities: Visitor centre and toilets open daily Apr-Oct.
Public transport: Nearest rail station is Berwick-upon-Tweed. Bus service from Berwick, tel 01289 308 719.
Habitat: Cliffs, coastal grasslands and freshwater loch.
Key birds: Apr-Aug: Seabird colonies with large numbers of Kittiwake, auks, Shag, Fulmar, migrants. *Apr-May and Sept-Oct*: Good autumn seawatching.
Other notable flora and fauna: Northern brown argus butterfly. Rock-rose, purple milk-vetch, spring sandwort.
Contact: Kevin Rideout, Rangers Cottage, Northfield, St Abbs, Borders TD14 5QF. 0844 493 2256.
e-mail:krideout@nts.org.uk www.nts.org.uk

4. THE HIRSEL

The Estate Office, The Hirsel.
Location: NT 827 403. Signed off the A698 on the outskirts of Coldstream.
Access: Open all year. Private estate so please stay on the public paths. Coaches by appointment.
Facilities: Car parks, visitor centre, toilets, hide, walks, tea-room.
Public transport: Bus: Coldstream, Kelso, Berwick-upon-Tweed, Edinburgh.
Habitat: Freshwater loch, reeds, woods.
Key birds: *Spring/summer*: Redstart, Garden Warbler, Blackcap, flycatchers, possible Water Rail, wildfowl. *Autumn*: Wildfowl, Goosander, possible Green Sandpiper. *Winter*: Whooper Swan, Pink-footed Goose, Wigeon, Goldeneye, Pochard, occasional Smew, Scaup, Slavonian Grebe.
Other notable flora and fauna: Rhododendrons.
Contact: The Managing Factor — Roger Dodd, Bridge Street, Kelso ATD5 7JD. 01573 224 144.

Dumfries and Galloway

5. CAERLAVEROCK WETLAND CENTRE

The Wildfowl and Wetlands Trust.
Location: NY 051 656. Overlooks the Solway. From Dumfries take B725 towards Bankend.
Access: Open daily (10am-5pm), except Christmas Day.
Facilities: 20 hides, heated observatory, four towers,

Salcot Merse Observatory, sheltered picnic area. Self-catering accommodation and camping facilities. Nature trails in summer. Old Granary visitor building with fair-trade coffee shop serving light meals and snacks; natural history bookshop; binoculars and telescopes for sale. Theatre/conference room. Binoculars for hire. Parking for coaches.
Public transport: Bus 371 from Dumfries stops 30 mins walk from reserve. Stagecoach 01387 253 496.
Habitat: Saltmarsh, grassland, wetland.
Key birds: *Winter:* Wildfowl esp. Barnacle Geese (max 30,000) and Whooper Swans. *Summer:* Osprey, Barn Owl, Sky Lark.
Other notable flora and fauna: Natterjack toads. Northern marsh, common spotted and twayblade orchids.
Contact: The Wildfowl and Wetlands Trust, Eastpark Farm, Caerlaverock DG1 4RS. 01387 770 200.

6. KEN/DEE MARSHES

RSPB (South and West Scotland Office).
Location: NX 699 684. Six miles from Castle Douglas — good views from A762 and A713 roads to New Galloway.
Access: From car park at entrance to farm Mains of Duchrae. Open during daylight hours. No dogs.
Facilities: Hides, nature trails. Three miles of trails available. Closer parking for elderly and disabled is available, but phone warden first. Part of Red Kite trail.
Public transport: None.
Habitat: Marshes, woodlands, open water.
Key birds: *All year:* Mallard, Grey Heron, Buzzard, Nuthatch, Willow Tit. *Spring/summer:* Pied Flycatcher, Redstart, Tree Pipit, Sedge Warbler. *Winter:* Greenland White-fronted and Greylag Geese, birds of prey (Hen Harrier, Peregrine, Merlin, Red Kite).
Other notable flora and fauna: Red squirrel.
Contact: Gus Keys, RSPB Scotland, 01671 404 975.

7. KIRKCONNELL MERSE

RSPB (South and West Scotland Office).
Location: NX990 690. Lies between Dumfries and Glencaple (B725) on banks of River Nith.
Access: None. View reserve from B725 on east side of River Nith.
Facilities: None. **Public transport:** None.
Habitat: Saltmarsh, inter-tidal sand flats and grassland.
Key birds: *Winter:* Whooper Swan, Pink-footed and Barnacle Geese, Pintail, waders.
Contact: Dave Fairlamb, RSPB Scotland, Mersehead Reserve, Southwick DG2 8AH. 01387 780 579

8. MERSEHEAD

RSPB (South and West Scotland Office).
Location: From Dumfries, take A710 Solway Coast road, passing through several villages, reserve is signposted just before Caulkerbush on L. Single track road with passing places runs for a mile down

to car park by visitor centre. From Castle Douglas, take A745, then A711 to Dalbeattie before joining the A710 Solway Coast road, reserve is signposted just after Caulkerbush bridge, on R. Follow above directions for single track road to reserve.
Access: Open at all times.
Facilities: Hide, nature trails, information centre and toilets.
Habitat: Wet grassland, arable farmland, saltmarsh, inter-tidal mudflats.
Key birds: *Winter:* Up to 9,500 Barnacle Geese, 4,000 Teal, 2,000 Wigeon, 1,000 Pintail, waders (inc. Dunlin, Knot, Oystercatcher). *Summer:* Breeding birds include Lapwing, Redshank, Sky Lark.
Contact: Eric Nielson, Mersehead, Southwick, Mersehead, Dumfries DG2 8AH. 01387 780 298.

9. MULL OF GALLOWAY

RSPB (South and West Scotland Office).
Location: NX 156 304. Most southerly tip of Scotland — five miles from village of Drummore, S of Stranraer.
Access: Open at all times. Access suitable for disabled. Disabled parking by centre. Centre open summer only (Apr-Oct).
Facilities: Visitor centre, toilets, nature trails, CCTV on cliffs.
Habitat: Sea cliffs, coastal heath.
Key birds: *Spring/summer:* Guillemot, Razorbill, Kittiwake, Black Guillemot, Puffin, Fulmar, Raven, Wheatear, Rock Pipit, Twite. Migrating Manx Shearwater. *All year:* Peregrine.
Contact: Gus Keys, RSPB Scotland, 01671 404 975.

10. WIGTOWN BAY LNR

Dumfries and Galloway Council.
Location: NX 465 545. Between Wigtown and Creetown, S of Newton Stewart. It is the largest LNR in Britain at 2,845 ha. The A75 runs along E side with A714 S to Wigtown and B7004 providing superb views of the LNR.
Access: Reserve open at all times. The hide is disabled-friendly. Main accesses: Roadside lay-bys on A75 near Creetown and parking at Martyr's Stake and Wigtown Harbour. All suitable for coaches. Visitor Centre in Wigtown County Building has coach parking and welcomes groups. It has full disabled access, including lift and toilets.
Facilities: Hide at Wigtown Harbour overlooking River Bladnoch, saltmarsh and fresh water wetland has disabled access from harbour car park. Walks and interpretation in this area. Visitor centre has a commanding view of the bay. CCTV of Ospreys breeding in Galloway during summer and wetland birds in winter. Open Mon-Sat (10am-5pm, later some days). Sun (2pm-5pm).
Public transport: Travel Information Line 08457 090 510 (local rate 9am-5pm Mon-Fri). Bus No 415 for Wigtown and W side. Bus No 431 or 500 X75 for Creetown and E side.
Habitat: Estuary with extensive saltmarsh/merse and mudflats with developed fresh water wetland at Wigtown Harbour.

Key birds: *Winter*: Internationally important for Pink-footed Goose, nationally important for Curlew, Whooper Swan and Pintail, with major gull roost and other migratory coastal birds. *Summer*: Breeding waders and duck.

Other notable flora and fauna: Fish including smelt and shad. Lax-flowered sea-lavender, thrift, sea aster.

Contact: Elizabeth Tindal, Countryside Ranger, Wigtown Bay Visitor Centre, 01988 402 401, mobile 07702 212 728. e-mail:wbLNR@dumgal.gov.uk www.dgcommunity.net/wblr

11. WOOD OF CREE

RSPB (South and West Scotland Office).

Location: NX 382 708. Four miles N of Newton Stewart on minor road from Minnigaff, parallel to A714.

Access: Open during daylight hours. Dogs on lead. Not suitable for disabled.

Facilities: Nature trails.

Habitat: Oak woodland, marshes, river.

Key birds: *Spring/summer:* Pied Flycatcher, Wood Warbler, Tree Pipit, Redstart, Buzzard, Great Spotted Woodpecker.

Other notable flora and fauna: Red squirrel, otter, Leisler's bat, carpet of bluebells and other spring wildflowers.

Contact: Gus Keys, RSPB Scotland, 01671 404 975.

Central Scotland

Argyll, Ayrshire, Clyde, Fife, Forth, Lothian

Argyll

1. COLL RESERVE

RSPB (South and West Scotland Office).

Location: NM 167 563. By ferry from Oban to island of Coll. Take the B8070 W from Arinagour for five miles. Turn R at Arileod. Continue for about one mile. Park at end of the road. Reception point at Totronald.

Access: Open all year. A natural site with unimproved paths not suitable for wheelchairs. Please avoid walking through fields and crops.

Facilities: Car park, information bothy at Totronald, guided walks in summer. Corn Crake viewing bench.

Public transport: None.

Habitat: Sand dunes, beaches, machair grassland, moorland, farmland.

Key birds: *Spring:* Gt Northern Diver offshore. Corn Crake arrive in late April. Displaying waders, inc Redshank, Lapwing, Snipe. *Summer:* Auks offshore, plus Gannet, shearwaters and terns. *Autumn:* Barnacle and Greenland White-fronted Geese arrive, thrushes on passage. Waders inc Purple Sandpiper. *Winter:* Long-tailed Duck, divers offshore. Hunting Hen Harrier and Merlin. Twite.

Other notable flora and fauna: Good for ceteceans and basking shark. Otter, 300-plus machair wildflowers inc rare orchids, great yellow bumblebee.

Contact: RSPB Coll Nature Reserve, 01879 230 301.

2. LOCH GRUINART, ISLAY

RSPB (South and West Scotland Office).

Location: NR 275 672. Sea loch on N coast of Islay, seven miles NW from Bridgend.

Access: Hide open all hours, visitor centre open (10am-5pm), disabled access to hide, viewing area

and toilets. Assistance required for wheelchair users. Coach parking at visitor centre only. No dogs in hides.

Facilities: Toilets (inc disabled), visitor centre (offers hot drinks), hide, trail. Two car parks — the one opposite the viewpoint is level and made from rolled stone. Group bookings accepted.

Public transport: Nearest bus stops 3 miles from reserve.

Habitat: Lowland wet grasslands, sea loch, moorland.

Key birds: *Oct-Apr:* Large numbers of Barnacle and White-fronted Geese, plus other wildfowl and waders. *May-Aug:* Breeding and displaying waders and Corn Crake. *Sept-Nov:* Many passage migrants and arriving wildfowl. Birds of prey are present all year, esp Hen Harrier and Peregrine, while Chough can be seen feeding in nearby fields. *Spring:* Displaying Snipe, Lapwing, Curlew and Redshank.

Other notable flora and fauna: Good chance of seeing otter, red and roe deer. Marsh fritillary butterflies during May and June. Herb-rich meadows.

Contact: Liz Hathaway, RSPB Scotland, Bushmills Cottage, Gruinart, Isle of Islay PA44 7PP. 01496 850 505, e-mail:loch.gruinart@rspb.org.uk www.rspb.org.uk/scotland

3. MACHRIHANISH SEABIRD OBSERVATORY

(sponsored by SNH and Leader+) John McGlynn, Nancie Smith and Eddie Maguire.

Location: NR 628 209. Southwest Kintyre, Argyll. Six miles W of Campbeltown on A83, then B843.

Access: Daily April-Oct. Wheelchair access. Dogs welcome. Parking for three cars. Digiscoping facilities include electricity and monitor.

Facilities: Seawatching hide, toilets in nearby village. Coach parking.

Public transport: Regular buses from Campbeltown (West Coast Motors, tel 01586 552 319).

Habitat: Marine, rocky shore and upland habitats.
Key birds: *Summer*: Golden Eagle, Peregrine, Storm Petrel and Twite. *Autumn*: Passage seabirds and waders. On-shore gales often produce inshore movements of Leach's Petrel and other scarce seabirds, including Balearic Shearwater, Sabine's Gull and Grey Phalarope. *Winter*: Great Northern Diver, Purple Sandpiper, Ruddy Turnstone with occasional Glaucous and Iceland Gulls.
Other notable flora and fauna: Grey and common seals, otter, wild goat.
Contact: Eddie Maguire, Warden, Seabird and Wildlife Observatory, Lossit Park, Machrihanish, SW Kintyre, Argyll PA28 6PZ. 07919 660 292.
e-mail:machrihanishbirds@btinternet.com
www.machrihanishbirds.org.uk

4. THE OA, ISLE OF ISLAY

RSPB (South and West Scotland Office).
Location: NR 282 423. Six miles SW of Port Ellen, Islay.
Access: Open all year.
Facilities: Car park and waymarked trail. No toilets or other facilities. Weekly guided walks every Tuesday at 10am (April to September).
Public transport: None.
Habitat: Open moorland, freshwater loch, seacliffs, coastal grassland and heath.
Key birds: Breeding Golden Eagle, Red-throated Diver, Peregrine, Hen Harrier, Chough, Corn Crake and farmland birds. *Winter*: Greenland White-fronted Geese and winter thrushes.
Other notable flora and fauna: Narrow-bordered bee hawkmoth, feral goats on cliffs.
Contact: Andy Schofield, RSPB Scotland, Kinnabus Farm, The Oa, Port Ellen PA42 7AU, 01496 300 118.

Ayrshire

5. AILSA CRAIG

RSPB (South and West Scotland Office).
Location: NX 020 998. Island is nine miles offshore, nearest town on mainland is Girvan.
Access: Accessible only by boat – no landing possible. Boat trips on the MFV Glorious (tel: 01465 713 219) or Kintyre Express (tel: 01294 270 160) from Girvan during the summer period. Also from Campbeltown by Mull of Kintyre Seatours' fast rib (Tel: 07785 542 811).
Facilities: None. **Public transport:** None.
Habitat: Dramatic seacliffs.
Key birds: Ailsa Craig is the third largest gannetry in the UK and supports 73,000 breeding seabirds, including Guillemont, Razorbill, Puffin, Black Guillemot, Kittiwake and up to 36,000 pairs of Gannets. Twite can also be found here.
Other notable flora and fauna: Slow worm.
Contact: RSPB South and West Scotland Office, 0141 331 0993, e-mail:glasgow@rspb.org.uk

6. CULZEAN CASTLE COUNTRY PARK

National Trust for Scotland.
Location: NS 234 103. 12 miles SW of Ayr on A719.
Access: Country Park open all year during daylight hours. Restaurant/shops open daily between April and Oct and weekends Nov-March. Access leaflet available.
Facilities: Car park, visitor centre, children's playground, picnic areas, 21 miles of footpath and estate tracks, ranging from unsurfaced woodland paths to metalled roads.
Public transport: Stagecoach bus No 60 (Ayr to Girvan) stops at site entrance. One mile walk downhill to visitor centre and castle. (Stagecoach 01292 613 700)
Habitat: Shoreline, parkland, woodland, gardens, streams, ponds.
Key birds: *All year*: Good populations of common woodland species, inc Jay, Great Spotted Woodpecker and thrushes, recent new resident – Nuthatch. *Spring/summer*: Arriving migrants, esp Blackcap, Chiffchaff and Willow Warbler. Nesting Raven and Fulmar on cliffs, Gannet and terns offshore. *Autumn/winter*: Regular flocks of Redwing and Fieldfare, Waxwing, crossbills. Wildfowl on pond inc Little Grebe, Tufted Duck, Goldeneye. Offshore divers and Eider.
Other notable flora and fauna: The high diversity of flora and fauna due to range of habitats merits site being listed as SWT Wildlife Site. Roe deer, otter, water vole, several species of bat. Shoreline SSSI rich in rock pool life.
Contact: The Ranger Service, Culzean Castle and Country Park, Maybole KA19 8LE. 0844 493 2148.

Clyde

7. BARON'S HAUGH

RSPB (South and West Scotland Office).
Location: NS 756 553. On SW edge of Motherwell, overlooking River Clyde. Via Adele Street, then lane off North Lodge Avenue.
Access: Open all year. Most paths suitable for wheelchairs, except circular nature trail, which has some steep sections.
Facilities: Four hides, information board in car park.
Habitat: Marshland, flooded areas, woodland, parkland, meadows, scrub, river.
Key birds: *Summer*: Breeding Gadwall, warblers (inc. Garden, Grasshopper); Whinchat, Common Sandpiper, Kingfisher, Sand Martin. *Autumn*: Excellent for waders (22 species). *Winter*: Whooper Swan, Pochard, Wigeon, Sparrowhawk.
Contact: RSPB, 0141 331 0993.

8. FALLS OF CLYDE

Scottish Wildlife Trust.
Location: NS 88 34 14. Approx one mile S of Lanark. Directions from Glasgow – travel S on M74 until J7 then along A72, following signs for Lanark and New

Lanark.
Access: Open during daylight hours all year. Disabled access limited.
Facilities: Visitor centre open 11am-5pm Mar-Dec, 12-4pm Jan-Feb. Toilets and cafeteria on site. Seasonal viewing facility for Peregrines. Numerous walkways and ranger service offers comprehensive guided walks programme.
Public transport: Scotrail trains run to Lanark (0845 7484 950). Local bus service from Lanark to New Lanark.
Habitat: River Clyde gorge, waterfalls, mixed woodland and broadleaved riparian gorge, meadow, pond.
Key birds: More than 100 species of bird recorded on the reserve, including unrivalled views of breeding Peregrine. Others include Tawny Owl, Kingfisher, Dipper, Great Spotted Woodpecker, Spotted Flycatcher and Goosander.
Contact: Miss Lindsay Cook, The Falls of Clyde Visitor Centre, New Lanark, South Lanark ML11 9DB. 01555 665 262; E-mail:fallsofclyde@swt.co.uk

9. LOCHWINNOCH

RSPB (South and West Scotland Office).
Location: NS 358 582. 18 miles SW of Glasgow, adjacent to A760.
Access: Open every day except Christmas and Boxing Day, Jan 1 and Jan 2. (10am-5pm).
Facilities: Special facilities for schools and disabled. Refreshments available. Visitor centre, hides.
Public transport: Rail station adjacent, bus services nearby.
Habitat: Shallow lochs, marsh, mixed woodland.
Key birds: _Winter:_ Wildfowl (esp. Whooper Swan, Wigeon, Goosander, Goldeneye). Occasional passage migrants inc. Whimbrel, Greenshank. _Summer:_ Breeding Great Crested Grebe, Water Rail, Sedge and Grasshopper Warblers, Reed Bunting.
Contact: RSPB Nature Centre, Largs Road, Lochwinnoch PA12 4JF. 01505 842 663; e-mail lochwinnoch@rspb.org.uk.

Fife

10. EDEN ESTUARY LNR

Fife Council.
Location: 470 195 (centre of site). The LNR can be accessed from Guardbridge, St Andrews (one mile) on A91, and from Leuchars via Tentsmuir Forest

off A919 (four miles). Use Outhead at St Andrews off West Sands beach to access Balgove Bay. Tentsmuir Forest car park best for northern access and Guardbridge village best for the River Eden section of reserve. Coble Shore southern access at GR 467 188.
Access: Eden Estuary Centre, Guardbridge: open (9am-5pm) all days except Dec 25, Jan 1 and Leuchars Airshow day. Evans Hide: at GR 483 183, parking at Pilmuir Links golf course car park. Combination number required from ranger service.
Facilities: Visitor centre at Guardbridge. Information panels at Outhead. Hide at Balgove Bay (key from Ranger Service).
Public transport: Leuchars train station (1.5 miles), regular bus service from Cupar and Dundee. Tel 08457 484 950.
Habitat: Intertidal mudflats, saltmarsh, river, reed, sand dunes and wetland.
Key birds: _Winter and passage:_ Significant numbers of waders and wildfowl. Outer estuary is good place for sea duck such as scoters, Eider and Long-tailed Duck, plus Gannet, terns and skuas. Mudflats ideal for godwits, plovers, sandpipers and Shelduck. River good for Kingfisher, Common Sandpiper and Goosander. Surrounding area is good for Short- and Long-eared Owl, Peregrine, Marsh Harrier and Merlin. Osprey are regular visitors, daily throughout the season.
Other notable flora and fauna: Northern marsh orchid, dune grasses, herbs, maiden pink, saltmarsh grasses and reed systems. Common harbour seal, bottle-nosed dolphin, porpoise, brown hare, stoat. Butterflies include comma, grayling, small pearl-bordered, dark green fritilliary, painted lady and orange tip.
Contact: Ranald Strachan, Fife Ranger Service, Harbourmaster House, Hot Pot Wynd, Dysart, KY1 2TQ. 01592 656 080, mobile: 07985 707 593. E-mail: Ranald.Strachan@fife.gov.uk

11. ISLE OF MAY NNR
Scottish Natural Heritage.
Location: NT 655 995. This small island lying six miles off Fife Ness in the Firth of Forth is a NNR.
Access: Boats run from Anstruther and North Berwick. Contact SNH for details 01334 654038. Keep to paths. RIB from Anstruther arranged for those using Observatory accommodation. Delays are possible, both arriving and leaving, because of weather.
Facilities: A small visitor centre. A permit is required to carry out research, filming or photography. Permit application forms can be obtained from SNH.
Public transport: Regular bus service to Anstruther and North Berwick harbour.
Habitat: Sea cliffs, rocky shoreline.
Key birds: Early *Summer*: Breeding auks and terns, Kittiwake, Shag, Eider, Fulmar. More than 45,000 pairs of Puffins. *Autumn/spring*: Weather-related migrations include rarities each year.
Other notable flora and fauna: Breeding grey seal colony.
Contact: For Observatory accomodation: David Thorne, Craigurd House, Blyth Bridge, West Linton, Peeblesshire EH46 7AH. For all other enquiries: SNH, 46 Crossgate, Cupar, Fife KY15 5HS. www.nnr-scotland.org

Forth

12. CAMBUS POOLS
Scottish Wildlife Trust.
Location: NS 846 937. Take A907 from Stirling towards Alloa, then Station Road to Cambus village. Park by river in village.
Access: Cross River Devon by bridge at NS 853 940 and walk down stream on R bank past bonded warehouses. Open all year.
Facilities: Bench on S side of western pool.
Public transport: None.
Habitat: Wet grassland with two salty pools.
Key birds: Used extensively by migrants in spring and autumn, inc. wildfowl and waders such as Black-tailed Godwit and Greenshank. Gadwall have bred here and Kingfisher is seen regularly.
Other notable flora and fauna: Brown hare, stoat, short-tailed vole, 115 species of vascular plants. Harbour porpoise seen in Forth.
Contact: SWT headquarters, 01313 127 765.

13. INVERSNAID
RSPB (South and West Scotland Office).
Location: NN 337 088. On E side of Loch Lomond. Via B829 W from Aberfoyle, then along minor road to car park by Inversnaid Hotel.
Access: Open all year.
Facilities: New car park and trail at Garrison Farm (NN 348 095).
Habitat: Deciduous woodland rises to craggy ridge and moorland.
Key birds: *Summer*: Breeding Black Grouse, Snipe,

Cuckoo, Wheatear and Twite. Raven, Grey Wagtail, Dipper, Wood Warbler, Redstart, Pied Flycatcher, Tree Pipit. The loch is on a migration route, especially for wildfowl and waders. Look for Red-throated and Black-throated Divers in spring. *Winter*: Hen Harrier and thrushes.
Other notable flora and fauna: Pine marten, slow worm, 17 species of butterfly inc small pearl-bordered fritillary on nature trail at Inversaid. Wilson's and Tunbridge filmy ferns on boulders through woodland.
Contact: RSPB South and West Scotland Office, 01413 310 993.

Lothian

14. ABERLADY BAY
East Lothian Council (LNR).
Location: NT 472 806. From Edinburgh take A198 E to Aberlady. Reserve is 1.5 miles E of Aberlady village.
Access: Open at all times. Please stay on footpaths to avoid disturbance. Disabled access from reserve car park. No dogs please.
Facilities: Small car park and toilets. Notice board with recent sightings at end of footbridge. SOC HQ, Waterston House, located W of Aberlady village. Includes shop, library, hot and cold drinks.
Public transport: Edinburgh to N Berwick bus service stops at reserve (request), service no 124. Nearest train station 4 miles away at Longniddry.
Habitat: Tidal mudflats, saltmarsh, freshwater marsh, dune grassland, scrub, open sea.
Key birds: *Summer*: Breeding birds include Shelduck, Eider, Reed Bunting and up to eight species of warbler. Passage waders inc. Green, Wood and Curlew Sandpipers, Little Stint, Greenshank, Whimbrel, Black-tailed Godwit. *Winter*: Divers (esp. Red-throated), Red-necked and Slavonian Grebes and geese (large numbers of Pink-footed roost); sea-ducks, waders.
Contact: John Harrison, Reserve Warden, Landscape and Countryside Management, East Lothian Council, 01875 870 588. email:jharrison@eastlothian.gov.uk www.aberlady.org

15. ALMONDELL & CALDERWOOD COUNTRY PARK
West Lothian Council.
Location: NT 091 697. North entrance, the closest to the visitor centre is signposted off A89, two miles S of Broxburn.
Access: Open all year. Parking available at N entrance. S entrance at East Calder. Mid Calder and Oakbank on A71 (furthest from visitor centre). Disabled car park at visitor centre. Coach parking available with prior notice.
Facilities: Car park, picnic area,hot and cold drinks, toilets, pushchair access, partial access for wheelchairs, visitor centre (open every day), gift shop, countryside ranger service.
Habitat: Woodland, river.
Key birds: *Spring/summer*: Woodcock, Tawny Owl,

Grasshopper Warbler, Yellowhammer, Blackcap, Garden Warbler. *Winter*: Goldcrest, Redpoll, Willow Tit. *All year*: Dipper, Grey Wagtail, Sparrowhawk.
Contact: Head Ranger, Visitor Centre, Broxburn, West Lothian, EH52 5PE, 01506 882 254;
www.beecraigs.com
e-mail:almondellandcalderwood@westlothian.gov.uk

16. BASS ROCK

Location: NT 605 875. Island NE of North Berwick.
Access: Private property. Regular daily sailings from N Berwick around Rock; local boatman has owner's permission to land individuals or parties by prior arrangement. For details contact 01620 892 838 or The Scottish Seabird Centre 01620 890 202; www.seabird.org
Facilities: None. **Habitat:** Sea cliffs.
Key birds: The spectacular cliffs hold a large Gannet colony, (up to 9,000 pairs), plus auks, Kittiwake, Shag and Fulmar.

17. BAWSINCH & DUDDINGSTON LOCH

Scottish Wildlife Trust.
Location: NT 284 725. Centre of Edinburgh, below Arthur's Seat. Use car park on Duddingston Road West and Holyrood Park Gate.
Access: Open access to north shore of loch and Cavalry ground to SE. Remainder of site and hide by

prior arrangement with C.McLean, 88 Gilmore Place, Edinburgh.
Facilities: Hide with bird and plant lists.
Habitat: Reedbed, marsh, loch, ponds, mixed woodland, flower meadow and scrub. Developed from former waste area.
Key birds: Heronry. Loch has breeding swans, geese, ducks and grebes. Summer migrants, winter-roosting wildfowl.
Other notable flora and fauna: Fox and otter. Damselfly, four species of amphibian.
Contact: SWT headquarters, 01313 127 765.

18. GLADHOUSE RESERVOIR

Scottish Water.
Location: NT 295 535. S of Edinburgh off the A703.
Access: Open all year although there is no access to the reservoir itself. Most viewing can be done from the road (telescope required).
Facilities: Small car park on north side. Not suitable for coaches.
Habitat: Reservoir, grassland, farmland.
Key birds: *Spring/summer*: Oystercatcher, Lapwing, Curlew. Possible Black Grouse. *Winter*: Geese, including Pinkfeet, Twite, Brambling, Hen Harrier.
Contact: Scottish Water, PO Box 8855, Edinburgh, EH10 6YQ, 084 6 018 855.
e-mail:customer.service@scottishwater.co.uk
www.scottishwater.co.uk

Eastern Scotland

Angus & Dundee, Moray & Nairn, NE Scotland, Perth & Kinross

Angus & Dundee

1. BALGAVIES LOCH

Scottish Wildlife Trust.
Location: NO523 516. From car park on A932, four miles E of Forfar.
Access: All areas apart from hide restricted. Groups should apply in advance.
Facilities: Hide, path.
Public transport: None.
Habitat: Loch, fen and woodland.
Key birds: *Winter*: Wildfowl and wetland breeding birds.
Contact: Montrose Basin Wildlife Centre, 01674 676 336.

2. LOCH OF LINTRATHEN

Scottish Wildlife Trust.
Location: NO 278 550. Seven miles W of Kirriemuir.

Take B951 and choose circular route on unclassified roads round loch.
Access: Two public hides (one wheelchair-accessible) open 24 hours a day. Rest of reserve is private, but good viewing is possible from several places along unclassified roads.
Facilities: Viewpoint can accommodate five cars.
Public transport: None.
Habitat: Mesotrophic loch designated a Ramsar site because of its value to waterbirds. Surrounded by mainly coniferous woodland.
Key birds: *Summer*: Grey Heron, Great Crested Grebe and other water birds. Osprey. *Winter*: Internationally-important numbers of Icelandic Greylag Geese, plus Goosander, Whooper Swan, Wigeon, Teal and other wildfowl.
Other notable flora and fauna: Red squirrel.
Contact: Robert Potter, Reserves Manager North East, SWT, The Kennels, Nr Cortachy, by Kirriemuir, Angus DD8 4QE. 01575 540 396; (M)07920 468 568.
e-mail:rpotter@swt.org.uk

Moray & Nairn

3. CULBIN SANDS

RSPB (North Scotland Office).
Location: NH 900 576. Approx ½ mile NE of Nairn, overlooking Moray Firth. Access to parking at East Beach car park, signed off A96.
Access: Open at all times. 750m path to Minster's Pool suitable for all abilities.
Facilities: Toilets (inc disabled) and bike racks at car park. Track along dunes and saltmarsh.
Public transport: Buses stop in St Ninian's Road, Nairn, half mile W of site. Call Rapsons on 0870 608 2608 or Stagecoach on 01862 892 683. Train station in Nairn three-quarters mile W of reserve.
Habitat: Saltmarsh, sandflats, dunes.
Key birds: *Winter:* Flocks of Common Scoter, Long-tailed Duck, Knot, Bar-tailed Godwit, Red-breasted Merganser. Raptors including Peregrine, Merlin and Hen Harrier attracted by wader flocks. Roosting geese, Snow Bunting flocks. *Spring:* Tern flock, esp Sandwich, passage waders. *Summer:* Breeding Ringed Plover and Oystercatcher. Osprey on passage.
Other notable flora and fauna: Dolphins in Firth. Otters sometimes seen.
Contact: RSPB North Scotland Office, 01463 715 000. e-mail:nsro@rspb.org.uk www.rspb.org.uk

4. SPEY BAY

Scottish Wildlife Trust.
Location: NJ 335 657. Eight miles NE of Elgin. From Elgin take A96 and B9015 to Kingston. Reserve is immediately E of village. Car parks at Kingston and Tugnet.
Access: Open all year.
Facilities: Car park, information board.
Public transport: None.
Habitat: Shingle, rivermouth and coastal habitats.
Key birds: *Summer:* Osprey, waders, wildfowl. *Winter:* Seaduck and divers offshore, esp. Long-tailed Duck, Common and Velvet Scoters, Red-throated Diver.
Other notable flora and fauna: Otter, plus dolphin offshore. Good range of dragonflies.
Contact: Robert Potter, Gardener's Cottage, Balhary Estate, Alyth PH11 8LT. 07920 468 568, e-mail:rpotter@swt.org.uk

5. TROUP HEAD

RSPB (East Scotland).
Location: NJ 825 672. Troup Head is between Pennan and Gardenstown on B9031, E along coast from Macduff. It is signposted off B9031. Look for small RSPB signs which direct you past the farm buildings to car park.
Access: Unrestricted, but not suitable for wheelchair users.
Facilities: Parking for small number of cars. Not suitable for coaches. Live pictures are beamed from the reserve to the Macduff Marine Aquarium during the summer with free entry to the aquarium for RSPB members on Tuesdays between April — August. Boat trips run from Macduff (contact Puffin Cruises 07900 920 445) and Banff or Gardenstown (contact North 58⁰ Sea Adventures) 01261 819 900).
Habitat: Sea cliffs, farmland.
Key birds: Spectacular seabird colony, including Scotland's only mainland nesting Gannets. Bonxies linger in summer. Migrants occur during spring/ autumn.
Other notable flora and fauna: Impressive common flower assemblage in spring. Ceteceans possible offshore in summer including minke whale. Brown hare common.
Contact: RSPB Troup Head warden, c/o Starnafin Farmhouse, Crimond, Fraserburgh AB43 8QN. 01346 532 017. E-mail:troup@rspb.org.uk

NE Scotland

6. CORRIE FEE NNR

Scottish Natural Heritage.
Location: NO 283 761. Take the B955 from Kirriemuir to the Ranger Base in Glen Doll at the head of Glen Clova (car park with a small charge).
Access: Walk 3 km up through Glen Doll Forest to Corrie Fee. Also path up through Corrie Fee itself.
Facilities: Ranger Base, toilets (24hr), picnic benches and paths, accessible from the Glen Doll car park.
Public transport: Post bus.
Habitat: Upland habitats.

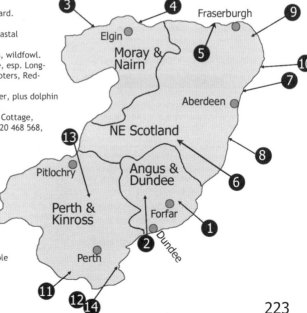

Key birds: *Summer*: Golden Eagles nest nearby, Peregrines, Ravens, cliff-nesting House Martins nest in the Corrie. Also Ring Ouzel, Twite.
Other notable flora and fauna: Very rare Arctic-alpine plants including UK's largest population of dwarf willows (woolly and downy) plus, other more common species like tormentil, opposite leaved saxifrage, chickweed wintergreen and mountain everlasting, can often be seen from the path.
Contact: Shona Hill, SNH, West Lodge, Airlie, Kirriemuir, DD8 5NP. 01575 530 333.
www.snh.org.uk

7. FORVIE NNR

Scottish Natural Heritage.
Location: NK 034 289. 12 miles N of Aberdeen. Through Newburgh off A975 road.
Access: Reserve open at all times but ternery closed Apr 1 to end of Aug annually. Stevenson Forvie Centre open every day (Apr-Sept) and, outside these months when staff are available. Centre and short trail are wheelchair-accessible.
Facilities: Interpretive display and toilets at Stevenson Forvie Centre. Bird hide, waymarked trails. Coach parking at Waterside car park and Stevenson Forvie Centre.
Public transport: Bluebird No 263 to Cruden Bay. Ask for the Newburgh or Collieston Crossroads stop. Tel: 01224 591 381.
Habitat: Estuary, dunes, coastal heath.
Key birds: *Spring/summer*: Breeding Eider and terns. Migrant waders and seabirds offshore. *Autumn*: Pink-footed Goose, migrant seabirds, waders and passerines inc occasional scarce species or rarity. *Winter*: Waders and wildfowl, inc Whooper Swan, Long-tailed Duck and Golden Plover.
Other notable flora and fauna: Occasional cetaceans offshore, esp in summer.
Contact: Annabel Drysdale (Reserve Manager), Scottish Natural Heritage, Stevenson Forvie Centre, Little Collieston Croft, Collieston, Aberdeenshire AB41 8RU. 01358 751 330; www.nnr-scotland.org

8. FOWLSHEUGH

RSPB
Location: NO 879 80. Cliff top path N from Crawton, signposted from A92, three miles S of Stonehaven.
Access: Unrestricted. Not suitable for wheelchair users.
Facilities: Car park with 12 spaces, 200 yards from reserve.
Public transport: Request bus stop (Stonehaven to Johnshaven route). Mile walk to reserve entrance. Details at www.travelinescotland.com.
Habitat: Sea cliffs.
Key birds: Spectacular 130,000-strong seabird colony, mainly Kittiwake and Guillemot plus Razorbill, Fulmar and Puffin. Gannet, Eider and skuas offshore, inc Bonxies lingering in summer. *Autumn*: Red-throated Diver on sea, terns on passage.
Other notable flora and fauna: Grey and common

seals, bottle-nosed dolphin regular, white-beaked dolphin and minke whale occasional in summer. Spring flowers, common butterflies and moths.
Contact: The Warden, c/o Starnafin Farmhouse, Crimond, Fraserburgh AB43 8QN. 01346 532 017, e-mail:strathbeg@rspb.org.uk

9. LOCH OF STRATHBEG

RSPB.
Location: NK 057 581. Britain's largest dune loch is near Crimond on the A90, nine miles S of Fraserburgh.
Access: Visitor Centre open daily 10am-4pm (Nov-Feb), 8am-6pm (later if staff time allows – check website for details) (Mar-Oct). Tower Pool, Bay and Fen Hides open dawn-dusk. Visitor centre wheelchair accessible. Coach parking available – book in advance.
Facilities: Visitor centre, with telescope, toilets, baby changing table and coffee machine. Tower Pool hide accessible via 700 metre footpath. Two hides overlooking Loch accessed via short drive to Airfield. Coastal section of reserve accessed from track behind Tufted Duck hotel in St Combs village. Wildlife garden, indoor children's area – kid's backpacks.
Public transport: Access to whole reserve difficult without vehicle. Buses from Fraserburgh and Peterhead to Crimond, one mile from centre. Details at www.travelin escotland.com.
Habitat: Dune loch with surrounding marshes, reedbeds, grasslands and dunes.
Key birds: 200 species a year. Breeding wetland species, passage waders, internationally important numbers of wintering wildfowl. Scarcities year round. *Winter*: Pink-footed and Barnacle Geese, Whooper Swan, large numbers of duck. Snow Goose and Slavonian Grebe annual. Raptors including Hen and Marsh Harriers. Great Northern Diver offshore. *Summer*: Common Tern, Water Rail, Corn Bunting. *Spring/autumn*: Little Egret, Spoonbill, Avocet, Marsh Harrier, Garganey, Little Gull, Pectoral Sandpiper.
Other notable flora and fauna: Otter, badger, stoat, roe deer. Early purple, butterfly and northern marsh orchids, dark green fritillary butterfly.
Contact: RSPB Loch of Strathbeg, Starnafin, Crimond, Fraserburgh, AB43 8QN. 01346 532 017. e-mail:strathbeg@rspb.org.uk

10. LONGHAVEN CLIFFS

Scottish Wildlife Trust.
Location: NK 116 394. 3.8 miles S of Peterhead. Take A952 S from Peterhead and then A975 to Bullers of Buchan (gorge).
Access: Access from car park at Blackhills quarry or Bullers of Buchan.
Facilities: Leaflet available. Parking.
Habitat: Rugged red granite cliffs and cliff-top vegetation.
Key birds: Nine species of breeding seabird, including Kittiwake, Shag, Guillemot, Razorbill, Puffin.
Other notable flora and fauna: Unusual form of coastal heath has developed, with plants such as bell

heather, crowberry, devil's-bit scabious and grass-of-Parnassus. Grey seals in sheltered inlets. Porpoise, dolphin and minke whale occasionally seen.
Contact: SWT headquarters 0131 312 7765.

Perth & Kinross

11. DOUNE PONDS

Stirling Council.
Location: NN 726 019. Take A820 Dunblane road E from the junction with the A84 Callander-Stirling road. Turn L onto Moray Street just before Doune Church.
Access: Wheelchair access to both hides and 1,000 metres of path. Open all year.
Facilities: Information board, paths, hides. Leaflet from local tourist information offices, local library.
Public transport: Bus: from Stirling and Callander to Doun e. Traveline 0870 608 2608.
Habitat: Pools, scrape, birch and willow woodlands created from old sand and gravel quarry.
Key birds: *All year*: Grey Heron, Buzzard, Snipe, Goldcrest, Siskin, Red Kite. *Spring/summer*: Common Sandpiper, Whitethroat, warblers.
Other notable flora and fauna: Good site for fungi
Contact: Stirling Council Countryside Ranger Service, Viewforth, Stirling FK8 2ET. 0845 2777 000.

12. LOCH LEVEN NNR

SNH, Loch Leven Laboratory.
Location: NO 150 010. Head S from Perth and leave M90 at exit 6, Kinross.
Access: An all abilities trail covers 8 miles of the western shore between Kinross and Vane Farm. Access with car parking is available at Kinross, Burleigh, Findatie and RSPB Vane Farm Local access guidance is in place at the site see www.snh.org.uk for details or pick up leaflet locally.
Facilities: Viewing hides at Kirkgate, Burleigh, Kinross, and RSPB Vane Farm. Seasonal tourist information, toilets and facilities available at the pier Kinross. Further toilets and facilities available at Findatie and Channel Farm. RSPB Vane farm has observation room, natural trail, cafe, shop and toilets (see www.rspb.org.uk/vanefarm).
Public transport: Bus from Perth or Edinburgh to Kinross.
Habitat: Lowland loch with islands.
Key birds: Flocks of geese (more than 20,000 Pinkfeet), huge numbers of the full range of ducks, Whooper Swan. *Summer*: Greatest concentration of inland breeding ducks in Britain (10 species), Osprey and grebes. *Passage*: Waders and hirundines.
Other notable flora and fauna: Lesser butterfly orchid, otter.
Contact: SNH, Loch Leven Laboratory, The Pier, Kinross KY13 8UF. 01577 864 439, www.snh.org.uk

13. LOCH OF THE LOWES

Scottish Wildlife Trust.
Location: NO 042 435. Sixteen miles N of Perth, two miles NE of Dunkeld, just off A923 (signposted).
Access: Visitor centre open all year (10am-5pm). Observation hide open all year during daylight hours. No dogs allowed. Full access for wheelchairs.
Facilities: Visitor centre, toilets, observation hide.
Public transport: Railway station at Birnam/Dunkeld, three miles from reserve. Bus from Dunkeld two miles from reserve.
Habitat: Freshwater loch with fringing woodland.
Key birds: Breeding Ospreys (Apr-end Aug). Nest in view, 200 metres from hide. Wildfowl and woodland birds. Greylag roost (Oct-Mar).
Other notable flora and fauna: Red squirrels.
Contact: Peter Ferns, (Manager), Scottish Wildlife Trust, Loch of the Lowes, Visitor Centre, Dunkeld, Perthshire PH8 0HH. 01350 727 337.

14. VANE FARM (LOCH LEVEN NNR)

RSPB Scotland
Location: NT 160 990. Part of Loch Leven NNR. Seven miles from Cowdenbeath, signposted two miles E of J5 from M90 onto B9097. Drive for approx two miles. Car park on R.
Access: Open daily (10am-5pm) except Christmas Day, Boxing Day, Jan 1 and Jan 2. Cost £3 adults, £2 concessions, 50p children, £6 family. Free to members. Disabled access to shop, coffee shop, observation room and toilets. Coach parking available for up to two coaches. Free car parking.
Facilities: Shop, coffee shop and observation room with five telescopes overlooking Loch Leven and the reserve. There is a 1.25 mile hill trail through woodland and moorland. Wetland trail with three observation hides. Toilets, including disabled. binoculars can be hired from shop.
Public transport: Trains to Cowdenbeath (7 miles), but no bus service from here. Limited bus service (204) runs to the reserve from Kinross (4 miles) on Wednesdays, Saturdays and Sundays. Contact Stagecoach Fife on 01383 511 911 for further details. Eight-mile cycle path around loch.
Habitat: Wet grassland and flooded areas by Loch Leven. Arable farmland. Native woodland and heath moorland.
Key birds: *Spring/summer*: Breeding and passage waders (including Lapwing, Redshank, Snipe, Curlew). Farmland birds (including Sky Lark and Yellowhammer), Tree Pipit. *Autumn*: Migrating waders on exposed mud. *Winter*: Whooper Swan, Bewick's Swan, Pink-footed Goose, finch and tit flocks.
Other notable flora and fauna: 237 butterfly and moth species. 25 mammal species including pipstrelle bat and roe deer.
Contact: Uwe Stoneman, Business Manager, Vane Farm Nature Centre, Kinross, Tayside KY13 9LX. 01577 862 355; e-mail:vanefarm@rspb.co.uk

Highlands & Islands

Caithness, Highlands and Sutherland

1. BEINN EIGHE

Scottish Natural Heritage (East Highland Area).
Location: NG 990 620. By Kinlochewe, Wester Ross, 50 miles from Inverness and 20 miles from Gairloch on A832.
Access: Reserve open at all times, no charge. Visitor centre open Easter-Oct (10am-5pm).
Facilities: Visitor centre, toilets, woodland trail and mountain trail (self-guided with leaflets from visitor centre). Trails suitable for all abilities.
Public transport: Very limited.
Habitat: Caledonian pine forest, dwarf shrub heath, mountain tops, freshwater loch shore.
Key birds: *All year*: Golden Eagle, Scottish Crossbill, Ptarmigan, Red Grouse, Siskin. *Summer*: Black-throated Diver, Redwing, Snow Bunting.
Other notable flora and fauna: Wide range of dragonflies, including golden ringed and common hawker.
Contact: Eoghain Maclean, Reserve Manager, SNH, Anancaun, Kinlochewe, Ross-shire IV22 2PD. 01445 760 254; e-mail:eoghain.maclean@snh.gov.uk

2. CORRIMONY

RSPB (North Scotland Office).
Location: NH 379 304. Lies SW of Inverness between Glen Affric and Loch Ness, off A 831.
Access: Open at all times. Unimproved paths, so terrain may not be suitable for disabled visitors.
Facilities: Way-marked trail (8.5 miles long) passes through farm. Please leave gates as you find them. Guided minibus safaris to see Black Grouse leks in April and May.
Public transport: No 17 bus from Inverness to Cannich stops 1.5 miles from reserve.
Habitat: Pine woodland, moorland, blanket bog.
Key birds: Black Grouse, Crested Tit, crossbill species, occasional Golden Eagle and Osprey. Breeding Greenshank, Red Grouse, Black-throated Diver. *Autumn*: Whooper Swan, Pinkfooted Goose, Woodcock.
Other notable flora and fauna: Red deer, pine marten. Many orchids in July.
Contact: RSPB North Scotland Office, 01463 715 000. e-mail:nsro@rspb.org.uk

3. FAIRY GLEN

RSPB (North Scotland Office).
Location: NH 732 580. On the Black Isle, by Rosemarkie on the A832.
Access: Open all year.
Facilities: Car park, nature trail. Coach parking available.

Public transport: Buses between Inverness and Cromarty stops in reserve car park). Bus info: Rapsons on 0870 608 2608.
Habitat: Broadleaved woodland in a steep-sided valley, stream, waterfalls.
Key birds: *All year*: Large rookery, Dipper, Buzzard, Grey Wagtail, usual woodland species. Migrant warblers in spring/summer.
Other notable flora and fauna: Roe deer. Range of dragonflies, pipistrelle bat, bluebells and other spring woodland plants.
Contact: RSPB North Scotland Office, 01463 715 000. e-mail:nsro@rspb.org.uk

4. FORSINARD

RSPB (North Scotland Office).
Location: NC 890 425. 30 miles SW of Thurso on A897. Turn off at Helmsdale from S (24 miles) or A836 at Melvich from N coast road (14 miles).
Access: Open at all times. Contact reserve office during breeding season (mid-Apr to end Jul) and during deerstalking season (Jul 1 to Feb 15) for advice. Families welcome. Self-guided trail open all year, requested no dogs, no suitable for wheelchairs.
Facilities: Visitor centre open Apr 1 to Oct 31 (9am-5.30pm), seven days per week. Static and AV displays, Hen Harrier nest CCTV. Wheelchair access to centre and toilet. Guided walks Tue and Thu afternoon, May-Aug. Hotel and B&B nearby.
Public transport: Train from Inverness and Thurso (08457 484 950). RSPB visitor centre is in former Forsinard Station building.
Habitat: Blanket bog, upland hill farm.
Key birds: The best time to visit for birds is May-July. Join a guided walk for the best chance of views of Red-throated Diver, Golden Plover, Greenshank, Dunlin, Hen Harrier, Merlin, Short-eared Owl. Few birds between Sep-Feb.
Other notable flora and fauna: Red deer, azure hawker dragonfly, emperor moth.
Contact: RSPB, Forsinard Flows Reserve Office, Forsinard, Sutherland KW13 6YT. 01641 571 225. e-mail:forsinard@rspb.org.uk www.rspb.org.uk

5. HANDA

Scottish Wildlife Trust.
Location: NC 138 480. Island accessible by boat from Tarbet, near Scourie — follow A894 N from Ullapool 40 miles. Continue another three miles, turn L down single track road another three miles to Tarbet.
Access: Open April-Sept. Boats leave 9.30am-2pm (last boat back 5pm). Dogs not allowed. Visitors are asked for a contribution of £2 towards costs. Not suitable for disabled due to uneven terrain.
Facilities: Three mile circular path, shelter (no toilets on island — use those in Tarbet car park). Visitors are given introductory talk and a leaflet with map on arrival.

NATURE RESERVES - HIGHLANDS AND ISLANDS

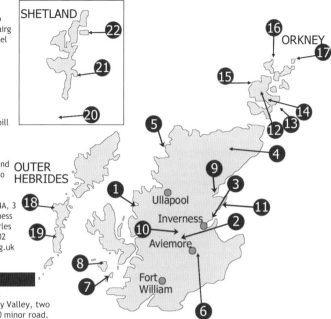

Public transport: Post bus to Scourie (tel 01549 402 357 Lairg Post Office). Train to Lairg (tel 0845 484 950 National Train enquiries). No connecting public transport between Scourie and Tarbet.
Habitat: Sea cliffs, blanket bog.
Key birds: *Spring/summer*: Biggest Guillemot and Razorbill colony in Britain and Ireland. Also nationally important for Kittiwakes, Arctic and Great Skuas. Puffin, Shag, Fulmar and Common and Arctic Terns also present.
Contact: Mark Foxwell, Conservation Manager, Unit 4A, 3 Carsegate Road North, Inverness IV3 8PU. 01463 714 746. Charles Thomson (Boatman) 01971 502 347. e-mail:mfoxwell@swt.org.uk www.swt.org.uk

6. INSH MARSHES

RSPB (North Scotland Office).
Location: NN 775 998. In Spey Valley, two miles NE of Kingussie on B970 minor road.
Access: Open at all times. No disabled access. Coach parking available along access road to car park.
Facilities: Information viewpoint, two hides, three nature trails. Access for disabled to Information Viewpoint only. No toilets.
Public transport: Nearest rail station and bus stop at Kingussie (two miles).
Habitat: Marshes, woodland, river, open water.
Key birds: *Spring/summer*: Waders (Lapwing, Curlew, Redshank, Snipe), wildfowl (including Goldeneye and Wigeon), Osprey, Wood Warbler, Redstart, Tree Pipit. *Winter*: Hen Harrier, Whooper Swan, other wildfowl.
Other notable flora and fauna: Black and highland darter dragonflies along Invertromie trail plus northern brown argus butterflies. Five species of orchid in Tromie Meadow. Roe deer.
Contact: Pete Moore, Ivy Cottage, Insh, Kingussie, Inverness-shire PH21 1NT. 01540 661 518. e-mail:pete.moore@rspb.org.uk www.visitkincraig.com

7. ISLE OF EIGG

Scottish Wildlife Trust.
Location: NM 38 48. Small island S of Skye, reached by ferry from Mallaig or Arisaig (approx 12 miles).
Access: Ferries seven days per week (weather permitting) during summer. Four days per week (weather permitting) between Sept-Apr. Coach parties would need to transfer to ferries for visit to Eigg. Please contact ferry companies prior to trip. Mix of roads, hardcore tracks and rough paths on island.
Facilities: Pier centre: shop/post office, tea-room,

craftshop, toilets.
Public transport: Train service from Glasgow, via Arisaig to Mallaig. Cal-Mac (01687 462 403) ferries (no sailing Wed and sun), MV Sheerwater (no sailing Thurs, tel: 01687 450 224). Island minibus/taxi usually available at the pier.
Habitat: Moorland (leading to Sgurr pitchstone ridge), extensive woodland and scrub, marshland, and bog, hay meadows, sandy bays and rocky shorelines.
Key birds: *All year*: Resident species include Red-throated Diver, Golden Eagle, Hen Harrier, Woodcock and Raven. *Summer*: Cuckoo, Wheatear, Whitethroat, Whinchat, Sedge and Willow Warblers, Twite. Large numbers of Manx Shearwaters offshore with Storm-petrels regularly seen from boats between June-Sept.
Other notable flora and fauna: 17 species of butterfly recorded, including green hairstreak, small pearl-bordered and dark green fritillaries. Nine species of damsel/dragonfly occur with golden ringed, common hawker and highland darter the most numerous. Approx 500 species of 'higher' plants listed, including 12 species of orchid, and alpine/arctic species such as mountain aven and moss campion. Carpet of primroses, bluebells and wild garlic in spring. Otters not uncommon and minke whales, bottle-nosed and common dolphins and harbour porpoises regularly recorded offshore. Basking sharks can be quite numerous in early summer.
Contact: John Chester, Millers Cottage, Isle of Eigg, Small Isles PH42 4RL. 01687 482 477. www.isleofeigg.org

8. ISLE OF RUM

Scottish Natural Heritage
Location: NM 370 970. Island lying S of Skye.
Passenger ferry from Mallaig, take A830 from Fort
William.
Access: Contact Reserve Office for details of special
access arrangements relating to breeding birds, deer
stalking and deer research.
Facilities: Kinloch Castle Hostel, 01687 462 037, Lea
Cottage B&B, 01687 462 036. General store and post
office, Kinloch Castle tea shop and bar. Guided walks
in summer.
Public transport: The Shearwater boat from Arisaig -
01687 450 224, also Caledonian MacBrayne ferry from
Mallaig, 01687 450224, www.arisaig.co.uk
Habitat: Coast, moorland, woodland restoration,
montane.
Key birds: *Summer*: Unique mountain-top Manx
Shearwater colony (a third of the world population).
Seabird breeding colony including auks, Kittiwake,
Fulmar, Eider, Shag. Gull colonies including Common,
Herring, Lesser and Greater Black-backed. Upland
breeding species including Golden Plover, Wheatear,
Merlin, Kestrel. *Late autumn/spring*: Thrush passage.
Winter: Greylag Geese, Oystercatcher, Red-breasted
Merganser.
Other notable flora and fauna: Butterflies including
small white, green veined, large white, green
hairstreak, small copper, common blue, red admiral,
small tortoiseshell, dark green fritillary, peacock
etc. Various dragonflies. Heath spotted orchid. Feral
goat, red deer, otter, Rhum highland pony, palmate
newt, lizard.
Contact: SNH Reserve Office, Isle of Rum, PH43 4RR.
01687 462 026; www.nnr-scotland.org

9. LOCH FLEET

Scottish Wildlife Trust.
Location: NH 794 965. Site lies two miles S of Golspie
on the A9 and five miles N of Dornoch. View across
tidal basin from A9 or unclassified road to Skelbo.
Access: Park at Little Ferry or in lay-bys around the
basin.
Facilities: Guided walks in summer. Interpretive
centre.
Public transport: None.
Habitat: Tidal basin, sand dunes, shingle, woodland,
marshes.
Key birds: *Winter*: Important feeding place for ducks
and waders. The sea off the mouth of Loch Fleet is a
major wintering area for Long-tailed Duck, Common
and Velvet Scoters, Eider Duck. In pine wood off
minor road S from Golspie to Little Ferry: Crossbill,
occasional Crested Tit.
Contact: SWT headquarters, 01313 127 765.

10. LOCH RUTHVEN

RSPB (North Scotland Office).
Location: NH 638 280. From Inverness, take A9 SE to
junction with B851. Head SW until the minor road NE
at Craochy (reserve is signposted); car park one mile.

Access: Open at all times. **Facilities:** Hide, car park.
Public transport: Nearest bus-stop at Craochy (one
mile from reserve). Service is not frequent.
Habitat: Freshwater loch and woodland.
Key birds: Best breeding site in Britain for Slavonian
Grebe, which arrive in late March. *Spring/summer*:
Red-throated Diver and Osprey. Teal, Wigeon and
other wildfowl breed. Peregrine, Buzzard often seen.
Other notable flora and fauna: Toad (mid-April).
Contact: RSPB North Scotland Office. 01463 715 000.
e-mail:nsro@rspb.org.uk

11. UDALE BAY RSPB RESERVE

RSPB (North Scotland Office).
Location: NH 712 651. On the Black Isle, one mile W
of Jemimaville on the B9163.
Access: Open all year. View wader roost from lay-
by. Nearest adapted unisex toilet in Allen Street,
Cromarty (one mile away).
Facilities: Hide, large lay-by. No coach parking.
Public transport: No 26 bus stops in Jemimaville six
times a day (approx 5 min walk to reserve). Bus Info
Contact: Rapsons, 0870 608 2608 or Stagecoach on
01862 892 683.
Habitat: Mudflat, saltmarsh and wet grassland.
Key birds: *Spring/summer*: 10,000 Pinkfeet on
passage each year, other wildfowl, Oystercatcher,
Redshank, waders. Possible Osprey fishing. *Autumn/
winter*: Large flocks of wildfowl (approx 10,000
Wigeon), geese, waders.
Contact: RSPB North Scotland Office, 01463 715 000.
e-mail:nsro@rspb.org.uk

Orkney

12. BRODGAR

RSPB (East Scotland).
Location: HY 296 134. Reserve surrounds the Ring
of Brodgar, part of the Heart of Neolithic Orkney
World Heritage Site on the B9055 off the Stromness-
Finstown Road.
Access: Open all year.
Facilities: Footpath, circular route approx one mile.
Public transport: Orkney Coaches. Service within
0.5 mile of reserve. Tel: 01856 870 555. Occasional
service past reserve.
Habitat: Wetland and farmland including species-rich
grassland, loch shores.
Key birds: *Spring/summer*: Breeding waterfowl on
farmland and nine species of waders breed here.
The farmed grassland is suitable for Corn Crake and
provides water, food and shelter for finches, larks and
buntings. *Winter*: large numbers of Golden Plover,
Curlew and Lapwing.
Other notable flora and fauna: A hotspot for great
yellow bumblebee in August. Possibility of otter,
while common seals haul out nearby on Loch of
Stenness.
Contact: The Warden,12/14 North End Road,
Stromness, Orkney KW16 3AG. 01856 850 176.
e-mail:orkney@rspb.org.ukwww.rspb.co.uk

NATURE RESERVES - HIGHLANDS AND ISLANDS

13. COPINSAY

RSPB (East Scotland).
Location: HY 610 010. Small island accessed by private boat or hire boat from mainland Orkney.
Access: Open all year round.
Facilities: House on island open to visitors, but no facilities. No toilets or hides.
Habitat: Sea cliffs, farmland.
Key birds: *Summer:* Stunning seabird-cliffs with breeding Kittiwake, Guillemot, Black Guillemot, Puffin, Razorbill, Shag, Fulmar, Rock Dove, Eider, Twite, Raven and Greater Black-backed Gull, Great Skua (new breeding species in recent years). Passage migrants esp. during periods of E winds.
Other notable flora and fauna: The island is a key breeding location for Atlantic grey seals from Oct-Dec. 2,385 pups counted in 2006.
Contact: The Warden, 12/14 North End Road, Stromness, Orkney KW16 3AG. 01856 850 176. e-mail:orkney@rspb.org.ukwww.rspb.co.ukS Foubisher (boatman) 01856 741252 — cannot sail if wind is in the east.

14. HOBBISTER

RSPB (East Scotland).
Location: HY 396 070 or HY 381 068. Near Kirkwall.
Access: Open access between A964 and the sea. Dogs on leads please.
Facilities: A council-maintained footpath to Waulkmill Bay, two car parks. New circular walk from RSPB car park along cliff top and Scapa Flow.
Public transport: Orkney Coaches, 01856 877 500.
Habitat: Orkney moorland, bog, fen, saltmarsh, coastal cliffs, scrub.
Key birds: *Summer:* Breeding Hen Harrier, Merlin, Short-eared Owl, Red Grouse, Red-throated Diver, Eider, Merganser, Black Guillemot. Wildfowl and waders at Waulkmill Bay. *Autumn/winter:* Waulkmill for sea ducks, divers, auks and grebes (Long-tailed Duck, Red-throated, Black-throated and Great Northern Divers, Slavonian Grebe).
Other notable flora and fauna: Otter occasionally seen from the Scapa trail. Grey and common seal both possible from footpath looking towards Scapa Flow.
Contact: The Warden, 12/14 North End Road, Stromness, Orkney KW16 3AG. 01856 850 176. e-mail:orkney@rspb.org.uk www.rspb.co.uk

15. MARWICK HEAD

RSPB (East Scotland).
Location: HY 229 242. On W coast of mainland Orkney, near Dounby. Path N from Marwick Bay, or from council car park at Cumlaquoy at HY 232 252.
Access: Open all year. Rough terrain not suitable for wheelchairs.
Facilities: Cliff top path.
Public transport: Orkney Coaches (01856 877 500), nearest stop one mile from reserve.
Habitat: Rocky bay, sandstone cliffs. Beach path good place for great yellow bumblebee in Aug.

Key birds: May-Jul best. Huge numbers of Kittiwakes and auks, inc. Puffins, also nesting Fulmar, Rock Dove, Raven, Rock Pipit.
Other notable flora and fauna: Cetaceans are a possibility from Marwick with porpoise and minke whale occasionally seen.
Contact: The Warden, 12/14 North End Road, Stromness, Orkney KW16 3AG. 01856 850 176. e-mail:orkney@rspb.org.uk www.rspb.co.uk

16. NORTH HILL, PAPA WESTRAY

RSPB (East Scotland).
Location: HY 496 538. Small island lying NE of Westray, reserve at N end of island's main road.
Access: Access at all times. During breeding season report to summer warden at Rose Cottage, 650 yards S of reserve entrance (Tel 01857 644 240) or use trail guide.
Facilities: Nature trails, hide/info hut.
Public transport: Orkney Ferries (01856 872 044), Loganair (01856 872 494).
Habitat: Sea cliffs, maritime heath.
Key birds: *Summer:* Close views of colony of Puffin, Guillemot, Razorbill and Kittiwake. Black Guillemot nest under flagstones around reserve's coastline. One of UK's largest colonies of Arctic Tern, also Arctic Skua.
Other notable flora and fauna: North Hill is one of the best areas to see 'Scottish primrose' (*primula scotica*) which has two flowering periods that just overlap (May-Aug).
Contact: Apr-Aug, The Warden at Rose Cottage, Papay Westray DW17 2BU. 01857 644 240 or RSPB Orkney Office, 12/14 North End Road, Stromness, Orkney KW16 3AG. 01856 850 176. e-mail:orkney@rspb.org.uk www.rspb.co.uk

17. NORTH RONALDSAY BIRD OBSERVATORY

Location: HY 64 52. 35 miles from Kirkwall, Orkney mainland.
Access: Open all year except Christmas.
Facilities: Three star guest house and hostel accommodation, restaurant, cafe, fully licenced, croft walk.
Public transport: Daily subsidised flights from Kirkwall (Loganair 01856 872 494). Once weekly ferry from Kirkwall (Fri or Sat), Tuesday and some Sunday sailings in summer (Orkney Ferries Ltd 01856 872 044).
Habitat: Crofting island with a number of eutrophic and oligotrophic wetlands. Coastline has both sandy bays and rocky shore. Walled gardens concentrate passerines.
Key birds: *Spring/Autumn:* Prime migration site including regular BBRC species. Wide variety of breeding seabirds, wildfowl and waders. *Winter:* Waders and wildfowl include Whooper Swan and hard weather movements occur.
Contact: Alison Duncan, North Ronaldsay Bird Observatory, Twingness, North Ronaldsay, Orkney KW17 2BE. 01857 633 200. e-mail:alison@nrbo.prestel.co.uk www.nrbo.f2s.com

Outer Hebrides

18. BALRANALD

RSPB (North Scotland Office).
Location: NF 705 707. From Skye take ferry to Lochmaddy, North Uist. Drive W on A865 for 20 miles to reserve. Turn off main road three miles NW of Bayhead at signpost to Houghharry.
Access: Open at all times, no charge. Dogs on leads. Circular walk not suitable for wheelchairs.
Facilities: Visitor Centre and toilets (disabled access). Marked nature trail. Group bookings welcome.
Public transport: Post bus service (tel 01876 560 244).
Habitat: Freshwater loch, machair, coast and croft lands.
Key birds: *Spring:* Skuas and divers at sea, Purple Sandpiper and other waders on shore. Dotterel. *Summer:* Corn Crake, Corn Bunting, Lapwing, Oystercatcher, Dunlin, Ringed Plover, Redshank, Snipe, terns. *Autumn:* Hen Harrier, Peregrine, Greylag Goose. *Winter:* Twite, Snow Bunting, Whooper Swan, Greylag Goose, Wigeon, Teal, Shoveler, sightings of Golden and White-tailed Eagles becoming commoner. *Passage:* Barnacle Goose, Pomarine Skua, Long-tailed Skua.
Other notable flora and fauna: Blanket bog and machair plants reach their peak in July.
Contact: Jamie Boyle, 9 Grenitote, Isle of North Uist, H56 5BP. 01876 560 287.
e-mail:james.boyle3@btinternet.com

19. LOCH DRUIDIBEG NNR

SNH (Western Isles Area).
Location: NF 782 378. Reserve of 1,577 ha on South Uist. Turn off A865 at B890 road for Loch Sgioport. Track to reserve is 1.5 miles further on — park at side of road.
Access: Open all year. Several tracks and one walk covering a range of habitats — most not suitable for wheelchair use. Stout footwear essential. Observe Scottish Outdoor Access Code in all areas with livestock. View E part of reserve from public roads but parking and turning areas for coaches is limited.
Facilities: None.
Public transport: Regular bus service stops at reserve. Hebridean Coaches 01870 620 345, MacDonald Coaches 01870 620 288. Large print timetable — call 01851 709 592.
Habitat: Range of freshwater lochs and marshes, machair, coast and moorland.
Key birds: *Summer:* Breeding waders, Corn Crake, wildfowl, terns and raptors. *Spring and autumn:* Migrant waders and wildfowl. *Winter:* Waders, wildfowl and raptors.
Contact: SNH Area Officer, SNH Office, Stilligarry, South Uist, HS8 5RS. 01870 620 238; Fax 01870 620 350; e-mail:western.isles@snh.gov.uk
www.nnr-scotland.org.uk

Shetland

20. FAIR ISLE BIRD OBSERVATORY

Fair Isle Bird Observatory.
Location: HZ 2172. Famous island for rarities located SE of mainland Shetland.
Access: Open from end Apr-end Oct. No access restrictions.
Facilities: Public toilets at Airstrip and Stackhoull Stores (shop). Accommodation at Fair Isle Bird Observatory (phone/e-mail: for brochure/details). Guests can be involved in observatory work and get to see birds in the hand. Slide shows, guided walks through Ranger Service.
Public transport: Tue, Thurs, Sat — ferry (12 passengers) from Grutness, Shetland. Tel: Neil or Pat Thomson on 01595 760 363. Mon, Wed, Fri, Sat — air (7 seater) from Tingwall, Shetland. Tel: Direct Flight 01595 840 246.
Habitat: Heather moor and lowland pasture/crofting land. Cliffs.
Key birds: Large breeding seabird colonies (auks, Gannet, Arctic Tern, Kittiwake, Shag, Arctic Skua and Great Skua). Many common and rare migrants Apr/May/early Jun, late Aug-Nov.
Other notable flora and fauna: Northern marsh, heath spotted and frog orchid, lesser twayblade, small adders tongue, oyster plant. Orcas, minke whale, white-backed, white-sided and Risso's dolphins. Endemic field mouse.
Contact: Deryk Shaw (Warden), Hollie Shaw (Administrator), Fair Isle Bird Observatory, Fair Isle, Shetland ZE2 9JU. 01595 760 258.
e-mail:fairisle.birdobs@zetnet.co.uk
www.fairislebirdobs.co.uk

21. FETLAR

RSPB Scotland
Location: HU 603 917. Small island lying E of Yell. Take car ferry from Gutcher, N Yell. Booking advised. Tel: 01957 722 259.
Access: Apart from the footpath to Hjaltadance circle, Vord Hill, the Special Protection Area is closed mid May to end July. Entry during this period is only by arrangement with warden.
Facilities: Hide at Mires of Funzie open Apr-Nov. Toilets and payphone at ferry terminal, interpretive centre at Houbie, campsite, shop.
Public transport: None.
Habitat: Serpentine heath, rough hill lane, upland mire.
Key birds: *Summer:* Breeding Red-throated Diver, Eider, Shag, Whimbrel, Golden Plover, Dunlin, skuas, Manx Shearwater, Storm Petrel. Red-necked Phalarope on Loch of Funzie (HU 655 899) viewed from road or RSPB hide overlooking Mires of Funzie.
Other notable flora and fauna: Heath spotted orchid and autumn gentian. Otters are common, harbour and grey seals breed.
Contact: RSPB North Isles Warden, Bealance, Fetlar,

Shetland ZE2 9DJ. Tel/Fax: 01957 733 246.
e-mail:malcolm.smith@rspb.org.uk

22. NOSS NNR

Scottish Natural Heritage (Shetland Office).
Location: HU 531 410. Take car ferry to Bressay from Lerwick and follow signs for Noss (5km). At end of road walk to shore (600 mtrs) where inflatable ferry (passenger only) to island will collect you (if red flag is flying, island is closed due to sea conditions). Information updated daily in season on 0800 107 7818.
Access: Access (Tue, Wed, Fri, Sat, Sun) 10am-5pm, late Apr-late Aug. Access by zodiac inflatable. Sorry, no dogs allowed on ferry. Steep rough track down to ferry. Groups or anyone requiring asistance to board ferry should contact SNH as far in advance as possible.
Facilities: Visitor centre, toilets. Bike rack/car park

on Bressay side. Parking for small coaches.
Public transport: None. Cycle hire in Lerwick.
Habitat: Dune and coastal grassland, moorland, heath, blanket bog, sea cliffs.
Key birds: *Spring/summer:* Breeding Fulmar, Shag, Gannet, Arctic Tern, Kittiwake, Herring and Great Black-backed Gull, Great Skua, Arctic Skua, Guillemot, Razorbill, Puffin, Black Guillemot, Eider, Lapwing, Dunlin, Snipe, Wheatear, Twite plus migrant birds at any time.
Other notable flora and fauna: Grey and common seals, otter porpoise regularly seen, killer whales annual in recent years.
Contact: Glen Tyler, Scottish Natural Heritage, Stewart Building, Alexandra Wharf, Lerwick, Shetland ZE1 0LL. 01595 693 345.
e-mail:noss_nnr@snh.gov.uk
www.nnr-scotland.org

Eastern Wales

Breconshire, Montgomeryshire, Radnorshire

1. BAILEY EINON LNR

Radnorshire Wildlife Trust.
Location: SO 083 613. From Llandrindod Wells, take the Craig Road leading to Cefnllys Lane. Down this road is Shaky Bridge with a car park and picnic site. A kissing-gate downstream from the picnic site marks the reserve entrance. Please do not park in front of the kissing-gate.
Access: Open all year.
Facilities: Car park, picnic site, waymarked trail.
Public transport: None.
Habitat: Woodland, river.
Key birds: *Spring/summer:* Pied Flycatcher, Redstart, Wood Warbler. *All year:* Great Spotted Woodpecker, Buzzard, usual woodland birds.
Other notable flora and fauna: Orange tip and ringlet butterflies. Red campion, yellow archangel.
Contact: Radnorshire Wildlife Trust, Warwick House, High Street, Llandrindod Wells, Powys, LD1 6AG, 01597 823 298, e-mail:info@rwtwales.org
www.radnorshirewildlifetrust.org.uk

2. BRECHFA POOL

Brecknock Wildlife Trust.
Location: SO 118 377. Travelling NE from Brecon look for lane off A470, 1.5 miles SW of Llyswen; on Brechfa Common, pool is on R after cattle grid.
Access: Open dawn to dusk. Road runs around three-quarters of pool, giving good access.
Facilities: None.
Public transport: None.
Habitat: Marshy grassland, large shallow pool.
Key birds: Good numbers of wintering wildfowl are

replaced by breeding gulls and commoner waterfowl. Species recorded inc Teal, Gadwall, Tufted Duck, Shoveler, Wigeon, Little Grebe, Black-headed Gull, Lapwing, Dunlin, Redshank, Kestrel.**Other notable flora and fauna:** Rare pillwort around pond margins, plus crowfoot, penny royal and orange foxtail.
Contact: Trust HQ, Lion House, Bethel Square, Brecon, Powys LD3 7AY. 01874 625 708.
e-mail:enquiries@bricknockwildlifetrust.org.uk
www.brecknockwildlifetrust.org.uk

3. CARNGAFALLT

RSPB Wales
Location: SN 935 653. From Rhayader take the B4518 W to Elan village. Turn into village and carry on over bridge into Elan village. Continue through village to cattle grid where nature trail starts.
Access: The nature trail is open at all times.
Facilities: None apart from trail.
Public transport: None.
Habitat: Ancient oak woodland, grassland and moorland. Spectacular upland scenery.
Key birds: Red Kite, Buzzard, Sparrowhawk, Peregrine, Raven, Green Woodpecker, Grey Wagtail and Marsh Tit are joined in the summer by Pied Flycatcher, Spotted Flycatcher, Wood Warbler, Redstart, Tree Pipit and Cuckoo.**Other notable flora and fauna:** Golden-ringed dragonfly, silver-washed, small pearl-bordered and dark-green fritillaries and purple hairstreak butterflies.
Contact: RSPB Ynys-Hir Reserve, Eglwys-fach, Machynlleth, Powys SY20 8TA. 01654 700 222.
e-mail:ynyshir@rspb.org.uk

NATURE RESERVES - EASTERN WALES

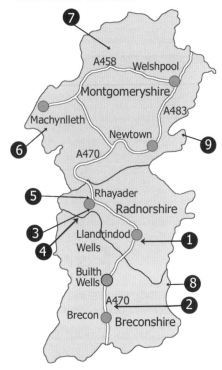

4. ELAN VALLEY

Dwr Cymru /Welsh Water.
Location: SN 928 646 (visitor centre). Three miles SW of Rhayader, off B4518.
Access: Mostly open access.
Facilities: Visitor centre and toilets (open between mid Mar-end Oct), nature trails all year and hide at SN 905 617.
Public transport: Local bus service discontinued.
Habitat: 45,000 acres of moorland, woodland, river and reservoir.
Key birds: *Spring/summer*: Birds of prey, upland birds including Golden Plover and Dunlin. Woodland birds include Redstart and Pied Flycatcher.
Other notable flora and fauna: Internationally important oak woodlands. More than 3,000 species of flora and fauna recorded.
Contact: Pete Jennings, Rangers Office, Elan Valley Visitor Centre, Rhayader, Powys LD6 5HP. 01597 810 880, e-mail:peter.jennings@dwrcymru.com www.elanvalley.org.uk

5. GILFACH

Radnorshire Wildlife Trust.
Location: SN 952 714. Two miles NW from Rhayader/ Rhaeadr-Gwy. Take minor road to St Harmon from A470 at Marteg Bridge.
Access: Open every day, all year.
Facilities: Visitor centre opening times may vary — contact Trust for details.
Public transport: None.
Habitat: Upland hill farm, river, oak woods, meadows, hill-land.
Key birds: *Spring/summer*: Pied Flycatcher, Redstart. *All year*: Dipper, Red Kite.
Other notable flora and fauna: Green hairstreak, wall brown and ringlet butterflies, mountain pansy, bloody-nosed beetle.
Contact: Reserve manager, St Harmon, Gilfach, St Harmon, Rhaeadr-Gwy, Powys LD6 5LF. 01597 823 298, e-mail:info@rwtwales.org www.radnorshirewildlifetrust.org.uk

6. GLASLYN, PLYNLIMON

Montgomeryshire Wildlife Trust.
Location: SN 826 941. Nine miles SE of Machynlleth. Off minor road between the B4518 near Staylittle and the A489 at Machynlleth. Go down the track for about a mile to the car park.
Access: Open at all times — dogs on lead at all times.
Facilities: Footpath.
Public transport: None.
Habitat: Heather moorland and upland lake.
Key birds: Red Grouse, Short-eared Owl, Meadow Pipit, Sky Lark, Wheatear and Ring Ouzel, Red Kite, Merlin, Peregrine. Goldeneye occasional.
Contact: Montgomeryshire Wildlife Trust, Collot House, 20 Severn Street, Welshpool, Powys SY21 7AD. 01938 555 654, e-mail:info@montwt.co.uk www.montwt.co.uk

7. LAKE VYRNWY

RSPB (North Wales Office).
Location: SJ 020 193. Located WSW of Oswestry. Nearest village is Llanfyllin on A490. Take B4393 to lake.
Access: Reserve open all year. Visitor centre open Apr-Dec (10.30am-4.30pm), Dec-Apr weekends only (10.30am-4.30pm).
Facilities: Toilets, visitor centre, hides, nature trails, coffee shop, RSPB shop, craft workshops.
Public transport: Train and bus Welshpool (25 miles away).
Habitat: Heather moorland, woodland, meadows, rocky streams and large reservoir.
Key birds: Dipper, Kingfisher, Pied Flycatcher, Wood Warbler, Redstart, Peregrine and Buzzard.**Other notable flora and fauna:** Mammals include otter, mink, brown hare. Golden-ringed dragonflies frequent in summer.
Contact: Centre Manager,, RSPB Lake Vyrnwy Reserve, Bryn Awel, Llanwddyn, Oswestry, Salop SY10 0LZ. 01691 870 278.
e-mail:lake.vyrnwy@rspb.org.uk

8. PWLL-Y-WRACH

Brecknock Wildlife Trust.
Location: SO 165 326. From Talgarth town centre

take Bell Street and then Hospital Road. After 1.5 miles, reserve is on the right.
Access: Reserve open all year. Please keep to footpaths. Level wheelchair-friendly path runs half way into site. Elsewhere, paths can be muddy and there are steps in places.
Facilities: No facilities.
Public transport: No local services.
Habitat: 8.5 hectares of ancient woodland, river and spectacular waterfall.
Key birds: Large variety of resident woodland birds, with migrant boost in spring. Dipper, Kingfisher, Pied Wagtail, Great Spotted Woodpecker, Chiffchaff, Wood Warbler, Pied Flycatcher, Mistle and Song Thrushes, Nuthatch.
Other notable flora and fauna: Otter, dormouse, bats, common lizard. Early purple and birds' nest orchids, herb paris, bluebell, wood anenome.
Contact: Trust HQ. 01874 625 708.
e-mail: enquiries@brecknockwildlifetrust.org.uk

9. ROUNDTON HILL

Montgomeryshire Wildlife Trust.
Location: SO 293 947. SE of Montgomery. From Churchstoke on A489, take minor road to Old Churchstoke, R at phone box, then first R.
Access: Open access. Tracks rough in places. Dogs on lead at all times.
Facilities: Car park. Waymarked trails.
Public transport: None.
Habitat: Ancient hill grassland, woodland, streamside wet flushes, scree, rock outcrops.
Key birds: Buzzard, Raven, Wheatear, all three woodpeckers, Tawny Owl, Redstart, Linnet, Goldfinch.
Contact: Montgomeryshire Wildlife Trust, Collot House, 20 Severn Street, Welshpool, Powys SY21 7AD. 01938 555 654; e-mail:info@montwt.co.uk
www.montwt.co.uk

Northern Wales

Anglesey, Caernarfonshire, Denbighshire, Flintshire, Merioneth

1. BARDSEY BIRD OBSERVATORY

Bardsey Bird Observatory.
Location: SH 11 21. Private 444 acre island. Twenty minute boat journey from Aberdaron.
Access: Mar-Nov. No dogs. Visitor accommodation in 150-year-old farmhouse (two single, two double, one x four bed dorm). To stay at the Observatory contact Alicia Normand (tel 01626 773 908) e-mail: bookings@ bbfo.org.uk. Day visitors by Bardsey Ferries (07971 769 895).
Facilities: Public toilets available for day visitors. Three hides, one on small bay, two seawatching. Gift shops and payphone.
Public transport: Trains from Birmingham to Pwllheli. Tel: 0345 484 950. Arriva bus from Bangor to Pwllheli. Tel: 0870 6082 608.
Habitat: Sea-birds cliffs viewable from boat only. Farm and scrubland, Spruce plantation, willow copses and gorse-covered hillside.
Key birds: *All year*: Chough, Peregrine. *Spring/ summer*: Manx Shearwaters (16,000 pairs), other seabirds. Migrant warblers, chats, Redstart, thrushes. *Autumn*: Many rarities including Eye-browed Thrush, Lanceolated Warbler, American Robin, Yellowthroat, Summer Tanager.
Other notable flora and fauna: Autumn ladies' tresses.
Contact: Steven Stansfield, Cristin, Ynys Enlli (Bardsey), off Aberaron, via Pwllheil, Gwynedd LL53 8DE. 07855 264 151; e-mail:warden@bbfo.org.uk
www.bbfo.org.uk

2. CEMLYN

North Wales Wildlife Trust.
Location: SH 329 936 and SH 336 932. Cemlyn is signposted from Tregele on A5025 between Valley and Amlwch on Anglesey.
Access: Open all the time. Dogs on leads. No wheelchair access. During summer months walk on seaward side of ridge and follow signs.
Facilities: Car parks at either end of reserve.
Public transport: None within a mile.
Habitat: Brackish lagoon, shingle ridge, salt marsh, mixed scrub.
Key birds: Wintering wildfowl and waders, breeding terns, gulls and warblers, pipits and passing migrants. *Spring*: Wheatear, Whitethroat, Sedge Warbler, Manx Shearwater, Sandwich Tern, Whimbrel, Dunlin, Knot and Black-tailed Godwit. *Summer*: Breeding Arctic, Common and Sandwich Terns, Black-headed Gull, Oystercatcher and Ringed Plover. *Autumn*: Golden Plover, Lapwing, Curlew, Manx Shearwater, Gannet, Kittiwake, Guillemot. *Winter*: Little and Great Crested Grebes, Shoveler, Shelduck, Wigeon, Red-breasted Merganser, Coot, Turnstone, Purple Sandpiper.
Other notable flora and fauna: 20 species of butterfly recorded. Sea kale, yellow horned poppy, sea purselane, sea beet, glasswort. Grey seal, harbour porpoise, bottlenose dolphin.
Contact: Trust HQ. 01248 351 541.
e-mail: nwwt@wildlifetrustswales.org
www.wildlifetrust.org.uk/northwales

3. CONNAHS QUAY POWER STATION NATURE RESERVE

Deeside Naturalists' Society and Eon UK.

Location: SJ 275 715. From England: Take A550 from Liverpool/N Wirral or A5117 from Ellesmere Port/ M56, follow road to Queensferry. 200 metres after junction of A550 and A5117, turn L at A548 and follow signs to Flint. Cross Dee Bridge and turn off dual carriageway at B5129, Connah's Quay exit.Turn R under A548 then L, following signs to power station. From Flint: Take A548 towards Connah's Quay/ Queensferry. After 2.5 miles, take B5129 (Connah's Quay exit). Turn L following signs to power station. From Connah's Quay: Take B5129 towards Flint. Go under A548, turn L following signs to power station.

Access: Advance permit required (group bookings only). Wheelchair access. Public welcome on open days — see website for details.

Facilities: Field studies centre, five hides.

Public transport: Contact Arriva Cymru on 01745 343 492.

Habitat: Saltmarsh, mudflats, grassland scrub, open water, wetland meadow.

Key birds: *Summer:* Small roosts of non-breeding estuarine birds. *Winter:* High water roosts of waders and wildfowl including, Black-tailed Godwit, Oystercatcher, Redshank, Spotted Redshank, Curlew, Lapwing, Teal, Pintail and Wigeon.

Contact: Secretary, Deeside Naturalists' Society, 21 Woodlands Court, Hawarden, Deeside, Flintshire CH5 3NB. 01244 537 440, www.deesidenaturalists.org.uk email:deenaturalists@btinternet.com

4. CONWY

RSPB (North Wales Office).

Location: SH 799 773. On E bank of Conwy Estuary. Access from A55 at exit 18 signed to Conwy and Deganwy. Footpath and cycleway accessed from Conwy Cob.

Access: Open daily (9.30am-5pm). Closed for Christmas Day. Ample parking for coaches. Toilets, buildings and trails accessible to pushchairs and wheelchairs.

Facilities: Visitor centre, gift shop, coffee shop, toilets including disabled. Four hides (accessible to wheelchairs) two viewing screens. Trails firm and level, though a little rough in places and wet in winter.

Public transport: Train service to Llandudno Junction, 10 minute walk. Bus service to Tesco supermarket, Llandudno Junction 5 minutes walk. Tel: 0871 200 2233.

Habitat: Lagoons, islands, reedbed, scrub, estuary.

Key birds: Wildfowl and waders in winter, warblers and wetland breeding birds in summer. *Spring:* Passage waders, hirundines and wagtails. *Summer:* Lapwing, waterbirds and warblers. *Winter:* Kingfisher, Goldeneye, Water Rail, Red-breasted Merganser, wildfowl, huge Starling roost.

Other notable flora and fauna: Common butterflies through summer, especially common blues. Great display of cowslips in March, bee orchids in June. Otters seen early mornings.

Contact: Conwy RSPB Nature Reserve, Llandudno Junction, Conwy LL31 9XZ. 01492 584 091.

5. GORS MAEN LLWYD

North Wales Wildlife Trust.

Location: SH 975 580. Follow A5 to Cerrigydrudion (seven miles S of site), then take B4501 and go past the Llyn Brennig Visitor Centre. Approx two miles beyond centre, turn R (still on B4501). First car park on R approx 300 yards after the cattle grid.

Access: Open all the time. Dogs on leads. Rare breeding birds on the heather so keep to paths.

Facilities: In second car park by lake shore there are toilets and short walk to bird hide. Paths are waymarked, but can be very wet and muddy in poor weather.

Habitat: Heathland. Heather and grass overlooking large lake.

Key birds: *Summer:* Red and Black Grouse, Hen Harrier, Merlin, Sky Lark, Curlew. *Winter:* Wildfowl on lake.

Contact: Graham Berry, Trust HQ, 01248 351 541; e-mail: nwwt@wildlifetrustswales.org www.wildlifetrust.org.uk/northwales

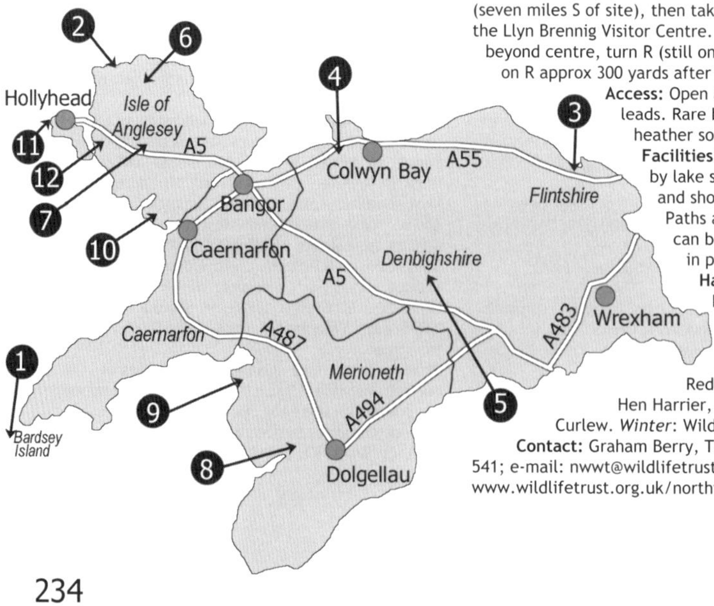

Map of Northern Wales showing: Hollyhead, Isle of Anglesey, Bangor, Caernarfon, Colwyn Bay, Flintshire, Denbighshire, Merioneth, Wrexham, Dolgellau, Bardsey Island, A5, A55, A487, A494, A483. Numbered location markers 1–12.

6. LLYN ALAW

Welsh Water/United Utilities.
Location: SH 390 865. North Anglesey, SW of Amlwch. Signposted from J5 of A55. Car park at SH375 856.
Access: Open all year. No dogs to hides or sanctuary area but dogs allowed (maximum two per adult) other areas. Limited wheelchair access. Coach parking in main car park (SH 373 856).
Facilities: Visitor centre, Toilets (including disabled), earth paths, boardwalks. Two hides, car parks, network of mapped walks, picnic sites, information boards. Coach parking at main car park.
Public transport: Not to within a mile.
Habitat: Large area of standing water, shallow reedy bays, hedges, scrub, woodland, marsh, grassland.
Key birds: *Winter*: Wildfowl and thrushes, breeding warblers/waterfowl. *Summer*: Lesser Whitethroat, Sedge and Grasshopper Warblers, Little and Great Crested Grebes, Tawny Owl, Barn Owl, Buzzard. *Winter*: Whooper Swan, Goldeneye, Hen Harrier, Short-eared Owl, Redwing, Fieldfare, Peregrine, Raven. *All year*: Bullfinch, Siskin, Redpoll, Goldfinch, Stonechat. *Passage waders*: Ruff, Spotted Redshank, Curlew Sandpiper, Green Sandpiper.
Other notable flora and fauna: Bee and northern marsh orchid, royal fern, skullcap, needle spikerush. Migrant hawker, hairy, four-spotted chaser dragonflies, banded demoiselle, wall brown, gatekeeper, clouded yellow and orange tip butterflies. Brown hare, water vole.
Contact: The Warden, Llyn Alaw, Llantrisant, Holyhead LL65 4TW. 01407 730 762.

7. LLYN CEFNI

Welsh Water/Forestry Commission/United Utilities.
Location: Entrance at Bodffordd SH 433 775 and Rhosmeirch SH 451 783. A reservoir located two miles NW of Llangefni, in central Anglesey. Follow B5111 or B5109 from the village.
Access: Open at all times. Dogs allowed except in sanctuary area. Good footpath (wheelchair accessible) for most of the site, bridges over streams.
Facilities: Two picnic sites, good footpath, coach parking at Rhosmeirch car prk SH451 783.
Public transport: Bus 32, 4 (44 Sun only, 52 Thu only). Tel 0871 200 2233 for information.
Habitat: Large area of open water, reedy bays, coniferous woodland, scrub, carr.
Key birds: *Summer*: Sedge and Grasshopper Warblers, Whitethroat, Buzzard, Tawny Owl, Little Grebe, Gadwall, Shoveler, Kingfisher. *Winter*: Waterfowl (Whooper Swan, Goldeneye), Crossbill, Redpoll, Siskin, Redwing. *All year*: Stonechat, Treecreeper, Song Thrush.
Other notable flora and fauna: Northern marsh orchid, rustyback fern, needle spikerush. Banded demoiselle, migrant hawker, golden ringed dragonfly, emerald damselfly. Ringlet, gatekeeper, clouded yellow and wall butterflies. Bloody nose beetle.
Contact: The Warden, Llyn Alaw, Llantrisant, Holyhead LL65 4TW. 01407 730 762.

8. MAWDDACH VALLEY

RSPB (North Wales Office).
Location: Coed Garth Gell (SH 688 192) is adjacent to the main Dolgellau to Barmouth road (A496) near Taicynhaeaf. No reserve parking is available but lay-bys are found close to the reserve's entrances. Arthog Bog (SH630138) is off the main Dolgellau to Tywyn road (A493) west of Arthog. Parking is available near by at the Morfa Mawddach station.
Access: Nature trails are open at all times.
Facilities: Nature trails and information boards.
Public transport: A regular bus service runs between Dolgellau and Barmouth and stops close to the reserve entrance at Coed Garth Gell. The Arthog Bog part of the reserve is served by the Dolgellau to Tywyn bus services which stops close by at Arthog. The Arthog Bog reserve is a short distance from the Morfa Mawddach railway station.
Habitat: Oak woodland, bracken and heathland at Coed Garth Gell. Willow and alder scrub and raised bog at Arthog bog.
Key birds: At Coed Garth Gell: Buzzard, Sparrowhawk, Peregrine, Raven, Lesser Spotted Woodpecker, Grey Wagtail, Dipper and Hawfinch are joined in the summer by Pied Flycatcher, Spotted Flycatcher, Wood Warbler, Redstart, Tree Pipit and Cuckoo. At Arthog bog Buzzard, Sparrowhawk, Peregrine, Raven are resident. Summer migrants include Tree Pipit, Grasshopper Warbler and Cuckoo. In winter flocks of Redpolls and Siskins are common and Red-breasted Merganser, Pintail and Little Egret are on the nearby estuary.
Other notable flora and fauna: Coed Garth Gell has Tunbridge filmy and beech ferns and a wide variety of butterflies. Golden-ringed dragonflies are regular at both reserves.
Contact: RSPB Ynys-Hir Reserve, Eglwys-fach, Machynlleth, Powys SY20 8TA. 01654 700 222. e-mail:ynyshir@rspb.org.uk

9. MORFA HARLECH NNR

CCW (North West Area).
Location: SH 574 317, NW of Harlech. On the A496 Harlech road.
Access: Open all year.
Facilities: Car park. Disabled parking bays and three coach parking spaces.
Public transport: The site is served by both bus and train. Train stations are at Harlech and Ty Gwyn (Ty Gwyn is near the saltmarsh wintering birds.) Contact Arriva for details (0844 8004 411).
Habitat: Shingle (except at Harlech), coast, marsh, dunes. Also forestry plantation, grassland, swamp.
Key birds: *Spring/summer*: Whitethroat, Spotted Flycatcher, Grasshopper Warbler, migrants. *Passage*: Waders, Manx Shearwater, ducks. *Winter*: Divers, Whooper Swan, Wigeon, Teal, Pintail, Scaup, Common Scoter, Hen Harrier, Merlin, Peregrine, Short-eared Owl, Little Egret, Water Pipit, Snow Bunting, Twite. *All year/breeding*: Redshank, Lapwing, Ringed Plover, Snipe, Curlew, Shelduck, Oystercatcher, Stonechat,

Whinchat, Wheatear, Linnet, Reed Bunting, Sedge Warbler. Also Red-breasted Merganser, Kestrel, gulls.
Other notable fauna: Sand lizard, otter, water vole.
Contact: CCW, 0845 1306 229; www.ccw.gov.uk
e-mail:enquiries@ccw.gov.uk

10. NEWBOROUGH WARREN & YNYS LLANDDWYN NNR

CCW (North Region).
Location: SH 406 670/430 630. In SE corner of Anglesey. From Menai Bridge head SW on A4080 to Niwbwrch or Malltraeth.
Access: Permit required for places away from designated routes. Disabled access from main car park in Newborough Forest.
Facilities: Toilets and shop in village. Bird hide in Llyn Rhosddu.
Public transport: Arriva Wales bus service.
Habitat: Sandhills, estuaries, saltmarshes, dune grasslands, rocky headlands.
Key birds: Wildfowl and waders at Malltraeth Pool (visible from road), Braint and Cefni estuaries (licensed winter shoot on marked areas of Cefni estuary administered by CCW); waterfowl at Llyn Rhosddu (public hide). Key site for Raven, also Curlew and other waders.
Other notable flora and fauna: Spectacular display of orchids, inc early marsh and northern marsh, plus marsh helleborine. Patch of dune helleborine located near Newborough Forest car park. Other plants inc dune pansy, yellow wort and grass of Parnassus.
Contact: CCW North Region, 0845 1306 229;
www.ccw.gov.uk e-mail:enquiries@ccw.gov.uk

11. SOUTH STACK CLIFFS

RSPB (North Wales Office).
Location: RSPB Car Park SH 211 818, Ellins Tower information centre SH 206 820. Follow A55 to W end in Holyhead, proceed straight on at roundabout, continue straight on through traffic lights. After another half mile turn L and follow the Brown Tourist signs for RSPB Ynys Lawd/South Stack.

Access: RSPB car park with disabled parking, 'Access for all' track leading to a viewing area overlooking the lighthouse adjacent to Ellins Tower Visitor centre. Access to Ellins Tower gained via staircase. Reserve covered by an extensive network of paths, some of which are steep and uneven. Coach parking by prior arrangement at The South Stack Kitchen Tel: 01407 762 181 (privately owned).
Facilities: Free access to Ellins Tower which has windows overlooking main auk colony open daily (10am-5.30pm Easter-Sep).
Public transport: Mainline station Holyhead. Infrequent local bus service, Holyhead-South Stack. Tel. 0870 608 2608.
Habitat: Sea cliffs, maritime grassland, maritime heath, lowland heath.
Key birds: Peregrine, Chough, Fulmar, Puffin, Guillemot, Razorbill, Rock Pipit, Sky Lark, Stonechat, Linnet, Shag, migrant warblers and passage seabirds.
Contact: Dave Bateson, Plas Nico, South Stack, Holyhead, Anglesey LL65 1YH. 01407 764 973.
www.rspb.org.uk

12. VALLEY WETLANDS

RSPB (North Wales Office).
Location: Off A5 on Anglesey, two miles S of Caergeilliog.
Access: Open all year.
Facilities: Nature trail. Small RSPB car park and information board to the south of Llyn Penrhyn (grid reference SH 312 765).
Public transport: Bus: Maes Awyr/RAF Valley daily from Bangor and Holyhead. Train: Valley (four miles)/ Rhosneigr (seven miles).
Habitat: Reed-fringed lakes, small rocky outcrops.
Key birds: *All year:* Grebes, ducks, geese, rails, Cetti's Warbler. *Summer:* Reed, Sedge and Grasshopper Warblers. *Winter:* Bittern recorded most years, but hard to see.
Other notable flora and fauna: Several species of dragonfly inc hairy dragonfly and variable damselfy.
Contact: RSPB North Wales Office, 01248 672 850.

Southern Wales

Glamorgan, Gower, Gwent

1. CWM CLYDACH

RSPB Wales
Location: SN 684 026. N of Swansea. Three miles N of J45 on M4, through the village of Clydach on B4291 to car park in Craig Cefn Parc.
Access: Open at all times along public footpaths and waymarked trails. Not suitable for wheelchairs. Coach parking not available.

Facilities: Two nature trails, car park, information boards.
Public transport: Hourly buses from Swansea stop at reserve entrance. Nearest railway station is in Swansea.
Habitat: Oak woodland on steep slopes lining the banks of the fast-flowing Lower Clydach River.
Key birds: Red Kite, Sparrowhawk, Buzzard, Peregrine, Raven, Green Woodpecker, Dipper, Grey

Wagtail and Marsh Tit are joined in the summer by Pied Flycatcher, Spotted Flycatcher, Wood Warbler, Redstart and Cuckoo. In winter Siskins and Lesser Redpolls are regular.
Other notable flora and fauna: Wood sorrel, silver-washed fritillary and speckled wood butterflies. Good range of fungi.
Contact: RSPB Ynys-Hir Reserve, Eglwys-fach, Machynlleth, Powys SY20 8TA. 01654 700 222.
e-mail:ynyshir@rspb.org.uk

2. CWM COL-HUW

The Wildlife Trust of South and West Wales.
Location: SS 957 674. SE from Bridgend, site includes Iron Age fort, overlooking Bristol Channel. From Bridgend take B4265 S to Llanwit Major. Follow beach road from village.
Access: Park in seafront car park. Climb steps. Open all year.
Facilities: All year toilets and café. Information boards.
Public transport: None.
Habitat: Unimproved grassland, woodland, scrub and Jurassic blue lias cliff.
Key birds: Cliff-nesting House Martin colony, breeding Fulmar, Grasshopper Warbler. Large autumn passerine passage. Peregrine. Seawatching vantage point. Occasional Chough.
Contact: Trust HQ, 01656 724 100.
e-mail:information@wtsww.cix.co.uk

3. KENFIG NNR

Bridgend County Borough Council.
Location: SS 802 811. Seven miles W of Bridgend. From J37 on M4, drive towards Porthcawl, then North Cornelly, then follow signs.
Access: Open at all times. Unsurfaced sandy paths, not suitable for wheelchairs. Flooding possible in winter and spring. Coach parking available.
Facilities: Toilets, hides, free car parking and sign-posted paths. Visitor centre and shop open weekends and holidays (10am-4.30pm), weekdays (2pm-4.30pm). Rooms available for hire.
Public transport: Local bus service: contact reserve for details.
Habitat: 1,300 acre sand dune system, freshwater lake with reeds, numerous wet dune slacks, sandy coastline with some rocky outcrops.
Key birds: *Summer:* Warblers and migrants including Cetti's, Grasshopper, Sedge, Reed, Lesser Whitethroat and Whitethroat. *Winter:* coastal waders and divers, wildfowl, Water Rail, Bittern and Merlin.
Other notable flora and fauna: 16 species of orchid, hairy dragonfly, red-veined and ruddy darters, small blue, dark green

fritillary, grayling, brown argus butterflies.
Contact: David Carrington, Ton Kenfig, Bridgend, CF33. 4PT01656 743 386.
e-mail:david.carrington@bridgend.gov.uk

4. MAGOR MARSH

Gwent Wildlife Trust.
Location: ST 427 867. Magor can be reached from junctions 23 and 23A of the M4 motorway. Reserve lies to S of Magor. Leave M4 at exit 23, turning R onto B4245. Follow signs for Redwick in Magor village. Take first L after railway bridge. Reserve entrance is half mile further on R.
Access: Open all year. Keep to path. Wheelchair access to bird hide..
Facilities: Hide. Car park, footpaths and boardwalks.
Public transport: Bus service to Magor village. Reserve is approx 10 mins walk along Redwick road.
Habitat: Sedge fen, reedswamp, willow carr, damp hay meadows and open water.
Key birds: Important for wetland birds. *Spring:* Reed, Sedge and Grasshopper Warblers, occasional Garganey and Green Sandpiper on passage, Hobby. *Winter:* Teal, Peregrine, Jack Snipe, Snipe, occasional Shoveler and Gadwall, Bittern records in two recent years. *All year:* Little Egret, Little Grebe, Reed Bunting, Cetti's Warbler and Water Rail.
Contact: Gwent Wildlife Trust, Seddon House, Dingestow, Monmouth NP25 4DY. 01600 740 358;
e-mail:info@gwentwildlife.co.uk
www.gwentwildlife.org

5. NEWPORT WETLANDS NNR

CCW/ RSPB/ Newport City Council.
Location: ST 334 834. SW of Newport. Reserve car park on West Nash Road, just before entrance to Uskmouth power station. From M4 J 24 take the A48 to Newport Retail Park, turn towards steelworks and follow brown 'duck' signs to the reserve car park.
Access: Free entry 9am to 5pm each day apart from Dec 25. Six disabled parking bays. All nature trails are accessible by wheelchair. Dogs only on perimeter footpath.
Facilities: Information centre, tea-rooms, shop, toilets (inc disabled), viewing screens.

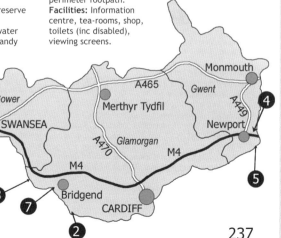

Public transport: No 65 bus from Queensway bus station in Newport stops at West Nash Community Hall, a 15 min walk from reserve. Contact Newport bus services, tel: 01633 263 600. Nearest train station: Newport.
Habitat: 438 hectares of wet meadows, saline lagoons, reedbed, scrub and mudflats on Severn estuary.
Key birds: *Spring/ summer:* Breeding waders such as Lapwing and Oystercatcher, Bearded Tit, Cetti's Warbler, Cuckoo and regular migrants on passage. *Autumn:* Large numbers of migrating wildfowl and waders arrive at the reserve — regulars include Curlew, Dunlin, Ringed Plover, Shoveler. *Winter:* Massive Starling roost (up to 50,000 birds). Bittern, nationally important numbers of Black-tailed Godwit, Shoveler and Dunlin.
Other notable flora and fauna: Badger, wood mouse, otter. Great crested newt. Orchids in spring, 16 species of dragonfly, 23 species of butterfly and around 200 species of moth.
Contact: Newport Wetlands Reserve, West Nash Road, Newport NP18 2BZ. RSPB visitor centre — 01633 636 363.

6. OXWICH

CCW (Swansea Office).
Location: SS 872 773. 12 miles from Swansea, off A4118.
Access: NNR open at all times. No permit required for access to foreshore, dunes, woodlands and facilities.
Facilities: Private car park, summer only. Toilets

summer only. Marsh boardwalk and marsh lookout. No visitor centre, no facilities for disabled visitors.
Public transport: Bus service Swansea/Oxwich. First Cymru, tel 01792 580 580.
Habitat: Freshwater marsh, saltmarsh, foreshore, dunes, woodlands.
Key birds: *Summer:* Breeding Reed, Sedge and Cetti's Warblers, Treecreeper, Nuthatch, woodpeckers. *Winter:* Wildfowl.
Contact: Countryside Council for Wales, RVB House, Llys Tawe, King's Road, Swansea SA1 8PG. 01792 634 960.e-mail:enquiries@ccw.gov.uk www.ccw.gov.uk

7. PARC SLIP NATURE PARK

The Wildlife Trust of South and West Wales.
Location: SS 880 840. Tondu, half mile W of Aberkenfig. From Bridgend take A4063 N, turning L onto B4281 after passing M4. Reserve is signposted from this road.
Access: Open dawn to dusk. Space for coach parking.
Facilities: Three hides, nature trail, interpretation centre.
Public transport: None.
Habitat: Restored opencast mining site, wader scrape, lagoons.
Key birds: *Summer:* Breeding Tufted Duck, Lapwing, Sky Lark. Migrant waders (inc. Little Ringed Plover, Green Sandpiper), Little Gull. Kingfisher, Green Woodpecker.
Contact: Trust HQ, 01656 724 100.
e-mail:info@welshwildlife.org

Western Wales

Carmarthenshire, Ceredigion, Pembrokeshire

1. CASTLE WOODS

The Wildlife Trust of South and West Wales.
Location: SN 615 217. About 60 acres of woodland overlooking River Tywi, W of Llandeilo town centre.
Access: Open all year by footpath from Tywi Bridge, Llandeilo (SN 627 221).
Facilities: Castle at W edge of woods open to visitors.
Public transport: None.
Habitat: Old mixed deciduous woodlands containing many large 'veteran' trees.
Key birds: All three woodpeckers, Buzzard, Raven, Sparrowhawk, Nuthatch and Treecreeper. *Summer:* Pied and Spotted Flycatchers, Redstart, Wood Warbler. *Winter:* On water meadows, look for Teal, Wigeon, Goosander, Shoveler, Tufted Duck and Pochard.
Other notable flora and fauna: Fallow deer.

Contact: Trust HQ, 01656 724 100.
e-mail:info@welshwildlife.org
www.welshwildlife.org

2. CORS CARON

CCW (West Wales Area).
Location: SN 692 625 (car park). Reached from B4343 N of Tregaron.
Access: Open access to S of car park along the railway to boardwalk (which is wheelchair accessible), out to SE bog. Access to rest of the reserve by permit. Dogs (on lead) allowed on boardwalk and old railway line walk but not on Riverside Walk. Access for coaches.
Facilities: New car park with toilets (one with disabled access) and picnic space. Bird hide along boardwalk. Riverside walk is open access. For access

to the rest of the reserve please contact the reserve manager.

Public transport: None.
Habitat: Raised bog, river, fen, wet grassland, willow woodland, reedbed.
Key birds: *Summer:* Lapwing, Redshank, Curlew, Red Kite, Hobby, Grasshopper Warbler, Whinchat. *Winter:* Teal, Wigeon, Whooper Swan, Hen Harrier, Red Kite.
Other notable flora and fauna: Small red damselfly among the abundant dragonflies which can be seen from boardwalk.
Contact: CCW, 01974 298 480;
e-mail:p.culyer@ccw.gov.uk www.ccw.gov.uk

3. GWENFFRWD & DINAS

RSPB Wales
Location: SN 788 471. North of Llandovery.From A483 take B road signposted to Llyn Brianne Reservoir.
Access: Public nature trail at Dinas open at all times.
Facilities: Nature trail including a board walk. Other parts of the trail are rugged. Car park and information board at start of trail. Coach parking can be arranged.
Public transport: Nearest station at Llandovery, 10 miles away.
Habitat: Hillside oak woods, streams and bracken slopes. Spectacular upland scenery.
Key birds: Upland species such as Red Kite, Buzzard, Peregrine, Raven, Goosander, Dipper and Grey Wagtail are joined in the summer by Pied Flycatcher, Spotted Flycatcher, Wood Warbler, Redstart, Tree Pipit, Common Sandpiper And Cuckoo. Marsh Tit and all three woodpecker species are present.
Other notable flora and fauna: Golden-ringed dragonfly, purple hairstreak, silver-washed fritillary and Wilson's filmy fern.
Contact: RSPB Ynys-Hir Reserve, Eglwys-fach, Machynlleth, Powys SY20 8TA. 01654 700 222.
e-mail:ynyshir@rspb.org.uk

4. DYFI

CCW (West Wales Area).
Location: SN 610 942. Large estuary area W of Machynlleth. Public footpaths off A493 E of Aberdyfi, and off B4353 (S of river); minor road from B4353 at Ynyslas to dunes and parking area.
Access: Ynyslas dunes and the estuary have unrestricted access. No access to Cors Fochno (raised bog) for casual birdwatching; permit required for study and research purposes. Good views over the bog and Aberleri marshes from W bank of Afon Leri.
Facilities: Public hide overlooking marshes beside footpath at SN 611 911.
Public transport: None.
Habitat: Sandflats, mudflats, saltmarsh, creeks, dunes, raised bog, grazing marsh.
Key birds: *Winter:* Greenland White-fronted Goose, wildfowl, waders and raptors. *Summer:* Breeding wildfowl

and waders (inc. Teal, Shoveler, Merganser, Lapwing, Curlew, Redshank).
Contact: CCW Warden, Plas Gogerddan, Aberystwyth, Ceredigion SY23 3EE. 01970 821 100.

5. NATIONAL WETLANDS CENTRE WALES

The Wildfowl & Wetlands Trust.
Location: SS 533 984. Overlooks the Burry Inlet near Llanelli. Leave M4 at junction 48. Signposted from A484, E of Llanelli.
Access: Open daily 9.30am-5pm, except Christmas Eve and Christmas Day. Grounds are open until 6pm in summer. The centre is fully accessible with disabled toilets. Mobility scooters and wheelchairs are free to hire.
Facilities: Visitor centre with toilets, hides, restaurant, shop, education facilities, free car and coach parking. The centre has level access and hard-surfaced paths.
Public transport: Bus from Llanelli to Lllwydhendy, approx 1 mile from the centre. Telephone Traveline Cymru 0871 200 2233 (7am-10pm daily).
Habitat: Inter-tidal mudflats, reedbeds, pools, marsh, waterfowl collection.
Key birds: Large flocks of Curlew, Oystercatcher, Redshank on saltmarsh. *Winter:* Pintail, Wigeon, Teal. Also Little Egret, Short-eared Owl, Peregrine.**Other notable flora and fauna:** Bee and southern marsh orchids, yellow bartisa. Damselflies and dragonflies, water voles and otters.
Contact: Centre Manager, WWT National Wetlands Centre Wales, Llwynhendy, Llanelli SA14 9SH. 01554 741 087; e-mail:info.llanelli@wwt.org.uk www.wwt.org.uk

6. RAMSEY ISLAND

RSPB (CYMRU).
Location: SM 706 237. One mile offshore from St Justinians lifeboat station. Two miles west of St Davids, Pembrokeshire.
Access: Open every day, weather

permitting, Easter-Oct 31. No wheelchair access. Coach parking available at St Justinians. For boat bookings Contact: Thousand Island Expeditions, 01437 721721; e-mail. sales@thousandislands.co.uk
Facilities: Toilets, small RSPB shop selling snacks and hot and cold drinks. Self-guiding trail with introduction from resident wardens. Guided walks are also available.
Public transport: Trains to Haverfordwest Station. Hourly buses to St Davids and then Celtic Coaster shuttle bus to boat embarkation point (Tel 01348 840539)
Habitat: Acid grassland, maritime heath, seacliffs.
Key birds: *Spring/summer*: Cliff-nesting auks (Guillemot, Razorbill), Kittiwake, Fulmar, Lesser, Great Black-backed and Herring Gulls, Shag, Wheatear, Stonechat. Sky Lark, Linnet. *All year*: Peregrine, Raven, Chough, Lapwing.
Other notable flora and fauna: Grey seal, red deer, harbour porpoise.
Contact: The Warden: 07836 535 733.
www.rspb.org.uk/ramseyisland

7. SKOKHOLM ISLAND

The Wildlife Trust of South and West Wales.
Location: SM 735 050. Island lying S of Skomer.
Access: Occasional day visits, also 3 or 4 night stays available. Weekly accomm. Apr-Sep, tel 01239 621 212 for details and booking.
Facilities: Call for details.
Public transport: None.
Habitat: Cliffs, bays and inlets.
Key birds: *Summer*: Large colonies of Razorbill, Puffin, Guillemot, Manx Shearwater, Storm Petrel, Lesser Black-backed Gull. Migrants inc. rare species.
Contact: 01239 621 212.

8. SKOMER ISLAND

The Wildlife Trust of South and West Wales.
Location: SM 725 095. Fifteen miles from Haverfordwest. Take B4327 turn-off for Marloes, embarkation point at Martin's Haven, two miles past village.
Access: Apr 1-Oct 31. Boats sail at 10am, 11am and noon every day except Mon (Bank Holidays excluded). Closed four days beginning of Jun for seabird counts. Not suitable for infirm (steep landing steps and rough ground).
Facilities: Information centre, toilets, two hides, wardens, booklets, guides, nature trails.
Habitat: Maritime cliff, heathland, freshwater ponds.
Key birds: Largest colony of Manx Shearwater in the world. Puffin, Guillemot, Razorbill (Apr-end Jul). Kittiwake (until end Aug), Fulmar (absent Oct), Short-eared Owl (during day Jun and Jul), Chough, Peregrine, Buzzard (all year), migrants.
Contact: Skomer Island, Marloes, Pembs SA62 2BJ. 07971 114 302; e-mail: skomer@wtww.co.uk

9. WELSH WILDLIFE CENTRE

The Wildlife Trust of South and West Wales.
Location: SN 188 451. Two miles SE of Cardigan. River Teifi is N boundary. Sign-posted from Cardigan to Fishguard road.
Access: Open 10.30am-5pm all year. Free parking for WTSWW members, £3 non-members. Dogs on leads welcome. Disabled access to visitor centre, paths, four hides.
Facilities: Visitor centre, restaurant, network of paths and seven hides.
Public transport: Train station, Haverfordwest (23 miles). Bus station in Cardigan. Access on foot from Cardigan centre, ten mins.
Habitat: Wetlands, marsh, swamp, reedbed, open water, creek (tidal), river, saltmarsh, woodland.
Key birds: Cetti's Warbler, Kingfisher, Water Rail, Great Spotted Woodpecker, Dipper, gulls, Marsh Harrier, Sand Martin, Hobby, Redstart, occasional Bittern and Red Kite.
Contact: The Welsh Wildlife Centre, Cilgerran, Cardigan SA43 2TB. 01239 621 212.
e-mail:wwc@welshwildlife.org
www.welshwildlife.org

10. YNYS-HIR

RSPB (CYMRU).
Location: SN 68 29 63. Off A487 Aberystwyth — Machynlleth road in Eglwys-fach village. Six miles SW of Machynlleth.
Access: Open every day (9am-9pm or dusk if earlier) except Christmas Day. Visitor centre open daily Apr-Oct (10am-5pm), Wed-Sun Nov-Mar (10am-4pm). Coaches welcome but please call for parking information. Sorry, no dogs allowed.
Facilities: Visitor centre and toilets. Numerous trails, six hides, drinks machine.
Public transport: Bus service to Eglwys-fach from either Machynlleth or Aberystwyth, tel. 01970 617 951. Rail service to Machynlleth.
Habitat: Estuary, freshwater pools, woodland and wet grassland.
Key birds: Large numbers of wintering waders, wildfowl and birds of prey on the estuary are replaced with breeding woodland birds in spring and summer. *All year*: Red Kite, Buzzard, Little Egret, Lapwing, Teal. *Spring*: Wood Warbler, Redstart, Pied Flycatcher, nine species of warbler. *Winter*: Greenland white-fronted Goose, Barnacle Goose, Wigeon, Hen Harrier.
Other notable flora and fauna: Sixteen species of dragonfly and damselfly include small red damselfly and golden-ringed dragonfly. Butterflies include dark green fritillary, brimstone and speckled wood. Otters and brown hares are resident though the former are rarely seen.
Contact: RSPB Ynys-Hir Reserve, Eglwys-fach, Machynlleth, Powys SY20 8TA. 01654 700 222.
e-mail:ynyshir@rspb.org.uk

COUNTY DIRECTORY

David Cromack

Though Reed Buntings are widely distributed throughout the UK, their declining numbers means they are now on the conservation Red List.

ENGLAND

THE INFORMATION in the directory has been obtained either from the persons listed or from the appropriate national or other bodies. In some cases, where it has not proved possible to verify the details directly, alternative responsible sources have been relied upon. When no satisfactory record was available, previously included entries have sometimes had to be deleted. Readers are requested to advise the editor of any errors or omissions.

AVON
See Somerset.

BEDFORDSHIRE

Bird Atlas/Avifauna
An Atlas of the Breeding Birds of Bedfordshire 1988-92 by R A Dazley and P Trodd (Bedfordshire Natural History Society, 1994).

Bird Recorders
Steve Blain, 34 Southill Road, Broom, Bedfordshire SG18 9NN. 07979 606 300;
e-mail: recorder@bedsbirdclub.org.uk

Bird Report
BEDFORDSHIRE BIRD REPORT (1946-), from Mary Sheridan, 28 Chestnut Hill, Linslade, Leighton Buzzard, Beds LU7 2TR. 01525 378 245;
e-mail: membership@bnhs.org.uk

BTO Regional Representative
RR. Nigel Willits, Orchard Cottage, 68 High Street, Wilden, Beds MK44 2QD. 01234 771 948;
e-mail: willits1960@hotmail.com

Club
BEDFORDSHIRE BIRD CLUB. (1992; 300). Miss Sheila Alliez, Flat 61 Adamson Court, Adamson Walk, Kempston, Bedford MK42 8QZ.
E-mail: alliezsec@peewit.
freeserve.co.uk
www.bedsbirdclub.org.uk
Meetings: 8.00pm, last Tuesday of the month (Sep-Mar), Maulden Village Hall, Maulden, Beds.

Ringing Groups
IVEL RG. Graham Buss, 11 Northall Close, Eaton Bray, Dunstable, LU6 2EB. 01525 221 023;
e-mail: g1j2buss@yahoo.co.uk

RSPB. WB Kirby. E-mail: will.kirby@rspb.org.uk

RSPB Local Groups
BEDFORD. (1970; 80). Bob Montgomery, 36 Princes Road, Bromham, Beds MK43 8QD. 01234 822 035;
e-mail: montgomery547@btinternet.com
www.rspb.org.uk/groups/bedford/
Meetings: 7.30pm, 3rd Thursday of the month, A.R.A. Manton Lane, Bedford.

LUTON AND SOUTH BEDFORDSHIRE. (1973; 120+).
Allyn Hill, 01582 666 297;
e-mail: cah_halfmoon@yahoo.com
www.rspb.org.uk/groups/luton
Meetings: 7.45pm, 2nd Wednesday of the month, Houghton Regis Social Cnetre, Parkside Drive, Houghton Regis, LU5 5QN.

Wetland Bird Survey Organiser
BEDFORDSHIRE. Mr R I Bashford, 6 Brook Road, St Neots, Cambridgeshire PE19 7AX;
e-mail: richard.bashford@rspb.org.uk

Wildlife Trust
See Cambridgeshire,

BERKSHIRE

Bird Atlas/Avifauna
The Birds of Berkshire by P E Standley et al (Berkshire Atlas Group/Reading Ornithological Club, 1996).

Bird Recorder
RECORDER (Records Committee and rarity records). Chris DR Heard, 3 Waterside Lodge, Ray Mead Road, Maidenhead, Berkshire SL6 8NP. 01628 633 828;
e-mail: chris.heard@virgin.net

Bird Reports
BERKSHIRE BIRD BULLETIN (Monthly, 1986-), from Brian Clews, 118 Broomhill, Cookham, Berks SL6 9LQ. 01628 525314; e-mail: brian.clews@btconnect.com

BIRDS OF BERKSHIRE (1974-), from Secretary of the Berkshire Ornithological Club,
e-mail: mike.turton@berksoc.org.uk
www.berksoc.org.uk

BIRDS OF THE THEALE AREA (1988-), from Secretary, Theale Area Bird Conservation Group.

NEWBURY DISTRICT BIRD REPORT (1959-) - covering West Berkshire (approx 12 miles from centre of Newbury), plus parts of north Hants, south Oxon, from Secretary, Newbury District Ornithological Club.

BTO Regional Representatives
RR. Sarah Priest and Kent White,. 01635 268 442;
e-mail: btoberks.ken.sarah@googlemail.com

Clubs
BERKSHIRE BIRD BULLETIN GROUP. (1986; 100). Berkshire Bird Bulletin Group, PO Box 680,

Maidenhead, Berks, SL6 9ST. 01628 525314; e-mail: brian.clews@btconnect.com

BERKSHIRE ORNITHOLOGICAL CLUB. (1947; 320). Mike Turton, 7, Fawcett Crescent, Woodley, Reading, RG5 3HX. 07815 644 385; www.berksoc.org.uk e-mail: mike.turton@berksoc.org.uk **Meetings:** 8pm, alternate Wednesdays (Oct-Mar). University of Reading.

NEWBURY DISTRICT ORNITHOLOGICAL CLUB. (1959; 110). Mr Jonathan Wilding, 4 Eliot Close, Thatcham, Berkshire RG18 3UG01635 827 088; e-mail: info1@ndoc.org.uk www.ndoc.org.uk

BERKSHIRE ORNITHOLOGICAL CLUB. (1947; 320). Mike Turton, 7, Fawcett Crescent, Woodley, Reading, RG5 3HX. 07815 644 385; www.berksoc.org.uk e-mail: mike.turton@berksoc.org.uk **Meetings:** 8pm, alternate Wednesdays (Oct-Mar). University of Reading.

THEALE AREA BIRD CONSERVATION GROUP. (1988; 75). Catherine McEwan, Secretary. 01189 415 792; e-mail: catherine_j_mcewan@fsmail.net www.freewebs.com/tabcg/index.htm **Meetings:** 8pm, 1st Tuesday of the month, Englefield Social Club.

Ringing Groups
NEWBURY RG. J Legg, 31 Haysoms Drive, Greenham, Thatcham, Nr Newbury, Berks RG19 8EY. E-mail: janlegg@btinternet.com www.newburyrg.co.uk

RUNNYMEDE RG. D G Harris, 22 Blossom Waye, Hounslow, TW5 9HD. http://rmxrg.org.uk E-mail: daveharris@tinyonline.co.uk

RSPB Local Groups
EAST BERKSHIRE. (1974; 200). Gerry Studd, 5 Cherry Grove, Holmer Green, High Wycombe, Bucks HP15 6RG. 01494 715 609; e-mail: gerrystudd@aol.com www.eastberksrspb.org.uk **Meetings:** 7.30pm, Thursdays (Sept-April), Methodist Church Hall, High Street, Maidenhead.

READING. (1986; 80). Carl Feltham. 0118 941 1713; e-mail: carl.feltham@virginmedia.com www.reading-rspb.org.uk

WOKINGHAM & BRACKNELL. (1979; 200). Les Blundell, Folly Cottage, Buckle Lane, Warfield, RG42 5SB. 01344 861964; e-mail: lesblundell@ymail.com www.rspb.org.uk/groups/wokinghamandbracknell **Meetings:** 8.00pm, 2nd Tuesday of the month (Sep-Jun), Finchampstead Memorial Hall, Wokingham, RG40 4JU.

Wetland Bird Survey Organisers
BERKSHIRE. Mr G Foster, 37 Park Road, Henley-on-Thames, Oxfordshire RG9 1DB. 07738 319 206; e-mail: websberkshire@aol.co.uk

Wildlife Hospitals
LIFELINE. Wendy Hermon, Treatment Centre Co-ordinator, Swan Treatment Centre, Cuckoo Weir Island, South Meadow Lane, Eton, Windsor, Berks SL4 6SS. 01753 859 397 (fax) 01753 622 709;

e-mail: wendyhermon@swanlifeline.org.uk www.swanlifeline.org.uk Registered charity. Thames Valley 24-hour swan rescue and treatment service. Veterinary support and hospital unit. Operates membership scheme.

Wildlife Trust
Director, See Oxfordshire.

BUCKINGHAMSHIRE

Bird Atlas/Avifauna
The Birds of Buckinghamshire ed by P Lack and D Ferguson (Buckinghamshire Bird Club, 1993). Now out of print.

Bird Recorder
Andy Harding, 93 Deanshanger Lane, Old Stratford, Milton Keynes MK19 6AX. 01908 565 896 (home/ evening/weekends) 01908 653 328 (work/weekdays); e-mail: a.v.harding@open.ac.uk

Bird Reports
AMERSHAM BIRDWATCHING CLUB ANNUAL REPORT (1975-), from Secretary.

BUCKINGHAMSHIRE BIRD REPORT (1980-), from John Gearing, Valentines, Dinton, Aylesbury, Bucks, HP17 8UW. E-mail: john_gearing@hotmail.com

NORTH BUCKS BIRD REPORT (12 pa), from John Gearing, 01296 748 245; e-mail: clubrecorder@bucksbirdclub.co.uk

BTO Regional Representatives
RR. Position Vacant

BTO Garden BirdWatch Ambassador
Mrs S Plaster, e-mail: steph.plaster@googlemail.com

Clubs
BUCKINGHAMSHIRE BIRD CLUB. (1981; 340). Neill Foster, Secretary. 01296 748 597; e-mail: Secretary@bucksbirdclub.co.uk www.bucksbirdclub.co.uk

NORTH BUCKS BIRDERS. (1977; 30). Ted Reed, c/o AACS, The Open University, Walton Hall, Milton Keynes MK7 6AA. 01908 653 517 (work); e-mail: E.J.Reed@open.ac.uk **Meetings:** No meetings. Contact is via North Bucks email group. To join contact the Group Administrator, Simon Nichols (si.nich@yahoo.com)

RSPB Local Groups
See also Herts: Chorleywood,

ENGLAND

AYLESBURY. (1981; 220). Brian Fisher
01844 215 924; e-mail: brian.fisher45@yahoo.co.uk
Website: www.rspb.org.uk/groups/aylesbury

NORTH BUCKINGHAMSHIRE. (1976; 440). Chris Ward,
41 William Smith Close, Woolstone, Milton Keynes,
MK15 0AN. 01908 669 448;
e-mail: northbucksrspb@hotmail.com
www.rspb.org.uk/groups/northbucks
Meetings: 8.00pm, 2nd Thursday of the month, Cruck
Barn, City Discovery Centre, Bradwell Abbey, MK13
9AP.

Wetland Bird Survey Organisers
BUCKINGHAMSHIRE. Graeme Taylor, Field House, 54
Halton Lane, Wendover, Aylesbury, Buckinghamshire
HP22 6AU. 01296 625 796.

Wildlife Hospitals
WILDLIFE HOSPITAL TRUST. St Tiggywinkles, Aston
Road, Haddenham, Aylesbury, Bucks, HP17 8AF.
01844 292 292 (24hr helpline);
e-mail: mail@sttiggywinkles.org.uk
www.sttiggywinkles.org.ukRegistered charity. All
British species. Veterinary referrals and helpline
for vets and others on wild bird treatments. Full
veterinary unit and staff. Pub: Bright Eyes (free to
members - sae).

Wildlife Trust
Director, See Oxfordshire,

CAMBRIDGESHIRE

Bird Atlas/Avifauna
*An Atlas of the Breeding Birds of Cambridgeshire (VC
29)* P M M Bircham et al (Cambridge Bird Club, 1994).

The Birds of Cambridgeshire: checklist 2000
(Cambridge Bird Club)

Bird Recorders
CAMBRIDGESHIRE. Mark Hawkes, 7 Cook Drive,
Eynesbury, St Neots, Cambs PE19 2JU. 01480 215 305;
e-mail: marklhawkes@yahoo.co.uk

Bird Reports
CAMBRIDGESHIRE BIRD REPORT (1925-), from Bruce
Martin, 178 Nuns Way, Cambridge, CB4 2NS. (H)01223
700 656; e-mail: bruce.s.martin@ntlworld.com

PETERBOROUGH BIRD CLUB REPORT (1999-), from
Secretary, Peterborough Bird Club.

BTO Regional Representatives
CAMBRIDGESHIRE RR. Position vacant.

HUNTINGDON & PETERBOROUGH. Phillip Todd. 01733
810 832; e-mail: huntspbororr@yahoo.co.uk

Clubs
CAMBRIDGESHIRE BIRD CLUB. (1925; 329). John
Harding, 3 Cotton's Field, Dry Drayton, Cambs CB23
8DG. E-mail: johnharding44@googlemail.com
Meetings: 2nd Friday of the month, St John's Church

Hall, Hills Road, Cambridge/Cottenham Village
College.

PETERBOROUGH BIRD CLUB. (1999; 210) Keith
Stapleford, 15 Derby Drive, Peterborough PE1 4NG.
01733 555 793; e-mail: keith.stapleford@talktalk.net
www.peterboroughbirdclub.co.uk
Meetings: Last Tuesday each month (Sep-Nov and Jan
-Apr) at 7.30pm at Post Office Social Club, Bourges
Boulevard, Peterborough. Outdoor meetings monthly
throughout most of year. Non-members welcome.

THE FRIENDS OF PAXTON PITS. (1995; 2,200+).
Membership enquiries, Marilyn McDonough, 01480 351
823; www.paxton-pits.org.uk
Meetings: No set days or venues - visit website for
details.

Ringing Group
WICKEN FEN RG. Dr C J R Thorne, 17 The Footpath,
Coton, Cambs CB23 7PX. 01954 210 566;
e-mail: cjrt@cam.ac.uk

RSPB Local Groups
CAMBRIDGE. (1977; 150). Melvyn Smith. 01799 500
482; e-mail: mel_brensmith@hotmail.co.uk
www.RSPB.org.uk/groups/cambridge
Meetings: 3rd Wednesday of every month Jan-May
and Sept-Dec 8pm. Chemistry Labs, Lensfield Road,
Cambridge.

HUNTINGDONSHIRE. (1982; 180). Martyn Williams,
1487 710 456; e-mail: edunit@edunit.plus.com
www.rspb.org.uk/groups/huntingdonshire
Meetings: 7.30pm, last Wednesday of the month
(Sep-Apr), Free Church, St Ives.

Wetland Bird Survey Organisers
CAMBRIDGESHIRE (including Huntingdonshire). Bruce
Martin, 178 Nuns Way, Cambridge, CB4 2NS. (H)01223
700 656; e-mail: bruce.s.martin@ntlworld.com

NENE WASHES. Charlie Kitchin, RSPB Nene Washes,
21a East Delph, Whittlesey, Cambs PE7 1RH. 01733
205 140; e-mail: Charlie.kitchin@rspb.org.uk

OUSE WASHES. Paul Harrngton, Ouse Washes RSPB
Reserve, e-mail: paul.harrington@rspb.org.uk

SOUTH LINCOLNSHIRE/PETERBOROUGH (inland). Bob
Titman, 01733 583 254; e-mail: titman@nildram.co.uk

Wildlife Trust
THE WILDLIFE TRUST FOR BEDFORDSHIRE,
CAMBRIDGESHIRE, NORTHAMPTONSHIRE AND
PETERBOROUGH. (1990; 33,000). The Manor House,
Broad Street, Great Cambourne, Cambridgeshire CB23
6DH. 01954 713 500; www.wildlifebcnp.org
e-mail: cambridgeshire@wildlifebcnp.org

CHESHIRE

Bird Atlas/Avifauna
*Birds in Cheshire and Wirral - A Breeding and
Wintering Atlas 2004-2007* by Professor David

ENGLAND

Norman, Liverpool University Press, Autumn 2008.

The Birds of Sandbach Flashes 1935-1999 by Andrew Goodwin and Colin Lythgoe (The Printing House, Crewe, 2000).

Bird Recorder (inc Wirral)
CHESHIRE & WIRRAL. Hugh Pulsford, 6 Buttermere Drive, Great Warford, Alderley Edge, Cheshire SK9 7WA. 01565 880 171; e-mail: countyrec@cawos.org

Bird Report
CHESHIRE & WIRRAL BIRD REPORT (1969-), from Andrew Duncalf, 25 Monarch Drive, Northwich, Cheshire CW9 8UN. 07771 774 5210;
e-mail: andrewduncalf@cawos.org
www.cawos.org

SOUTH EAST CHESHIRE ORNITHOLOGICAL SOCIETY BIRD REPORT (1985-), from The Secretary, South East Cheshire Ornithol Soc. 01270 5826 42.

BTO Regional Representatives & Regional Development Officer
MID RR. Paul Miller. 01928 787 535;
e-mail: huntershill@worldonline.co.uk

NORTH & EAST RR. Mark Eddowes, 59 Westfield Drive, Knutsford, Cheshire WA16 0BH. 01925 843 422; e-mail: mark.eddowes@esrtechnology.com

SOUTH RR & RDO. Charles Hull, Edleston Cottage, Edleston Hall Lane, Nantwich, Cheshire CW5 8PL. 01270 628194; e-mail: edleston@yahoo.co.uk

BTO Garden BirdWatch Ambassador
Mr G J Pilkington,
e-mail: george.pilkington@ntlworld.com

Clubs
CHESHIRE & WIRRAL ORNITHOLOGICAL SOCIETY. (1988; 375). Dr Ted Lock, 2 Bourne Street, Wilmslow, Cheshire, SK9 5HD. 01625 540 466;
e-mail: secretary@cawos.org www.cawos.org
Meetings: 7.45pm, 1st Friday of the month, Knutsford Civic Centre.

CHESTER & DISTRICT ORNITHOLOGICAL SOCIETY. (1967; 50). David King, 13 Bennett Close, Willaston, South Wirral, CH64 2XF. 0151 327 7212;
Meetings: 7.30pm, 1st Thursday of the month (Oct-Mar), Caldy Valley Community Centre.

KNUTSFORD ORNITHOLOGICAL SOCIETY. (1974; 45). Derek A Pike, 2 Lilac Avenue, Knutsford, Cheshire, WA16 0AZ. 01565 653 811;
e-mail: tony@mobberley.eu www.10x50.com
Meetings: 7.30pm, 4th Friday of the month (not Dec), Jubilee Hall, Stanley Road, Knutsford.

LANCASHIRE & CHESHIRE FAUNA SOCIETY. (1914; 140). Dave Bickerton, 64 Petre Crescent, Rishton, Blackburn, Lancs, BB1 4RB. 01254 886 257;
e-mail: bickertond@aol.com www.lacfs.org.uk

LYMM ORNITHOLOGY GROUP. (1975; 60). Mandy Tongue; email: mandy.tonge@zetnet.co.uk

www.users.zetnet.co.uk/lymmog/
Meetings: 8.00pm, last Friday of the month (Aug-May), Lymm Village Hall.

MID-CHESHIRE ORNITHOLOGICAL SOCIETY. (1963; 80). John Drake, 17 Wisenholme Close, Beechwood West, Runcorn, Cheshire WA7 2RU. 01928 561 133; e-mail: contact@midcheshireos.co.uk
www.midcheshireos.co.uk
Meetings: 7:30pm, 2nd Friday of the month (Oct-Mar), Cuddington and Sandiway Village Hall.

SOUTH EAST CHESHIRE ORNITHOLOGICAL SOCIETY. (1964; 140). Colin Lythgoe, 11 Waterloo Road, Haslington, Crewe, CW1 5TF. 01270 582 642;
www.secos.org.uk
Meetings: 2nd Friday (Sept-Apr), 7.30pm, Ettiley Heath Church Community Centre, Sandbach.

WILMSLOW GUILD BIRDWATCHING GROUP. (1965; 67). Tom Gibbons, Chestnut Cottage, 37 Strawberry Lane, Wilmslow, Cheshire SK9 6AQ. 01625 520 317;
http://wgbw.wikidot.com
Meetings: 7.30pm last Friday of the month, Wilmslow Guild, Bourne St, Wilmslow.

Ringing Groups
CHESHIRE SWAN GROUP. David Cookson, 01270 567 526; e-mail: Cheshireswans@aol.com
www.record-lrc.co.uk (then follow link to Cheshire Swans Group).

MERSEYSIDE RG. Bob Harris, 3 Mossleigh, Whixalll, Whitchurch, Shropshire SY13 2SA. Work 0151 706 4311; e-mail: harris@liv.ac.uk

SOUTH MANCHESTER RG. Mr N.B. Powell; e-mail: neville.powell@tiscali.co.uk

RSPB Local Groups
CHESTER. (1988; 220). Liz McClure. 01829 782 237; e-mail: chester1RSPB@btinternet.com
www.rspb.org.uk/groups/chester
Meetings: 7.30pm, 3rd Wednesday of the month (Sep-Apr), St Mary's Centre, Chester.

MACCLESFIELD. (1979; 300). Anne Bennett. 01260 271 231; e-mail: secretary@macclesfieldrspb.org.uk
www.macclesfieldrspb.org.uk
Meetings: 7.45pm, 2nd Tuesday of the month (Sept-May), Senior Citizens Hall, Duke Street, MACCLESFIELD, Cheshire, SK11 6UR

NORTH CHESHIRE. (1976; 100). Paul Grimmett. 01925 268 770; e-mail: paulwtwitcher@hotmail.com
www.rspb.org.uk/groups/north_cheshire
Meetings: 7.45pm, 3rd Friday (Jan-April and Sept-Nov), Appleton Parish Hall, Dudlow Green Road, Appleton, Warrington.

Wetland Bird Survey Organiser
CHESHIRE SOUTH. David Cookson, 01270 567 526; e-mail: cheshireswans@aol.com

Wildlife Hospitals
RSPCA STAPELEY GRANGE WILDLIFE CENTRE. London

Road, Stapeley, Nantwich, Cheshire, CW5 7JW. 0300 123 0722. All wild birds. Oiled bird wash facilities and pools. Veterinary support.

Wildlife Trust
CHESHIRE WILDLIFE TRUST. (1962; 13,100). Bickley Hall Farm, Bickley, Malpas, Cheshire SY14 8EF. 01948 820 728; e-mail: info@cheshirewt.org.uk
www.cheshirewildlifetrust.co.uk

CLEVELAND

Bird Atlas/Avifauna
The Breeding Birds of Cleveland. Teesmouth Bird Club, 2008.

Bird Recorder
CLEVELAND. Tom Francis.
E-mail: mot.francis@ntlworld.com

Bird Report
CLEVELAND BIRD REPORT (1974-), from Mr J Fletcher, 43 Glaisdale Avenue, Middlesbrough TS5 7PF. 01642 818 825;

BTO Regional Representative
CLEVELAND RR. Vic Fairbrother, 8, Whitby Avenue, Guisborough, Cleveland, TS14 7AP. 01287 633 744; e-mail: vic.fairbrother@ntlworld.com

Club
TEESMOUTH BIRD CLUB. (1960; 425). Chris Sharp (Hon Sec.), 20 Auckland Way, Hartlepool, TS26 0AN. 01429 865 163; www.teesmouthbc.com
Meetings: 7.30pm, 1st Monday of the month (Sep-Apr), Stockton Library, Church Road, Stockton.

Ringing Groups
TEES RG. Mr A.Snape;
e-mail: allan.snape@talktalk.net

SOUTH CLEVELAND RG. W Norman, 2 Station Cottages, Grosmont, Whitby, N Yorks YO22 5PB. 01947 895 226; e-mail: wilfgros@lineone.net

RSPB Local Group
CLEVELAND. (1974; 150). Terry Reeve.
E-mail: ClevelandRSPB@googlemail.com
www.rspb.org.uk/groups/cleveland
Meetings: 7.00 for 7.30pm, 2nd Monday of each month (Sep-Apr), Nature's World, Ladgate Lane, Middlesbrough, Cleveland.

Wetland Bird Survey Organisers
CLEVELAND (excl. Tees Estuary). Chris Sharpe, 01429 865 163; e-mail: chrisandlucia@ntlworld.com

TEES ESTUARY. Mike Leakey, c/o Natural England, British Energy, Tees Road, Hartlepool TS25 2BZ. 01429 853 325;
e-mail: mike.leakey@naturalengland.org.uk

Wildlife Trust
TEES VALLEY WILDLIFE TRUST. (1979; 5,000). Margrove Heritage Centre, Margrove Park, Boosbeck,

Saltburn-by-the-Sea, TS12 3BZ. 01287 636 382;
e-mail: info@teeswildlife.org
www.teeswildlife.org

CORNWALL

Bird Atlas/Avifauna
The Essential Guide to Birds of The Isles of Scilly 2007 by RL Flood, N Hudson and B Thomas, published by authors.

Bird Recorders
CORNWALL. Darrell Clegg, 55 Lower Fore Street, Saltash, Cornwall PL12 6JQ.
E-mail: darrell@bluetail.fsnet.co.uk

ISLES OF SCILLY. Nigel Hudson, Carn Ithen, Trench Lane, Old Town, St Mary's, Isles of Scilly TR21 0PA. 01720 42 917; e-mail: nigel@carnithen.co.uk

Bird Reports
BIRDS IN CORNWALL (1931-), from Gary Lewis, 40 Podfield Road, Saltash PL12 4UA. £11.00 (UK) including p&p, cheques made out to CBWPS.

ISLES OF SCILLY BIRD REPORT and NATURAL HISTORY REVIEW 2000 (1969-), see website;
www.scilly-birding.co.uk

BTO Regional Representative
CORNWALL. Stephen Jackson, 2, Trelawney Cottages, Falmouth, Cornwall TR11 3NY. 01326 313 533;
e-mail: stephen.f.jackson@btinternet.com

ISLES OF SCILLY RR & RDO. Will Wagstaff, 42 Sally Port, St Mary's, Isles of Scilly, TR21 0JE. 01720 422 212; e-mail: william.wagstaff@virgin.net

Clubs
CORNWALL BIRDWATCHING & PRESERVATION SOCIETY. (1931; 762). Tony Bertenshaw, (Honorary Secretary), Hantergantick, St. Breward, CornwallPL30 4NH. 01208 850 419; e-mail: secretary@cbwps.org.uk
www.cbwps.org.uk

CORNWALL WILDLIFE TRUST PHOTOGRAPHIC GROUP. (40). David Chapman, 41 Bosence Road, Townshend, Nr Hayle, Cornwall TR27 6AL. 01736 850287;
e-mail: david@ruralimages.freeserve.co.uk
www.ruralimages.freeserve.co.uk
Meetings: Mixture of indoor and outdoor meetings, please phone for details.

ISLES OF SCILLY BIRD GROUP. (2000; 510). Membership Secretary, e-mail: danni@carnithen.co.uk
www.scilly-birding.co.uk

Ringing Group
SCILLONIA SEABIRD GROUP. Peter Robinson, Secretary, 19 Pine Park Road, Honiton, Devon EX14 2HR. (Tel/(fax) 01404 549 873 (M)07768 538 132; e-mail: pjrobinson2@aol.com
www.birdexpertuk.com

ENGLAND

RSPB Local Group
CORNWALL. (1972; 600). Roger Hooper, 01209 820
610; e-mail: rogerhooper@talktalk.net
www.RSPBcornwall.org.uk
Meetings: Indoor meetings (Oct-Apr), outdoor
throughout the year.

Wetland Bird Survey Organisers
CORNWALL (excl. Tamar Complex). Dr I Maclean,
07966 693 552; e-mail: i.m.d.maclean@exeter.ac.uk

TAMAR COMPLEX. Gladys Grant, 18 Orchard Crescent,
Oreston, Plymouth, PL9 7NF. 01752 406 287;
e-mail: gladysgrant@talktalk.net

Wildlife Hospital
MOUSEHOLE WILD BIRD HOSPITAL & SANCTUARY
ASSOCIATION LTD. Raginnis Hill, Mousehole,
Penzance, Cornwall, TR19 6SR. 01736 731 386. All
species. No ringing.

Wildlife Trust
CORNWALL WILDLIFE TRUST. (1962; 14,000). Five
Acres, Allet, Truro, Cornwall, TR4 9DJ. 01872 273
939; e-mail: info@cornwallwildlifetrust.org.uk
www.cornwallwildlifetrust.org.uk

THE ISLES OF SCILLY WILDLIFE TRUST. (462) Carn
Thomas, Hugh Town, St Marys, Isles of Scilly TR21
0PT.01720 422 153 (fax) 01720 422153;
e-mail: enquiries@ios-wildlifetrust.org.uk
www.ios-wildlifetrust.org.uk

CUMBRIA

Bird Atlas/Avifauna
The Breeding Birds of Cumbria by Stott, Callion,
Kinley, Raven and Roberts (Cumbria Bird Club, 2002).

Bird Recorders
CUMBRIA. Colin Raven, 18 Seathwaite Road, Barrow-
in-Furness, Cumbria, LA14 4LX.
E-mail: colin@walneyobs.fsnet.co.uk

NORTH WEST (Allerdale & Copeland). Derek McAlone,
88 Whinlatter Road, Mirehouse, Whitehaven, Cumbria
CA28 8DQ. 01946 691 370;
e-mail: derekmcalone@hotmail.co.uk

SOUTH (South Lakeland & Furness). Ronnie Irving. 24
Birchwood Close, Vicarage Park, Kendal, Cumbria LA9
5BJ E-mail: ronnie@fenella.fslife.co.uk

Bird Reports
BIRDS AND WILDLIFE IN CUMBRIA (1970-), from Dave
Piercy, Secretary (see Cumbria Bird Club)
e-mail: daveandkathypiercy@tiscali.co.uk

WALNEY BIRD OBSERVATORY REPORT, from Warden,
see Reserves.

BTO Regional Representatives
CUMBRIA. Clive Hartley, Undercragg, Charney Well
La, Grange Over Sands, LA11 6DB. 01539 532 856;
e-mail: clive.hartley304@btinternet.com

Clubs
ARNSIDE & DISTRICT NATURAL HISTORY SOCIETY.
(1967; 221). Jane Phillips. 01524 782 582;
Meetings: 7.30pm, 2nd Tuesday of the month (Sept-
Apr). WI Hall, Arnside. (Also summer walks).

CUMBRIA BIRD CLUB. (1989;
230). Dave Piercy, Secretary,
Derwentwater Youth Hostel,
Borrowdale, Keswick CA12 5UR.
01768 777 909;
e-mail: daveandkathypiercy@
tiscali.co.uk
www.cumbriabirdclub.org.uk
Meetings: Various evenings and venues (Oct-Mar)
check on website for further details. £2 for non-
members.

Ringing Groups
EDEN RG. G Longrigg, 1 Spring Cottage, Heights,
Appleby-in-Westmorland, Cumbria CA16 6EP.

WALNEY BIRD OBSERVATORY. K Parkes, 176 Harrogate
Street, Barrow-in-Furness, Cumbria, LA14 5NA. 01229
824 219.

RSPB Local Groups
CARLISLE. (1974; 400). Bob Jones, 130 Greenacres,
Wetheral, Carlisle, 01225 561 684;
e-mail: bob@onethirty.force9.co.uk
www.rspb.org.uk/groups/carlisle
Meetings: 7.30pm, Wednesday monthly (Sep-Mar),
Tithe Barn, (Behind Marks And Spencer's), West
Walls, CARLISLE, Cumbria, CA3. Also monthly field
trips except August.

SOUTH LAKELAND. (1973; 305). Mr Martin Baines, 101
Serpentine Road, Kendal, Cumbria, LA9 4PD. 01539
732 214;
Meetings: Contact above.

WEST CUMBRIA. (1986; 270). Marjorie Hutchin,
3 Camerton Road, Gt Broughton, Cockermouth,
Cumbria CA13 0YR. 01900 825 231;
e-mail: majorie.hutchin@btinternet.com
www.rspb.org.uk/groups/westcumbria
Meetings: 7.30pm, 1st Tuesday (Sept-Apr), United
Reformed Church, Main St, Cockermouth

Wetland Bird Survey Organiser
CUMBRIA (excl estuaries). Dave Shackleton,
e-mail: dave.shack@care4free.net

DUDDON ESTUARY. Rosalyn Gay, 8 Victoria Street,
Millom, Cumbria LA18 5AS. 01229 773 820;
e-mail: rosaatmillom@aol.com

IRT/MITE/ESK ESTUARY. Mike Douglas, Cumbria
WildlifeTrust,
e-mail: miked@cumbriawildlifetrust.org.uk

SOLWAY ESTUARY SOUTH. Norman Holton, 01697 351
330; e-mail: norman.holton@rspb.org.uk

Wildlife Trust
CUMBRIA WILDLIFE TRUST. (1962; 15,000).

Plumgarths, Crook Road, Kendal, Cumbria LA8 8LX. 01539 816 300 (fax) 01539 816 301; e-mail: mail@cumbriawildlifetrust.org.uk www.cumbriawildlifetrust.org.uk

DERBYSHIRE

Bird Atlas/Avifauna
The Birds of Derbyshire, ed. RA Frost (in preparation)
Bird Recorders
1. JOINT RECORDER. Roy A Frost, 66 St Lawrence Road, North Wingfield, Chesterfield, Derbyshire S42 5LL. 01246 850 037; e-mail: frostra66@btinternet.com

2. Records Committee & rarity records. Rodney W Key, 3 Farningham Close, Spondon, Derby, DE21 7DZ. 01332 678571; e-mail: r_key@sky.com

3. JOINT RECORDER. Richard M R James, 10 Eastbrae Road, Littleover, Derby, DE23 1WA. 01332 771 787; e-mail: rmrjames@yahoo.co.uk

Bird Reports
CARSINGTON BIRD CLUB ANNUAL REPORT, from the Secretary.

DERBYSHIRE BIRD REPORT (1954-), from Bryan Barnacle, Mays, Malthouse Lane, Froggatt, Hope Valley, Derbyshire S32 3ZA. 01433 630 726; e-mail: barney@mays1.demon.co.uk

OGSTON BIRD CLUB REPORT (1970-), from contact for Ogston Bird Club below.

BTO Regional Representatives
NORTH and SOUTH RR. Dave Budworth, 121 Wood Lane, Newhall, Swadlincote, Derbys DE11 0LX. 01283 215 188; e-mail: dbud01@aol.com

Clubs
BAKEWELL BIRD STUDY GROUP. (1987; 80). Ken Rome, View Cottage, Wensley, Matlock, Derbys DE4 2LH. E-mail: viewcottage@lineone.net www.bakewellbirdstudygroup.co.uk **Meetings:** 7.30pm, 2nd Monday of the month, Friends Meeting House, Bakewell.

BUXTON FIELD CLUB. (1946; 68). B Aries, 1 Horsefair Avenue, Chapel-en-le-Frith, High Peak, Derbys SK23 9SQ. 01298 815 291; e-mail: brian.aries@btinternet.com **Meetings:** 7.30pm, Saturdays fortnightly (Oct-Mar), Methodist Church Hall, Buxton.

CARSINGTON BIRD CLUB. (1992; 257). Paul Hicking (Secretary), 12 Beaurepaire Crescent, Belper, Derbyshire DE5 1HR. 01629 823 693; e-mail: membership@ carsingtonbirdclub.co.uk www.carsingtonbirdclub.co.uk **Meetings:** 3rd Tuesday of the month (Sep-Mar), Hognaston Village Hall, (Apr-Aug), outdoors.

DERBYSHIRE ORNITHOLOGICAL SOCIETY. (1954; 550). Steve Shaw, 84 Moorland View Road, Walton, Chesterfield, Derbys S40 3DF. 01246 236 090; e-mail: steveshaw84mrr@btinternet.com www.derbyshireOS.org.uk **Meetings:** 7.30pm, last Friday of the winter months, various venues.

OGSTON BIRD CLUB. (1969; 1,126). Malcolm Hill, 2 Sycamore Avenue, Glapwell, Chesterfield, S44 5LH. 01623 812 159; e-mail: aamahaamah@yahoo.co.uk www.ogstonbirdclub.co.uk

SOUTH PEAK RAPTOR STUDY GROUP. (1998; 12). M E Taylor, 76 Hawksley Avenue, Newbold, Chesterfield, Derbys S40 4TL. 01246 277 749;

Ringing Groups
DARK PEAK RG. W M Underwood, Ivy Cottage, 15 Broadbottom Road, Mottram-in-Longdendale, Hyde, Cheshire SK14 6JB.
E-mail: w.m.underwood@talk21.com

SORBY-BRECK RG. Dr Geoff P Mawson, Moonpenny Farm, Farwater Lane, Dronfield, Sheffield S18 1RA. E-mail: moonpenny@talktalk.net www.sorbybreckringinggroup.co.uk

SOUDER RG. Dave Budworth, 121 Wood Lane, Newhall, Swadlincote, Derbys DE11 0LX. E-mail: dbud01@aol.com

RSPB Local Groups
CHESTERFIELD. (1987; 274). Ann and Pete Furniss. 0114 248 5261; e-mail: annfurniss@supanet.com www.rspb.org.uk/groups/chesterfield **Meetings:** 7.15pm, usually 3rd Monday of the month, Winding Wheel, New Exhibition Centre, 13 Holywell Street, Chesterfield.

DERBY LOCAL GROUP. (1973; 500). Chris Hunt, 38 Spenbeck Drive, Allestree, Derby, DE22 2UH. 01332 551 701; e-mail: chris.hunt42@ntlworld.com www.rspb.org.uk/groups/derby **Meetings:** 7.30pm, 2nd Wednesday of the month (Sep-Apr), Broughton Suite, Grange Banqueting Suite, 457 Burton Road, Littleover, Derby DE23 6FL.

HIGH PEAK. (1974; 160). Jim Jeffery. 0161 494 5367; e-mail: henrygordon@live.co.uk www.rspb.org.uk/groups/highpeak **Meetings:** 7.30pm, 3rd Monday of the month (Sep-May), Marple Senior Citizens Hall, Memorial Park, Marple, STOCKPORT SK6 6BA.

Wildlife Trust
DERBYSHIRE WILDLIFE TRUST. (1962; 14,000). East Mill, Bridge Foot, Belper, Derbyshire DE56 1XH. 01773 881 188 (fax) 01773 821 826; e-mail: enquiries@derbyshirewt.co.uk www.derbyshirewildlifetrust.org.uk

ENGLAND

DEVON

Bird Atlas/Avifauna
Tetrad Atlas of Breeding Birds of Devon by H P Sitters (Devon Birdwatching & Preservation Society, 1988).

The Birds of Lundy by Tim Davis and Tim Jones 2007. Available from R M Young (Bookseller) on 01769 573 350 (see www.birdsoflundy.org.uk for further details).

Bird Recorder
The Recorder (name not available at the time of publication), e-mail: devon-birdrecorder@lycos.com

Bird Reports
DEVON BIRD REPORT (1971) Previous annual reports since 1929, from DBWPS, PO Box 71, Okehampton, Devon EX20 1WF.

LUNDY FIELD SOCIETY ANNUAL REPORT (1946-). £3 each inc postage, check website for availability, from Frances Stuart, 3 Lower Linden Road, Clevedon, North Somerset BS21 7SU. E-mail: lfssec@hotmail.co.uk

BTO Regional Representative
Dr J.P.A. Twyford, 01392 264 771;
e-mail: bto.devon@hotmail.com

BTO Garden BirdWatch Ambassador
DEVON (north) Mr D Gayton,
e-mail: gayton881@btinternet.com

DEVON (south) Mr M K Overy,
e-mail: martin@martin-overy.co.uk

Clubs
DEVON BIRD WATCHING & PRESERVATION SOCIETY. (1928; 1200). Mrs Joy Vaughan, 28 Fern Meadow, Okehampton, Devon, EX20 1PB. 01837 533 60; e-mail: joy@vaughan411.freeserve.co.uk www.devonbirds.org

KINGSBRIDGE & DISTRICT NATURAL HISTORY SOCIETY. (1989; 130). Martin Catt, Migrants Rest, East Prawle, Kingsbridge, Devon TQ7 2DB. 01548 511 443; e-mail: martin.catt@btinternet.com
Meeting:4th Monday of Sept-Apr, 7.30pm phone for venue.

LUNDY FIELD SOCIETY. (1946; 450). Mr Paul James, Hibernia,New Road, Pamber Green, Tadley RG26 3AG. E-mail: lfssec@hotmail.co.uk www.lundy.org.uk
Meeting: AGM 1st Saturday in March, 1.45pm, Exeter University.

TOPSHAM BIRDWATCHING & NATURALISTS' SOCIETY. (1969; 140). Mrs M Heal, 5 Majorfield Road, Topsham, Exeter, EX3 0ES. E-mail: tbnsociety@hotmail.com www.topsham.org/tbns
Meetings: 7.30pm, 2nd Friday of the month (Sep-May), Matthews Hall, Topsham.

Ringing Groups
AXE ESTUARY RINGING GROUP. Mike Tyler, The Acorn, Shute Road, Kilmington, Axminster EX13 7ST. 01297 349 58; e-mail: mwtyler2@googlemail.com

DEVON & CORNWALL WADER RG. R C Swinfen, 72 Dunraven Drive, Derriford, Plymouth, PL6 6AT. 01752 704 184.

LUNDY FIELD SOCIETY. A M Taylor, 26 High Street, Spetisbury, Blandford, Dorset DT11 9DJ. 01258 857336; e-mail: ammataylor@yahoo.co.uk

SLAPTON BIRD OBSERVATORY. R C Swinfen, 72 Dunraven Drive, Derriford, Plymouth, PL6 6AT. 01752 704 184.

RSPB Local Groups
EXETER & DISTRICT. (1974; 466). Roger Tucker. 01392 860 518; e-mail: parrog@aol.com
www.exeter-rspb.org.uk
Meetings: 7.30p, various evenings, Southernhay United Reformed Church Rooms, Dix's Field, EXETER.

PLYMOUTH. (1974; 600). Mrs Eileen Willey, 11 Beverstone Way, Roborough, Plymouth, PL6 7DY. 01752 208 996;

Wetland Bird Survey Organiser
DEVON other sites. Peter Reay, Crooked Fir, Moorland Park, South Brent, Devon TQ10 9AS. 01364 73293; e-mail: peter.p.j.reay@btinternet.com

TAMAR COMPLEX. Gladys Grant, 18 Orchard Crescent, Oreston, Plymouth, PL9 7NF. 01752 406 287; e-mail: gladysgrant@talktalk.net

TAW/TORRIDGE ESTUARY. Terry Chaplin, 01271 342 590; e-mail: terry@chaplin.eclipse.co.uk

Wildlife Hospitals
BIRD OF PREY CASUALTY CENTRE. Mrs J E L Vinson, Crooked Meadow, Stidston Lane, South Brent, Devon, TQ10 9JS. 01364 72174; Birds of prey, with emergency advice on other species. Aviaries, rehabilitation facilities. Veterinary support.

Wildlife Trust
DEVON WILDLIFE TRUST. (1962; 33,000). Cricklepit, Commercial Road, Exeter, EX2 4AB. 01392 279 244; e-mail: contactus@devonwildlifewt.org
www.devonwildlifetrust.org

DORSET

Bird Atlas/Avifauna
Dorset Breeding Bird Atlas (working title). In preparation.

The Birds of Dorset by Dr George Green (Christopher Helm 2004)

Bird Recorder
Kevin Lane, e-mail: kevin@broadstone heath.co.uk

Bird Reports
DORSET BIRDS (1977-), from Neil Gartshore, Moor Edge, 2 Bere Road, Wareham, Dorset BH20 4DD. 01929 552 560; e-mail: enquiries@callunabooks.co.uk

THE BIRDS OF CHRISTCHURCH HARBOUR (1956-), from Ian Southworth, 1 Bodowen Road, Burton, Christchurch, Dorset BH23 7JL. E-mail: ianbirder@aol.com

PORTLAND BIRD OBSERVATORY REPORT, from Warden, see Reserves.

BTO Regional Representatives
Position vacant, please contact BTO Thetford.

Clubs
CHRISTCHURCH HARBOUR ORNITHOLOGICAL GROUP. (1956; 275). Mr. I.H. Southworth, Membership Secretary, 1 Bodowen Road, Burton, Christchurch, Dorset BH23 7JL. 01202 478 093; www.chog.org.uk

DORSET BIRD CLUB. (1987; 525). Mrs Diana Dyer, The Cedars, 30 Osmay Road, Swanage, Dorset BH19 2JQ. 01929 421 402; e-mail: richarddiana@tiscali.com www.dorsetbirdclub.org.uk

DORSET NATURAL HISTORY & ARCHAEOLOGICAL SOCIETY. (1845; 2188). Dorset County Museum. High West Street, Dorchester, Dorset DT1 1XA. 01305 262 735; e-mail: secretary@dorsetcountymuseum.org www.dorsetcountymuseum.org

Ringing Groups
CHRISTCHURCH HARBOUR RS. E C Brett, 3 Whitfield Park, St Ives, Ringwood, Hants, BH24 2DX. E-mail: ed_brett@lineone.net

PORTLAND BIRD OBSERVATORY. Martin Cade, Old Lower Light, Portland Bill, Dorset, DT5 2JT. 01305 820 553; e-mail: obs@btinternet.com www.portlandbirdobs.org.uk

STOUR RG. R Gifford, 62 Beacon Park Road, Upton, Poole, Dorset BH16 5PE.

RSPB Local Groups
BLACKMOOR VALE. (1981; 130). Alison Rymell, Group Leader, 01985 844 819; e-mail: alisonrymell@yahoo.co.uk www.rspb.org.uk/groups/blackmoorvale Meetings: 7.30pm, 3rd Friday in the month, Gillingham Primary School.

EAST DORSET. (1974; 435). Hugh Clark. 01202 532595; e-mail: jammy.jan@hotmail.com www.rspb.org.uk/groups/eastdorset Meetings: 7.30pm, 2nd Wednesday of the month, St Mark's Church Hall, Talbot Village, Wallisdown, Bournemouth.

POOLE. (1982; 305). John Derricott, 49 Medbourne Close, Blandford, Dorset DT11 7UA. 01258 450 927; e-mail: jd461@btinternet.com www.rspb.org.uk/groups/poole Meetings: 7.30pm, Upton Community Centre, Poole Road, Upton.

SOUTH DORSET. (1976; 422). Andrew Parsons. 01305 772 678; e-mail: andrew_parsons_141@yahoo.co.uk www.rspb.org.uk/groups/southdorset Meetings: 3rd Thursday of each month (Sep-Dec 2009), Dorchester Town Hall. (Jan-Apr 2010) St Georges Church Hall, Fordington, Dorchester.

Wetland Bird Survey Organisers
DORSET (excl estuaries). John Jones, e-mail: blackbirdcott@tiscali.co.uk

POOLE HARBOUR. Harold Lilley, 01202 889 633; e-mail: halilley@tiscali.co.uk

THE FLEET & PORTLAND HARBOUR. Steve Groves, Abbotsbury Swannery, New Barn Road, Abbotsbury, Dorset DT3 4JG. (W)01305 871 684; e-mail: swannery@gotadsl.co.uk

RADIPOLE & LODMOOR. Nick Tomlinson, Site Manager, RSPB Weymouth Reserves, e-mail: nick.tomlinson@rspb.org.uk

Wildlife Hospital
SWAN RESCUE SANCTUARY. Ken and Judy Merriman, The Wigeon, Crooked Withies, Holt, Wimborne, Dorset BH21 7LB. 01202 828 166; www.swan.jowebdesign.co.uk 24 hr rescue service for swans. Large sanctuary of 40 ponds and lakes. Hospital and intensive care. Veterinary support. Free advice and help line. Three fully equipped rescue ambulances. Rescue water craft for all emergencies. Viewing by appointment only.

Wildlife Trust
DORSET WILDLIFE TRUST. (1961; 25,000). Brooklands Farm, Forston, Dorchester, Dorset, DT2 7AA. 01305 264 620; e-mail: enquiries@dorsetwildlife.co.uk www.dorsetwildlife.co.uk

DURHAM

Bird Atlas/Avifauna
A Summer Atlas of Breeding Birds of County Durham by Stephen Westerberg/Kieth Bowey. (Durham Bird Club, 2000).

Bird Recorders
Mark Newsome, 69 Cedar Drive, Jarrow, NE32 4BF. E-mail: mvnewsome@hotmail.com

Bird Reports
BIRDS IN DURHAM (1971-), from D Sowerbutts, 9 Prebends Field, Gilesgate Moor, Durham, DH1 1HH. H:0191 386 7201; e-mail: david.sowerbutts@dunelm.org.uk

BTO Regional Representatives
David L Sowerbutts, 9 Prebends Field, Gilesgate Moor,

ENGLAND

Durham, DH1 1HH. H:0191 386 7201;
e-mail: david.sowerbutts@dunelm.org.uk

Clubs
DURHAM BIRD CLUB. (1975; 320). Paul Anderson, Chairman, 2 Hawsker Close, Tunstall Village, Sunderland SR3 2YD. E-mail: paulandcath29@aol.com
www.durhambirdclub.org
Meetings: Monthly indoor meetings (Sept-Apr), in Durham and Sunderland.
SUMMERHILL (HARTLEPOOL) BIRD CLUB. (2000; 75). George Smith, 01429 420 593 (M)07500 867 626;
e-mail: george.smith8@ntlworld.com
www.summerhillbirdclub.co.uk
Meetings: 7pm, 2nd Tuesday of the month (Sept-May), Summerhill Visitors Centre, Catcote Road, Hartlepool.

Ringing Groups
NORTHUMBRIA RG. Richard Barnes, 12 Thorp Cottages, Bar Moor, Ryton, Tyne & Wear NE40 3AU. 0191 413 3846.

DURHAM DALES RG. J R Hawes, Fairways, 5 Raby Terrace, Willington, Crook, Durham DL15 0HR.

RSPB Local Group
DURHAM. (1974; 125). Richard Cowen, 0191 377 2061;
e-mail: richardcowen2002@yahoo.co.uk
www.durham-rspb.org.uk
Meetings: 7.30pm, 2nd Tuesday of the month (Oct-Mar), Room CG83, adjacent to Scarborough Lecture Theatre, University Science Site, Stockton Road entrance.

Wildlife Trust
DURHAM WILDLIFE TRUST. (1971; 4,000). Rainton Meadows, Chilton Moor, Houghton-le-Spring, Tyne & Wear DH4 6PU. 0191 584 3112;
e-mail: mail@durhamwt.co.uk
www.durhamwt.co.uk

ESSEX

Bird Atlas/Avifauna
The Birds of Essex
by Simon Wood (A&C Black, August 2007).

The Breeding Birds of Essex by M K Dennis (Essex Birdwatching Society, 1996).

Bird Recorder
RECORDER. Les Steward, 6 Creek View, Basildon, Essex SS16 4RU. 01268 551 464,
e-mail: les.steward@btinternet.com

Bird Report
ESSEX BIRD REPORT (inc Bradwell Bird Obs records) (1950-), from Peter Dwyer, Sales Officer, 48 Churchill Avenue, Halstead, Essex, CO9 2BE. Tel/(fax) 01787 476524; e-mail: petedwyer@petedwyer.plus.com

BTO Regional Representatives
NORTH-EAST Mr M Shuter;
e-mail: btoexne@gmail.com

NORTH-WEST RR. Graham Smith. 01277 354 034;
e-mail: silaum.silaus@tiscali.co.uk

SOUTH RR. Positions vacant.

Club
ESSEX BIRDWATCHING SOCIETY. (1949; 700). Roy Ledgerton, 25 Bunyan Road, Braintree, Essex CM7 2PL. E-mail: r.ledgerton@virgin.net
www.essexbirdwatchsoc.co.uk
Meetings: 1st Friday of the month (Oct-Mar), Friends' Meeting House, Rainsford Road, Chelmsford.

Ringing Groups
ABBERTON RG. C P Harris, Wyandotte, Seamer Road, Southminster, Essex, CM0 7BX.

BRADWELL BIRD OBSERVATORY. C P Harris, Wyandotte, Seamer Road, Southminster, Essex, CM0 7BX.

RSPB Local Groups
CHELMSFORD AND CENTRAL ESSEX. (1976; 1200). Mike Logan Wood, Highwood, Ishams Chase, Wickham Bishops, Essex, CM8 3LG. 01621 892 045;
e-mail: mike.lw@tiscali.co.uk
www.rspb.org.uk/groups/chelmsford
Meetings: 8pm, Thursdays, eight times a year. The Cramphorn Theatre, Chelmsford.

COLCHESTER. (1981; 220). Mr Russell Leavett, 10 Grove Road, Brantham, Manningtree, Essex CO11 1TX. 01206 399 059; e-mail: rleavett@btinternet.com
www.rspb.org.uk/groups/colchester
Meetings: 7.45pm, 2nd Thursday of the month (Sep-Apr), Shrub End Community Hall, Shrub End Road, Colchester. Regular coach and car trips to local birding sites and those further afield.

SOUTH EAST ESSEX. (1983; 200). Graham Mee, 34 Park View Drive, Leigh on Sea, Essex SS9 4TU. 01702 525 152; e-mail: grahamm@southendrspb.co.uk
www.southendrspb.co.uk
Meetings: 7.30pm, usually 1st Tuesday of the month (Sep-May), Belfairs School Hall, School Way, Leigh-on-Sea SS9 4HX.

Wetland Bird Survey Organiser
CROUCH/ROACH ESTUARY and SOUTH DENGIE. Peter Mason, 32 Providence, Burnham on Crouch, Essex CM0 8JU; e-mail: Petermason32@waitrose.com

HAMFORD WATER. Julian Novorol, 01255 880 552.

LEE VALLEY. Cath Patrick. Myddelton House, Bulls Cross, Enfield, Herts EN2 9HG. 01992 717 711;
e-mail: cpatrick@leevalleypark.org.uk

NORTH BLACKWATER. John Thorogood. 01206 768 771.

SOUTH BLACKWATER AND NORTH DENGIE. Anthony Harbott, 01992 575 213;
e-mail: anthonyharbott@talktalk.net

251

STOUR ESTUARY. Rick Vonk, RSPB, Unit 13 Court Farm, 3 Stutton Road, Brantham Suffolk CO11 1PW. (D)01473 328 006; e-mail: rick.vonk@rspb.org.uk

THAMES ESTUARY — Foulness. Chris Lewis, e-mail: cpm.lewis@ukonline.co.uk

Wildlife Trust
ESSEX WILDLIFE TRUST. (1959; 36,000). The Joan Elliot Visitor Centre, Abbots Hall Farm, Great Wigborough, Colchester, CO5 7RZ. 01621 862 960; e-mail: admin@essexwt.org.uk www.essexwt.org.uk

GLOUCESTERSHIRE

Bird Atlas/Avifauna
Atlas of Breeding Birds of the North Cotswolds. (North Cotswold Ornithological Society, 1990).

Birds of The Cotswolds (Liverpool University Press 2009).

Bird Recorder
GLOUCESTERSHIRE EXCLUDING S.GLOS (AVON). Richard Baatsen. E-mail: baatsen@surfbirder.com

Bird Reports
CHELTENHAM BIRD CLUB BIRD REPORT (1998-2001) - no longer published, back copies from Secretary.

GLOUCESTERSHIRE BIRD REPORT (1953-). £7.50 including postage, from David Cramp, 2 Ellenor Drive, Alderton, Tewkesbury, GL20 8NZ.
E-mail: djcramp@btinternet.com

NORTH COTSWOLD ORNITHOLOGICAL SOCIETY ANNUAL REPORT (1983-), from T Hutton, 15 Green Close, Childswickham, Broadway, Worcs, WR12 7JJ. 01386 858 511.

BTO Regional Representative
Mike Smart, 143 Cheltenham Road, Gloucester, GL2 0JH. 01452 421 131;
e-mail: smartmike@btinternet.com

Clubs
CHELTENHAM BIRD CLUB. (1976; 94). Mr Peter Ridout, 64 Prestbury Road, Cheltenham, GL52 2DA. 01242 517 424; www.cheltenhambirdclub.org.uk
Meetings: 7.15pm, Mondays (Oct-Mar), Bournside School, Warden Hill Road, Cheltenham.

DURSLEY BIRDWATCHING & PRESERVATION SOCIETY. (1953; 350). Jennifer Rogers, 15 Shadwell, Uley, Dursley, Glos GL11 5BW. 01453 860 128; www. dursleybirdwatchers.btik.com e-mail: j.rogers1@btinternet.com
Meetings: 7.45pm, 2nd and 4th Monday (Sept-Mar), Dursley Community Centre.

GLOUCESTERSHIRE NATURALISTS' SOCIETY. (1948; 500). Mike Smart, 143 Cheltenham Road, Gloucester,

GL2 0JH. 01452 421 131; www.glosnats.org.uk
e-mail: smartmike@btinternet.com

NORTH COTSWOLD ORNITHOLOGICAL SOCIETY. (1982; 70). T Hutton, 15 Green Close, Childswickham, Broadway, Worcs WR12 7JJ. 01386 858 511;
Meetings: Monthly field meetings, usually Sundays.

Ringing Groups
COTSWOLD WATER PARK RG. John Wells, 25 Pipers Grove, Highnam, Glos, GL2 8NJ.
E-mail: john.wells2@btinternet.com
SEVERN ESTUARY GULL GROUP. M E Durham, 6 Glebe Close, Frampton-on-Severn, Glos, GL2 7EL. 01452 741 312.

WILDFOWL & WETLANDS TRUST. Richard Hearn, Wildfowl & Wetlands Trust, Slimbridge, Glos, GL2 7BT. E-mail: richard.hearn@wwt.org.uk

RSPB Local Group
GLOUCESTERSHIRE. (1972; 600). David Cramp, 2 Ellenor Drive, Alderton, Tewkesbury, GL20 8NZ. 01242 620 281; e-mail: djcramp@btinternet.com www.rspbgloucestershire.co.uk
Meetings: 7.30pm, 3rd Tuesday of the month, Gala Club, Longford, Gloucester.

Wildlife Hospital
VALE WILDLIFE RESCUE - WILDLIFE HOSPITAL + REHABILITATION CENTRE. Any staff member, Station Road, Beckford, Tewkesbury, Glos GL20 7AN. 01386 882 288; e-mail: info@valewildlife.org.uk www.valewildlife.org.uk All wild birds. Intensive care. Registered charity. Veterinary support.

Wetland Bird Survey Organisers
GLOUCESTERSHIRE (Inland). Mike Smart, 143 Cheltenham Road, Gloucester, GL2 0JH. 01452 421 131; e-mail: smartmike@btinternet.com

COTSWOLD WATER PARK. Gareth Harris, Cotswold Water Park Society, Cotswold House, Down Ampney Estate, Cirencester, Glos GL7 5QF. 01793 752 413 or 01793 752 730; e-mail: gareth.harris@waterpark.org www.waterpark.org

Wildlife Trust
GLOUCESTERSHIRE WILDLIFE TRUST. (1961; 23,000). Conservation Centre, Robinswood Hill Country Park, Reservoir Road, Gloucester, GL4 6SX. 01452 383 333 (fax) 01452 383334; e-mail: info@gloucestershirewildlifetrust.co.uk www.gloucestershirewildlifetrust.co.uk

HAMPSHIRE

Bird Atlas/Avifauna
Birds of Hampshire by J M Clark and J A Eyre (Hampshire Ornithological Society, 1993).

Bird Recorder
RECORDER. Keith Betton.
E-mail: keithbetton@hotmail.com

ENGLAND

Bird Reports
HAMPSHIRE BIRD REPORT (1955-). 2008 edition £12.10
inc postage, from Mrs Margaret Boswell, 5 Clarence
Road, Lyndhurst, Hants, SO43 7AL. 023 8028 2105;
e-mail: mag_bos@btinternet.com
www.hos.org.uk

BTO Regional Representatives
RR. Glynne C Evans, Waverley, Station Road,
Chilbolton, Stockbridge, Hants SO20 6AL. H:01264 860
697; e-mail: hantsbto@hotmail.com

BTO Garden BirdWatch Ambassador
Prof A Jones, e-mail: gbwhants@btinternet.com

Clubs
HAMPSHIRE ORNITHOLOGICAL SOCIETY. (1979; 1,200).
John Shillitoe, Honarary
Secretary, Westerly,
Hundred Acres Road,
Wickham, Hampshire PO17
6HY. 01329 833 086; e-mail:
john@shillitoe.freeserve.
co.uk
www.hos.org.uk

Ringing Groups
FARLINGTON RG. D A Bell, 38 Holly Grove, Fareham,
Hants, PO16 7UP.

ITCHEN RG. W F Simcox, 10 Holdaway Close,
Kingsworthy, Winchester, SO23 7QH.
E-mail: wilfsimcox@gmx.com

RSPB Local Groups
BASINGSTOKE. (1979; 90). Peter Hutchins, 35
Woodlands, Overton, Whitchurch, RG25 3HN. 01256
770 831; e-mail: fieldfare@jaybry.gotadsl.co.uk
www.rspb.org.uk/groups/basingstoke
Meetings: 7.30pm 3rd Wednesday of the month (Sept-
May), The Barn, Church Cottage, St Michael's Church,
Church Square, Basingstoke.

NEW FOREST
Steve Lankester, 01590 682 421;
e-mail: steve.lankester@virgin.net
www.rspb.org.uk/groups/newforest
Meetings: 7.30, 2nd Wednesday of the month (Sep-
Jun), Lyndhurst Community Centre, High Street,
Lyndhurst SO43 7NY.

NORTH EAST HAMPSHIRE. (1976; 215). Sue Radbourne,
01276 29 434;
e-mail: Mailto@northeasthantsRSPB.org.uk
www.northeasthantsrspb.org.uk
Meetings: See website.

PORTSMOUTH. (1974; 210). Gordon Humby, 19
Charlesworth Gardens, Waterlooville, Hants, PO7
6AU. 02392 353 949;
e-mail: PortsmouthRSPB@googlemail.com
www.rspb.org.uk/groups/portsmouth
Meetings: 7.30pm, 4th Saturday of every month.
Colmans' Church Hall, Colman's Ave, Cosham.

Programme and news letter issued to paid up
members of the group who must be RSPB members.

WINCHESTER & DISTRICT LOCAL GROUP. (1974; 175).
Pam Symes. 01962 851 821;
e-mail: psymes033@gmail.com
www.rspb.org.uk/groups/winchester
Meetings: 7.30pm, 1st Wednesday of the month (not
Jan or Aug), Shawford Parish Hall, Pearson Lane,
Shawford.

Wetland Bird Survey Organisers
AVON VALLEY. John Clark, 4 Cygnet Court, Old Cove
Road, Fleet, Hants GU51 2RL. 01252 623 397;
e-mail: johnclark50@sky.com

HAMPSHIRE (estuaries/coastal). John Shillitoe, 01329
833 086; e-mail: john@shillitoe.freeserve.co.uk

HAMPSHIRE (Inland - excluding Avon Valley). Keith
Wills, 51 Peabody Road, Farnborough, GU14 6EB.
01252 548 408; e-mail: keithb.wills@ukgateway.net

ISLE OF WIGHT. Jim Baldwin, 01983 202 223;
e-mail: jimr.baldwin@tiscali.co.uk

Wildlife Trust
HAMPSHIRE & ISLE OF WIGHT WILDLIFE TRUST. (1960;
27,000). Beechcroft House, Vicarage Lane, Curdridge,
Hampshire SO32 2DP. 01489 774 400 (fax) 01489 774
401; e-mail: feedback@hwt.org.uk
www.hwt.org.uk

HEREFORDSHIRE

Bird Report
THE BIRDS OF HEREFORDSHIRE (2008 -), from Mr WJ
Marler, Cherry Tree House, Walford, Leintwardine,
Craven Arms, Shropshire SY7 0JT

*THE YELLOWHAMMER - Herefordshire Ornithological
Club annual report, (1951-),* from the secretary,
Herefordshire Ornithological Club.

Bird Recorder
Steve Coney, 5 Springfield Road, Withington,
Hereford, HR1 3RU. 01432 850 068;
e-mail: coney@bluecarrots.com

BTO Regional Representative
Steve Coney, 5 Springfield Road, Withington,
Hereford, HR1 3RU. 01432 850 068;
e-mail: coney@bluecarrots.com

Club
HEREFORDSHIRE ORNITHOLOGICAL CLUB. (1950; 439).
TM Weale, Foxholes, Bringsty
Common, Worcester, WR6 5UN.
01886 821 368;
e-mail: weale@tinyworld.co.uk
www.herefordshirebirds.org
Meetings: 7.30pm, 2nd Thursday
of the month (Autumn/winter),
Holmer Parish Centre, Holmer,
Hereford.

Ringing Group
LLANCILLO RG. Dr G R Geen, Little Langthorns, High Cross Lane, Little Canfield, Dunmow, Essex CM6 1TD. 01371 873 628; e-mail: graham.geen@gsk.com

Wetland Bird Survey Organiser
HEREFORDSHIRE. Steve Coney, 5 Springfield Road, Withington, Hereford, HR1 3RU. 01432 850 068; e-mail: coney@bluecarrots.com

Wildlife Trust
HEREFORDSHIRE NATURE TRUST. (1962; 2,535). Lower House Farm, Ledbury Road, Tupsley, Hereford, HR1 1UT. 01432 356 872 (fax) 01432 275 489; e-mail: enquiries@herefordshirewt.co.uk www.herefordshirewt.org

HERTFORDSHIRE

Bird Atlas/Avifauna
Birds at Tring Reservoirs by R Young et al (Hertfordshire Natural History Society, 1996).

Mammals, Amphibians and Reptiles of Hertfordshire by Hertfordshire NHS in association with Training Publications Ltd, 3 Finway Court, Whippendell Road, Watford WD18 7EN, (2001).

The Breeding Birds of Hertfordshire by K W Smith et al (Herts NHS, 1993). Purchase from HNHS at £5 plus postage. E-mail: herts.naturalhistorysociety@aol.com

Bird Recorder
Tony Blake, 9 Old Forge Close, Stanmore, Middx HA7 3EB. E-mail: recorder@hertsbirdclub.org.uk www.hnhs.org/birds

Bird Report

HERTFORDSHIRE BIRD REPORT (1908-2006), from Linda Smith, 24 Mandeville Road, Welwyn Garden City, Herts AL8 7JU. E-mail: herts.naturalhistorysociety@ntlworld.com www.hnhs.org and www.hertsbirdclub.org.uk

BTO Regional Representative & Regional Development Officer
RR & RDO Chris Dee, 26 Broadleaf Avenue, Thorley Park, Bishop's Stortford, Herts, CM23 4JY. H:01279 755 637; e-mail: hertsbto@hotmail.com

BTO Garden BirdWatch Ambassadors
Ms J Crystal, e-mail: jeanlcrystal@aol.com

Mr S L Jones, e-mail: simon.l.jones@ntlworld.com

Miss C L M Fellingham, e-mail: chfellingham@aim.com

Ms M Campbell, e-mail: myra42campbell@googlemail.com

Clubs
FRIENDS OF TRING RESERVOIRS. (1993; 350). Membership Secretary, PO Box 1083, Tring HP23 5WU. 01442 822 471; e-mail: keith@fotr.org.uk www.fotr.org.uk
Meetings: See website.

HERTFORDSHIRE NATURAL HISTORY SOCIETY AND HERTS BIRD CLUB. (1875; 320) Linda Smith, 24 Mandeville Rise, Welwyn Garden City, Herts, AL8 7JU. 01707 330 405; e-mail: secretary@hnhs.org www.hnhs.org and www. hertsbirdclub.org.uk **Meetings:**Saturday afternoon, Nov and Mar (date and venue varies).

Ringing Groups
MAPLE CROSS RG. P Delaloye. E-mail: pdelaloye@tiscali.co.uk

RYE MEADS RG. Chris Dee, 26 Broadleaf Avenue, Thorley Park, Bishop's Stortford, Herts CM23 4JY. H:01279 755 637; e-mail: ringingsecretary@rmrg.org.uk

TRING RG. Mick A'Court, 6 Chalkshire Cottages, Chalkshire road, Butlers Cross, Bucks HP17 0TW. H:01296 623 610 W:01494 462 246; e-mail: mick_acourt@o2.co.uk

RSPB Local Groups
CHORLEYWOOD & DISTRICT. (1977; 142). Carol Smith, 24 Beacon Way, Rickmansworth, Herts WD3 7PE. 01923 897 885; e-mail: carolsmithuk@hotmail.com www.rspb.org.uk/groups/chorleywood **Meetings:** 8pm, 3rd Thursday of the month (Sept-Nov, Jan-May), 2nd Thursday (Dec), Russell School, Brushwood Drive, Chorleywood.

HARPENDEN. (1974; 1000). Geoff Horn, 41 Ridgewood Drive, Harpenden, Herts AL5 3LJ. 01582 765 443; e-mail: geoffrhorn@yahoo.co.uk **Meetings:** 8pm, 2nd Thursday of the month (Sept-June), All Saint's Church Hall, Station Road, Harpenden.

HEMEL HEMPSTEAD. (1972; 150). Paul Green, 207 Northridge Way, Hemel Hempstead, Herts, HP1 2AU. 01442 266637; paul@310nrwhh.freeserve.co.uk www.hemelrspb.org.uk **Meetings:** 8pm, 1st Monday of the month (Sep-Jun),The Cavendish School.

HITCHIN & LETCHWORTH. (1973; 100). Dr Martin Johnson, 1 Cartwright Road, Royston, Herts SG8 9ET. 01763 249459; e-mail: martinrjspc@hotmail.com **Meetings:** 7.30pm, 1st Friday of the month, The Settlement, Nevells Road, Letchworth SG6 4UB.

POTTERS BAR & BARNET. (1977; 1400). Lesley Causton, 57 Lakeside Crescent, East Barnet, Herts EN4 8QH. 0208 440 2038; e-mail: lesleycauston@talktalk.net

ENGLAND

www.pottersbar-rspb.org.uk
Meetings: 2.00pm, 2nd Wednesday of the month, St Johns URC Hall, Mowbray Road, Barnet. Evening meetings, 3rd Friday of the month (not Jul, Aug or Dec) 8.00pm, Potters Bar United Reform Church, Tilbury Hall, Darkes Lane, Potters Bar, EN6 1BZ.

ST ALBANS. (1979; 1550 in catchment area). Peter Antram, 6 Yule Close, Bricket Wood, St Albans, Herts AL2 3XZ. 01923 678 534;
e-mail: peter@antram.demon.co.uk
www.rspb.org.uk/groups/stalbans
Meetings: 8.00pm, 2nd Tuesday of the month (Sep-May), St Saviours Church Hall, Sandpit Lane, St Albans.

SOUTH EAST HERTS. (1971; 2,400 in catchment area). Terry Smith, 31 Marle Gardens, Waltham Abbey, Essex, EN9 2DZ. 01992 715634;
e-mail: se_herts_rspb@yahoo.co.uk
www.rspb.org.uk/groups/southeasthertfordshire
Meetings: 7.30pm, usually last Tuesday of the month (Sept-June), URC Church Hall, Mill Lane, Broxbourne EN10 7BQ.

STEVENAGE. (1982; 1300 in the catchment area). Mrs Ann Collis, 16 Stevenage Road, Walkern, Herts, 01483 861 547; e-mail: p.collis672@btinternet.com
www.rspb.org.uk/groups/stevenage
Meetings: 7.30pm, 3rd Tuesday of the month, Friends Meeting House, Cuttys Lane, Stevenage.

WATFORD. (1974; 590). Janet Reynolds. 01923 249 647; e-mail: janet.reynolds@whht.nhs.uk
www.rspb.org.uk/groups/watford
Meetings: 7.30pm, 2nd Wednesday of the month (Sep-Jun), St Thomas' Church Hall, Langley Road, Watford.

Wetland Bird Survey Organiser
HERTFORDSHIRE (excl. Lee Valley). Jim Terry, e-mail: jimjoypaddy@virginmedia.com

LEE VALLEY. Cath Patrick. Myddelton House, Bulls Cross, Enfield, Herts EN2 9HG. 01992 717 711;
e-mail: cpatrick@leevalleypark.org.uk

Wildlife Trust
HERTS & MIDDLESEX WILDLIFE TRUST. (1964; 18,500). Grebe House, St Michael's Street, St Albans, Herts, AL3 4SN. 01727 858 901; e-mail: info@hmwt.org
www.wildlifetrust.org.uk/herts/

ISLE OF WIGHT

Bird Recorder
Robin Attrill, e-mail: robin@rpattrill.freeserve.co.uk

Bird Reports
ISLE OF WIGHT BIRD REPORT (1986-) (Pre-1986 not available), from Mr DJ Hunnybun, 40 Churchill Road, Cowes, Isle of Wight, PO31 8HH. 01983 292 880;
e-mail: davehunnybun@hotmail.com

BTO Regional Representative
James C Gloyn, 3 School Close, Newchurch, Isle of Wight, PO36 0NL. 01983 865 567;
e-mail: gloynjc@yahoo.com

Clubs
ISLE OF WIGHT NATURAL HISTORY & ARCHAEOLOGICAL SOCIETY. (1919; 500). The Secretary, Salisbury Gardens, Dudley Road, Ventnor, Isle of Wight PO38 1EJ. 01983 855 385;
www.iwnhas.org

ISLE OF WIGHT ORNITHOLOGICAL GROUP. (1986; 155). Mr DJ Hunnybun, 40 Churchill Road, Cowes, Isle of Wight, PO31 8HH. 01983 292 880;
e-mail: davehunnybun@hotmail.com

Wildlife Trust
Director, See Hampshire,

KENT

Bird Atlas/Avifauna
Birding in Kent by D W Taylor et al 1996. Pica Press

Bird Recorder
Barry Wright, 6 Hatton Close, Northfleet, Kent DA11 8SD. 01474 320 918 (M)07789 710 555;
e-mail: barrybirding@tiscali.co.uk

Bird Reports
DUNGENESS BIRD OBSERVATORY REPORT (1989-), from Warden, see Reserves.

KENT BIRD REPORT (1952-), from Chris Roome, Rowland House, Station Road, Staplehurst, KentTN12 0PY. 01580 891 686;
e-mail: chris.roome@zulogic.co.uk

SANDWICH BAY BIRD OBSERVATORY REPORT, from Warden, see Reserves,

BTO Regional Representatives
RR. Sally Hunter. 01304 612 425;
e-mail: sally.hunter@tesco.net

Club
KENT ORNITHOLOGICAL SOCIETY. (1952; 650). Mr Martin Coath, 14A Mount Harry Road, Sevenoaks, Kent TN13 3JH. 01732 460 710; e-mail: crag_martin2000@yahoo.co.uk
www.kentos.org.uk
Meetings: Indoor: October-April at various venues; the AGM in April is at Grove Green community Hall, Grovewood Drive, Maidstone ME14 5TQ. See website for details: www.kentos.org.uk

Ringing Groups
DARTFORD RG. PE Jones.
E-mail: philjones@beamingbroadband.com

DUNGENESS BIRD OBSERVATORY. David Walker, Dungeness Bird Observatory, Dungeness, Romney

Marsh, Kent TN29 9NA. 01797 321 309; e-mail: dungeness.obs@tinyonline.co.uk www.dungenessbirdobs.org.uk

RECULVER RG. Chris Hindle, 42 Glenbervie Drive, Herne Bay, Kent, CT6 6QL. 01227 373 070; e-mail: christopherhindle@hotmail.com

SANDWICH BAY BIRD OBSERVATORY. Mr KB Ellis, 6 Alderney Gardens, St Peters, Broadstairs, Kent CT10 2TN. 01304 617 341; e-mail: keithjulie@talktalk.net

SWALE WADER GROUP. Rod Smith, 67 York Avenue, Chatham, Kent, ME5 9ES. 01634 865 836; www.swalewaders.co.uk

RSPB Local Groups

CANTERBURY. (1973; 216). Chris Sproul. 01227 450 655; e-mail: cyasproul@yahoo.co.uk www.rspb.org.uk/groups/canterbury Meetings: 8.00pm, 2nd Tuesday of the month (Sept-Apr), Chaucer Social Club, Off Chaucer Drive, Canterbury, CT1 1YW.

GRAVESEND & DISTRICT. (1977; 278). Jeffrey Kirk, 01474 365 757; e-mail: jeffandwendy28@btopenworld.com www.rspbgravesend.org.uk Meetings: 7.45pm, 2nd Wednesday of the month (Sep-May), St Botolph's Hall, North Fleet, Gravesend.

MAIDSTONE. (1973; 250). Dick Marchese, 11 Bathurst Road, Staplehurst, Tonbridge, Kent TN12 0LG. 01580 892 458; e-mail: marchese8@aol.com http://maidstone.localrspb.org.uk/ Meetings: 7.30pm, 3rd Thursday of the month, Grove Green Community Hall, Penhurst Close, Grove Green, opposite Tesco's.

MEDWAY. (1974; 230). Marie Tilley, 01634 387 431; e-mail: marie.tilley@btinternet.com www.medway-rspb.pwp.blueyonder.co.uk Meetings: 7.45pm 3rd Tuesday of the month (except Aug), Strood Library, Bryant Road, Strood.

SEVENOAKS. (1974; 265). Anne Chapman, 01732 456 459; e-mail: anneanddave.chapman@virgin.net www.rspb.org.uk/groups/sevenoaks Meetings: 7.45pm 1st Thursday of the month, Otford Memorial Hall.

THANET. (1975; 119). Peter Radclyffe, Cottage of St John, Caterbury Road, Sarre, Kent CT7 0JY. 01843 847 345; e-mail: Hazel.johnson1@sky.com www.rspb.org.uk/groups/thanet Meetings: 7.30pm last Tuesday of the month (Jan-Nov), Portland Centre.

TONBRIDGE. (1975; 150 reg attendees/1700 in catchment). Stephen Daniell, 01892 546 699; e-mail: stephen_daniell@O2.co.uk www.rspb.org.uk/groups/tonbridge Meetings: 7.45pm 3rd Wednesday of the month (Sept-Apr), St Phillips Church, Salisbury Road.

Wetland Bird Survey Organisers

DUNGENESS AREA. David Walker, Dungeness Bird Observatory, Dungeness, Romney Marsh, Kent TN29 9NA. 01797 321 309; e-mail: dungeness.obs@tinyonline.co.uk

EAST KENT. Ken Lodge, 14 Gallwey Avenue, Birchington, Kent CT7 9PA. 01843 843 105; e-mail: lodge9pa@btinternet.com

PEGWELL BAY. Pete Findley, c/o Sandwich Bay Bird Observatory, 01304 379 074; e-mail: pwjfindley@hotmail.com

Wildlife Hospital

RAPTOR CENTRE. Eddie Hare, Ivy Cottage, Groombridge Place, Groombridge, Tunbridge Wells, Kent TN3 9QG. 01892 861 175; e-mail: raptorcentre@btconnect.com www.raptorcentre.co.uk Birds of prey. Veterinary support. 24hr rescue service for sick and injured birds of prey that covers the South-East.

Wildlife Trust

KENT WILDLIFE TRUST. (1958; 10500). Tyland Barn, Sandling, Maidstone, Kent, ME14 3BD. 01622 662 012; e-mail: info@kentwildlife.org.uk www.kentwildlifetrust.org.uk

LANCASHIRE

Bird Atlas/Avifauna

An Atlas of Breeding Birds of Lancaster and District by Ken Harrison (Lancaster & District Birdwatching Society, 1995).

Birds of Lancashire and North Merseyside by White, McCarthy and Jones (Hobby Publications 2008).

Breeding Birds of Lancashire and North Merseyside (2001), sponsored by North West Water. Contact: Bob Pyefinch, 12 Bannistre Court, Tarleton, Preston PR4 6HA.

Bird Recorder

(See also Manchester).

LANCASHIRE (inc North Merseyside). Steve White, 102 Minster Court, Crown Street, Liverpool, L7 3QD. 0151 707 2744; e-mail: stevewhite102@btinternet.com

Bird Reports

BIRDS OF LANCASTER & DISTRICT (1959-), from Kevin Briggs, The Bramblings, 1 Washington Drive, Warton LA5 9RA, Email: ldbws@yahoo.co.uk www.lancasterbirdwatching.org.uk

EAST LANCASHIRE ORNITHOLOGISTS' CLUB BIRD REPORT (1982-) Members £2.50, Non-members £5.50, from Tony Cooper, 28 Peel Park Ave, Clitheroe BB7 1ET. www.eastlancashireornithologists.org.uk

ENGLAND

CHORLEY AND DISTRICT NATURAL HISTORY SOCIETY ANNUAL REPORT (1979 -), published on website www.chorleynats.org.uk

BLACKBURN & DISTRICT BIRD CLUB ANNUAL REPORT (1992-), from Doreen Bonner, 6 Winston Road, Blackburn, BB1 8BJ. 01254 261 480;
e-mail: webmaster@blackburnbirdclub.co.uk
www.blackburnbirdclub.co.uk

FYLDE BIRD REPORT (1983-), from Paul Ellis, 18 Staining Rise, Blackpool, FY3 0BU.
www.fyldebirdclub.org

LANCASHIRE BIRD REPORT (1914-), from Secretary, Lancs & Cheshire Fauna Soc,

ROSSENDALE ORNITHOLOGISTS' CLUB BIRD REPORT (1977-).from Secretary, Rossendale Ornithologists Club, 25 Church St, Newchurch, Rossendale, Lancs BB4 9EX. Email: info@rossendalebird.freeuk.com
www.rossendalebird.freeuk.com

BTO Regional Representatives
EAST RR. Tony Cooper, 28 Peel Park Avenue, Clitheroe, Lancs, BB7 1ET. 01200 424 577;
e-mail: anthony.cooper@talktalk.net

NORTH & WEST RR. Jean Roberts. 01524 770 295;
e-mail: JeanRbrts6@aol.com

SOUTH RR. Stephen Dunstan,
e-mail: stephen-dunstan@tiscali.co.uk

Clubs
BLACKBURN & DISTRICT BIRD CLUB. (1991; 134). Jim Bonner, 6 Winston Road, Blackburn, BB1 8BJ. 01254 261 480; e-mail: webmaster@blackburnbirdclub.co.uk
www.blackburnbirdclub.co.uk
Meetings: Normally 7.30pm, 1st Monday of the month, (Sept-Apr), Church Hall, Preston New Road. Check website for all indoor and outdoor meetings.

CHORLEY & DISTRICT NATURAL HISTORY SOCIETY. (1979; 170). Phil Kirk, Millend, Dawbers Lane, Euxton, Chorley, Lancs PR7 6EB. 01257 266783;
e-mail: secretary@chorleynats.org.uk
www.chorleynats.org.uk
Meetings: 7.30pm, 3rd Thursday of the month (Sept-Apr), St Mary's Parish Centre, Chorley

EAST LANCASHIRE ORNITHOLOGISTS' CLUB. (1955; 45). Dr J Plackett, 71 Walton Lane, Nelson, Lancs BB9 8BG. 01282 612 870;
e-mail: john.plackett@eastlancsornithologists.org.uk
www.eastlancsornithologists.org.uk
Meetings: 7.30pm, 1st Monday of the month (Check website or local press), St Anne's Church Hall, Fence, Nr Burnley.

FYLDE BIRD CLUB (Registered charity number 1102961). (1982; 110). Paul Ellis, 18 Staining Rise, Blackpool, FY3 0BU. 01253 891281; e-mail: paul. ellis24@btopenworld.com or KBeaver@uclan.ac.uk

www.fyldebirdclub.org
Meetings: 7.45pm, 4th Tuesday of the month, River Wyre Hotel, Breck Road, Poulton le Fylde.

FYLDE NATURALISTS' SOCIETY. (1946; 140). Julie Clarke, 7 Cedar Avenue, Poulton-le-Fylde, Blackpool, FY6 8DQ. 01253 883 785; e-mail: secretary@ fyldenaturalists.co.uk
www.fyldenaturalists.co.uk
Meetings: 7.30pm, fortnightly (Sep-Mar), Fylde Coast Alive, Church Hall, Raikes Parade, Blackpool unless otherwise stated in the Programme.

LANCASHIRE & CHESHIRE FAUNA SOCIETY. (1914; 150). Dave Bickerton, 64 Petre Crescent, Rishton, Lancs, BB1 4RB. 01254 886 257;
e-mail: bickertond@aol.com
www.lacfs.org.uk

LANCASTER & DISTRICT BIRD WATCHING SOCIETY. (1959; 200). Kevin Briggs,The Bramblings,1 Washington Drive,Warton LA5 9RA,
e-mail: ldbws@yahoo.co.uk
www.lancasterbirdwatching.org.uk
Meetings: 7.30pm, last Monday of the month (Sep-Nov, Feb-Mar), Bare Methodist Church Hall, St Margarets Road, Morecambe; (Jan and Apr) the Hornby Institute, Hornby.

PRESTON BIRD WATCHING & NATURAL HISTORY SOCIETY. (1876 as the Preston Scientific Society; 110). Stephen R. Halliwell, 3 Baillie Street, Williams Lane, Fulwood Park, Preston. 01772 705 468; e-mail: stephenhalliwell@supanet.com
www.prestonsociety.co.uk
Meetings: Check website for details.

ROSSENDALE ORNITHOLOGISTS' CLUB. (1976; 35). Ian Brady, 25 Church St, Newchurch, Rossendale, Lancs BB4 9EX. 01706 222 120;
e-mail: info@rossendalebird.freeuk.com
www.rossendalebird.freeuk.com
Meetings: 7.30pm, 3rd Monday of the month, Weavers Cottage, Bacup Road, Rawtenstall.

Ringing Groups
FYLDE RG. Mr S. Eaves,
e-mail: seumus@rootstobranches.co.uk

NORTH LANCS RG. John Wilson BEM, 40 Church Hill Avenue, Warton, Carnforth, Lancs LA5 9NU.
E-mail: johnwilson711@btinternet.com

SOUTH WEST LANCASHIRE RG. I H Wolfenden, 35 Hartdale Road, Thornton, Liverpool, Merseyside L23 1TA. 01519 311 232;

RSPB Local Groups
BLACKPOOL. (1983; 170). Alan Stamford, 6 Kensington Road, Cleveleys, FY5 1ER. 01253 859 662;
e-mail: alanstamford140@msn.com
Meetings: 7.30pm, 2nd Friday of the month (Sept-June), Frank Townend Centre, Beach Road, Cleveleys.

257

LANCASTER. (1972; 176). Jill Blackburn, 13 Coach Road, Warton, Carnforth, Lancs LA5 9PR.
E-mail: jill.blackburn@dsl.pipex.com
www.rspb.org.uk/localgroups/lancaster

Wetland Bird Survey Organisers
MORECAMBE BAY NORTH. Clive Hartley, 01539 536 824; e-mail: clive.hartley304@btinternet.com

MORECAMBE BAY SOUTH. Jean Roberts. 07815 979 856; e-mail: JeanRbrts6@aol.com

NORTH LANCASHIRE (Inland). Mr Pete Marsh, Leck View Cottage, Ashley's farm, High Tatham, Lancaster LA2 8PH. 07989 866 487; e-mail: pmrsh123@aol.com

RIBBLE ESTUARY. Ken Abram,
e-mail: k.abram@btinternet.com

RIVER LUNE. Jean Roberts. 07815 979 856;
e-mail: JeanRbrts6@aol.com

Wildlife Trust
THE WILDLIFE TRUST FOR LANCASHIRE, MANCHESTER AND NORTH MERSEYSIDE. (1962; 18,000). Mr James Ellaby, Communications Officer, The Barn, Berkeley Drive, Bamber Bridge, Preston PR5 6BY. 01772 324 129 (fax): 01772 628 849; e-mail: info@lancswt.org.uk
www.lancswt.org.uk

LEICESTERSHIRE & RUTLAND

The Birds of Leicestershire and Rutland by Rob Fray et al. (A&C Black, due August 2009)

Bird Recorder
Steve Lister, 6 Albert Promenade, Loughborough,, Leicestershire LE11 1RE. 01509 829 495;
e-mail: stevelister@surfbirder.com

Bird Reports
*LEICESTERSHIRE & RUTLAND
BIRD REPORT (1941-)*, from Mrs
S Graham, 5 Lychgate Close,
Cropston, Leicestershire LE7 7HU.
0116 236 6474;
e-mail: JSGraham83@aol.com

*RUTLAND NAT HIST SOC ANNUAL
REPORT (1965-)*, from Secretary, 01572 747302.

BTO Regional Representative
LEICESTER & RUTLAND RR. Tim Grove, 35 Clumber Street, Melton Mowbray, Leicestershire, LE13 0ND. 01664 850766; e-mail: k.grove1@ntlworld.com

Clubs
BIRSTALL BIRDWATCHING CLUB. (1976; 50). Mr KJ Goodrich, 6 Riversdale Close, Birstall, Leicester, LE4 4EH. 0116 267 4813;
Meetings: 7.30pm, 2nd Tuesday of the month (Oct-Apr), The Rothley Centre, Mountsorrel Lane, Rothley, Leics LE7 7PR.

LEICESTERSHIRE & RUTLAND ORNITHOLOGICAL SOCIETY. (1941; 580). Mrs Rosemary Rowley, 4

Orchard View, Mountsorrel, Leicester, LE12 7HW.
0116 230 2747; e-mail: rowleyrosemary@hotmail.com
www.lros.org.uk
Meetings: 7.30pm, 1st Friday of the month (Oct-May), Oadby Methodist Church, off Central Car Park, alternating with The Rothley Centre, Mountsorrel Lane, Rothley. Additional meeting at Rutland Water Birdwatching Cntr.

SOUTH LEICESTER BIRDWATCHERS. (2006; 60). Paul Seaton, 76 Roehampton Drive, Wigston, Leics, LE18 1HU. 07969 387 914;
e-mail: paul.lseaton@btinternet.com
Meetings: 7.30 pm, 2nd Wednesday of the month (Sep-Jun), County Scout Centre, Winchester Road, Blaby, Leicester LE8 4HN.

RUTLAND NATURAL HISTORY SOCIETY. (1964; 256). Mrs L Worrall, 6 Redland Close, Barrowden, Oakham, Rutland, LE15 8ES. 01572 747 302;
www.rnhs.org.uk
Meetings: 7.30pm, 1st Tuesday of the month (Oct-Apr), Oakham CofE School, Burley Road, Oakham.

Ringing Groups
RUTLAND WATER RG. Mr M Kerman
e-mail:kerman.martin@ntlworld.com

STANFORD RG. John Cranfield, 41 Main Street, Fleckney, Leicester, LE8 8AP. 0116 240 4385;
e-mail: JacanaJohn@talktalk.net

RSPB Local Groups
LEICESTER. (1969; 1600 in catchment area). Chris Woolass, 136 Braunstone Lane, Leicester, LE3 2RW. 0116 2990078; e-mail: j.woolass1@ntlworld.com
www.rspb.org.uk/groups/leicester
Meetings: 7.30pm, 3rd Friday of the month (Sep-May), Trinity Methodist Hall, Harborough Road, Oadby, LEICESTER, LE2 4LA

LOUGHBOROUGH. (1970; 300). Robert Orton, 01509 413 936; e-mail: Lboro.RSPB@virgin.net
www.rspb.org.uk/groups/loughborough
Meetings: Monthly Friday nights, Loughborough University.

Wetland Bird Survey Organisers
LEICESTERSHIRE & RUTLAND (excl Rutland Water). Tim Grove, 35 Clumber Street, Melton Mowbray, Leics LE13 0ND. 01664 850 766;
e-mail: k.grove1@ntlworld.com

RUTLAND WATER. Tim Appleton, Reserve Manager, Egleton, Oakham, Rutland LE15 8BT;
e-mail: tim@rutlandwater.org.uk

Wildlife Trust
LEICESTERSHIRE & RUTLAND WILDLIFE TRUST. (1956; 14,000). Brocks Hill Environment Centre, Washbrook Lane, Oadby, Leicestershire LE2 5JJ. 0116 272 0444 (fax) 0116 272 0404; e-mail: info@lrwt.org.uk
www.lrwt.org.uk

ENGLAND

LINCOLNSHIRE

Bird Recorders
Steve Keightley, Redclyffe, Swineshead Road,
Frampton Fen, Boston PE20 1SG. 01205 290 233;
e-mail: steve.keightley@btinternet.com

Bird Reports
*LINCOLNSHIRE BIRD REPORT (1979-), 1990 is now
sold out, 2008 is the latest report, £13.75 including
postage*, from Bill Sterling, Newlyn, 5 Carlton Avenue,
Healing, NE Lincs DN41 7PW.
E-mail: wbsterling@hotmail.com

*LINCOLNSHIRE RARE AND SCARCE BIRD REPORTS
(1997-1999) & (2000-2002), £13.75 each including
postage.*,Bill Sterling, Newlyn, 5 Carlton Avenue,
Healing, NE Lincs DN41 7PW.
E-mail: wbsterling@hotmail.com

*SCUNTHORPE & NORTH WEST LINCOLNSHIRE BIRD
REPORT (1973-)*, from Secretary, Scunthorpe Museum
Society, Ornithological Section, (Day)01724 402 871
(Eve)01724 734 261.

BTO Regional Representatives
EAST RR. Mr P M J Espin,
e-mail: philespin@live.co.uk

NORTH RR. Chris Gunn, 01777 707 888;
e-mail: chris@cgtraining.co.uk

SOUTH RR. Richard & Kay Heath, 56 Pennytoft Lane,
Pinchbeck, Spalding, Lincs PE11 3PQ. 01775 767055;
e-mail: heathsrk@ukonline.co.uk

WEST RR. Peter Overton, Hilltop Farm, Welbourn,
Lincoln, LN5 0QH. Work 01400 273 323;
e-mail: nyika@biosearch.org.uk
Sponsoring the Kestrel in the Bird Atlas through
Biosearch Expeditions, www.biosearch.org.uk

RDO. Nicholas Watts, Vine House Farm, Deeping St
Nicholas, Spalding, Lincs PE11 3DG. 01775 630 208;

Club
LINCOLNSHIRE BIRD CLUB. (1979;
220). Janet Eastmead, Garlicroft
Cottage, 89 Main Road, Hundleby,
Spilsby PE23 5ND. E-mail:
secretary@lincsbirdclub.co.uk
www.lincsbirdclub.co.uk
Meetings: Local groups hold winter
evening meetings (contact Secretary for details).

SCUNTHORPE MUSEUM SOCIETY (Ornithological
Section). (1973; 50). Keith Parker, 7 Ryedale Avenue,
Winterton, Scunthorpe, Lincs DN15 9BJ.
Meetings: 7.15pm, 3rd Monday of the month (Sep-
Apr), Scunthorpe Museum, Oswald Road.

Ringing Groups
GIBRALTAR POINT BIRD OBSERVATORY. Mr M.R.
Briggs. E-mail: mbriggs@gibobs.fsworld.co.uk

MID LINCOLNSHIRE RG. Miss D.M.Staples,
e-mail: donnamstaples@hotmail.com

WASH WADER RG. P L Ireland, 27 Hainfield Drive,
Solihull, W Midlands, B91 2PL. 0121 704 1168;
e-mail: pli@blueyonder.co.uk

RSPB Local Groups
GRIMSBY. (1986; 2200 in catchment area). Jenny
Curtis, 01472 232 632;
e-mail: GrimsbyRSPB@gmail.com
www.rspb.org.uk/groups/grimsby
Meetings: 7.30pm, 1st Monday of the month (Sept-
May), Corpus Christi Church Hall, Grimsby Road,
Cleethorpes, DN35 7LJ.

LINCOLN. (1974; 250). Peter Skelson, 26 Parksgate
Avenue, Lincoln, LN6 7HP. 01522 695 747;
e-mail: peter.skelson@lincolnrspb.org.uk
www.lincolnrspb.org.uk
Meetings: 7.30pm, 2nd Thursday of the month (not
Jun, Jul, Aug, Dec), The Lawn, Union Road, Lincoln.

SOUTH LINCOLNSHIRE. (1987; 350). Anne Algar. 01529
460 877; e-mail: info@southlincsrspb.org.uk
www.southlincsrspb.org.uk
Meetings: Contact group.

Wetland Bird Survey Organisers
HUMBER ESTUARY - Inner South.Keith Parker, e-mail:
Keith.Parker@corusgroup.com

HUMBER ESTUARY - Outer South.John Walker, e-mail:
dunewalker@btopenworld.com

SOUTH LINCOLNSHIRE/PETERBOROUGH (inland). Bob
Titman, 01733 583 254; e-mail: titman@nildram.co.uk

Wildlife Trust
LINCOLNSHIRE WILDLIFE TRUST. (1948; 26,000).
Banovallum House, Manor House Street, Horncastle,
Lincs, LN9 5HF. 01507 526 667 (fax) 01507 525 732;
e-mail: info@lincstrust.co.uk
www.lincstrust.org.uk

LONDON, GREATER

Bird Atlas/Avifauna
*The Breeding Birds Illustrated magazine of the
London Area, 2002.* ISBN 0901009 121 ed Jan
Hewlett(London Natural History Society).

Two Centuries of Croydon's Birds by John Birkett
(RSPB Croydon Local Group 2007). £10 plus p&p.

Bird Recorder see also Surrey
Andrew Self, 16 Harp Island Close, Neasden, London,
NW10 0DF. 07889 761 828; e-mail: a-self@sky.com
http://londonbirders.wikia.com

Bird Report
CROYDON BIRD SURVEY (1995), from Secretary,
Croydon RSPB Group, 020 8640 4578;
e-mail: johndavis.wine@care4free.net
www.croydon-rspb.org.uk

259

ENGLAND

LONDON BIRD REPORT (20-mile radius of St Paul's Cath) (1936-), from Catherine Schmitt, Publications Sales, London Natural History Society, 4 Falkland Avenue, London N3 1QR. 020 8346 4359.

BTO Regional Representatives
LONDON, NORTH. Ian Woodward, 245 Larkshall Road, Chingford, London, E4 9HY. 07947 321 889; e-mail: ianw_bto_nlon@hotmail.co.uk

LONDON, SOUTH. Richard Arnold. 020 8224 1135; e-mail: bto@thomsonecology.com

Clubs
THE LONDON BIRD CLUB (formerly the Ornithological Section of the London Natural History Society). (1858; 1000). Mrs Angela Linnell, 20 Eleven Acre Rise, Loughton, Essex, IG10 1AN. 020 8508 2932; e-mail: angela.linnell@phonecoop.coop
www.lnhs.org.uk
Meetings: See website.

MARYLEBONE BIRDWATCHING SOCIETY. (1981; 110). Marion Hill, 20 Howitt Close, Howitt Road, London NW3 4LX. E-mail: birdsmbs@yahoo.com
www.birdsmbs.org.uk
Meeting:2nd Friday of month (Sept-May), 7.15pm Gospel Oak Methodist Church, Lisburne Road, London NW3 2NR. Also programme of Saturday local and coach outings and weekly walks on Hampstead Heath.

Ringing Groups
LONDON GULL STUDY GROUP - (SE including Hampshire, Surrey, Susex, Berkshire and Oxfordshire). This group is no longer active but still receiving sightings/recoveries of ringed birds. (Also includes Hampshire, Surrey, Sussex, Berkshire and Oxfordshire). No longer in operation but able to give information on gulls. Mark Fletcher, 24 The Gowans, Sutton-on-the-Forest, York, YO61 1DJ.
E-mail: mark.fletcher@fera.gsi.gov.uk

RUNNYMEDE RG. D G Harris, 22 Blossom Waye, Hounslow, TW5 9HD; http://rmxrg.org.uk
E-mail: daveharris@tinyonline.co.uk

RSPB Local Groups
BEXLEY. (1979; 180). Tony Banks, 15 Boundary Road, Sidcup, Kent DA15 8SS. 020 8859 3518; e-mail: tonybanks@fsmail.net
www.bexleyrspb.org.uk
Meetings: 7.30pm, 3rd Friday of the month, Hurstmere School Hall, Hurst Road, Sidcup.

BROMLEY. (1972; 285). Val Bryant, 11 Hastings Road, Bromley, Kent BR2 8NZ. 0208 462 6330; e-mail: valbryant5@gmail.comt
www.rspb.org.uk/groups/bromley
Meetings: 2nd Wednesday of the month (Sep-Jun), Large Hall, Bromley Central Library Building, Bromley High Street.

CENTRAL LONDON. (1974; 250). Margaret Blackburn, 0208 866 5853; e-mail: mblackburn@tesco.net
www.janja.dircon.co.uk/rspb
Meetings: (Indoor) 2nd Thursday of the month (Sep-May), St Columba's Church Hall, Pont St, London SW1. See website for details of field meetings.

CROYDON. (1973; 4000 in catchment area). John Davis, 9 Cricket Green, Mitcham, CR4 4LB. 020 8640 4578; e-mail johndavis.wine@care4free.net
www.croydon-rspb.org.uk
Meetings: 2nd Monday of each month at 2pm-4pm and again at 8pm-10pm at Old Whitgiftian Clubhouse, Croham Manor Road, South Croydon.

ENFIELD. (1971; 2700). Norman G Hudson, 125 Morley Hill, Enfield, Middx, EN2 0BQ. 020 8363 1431; e-mail: dorandnor@tiscali.co.uk
www.rspb.org.uk/groups/enfield
Meetings: 8pm, 1st Thursday of the month, St Andrews Hall, Enfield Town.

HAVERING. (1972; 270). Martin Runchman, 01767 690 093; e-mail: mrunchman@yahoo.com
www.rspb.org.uk/groups/havering/
Meetings: 8pm, 2nd Friday of the month, Hornchurch Library, North Street, Hornchurch.

NORTH EAST LONDON. David Littlejohns, 0208 989 4746; e-mail: NelondonRSPB@yahoo.co.uk
www.rspb.org.uk/groups/northeastlondon
Meetings: 7.30pm, 2nd Tuesday of every month, Snaresbrook Primary School, Meadow Walk, South Woodford, London, E18 2EN

NW LONDON RSPB GROUP. (1983; 2000 in catchment area). Bob Husband, The Firs, 49 Carson Road, Cockfosters, Barnet, Herts EN4 9EN. 020 8441 8742; e-mail: bobhusband@hotmail.co.uk
www.rspb.org.uk/groups/nwlondon
Meetings: 8pm, Usually last Tuesday of the month, (Sep-Mar), Wilberforce Centre, St Paul's Church, The Ridgeway, Mill Hill, London, NW7 1QU.

PINNER & DISTRICT. (1972; 300). Dennis Bristow, 118 Crofts Road, Harrow, Middx, HA1 2PJ. 020 8863 5026; e-mail: dennisbristow789@btinternet.com
www.rspb.org.uk/groups/pinner/
Meetings: 8pm, 2nd Thursday of the month (Sept-May), Church Hall, St John The Baptist Parish Church, Pinner HA5 3AS.

RICHMOND & TWICKENHAM. (1979; 285). Jenny Shalom, 0208 392 9938; e-mail: RichmondRSPB@yahoo.co.uk
www.rspb.org.uk/groups/richmond
Meetings: 8.00pm, 1st Wednesday of the month, York House, Twickenham.

Wetland Bird Survey Organiser
GREATER LONDON (excl. Thames Estuary). Helen Baker, e-mail: helen.baker60@tiscali.co.uk

LEE VALLEY. Cath Patrick. Myddelton House, Bulls Cross, Enfield, Herts EN2 9HG. 01992 717 711; e-mail: cpatrick@leevalleypark.org.uk

ENGLAND

Wildlife Trust
LONDON WILDLIFE TRUST. (1981; 7500). Skyline House, 200 Union Street, London, SE1 0LX. 0207 261 0447 (fax) 0207 633 0811;
e-mail: enquiries@wildlondon.org.uk
www.wildlondon.org.uk

MANCHESTER, GREATER

Bird Atlas/Avifauna
Breeding Birds in Greater Manchester by Philip Holland et al (1984).

Bird Recorder
RECORDER AND REPORT EDITOR. Mrs A Judith Smith, e-mail: ajudithsmith@gmail.com
www.manchesterbirding.com

ASSISTANT RECORDER (Rarities). Ian McKerchar, 42 Green Ave, Astley, Manchester, M29 7EH. 01942 701 758; e-mail: ianmckerchar1@gmail.com
www.manchesterbirding.com

Bird Reports
BIRDS IN GREATER MANCHESTER (1976-) from County Recorder.

LEIGH ORNITHOLOGICAL SOCIETY BIRD REPORT (1971-), from Mr D Shallcross, 28 Surrey Avenue, Leigh, Lancs, WN7 2NN. www.leighos.org.uk
E-mail: chairman@leighos.org.uk

BTO Regional Representatives
MANCHESTER. Steve Suttill, 94 Manchester Road, Mossley, Ashton-under-Lyne, Lancashire OL5 9AY. 01457 836 360; e-mail: suttill.parkinson@virgin.net

Clubs
ALTRINGHAM AND DISTRICT NATURAL HISTORY SOCIETY. Claire Joures (Secretary), 0161 928 4513;
Meetings: 7:30pm, Tuesdays, Hale Methodist Church Hall, Oak Road, off Hale Road, Hale. 50p charge includes refreshments.

GREATER MANCHESTER BIRD RECORDING GROUP. (2002: 40) Restricted to contributors of the county bird report. Mrs A Judith Smith;
e-mail: ajudithsmith@gmail.com
www.manchesterbirding.com

LEIGH ORNITHOLOGICAL SOCIETY. (1971; 118). Mr D Shallcross, 28 Surrey Avenue, Leigh, Lancs, WN7 2NN. E-mail: chairman@ leighos.org.uk
www.leighos.org.uk
Meetings: 7.15pm, Fridays, Leigh Library (check website for details).

ROCHDALE FIELD NATURALISTS' SOCIETY. (1970; 90). Mrs D Francis, 20 Hillside Avenue, Shaw, Oldham OL2 8HR. 01706 843 685; e-mail: secretary@ rochdalefieldnaturalistssociety.co.uk
www.rochdalefieldnaturalistssociety.co.uk

Meetings: 7.30pm (Sept-Apr) at Cutgate Baptist Church, Edenfield Rd, Rochdale. Yearly syllabus (out after AGM in Sept) states dates of lectures and outings.

STOCKPORT BIRDWATCHING SOCIETY. (1972; 80). Dave Evans, 36 Tatton Road South, Stockport, Cheshire, SK4 4LU. 0161 432 9513;
e-mail: windhover@ntlworld.com
Meetings: 7.30pm, last Wednesday of the month, The Heatons Sports Club, Heaton Moor Stockport.

Ringing Groups
LEIGH RG. A J Gramauskas, 21 Elliot Avenue, Golborne, Warrington, WA3 3DU. 0151 929 215;

SOUTH MANCHESTER RG. Mr N.B. Powell.
E-mail: neville.powell@tiscali.co.uk

RSPB Local Groups
BOLTON. (1978; 320). Anthony Johnson, 01204 468 850; e-mail: anthony@ajohnson65.fsbusiness.co.uk
http://boltonrspb.users.btopenworld.com
Meetings: 7.30pm, Thursdays (dates vary), Main Hall, Smithills School, Smithills Dean Road, Bolton.

MANCHESTER. (1972;3600 in catchment area). Peter Wolstenholme, 31 South Park Road, Gatley, Cheshire, SK8 4AL. 0161 428 2175; www.rspbmanchester.org.uk
Meetings: 7.30 pm, St James Parish Hall, Gatley Green, Church Road, Cheadle.

STOCKPORT LOCAL GROUP. (1979; 120). Gay Crossley, 5 Broadhill Close, Bramhall, Stockport, Cheshire SK7 3BY. 0161 439 3210;
e-mail: StockportRSPB@googlemail.com
www.rspb.org.uk/groups/stockport
Meetings: 7.30pm, 2nd Monday of the month (Sep-Apr), Stockport College of Technology, Lecture Theatre B.

WIGAN. (1973; 80). Neil Martin. 01695 624 860;
e-mail: neimaz07@yahoo.co.uk
www.rspb.org.uk/groups/wigan
Meetings: 7.45pm. St Anne's Parish Hall, Church Lane, Shevington, Wigan, Lancashire, WN6 8BD.

Wetland Bird Survey Organiser
GREATER MANCHESTER. Adrian Dancy. 0161 234 3537;
e-mail: a.dancy@ntlworld.com

Wildlife Trust
See Lancashire.

MERSEYSIDE & WIRRAL

Bird Atlas see Cheshire

Bird Recorders see Cheshire; Lancashire

Bird Reports see also Cheshire
HILBRE BIRD OBSERVATORY REPORT, from Warden, see Reserves.

BTO Regional Representatives
MERSEYSIDE RR and RDO. Bob Harris, 3 Mossleigh,

Whixalll, Whitchurch, Shropshire SY13 2SA. Work 0151 706 4311; e-mail: harris@liv.ac.uk

WIRRAL RR. Paul Miller. 01928 787 535; e-mail: huntershill@worldonline.co.uk

BTO Garden BirdWatch Ambassador
Miss J Grant, e-mail: janet.grant1967@tiscali.co.uk

Clubs
MERSEYSIDE NATURALISTS' ASSOCIATION. (1938; 150). David Bryant, Chairman, 13, Strafford Drive, Bootle, Merseyside L20 9JN. 0151 523 5240; e-mail: chairman@mnapage.info www.mnapage.info
Meetings: 2-4pm, Saturday afternoons (Feb, Oct and Nov), Bootle Cricket Club, check website for details. 7-8 coach outings per year.

WIRRAL BIRD CLUB. (1977; 150). The Secretary. E-mail: info@wirralbirdclub.com www.wirralbirdclub.com

Ringing Groups
MERSEYSIDE RG. Bob Harris, 3 Mossleigh, Whixalll, Whitchurch, Shropshire SY13 2SA. Work 0151 706 4311; e-mail: harris@liv.ac.uk

SOUTH WEST LANCASHIRE RG. I H Wolfenden, 35 Hartdale Road, Thornton, Liverpool, Merseyside L23 1TA. 01519 311 232;

RSPB Local Groups
LIVERPOOL. (1966; 162). Chris Tynan, 10 Barker Close, Huyton, Liverpool, L36 0XU. 0151 480 7938 (M)07831 352 870; e-mail: christtynan@aol.com www.rspbliverpool.org.uk
Meetings: 7 for 7.30pm, 3rd Monday of the month (Sep-Apr), Mossley Hill Parish Church, Junc. Rose Lane and Elmswood Rd.

SOUTHPORT. (1974; 300). Alan Toms, 01704 871 540; e-mail: tomsrspb@talktalk.net www.rspb.org.uk/groups/southport
Meetings: 7.45pm, 3rd Friday of the month, Lord Street West Church Hall, Duke Street, SOUTHPORT.

WIRRAL. (1982; 120). Jeremy Bradshaw. 0151 632 2364; e-mail: Info@wirralRSPB.org.uk www.rspb.org.uk/groups/wirral
Meetings: 7.30pm, 1st Thursday of the month, Bromborough Civic Centre, 2 Bromborough Village Road, WIRRAL.

Wetland Bird Survey Organiser
ALT ESTUARY. Steve White, 102 Minster Court, Crown Street, Liverpool, L7 3QD. 0151 707 2744; e-mail: swhite@lancswt.org.uk

DEE ESTUARY. Colin Wells, Burton Farm Point, Station Road, Nr Neston, South Wirra CH64 5SB. 01513 367 681; e-mail: colin.wells@rspb.org.uk

MERSEY ESTUARY. Graham Thomason, 110 Coroners Lane, Widnes, Cheshire WA8 9HZ.

MERSEYSIDE (inland). Stephen Birch, 07779 862 821; e-mail: stevebirch1@live.co.uk

Wildlife Trust
See Lancashire.

NORFOLK

Bird Atlas/Avifauna
The Birds of Norfolk by Moss Taylor, Michael Seago, Peter Allard & Don Dorling (Pica Press, 1999).

Bird Recorder
JOINT COUNTY RECORDERS. Dave and Jacquie Bridges, 27 Swan Close, Hempstead Road, Holt, Norfolk NR25 6DP. 01263 713 249; e-mail: dnjnorfolkrec@aol.com

Bird Reports
CLEY BIRD CLUB 10-KM SQUARE BIRD REPORT (1987-), from Peter Gooden, 45 Charles Road, Holt, Norfolk, NR25 6DA. 01263 712 368;

NAR VALLEY ORNITHOLOGICAL SOCIETY ANNUAL REPORT (1976-), from The Chairman, Ian Black.

NORFOLK BIRD & MAMMAL REPORT (1953-), from DL Paull, 8 Lindford Drive, Eaton, Norwich NR4 6LT; e-mail: info@nnns.org.uk www.NNNS.org.uk

NORFOLK ORNITHOLOGISTS' ASSOCN ANNUAL REPORT (1961-), from Holme Bird Observatory, 01485 525 406, or NOA, Broadwater Road, Holme Next the Sea, Hunstanton, Norfolk, PE36 6LQ. E-mail: info@noa.org.uk

WENSUM VALLEY BIRDWATCHING SOCIETY (2003-) from the secretary, e-mail: admin@wvbs.co.uk www.wvbs.co.uk

BTO Regional Representatives
NORTH-EAST RR. Chris Hudson, Cornerstones, 5 Ringland Road, Taverham, Norwich, NR8 6TG. 01603 868 805 (M)07771 635 844; e-mail: Chris697@btinternet.com

NORTH-WEST RR. Allan Hale. 01366 328 421; e-mail: allan@ajhale.plus.com

SOUTH-EAST RR. Rachel Warren. 01603 593 912; e-mail: campephilus@btinternet.com

SOUTH-WEST RR. Vince Matthews, Rose's Cottage, The Green, Merton, Thetford, Norfolk IP25 6QU. e-mail: norfolksouthwest@tiscali.co.uk

Clubs
CLEY BIRD CLUB. (1986; 500). Peter Gooden, 45 Charles Road, Holt, Norfolk, NR25 6DA. 01263 712368;
Meetings: 8.00pm, Wednesdays, monthly (Dec-Feb), White Horse Hotel, Blakeney.

GREAT YARMOUTH BIRD CLUB. (1989; 30). Keith R Dye, 104 Wolseley Road, Great Yarmouth, Norfolk, NR31 0EJ. 01493 600 705; www.gybc.org.uk

Meetings: 7.45pm, 4th Monday of the month, Rumbold Arms, Southtown Road.

NAR VALLEY ORNITHOLOGICAL SOCIETY. (1976; 125). Ian Black, Three Chimneys, Tumbler Hill, Swaffham, Norfolk, PE37 7JG. 01760 724 092; e-mail: ian_a_black@hotmail.com www.accessbs.com/narvos
Meetings: 7.30pm, last Tuesday of the month (Jul-Nov and Jan-May), Barn Theatre, Convent of The Sacred Heart, Mangate Street, Swaffham, PE37 7QW.

NORFOLK & NORWICH NATURALISTS' SOCIETY. (1869; 630). DL Paull. 8 Lindford Drive, Eaton, Norwich NR4 6LT. 01603 457 270; e-mail: info@nnns.org.uk www.NNNS.org.uk
Meetings: 7.30pm, 3rd Tuesday of the month (Oct-Mar), St Andrew's Church Hall, Church Lane, Norwich

NORFOLK ORNITHOLOGISTS' ASSOCIATION. (1962; 1100). Jed Andrews, Broadwater Road, Holme-next-Sea, Hunstanton, Norfolk PE36 6LQ. 01485 525 406; e-mail: info@noa.org.uk www.noa.org.uk

WENSUM VALLEY BIRDWATCHING SOCIETY. (2003; 125). Colin Wright, 7 Hinshalwood Way, Old Costessey, Norwich, Norfolk NR8 5BN. 01603 740548; e-mail: admin@wvbs.co.uk www.wvbs.co.uk
Meetings: 7.30pm, 3rd Thursday of the month, Weston Longville village hall.

Ringing Groups
BTO NUNNERY RG. Kate Risely, c/o BTO, The Nunnery, Thetford, Norfolk IP24 2PU. E-mail: kate.risely@bto.org

HOLME BIRD OBSERVATORY. Miss SA Barker. E-mail: info@noa.org.uk

NORTH NORFOLK FARMLAND STUDY & RINGING GROUP. Keith Herber, Laleham, 60 Dale End, Brancaster Staithe, King's Lynn PE31 8DA. 01485 210 980; e-mail: keith.herber@btinternet.com

NORTH WEST NORFOLK RG. Mr J L Middleton, 8 Back Lane, Burnham Market, Norfolk PE31 8EY. E-mail: johnmiddleton@bmarket.freeserve.co.uk

SHERINGHAM RG. D Sadler, 26 Abbey Road, Sheringham, Norfolk, NR26 8NN. 01263 821 904;

WASH WADER RG. P L Ireland, 27 Hainfield Drive, Solihull, W Midlands, B91 2PL. 0121 704 1168; e-mail: pli@blueyonder.co.uk

RSPB Local Groups
NORWICH. (1971; 360). Robert Pindar. 01692 582 689; e-mail: r.pindar@uea.ac.uk www.rspb.org.uk/groups/norwich
Meetings: 7.30pm, 2nd Monday of the month (except Aug), Hellesdon Community Centre, Middletons Lane, Hellesdon, Norwich (entrance of Woodview Road).

WEST NORFOLK. (1977; 247). Stuart Hall, 01553 670 208; e-mail: shall19@sky.com www.rspb-westnorfolk.org
Meetings: 7.30pm, 3rd Wednesday of the month (Sep-Apr), South Wootton Village Hall, Church Lane, South Wootton, King's Lynn.

Wetland Bird Survey Organisers
NORTH NORFOLK COAST. Michael Rooney, Natural England, Hill Farm Offices, Main Road, Well-next-the -Sea Norfolk NR23 1AB. 01328 711 635; e-mail: michael.rooney@naturalengland.org.uk

NORFOLK (excl. estuaries). Tim Strudwick, RSPB Strumpshaw Fen, Staithe Cottage, Low Road, Strumpshaw Norfolk NR13 4HS. 01603 462 128; e-mail: tim.strudwick@rspb.org.uk

THE WASH. Jim Scott, 01485 545 261; e-mail: jim.scott@rspb.org.uk

Wildlife Trust
NORFOLK WILDLIFE TRUST. (1926; 35,000). Bewick House, 22 Thorpe Road, Norwich, Norfolk NR1 1RY. 01603 625 540; www.norfolkwildlifetrust.org.uk e-mail: info@norfolkwildlifetrust.org.uk

NORTHAMPTONSHIRE

Bird Recorder
Position vacant, Enquiries to Mike Alibone, 25 Harrier Park, East Hunsbury, Northants NN4 0QG. E-mail: northantsbirds@ntlworld.com

Bird Report
NORTHAMPTONSHIRE BIRD REPORT (1969-), from Mr John Coleman, 2 Marsons Drive, Crick, Northants NN6 7TD.01788 822 905; http://northamptonshirebirdclub.ning.com

BTO Regional Representatives
RR. Barrie Galpin. 01780 444 351; e-mail: barrie.galpin@zen.co.uk

BTO Garden BirdWatch Ambassador
Mr J A & Mrs L Tyler, e-mail: linda.john_gbw@yahoo.co.uk

Clubs
NORTHAMPTONSHIRE BIRD CLUB. (1973; 100). Mrs Eleanor McMahon, Oriole House, 5 The Croft, Hanging Houghton, Northants, NN6 9HW. 01604 880 009; e-mail: eleanor1960@btinternet.com http://sites.google.com/site/northantsbirdclub
Meetings: 7.30pm, 1st Wednesday of the month. Village Hall, Pound Lane, Moulton, Northants.

Ringing Group
NORTHANTS RG. D M Francis, 2 Brittons Drive, Billing Lane, Northampton, NN3 5DP.

ENGLAND

STANFORD RG. John Cranfield, 41 Main Street, Fleckney, Leicester, LE8 8AP. 0116 240 4385; e-mail: JacanaJohn@talktalk.net

RSPB Local Groups
MID NENE. (1975; 350). Hilary Guy. 01536 516 422; e-mail: hilary@snowdrop.demon.co.uk
www.rspb.org.uk/groups/midnene
Meetings: 7.30pm, 2nd or 3rd Thursday of the month (Sep-Apr), The Saxon Hall, Thorpe Street/Brook Street, Raunds.

NORTHAMPTON. (1978; 3000). Liz Wicks, 6 Waypost Court, Lings, Northampton, NN3 8LN. 01604 513 991; e-mail: lizydrip@ntlworld.com
Meetings: 7.30pm, 2nd Thursday of the month, Northants County Council staff sports and social club (Wootton Hall Pavilion), Wootton Hall Park, Wootton NN4 0JA

Wetland Bird Survey Organiser
Jim Williams, Langsend, Newnham, Nr Daventry, Northants NN11 3HQ. 01203 402 121; e-mail: jim.williams4@btinternet.com

Wildlife Trust
Director, See Cambridgeshire,

NORTHUMBERLAND

Bird Atlas/Avifauna
The Atlas of Breeding Birds in Northumbria edited by J C Day et al (Northumberland and Tyneside Bird Club, 1995).

Bird Recorder
Tim Dean, 2 Knocklaw Park, Rothbury, Northumberland NE65 7PW. 01669 621 460 (M)07766 263 167; e-mail: t.r.dean@btopenworld.com

Bird Reports
BIRDS IN NORTHUMBRIA (1970-), from Trevor Blake, 6 Glenside, Ellington, Morpeth, Northumberland NE61 5LS. 01670 862 635; e-mail: trevor.1958@live.co.uk

BIRDS ON THE FARNE ISLANDS (1971-), from Secretary, Natural History Society of Northumbria, 0191 2326386; e-mail: nhsn@ncl.ac.uk
www.nhsn.ncl.ac.uk

BTO Regional Representative & Regional Development Officer
RR. Tom Cadwallender, 22 South View, Lesbury, Alnwick, Northumberland NE66 3PZ. H:01665 830 884 M: 07980 341 9412;
e-mail: tomandmurielcadwallender@hotmail.com

RDO. Muriel Cadwallender, 22 South View, Lesbury, Alnwick, Northumberland NE66 3PZ. 01665 830 884; e-mail: tomandmurielcadwallender@hotmail.com

BTO Garden BirdWatch Ambassador
Dr V L Tuck, e-mail: val.tuck@hotmail.co.uk

Clubs
NORTH NORTHUMBERLAND BIRD CLUB. (1984; 210). Richard Narraway, Workshop Cottage, The Friary, Bamburgh, NE69 7AE. 01668 214 759; e-mail: ringouzel@northnorthumberlandbirdclub.co.uk
www.northnorthumberlandbirdclub.co.uk
Meetings: 7.30pm, 1st Friday of the month(Sept), 2nd Friday (Oct-Jun), Bamburgh Pavilion (below castle).

NORTHUMBERLAND & TYNESIDE BIRD CLUB. (1958; 270). Alan Watson, Secretary, 3 Green Close, Whitley Bay, Northumberland NE25 9SH. 0191 252 2744; e-mail: apusx@blueyonder.co.uk
www.ntbc.org.uk
Meetings: 7.00pm, 2nd Thursday of the month (Sep-Apr), Newcastle Falcons Rugby Club, Brunton Road, Kenton Bank Foot, Newcastle upon Tyne NE13 8AF.

Northumberland & Tyneside Bird Club

NATURAL HISTORY SOCIETY OF NORTHUMBRIA. (1829; about 950). Dr C P F Redfern, Natural History Society of Northumbria, Great North Museum: Hancock, Barras Bridge, Newcastle upon Tyne NE2 4PT. 0191 232 6386; e-mail: nhsn@ncl.ac.uk
www.nhsn.ncl.ac.uk

Ringing Groups
NORTHUMBRIA RG. Secretary. B Galloway, 34 West Meadows, Stamfordham Road, Westerhope, Newcastle upon Tyne NE5 1LS. 0191 286 4850;

Wetland Bird Survey Organisers
LINDISFARNE. Andrew Craggs, Lindisfarne NNR, Beal Station, Beal, Berwick Upon Tweed TD15 2SP. 01289 381 470.

NORTHUMBERLAND COAST. J Roper, 1 Long Row, Howick, Alnwick, Northumberland NE66 3LQ. E-mail: roperjuliea@hotmail.com

NORTHUMBERLAND (Inland). Steve Holliday, 2 Larriston Place, Cramlington, Northumberland NE23 8ER. 01670 731 963; e-mail: steveholliday@hotmail.co.uk

Wildlife Hospitals
BERWICK SWAN & WILDLIFE TRUST. The Honorary Secretary, Windmill Way East, Ramparts Business Park, Berwick-upon-Tweed TD15 1TU. 01289 302882; e-mail: swan-trust@hotmail.co.uk
www.swan-trust.org Registered charity. All categories of wildlife. Pools for swans and other waterfowl. Veterinary support.

Wildlife Trust
NORTHUMBERLAND WILDLIFE TRUST. (1962; 13,000). The Garden House, St Nicholas Park, Jubilee Road, Gosforth, Newcastle upon Tyne, NE3 3XT. 0191 284 6884 (fax) 0191 284 6794; e-mail: mail@northwt.org.uk
www.nwt.org.uk

NOTTINGHAMSHIRE

Bird Recorders
Andy Hall, e-mail: andy.h11@ntlworld.com

Bird Reports
LOUND BIRD REPORT (1990-) latest 2007 report £4,
from Gary Hobson, 18 Barnes Avenue, Wrenthorpe,
Wakefield, WF1 2BH. 01924 384 419;
e-mail: gary.lbc1@tiscali.co.uk

BIRDS OF NOTTINGHAMSHIRE (1943-). £4 for previous
issues, plus p&p, from Ms Jenny Swindells, 21
Chaworth Road, West Bridgford, Nottingham NG2 7AE.
0115 9812 432; e-mail: j.swindells@btinternet.com
www.nottsbirders.net

NETHERFIELD WILDLIFE GROUP ANNUAL REPORT
(1990-). £5 inc postage, from Mr N Matthews, 4
Shelburne Close, Heronridge, Nottingham, NG5 9LL.
www.netherfieldwildlife.org.uk

BTO Regional Representatives
RR. Mrs Lynda Milner, 6 Kirton Park, Kirton, Newark,
Notts NG22 9LR. 01623 862 025;
e-mail: milner.lynda@googlemail.com

BTO Garden BirdWatch Ambassador
Mr C Harwood, **e-mail:** C.Harwood1@btinternet.com

Clubs
LOUND BIRD CLUB. (1991; 50). Gary Hobson, 18
Barnes Avenue, Wrenthorpe, Wakefield, WF1 2BH.
01924 384 419; e-mail: gary.lbc1@tiscali.co.uk
http://loundbirdclub.webs.com
Meetings: Various walks and talks throughout the
year, see website for details.

NETHERFIELD WILDLIFE GROUP. (1999; 130). Philip
Burnham, 57 Tilford Road, Newstead Village,
Nottingham, NG15 0BU. 01623 401 980 (M)07765 369
590; e-mail: philb50@fastmail.fm
www.netherfieldwildlife.org.uk

NOTTINGHAMSHIRE
BIRDWATCHERS. (1935;
370). Ms Jenny Swindells,
21 Chaworth Road, West
Bridgford, Nottingham, NG2
7AE. 0115 9812 432; e-mail:
j.swindells@btinternet.com
www.nottsbirders.net
Meetings and events: Please
see website for details.

WOLLATON NATURAL HISTORY SOCIETY. (1976; 86).
Mrs P Price, 33 Coatsby Road, Hollycroft, Kimberley,
Nottingham NG16 2TH. 0115 938 4965;
Meetings: 7.30pm, 3rd Wednesday of the month, St
Leonards Community Centre, Wollaton Village, HG8
2ND.

Integrated Population Monitoring Group
TRESWELL WOOD INTEGRATED POPULATION
MONITORING GROUP. Chris du Feu, 66 High Street,

Beckingham, Notts, DN10 4PF.
E-mail: chris@chrisdufeu.force9.co.uk

Ringing Groups
BIRKLANDS RG. A Ashley, 39 Winkburn Road,
Mansfield, Notts NG19 6SJ. 07794 179 494;
e-mail: alowe@nottswt.co.uk

NORTH NOTTS RG. Adrian Blackburn, Willows End, 27
Palmer Road, Retford, Notts DN22 6SS. 01777 706 516
(M)07718 766 873.

SOUTH NOTTINGHAMSHIRE RG. K J Hemsley, 8 Grange
Farm Close, Toton, Beeston, Notts NG9 6EB.
E-mail: k.hemsley@ntlworld.com

RSPB Local Groups
MANSFIELD LOCAL GROUP. (1986; 200). John Barlow,
240 Southwell Road West, Mansfield NG18 4LB. 01623
626 647; e-mail: Terri-Cumberland@supanet.com
www.rspb.org.uk/groups/mansfield
Meetings: 7pm, 1st Wednesday of the month (Sep-
Jun), Bridge St Methodist Church, Rock Valley,
Mansfield.

NOTTINGHAM. (1974; 395). Penny Cross, 93 Hilton
Road, Nottingham, NG3 6AQ. 0115 960 4205;
e-mail: pennyguilbert@hotmail.com
www.notts-rspb.org.uk
Meetings: 7.30pm, 1st Wed of month (Sept -
May). Nottingham Mechanics, North Sherwood St.
Nottingham, NG1 4EZ.

Wetland Bird Survey Organiser
Gary Hobson, 18 Barnes Avenue, Wrenthorpe,
Wakefield, WF1 2BH. 01924 384 419;
e-mail: gary.lbc1@tiscali.co.uk

Wildlife Trust
NOTTINGHAMSHIRE WILDLIFE TRUST. (1963; 4,300).
The Old Ragged School, Brook Street, Nottingham,
NG1 1EA. 0115 958 8242; e-mail: info@nottswt.co.uk
www.nottinghamshirewildlife.org.uk

OXFORDSHIRE

Bird Atlas/Avifauna
Birds of Oxfordshire by J W Brucker et al (Oxford,
Pisces, 1992).

The New Birds of the Banbury Area by T G
Easterbrook (Banbury Ornithological Society, 1995).

Bird Recorder
Ian Lewington, 119 Brasenose Road, Didcot, Oxon,
OX11 7BP. 01235 819 792;
e-mail: ian@recorder.fsnet.co.uk

Bird Reports
BIRDS OF OXFORDSHIRE (1921-), from Barry Hudson,
Pinfold, 4 Bushy Row, Bampton, Oxon OX18 2JU.
01865 775 632.

BANBURY ORNITHOLOGICAL SOCIETY ANNUAL REPORT
(1952-). £5 each including postage, from

MJ Lewis, Old Mill Cottage, Avon Dassett, Southam, Warwickshire, CV47 2AE. 01295 690 643; e-mail: mikelewisad@hotmail.com

BTO Regional Representatives & Regional Development Officer
NORTH. Frances Buckel, Witts End, Radbones Hill, Over Norton, Chipping Norton, Oxon OX7 5RA. 01608 644 425; e-mail: fran.buckel@binternet.com

SOUTH RR & RDO. Mr John Melling, 17 Lime Grove, Southmoor, Nr Abingdon, Oxon OX13 5DN. E-mail: bto-rep@oos.org.uk

Clubs
BANBURY ORNITHOLOGICAL SOCIETY. (1952; 100). Frances Buckel, Witts End, Radbones Hill, Over Norton, Chipping Norton, Oxon OX7 5RA. 01608 644 425; e-mail: fran.buckel@binternet.com www.banburyornithologicalsociety.org.uk
Meetings: 7.30pm, 2nd Monday of the month, Freemason's Hall, Marlborough Road, Banbury.

OXFORD ORNITHOLOGICAL SOCIETY. (1921; 330). Barry Hudson, Pinfold, 4 Bushy Row, Bampton, Oxon OX18 2JU. 01993 852 028; e-mail: secretary@oos.org.uk www.oos.org.uk
Meetings: 7.45pm, various dates, Stratfield Brake, Kidlington.

Ringing Group
EDWARD GREY INSTITUTE. Dr A G Gosler, c/o Edward Grey Institute, Department of Zoology, South Parks Road, Oxford OX1 3PS. 01865 271 158; e-mail: andrew.gosler@zoo.ox.ac.uk

RSPB Local Groups
OXFORD. (1977; 100). Ian Kilshaw, 6 Queens Court, Bicester, Oxon, OX26 6JX. 01869 601 901; e-mail: ian.kilshaw@ntlworld.com www.rspb-oxford.org.uk
Meetings: 7.45pm, normally 1st Thursday of the month, Sandhills Primary School, Terret Avenue, Headington, Oxford (opposite Thornhill park and ride).

VALE OF WHITE HORSE. (1977; 330). Philip Morris. 01367 710 285; www.rspb-vwh.org.uk
Meetings: 7.30pm, 3rd Monday of the month (Sep-May). Didcot Civic Hall.

Wetland Bird Survey Organiser
OXFORDSHIRE (North) Sandra Bletchly, e-mail: sandra@banornsoc.fsnet.co.uk

OXFORDSHIRE (South) Ian Lees, 01865 256 370. E-mail: ianlees@me.com

Wildlife Trust
BBOWT. (1959; 24,000). The Lodge, 1 Armstrong Road, Littlemore, Oxford, OX4 4XT. 01865 775 476; e-mail: info@bbowt.org.uk www.bbowt.org.uk

SHROPSHIRE

Bird Atlas/Avifauna
Atlas of the Breeding Birds of Shropshire (Shropshire Ornithological Society, 1995).

Bird Recorder
Geoff Holmes, 22 Tenbury Drive, Telford Estate, Shrewsbury, SY2 5YF. 01743 364 621; e-mail: geoff.holmes.4@btinternet.com

Bird Report
SHROPSHIRE BIRD REPORT (1956-) Annual, from Helen Griffiths (Hon Secretary), 104 Noel Hill Road, Cross Houses, Shrewsbury SY5 6LD. 01743 761 507; e-mail: helen.griffiths@naturalengland.org.uk www.shropshirebirds.com

BTO Regional Representative
RR. Allan Dawes, Rosedale, Chapel Lane, Trefonen, Oswestry, Shrops SY10 9DX. 01691 654245; e-mail: allandawes@btinternet.com

BTO Garden BirdWatch Ambassadors
Mr A J Arnfield, e-mail: arnfield.2@osu.edu

Mr T R Blackshaw, e-mail: trevor.blackshaw@ssesurf.co.uk

Dr C R Price, e-mail: Cath_Price@btinternet.com

Club
SHROPSHIRE ORNITHOLOGICAL SOCIETY. (1955; 800). Helen Griffiths, 104 Noel Hill Road, Cross Houses, Shrewsbury, SY5 6LD. 01743 761 507; e-mail: helen.griffiths@naturalengland.org.uk www.shropshirebirds.com
Meetings: 7.15pm, 1st Thursday of month (Oct-Apr), Shirehall, Shrewsbury.

RSPB Local Group
SHROPSHIRE. (1992; 320). Roger M Evans, 01295 253 330; www.rspb.org.uk/groups/shropshire
Meetings: 4th Wednesday of the month (Sep-Apr), Council Chamber, Shirehall, Shrewsbury. Also field trip year round. 3rd Wednesday in the month (Oct-March) Secret Hills Centre Craven Arms.

SOUTH SHROPSHIRE. Alvin Botting (Group Leader). 01547 540 176; e-mail: Christinelbateman@yahoo.com www.rspbsouthshropshire.co.uk
Meetings: 7.30pm (Sep-Apr), Shropshire Hills Discovery Centre (Secret Hills), Craven Arms.

Wetland Bird Survey Organiser
SHROPSHIRE. Michael Wallace, 01743 369 035; e-mail: michael@wallace7536.freeserve.co.uk

Wildlife Trust
SHROPSHIRE WILDLIFE TRUST. (1962; 10,000). 193 Abbey Foregate, Shrewsbury, Shropshire SY2 6AH. 01743 284 280 (fax) 01743 284281; e-mail: shropshirewt@cix.co.uk www.shropshirewildlifetrust.org.uk

SOMERSET & BRISTOL

Atlas of Breeding Birds in Avon 1988-91 by R L Bland and John Tully (John Tully, 6 Falcondale Walk, Westbury-on-Trym, Bristol BS9 3JG, 1992).

Bristol Ornithology no. 29 by Robin Prythock (Bristol Ornithological Club 2008).

Bird Atlas/Avifauna
The Birds of Exmoor and the Quantocks by DK Ballance and BD Gibbs. (Isabelline Books, 2 Highbury House, 8 Woodland Crescent, Falmouth TR11 4QS. 2003).

Bird Recorders
Brian D Gibbs, 23 Lyngford Road, Taunton, Somerset, TA2 7EE. 01823 274 887;
e-mail: brian.gibbs@somersetbirds.net
www.somersetbirds.net

BRISTOL, S GLOUCESTERSHIRE, BATH AND NE SOMERSET, NORTH SOMERSET. John Martin, 34 Cranmore Green, Pilning, Bristol BS35 4QF. 01454 633 040; e-mail: avonbirdrecorder@googlemail.com

Bird Reports
AVON BIRD REPORT (1977-), £8 plus postage, from Harvey Rose, 12 Birbeck Road, Bristol, BS9 1BD. 0117 968 1638; e-mail: h.e.rose@bris.ac.uk

EXMOOR NATURALIST (1974-), from Secretary, Exmoor Natural History Society.E-mail: carol.enhs@virgin.net

SOMERSET BIRDS (1912-) £7.50 inc p&p, from Somerset Ornithological Society, c/o Flat 2, Dunboyne, Bratton Lane, Minehead, Somerset TA24 8SQ. 01643 706 820;

BTO Regional Representatives
AVON RR. Richard L Bland, 11 Percival Road, Bristol, BS8 3LN. Home/W:01179 734 828;
e-mail: richardbland@blueyonder.co.uk

AVON ASSISTANT REGIONAL REPRESENTATIVE. John Tully, 6 Falcondale Walk, Westbury-on-Trym, Bristol, BS9 3JG. 0117 950 0992; e-mail: johntully4@aol.com

SOMERSET RR. Eve Tigwell, Hawthorne Cottage, 3 Friggle Street, Frome, Somerset BA11 5LP. 01373 451630; e-mail: eve.tigwell@zen.co.uk

Clubs
BRISTOL NATURALISTS' SOCIETY (Ornithological Section). (1862; 550). Becky Coffin, 33 London Street, Kingswood, Bristol, BS15 1RA. 07773 188 286;
e-mail: beckycoffin@yahoo.com
www.bristolnats.org.uk
Meetings: 7.30pm, 2nd Wednesday in the mohth (check for dates, Oct-Mar), Westmorland Hall, Westmorland Road, Bristol.

BRISTOL ORNITHOLOGICAL CLUB. (1966; 670). Mrs Judy Copeland, 19 St George's Hill, Easton-in-Gordano, North Somerset, BS20 0PS. Tel/(fax) 01275 373554; e-mail: judy.copeland@tiscali.co.uk
www.boc-bristol.org.uk
Meetings: 7.30pm, 3rd Thursday of the month, Newman Hall, Grange Court Road, Westbury-on-Trym.

CAM VALLEY WILDLIFE GROUP. (1994: 356). Diana Walker, Membership Secretary,
8 Grovewood Road, Haydon, Radstock, Somerset, BA3 3QZ Tel: 01761 433 688;
e-mail: enquiries@cvwg.org.uk
www.somersetmade.co.uk/cvwg/

EXMOOR NATURAL HISTORY SOCIETY. (1974; 480). Miss Caroline Giddens, 12 King George Road, Minehead, Somerset, TA24 5JD. 01643 707 624;
e-mail: carol.enhs@virgin.net
www.enhs.org.uk
Meetings: 7.30pm, 1st Wednesday of the month (Oct-Mar), Methodist Church Hall, The Avenue, Minehead.

SOMERSET ORNITHOLOGICAL SOCIETY. (1974; 350). Mr JA Hazell, Membership Secretary, 9 Hooper Road, Street, Somerset BA16 0NP. 01458 443 780;
e-mail: jeff.hazell@somersetbirds.net
www.somersetbirds.net
Meetings: 7.30pm, various Thursdays (Oct-Apr), Ruishton Village Hall, Taunton.

Ringing Groups
CHEW VALLEY RS. Mr A Ashman.
E-mail: alan.ashman@talktalk.net

GORDANO VALLEY RG. Lyndon Roberts, 20 Glebe Road, Long Ashton, Bristol, BS41 9LH. 01275 392 722; e-mail: mail@lyndonroberts.com

RSPCA. Mr K Leighton. E-mail: kleighton@rspca.org.uk

RSPB Local Groups
BATH AND DISTRICT. (1989; 220). Alan Barrett. 01225 310 905; e-mail: alan_w_h_barrett@yahoo.co.uk
www.rspb.org.uk/groups/bath
Meetings: 7.30pm, 3rd Wednesday of the month (Sep-Mar), Bath Society Meeting Room, Green Park Station, Bath.

CREWKERNE & DISTRICT. (1979; 320). Denise Chamings, Daniels Farm, Lower Stratton, South Petherton, Somerset TA13 5LP. 01460 240 740;
e-mail: denise.chamings@talktalk.net
www.rspb.org.uk/groups/crewkerne
Meetings: 7.30pm, 3rd Thursday of the month (Sep-Apr), The Henhayes Centre, Crewkerne.

TAUNTON. (1975; 148). Frances Freeman. 01823 674 182; e-mail: francesfreeman@yahoo.com
www.rspb.org.uk/groups/taunton
Meetings: 7.30pm, last Friday of the month, Trull Memorial Hall, Church Road, Trull, TAUNTON TA3 7JZ

WESTON-SUPER-MARE (N SOMERSET). (1976; 215). Don Hurrell, Freeways, Star, Winscombe, BS25 1PS. 01934

842 717; e-mail: hurrell@cpsmail.co.uk
www.rspb.org.uk/groups/westonsupermare
Meetings: 7.45pm, 1st Thursday of the month (Sep-Apr), St Pauls Church Hall, Walliscote Road, Weston-Super-Mare.

Wetland Bird Survey Organisers
SEVERN ESTUARY - SOUTHERN COAST. Harvey Rose, 12 Birbek Road, Stoke Bishop, Bristol, BS9 1BD. 0117 968 1638; e-mail: h.e.rose@bris.ac.uk

SOMERSET (other sites) and SOUTH AVON (inland). Keith Fox, e-mail: keith@kfox.wanadoo.co.uk
SOMERSET LEVELS. Steve Meen, RSPB West Sedgemoor, Dewlands Farm, Redhill, Curry Rivel, Langport Somerset TA10 0PH. 01458 252 805; e-mail: steve.meen@rspb.org.uk

Wildlife Trusts
AVON WILDLIFE TRUST. (1980; 17,000). 32 Jacobs Wells Road, Bristol, BS8 1DR. 0117 917 7270 (fax) 0117 929 7273; e-mail: mail@avonwildlifetrust.org.uk
www.avonwildlifetrust.org.uk

SOMERSET WILDLIFE TRUST. (1964; 21,000). Tonedale Mill,Tonedale,Wellington,Somerset TA21 0AW. 01823 652 400 (fax) 01823 652 411;
e-mail: enquiries@somersetwildlife.org
www.somersetwildlife.org

STAFFORDSHIRE

Bird Report
See West Midlands.

Bird Recorder
Nick Pomiankowski,22 The Villas, West End, Stoke ST4 5AQ; 01782 849 682;
e-mail: staffs-recorder@westmidlandbirdclub.com

BTO Regional Representatives
NORTH EAST. Martin Godfrey, 01785 229 713;
e-mail: martinandrosie@aol.com

SOUTH & CENTRAL. Martin Godfrey, 01785 229 713;
e-mail: martinandrosie@aol.com

WEST. Martin Godfrey, 01785 229 713;
e-mail: martinandrosie@aol.com

Clubs
SOUTH PEAK RAPTOR STUDY GROUP. (1998; 12). M E Taylor, 76 Hawksley Avenue, Newbold, Chesterfield, Derbys S40 4TL. 01246 277 749;

WEST MIDLAND BIRD CLUB (STAFFORD BRANCH). Gerald Ford. 01630 673 409;
e-mail: gerald.ford@westmidlandbirdclub.com
www.westmidlandbirdclub.com/stafford
Meetings: 7.30pm, 2nd Friday of the month (Oct-Mar), at Perkins Engines Sports & Social Club, Tixall Road, Stafford.

WEST MIDLAND BIRD CLUB (TAMWORTH BRANCH). (1992). Barbara Stubbs, 19 Alfred Street, Tamworth,

Staffs, B79 7RL. 01827 57865;
e-mail: tamworth@westmidlandbirdclub
www.westmidlandbirdclub.com/tamworth
Meetings: 7.30pm, 3rd Friday of the month (Sep-Apr), Phil Dix Centre, Corporation Street, Tamworth.

RSPB Local Groups
BURTON-ON-TRENT AND SOUTH DERBYSHIRE. (1973; 50). Dave Lummis, 121 Wilmot Road, Swadlincote, Derbys, DE11 9BN. 01283 219 902;
e-mail: davelummis@hotmail.co.uk
www.basd-rspb.co.uk
Meetings: 7.30pm 1st Wednesday of the month, All Saint's Church, Branston Road, Burton.

LICHFIELD & DISTRICT. (1977; 1150). Bob Russon, 108 Walsall Road, Lichfield, Staffs, WS13 8AF. 01543 252 547; e-mail: LichfieldRSPB@hotmail.co.uk
Meetings: 7.30pm, 2nd Tuesday of the month (Jan-May, Sept-Dec), St Mary's Centre, Lichfield.

NORTH STAFFS. (1982; 198). John Booth, 32 St Margaret Drive, Sneyd Green, Stoke-on-Trent, ST1 6EW. 01782 262 082; e-mail: daylateuk@yahoo.co.uk
www.rspb.org.uk/groups/northstaffords
Meetings: 7.30pm, normally 3rd Wednesday of the month, North Staffs Conference Centre (Medical Institute).

SOUTH WEST STAFFORDSHIRE. (1972; 182). Mrs Theresa Dorrance, 39 Wilkes Road, Codsall, Wolverhampton, WV8 1RZ. 01902 847 041;
e-mail: stevedorrance@googlemail.com
Meetings: 8.00pm, 2nd Tuesday of the month (Sep-May), Codsall Village Hall.

Wetland Bird Survey Organisers
STAFFORDSHIRE. Steven Turner, c/o WeBS Office, BTO, The Nunnery, Thetford, Norfolk IP24 2PU.

Wildlife Hospitals
BRITISH WILDLIFE RESCUE CENTRE. Alfred Hardy, Amerton Working Farm, Stowe-by-Chartley, Stafford, ST18 0LA. 01889 271 308; e-mail:
joyce.hardy351@ntlworld.com
www.britishwildliferescue.co.uk
On A518 Stafford/Uttoxeter road. All species, including imprints and permanently injured. Hospital, large aviaries and caging. Open to the public every day. Veterinary support.

GENTLESHAW BIRD OF PREY HOSPITAL. Jenny Smith, Gentleshaw Wildlife Centre, Fletcher's Country Garden Centre, Stone Road, Eccleshall, Staffs ST21 6JY. 01785 850 379;
e-mail: info@gentleshawwildlife.co.uk
www.gentleshawwildlife.co.uk Registered charity. All birds of prey (inc. owls). Hospital cages and aviaries; release sites. Veterinary support. Also GENTLESHAW BIRD OF PREY AND WILDLIFE CENTRE, Fletchers Country Garden Centre, Stone Road, Eccleshall, Stafford. 01785 850 379 (10.00-17.00).

Wildlife Trust
STAFFORDSHIRE WILDLIFE TRUST. (1969; 14,000). The Wolseley Centre, Wolseley Bridge, Stafford, ST17 0WT. 01889 880 100; e-mail: staffs-wildlife.org.uk www.staffs-wildlife.org.uk

SUFFOLK

Bird Atlas/Avifauna
Birds of Suffolk by S H Piotrowski (February 2003) Quatermelon.

Bird Recorders
NORTH EAST. David Fairhurst.
E-mail: davidfairhurst@lycos.com

SOUTH EAST (inc. coastal region from Slaughden Quay southwards). Eddie Marsh.
E-mail: marshharrier@btinternet.com

WEST (whole of Suffolk W of Stowmarket, inc. Breckland). Colin Jakes, 7 Maltward Avenue, Bury St Edmunds, Suffolk IP33 3XN. 01284 702 215; e-mail: colin.jakes@stedsbc.gov.uk

Bird Report
SUFFOLK BIRDS (inc Landguard Bird Observatory Report) (1950-), from Ipswich Museum, High Street, Ipswich, Suffolk.

BTO Regional Representative
Mick T Wright, 15 Avondale Road, Ipswich, IP3 9JT. 01473 710 032; e-mail: micktwright@btinternet.com

BTO Garden BirdWatch Ambassador
Mr C R Powell,
e-mail: carlann.powell@tiscali.co.uk

Clubs
LAVENHAM BIRD CLUB. (1972; 54). Mr G Pattrick, Brights Farmhouse, Brights Lane, Lavenham, Suffolk CO10 9PH. 01787 248 128;
Meetings: 7.30pm, normally 3rd Saturday (Sep-Mar, except Dec), Lavenham Guildhall.

SUFFOLK ORNITHOLOGISTS' GROUP. (1973; 650). Paul Gowen, 14 Two Acres, Capel St Mary, Ipswich, Suffolk IP9 2XP. 01473 311 263; e-mail: info@sogonline.org.uk www.sogonline.org.uk
Meetings: Last Thursday of the month (Jan-Mar, Oct-Nov), London Road Holiday Inn (IP2 0UA) on the SW side of Ipswich near the A14/A12 Copdock roundabout.

Ringing Groups
DINGLE BIRD CLUB. Dr D Pearson, 4 Lupin Close, Reydon, Southwold, Suffolk IP18 6NW. 01502 722 348;

LACKFORD RG. Dr Peter Lack, 11 Holden Road, Lackford, Bury St Edmunds, Suffolk IP28 6HZ.
E-mail: bee.eaters@btinternet.com

LANDGUARD RG. Landguard Ringing Group, Landguard

Bird Observatory, Mr M.C. Marsh,
e-mail: mike@imafxt.co.uk
www.lbo.co.uk

MARKET WESTON RG. Dr R H W Langston, Walnut Tree Farm, Thorpe Street, Hinderclay, Diss, Norfolk IP22 1HT. E-mail: rlangston@wntfarm.demon.co.uk

RSPB Local Groups
BURY ST EDMUNDS. (1982; 150). Terry Fordham. 01449 616 292; e-mail: terry.fordham16@sky.com www.rspb.org.uk/groups/burystedmunds
Meetings: 7.30pm, 3rd Tuesday of the month (Sep-May), County Upper School, Beetons Way, Bury St Edmunds.

IPSWICH. (1975; 210). Mr Chris Courtney, St Elmo, 19 Marlborough Road, Ipswich, Suffolk IP4 5AT. 01473 423 213; e-mail: chrisc.courtney@yahoo.co.uk www.rspb.org.uk/groups/ipswich
Meetings: 7.30pm, 2nd Thursday of the month (Sep-Apr), Sidegate Lane Primary School, Sidegate Lane, Ipswich. Please note, Apr 2011 meeting on 4th Tuesday (28th).

LOWESTOFT & DISTRICT. (1976; 130). Howard Bayliss, 01502 539 030; e-mail: leader.group@tesco.net www.rspb.org.uk/groups/lowestoft
Meetings: Friday 7.15pm 1st Monday in the month, St Marks Church Hall, Oulton Broad.

WOODBRIDGE. (1987; 450). Malcolm Key, Riverside, Parham, Suffolk, IP13 9LZ. 01728 723 155; e-mail: malcolm.key@btopenworld.com
Meetings: 7.30pm, 1st Thursday of the month (Oct-May), Woodbridge Community Hall.

Wetland Bird Survey Organisers
ALDE COMPLEX. Mr I Castle, 01394 450 188; e-mail: ic.pda@the-pda.com

ALTON WATER. Mr J A Glazebrook, 61 Woodlands, Chelmondiston, Ipswich, Suffolk IP9 1DU.

ORWELL ESTUARY. Mick T Wright, 15 Avondale Road, Ipswich, IP3 9JT. 01473 710 032; e-mail: micktwright@btinternet.com

DEBEN ESTUARY. Nick Mason, 8 Mallard Way, Hollesley, Nr Woodbridge, Ipswich IP12 3QJ. (H)01359 411 150; e-mail: nick.mason4@btinternet.com

STOUR ESTUARY. Rick Vonk, RSPB, Unit 13 Court Farm, 3 Stutton Road, Brantham Suffolk CO11 1PW. (D)01473 328 006; e-mail: rick.vonk@rspb.org.uk

SUFFOLK (other sites). Alan Miller, Suffolk Wildlife Trust, Moonrakers, Back Lane, Wenhaston, Halesworth, Suffolk, IP19 9DY.
E-mail: alan.miller@suffolkwildlifetrust.org

Wildlife Trust
SUFFOLK WILDLIFE TRUST. (1961; 25,000). Brooke House, The Green, Ashbocking, Ipswich, IP6 9JY. 01473 890 089; e-mail: info@suffolkwildlifetrust.org www.suffolkwildlifetrust.org

SURREY

Bird Atlas/Avifauna
Birds of Surrey by Jeffery Wheatley (Surrey Bird Club 2007).

Bird Recorder (inc London S of Thames & E to Surrey Docks)
SURREY (includes Greater London south of the Thames and east to the Surrey Docks, excludes Spellthorne). Position vacant. 01252 702 450 (for enquiries) or www.surreybirdclub.org.uk

Bird Report
SURBITON AND DISTRICT BIRD WATCHING SOCIETY (1972-), from Thelma Caine, 21 More Lane, Esher, Surrey KT10 8AJ; e-mail: sdbws@encief.co.uk
www.encief.co.uk/sdbws

SURREY BIRD REPORT (1952-), from J Gates, 5 Hillside Road, Weybourne, Farnham, Surrey GU9 9DW. 01252 315 047; e-mail: jeremygates@live.com

BTO Regional Representative
RR. Position vacant.

Clubs
SURBITON & DISTRICT BIRDWATCHING SOCIETY. (1954; 140). Gary Caine, 21 More Lane, Esher, Surrey, KT10 8AJ. 01372 468 432; e-mail: sdbws@encief.co.uk
www.encief.co.uk/sdbws
Meetings: 7.30pm, 3rd Tuesday of the month, Surbiton Library Annex.

SURREY BIRD CLUB. (1957; 350).
Penny Williams, Bournbrook House, Sandpit Hall Lane, Chobham Surrey GU24 8HA. 07973 382 210; e-mail: penny@waxwing.plus.com
www.surreybirdclub.org.uk
Meetings: See website for details.

Ringing Groups
HERSHAM RG. A J Beasley, 29 Selbourne Avenue, New Haw, Weybridge, Surrey KT15 3RB.
E-mail: abeasley00@hotmail.com

RUNNYMEDE RG. D G Harris, 22 Blossom Waye, Hounslow, TW5 9HD, http://rmxrg.org.uk
E-mail: daveharris@tinyonline.co.uk

RSPB Local Groups
DORKING & DISTRICT. (1982; 230). John Burge, Broughton Norrels Drive, East Horsley, Leatherhead, KT24 5DR. 01483 283 803;
e-mail: burgejs@googlemail.com
www.rspb.org.uk/groups/dorkinganddistrict
Meetings: 8.00pm, Fridays once a month (Sep-Apr), Christian Centre, next to St Martin's Church, Dorking.

EAST SURREY. (1984; 2800 plus in catchment area). John Lawrence, 123 Chaldon Way, Coulsdon, Surrey CR5 1DN. 01737 553 316;
e-mail: jfjlawrence@gmail.com
www.eastsurreyrspb.co.uk
Meetings: 8.00pm, 2nd Wednesday of the month (except August), White Hart Barn, Godstone, RH9 8DT.

EPSOM & EWELL. (1974; 168). Janet Gilbert, 78 Fairfax Avenue, Ewell, Epsom, Surrey KT17 2QQ. 0208 394 0405; e-mail: janetegilbert@btinternet.com
www.rspb.org.uk/groups/epsom
Meetings: 7.45pm, 2nd Friday of the month, All Saints Church Hall, Fulford Road, West Ewell.

GUILDFORD AND DISTRICT. (1974; 550). Roger Beck, 14 Overbrook, West Horsley, KT24 6BH. 01483 282 417; e-mail: rogerbeck@beck40.fsnet.co.uk
www.rspb.org.uk/groups/guildford
Meetings: 2.15pm 2nd Thursday and 7.45pm 4th Wednesday (Oct-Apr), Onslow Village Hall, Guildford.

NORTH WEST SURREY. (1973; 150). Dave Braddock, 20 Meadway Drive, New Haw, Surrey, KT15 2DT. 01932 858 692; e-mail: dave@utter-chaos.co.uk
www.rspb.org.uk/groups/nwsurrey
Meetings: 7.45pm, 4th Wednesday of the month (not Dec, Jul, Aug), Sir William Perkin's School, Chertsey KT16 9BN.

Wetland Bird Survey Organiser
SURREY (includes Greater London south of the Thames and east to the Surrey Docks, excludes Spellthorne). Jeffery Wheatley, 9 Copse Edge, Elstead, Godalming, Surrey GU8 6DJ. 01252 702 450; e-mail: j.j.wheatley@btinternet.com

Wildlife Hospitals
THE SWAN SANCTUARY. See National Directory

WILDLIFE AID. Randalls Farm House, Randalls Road, Leatherhead, Surrey, KT22 0AL. 01372 377 332 24-hr emergline 09061 800 132 (50p/min) (fax) 01372 375183; e-mail: wildlife@pncl.co.uk
www.wildlifeaid.com Registered charity. Wildlife hospital and rehabilitation centre helping all native British species. Special housing for birds of prey. Membership scheme and fund raising activities. Veterinary support.

Wildlife Trust
SURREY WILDLIFE TRUST. (1959; 25,700). School Lane, Pirbright, Woking, Surrey, GU24 0JN. 01483 795 440 (fax) 01483 486 505;
e-mail: info@surreywt.org.uk
www.surreywildlifetrust.org

SUSSEX

Bird Atlas/Avifauna
The Birds of Selsey Bill and the Selsey Peninsular (a checklist to year 2000) From: Mr O Mitchell, 21 Trundle View Close, Barnham, Bognor Regis, PO22 0JZ.

Birds of Sussex ed by Paul James (Sussex Ornithological Society, 1996).

Fifty Years of Birdwatching, a celebration of the acheivements of the Shoreham District OS from 1953 onwards. from Shoreham District Ornithological Society, 7 Berberis Court, Shoreham by Sea, West Sussex BN43 6JA. £15 plus £2.50 p&p.

Henfield Birdwatcher Reports 2000 and 2005 ed Mike Russell et al, Henfield Birdwatch

Bird Recorder
Mr Nick Paul, Old Durfold, Warnham, Horsham, West Sussex RH15 3RY. 01403 264 762;
e-mail: recorder@sos.org www.sos.org

Bird Reports
BIRDS OF RYE HARBOUR NR ANNUAL REPORT (1977-published every 5 years), from Dr Barry Yates, see Clubs.

PAGHAM HARBOUR LOCAL NATURE RESERVE ANNUAL REPORT, from Warden, see Reserves,

SHOREHAM DISTRICT ORNITHOLOGICAL SOCIETY ANNUAL REPORT (1952-) - back issues available at £3.50 + P&P at current rates, from Mrs. Shena Maskell, SDOS Membership Secretary, 41 St. Lawrence Avenue, Worthing, West Sussex BN14 7JJ, or through website - www.sdos.org

SUSSEX BIRD REPORT (1963-), from J E Trowell, Lorrimer, Main Road, Icklesham, Winchelsea, E Sussex, TN36 4BS. E-mail: membership@sos.org.uk www.sos.org.uk

BTO Regional Representative
Dr Helen Crabtree, 01444 441 687;
e-mail: hcrabtree@gmail.com

Clubs
FRIENDS OF RYE HARBOUR NATURE RESERVE. (1973; 1800). Dr Barry Yates, 2 Watch Cottages, Nook Beach, Winchelsea, E Sussex TN36 4LU. 01797 223 862;
e-mail: rhnr.office@eastsussex.gov.uk
www.wildrye.info
Meetings: Monthly talks in winter, monthly walks all year.

HENFIELD BIRDWATCH. (1999; 135). Mike Russell, 31 Downsview, Small Dole, Henfield, West Sussex BN5 9YB. 01273 494311;
e-mail: mikerussell@sussexwt.org.uk

SHOREHAM DISTRICT ORNITHOLOGICAL SOCIETY. (1953; 180). Mrs. Shena Maskell, SDOS Membership Secretary, 41 St. Lawrence Avenue, Worthing, West Sussex BN14 7JJ. or through website - www.sdos.org
Meetings: 7.30pm, 2nd Tuesday of the month (Oct-Apr), St Peter's Church Hall, Shoreham-by-Sea. (7 indoor meetings, 18+ field outings).

SUSSEX ORNITHOLOGICAL SOCIETY. (1962; 1600). Val Bentley, Chetsford, London Road, Henfield, West Sussex BN5 9JJ. 01273 494 723;
e-mail: secretary@sos.org.uk www.sos.org.uk

Ringing Groups
BEACHY HEAD RS. R D M Edgar, 32 Hartfield Road, Seaford, E Sussex BN25 4PW.

CUCKMERE RG. Tim Parmenter, 18 Chapel Road, Plumpton Green, East Sussex, BN7 3DD. 01273 891 881;

RYE BAY RG. P Jones,
e-mail: philjones@beamingbroadband.com

STEYNING RINGING GROUP. B R Clay, Meghana, Honeysuckle Lane, High Salvington, Worthing, West Sussex BN13 3BT. E-mail: brian.clay@ntlworld.com

RSPB Local Groups
BATTLE. (1973; 80). Mr Dave Yates, 5 London Road, Battle, E Sussex TN33 0EU. 01424 773 826;
e-mail: familyatbattle@yahoo.co.uk
www.battlerspb.org.uk
Meetings: 7.30pm, 4th Tuesday of the month, Battle and Langton Primary School, Battle.

BRIGHTON & DISTRICT. (1974; 260). Mark Weston, 07802 293 417, e-mail: mark.weston@RSPB.org.uk
www.rspb.org.uk/groups/brighton
Meetings: 7.30pm, 4th Thursday of the month, All Saints Church Hall, Eaton Road, Hove. Anyone is welcome, non-members should phone first as dates can vary.

CHICHESTER & SW SUSSEX. (1979; 245). David Hart, Heys Bridle Rd, Slindon Common, Arundel, BN18 0NA. 01243 814 497; www.rspb.org.uk/groups/chichester
Meetings: 7.30 pm 2nd Thursday of each month, Newell Centre, Newell Centre, Tozer Way, St Pancras, Chichester.

CRAWLEY & HORSHAM. (1978; 148). Andrea Saxton, 104 Heath Way, Horsham, W Sussex, RH12 5XS. 01403 242 218; e-mail: Andrea.saxton@sky.com
www.rspb.org.uk/groups/crawley
Meetings: 8.00pm, 3rd Wednesday of the month (Sept-Apr), The Friary Hall, Crawley.

EAST GRINSTEAD. (1998; 185). Nick Walker, 14 York Avenue, East Grinstead, W Sussex RH19 4TL. 01342 315 825; e-mail: nickwalker55@btinternet.com
www.rspb.org.uk/groups/egrinstead
Meetings: 8.00pm, last Wednesday of the month, Large Parish Hall, De La Warr Road, East Grinstead.

EASTBOURNE & DISTRICT. (1993; 320). Ian Muldoon. 01273 476852; e-mail: ian1muldoon@yahoo.co.uk
www.rspb.org.uk/groups/eastbourne
Meetings: 2.15 pm and 7.30 pm,1st Wednesday of the month (Sep-Jun), St. Wilfrid's Church Hall, Eastbourne Road, Pevensey Bay.

HASTINGS & ST LEONARDS. (1983; 110). Richard Prebble, 01424 751 790.

Meetings: 7.30pm, 3rd Friday of the month, Taplin Centre, Upper Maze Hill.

Wetland Bird Survey Organiser
CHICHESTER HARBOUR.Mr E Rowsell, 01243 510 985; e-mail: edward@conservancy.co.uk

OTHER SITES. Richard Bown,
e-mail: hr.bown@btinternet.com

Wildlife Hospital
BRENT LODGE BIRD & WILDLIFE TRUST. Penny Cooper, Brent Lodge, Cow Lane, Sidlesham, Chichester, West Sussex, PO20 7LN. 01243 641 672 (emergency number); www.brentlodge.org All species of wild birds and small mammals. Full surgical and medical facilities (inc. X-ray) in conjunction with veterinary support. Purpose-built oiled bird washing unit. Veterinary support.

Wildlife Trust
SUSSEX WILDLIFE TRUST. (1961; 26,000). Woods Mill, Shoreham Road, Henfield, W Sussex, BN5 9SD. 01273 492630 (fax) 01273 494500;
e-mail: enquiries@sussexwt.org.uk
www.sussexwt.org.uk

TYNE & WEAR

Bird Report
See Durham; Northumberland.

Bird Recorders
See Durham; Northumberland.

Clubs
GATESHEAD BIRDERS.
www.gatesheadbirders.co.uk

NATURAL HISTORY SOCIETY OF NORTHUMBRIA. (1829; 900). The Natural History Society of Northumbria, Great North Museum: Hancock, Newcastle upon Tyne, NE2 4PT. 0191 232 6386; e-mail: nhsn@ncl.ac.uk
www.NHSN.ncl.ac.uk
Meetings: 7.00pm, every Friday (Oct-Mar), Percy Building, Newcastle University.

NORTHUMBERLAND & TYNESIDE BIRD CLUB. (1958; 270). Alan Watson, Secretary, 3 Green Close, Whitley Bay, Northumberland NE25 9SH.

0191 252 2744; e-mail: apusx@blueyonder.co.uk
www.ntbc.org.uk

RSPB Local Groups
NEWCASTLE UPON TYNE. (1969; 250). Brian Moorhead. 07903 387 429;
e-mail: ncastlerspbgroup@btinternet.com
www.rspb.org.uk/groups/newcastle
Meetings: 7pm, (Mar, Jun, Sep, Nov), Northumbria University, Ellison Place, Newcastle upon Tyne.

WARWICKSHIRE

Bird Report See West Midlands.

Bird Recorder
Jonathan Bowley, 17 Meadow Way, Fenny Compton, Southam, Warks, CV47 2WD. 01295 770 069; e-mail: warks-recorder@westmidlandbirdclub.com

BTO Regional Representatives
WARWICKSHIRE. Mark Smith. 01926 735 398;
e-mail: mark.smith36@ntlworld.com

Clubs
NUNEATON & DISTRICT BIRDWATCHERS' CLUB. (1950; 78). Alvin K Burton, 23 Redruth Close, Horeston Grange, Nuneaton, Warwicks CV11 6FG. 024 7664 1591; http://ndbwc.webs.com/
Meetings: 7.30pm, 3rd Thursday of the month (Sep-Jun), Hatters Space Community Centre, Upper Abbey Street, Nuneaton.

Ringing Groups
ARDEN RG. Roger J Juckes, 24 Croft Lane, Temple Grafton, Alcester, Warks B49 6PA. 01789 778 748;

BRANDON RG. David Stone, Overbury, Wolverton, Stratford-on-Avon, Warks CV37 0HG. 01789 731488;

RSPB Local Group
See West Midlands.

Wildlife Trust
WARWICKSHIRE WILDLIFE TRUST. (1970; 13,000). Brandon Marsh Nature Centre, Brandon Lane, Coventry, CV3 3GW. 024 7630 2912 (fax) 024 7663 9556; e-mail: enquiries@wkwt.org.uk
www.warwickshire-wildlife-trust.org.uk

WEST MIDLANDS

Bird Atlas/Avifauna
The New Birds of the West Midlands edited by Graham and Janet Harrison (West Midland Bird Club, 2005). Available from 147 Worlds End Lane, Quinton, Birmingham B32 1JX.

Bird Recorder
Kevin Clements, 26 Hambrook Close, Dunstall Park, Wolverhampton, West Midlands WV6 0XA. 01902 568 997; e-mail: west-mids-recorder@westmidlandbirdclub.com

Bird Reports
THE BIRDS OF SMESTOW VALLEY AND DUNSTALL PARK (1988-), from Secretary, Smestow Valley Bird Group.

WEST MIDLAND BIRD REPORT (inc Staffs, Warks, Worcs and W Midlands) (1934-), from Barbara Oakley, 147 Worlds End, Quinton, Birmingham B32 1JX.
E-mail: secretary@westmidlandbirdclub.com
westmidlandbirdclub.com

ENGLAND

BTO Regional Representative
BIRMINGHAM & WEST MIDLANDS. Steve Davies. 07882 891 726; e-mail: stevendavies907@btinternet.com

BTO Garden BirdWatch Ambassador
Mr M Hope-Urwin, e-mail: mandm@greenbee.net

Clubs
SMESTOW VALLEY BIRD GROUP. (1988; 46). Frank Dickson, 11 Bow Street, Bilston, Wolverhampton, WV14 7NB. 01902 493 733;

WEST MIDLAND BIRD CLUB - serving Ornithologists in Staffs, Warks, Worcs and the West Midlands County. (1929; 2000). Barbara Oakley.
E-mail: secretary@westmidlandbirdclub.com
www.westmidlandbirdclub.com
Meetings: Check website for details of the different branches and their events.

WEST MIDLAND BIRD CLUB (BIRMINGHAM BRANCH). (1995; 800). Andy Mabbett. E-mail:
birmingham@westmidlandbirdclub.com
www.westmidlandbirdclub.com/birmingham
Meetings: 7.30pm, usually last Tuesday (Oct-Apr), Birmingham Medical Institute, in Harborne Road, Edgbaston, near Five Ways.

WEST MIDLAND BIRD CLUB (SOLIHULL BRANCH). (1973). Raymond Brown, The Spinney, 63 Grange Road, Dorridge, Solihull B93 8QS. 01564 772 550; e-mail: solihull@westmidlandbirdclub www.westmidlandbirdclub.com/solihull
Meetings: 7.30 pm, Fridays (usually 1st of month), Guild House, Knowle, Solihull, West Midlands B93 0LN.

Ringing Groups
MERCIAN RG (Sutton Coldfield). Mr DJ Clifton. 59 Daisybank Crescent, Walsall, WS5 3BH. 01922 628 572.

RSPB Local Groups
BIRMINGHAM. (1975; 100). John Bailey, 52 Gresham Road, Hall Green, Birmingham, B28 0HY. 0121 777 4389; e-mail: jvbailey@btinternet.com
www.rspb-birmingham.org.uk
Meetings: 7.30pm, 3rd Thursday of the month (Sep-Jun), Salvation Army Citadel, St Chads, Queensway, Birmingham.

COVENTRY & WARWICKSHIRE. (1969; 130). Ron Speddings.01926 428 365;
e-mail: Ron@speddings.spacomputers.com
www.rspb.org.uk/groups/coventryandwarwickshire
Meetings: 7.30pm, 4th Friday of the month, (Sep-May unless otherwise stated), Warwick Arts Centre And Baginton Village Hall.

SOLIHULL. (1983; 2600). John Roberts, 115 Dovehouse Lane, Solihull, West Midlands, B91 2EQ. 0121 707 3101; e-mail: johnbirder@care4free.net
www.rspb.org.uk/groups/solihull
Meetings: 7.30pm, usually 2nd Tuesday of the month (Sep-Apr), Oliver Bird Hall, Church Hill Road, Solihull.

STOURBRIDGE. (1978; 150). David Ackland. 01384 293 090; e-mail: davidackland@blueyonder.co.uk
www.rspb.org.uk/groups/stourbridge
Meetings: 2nd Wednesday of the month (Sep-May), Wollaston Suite, Stourbridge Town Hall, Crown Centre, Stourbridge, West Midlands, DY8 1YE

SUTTON COLDFIELD. (1986; 250). Martin Fisher. 0121 308 4400; e-mail: martinjfisher@care4free.net
www.rspb.org.uk/groups/suttoncoldfield
Meetings: 7.30pm, 1st Monday of the month, Bishop Vesey's Grammer School.

WALSALL. (1970). Mike Pittaway, 2 Kedleston Close, Bloxwich, Walsall, WS3 3TW. 01922 710 568;
e-mail: michaelp@kedclose.freeserve.co.uk
www.rspb-walsall.org.uk
Meetings: 7.30pm, 3rd Wednesday of the month, St Marys School, Jesson Road, Walsall.

WOLVERHAMPTON. (1974; 110). Barry Proffitt. 07900 431 820; e-mail: RSPBwolverhampton@hotmail.co.uk
www.rspb.org.uk/groups/wolverhampton
Meetings: 7.30pm, 2nd Wednesday of the month (Sept-Apr), The Newman Centre, Haywood Drive, Tettenhall, Wolverhampton. Also monthly field-trips (Sep-Jun).

Wildlife Trust
THE WILDLIFE TRUST FOR BIRMINGHAM AND THE BLACK COUNTRY. (1980; 5,500). 28 Harborne Road, Edgbaston, Birmingham, B15 3AA. 0121 454 1199 (fax) 0121 454 6556; e-mail: info@bbcwildlife.org.uk
www.bbcwildlife.org.uk

WILTSHIRE

Bird Atlas/Avifauna
*Birds of Wiltshire*by James Ferguson-Lees 2007, Wiltshire Ornithological Society.

Bird Recorder
Rob Turner, 14 Ethendun, Bratton, Westbury, Wilts, BA13 4RX. 01380 830 862;
e-mail: robt14@btopenworld.com

Bird Report
HOBBY (journal of the Wiltshire OS) (1975-), from John Osborne, 4 Fairdown Avenue, Westbury, Wiltshire BA13 3HS. 01373 864 598;
e-mail: josb@talktalk.net
www.wiltshirebirds.co.uk

BTO Regional Representatives
NORTH and SOUTH. Bill Quantrill. 01225 866 245;
e-mail: william.quantrill@btinternet.com

Clubs

SALISBURY & DISTRICT NATURAL HISTORY SOCIETY. (1952; 146). Elisabeth Richmond, 15 Chantry Road, Wilton, Salisbury, SP2 0LT. 01722 742 755; e-mail: erichmond@madasafish.com
Meetings: 7.30pm, 3rd Thursday of the month (Sept-Apr), Lecture Hall, Salisbury Museum, Kings House, The Close, Salisbury.

WILTSHIRE ORNITHOLOGICAL SOCIETY. (1974; 450). Phil Deacon, 12 Rawston Close, Nythe, Swindon, Wilts SN3 3PW. 01793 528 930; e-mail: phil.deacon@ntlworld.com
www.wiltshirebirds.co.uk
Meetings: See website for details.

Ringing Group

COTSWOLD WATER PARK RG. John Wells, 25 Pipers Grove, Highnam, Glos, GL2 8NJ. E-mail: john.wells2@btinternet.com

WEST WILTSHIRE RG. Mr M.J. Hamzij, 13 Halfway Close, Trowbridge, Wilts BA14 7HQ. E-mail: m.hamzij@btinternet.com

RSPB Local Groups

NORTH WILTSHIRE. (1973; 115). 01793 349 262; e-mail: Raymond.thatcher@ntlworld.com
www.rspb.org.uk/groups/northwiltshire
Meetings: 7.30pm, 1st Tuesday of the month (Sep-Jun), Even Swindon Community Centre, Jennings St, Swindon SU 137 849.

SOUTH WILTSHIRE. (1986; 800). Tony Goddard, Clovelly, Lower Road, Charlton All Saints, Salisbury, SP5 4HQ. 01725 510 309; e-mail: goddard543@hotmail.com
www.rspb.org.uk/groups/southwiltshire
Meetings: 7.30pm, Tuesday evenings (monthly), Salisbury Arts Centre, Salisbury.

Wetland Birds Survey Organiser

COTSWOLD WATER PARK. Gareth Harris, Keynes Country Park, Spratsgate Lane, Shorncote, Glos GL7 6DF. 01793 752 413 or 01793 752 730; e-mail: gareth.harris@waterpark.org
www.waterpark.org

WILTSHIRE. Julian Rolls, c/o WeBS Office, BTO, The Nunnery, Thetford, Norfolk IP24 2PU.

Wildlife Trust

WILTSHIRE WILDLIFE TRUST. (1962; 18,500). Elm Tree Court, Long Street, Devizes, Wilts, SN10 1NJ. 01380 725 670 (fax) 01380 729 017; e-mail: info@wiltshirewildlife.org
www.wiltshirewildlife.org

Bird Report See West Midlands.

Bird Recorder

Brian Stretch, 13 Pitmaston Road, Worcester WR2 4HY. 01905 423 417; e-mail: worcs-recorder@westmidlandbirdclub.com
www.westmidlandbirdclub.com

BTO Regional Representative

G Harry Green MBE, Windy Ridge, Pershore Road, Little Comberton, Pershore, Worcs, WR10 3EW. 01386 710 377; e-mail: harrygreen_worcs@yahoo.co.uk or zen130501@zen.co.uk

Ringing Group

WYCHAVON RG. J R Hodson, 15 High Green, Severn Stoke, Worcester, WR8 9JS. 01905 371 333; e-mail: hodson77@btinternet.com

Club

WEST MIDLAND BIRD CLUB (KIDDERMINSTER BRANCH). Celia Barton, 28A Albert Street, Wall Heath, Kingswinford, DY6 0NA. 01384 839 838; e-mail: kidderminster@westmidlandbirdclub.com
Meetings: 7.30pm, 4th Wednesday of the month (Sep-Apr), St Oswalds Church Centre, Broadwaters, Kidderminster.

RSPB Local Group

WORCESTER & MALVERN. (1980; 300). Garth Lowe, Sunnymead, Old Storridge, Alfrick, Worcester WR6 5HT. 01886 833 362; e-mail: garthlowe@mypostoffice.co.uk
www.rspb.org.uk/groups/worcester
Meetings: 7.30pm, 2nd Wednesday in month (Sept-May), Powick Village Hall.

Wetland Birds Survey Organiser

WORCESTERSHIRE. Andrew Warr, 14 Bromsgrove Street, Barbourne, Worcester WR3 8AR; e-mail: andrew.warr3@btopenworld.com

Wildlife Hospital

VALE WILDLIFE RESCUE - WILDLIFE HOSPITAL + REHABILITATION CENTRE. Any staff member, Station Road, Beckford, Tewkesbury, Glos GL20 7AN. 01386 882 288; e-mail: info@valewildlife.org.uk
www.valewildlife.org.uk All wild birds. Intensive care. Registered charity. Veterinary support.

Wildlife Trust

WORCESTERSHIRE WILDLIFE TRUST. (1968; 9,000). Lower Smite Farm, Smite Hill, Hindlip, Worcester, WR3 8SZ. 01905 754 919 (fax) 01905 755868; e-mail: enquiries@worcestershirewildlifetrust.co.uk
www.worcswildlifetrust.co.uk
Charity no. 256618.

YORKSHIRE

Bird Atlas/Avifauna
Atlas of Breeding Birds in the Leeds Area 1987-1991
by Richard Fuller et al (Leeds Birdwatchers' Club, 1994).

The Birds of Halifax by Nick Dawtrey (only 20 left), 14 Moorend Gardens, Pellon, Halifax, W Yorks, HX2 0SD.

The Birds of Yorkshire by John Mather (Croom Helm, 1986).

*An Atlas of the Breeding Birds of the Huddersfield Area, 1987-1992.*by Brian Armitage et al (2000) - very few copies left.

Birds of Barnsley by Nick Addey (Pub by author, 114 Everill Gate Lane, Broomhill, Barnsley S73 0YJ, 1998).

Birds of The Huddersfield Area by Paul and Betty Bray (Huddersfield Birdwatchers Club 2008).

Breeding Bird Atlas for Barnsley in preparation.

County Bird Recorder
Craig Thomas, Sunnybank, Church Lane, Flamborough YO15 1PG. 01262 851 677;
e-mail: cragcthomas@yahoo.co.uk

Vice County Bird Recorders
VC61 (East Yorkshire) and Editor of *Yorkshire Bird Report*. Geoff Dobbs, 1 Priory Road, Beverley, East Yorkshire HU17 0EG. 07778 559 763;
e-mail: geoffdobbs@aol.com

VC62 (West Yorkshire)/HARROGATE & CRAVEN. Phil Bone, 11 Dorrington Close, Pocklington, York YO42 2GS. 0788 084 6905; e-mail: philsarab@aol.co.uk

VC63 (South & West Yorkshire). Covering the following groups - Barnsley Bird Study, Blacktoft Sands RSPB, Doncaster and District OS, Rotherham and District OS, Sheffield Bird Study and SK58 Birders. John Wint, 9 Yew Tree Park, Whitley, Goole, DN14 0NZ. 01977 662 826;
e-mail: j.wint114@btinternet.com

VC64 (Mid-West Yorkshire). Ian Court, 2 Burley Mews, Steeton, Keighley BT20 6TX. 01535 658 582;
e-mail: ian.court@mypostoffice.co.uk

VC65 (North Yorkshire West). Steve Worwood, 18 Coltsgate Hill, Ripon, HG4 2AB;
e-mail: steve@worwood.entadsl.com

Bird Reports
BARNSLEY & DISTRICT BIRD STUDY GROUP REPORT (1971-), from Waxwing Books, Sunnybank Cottage, Ruston Parva, Driffield YO25 4DG.

YORKSHIRE BIRD REPORT - formerly York Ornithological Club Annual Report (1970-), from Jill Warwick, Sharow Grange, Sharow, Ripon, HG4 5BN. 01765 602 832; e-mail: jill@swland.co.uk

YORKSHIRE NATURALISTS' UNION: BIRD REPORT (1940-). 2007 edition £12 including postage, from Jill Warwick, Sharow Grange, Sharow, Ripon, HG4 5BN. 01765 602 832; e-mail: jill@swland.co.uk

BRADFORD NATURALISTS' SOCIETY ANNUAL REPORT, from Mr I Hogg, 23 St Matthews Road, Bankfoot, Bradford, BD5 9AB. 01274 727 902.

BRADFORD ORNITHOLOGICAL GROUP REPORT (1987-) - after the 2008 issue, this report will only be available to paid up members of the group, from Jenny Barker, 3 Chapel Fold, Slack Lane, Oakworth, Keighley, BD22 0RQ.

FILEY BRIGG BIRD REPORT (1976-), from Mr C Court, 12 Pinewood Avenue, Filey, YO14 9NS.

HARROGATE & DISTRICT NATURALISTS' SOCIETY REPORT (1996-), from Jill Warwick, Sharow Grange, Sharow, Ripon, HG4 5BN. 01765 602 832; e-mail: jill@swland.co.uk

HULL VALLEY WILDLIFE GROUP REPORT (2000-) covering Hull Valley. from Roy Lyon, 670 Hotham Road South, Hull, HU5 5LE. 07754 439 496; www.hullvalleywildlifegroup.co.uk

BIRDS IN HUDDERSFIELD (1966-), from Mr M Wainman, 2 Bankfield Avenue, Taylor Hill, Huddersfield HD4 7QY.01484 305 054;
e-mail: brian.armitage@ntlworld.com

LEEDS BIRDWATCHERS' CLUB ANNUAL REPORT (1949-), from Peter Murphy, 12 West End Lane, Horsforth, Leeds LS18 5JP.

BIRDS OF ROTHERHAM (1975-) - cost £2.50 inc p&p, cheque payable to R.D.O.S., from The Secretary, Rotherham & District Bird Club,
e-mail: rdos@hotmail.co.uk
www.rotherhambirds.co.uk

BIRDS IN THE SHEFFIELD AREA (1973-), from Richard Hill, Honorary Secretary, 22 Ansell Road, Sheffield, South Yorkshire S11 7PE. E-mail: Secretary@sbsg.org www.sbsg.org

THE BIRDS OF SK58 (1993-), from Secretary, SK58 Birders. E-mail: recorder@sk58birders.com www.sk58birders.com

SORBY RECORD (1962-), from Ken Dorning, Sorby

NHSoc, c/o Room C12i, Dainton Building, Brook Hill, Sheffield S3 7HF.

SPURN BIRD OBSERVATORY ANNUAL REPORT, from Warden, see Reserves.

SWILLINGTON INGS BIRD GROUP - ANNUAL REPORT AND TWENTY YEAR REVIEW - 2008, from Chris Robinson, 43 Northfield Road, Sprotbrough, Doncaster, DN5 8AY. 07534 271 254; e-mail: GBFShrike@hotmail.com http://sibg1.wordpress.com

WINTERSETT AREA ANNUAL REPORT (1988-), from Steve Denny, 13 Rutland Drive, Crofton, Wakefield, WF4 1SA.01924 864487;

BTO Regional Representatives & Regional Development Officers
BRADFORD RR & RDO. Mike L Denton, 77 Hawthorne Terrace, Crosland Moor, Huddersfield, HD4 5RP. 01484 646 990.

EAST RR. Position vacant.

HULL RR. Geoff Dobbs, 1 Priory Road, Beverley, East Yorkshire HU17 0EG. 07778 559 763; e-mail: geoffdobbs@aol.com

LEEDS & WAKEFIELD RR. Position vacant.

NORTH-EAST RR. Mr and Mrs MJ Carroll. 01751 476 550.

NORTH-WEST RR. Gerald Light. 01756 753 720; e-mail: gerald@uwlig.plus.com

RICHMOND RR. John Edwards, 7 Church Garth, Great Smeaton, Northallerton, N Yorks DL6 2HW. H:01609 881 476; e-mail: john@jhedwards.plus.com

SOUTH-EAST AND SOUTH-WEST RR. David Gains. 28 Raleigh Road, Sheffield, S2 3AZ. 0114 255 7075; e-mail: bto-rep@fireflyuk.net

YORK RR. Rob Chapman, 12 Moorland Road, York, YO10 4HF. 01904 633 558; e-mail: robert.chapman@tinyworld.co.uk

YORKSHIRE (HARROGATE) RR. Mike Brown, 48 Pannal Ash Drive, Harrogate, N Yorks, HG2 0HU. 01423 567 382; e-mail: mike@thebrownsathome.plus.com
BTO Garden BirdWatch Ambassadors
Mr R G Wallace, e-mail: robert.g.wallace@btopenworld.com

Mrs E Learmont-Thom, e-mail: svelt127@hotmail.com

Mr J Preston, e-mail: johnpreston64@tiscali.co.uk

Ms L Clinton, e-mail: liztomclinton@aol.com

Mr T D Godson, e-mail: godson33@btinternet.com

Clubs
BARNSLEY BIRD STUDY GROUP. (1970; 35). Graham Speight, 58 Locke Avenue, Barnsley, South Yorkshire S70 1QH. 01226 321 300;

Meetings: 7.15pm, 1st Thursday in the month (Nov-Mar), RSPB Old Moor, Barnsley.

BRADFORD ORNITHOLOGICAL GROUP. (1987; 180). Shaun Radcliffe, 8 Longwood Avenue, Bingley, W Yorks, BD16 2RX. 01274 770 960; www.bradfordbirding.org
Meetings: 1st Tuesday of the month - see website for details.

CASTLEFORD & DISTRICT NATURALISTS' SOCIETY. (1956; 16). Michael J Warrington, 31 Mount Avenue, Hemsworth, Pontefract, W Yorks WF9 4QE. 01977 614 954; e-mail: michaelwarrington@talktalk.net
Meetings: 7.30pm, Tuesdays monthly (Sep-Mar), SkillsXchange Campus, Castleford. Check contact name for dates.

FILEY BRIGG ORNITHOLOGICAL GROUP. (1977; 100). Dr Sue Hull, 32 West Road, Filey, N Yorkshire YO14 9LP.01723 515 042; www.fbog.co.uk e-mail: secretary-at-fbog.co.uk

HARROGATE & DISTRICT NATURALISTS' SOCIETY. (1947; 350). Mrs Pat Cook, General Secretary, 1 Millbank Terrace, Shaw Mills, Harrogate, 01423 772 953; e-mail: gensec.hdns@talktalk.net www.knaresborough.co.uk/hdns/index.html
Meetings: 7.45pm, St. Roberts Centre, 2/3 Robert Street, Harrogate. The programme of meetings is sent out to members in September.

HORNSEA BIRD CLUB. (1967; 35). John Eldret, 44 Rolston Road, Hornsea, HU18 1UH. 01964 532 854;
Meetings: 7.30pm, 3rd Friday of the month (Sep-Mar), Hornsea Library. Monthly visits to local bird reserves.

HUDDERSFIELD BIRDWATCHERS' CLUB. (1966; 90). Chris Abell, 57 Butterley Lane, New Mill, Holmfirth, HD9 7EZ. 01484 681 499; e-mail: cdabell@gmail.com www.huddersfieldbirdwatchersclub.co.uk
Meetings: 7.30pm, Tuesday's fortnightly (Sep-May), The Old Court Room, Town Hall, Ramsden St, Huddersfield HD1 2TA.

HULL VALLEY WILDLIFE GROUP. (1997; 175). The Secretary, 29 Beech View, Cranswick, East Yorkshire YO25 9QQ. 01377 270 957. www.hullvalleywildlifegroup.co.uk

LEEDS BIRDWATCHERS' CLUB. (1949; 60). Peter Murphy, 12 West End lane, Horsforth, Leeds, LS18 5JP. 0113 293 0188; e-mail: pandbmurphy@ntlworld.com
Meetings: 7.15pm Monday fortnightly, Quaker Meeting House, Woodhouse Lane, Leeds.

ROTHERHAM & DISTRICT ORNITHOLOGICAL SOCIETY. (1974; 80). Malcolm Taylor, 18 Maple Place,

Chapeltown, Sheffield, S35 1QW. 0114 246 1848; e-mail: rdos@hotmail.co.uk

www.rotherhambirds.co.uk
Meetings: 7.30pm, 2nd Friday of the month, United Reform church hall, Herringthorpe.

SCARBOROUGH BIRDERS. (1993; 21). R.N.Hopper (Membership Secretary), 10A Ramshill Road, Scarborough, N Yorkshire YO11 2QE. 01723 369 537; www.scarboroughbirding. co.uk
Meetings: 3rd Thursday of the month (Sep-Nov) and (Jan-Apr). Check website for details.

SHEFFIELD BIRD STUDY GROUP. (1972; 160). Richard Dale, 22 Ansell Road, Sheffield, South Yorkshire S11 7PE. E-mail: rdhill@yahoo.com
www.sbsg.org
Meetings: 7.15pm, 2nd Wednesday of the month (Sep-Jun), Lecture Theatre 5, Sheffield University Arts Tower.

SK58 BIRDERS. (1993; 66). Andy Hirst, 15 Hunters Drive, Dinnington, Sheffield, S25 2TG. 07947 068 125; e-mail: contact@skbirders.com
www.sk58birders.com
Chair: Mick Clay, 2 High St, S.Anston, Sheffield. 01909 566 000.
Meetings: 7.30pm, last Wednesday of the month (except July, Aug & Dec (Christmas social)), Upstairs Room, Loyal Trooper pub, South Anston.

SOUTH PEAK RAPTOR STUDY GROUP. (1998; 12). M E Taylor, 76 Hawksley Avenue, Newbold, Chesterfield, Derbys S40 4TL. 01246 277 749;

SORBY NHS (ORNITHOLOGICAL SECTION). (1918; 400). The Secretary, C/O 100 Bole Hill Lane, Sheffield S10 1SD, e-mail: ornithology@sorby.org.uk
www.sorby.org.uk

SWILLINGTON INGS BIRD GROUP. (1989; 83). Chris Robinson, 43 Northfield Road, Sprotbrough, Doncaster, DN5 8AY. 07534 271 254;
e-mail: GBFShrike@hotmail.com
http://sibg1.wordpress.com
Meetings: 7.30pm, 1st Thursday of even months with informal social evenings 1st Thursday of odd months (please phone for details of venue).

WAKEFIELD NATURALISTS' SOCIETY. (1851; 32). Michael Warrington, 31 Mount Avenue, Hemsworth, Pontefract, W Yorks WF9 4QE. 01977 614 954;
e-mail: michaelwarrington@talktalk.net
Meetings: 7.30pm, 2nd Tuesday of the month (Sep-Apr), Friends Meeting House, Thornhill Street, Wakefield.

YORK ORNITHOLOGICAL CLUB. (1967; 80). Linda Newton, 5 Fairfields Drive, Skelton, York YO30 1YP, 01904 471 446; e-mail: secretary@yorkbirding.org.uk
www.yorkbirding.org.uk

Meetings: 7.30pm, 1st Tuesday of the month, Friends' Meeting House, Friargate, York (see website).

YORKSHIRE NATURALISTS' UNION (Bird Section). (1875; 500). Jim Pewtress, 31 Piercy End, Kirbymoorside, York, YO62 6DQ. 01751 431 001; e-mail: trivialis@operamail.com
www.ynu.org.uk

Ringing Groups
BARNSLEY RG. M C Wells, 715 Manchester Road, Stocksbridge, Sheffield, S36 1DQ. 0114 288 4211; e-mail: barnsleybsg.plus.com

SOUTH CLEVELAND RG. W Norman, 2 Station Cottages, Grosmont, Whitby, N Yorks YO22 5PB. 01947 895226; e-mail: wilfgros@lineone.net

DONCASTER RG. D Hazard, 41 Jossey Lane, Scawthorpe, Doncaster, S Yorks DN5 9DB. 01302 788 044; e-mail: dave.hazard@tiscali.co.uk

EAST DALES RG. P. Bone, 11 Dorrington Close, Pocklington, York, YO42 2GS.
E-mail: philsarab@aol.co.uk

EAST YORKSHIRE RG. Mr ICD Marshall, e-mail recording.fbo@ukf.net

SORBY-BRECK RG. Geoff P Mawson, Moonpenny Farm, Farwater Lane, Dronfield, Sheffield S18 1RA.
E-mail: moonpenny@talktalk.net

SPURN BIRD OBSERVATORY. Paul Collins, Kew Villa, Seaside Road, Kilnsea, Hull HU12 0UB. 01964 650 479; e-mail: pcnfa@hotmail.com

WINTERSETT RG. P Smith, 16 Templar Street, Wakefield, W Yorks, WF1 5HB. 01924 375 082;

RSPB Local Groups
AIREDALE AND BRADFORD. (1972; 3500 in catchment area). Ruth Porter. 01274 592 467;
e-mail: AbRSPB@blueyonder.co.uk
www.rspb.org.uk/groups/airedaleandbradford
Meetings: 7.30pm, monthly on Fridays, Room 3, Shipley Library.

CRAVEN & PENDLE. (1986; 300). Colin Straker. 01756 751 888; e-mail: colin.straker@btinternet.com
www.cravenandpendlerspb.org
Meetings: 7.30pm 2nd Wednesday of the month (Sep-May), St Andrews Church Hall, Newmarket Street, Skipton.

DONCASTER. (1984; 105). Sue Clifton, West Lodge, Wadworth Hall Lane, Wadworth, Doncaster, DN11 9BH. Tel/(fax) 01302 854 956;
e-mail: sue.cl.@waitrose.com
www.rspb.org.uk/groups/doncaster
Meetings: 7.30pm 2nd Wednesday of the month (Sept-May), Salvation Army Community Church, Lakeside.

277

EAST YORKSHIRE. (1986;120). Trevor Malkin, 9 Angus Drive, Driffield, E Yorks, YO25 5BQ. 01377 257 325; e-mail: eastyorksrspb@yahoo.co.uk
www.rspb.org.uk/groups/eastyorkshire
Meetings: 7.30pm, North Bridlington Library, Martongate, Bridlington (check website for details).

HUDDERSFIELD & HALIFAX. (1981; 140). David Hemingway, 267 Long Lane, Dalton, Huddersfield, HD5 9SH. 01484 301 920;
e-mail: d.hemingway@ntlworld.com
www.rspb.org.uk/groups/huddersfieldand halifax
Meetings: 7.30pm, Huddersfield Methodist Mission, 3-13 Lord Street, Huddersfield, HD1 1QA.

HULL & DISTRICT. (1983; 334). Betty Hilton. 01482 849 503; e-mail: betty_hilton@hotmail.com
Meetings: 7.30pm, Tuesdays (Sept-Apr), United Reformed Church, Southella Way, Kirkella, HULL. (£2 for Local Group Members and £2.50 for Non Members).

LEEDS. (1974; 450). Ian Willoughby;
e-mail: RSPBleeds@googlemail.com
www.rspb.org.uk/groups/leeds
Meetings: 7.30pm, 3rd Wednesday of the month (Sep-Apr), Lecture Theatre B, School of Mechanical Engineering, University of Leeds.

RICHMONDSHIRE & HAMBLE(2005) Jim Brettell 01748 850 272; E-mail: JGB@barneyschool.org.uk
www.communigate.co.uk/ne/rhrspb
Meetings: Check website.

SHEFFIELD. (1981; 500). Malcolm Dyke, Flat 5, 648 Abbeydale Road, Sheffield, S7 2BB. 07947 605 959; www.rspb-sheffield.org.uk
Meetings: 7.30pm 1st Thursday of the month (Sept-May), Central United Reformed Church, Norfolk St, Sheffield.

WAKEFIELD. (1987; 150). Duncan Stokoe, 12 New Road, Horbury, Wakefield, West Yorkshire WF4 5LR. E-mail: duncanstokoe@talktalk.net
www.rspb.org.uk/groups/wakefield

Meetings: 7.30pm, 4th Thursday of the month (Sep-Apr), Ossett War Memorial Community Centre, Prospect Road, Ossett, WF5 8AN.
YORK. (1972; 600). Chris Lloyd, 7 School Lane, Upper Poppleton, York, YO26 6JS. 01904 794865;
e-mail: rspb.calyork@btinternet.com
www.yorkrspb.org.uk
Meetings: 7.30pm, Tues, Wed or Thurs, Temple Hall, York St John University, Lord Mayors Walk, York.

Wetland Bird Survey Organiser
EAST YORKSHIRE AND SCARBOROUGH (excl. Humber). Mrs S Pashby, 10 Ambrey Close, Hunmanby, Filey, North Yorks YO14 0LZ. 01723 891 377.

HARROGATE AND YORKSHIRE DALES. Mr W G Haines, 07870 8289 788; e-mail: bill.haines@tiscali.co.uk
LEEDS AREA. Paul Morris, e-mail: pmorris@wyjs.org.uk

Wildlife Hospital
ANIMAL HOUSE WILDLIFE WELFARE. Mrs C Buckroyd, 14 Victoria Street, Scarborough, YO12 7SS. 01723 371 256 (please leave a message on the answer machine and callers will be contacted as soon as possible); e-mail: cynthiabuckroyd@talktalk.net or cindybuckroyd@hotmail.com All species of wild birds. Oiled birds given treatment before forwarding to cleaning stations. Incubators, hospital cages, heat pads, release sites. Birds ringed before release. Prior telephone call requested. Collection if required. Veterinary support. Charity shop at 127 Victoria Road.

Wildlife Trusts
SHEFFIELD WILDLIFE TRUST. (1985; 4,450). 37 Stafford Road, Sheffield, S2 2SF. 0114 263 4335 (fax) 0114 263 4345; e-mail: mail@wildsheffield.com
www.wildsheffield.com

YORKSHIRE WILDLIFE TRUST. (1946; 21,500). 1 St George's Place, Tadcaster Road, York YO24 1GN. 01904 659 570 (fax) 01904 613 467; e-mail: info@ywt.org.uk
www.ywt.org.uk

SCOTLAND

Bird Report
SCOTTISH BIRD REPORT, from: The SOC, The Scottish Birdwatching Resource Centre, Waterston House, Aberlady, East Lothian, EH32 0PY

Club
See Scottish Ornithologists' Club in National Directory.

ANGUS & DUNDEE

Bird Recorder
ANGUS & DUNDEE. Jon Cook, 76 Torridon Road, Broughty Ferry, Dundee, DD5 3JH. 01382 738 495; e-mail: 1301midget@tiscali.co.uk

Bird Report
ANGUS & DUNDEE BIRD REPORT (1974-), From The Secretary, Angus & Dundee Bird Club.

BTO Regional Representatives & Regional Development Officer
ANGUS RR & RDO. Bruce Lynch, 01382 737 528; e-mail: b_lynch1@sky.com

Clubs
ANGUS & DUNDEE BIRD CLUB. (1997; 220). Dorothy Fyffe, 33 Ireland Street, Carnoustie, Angus DD7 6AS. 1241 853 053. www. angusbirding.com
Meetings: 7.30pm, Tuesdays, Montrose Basin Wildlife Centre.

SOC TAYSIDE BRANCH. (145). Brian Boag, Birch Brae, Knapp, Inchture, Perthshire PH14 9SW. 01828 686 669 www.the-soc.org.uk

Ringing Group
TAY RG. Ms S Millar, Edenvale Cottage, 1 Lydox Cottages, Dairsie, Fife, KY15 4RN. e-mail: shirley@edenecology.co.uk

RSPB Members' Group
DUNDEE. (1972;110). Graham Smith, 01382 532 461; e-mail: grahamnjen@hotmail.com
www.RSPB.org.uk/groups/dundee
Meetings: 7.30 pm, monthly on a Wednesday (Sep-Mar), Methodist Church, 20, West Marketgait, Dundee. Admission £1.00 for all, including refreshments.

Wetland Bird Survey Organisers
ANGUS (excl Montrose Basin). Dr BM Lynch, 27 Luke Place, Broughty Ferry, Dundee DD5 3BN. e-mail: b_lynch1@sky.com

MONTROSE BASIN. Adam McClure, 01674 676 336; e-mail: amcclure@swt.org.uk

ARGYLL

Birds of Argyll (Argyll Bird Club 2007, £45 inc postage), available from Bob Furness, The Cnoc, Tarbert, Arrochar, Dunbartonshire G83 7DG. 01301 702 603

Bird Recorder
ARGYLL. Paul Daw, Tigh-na-Tulloch, Tullochgorm, Minard, Argyll, PA32 8YQ. 01546 886 260; e-mail: monedula@globalnet.co.uk

Bird Reports
ARGYLL BIRD REPORT (1984-), from Dr Bob Furness, The Cnoc, Tarbet, Dunbartonshire G83 7DG.01301 702 603; e-mail: r.furness@bio.gla.ac.uk

ISLE OF MULL BIRD REPORT (2004-), from Mr Alan Spellman, Maridon, Lochdon, Isle of Mull, Argyll. PA64 6AP. 01680 812 448; www.mullbirds.com
e-mail: mullbirds@btinternet.com

MACHRIHANISH SEABIRD OBSERVATORY REPORT (1992-), from the Observatory, see Reserves & Observatories.

BTO Regional Representatives
ARGYLL (MULL, COLL, TIREE AND MORVERN). Arthur Brown, 01688 400 415; 07780 600 367; e-mail: pamartbrown@btinternet.com

ARGYLL SOUTH, BUTE, GIGHA AND ARRAN. Richard Allen, e-mail: r.allan13@btinternet.com

ISLAY, JURA, COLONSAY RR. John S Armitage, Airigh Sgallaidh, Portnahaven, Isle of Islay, PA47 7SZ. 01496 860 396; e-mail: jsa@ornquest.plus.com
www.islaybirder.blogspot.com

Clubs
ARGYLL BIRD CLUB. (1983;270). Katie Pendreigh, The Whins, Farry Road, Tayinloan, Argyll PA37 1PT.01631 710 630. www.argyllbirdclub.org

ISLE OF MULL BIRD CLUB. (2001;160), Mrs Janet T Hall, Membership Secretary, Druim Mhor, Craignure, Isle of Mull, Argyll PA65 6AY.01680 812 441; e-mail: oystercatcher@dee-emm.co.uk
www.mullbirdclub.org.uk
Meetings: 7 for 7.30pm start, 3rd Friday of the month (Oct-Apr), Craignure Village Hall.

Ringing Group
TRESHNISH ISLES AUK RG. Robin Ward, e-mail: robin.ward2@virginmedia.com

RSPB Members' Group
HELENSBURGH. (1975; 62). Steve Chadwin, 01436 670 158.

Meetings: The Guide Halls, Lower John Street, HELENSBURGH.

Wildlife Hospital
WINGS OVER MULL. Richard and Sue Dewar, Auchnacroish House, Torosay, Craignure, Isle of Mull PA65 6AY. Tel/fax: 01680 812 594; e-mail: dewars@wingsovermull.com www.wingsovermull.com

Wetland Bird Survey Organisers
ARGYLL MAINLAND. Paul Daw, Tigh-na-Tulloch, Minard, Inveraray, Argyll PA32 8YQ. 01546 886 260; e-mail: monedula@globalnet.co.uk

MULL. Paul Daw, Tigh-na-Tulloch, Minard, Inveraray, Argyll PA32 8YQ. 01546 886 260; e-mail: monedula@globalnet.co.uk

TIREE & COLL. John Bowler, e-mail: john.bowler@rspb.org.uk

AYRSHIRE

Bird Recorder
AYRSHIRE. Fraser Simpson, 4 Inchmurrin Drive, Kilmarnock, Ayrshire KA3 2JD. e-mail: recorder@ayrshire-birding.org.uk

Bird Report
AYRSHIRE BIRD REPORT (1976-), from The Recorder or Dr RG Vernon, 29 Knoll Park, Ayr KA7 4RH. 01292 442 195; e-mail: rgv_mcv@tiscali.co.uk

BTO Regional Representatives
AYRSHIRE RR. Brian Broadley, 01290 424 241; e-mail: brianbroadley@onegreendoor.com

Club
SOC AYRSHIRE. (1962; 154). Anne Dick, Rowanmyle House,Tarbolton, Mauchline KA5 5LU. 01292 541 981. www.ayrshire-birding.org.uk www.the-soc.org.uk
Meetings: 7.30pm, Tuesdays monthly, Monkton Community Church, Monkton by Prestwick.

RSPB Members' Groups
CENTRAL AYRSHIRE LOCAL GROUP. (1978; 85). Ronnie Coombes (Group Leader), 01292 265 891; e-mail: ronnie.coombes@tesco.net www.ayrshire-birding.org.uk
Meetings: 7.40pm, 3rd Monday of the month (Sep-Apr), Carnegie Library, Main Street, Ayr.

NORTH AYRSHIRE. (1976; 180). Duncan Watt, 28 Greenbank, Dalry, Ayrshire, KA24 5AY. 01294 832 361; e-mail: duncan@spectrus.co.uk www.narspb.org.uk
Meetings: 7.30pm, various Fridays (Aug-Apr), Argyll Centre, Donaldson Avenue, Saltcoats, Ayrshire, KA21 5AG.

Wetland Bird Survey Organiser
AYRSHIRE. Mr David Grant, e-mail: david.grant@sac.ac.uk

ARRAN. Jim Cassels, Kilpatrick Kennels, Kilpatrick, Blackwaterfoot, Isle of Arran KA27 8EY. e-mail: james.cassels@virgin.net

Wildlife Hospital
HESSILHEAD WILDLIFE RESCUE CENTRE. Gay & Andy Christie, Gateside, Beith, Ayrshire, KA15 1HT. 01505 502 415; e-mail: info@hessilhead.org.uk www.hessilhead.org.uk; All species. Releasing aviaries. Veterinary support. Visits only on open days please.

THE SCOTTISH BORDERS

Bird Atlas/Avifauna
The Breeding Birds of South-east Scotland, a tetrad atlas 1988-1994 by R D Murray et al. (Scottish Ornithologists' Club, 1998).

Bird Recorder
Ray Murray, 4 Bellfield Crescent, Eddleston, Peebles, EH45 8RQ. 01721 730 677; e-mail: raymurray1@tiscali.co.uk

Bird Report
BORDERS BIRD REPORT (1979-), from Malcolm Ross, Westfield Cottage, Smailholm, Kelso TD5 7PN.01573 460 699; e-mail: eliseandmalcolm@btinternet.com

BTO Regional Representative
Graham Pyatt, The Schoolhouse, Manor, Peebles EH45 9JN. 01721 740 319; e-mail: d.g.pyatt@btinternet.com

Club
SOC BORDERS BRANCH. (100). Graham Pyatt, The Schoolhouse, Manor, Peebles EH45 9JN. 01721 740 319; www.the-soc.org.uk
Meetings:7.30pm, 2nd Monday of the month, George & Abbotsford Hotel, Melrose.

Ringing Group
BORDERS RG. (1991; 10). Dr T W Dougall, 38 Leamington Terrace, Edinburgh EH10 4JL. (Office) 0131 344 2600.

RSPB Members' Group
BORDERS. (1995; 94). John Marshall, 01896 850 564; e-mail: n-jmarshall@tiscali.co.uk
Meetings: 7.30pm, 3rd Wednesday of the month, The Corn Exchange, Market Square, MELROSE.

Wetland Bird Survey Organisers
BORDERS. Andrew Bramhall, 2 Abbotsferry Road, Tweedbank, Galashiels, Scottish Borders TD1 3RX; e-mail: andrew@atbramhall.go-plus.net

SCOTLAND

CAITHNESS

Bird Recorders
CAITHNESS. Stan Laybourne, Old Schoolhouse, Harpsdale, Halkirk, Caithness, KW12 6UN. 01847 841 244; e-mail: stanlaybourne@talk21.com

Bird Reports
CAITHNESS BIRD REPORT (1983-97). Now incorporated into The Highland Bird Report, From Alistair F McNee, Liathach, 4 Balnafettack Place, Inverness, IV3 8TQ. 01463 220 493; e-mail: aj.mcnee@care4free.net

BTO Regional Representative
CAITHNESS. D Omand, 9 Skiall, Shebster, Thurso, Caithness KW14 7YD. 01847 811 403; e-mail: achreamie@yahoo.co.uk

Clubs
SOC CAITHNESS BRANCH. (51). Stan Laybourne, Old Schoolhouse, Harpsdale, Halkirk, Caithness, KW12 6UN. 01847 841 244; e-mail: stanlaybourne@talk21.com www.the-soc.org.uk

CLYDE

Bird Atlas/Avifauna
A Guide to Birdwatching in the Clyde Area (2001)by Cliff Baister and Marin Osler (Scottish Ornithologists' Club, Clyde branch).

Clyde Breeding Bird Atlas (working title). In preparation.

Bird Recorder
CLYDE ISLANDS (ARRAN, BUTE & CUMBRAES). Bernard Zonfrillo, 28 Brodie Road, Glasgow,G21 3SB. e-mail: b.zonfrillo@bio.gla.ac.uk

CLYDE. Iain P Gibson, 8 Kenmure View, Howwood, Johnstone, Renfrewshire, PA9 1DR. 01505 705 874; e-mail: iaingibson.soc@btinternet.com

Bird Reports
CLYDE BIRDS (1973-), From Valerie Wilson, 76 Laigh Road, Newton Mearns, Glasgow, G77 5EQ. e-mail: wilsonval@btinternet.com

BTO Regional Representatives
LANARK, RENFREW, DUMBARTON. John Knowler, 0141 584 9117; e-mail: john.knowler@ntlworld.com

Club
SOC CLYDE BRANCH. (300). Hayley Douglas, Top Right, 35 Church Street, Lochwinnoch PA12 4AE. 07715 634 079. www.the-soc.org.uk

Ringing Groups
CLYDE RG. (1979; 18)I Livingstone, 57 Strathview Road, Bellshill, Lanarkshire, ML4 2UY.01698 749 844; e-mail: iainlivcrg@googlemail.com

RSPB Members' Groups
GLASGOW. (1972;141). Roger Adams. 0141 942 6920; e-mail: Rogerlpadams7@aol.com www.rspb.org.uk/groups/glasgow
Meetings: 7.30pm, generally 1st Wednesday of the month (Sep-Apr), Woodside Halls, Clarendon Street, off Maryhill Road, Glasgow, G20 7QD.

HAMILTON. (1976;90). Jim Lynch, 0141 583 1044; e-mail: birder45a@yahoo.co.uk www.baronshaugh.co.uk
Meetings: 7.30pm, 3rd Thursday of the month (Sept-May), Watersports Centre, Motherwell (next to Strathclyde Loch).

RENFREWSHIRE. (1986; 200). Iain Smeaton. e-mail: RenfrewRSPB@hotmail.co.uk www.rspb.org.uk/groups/renfrewshire
Meetings: 1st Friday of the month (Sep-Apr), The McMaster Centre, 2a Donaldson Drive, RENFREW

Wetland Bird Survey Organisers
CLYDE ESTUARY. John Clark, Laighfield, Station Road, Shandon, Helensburgh G84 8NX; e-mail: johnclark@jcmc.demon.co.uk

GLASGOW/RENFREWSHIRE/LANARKSHIRE/DUNBARTONSHIRE. John Clark, Laighfield, Station Road, Shandon, Helensburgh G84 8NX; e-mail: johnclark@jcmc.demon.co.uk

BUTE. Ian Leslie Hopkins, 2 Eden Place, 179 High Street, Rothesay, Isle of Bute PA20 9BS. 01700 504 042; e-mail: ian@hopkins0079.freeserve.co.uk

DUMFRIES & GALLOWAY

Bird Recorders
Paul Collin, Gairland, Old Edinburgh Road, Minnigaff, Newton Stewart, DG8 6PL. 01671 402 861; e-mail: pncollin@live.co.uk

Bird Report
DUMFRIES & GALLOWAY REGION BIRD REPORT (1985-), from Peter Swan, 3 Castle View, Glancaple, Castle Douglas, DG7 1BG. 01556 502 144.

BTO Regional Representatives
DUMFRIES RR. Edmund Fellowes, 01387 262 094; e-mail: edmundfellowes@aol.com

KIRKCUDBRIGHT RR and Atlas Co-ordinator. Andrew Bielinski, 41 Main Street, St Johns Town of Dalry, Castle Douglas, Kirkcudbright, DG7 3UP. 01644 430 418 (evening); e-mail: andrewb@bielinski.fsnet.co.uk

WIGTOWN RR. Geoff Sheppard, The Roddens, Leswalt, Stranraer, Wigtownshire, DG9 0QR. 01776 870 685; e-mail: geoff.roddens@btinternet.com

281

Clubs

SOC DUMFRIES BRANCH. (1961; 105). Mrs Pat Abery, East Daylesford, Colvend, Dalbeattie, Dumfries, DG5 4QA. 01556 630 483. www.the-soc.org.uk
Meetings: 7.30pm, 2nd Wednesday of the month (Sept-Apr), Cumberland St Day Centre.

SOC STEWARTRY BRANCH. (1976; 80). Miss Joan Howie, 60 Main Street, St Johns Town of Dalry, Castle Douglas, Kirkcudbrightshire, DG7 3UW. 01644 430 226 www.the-soc.org.uk
Meetings: 7.30pm, usually 2nd Thursday of the month (Sep-Apr), Kells School, New Galloway.

SOC WEST GALLOWAY BRANCH. (1975; 50). Geoff Sheppard, The Roddens, Leswalt, Stranraer, Wigtownshire, DG9 0QR. 01776 870 685; e-mail: geoff.roddens@btinternet.com www.the-soc.org.uk
Meetings: 7.30pm, 2nd Tuesday of the month (Oct-Mar), Stranraer Library.

Ringing Group

NORTH SOLWAY RG. Geoff Sheppard, The Roddens, Leswalt, Stranraer, Wigtownshire, DG9 0QR. 01776 870 685; e-mail: geoff.roddens@btinternet.com

RSPB Members' Group

GALLOWAY. (1985;150). Cynthia Douglas, Midpark, Balmaclellan, Castle Douglas, DG7 3PX. 01644 420 605; e-mail: cynthia@cdouglas.plus.com www.rspb.org.uk/groups/galloway
Meetings: 7.30pm 3rd Tuesday in the month, Castle Douglas High School.

Wetland Bird Survey Organisers

AUCHENCAIRN AND ORCHARDTON BAYS. Euan MacAlpine, Auchenshore, Auchencairn, Castle Douglas, Galloway DG7 1QZ . 01556 640 244; e-mail: js.eamm@sky.com

FLEET BAY. David Hawker. 01556 610 086; e-mail: dheco@dsl.pipex.com

LOCH RYAN. Geoff Shepherd, The Roddens, Leswalt, Stranraer, Wigtonshire DG9 0QR. 01776 870 685; e-mail: geoff.roddens@btinternet.com

ROUGH FIRTH. Judy Baxter, Saltflats Cottage, Rockcliffe, Dalbeattie, DG5 4QQ. 01556 630 262; e-mail: Jbaxter@nts.org.uk

WIGTOWN BAY. Paul Collin, Gairland, Old Edinburgh Road, Minnigaff, Newton Stewart, DG8 6PL. 01671 402 861; e-mail: pncollin@live.co.uk

DUMFRIES AND GALLOWAY (other sites). Andy Riches, 07792 142 446; e-mail: slioch69@aol.com

SOLWAY ESTUARY - NORTH. Andy Riches, 07792 142 446; e-mail: slioch69@aol.com

FIFE

Bird Atlas/Avifauna

The Fife Bird Atlas 2003 by Norman Elkins, et al. Available from Allan W. Brown (FOAG), 61 Watts Gardens, Cupar, Fife KY15 4UG, Tel. 01334 656 804, email: swans@allanwbrown.co.uk

Bird Recorders

FIFE REGION INC OFFSHORE ISLANDS (NORTH FORTH). Mr Malcolm Ware,15a King Street, Inverkeithing, Fife, KY11 1NB; e-mail: mw160598@hotmail.co.uk

ISLE OF MAY BIRD OBSERVATORY. Iain English, 19 Nethan Gate, Hamilton, S Lanarks, ML3 8NH; e-mail: i.english@talk21.com

Bird Reports

FIFE BIRD REPORT (1988-) (FIFE & KINROSS BR 1980-87), From Mr Malcolm Ware, 15a King Street, Inverkeithing, Fife, KY11 1NB.
e-mail: mw160598@hotmail.co.uk

ISLE OF MAY BIRD OBSERVATORY REPORT (1985-), From Iain English, 19 Nethan Gate, Hamilton, S Lanarks, ML3 8NH. e-mail: i.english@talk21.com

BTO Regional Representative

FIFE & KINROSS RR. Norman Elkins, 18 Scotstarvit View, Cupar, Fife, KY15 5DX. 01334 654 348; e-mail: jandnelkins@btinternet.com

Clubs

FIFE BIRD CLUB. (1985; 200). Mr Drew Crosbie, 14 Dunvegan Drive, Falkirk, Central Scotland FK2 7UG. www.fifebirdclub.org
Meetings: 7.30pm, (various evenings), Dean Park Hotel, Chapel Level, Kirkcaldy.

LOTHIANS AND FIFE SWAN & GOOSE STUDY GROUP. (1978) Allan & Lyndesay Brown, 61 Watts Gardens, Cupar, Fife, KY15 4UG. e-mail: swans@allanwbrown.co.uk

SOC FIFE BRANCH. (1956;170). Karen Dick,South Lodge,St Michaels,St Andrews KY16 0DU. 01334 848 278; e-mail: fifesoc@sky.com www.the-soc.org.uk
Meetings: 7.30pm, 2nd Wednesday of the month (Sep-Apr), St Andrews Town Hall.

Ringing Groups

ISLE OF MAY BIRD OBSERVATORY. David Grieve, 50 Main Street, Symington, Biggar, South Lanarkshire ML12 6LJ. 01899 309 176

TAY RG. Ms S Millar, Edenvale Cottage, 1 Lydox Cottages, Dairsie, Fife, KY15 4RN. e-mail: shirley@edenecology.co.uk

SCOTLAND

Wetland Bird Survey Organisers

FIFE (excluding estuaries). Grey Goose count organiser for Fife, Lothians and Borders. Allan Brown, 61 Watts Gardens, Cupar, Fife KY15 4UG; e-mail: swans@allanwbrown.co.uk

FORTH ESTUARY (North). Alastair Inglis, 5 Crowhill Road, Dalgety Bay, Fife KY11 5LJ. e-mail: aandjinglis@hotmail.com

TAY AND EDEN ESTUARIES. Norman Elkins, 18 Scotstarvit View, Cupar, Fife KY15 5DX. 01334 654 348; e-mail: jandnelkins@btinternet.com

Wildlife Hospital

SCOTTISH SPCA WILD LIFE REHABILITATION CENTRE. Middlebank Farm, Masterton Road, Dunfermline, Fife, KY11 8QN. 01383 412 520 All species. Open to visitors, groups and school parties. Illustrated talk on oiled bird cleaning and other aspects of wildlife rehabilitation available. Veterinary support.

FORTH

Bird Recorder

UPPER FORTH (Does not include parts of Stirling in Loch Lomondside/Clyde Basin). Chris Pendlebury, 3 Sinclair Street, Dunblane, FK5 0AH. 07798 711 134; e-mail: chris@upperforthbirds.co.uk

Bird Report

FORTH AREA BIRD REPORT (1975-) - enlarged report published annually in The Forth Naturalist and Historian, University of Stirling, From Dr Roy Sexton, Asst. Editor, Forth Naturalist and Historian, 22 Alexander Drive, Bridge of Allan, FK9 4QB.01786 833 409; e-mail: RoyGravedigger@AOL.com www.fnh.stir.ac.uk

BTO Regional Representative

CENTRAL RR. Neil Bielby, 56 Ochiltree, Dunblane, Perthshire, FK15 0DF. 01786 823 830; e-mail: n.bielby@sky.com

Club

SOC CENTRAL SCOTLAND BRANCH. (1968; 101). Mr RL Gooch, The Red House, Dollarfield, Dollar, Clacks FK14 7LX. 01259 742 326. www.the-soc.org.uk
Meetings: 7.30pm, 1st Thursday of the month (Sep-Apr), The Smith Art Gallery and Museum, Dumbarton Road, Stirling.

RSPB Members' Group

CENTRAL, FORTH VALLEY. (1995; 150). Tam Craig, 53 The Braes, Tullibody, Clackmannashire FK10 2TT. 01259 211 550; e-mail: tam_craig@btinternet.com www.forthrspb.org.uk
Meetings: 7.30pm, 3rd Thursday of the month (Sept-Apr), Hill Park Centre, Stirling.

Wetland Bird Survey Organiser

CENTRAL (excl Forth Estuary). Neil Bielby, 56 Ochiltree, Dunblane, Perthshire FK15 0DF. 01786 823 830; e-mail: n.bielby@sky.com

FORTH ESTUARY (Inner). Michael Bell, 48 Newton Crescent, Dunblane, Perthshire FK15 0DZ. 01786 73171; e-mail: mvbell34@tiscali.co.uk

Coordinator for the Icelandic breeding goose counts (Pinkfeet & Greylag) for inner Forth, Forth Valley & Perthshire. Michael Bell, 48 Newton Crescent, Dunblane, Perthshire FK15 0DZ. 01786 73171; e-mail: mvbell34@tiscali.co.uk

HIGHLAND

Bird Atlas/Avifauna

The Birds of Sutherland by Alan Vittery (Colin Baxter Photography Ltd, 1997).

Birds of Skye by Andrew Currie. In preparation.

Bird Recorder

ROSS-SHIRE, INVERNESS-SHIRE, SUTHERLAND, BADENOCH & STRATHSPEY, LOCHABER, LOCHALSH and SKYE. Kevin Davis, 14 Forsyth Place, Cromarty, Ross-shire IV11 8XW. 01381 600 545, (M)07881 522 967; e-mail: kjdshoebill@live.co.uk

Bird Reports

HIGHLAND BIRD REPORT (1991-). 2007 edition £9.50 inc p&p, from The Recorder. 2007 edition £8, 2009 £9.50 including p&p.

BTO Regional Representatives & Regional Development Officers

INVERNESS & SPEYSIDE RR & RDO. Hugh Insley, 1 Drummond Place, Inverness,IV2 4JT. 01463 230 652; e-mail: hugh.insley@btinternet.com

RUM, EIGG, CANNA & MUCK RR & RDO. Bob Swann, 14 St Vincent Road, Tain, Ross-shire, IV19 1JR. 01862 894 329; e-mail: robert.swann@homecall.co.uk

ROSS-SHIRE RR. Simon Cohen, e-mail: saraandsimon@hotmail.com

SUTHERLAND. Position vacant.

SKYE. Position vacant.

Clubs

EAST SUTHERLAND BIRD GROUP. (1976; 120). Tony Mainwood, 13 Ben Bhraggie Drive, Golspie, Sutherland KW10 6SX. 01408 633 247; e-mail: tony.mainwood@btinternet.com
Meetings: 7.30pm, Last Monday of the month (Oct, Nov, Jan, Feb, Mar), Golspie Community Centre.

SOC HIGHLAND BRANCH. (1955; 151). Ann Sime, 4 Culduthel House, Culduthel Road, Inverness, IV2 4HH. 01463 236 529. www.the-soc.org.uk
Meetings: 7.45pm, 1st Tuesday of the month (Sep-Mar), Culloden Library.

SCOTLAND

Ringing Groups
HIGHLAND RG. Bob Swann, 14 St Vincent Road, Tain, Ross-shire, IV19 1JR.
e-mail: robert.swann@homecall.co.uk

RSPB Members' Group
HIGHLAND. (1987; 214). Doreen Manson, Muirton Lodge, Urray, Muir of Ord, Ross-shire IV6. 01997 433 283; e-mail: john@jmanson2.wanadoo.co.uk
www.rspb.org.uk/groups/highland
Meetings: 7.30pm, last Thursday of the month (Sep-Apr), Kingsmill Hotel, Culcabock Road, Inverness.

Wetland Bird Survey Organisers
BADENOCH AND STRATHSPEY. Keith Duncan, Scottish Natural Heritage, Achantoul, Aviemore, Inverness-Shire PH22 1QD. 01479 810 477;
e-mail: keith.duncan@snh.gov.uk

LOCHABER. John Dye, e-mail: john.dye@virgin.net

SKYE & LOCHALSH. Bob McMillan, 11 Elgol, Nr Broadford, Isle of Skye IV49 9BL. 01471 866 305;
e-mail: bob@skye-birds.com

LOTHIAN

Bird Atlas/Avifauna
The Breeding Birds of South-east Scotland, a tetrad atlas 1988-1994 by R D Murray et al. (Scottish Ornithologists' Club, 1998).

Bird Recorder
David J Kelly, 01875 6140 72;
e-mail: dj_kelly@btinternet.com

Bird Reports
LOTHIAN BIRD REPORT (1979-), from Jacky Robinson, 141 Currievale Drive, Currie, Edinburgh, EH14 5RP. e-mail: jackyrobinson48@btinternet.com

BTO Regional Representative
Alan Heavisides, 9 Addiston Crescent, Balerno, Edinburgh, EH14 7DB. 0131 449 3816;
e-mail: alanheavisides@yahoo.com

BTO Garden BirdWatch Ambassador
Prof J I B Wilson, e-mail: jib4wilson@o2.co.uk

Clubs
EDINBURGH NATURAL HISTORY SOCIETY. (1869; 200). Mrs Joan McNaughton, 14 Relugas Road, Edinburgh EH9 2ND. 0131 477 0270. e-mail: enquiries@ edinburghnaturalhistorysociety.org.uk
www.edinburghnaturalhistorysociety.org.uk
Meetings: 7.30pm, 4th Wednesday of the month The Guide Hall, 33 Melville Street, Edinburgh.

LOTHIANS AND FIFE MUTE SWAN STUDY GROUP. (1978; 12)Allan & Lyndesay Brown, 61 Watts Gardens, Cupar, Fife, KY15 4UG.
e-mail: swans@allanwbrown.co.uk

LOTHIAN SOC. (1936; 570). Doreen Main;
e-mail: doreen.main@yahoo.com

www.the-soc.org.uk
Meetings: 7.30pm, 2nd Tuesday (Sep-Dec and Jan-Apr), Lounge 2, Meadowbank Sports Stadium.

Ringing Group
LOTHIAN RG. Mr M Cubitt, 12 Burgh Mills Lane, Linlithgow,West Lothian EH49 7TA.

RSPB Members' Group
EDINBURGH. (1974;480). Mark Stephen, 25 Newcroft Drive, Glasgow G44 5RT. 07796 538 837;
e-mail: markbirder@googlemail.com
www.rspb.org.uk/groups/edinburgh/
Meetings: 7.30pm, 3rd Tuesday or Wednesday of the month (Sep-Apr), Napier University, Craiglockhart Campus, Edinburgh.

Wetland Bird Survey Organisers
FORTH ESTUARY (Outer South). Duncan Priddle, 19c High Street, Haddington, East Lothian EH41 3ES. 01620 827 459; e-mail: dpriddle@eastlothian.gov.uk

LOTHIAN (excl estuaries). Joan Wilcox, 18 Howdenhall Gardens, Edinburgh, Midlothian EH16 6UN. (H)0131 664 8 893; e-mail: webs@bto.org

TYNINGHAME ESTUARY. Mr R Anderson, John Muir Country Park, East Lothian Countryside Ranger Service, Block C, Brewery Park, Haddington EH41 3HA. 01620 827 318;
e-mail: randerson@eastlothian.gov.uk

MORAY & NAIRN

Bird Atlas/Avifauna
The Birds of Moray and Nairn by Martin Cook (Mercat Press, 1992.

Bird Recorder
NAIRN. Martin J H Cook, Rowanbrae, Clochan, Buckie, Banffshire, AB56 5EQ. 01542 850 296;
e-mail: martin.cook99@btinternet.com

MORAY. Martin J H Cook, Rowanbrae, Clochan, Buckie, Banffshire, AB56 5EQ. 01542 850 296;
e-mail: martin.cook99@btinternet.com

Bird Reports
BIRDS IN MORAY AND NAIRN (1999-), from The Moray & Nairn Recorder, 01542 850 296;
e-mail: martin.cook99@btinternet.com

MORAY & NAIRN BIRD REPORT (1985-1998), From the Moray & Nairn Recorder, 01542 850 296;
e-mail: martin.cook99@btinternet.com

BTO Regional Representatives
NAIRN RR. Bob Proctor, 78 Marleon Field, Elgin, Moray, IV30 4GE.
e-mail: bobandlouise@proctor8246.fsnet.co.uk

MORAY RR. Bob Proctor, 78 Marleon Field, Elgin, Moray, IV30 4GE.
e-mail: bobandlouise@proctor8246.fsnet.co.uk

SCOTLAND

Wetland Bird Survey Organisers
LOSSIE ESTUARY. Bob Proctor, 78 Marleon Field, Silvercrest, Bishopmill, Elgin, IV30 4GE; e-mail: bobandlouise@proctor8246.fsnet.co.uk

MORAY & NAIRN (Inland). David Law, 01463 725 200; e-mail: jdavidlaw@btinternet.com

MORAY BASIN COAST. Bob Swann, 14 St Vincent Road, Tain, Ross-Shire IV19 1JR. 01862 894 329; e-mail: robert.swann@homecall.co.uk

NORTH EAST SCOTLAND

Bird Atlas/Avifauna
The Birds of North East Scotland by S T Buckland, M V Bell & N Picozzi (North East Scotland Bird Club, 1990).

Bird Recorder
NORTH-EAST SCOTLAND. Hywel Maggs, 4 Merlin Terrace, Newburgh, Ellon, Aberdeenshire AB41 6FA.01358 788 106; e-mail: hywelmaggs@hotmail.com

Bird Reports
NORTH-EAST SCOTLAND BIRD REPORT (1974-), From Dave Gill, Drakemyre Croft, Cairnorrie, Methlick, Aberdeenshire, AB41 7JN. 01651 806 252; e-mail: david@gilldavid1.orangehome.co.uk

NORTH SEA BIRD CLUB ANNUAL REPORT (1979-), from Andrew Thorpe, Ocean Laboratory and Centre for Ecology, Aberdeen University, Newburgh, Ellon, Aberdeenshire, AB41 6AA. 01224 274 428; e-mail: nsbc@abdn.ac.uk

BTO Regional Representatives
ABERDEEN. Paul Doyle, 01358 751 365; e-mail: paul@wildlifeweb.co.uk

KINCARDINE & DEESIDE. Graham Cooper, Westbank, Beltie Road, Torphins, Banchory, Aberdeen, AB31 4JT. 01339 882 706; e-mail: grm.cooper@btinternet.com

Clubs
SOC GRAMPIAN BRANCH. (1956; 110). Graham Cooper, Westbank, Beltie Road, Torphins, Banchory, Aberdeen, AB31 4JT. 01339 882 706; www.the-soc.org.uk
Meetings: 7.30pm, usually 1st Monday of the month (Sep-Apr), Sportsmans's Club, 11 Queens Road, Aberdeen.

Ringing Groups
ABERDEEN UNIVERSITY RG. Andrew Thorpe, e-mail: Andrew.Thorpe147@btinternet.com

GRAMPIAN RG. R Duncan, 86 Broadfold Drive, Bridge of Don, Aberdeen, AB23 8PP.
e-mail: Raymond@waxwing.fsnet.co.uk

RSPB Members' Group
ABERDEEN. (1975; 210). Rodney Payne, 2 Arbuthnott Court, Stonehaven,AB39 2GW. 01569 763 742; e-mail: rodney_payne@btopenworld.com
www.rspb.org.uk/groups/aberdeen
Meetings: 7.30pm, monthly in the winter, Lecture Theatre, Zoology Dept, Tillydrone Av, Aberdeen. Two birding trips monthly throughout the year.

Wildlife Hospital
GRAMPIAN WILDLIFE REHABILITATION TRUST. 40 High Street, New Deer, Turriff, Aberdeenshire, AB53 6SX. 01771 644 489; (M)07803 235 383; e-mail: laurence. brain@btconnect.com; Veterinary surgeon. Access to full practice facilities. Will care for all species of birds.

ORKNEY

Bird Atlas/Avifauna
The Birds of Orkney by CJ Booth et al (The Orkney Press, 1984).

Bird Recorder
Mr EJ Williams, Fairholm, Finstown, Orkney, KW17 2EQ. e-mail: jim@geniefea.freeserve.co.uk

Bird Report
ORKNEY BIRD REPORT (inc North Ronaldsay Bird Report) (1974-), from Mr EJ Williams, Fairholm, Finstown, Orkney, KW17 2EQ. e-mail: jim@geniefea.freeserve.co.uk

BTO Regional Representative
Colin Corse, Garrisdale, Lynn Park, Kirkwall, Orkney, KW15 1SL. 01856 874 484; e-mail: ccorse@aol.com

Club
SOC ORKNEY BRANCH. (1993; 15). Colin Corse, Garrisdale, Lynn Park, Kirkwall, Orkney, KW15 1SL. H:01856 874 484; e-mail: ccorse@aol.com
www.the-soc.org.uk

Ringing Groups
NORTH RONALDSAY BIRD OBSERVATORY. Ms A E Duncan, Twingness, North Ronaldsay, Orkney, KW17 2BE. e-mail: alison@nrbo.prestel.co.uk
www.nrbo.co.uk

ORKNEY RG. Colin Corse, Garrisdale, Lynn Park, Kirkwall, Orkney, KW15 1SL. H:01856 874 484; e-mail: ccorse@aol.com

SULE SKERRY RG. Dave Budworth, 121 Wood Lane, Newhall, Swadlincote, Derbys, DE11 0LX. 01283 215 188.

RSPB Members' Group
ORKNEY. (1985;300 in catchment area). Mrs Pauline Wilson, Sunnybank, Deerness, Orkney KW17 2QQ. 01856 741 382; e-mail: p.wilson410@btinternet.com
Meetings: Meetings advertised in newsletter and local press, held at St Magnus Centre, Kirkwall.

SCOTLAND

Wetland Bird Survey Organiser
ORKNEY. Eric Meek, Smyril, Stenness, Stromness, Orkney KW16 3JX. 01856 850 176;
e-mail: eric.meek@rspb.org.uk

OUTER HEBRIDES

Bird Recorder
OUTER HEBRIDES AND WESTERN ISLES. Brian Rabbitts, 6 Carinish, Isle of North Uist HS6 5HL. 01876 580 328;
e-mail: rabbitts@hebrides.net

Bird Report
OUTER HEBRIDES BIRD REPORT (1989-), From The Recorder. 6 Carinish, Isle of North Uist HS6 5HL01876 580 328; e-mail: rabbitts@hebrides.net

BTO Regional Representatives
BENBECULA & THE UISTS. Position vacant.

LEWIS & HARRIS RR. Chris Reynolds, 11 Reef, Isle of Lewis, HS2 9HU. 01851 672 376;
e-mail: cmreynolds@btinternet.com

Ringing Group
SHIANTS AUK RG. Jim Lennon, The Dovecote, Main Street, Fintham, Newark NG23 5LA. 01636 525 963.

Wetland Bird Survey Organiser
UISTS AND BENBECULA. Brian Rabbitts, 6 Carinish, Isle of North Uist HS6 5HL01876 580 328;
e-mail: rabbitts@hebrides.net

ISLAY, JURA AND COLONSAYJohn Armitage, Airigh Sgallaidh, Portnahaven, Isle of Islay PA47 7SZ01496 860 396; e-mail: jsa@ornquest.plus.com
www.islaybirder.blogspot.com/

PERTH & KINROSS

Bird Recorder
PERTH & KINROSS. Mike Martin,
e-mail: mwa.martin@btinternet.com

Bird Report
PERTH & KINROSS BIRD REPORT (1974-), from the Recorder.

BTO Regional Representatives & Regional Development Officer
PERTHSHIRE RR. Richard Paul. 01882 632 212;
e-mail: richard@rannoch.net
www.perthshire-birds.org.uk

Clubs
PERTHSHIRE SOCIETY OF NATURAL SCIENCE (Ornithological Section). (1964; 29). Miss Esther Taylor, 23 Verena Terrace, Perth,PH2 0BZ. 01738 621 986; www.psns.org.uk
Meetings: 7.30pm, Wednesdays monthly (Oct-Mar), Perth Museum. Summer outings.

Wetland Bird Survey Organiser
LOCH LEVEN. Jeremy Squire, c/o Scottish Natural Heritage, The Pier, Kinross, KY13 8UF.
e-mail: jeremy.squire@snh.gov.uk

TAY AND EDEN ESTUARIES. Norman Elkins, 18 Scotstarvit View, Cupar, Fife KY15 5DX. 01334 654 348; e-mail: jandnelkins@btinternet.com

SHETLAND

Bird Recorders
FAIR ISLE. Deryk Shaw, Bird Observatory, Fair Isle, Shetland, ZE2 9JU.
e-mail: fairisle.birdobs@zetnet.co.uk

SHETLAND. Mark Chapman, 55 Leaside, Firth, Mossbank, ShetlandZE2 9TF. 01806 242 401;
e-mail: msc.1@btinternet.com

Bird Reports
FAIR ISLE BIRD OBSERVATORY REPORT (1949-), from Scottish Ornithologists' Club, 21 Regent Terrace, Edinburgh, EH7 5BT. 0131 556 6042

SHETLAND BIRD REPORT (1969-) £10 inc p&p, no pre 1973 available, From Martin Huebeck, Shetland Bird Club, Sumburgh Lighthouse, Virkie, Shetland ZE3 9JN.
e-mail: martinheubeck@btinternet.com

BTO Regional Representative
RR and RDO. Dave Okill, Heilinabretta, Cauldhame, Trondra, Shetland, ZE1 0XL. 01595 880 450.
e-mail: david@auroradesign.plus.com

Club
SHETLAND BIRD CLUB. (1973; 200). Russ Haywood, Lamnaberg, Wester Quarff, Shetland ZE2 9EZ. 01950 477 471; e-mail: haywood712@ btinternet.com
www.nature-shetland.co.uk

Ringing Groups
FAIR ISLE BIRD OBSERVATORY. Deryk Shaw, Bird Observatory, Fair Isle, Shetland, ZE2 9JU.
e-mail: fairisle.birdobs@zetnet.co.uk

SHETLAND RG. Dave Okill, Heilinabretta, Cauldhame, Trondra, Shetland, ZE1 0XL. H:01595 880 450;
W:01595 696 926.

Wetland Bird Survey Organiser
SHETLAND. Paul Harvey, Shetland Biological Records Centre, Shetland Amenity Trust, 22-24 North Road, Lerwick, Shetland, ZE1 3NG. (Day)01595 694 688;
e-mail: sbrc@shetlandamenity.org

WALES

Bird Report
See Welsh Ornithological Society in National Directory

BTO Honorary Wales Officer
BTO WALES OFFICER. John Lloyd, Cynghordy Hall, Cynghordy, Llandovery, Carms SA20 0LN.
e-mail: the_lloyds@dsl.pipex.com

Club
See Welsh Ornithological Society in National Directory.

EAST WALES

Bird Atlas/Avifauna
Birds of Radnorshire. In preparation.

The Birds of Gwent by Venables et al, published by Helm on behalf of Gwent Ornithological Society.

The Gwent Atlas of Breeding Birds by Tyler, Lewis, Venables & Walton (Gwent Ornithological Society, 1987).

Bird Recorders
BRECONSHIRE. Andrew King, Heddfan, Pennorth, Brecon, Powys LD3 7EX. 01874 658 351;
e-mail: andrew.king53@virgin.net

GWENT. Chris Jones.
e-mail: countyrecorder@gwentbirds.org.uk

MONTGOMERYSHIRE. Brayton Holt, Scops Cottage, Pentrebeirdd, Welshpool, Powys SY21 9DL. 01938 500 266; e-mail: brayton.wanda@virgin.net

RADNORSHIRE. Pete Jennings, Penbont House, Elan Valley, Rhayader, Powys LD6 5HS. H:01597 811522; W:01597 810 880;
e-mail: radnorshirebirds@hotmail.com

Bird Reports
BRECONSHIRE BIRDS (1962-), from Brecknock Wildlife Trust.

GWENT BIRD REPORT (1964-), from Jerry Lewis, Y Bwthyn Gwyn, Coldbrook, Abergavenny, Monmouthshire NP7 9TD. (H)01873 855 091; (W)01633 644 856

MONTGOMERYSHIRE BIRD REPORT (1981-82-), from Montgomeryshire Wildlife Trust.

RADNOR BIRDS (1987/92-), from Radnorshire Recorder.

BTO Regional Representatives
BRECKNOCK RR. John Lloyd, Cynghordy Hall, Cynghordy, Llandovery, Carms, SA20 0LN.
e-mail: the_lloyds@dsl.pipex.com

GWENT RR. Jerry Lewis, Y Bwthyn Gwyn, Coldbrook, Abergavenny, Monmouthshire NP7 9TD. H:01873 855 091; W:01633 644 856.
e-mail: jerryLewis@monmouthshire.gov.uk

MONTGOMERY RR. Jane Kelsall, Clog y Fran, High Street, Borth, SY24 5HZ. 01970 872 019;
e-mail: janekelsall@phonecoop.coop

RADNORSHIRE RR. Brian Jones. 01547 560 175;
e-mail: jones.brn10@virgin.net

Clubs
THE GWENT ORNITHOLOGICAL SOCIETY. (1964; 420). T J Russell. 01600 716 266;
e-mail: secretary@ GwentBirds.org.uk
www.gwentbirds.org.uk
Meetings: 7.30pm, alternate Saturdays (Sept-Apr), Goytre Village Hall.

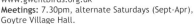

MONTGOMERYSHIRE WILDLIFE TRUST BIRD GROUP. (1997; 110). A M Puzey, Four Seasons, Arddleen, Llanymynech, Powys SY22 6RU. 01938 590 578.
www.montwt.co.uk/bird_group.html
Meetings: 7.30pm, 3rd Wednesday of the month (Jan-Mar) and (Sep-Dec), Welshpool Methodist Hall.

Ringing Groups
GOLDCLIFF RG. Mr RM Clarke.
e-mail: chykembro2@aol.com

LLANGORSE RG. (1987; 15). Jerry Lewis, Y Bwthyn Gwyn, Coldbrook, Abergavenny, Monmouthshire NP7 9TD. H:01873 855 091; W:01633 644 856

Wetland Bird Survey Organisers
BRECONSHIRE. Andrew King, Heddfan, Pennorth, Brecon LD3 7EX; e-mail: andrew.king53@virgin.net

GWENT (excl. Severn Estuary). Chris Jones, 22 Walnut Drive, Caerleon, Newport, Gwent NP18 3SB.
e-mail: chrisj22@talktalk.net

RADNORSHIRE. Peter Jennings, Pentbont House, Elan Valley, Rhayader, Powys LD6 5HS. H:01597 811 522; W:01597 810 880;
e-mail: radnorshirebirds@hotmail.com

Wildlife Trusts
BRECKNOCK WILDLIFE TRUST. (1963; 650). Lion House, Bethel Square, Brecon, Powys LD3 7AY. 01874 625 708;
e-mail: enquiries@brecknockwildlifetrust.org.uk
www.brecknockwildlifetrust.org.uk

GWENT WILDLIFE TRUST. (1963; 9,800). Seddon House, Dingestow, Monmouth, NP25 4DY. 01600 740 600; (fax) 01600 740 299;
e-mail: info@gwentwildlife.org
www.gwentwildlife.org

WALES

MONTGOMERYSHIRE WILDLIFE TRUST. (1982; 1000). Collot House, 20 Severn Street, Welshpool, Powys, SY21 7AD. 01938 555 654; (fax) 01938 556 161; e-mail: info@montwt.co.uk
www.montwt.co.uk

RADNORSHIRE WILDLIFE TRUST. (1987; 878). Warwick House, High Street, Llandrindod Wells, Powys LD1 6AG. 01597 823 298; (fax) 01597 823 274; e-mail: info@rwtwales.org
www.radnorshirewildlifetrust.org.uk

NORTH WALES

Bird Atlas/Avifauna
The Birds of Caernarfonshire by John Barnes (1998, from Lionel Pilling, 51 Brighton Close, Rhyl LL18 3HL).

Bird Recorders
ANGLESEY. Stephen Culley, 22 Cae Derwydd, Cemaes Bay, Anglesey, LL67 0LP. 01407 710 542; e-mail: SteCul10@aol.com

CAERNARFONSHIRE. John Barnes, Fach Goch, Waunfawr, Caernarfon, LL55 4YS. 01286 650 362

DENBIGHSHIRE & FLINTSHIRE. Ian Spence, 43 Blackbrook, Sychdyn, Mold, Flintshire CH7 6LT. Tel/fax: 01352 750 118; e-mail: ianspence.cr@btinternet.com
www.cbrg.org.uk

MEIRIONNYDD. Jim Dustow, Lake Vyrnwy/ Llyn Efyrnwy RSPB, Oswestry, Shropshire SY10 0LZ. e-mail: Jim.Dustow@rspb.org.uk

Bird Reports
BARDSEY BIRD OBSERVATORY ANNUAL REPORT, from the Warden, see Reserves.

CAMBRIAN BIRD REPORT (sometime Gwynedd Bird Report) (1953-), from Geoff Gibbs. 01248 681 936; e-mail: geoffkate.gibbs@care4free.net
www.welshos.org.uk/cambrian/

NORTH-EAST WALES BIRD REPORT (2004-), formerly *CLWYD BIRD REPORT (2002-2003)*, from Ian M Spence, 43 Blackbrook, Sychdyn, Mold, Flintshire CH7 6LT. 01352 750 118; e-mail: ianspence.cr@btinternet.com www.cbrg.org.uk

MEIRIONNYDD BIRD REPORT Published in Cambrian Bird Report (above).

WREXHAM BIRDWATCHERS' SOCIETY ANNUAL REPORT (1982-), from The Secretary, Wrexham Birdwatchers' Society.

BTO Regional Representatives
ANGLESEY RR. Tony White. 01407 710 137; e-mail: wylfor@treg5360.freeserve.co.uk

CAERNARFON RR. Geoff Gibbs. 01248 681 936; e-mail: geoffkate.gibbs@care4free.net

CLWYD EAST RR. Dr Anne Brenchley, Ty'r Fawnog, 43 Black Brook, Sychdyn, Mold, Flints CH7 6LT. 01352 750 118; e-mail: anne.brenchley@btinternet.com

CLWYD WEST RR. Mel ab Owain, 31 Coed Bedw, Abergele, Conwy, LL22 7EH. 01745 826 528; e-mail: melabowain@btinternet.com

MEIRIONNYDD RR. David Anning. 01654 700 222; e-mail: anning.ecology@tiscali.co.uk

Clubs
BANGOR BIRD GROUP. (1947; 100). Jane Prosser, 15 Victoria Street, Bangor, Gwynedd LL57 2HD. 01248 364 632.
Meetings: 7.30pm, Semester terms, Bramble Building, University of Bangor.

CAMBRIAN ORNITHOLOGICAL SOCIETY. (1952; 190). Geoff Gibbs. 01248 681 936; e-mail: geoffkate.gibbs@care4free.net
www.welshos.org.uk/cambrian/
Meetings: 7.30pm, 1st Friday of the month, Pensychnant Centre, Sychnant Pass.

CLWYD BIRD RECORDING GROUP (committee that produces the Bird Report). Ian Spence, Tel/fax 01352 750118; e-mail: ianspence.cr@btinternet.com
www.cbrg.org.uk

CLWYD ORNITHOLOGICAL SOCIETY. (1956; 45). Ms J Irving, 45, Plas Uchaf Avenue, Prestatyn, LL19 9NR, 45 Plas Uchaf Avenue, Prestatyn, Denbighshire LL19 9NR. 01745 854 132; e-mail: jacqui970irving@btinternet.com
Meetings: 7.30pm (Sep-Apr), Farmers Arms, Waen, St. Asaph.

DEE ESTUARY CONSERVATION GROUP. (1973; 25 grps). Richard Smith, Secretary, e-mail: decg@deeestuary.co.uk
www.deeestuary.co.uk/decg.htm

DEESIDE NATURALISTS' SOCIETY. (1973; 1,000). Secretary, 21 Woodlands Court, Hawarden, Deeside, Flints CH5 3NB. 01244 537 440; e-mail: deenaturalists@btinternet.com
www.deesidenaturalists.org.uk

WREXHAM BIRDWATCHERS' SOCIETY. (1974; 90). Miss Marian Williams, 10 Lake View, Gresford, Wrexham, Clwyd LL12 8PU. 01978 854 633.
Meetings: 7.30pm, 1st Friday of the month (Sep-Apr), Gresford Memorial Hall, Gresford.

Ringing Groups
BARDSEY BIRD OBSERVATORY. Steven Stansfield, Bardsey Island, off Aberdaron, Pwllheli, Gwynedd LL53 8DE. 07855 264151; e-mail: warden@bbfo.org.uk

CHESHIRE SWAN GROUP. David Cookson, 01270 567 526; e-mail:Cheshireswans@aol.com www.record-lrc.co.uk (then follow link to Cheshire Swans Group).

MERSEYSIDE RG. Bob Harris, 2 Dulas Road, Wavertree Green, Liverpool, L15 6UA. (Work)0151 706 4311; e-mail: harris@liv.ac.uk

SCAN RG. Dr D. Moss. e-mail: dorian@dorianmoss.com

RSPB Local Group
NORTH WALES. (1986; 80). Maureen Douglas, 57 Penrhyn Beach East, Penrhyn Bay, Llandudno, Conwy LL30 3RW. 01492 547 768; e-mail: Mary.clarke@clarren.freeserve.co.uk www.rspb.org.uk/groups/northwales
Meetings: 7.30pm, 3rd Friday of the month (Sep-Apr), St Davids Church Hall, Penrhyn Bay, Llandudno, Gwynedd, LL30 3EJ.

Wetland Bird Survey Organisers
ANGLESEY (other sites). Ian Sims, RSPB Malltraeth Marsh, Tai'r Gors, Pentre Berw, Gaerwen, Anglesey, LL60 6LB; e-mail: ian.sims@rspb.org.uk

ARTRO/MAWDDACH/TRAETH BACH/DYSYNNI ESTUARY. Jim Dustow, Lake Vyrnwy/ Llyn Efyrnwy RSPB, Oswestry, Shropshire SY10 OLZ. e-mail: Jim.Dustow@rspb.org.uk

CAERNARFONSHIRE. Rhion Pritchard, Pant Afonig, Hafod Lane, Bangor, Gwynedd LL57 4BU. (H)01248 671 301; e-mail: rhion678pritchard@btinternet.com

CLWYD (Coastal). Mr Peter Wellington, 4 Cheltenham Avenue, Rhyl, Clwyd LL18 4DN. (H)01745 354 232; e-mail: webs@bto.org

DEE ESTUARY. Colin Wells, Burton Point Farm, Station Road, Burton, Nr Neston, South Wirral CH64 5SB. 0151 336 7681.

FORYD BAY. Simon Hugheston-Roberts, Oakhurst, St David's Road, Caernarfon, LL55 1EL. e-mail: sm.roberts@ccw.gov.uk

MEIRIONNYDD (other sites). Trefor Owen, Crochendy Twrog, Maentwrog, Blaenau Ffestiniog, LL41 3YU.

Wildlife Trust
NORTH WALES WILDLIFE TRUST. (1963; 6,450). 376 High Street, Bangor, Gwynedd, LL57 1YE. 01248 351 541; e-mail: nwwt@wildlifetrustswales.org www.northwaleswildlifetrust.org.uk

SOUTH WALES

Bird Atlas/Avifauna
An Atlas of Breeding Birds in West Glamorgan by David M Hanford et al (Gower Ornithological Society, 1992).

Birds of Glamorgan by Clive Hurford and Peter Lansdown (Published by the authors, c/o National Museum of Wales, Cardiff, 1995)

Bird Recorders
GLAMORGAN (EAST). David RW Gilmore, 116, Donald Street, Roath, Cardiff, Glamorgan CF24 4TN. 7779 176 766; e-mail: d.gilmore2@ntlworld.com

GOWER (WEST GLAMORGAN). Robert Taylor, 285 Llangyfelach Road, Brynhyfryd, Swansea, SA5 9LB. 01792 464 780; (M) 07970 567 007; e-mail: rob@birding.freeserve.co.uk

Bird Reports
EAST GLAMORGAN BIRD REPORT (title varies 1963-95) 1996-2007, from Mr John D Wilson, 122 Westbourne Road, Penarth, Vale of Glamorgan, CF64 3HH. 029 2033 9424;
e-mail: john.wilson@glamorganbirds.org.uk www.glamorganbirds.org.uk

GOWER BIRDS (1965-) - covers Swansea, Neath and Port Talbot counties, from Barry Stewart, 36 Pencaecrwn Road, Gorseinon, Swansea SA4 4FU. e-mail: gowerbirdsf@hotmail.co.uk www.glamorganbirds.org.uk

BTO Regional Representatives
EAST GLAMORGAN (former Mid & South Glam) RR. Wayne Morris, 8 Hughes Street, Penygraig, Rhondda, CF40 1LX. e-mail: waynemorris@tiscali.co.uk

GLAMORGAN (WEST) RR. Bob Howells, Ynys Enlli, 14 Dolgoy Close, West Cross, Swansea SA3 5LT. e-mail: bobhowells31@hotmail.com

BTO Garden BirdWatch Ambassadors
Mr M Bailey, e-mail: mick@mickbailey.fsnet.co.uk

Miss A Skull, e-mail: gbw@hiafi.co.uk

Clubs
CARDIFF NATURALISTS' SOCIETY. (1867; 200). Stephen R Howe, National Museum of Wales, Cardiff, CF10 3NP. e-mail: steve.howe@museumwales.ac.uk www.cardiffnaturalists.org.uk
Meetings: 7.30pm, various evenings, Llandaff Campus Uwic, Western Avenue, Cardiff.

GLAMORGAN BIRD CLUB. (1990; 290). Laura Palmer, 2 Greenfield Terrace, Shwt, Bettws, BRIDGEND CF32 8UD. 01656 725 712 (home); 07799 565 237 (mobile) e-mail: chair@glamorganbirds.org.uk www.glamorganbirds.org.uk
Meetings: 7.30pm, 2nd Tuesday of winter months, Kenfig Reserve Centre.

GOWER ORNITHOLOGICAL SOCIETY. (1956; 120). Peter Douglas-Jones, 28 Brynfield Road, Langland, Swansea, SA3 4SX. 01792 360 287; e-mail: gowerbirds@hotmail.co.uk www.glamorganbirds.org.uk
Meetings: 7.15pm, last Friday of the month (Sep-Mar), The Environment Centre, Pier Street, Swansea.

WALES

Ringing Groups
FLAT HOLM RG. Brian Bailey, Tamarisk House, Wards Court, Frampton-on-Severn, Glos, GL2 7DY.
e-mail: brian.bailey@sandbservices.eclipse.co.uk

KENFIG RG. Mr D.G. Carrington, 44 Ogmore Drive, Nottage, Porthcawl, Mid Glamorgan CF36 3HR.

RSPB Local Groups
CARDIFF & DISTRICT. (1973:). Huw Moody-Jones.
01446 760 757; e-mail: huwmoodyjones@hotmail.com
www.RSPB.org.uk/groups/cardiff
Meetings: 7.30pm, various Fridays (Sept-May), Llandaff Parish Hall, Llandaff, Cardiff.

WEST GLAMORGAN. (1985; 346). Maggie Cornelius.
01792 229 244;
e-mail: RSPBwglamgrp@googlemail.com
www.rspb.org.uk/groups/westglamorgan
Meetings: 7.30pm, Environment Centre, Pier Street, Swansea, SA1 1RY

Wetland Bird Survey Organisers
EAST GLAMORGAN. Daniel Jenkins-Jones, 18 St. Margarets Road, Whitchurch, Cardiff, South Glamorgan CF14 7AA. (H)0292 062 1394; (M)07828 093 613.

SEVERN ESTUARY. Niall Burton, c/o BTO, The Nunnery, Thetford, Norfolk, IP24 2PU.
e-mail: niall.burton@bto.org

WEST GLAMORGAN. Bob Howells, Ynys Enlli, 14 Dolgoy Close, West Cross, Swansea SA3 5LT. 01792 405 363;
e-mail: bobhowells31@hotmail.com

Wildlife Hospital
GOWER BIRD HOSPITAL. Karen Kingsnorth and Simon Allen, Valetta, Sandy Lane, Pennard, Swansea, SA3 2EW. 01792 371 630;
e-mail: admin@gowerbirdhospital.org.uk
www.gowerbirdhospital.org.uk
All species of wild birds, also hedgehogs and small

mammals. Prior phone call essential. Gower Bird Hospital cares for sick, injured and orphaned wild birds and animals with the sole intention of returning them to the wild. Post release radio tracking projects, ringing scheme. Contact us for more information.

Wildlife Trust
WILDLIFE TRUST OF SOUTH AND WEST WALES. (2002; 6,000). Nature Centre, Parc Slip, Fountain Road, Tondu, Bridgend CF32 0EH. 01656 724 100; fax 01656 726 980; e-mail: info@welshwildlife.org
www.welshwildlife.org

WEST WALES

Bird Atlas/Avifauna
Birds of Ceredigion by Hywel Roderick and Peter Davis (2010).

The Birds of Carmarthenshire by John Lloyd (in preparation)

Birds of Pembrokeshire by Jack Donovan and Graham Rees (Dyfed Wildlife Trust, 1994).

Bird Recorders
CARMARTHENSHIRE. Owen Harris, 5 William Terrace, Burry Port, Carmarthenshire SA16 0PG.
e-mail: Owenharris@aol.com

CEREDIGION. Russell Jones, Bron y Gan, Talybont, Ceredigion, SY24 5ER. 07753 774 891;
e-mail: russell.jones@rspb.org.uk

PEMBROKESHIRE 2. Stephen Berry, Teifi House, Dolbadau Road, Cilgerran, Pembrokeshire SA43 2SS.
01348 872 233;
e-mail: stephen.berry16@btinternet.com

PEMBROKESHIRE 2. Jon Green, Crud Yr Awel, Bowls Road, Blaenporth, Ceredigion SA43 2AR. 01239 811 561; e-mail: jonrg@tiscali.co.uk

Bird Reports
CARMARTHENSHIRE BIRD REPORT (1982-), available online at www.carmarthenshirebirds.co.uk

CEREDIGION BIRD REPORT (biennial 1982-87; annual 1988-), from Wildlife Trust West Wales.

PEMBROKESHIRE BIRD REPORT (1981-), from Ms Barbara Priest, The Pines, Templeton, Pembs, SA67 8RT. e-mail: barbara.priest@tiscali.co.uk

BTO Regional Representatives
CARDIGAN RR. Moira Convery, 41 Danycoed, Aberystwyth, SY23 2HD.
e-mail: moira.convery@dsl.pipex.com

CARMARTHEN RR. Position vacant.

PEMBROKE RR. Annie and Bob Haycock, 1 Rushmoor, Martletwy, Narberth,Dyfed SA67 8BB. 01646 661 368;
e-mail: rushmoor1@tiscali.co.uk

Clubs
CARMARTHENSHIRE BIRD CLUB.
(2003; 120).Owen Harris, 5 William Terrace, Burry Port, Carmarthenshire SA16 0PG.
e-mail: Owenharris@aol.com
www.carmarthenshirebirds. co.uk
Meetings: Winter evenings at WWT Penclacwydd (check website for details).

WALES

PEMBROKESHIRE BIRD GROUP. (1993; 60). Ms Barbara Priest, The Pines, Templeton, Pembs, SA67 8RT.
e-mail: barbara.priest@tiscali.co.uk
Meetings: 7.30pm, 1st Monday of the month (Oct-Apr), The Patch, Furzy Park, Haverfordwest.

Ringing Group
PEMBROKESHIRE RG. J Hayes, 3 Wades Close, Holyland Road, Pembroke, SA71 4BN. 01646 687 036; e-mail: hayes313@btinternet.com

Wetland Bird Survey Organisers
CARDIGAN (incl Dyfi Estuary). Dick Squires, Cae'r Berllan, Eglwysfach, Machynlleth, Powys SY20 8TA.
e-mail: dick.squires@rspb.org.uk

CARMARTHEN, BAY AND INLAND. Ian Hainsworth, 23 Rhyd y Defaid Drive, Swansea, SA2 8AJ. 01792 205 693; e-mail: ian.hains@ntlworld.com

GWENT (excl. Severn Estuary). Chris Jones, 22 Walnut Drive, Caerleon, Newport, Gwent NP18 3SB.
e-mail: chrisj22@talktalk.net

PEMBROKESHIRE. Annie Haycock,
e-mail: rushmoor1@tiscali.co.uk
Annie Haycock, 1 Rushmoor, Martletwy, Pembrokeshire SA67 8BB.
e-mail: rushmoor1@tiscali.co.uk

Wildlife Trust
WILDLIFE TRUST OF SOUTH AND WEST WALES. (2002; 6,000). Nature Centre, Parc Slip, Fountain Road, Tondu, Bridgend CF32 0EH. 01656 724 100; fax 01656 726 980; e-mail: info@welshwildlife.org
www.welshwildlife.org

ISLE OF MAN

Bird Atlas/Avifauna
Manx Bird Atlas. 5-yr BBS and Winter Atlas research completed. (Liverpool University Press, 2007). From NHBS Environment Bookstore, 01803 865 913; www.nhbs.co.uk

Bird Recorder
Dr Pat Cullen, Troutbeck, Cronkbourne, Braddan, Isle of Man, IM4 4QA. Home: 01624 623 308 Work: 01624 676 774; E-mail: bridgeen@mcb.net

Bird Reports
MANX BIRD REPORT (1947-), published in *Peregrine.* From Mrs A C Kaye, Cronk Ny Ollee, Glen Chass, Port St Mary, Isle of Man IM9 5PL. 01624 834 015;

CALF OF MAN BIRD OBSERVATORY ANNUAL REPORT, from The Secretary, Manx National Heritage, Manx Museum, Douglas, Isle of Man, IM1 3LY.

BTO Regional Representatives
RR. Dr Pat Cullen, as above. 01624 623 308;

Club
MANX ORNITHOLOGICAL SOCIETY. (1967; 150). Mrs A C Kaye, Cronk Ny Ollee, Glen Chass, Port St Mary, Isle of Man IM9 5PL. 01624 834 015;
Meetings: 1st Tues in month, 7.30pm, Union Mills Hall.

Ringing Group
MANX RINGING GROUP. Mr Kevin Scott.
E-mail: kev@wm.im
www.manxringer.blogspot.com

Wetland Bird Survey Organiser
Pat Cullen, Troutbeck, Cronkbourne, Braddan, Isle of Man, IM4 4QA. (H)01624 623 308; (W)01624 676 774; E-mail: bridgeen@mcb.net

Wildlife Trust
MANX WILDLIFE TRUST. (1973; 900). The Courtyard, Tynwald Mills, St Johns, Isle of Man IM4 3AE. 01624 801 985 (fax) 01624 801022; e-mail: manxwt@cix.co.uk
www.manxwt.org.uk

Manx Bird Atlas
An Atlas of Breeding and Wintering Birds on the Isle of Man

CHANNEL ISLANDS

ALDERNEY

Bird Recorder
Mark Atkinson. E-mail:atkinson@cwgsy.net

Bird Report
ALDERNEY SOCIETY ORNITHOLOGY REPORT (1992-),
from The Recorder.

BTO Regional Representative
Philip Alexander. 01481 726 173;
e-mail:alybru@cwgsy.net

Wetland Birds Survey Organiser
Alderney Wildlife Trust Ecologist, Alderney Wildlife
Trust Office, 51 Victoria Street, St Anne Alderney GY9
3TA. 01481 822 935; e-mail:info@alderneywildlife.org

CHANNEL ISLANDS (inland). Glyn Young, 01534 860
000; e-mail:glyn.young@durrell.org

Wildlife Trust
ALDERNEY WILDLIFE TRUST. (2002; 460). Alderney
Wildlife Trust Office, 51 Victoria Street, St Anne
Alderney GY9 3TA. 01481 822 935 (fax)01481 822 935;
e-mail: info@alderneywildlife.org
www.alderneywildlife.org

GUERNSEY

Bird Atlas/Avifauna
Birds of the Bailiwick of Guernsey (working title). In
preparation.

Bird Recorder
Mark Lawlor E-mail:mplawlor@cwgsy.net

Bird Report
*REPORT & TRANSACTIONS OF LA SOCIETE
GUERNESIAISE (1882-)*, from The Recorder.

BTO Regional Representative
Philip Alexander. 01481 726 173;
E-mail:alybru@cwgsy.net

Clubs
LA SOCIÉTIÉ GUERNESIAISE (Ornithological Section).
(1882; 30). Secretary, La Société Guernesiaise,
Candie Gardens, St Peter Port, Port Guernsey GY1
1UG; e-mail:societe@cwgsy.net
www.societe.org.gg
Meetings: First Thurs of month, 8pm, Candie Gardens
lecture theatre.

RSPB Local Group
GUERNSEY. (1975; 350+). Michael Bairds, Les Quatre
Vents, La Passee, St Sampsons, Guernsey GY2 4TS.
01481 255 524; e-mail:mikebairds@cwgsy.nett

www.rspbguernsey.co.uk
Meetings: La Villette Hotel, St Martins, Guernsey,
GY4 6QG.

Wetland Bird Survey Organiser
GUERNSEY COAST. Mary Simmons, Les Maeures, Mont
d'Aval, Castel, Guernsey GY5 7UQ. 01481 256 016;
e-mail:msim@cwgsy.net

Wildlife Hospital
GUERNSEY. GSPCA ANIMAL
SHELTER. Mrs Jayne Le
Cras, Les Fiers Moutons, St
Andrews, Guernsey, Channel
Islands GY6 8UD. 01481 257
261; e-mail:jaynelecras@
gspca.org.gg
www.gspca.org.gg; All species. Modern cleansing
unit for oiled seabirds. 24-hour emergency service.
Veterinary support.

JERSEY

Bird Recorder
Tony Paintin, Cavok, 16 Quennevais Gardens, St
Brelade, Jersey, Channel Islands, JE3 8FQ. 01534 741
928; e-mail:cavokjersey@hotmail.com

Bird Report
JERSEY BIRD REPORT, from La Société Jersiaise, 7
Pier Road, St Helier, Jersey JE2 4XW.
e-mail:societe@societe-jersiaise.org

BTO Regional Representative
Tony Paintin, Cavok, 16 Quennevais Gardens, St
Brelade, Jersey, Channel Islands, JE3 8FQ. 01534 741
928; e-mail:cavokjersey@hotmail.com

Club
SOCIÉTIÉ JERSIAISE (Ornithological Section). (1948;
40). C/O La Société Jersiaise, 7 Pier Road, St Helier,
Jersey JE2 4XW. 01534 758 314;
e-mail:societe@societe-jersiaise.org
www.societe-jersiaise.org
Meetings: 8.00pm, alternate Thursdays throughout
the year, Museum in St.Helier.

Wetland Bird Survey Organiser
JERSEY COAST. Roger Noel,
E-mail:rogernoel1@googlemail.com

Wildlife Hospital
JERSEY. JSPCA ANIMALS' SHELTER. The Manager, 89
St Saviour·s Road, St Helier, Jersey, JE2 4GJ. 01534
724 331 (fax) 01534 871 797; e-mail:info@jspca.org.je
www.jspca.org.je All species. Expert outside support
for owls and raptors. Oiled seabird unit. Veterinary
surgeon on site. Educational Centre.

NORTHERN IRELAND

Bird Recorder
George Gordon, 2 Brooklyn Avenue, Bangor, Co Down, BT20 5RB. 028 9145 5763;
E-mail: gordon@ballyholme2.freeserve.co.uk

Bird Reports
NORTHERN IRELAND BIRD REPORT, from Secretary, Northern Ireland, Birdwatchers' Association (see National Directory).

IRISH BIRD REPORT, Included in Irish Birds, BirdWatch Ireland in National Directory.

COPELAND BIRD OBSERVATORY REPORT, from the Observatory.

BTO Regional Representatives
BTO IRELAND OFFICER. Shane Wolsey. 028 9146 7947;
E-mail: shane@swolsey.biz

ANTRIM & BELFAST. Position vacant.

ARMAGH. David W A Knight, 23 Richmond Drive, Ballymore Road, Tandragee, Co Armagh BT62 2JJ. 028 38 840 658; e-mail: david.knight@niwater.com

DOWN. Position vacant.

FERMANAGH. Position vacant.

LONDONDERRY. Charles Stewart, Bravallen, 18 Duncrun Road, Bellarena, Limavady, Co Londonderry BT49 0JD. 028 7775 0468;
e-mail: charles.stewart2@btinternet.com

TYRONE. Position vacant.

BTO Garden BirdWatch Ambassadors
COUNTY ARMAGH. Ms P A Flowerday,
E-mail: pflowerday@utvinternet.com

COUNTY DERRYMr P Smith,
e-mail: bto@pete-smith.co.uk

Clubs
NORTHERN IRELAND BIRDWATCHERS' ASSOCIATION See National Directory.

NORTHERN IRELAND ORNITHOLOGISTS' CLUB, see National Directory.

CASTLE ESPIE BIRDWATCHING CLUB (COMBER). (1995; 60). Dot Blakely, 8 Rosemary Park, Bangor, Co Down, BT20 3EX. 028 9145 0784;

Ringing Groups
COPELAND BIRD OBSERVATORY. C W Acheson, 28 Church Avenue, Dunmurry, Belfast, BT17 9RS.

NORTH DOWN RINGING GROUP. Mr D C Clarke. 07774 780 750; e-mail: declan.clarke@homecall.co.uk;

RSPB Local Groups
ANTRIM. (1977; 23). Brenda Campbell. 02893 323 657;
e-mail: brendacampbell@supanet.com
www.rspb.org.uk/groups/antrim
Meetings: 8pm, 2nd Monday of the month, College of Agriculture Food & Rural Enterprise, 22 Greenmount Road, Antrim.

BANGOR. (1973; 25). Fulton Somerville.
e-mail: fultonsomerville@yahoo.co.uk
Meetings: Trinity Presbyterian Church Hall, Main Street, Bangor, County Down.

BELFAST. (1970; 130). Ron Houston. 028 9079 6188;
Meetings: Cooke Centenary Church Hall, Cooke Centenary Church Hall, Ormeau Rd, Belfast.

COLERAINE. (1978; 45). Peter Robinson, 34 Blackthorn Court, Coleraine, Co Londonderry, BT52 2EX. 028 7034 4361; e-mail: robinson493@btinternet.com
Meetings: 7.30pm, third Monday of the month (Sept-Apr), St Patricks Church, Minor Church Hall, Corner of Brook St and Circular Road, Coleraine

FERMANAGH. (1977; 28). Barbara Johnston. 028 6634 1708; e-mail: johnston.cb@googlemail.com
Meetings: 7.30pm, 4th Tuesday of the month, St Macartans Church Hall.

LARNE. (1974; 35). Jimmy Christie, 314 Coast Road, Ballygally, Co Antrim, BT40 2QZ. 028 2858 3223;
e-mail: candjchristie@btinternet.com
Meetings: 7.30pm, 1st Wednesday of the month, Larne Grammar School.

LISBURN. (1978; 30). Peter Galloway. 028 9266 1982;
e-mail: peter.dolly@virgin.net
www.rspblisburn.com
Meetings: 7.30pm, 4th Monday of the month, Friends Meeting House, 4 Magheralave Road, LISBURN

LARNE LOUGH. Doreen Hilditch.
e-mail: 18brae@btinternet.com

Wetland Bird Survey Organisers
BANN ESTUARY. Hill Dick, 02870 329 720;
e-mail: webs@bto.org

BELFAST LOUGH. Shane Wolsey, 25 Ballyholme Esplanade, Bangor, County Down, BT20 5LZ. 07831 697 371; e-mail: shane@swolsey.biz

DUNDRUM BAY. Malachy Martin, Murlough NNR, Keel Point, Dundrum, Co. Down, BT33 0NQ. 028 4375 1467; e-mail: Malachy.Martin@nationaltrust.org.uk

LOUGH FOYLE. Matthew Tickner, 028 491 547;
e-mail: matthew.tickner@rspb.org.uk

STRANGFORD LOUGH. Kerry Mackie, WWT Castle Espie; e-mail: kerry.mackie@wwt.org.uk

Wildlife Hospital
TACT WILDLIFE CENTRE. Mrs Patricia Nevines, 2 Crumlin Road, Crumlin, Co Antrim, BT29 4AD. 028 9442 2900; e-mail: tactwildlife@btinternet.com www.tactwildlifecentre.org.uk All categories of birds treated and rehabilitated; released where practicable, otherwise given a home. Visitors (inc.

school groups and organisations) welcome by prior arrangement. Veterinary support.

Wildlife Trust
ULSTER WILDLIFE TRUST. (1978; 7.500). 3 New Line, Crossgar, Co Down, BT30 9EP. 028 4483 0282 (fax) 028 4483 0888; e -mail: info@ulsterwildlifetrust.org www.ulsterwildlifetrust.org

REPUBLIC OF IRELAND

Bird Recorders
BirdWatch Ireland, P.O. Box 12, Greystones, Co. Wicklow, Ireland. 353 (0)1 2819 878 (Fax) 353 (0)1 2810 997; e-mail: info@birdwatchireland.ie www.birdwatchireland.ie

Rarities. Paul Milne, 100 Dublin Road, Sutton, Dublin 13, +353 (0)1 832 5653; e-mail: paul.milne@oceanfree.net

CLARE. John Murphy; e-mail: jemurphy@esatclear.ie

CORK. Mark Shorten; e-mail: mshorten@indigo.ie

DONEGAL. Ralph Sheppard; e-mail: rsheppard@eircom.net

DUBLIN, LOUTH, MEATH AND WICKLOW. Declan Murphy; e-mail: dmurphy@birdwatchireland.ie

Dick Coombes; e-mail: rcoombes@birdwatchireland.ie

GALWAY. Tim Griffin; 74 Monalee Heights, Knocknacarra.

KERRY. Edward Carty; 3 The Orchard, Ballyrickard, Tralee.

LIMERICK. Tony Mee; Ballyorgan, Kilfinane, Co. Limerick.

MAYO. Tony Murray; National Parks and Wildlife, Lagduff More, Ballycroy, Westport; e-mail: murraytony@hotmail.com

MID-SHANNON. Stephen Heery; e-mail: sheery@eircom.net

MONAGHAN. Joe Shannon; e-mail: joeshan@eircom.net

WATERFORD. Paul Walsh; 16 Castlepoint, Crosshaven, Co. Cork, e-mail: pmwalsh@waterfordbirds.com

WEXFORD. Tony Murray, Wexford Wildfowl Reserve, North Slob, e-mail: murraytony@hotmail.com

Bird Reports
IRISH BIRD REPORT, contact BirdWatch Ireland in National, Directory).

CAPE CLEAR BIRD OBSERVATORY ANNUAL REPORT, from the observatory.

CORK BIRD REPORT (1963-71; 1976-), Cork Bird Report Editorial Team, Long Strand, Castlefreke, Clonakilty, Co. Cork; e-mail: cbr@corkecology.net

EAST COAST BIRD REPORT (1980-), Contact BirdWatch Ireland.

BirdWatch Ireland Branches
Branches may be contacted in writing via BirdWatch Ireland HQ (see entry in National Directory).

Ringing Groups
CAPE CLEAR B.O, Steve Wing, e-mail: steve.ccbo@gmail.com

GREAT SALTEE RINGING STATION, Mr O J Merne, 20 Cuala Road, Bray, Co Wicklow, Ireland, e-mail: omerne@eircom.net

MUNSTER RG, Mr K.P.C. Collins, Ballygambon, Lisronagh, Clonmel, County Tipperary, e-mail: kcsk@eircom.net

NATIONAL DIRECTORY

Want to make a contribution to the nations's bird knowledge? If you have access to bird boxes then you can submit records to the BTO's Nest Record Scheme (see page 311).

NATIONAL ORGANISATIONS

After the title of each organisation you will see (in brackets) the year the group was founded and, where known, the current membership figure.

ARMY ORNITHOLOGICAL SOCIETY (1960; 200)

Open to serving and retired MoD employees who have an interest in their local MoD estate. Activities include field meetings, expeditions, the preparation of checklists of birds on Ministry of Defence property, conservation advice and an annual bird count. Annual journal *Adjutant*.
Contact: Maj AJ Bray RLC, www.aos-uk.com
e-mail: secretary@aos.org.uk

ASSOCIATION OF COUNTY RECORDERS AND EDITORS (1993; 120)

The basic aim of ACRE is to promote best practice in the business of producing county bird reports, in the work of Recorders and in problems arising in managing record systems and archives. Organises periodic conferences and publishes *newsACRE*.
Contact: The Secretary; e-mail: countyrec@cawos.org

ASSOCIATION FOR THE PROTECTION OF RURAL SCOTLAND (1926)

Works to protect Scotland's countryside from unnecessary or inappropriate development, recognising the needs of those who live and work there and the necessity of reconciling these with the sometimes competing requirements of recreational use.
Contact: Association for the Protection of Rural Scotland, Gladstone's Land, 3rd Floor, 483 Lawnmarket, Edinburgh EH1 2NT. 0131 225 7012; e-mail: info@ruralscotland.org
www.ruralscotland.btik.com

BARN OWL TRUST (1988)

A registered charity dedicated to conserving the Barn Owl and its environment and is the main source of Barn Owl information in the UK. The Trust's educational work began in 1989 and it now runs training courses for ecological consultants and planning officers. It carries out surveys of old buildings due for development, and advises on Barn Owl mitigation measures. A booklet *Barn Owls on Site*, a guide for developers and planners, published by English Nature, is widely used by local authorities and other official bodies.
Published research projects cover subjects such as the effect of barn conversions on Barn Owls, road mortality, the survival of released Barn Owls, rehabilitation and release methods, as well as county surveys. The Trust has erected over 2,000 nestboxes

is are closely involved in habitat creation both on its own land and through farm visits.
Contact: Barn Owl Trust, Waterleat, Ashburton, Devon TQ13 7HU. 01364 653 026;
e-mail: info@barnowltrust.org.uk
www.barnowltrust.org.uk

BIRD OBSERVATORIES COUNCIL (1970)

Aims to provide a forum for establishing closer links and co-operation between individual observatories and to help co-ordinate the work carried out by them. All accredited bird observatories affiliated to the Council undertake a ringing programme and provide ringing experience to those interested, most also provide accommodation for visiting birdwatchers.
Contact: Peter Howlett, Bird Observatories Council, c/o Dept of Biodiversity, National Museum Wales, Cardiff CF10 3NP. 0292 057 3233; (Fax) 0292 023 9009; e-mail: info@birdobscouncil.org.uk
www.birdobscouncil.org.uk

BIRD STAMP SOCIETY (1986; 220)

Quarterly journal *Flight* contains philatelic and ornithological articles. Lists all new issues and identifies species. Runs a quarterly Postal Auction; number of lots range from 400 to 800 per auction. UK subs £14 per annum from 1st August. Under-16s half price.
Contact: Mrs R Bradley, Bird Stamp Society, 31 Park View, Crossway Green, Chepstow NP16 5NA. 01291 625412; e-mail: bradley666@lycos.co.uk
www.birdstampsociety.org

BIRDWATCH IRELAND (1968; 14,000 with a network of 20 branches)

The largest independent conservation organisation in Ireland. Its primary objective is the protection of wild birds and their habitats in Ireland through the efforts of their staff, members and volunteers alike. It carries out extensive research and survey work, operates applied conservation projects and manages a network of reserves nationwide. It prepares and advocates policies and recruits, retains and services a growing membership base. It publishes *Wings* magazine and an annual journal *Irish Birds*.
Contact: BirdWatch Ireland, Unit 20, Block D, Bullford Business Campus, Kilcoole, Co. Wicklow, Ireland. +353 (0)1 2819878 353 (0)1 281 9878; Fax: +353 (0)1 281 0997; e-mail: info@birdwatchireland.org
www.birdwatchireland.ie

BRITISH BIRDS RARITIES COMMITTEE (1959)

The Committee adjudicates records of species of rare occurrence in Britain (marked `R' in the Log Charts) and publishes its annual report in *British Birds*. The BBRC also assesses records from the Channel Islands. In the case of rarities trapped for ringing, records should be sent to the Ringing Office of the British Trust for Ornithology, who will in turn forward them to the BBRC.

Contact: The Hon Secretary, British Birds Rarities Committee, e-mail: secretary@bbrc.org.uk www.bbrc.org.uk

BRITISH DRAGONFLY SOCIETY (1983; 1,604)

The BDS aims to promote the conservation and study of dragonflies. Members receive two issues of *Dragonfly News* and *BDS Journal* each year in spring and autumn. There are countrywide field trips, an annual members day and training is available on aspects of dragonfly ecology. The BDS has published a booklet, *Dig a Pond for Dragonflies* containing advice on pond creation and maintenance to attract dragonflies, also *Managing Habitats for Dragonflies* which is aimed at countryside managers.
Contact: Mr H Curry, Hon Secretary, British Dragonfly Society, 23 Bowker Way, Whittlesey, Cambs PE7 1PY. e-mail: bdssecretary@dragonflysoc.org.uk www.dragonflysoc.org.uk

BRITISH FALCONERS' CLUB (1927; 1,200)

Largest falconry club in Europe, with regional branches. Its aim is to encourage responsible falconers and conserve birds of prey by breeding, holding educational meetings and providing facilities, guidance and advice to those wishing to take up the sport. Publishes *The Falconer* annually and newsletter twice yearly.
Contact: British Falconers' Club, Westfield, Meeting Hill, Worstead, North Walsham, Norfolk NR28 9LS. 01692 404 057;
e-mail: admin@britishfalconersclub.co.uk www.britishfalconersclub.co.uk

BRITISH NATURALISTS' ASSOCIATION (1905)

The association, a registered charity, was founded to promote the interests of nature lovers and bring them together. Today, it encourages and supports schemes and legislation for the protection of the country's natural resources. It organises meetings, field weeks, lectures and exhibitions to help popularise the study of nature. BNA publishes two magazines and copies of *Country-Side* are available to non-members at some libraries.
Contact: General Secretary, BNA, PO Box 5682, Corby, Northants NN17 2ZW. 0844 892 1817; e-mail: info@bna-naturalists.org www.bna-naturalists.org

BRITISH ORNITHOLOGISTS' CLUB (1892; 450)

A registered charity, the Club's objects are 'the promotion of scientific discussion between those interested in ornithology, and to facilitate the publication of scientific information in connection with ornithology'. The Club maintains a special interest in avian systematics, taxonomy and distribution. Publishes the *Bulletin of the British Ornithologists' Club* quarterly, also (since 1992) a continuing series of occasional publications. About eight lecture dinner meetings are held each year.
Contact: BOC Office, British Ornithologists' Club, PO Box 417, Peterborough, PE7 3FX. (Tel/Fax) 01733 844 820; e-mail: boc.admin@bou.org.uk www.boc-online.org

BRITISH ORNITHOLOGISTS' UNION (1858; 1,250)

The BOU is one of the world's oldest and most respected ornithological societies. It aims to promote ornithology within the scientific and birdwatching communities, both in Britain and around the world. This is largely achieved by the publication of its  quarterly international journal, *Ibis* (1859-), featuring work at the cutting edge of our understanding of the world's birdlife. It also publishes an ongoing series of country/island group 'checklists' (24 titles to date – see BOU website for details) and operates an active programme of meetings, seminars and conferences. Work being undertaken around the world can include research projects that have received financial assistance from the BOU's ongoing programme of Ornithological Research Grants. Copies of journals and offprints received and books reviewed in *Ibis* are held as part of the Alexander Library in the Zoology Department of the University of Oxford (see Edward Grey Institute). The BOU Records Committee maintains the official British List (see below)
Contact: Steve Dudley, British Ornithologists' Union, PO Box 417, Peterborough, PE7 3FX. (Tel/Fax) 01733 844 820; e-mail: bou@bou.org.uk www.bou.org.uk, www.ibis.ac.uk and www.bouproc.net

BRITISH ORNITHOLOGISTS' UNION RECORDS COMMITTEE

A standing committee of the British Ornithologists' Union (BOU), the BOURC's function is to maintain the British List, the official list of birds recorded in Great Britain. The up-to-date list can be viewed on the BOU website. Where vagrants are involved it is concerned only with those which relate to potential additions to the British List (ie first records). In this it differs from the British Birds Rarities Committee (qv) in maintaining the British List, it also differs from the BBRC in that it examines, where necessary, important pre-1950 records, monitors introduced species for possible admission to or deletion from the List, and reviews taxonomy and nomenclature relating to the List. BOURC reports are published in *Ibis* and are also available via the BOU website. Decisions which affect the List are also announced direct to the birdwatching public via e-groups, web forums and the popular birdwatching press.
Contact: Steve Dudley, BOURC, PO Box 417, Peterborough, PE7 3FX. (Tel/Fax) 01733 844 820; e-mail: bourc@bou.org www.bou.org.uk

BRITISH TRUST FOR ORNITHOLOGY (1933; 13,500)

A registered charity governed by an elected Council, BTO has a rapidly growing membership and enjoys the support of a large number of county and local

birdwatching clubs and societies through the BTO/Bird Clubs Partnership. Its aims are: `To promote and encourage the wider understanding, appreciation and conservation of birds through scientific studies using the combined skills and enthusiasm of its members, other birdwatchers and staff.' Through the fieldwork of its members and other birdwatchers, the BTO is responsible for the majority of the monitoring of British birds, British bird population and their habitats. BTO surveys include the National Ringing Scheme, the Nest Record Scheme, the Breeding Bird Survey (in collaboration with JNCC and RSPB), and the Waterways Breeding Bird Survey, which all contribute to an integrated programme of population monitoring. The BTO also runs projects on the birds of farmland and woodland, also (in collaboration with WWT, RSPB and JNCC) the Wetland Bird Survey, in particular Low Tide Counts. Garden BirdWatch, which started in 1995, now has more than 15,000 participants. The Trust has 140 voluntary regional representatives (see County Directory) who organise fieldworkers for the BTO's programme of national surveys in which members participate. The results of these co-operative efforts are communicated to government departments, local authorities, industry and conservation bodies for effective action. For details of current activities see National Projects. Members receive *BTO News* six times a year and have the option of subscribing to the thrice-yearly journal, *Bird Study* and twice yearly *Ringing & Migration*. Local meetings are held in conjunction with bird clubs and societies; there are regional and national birdwatchers' conferences, and specialist courses in bird identification and modern censusing techniques. Grants are made for research, and members have the use of a lending and reference library at Thetford and the Alexander Library at the Edward Grey Institute of Field Ornithology (qv)
Contact: British Trust for Ornithology, The Nunnery, Thetford, Norfolk IP24 2PU. 01842 750 050; (Fax)01842 750 030; e-mail: info@bto.org www.bto.org

BTO SCOTLAND (2000; 989)
BTO Scotland's main functions are to promote the work of the Trust and develop wider coverage for surveys in Scotland, by encouraging greater participation in survey work. It also seeks to develop contract research income within Scotland. BTO Scotland ensures that the Trust's work is not just related to the priorities of the UK as a whole but is also focused on the priorities of Scotland, with a landscape and wildlife so different from the rest of the UK.
Contact: BTO Scotland, British Trust for Ornithology, School of Biological and Environmental Sciences,

Cottrell Building, University of Stirling, Stirling FK9 4LA. 01786 466 560 (Fax)01786 466 561; e-mail: scot.info@bto.org www.bto.org

BRITISH LIBRARY SOUND ARCHIVE - WILDLIFE SOUNDS (1969)
(Formerly BLOWS - British Library of Wildlife Sounds) The most comprehensive collection of bird sound recordings in existence: over 150,000 recordings of more than 8,000 species of birds worldwide, available for free listening. Copies or sonograms of most recordings can be supplied for private study or research and, subject to copyright clearance, for commercial uses. Contribution of new material and enquiries on all aspects of wildlife sounds and recording techniques are welcome. Publishes *Bioacoustics* journal, CD guides to bird songs and other wildlife, including ambience titles. Comprehensive catalogue available on-line at http://cadensa.bl.uk/uhtbin/cgisirsi/x/x/0/49/
Contact: Cheryl Tipp, Curator, Wildlife Sounds, The British Library Sound Archive, 96 Euston Road, London NW1 2DB. 020 7412 7403; (Fax) 020 7412 7441; e-mail: wildlifesound@bl.uk
www.bl.uk/reshelp/findhelprestype/sound/wildsounds/wildlife.html

BRITISH WATERFOWL ASSOCIATION

The BWA is an association of enthusiasts interested in keeping, breeding and conserving all types of waterfowl, including wildfowl and domestic ducks and geese. It is a registered charity, without trade affiliations, dedicated to educating the public about waterfowl and the need for conservation as well as to raising the standards of keeping and breeding ducks, geese and swans in captivity.
Contact: Mrs Sue Schubert, British Waterfowl Association, PO Box 163, Oxted, RH8 0WP. 01892 740 212; e-mail: info@waterfowl.org.uk
www.waterfowl.org.uk

BRITISH WILDLIFE REHABILITATION COUNCIL (1987)
Promoting the care and rehabilitation of wildlife casualties through the exchange of information between people such as rehabilitators, zoologists and veterinary surgeons who are active in this field. Organises an annual symposium or workshop. Publishes a regular newsletter. Supported by many national bodies including the Zoological Society of London, the British Veterinary Zoological Society, the RSPCA, the SSPCA, and the Vincent Wildlife Trust.
Contact: To make a contribution - Janet Peto, BWRC, PO Box 8686, Grantham, Lincolnshire NG31 0AG; e-mail: janet@bwrc.org.uk
www.bwrc.org.uk

NATIONAL ORGANISATIONS

BTCV (formerly British Trust for Conservation Volunteers) (1959)

BTCV's mission is to create a more sustainable future by inspiring people and improving places. It aims to enrich the lives of people, through volunteering opportunities, employment, improved health, and life skills development; to improve the biodiversity and local environment of 75,000 places and to support active citizenship in 5,000 community-based groups. BTCV currently supports 300,000 volunteers to take practical action to improve their urban and rural environments. Publishes a quarterly magazine, *Roots*, a series of practical handbooks and a wide range of other publications.
Contact: BTCV, Sedum House, Mallard Way, Doncaster DN4 8DB. 01302 388 883; e-mail: Information@btcv.org.uk www.btcv.org.uk

BTCV CYMRU

Contact: The Conservation Centre, BTCV Cymru, Forest Farm Road, Whitchurch, Cardiff, CF14 7JJ. 029 2052 0990; e-mail: wales@btcv.org.uk www.btcvcymru.org

BTCV SCOTLAND

Runs 7-14 day Action Breaks in Scotland during which participants undertake conservation projects; weekend training courses in environmental skills; midweek projects in Edinburgh, Glasgow, Aberdeen, Stirling and Inverness.
Contact: BTCV Scotland, Balallan House, 24 Allan Park, Stirling FK8 2QG. 01786 479 697; e-mail: scotland@btcv.org.uk www2.btcv.org.uk/display/btcv_scotland

BTCV NORTHERN IRELAND (1983)

Contact: Conservation Volunteers Northern Ireland, Beech House, 159 Ravenhill Road, Belfast BT6 0BP. 028 9064 5169; e-mail: CVNI@btcv.org.uk www.cvni.org

BUGLIFE – THE INVERTEBRATE CONSERVATION TRUST (2000)

The first organisation in Europe devoted to the conservation of all invertebrates, actively engaged in halting the extinction of Britain's rarest slugs, snails, bees, wasps, ants, spiders, beetles and many more. It is working to achieve this through practical conservation projects; promoting the environmental importance of invertebrates  and raising awareness about the challenges to their survival; assisting in the development of helpful legislation and policy and encouraging and supporting invertebrate conservation initiatives by other organisations in the UK, Europe and worldwide.
Contact: Buglife (ICT), 1st Floor, 90 Bridge Street, Peterborough PE1 1DY. 01733 201 210; e-mail: info@buglife.org.uk www.buglife.org.uk

CAMPAIGN FOR THE PROTECTION OF RURAL WALES (1928; 2,800)

Its aims are to help the conservation and enhancement of the landscape, environment and amenities of the countryside, towns and villages of rural Wales and to form and educate opinion to ensure the promotion of its objectives. It gives advice and information upon matters affecting protection, conservation and improvement of the visual environment.
Contact: Ty Gwyn, 31 High Street, Welshpool, Powys SY21 7YD. 01938 552 525 or 01938 556 212; e-mail: info@cprwmail.org.uk www.cprw.org.uk

CENTRE FOR ECOLOGY & HYDROLOGY (CEH)

The work of the CEH, a component body of the Natural Environment Research Council, includes a range of ornithological research, covering population studies, habitat management and work on the effects of pollution. The CEH has a long-term programme to monitor pesticide and pollutant residues in the corpses of predatory birds sent in by birdwatchers, and carries out detailed studies on affected species. The Biological Records Centre (BRC), which is part of the CEH, is responsible for the national biological data bank on plant and animal distributions (except birds).
Contact: Centre for Ecology & Hydrology, Maclean Building, Crowmarsh Gifford, Wallingford, Oxfordshire OX10 8BB. 01491 692 371.
E-mail: enquiries@ceh.ac.uk www.ceh.ac.uk

CONSERVATION FOUNDATION (1982)

Created by David Bellamy and David Shreeve to provide a means for people in public, private and not-for-profit sectors to collaborate on environmental causes. Over the years its programme has included award schemes, conferences, promotions, special events, field studies, school programmes, media work, seminars and workshops etc. The Conservation Foundation has created and managed environmental award schemes of all kinds including the Ford European Awards, The Trust House Forte Community Chest, The PA Golden Leaf Awards, The Co-op Save Our Species Awards, the Pollution Abatement Technology Awards and many others. For information about how to apply for current award schemes visit the website.
Contact: Conservation Foundation, 1 Kensington Gore, London SW7 2AR. 020 7591 3111; e-mail: info@conservationfoundation.co.uk www.conservationfoundation.co.uk

COUNTRY LAND AND BUSINESS ASSOCIATION (1907; 36,000)

The CLA is at the heart of rural life and is the voice of the countryside for England and Wales, campaigning on issues which directly affect those who live and work in rural communities. Its members, ranging from some of the largest landowners, with interests in forest, moorland, water and agriculture, to some with little more than a paddock or garden, together

NATIONAL ORGANISATIONS

manage 50% of the countryside.
Contact: Country Land and Business Association, 16 Belgrave Square, London, SW1X 8PQ. 020 7235 0511; e-mail: mail@cla.org.uk
www.cla.org.uk

COUNTRYSIDE COUNCIL FOR WALES
The Government's statutory adviser on wildlife, countryside and maritime conservation matters in Wales and the executive authority for the conservation of habitats and wildlife. CCW champions the environment and landscapes of Wales and its coastal waters as sources of natural and cultural riches, as a foundation for economic and social activity, and as a place for leisure and learning opportunities.
Contact: Countryside Council for Wales, Maes-y-Ffynnon, Penrhosgarnedd, Bangor, Gwynedd LL57 2DL, 0845 1306 229; e-mail: enquiries@ccw.gov.uk
www.ccw.gov.uk

CPRE (formerly Council for the Protection of Rural England) (1926; 60,000)
Patron HM The Queen. CPRE now has 43 county branches and 200 local groups. It highlights threats to the countryside and promotes positive solutions. In-depth research supports active campaigning, and through reasoned argument and lobbying, CPRE seeks to influence public opinion and decision-makers at every level. Membership open to all.
Contact: CPRE National Office, 128 Southwark Street, London SE1 0SW. 020 7981 2800;
e-mail: info@cpre.org.uk www.cpre.org.uk

DEPARTMENT OF THE ENVIRONMENT FOR NORTHERN IRELAND
Responsible for the declaration and management of National Nature Reserves, the declaration of Areas of Special Scientific Interest, the administration of Wildlife Refuges, the classification of Special Protection Areas under the EC Birds Directive, the designation of Special Areas of Conservation under the EC Habitats Directive and the designation of Ramsar sites under the Ramsar Convention. It administers the Nature Conservation and Amenity Lands (Northern Ireland) Order 1985, the Wildlife (Northern Ireland) Order 1985, the Game Acts and the Conservation (Natural Habitats, etc) Regulations (NI) 1995 and the Environment (Northern Ireland) Order 2002.
Contact: Environment and Heritage Service, Klondyke Building, Cromac Avenue, Gasworks Business Park, Lower Ormeau Road, Belfast BT7 2JA. 0845 302 0008; (pollution hotline; 0800 807 060);
e-mail: nieainfo@doeni.gov.uk www.ehsni.gov.uk

DISABLED BIRDER'S ASSOCIATION (2000; 700)
The DBA is a registered charity and international movement, which aims to promote access to reserves and other birding places and to a range of services, so that people with different needs can follow the birding obsession as freely as able-bodied people. Membership is currently free and new members

are needed to help give a stronger message across to those who own and manage nature reserves to improve access when they are planning and improving facilities. DBA also seeks to influence those who provide birdwatching services and equipment. The DBA also runs overseas trips. Chairman, Bo Beolens.
Contact: The Membership Secretary, Margaret Read MBE, Disabled Birder's Association, 121 Lavernock Road, Penarth, Vale of Glamorgan CF64 3QG; e-mail: bo@fatbirder.com
www.disabledbirdersassociation.co.uk

EARTHWATCH INSTITUTE (1971)
Earthwatch developed the innovative idea of engaging the general public into the scientific process by bringing together individual volunteers and scientists on field research projects, thereby providing an alternative means of funding, as well as a dedicated labour force for field scientists. Last year, more than 3,500 volunteers had worked on Earthwatch projects, which have grown to 140 projects in over 50 countries around the world.
Contact: Earthwatch Institute (Europe), Mayfield House, 256 Banbury Road, Oxford 0X2 7DE. 01864 318 838; e-mail: info@earthwatch.co.uk
www.earthwatch.org/europe

EDWARD GREY INSTITUTE OF FIELD ORNITHOLOGY (1938)
The EGI takes its name from Edward Grey, first Viscount Grey of Fallodon, a life-long lover of birds and former Chancellor of the University of Oxford, who gave his support to an appeal for its foundation capital. The Institute now has a permanent research staff; it usually houses some 12-15 research students, five or six senior visitors and post-doctoral research workers. Field research is carried out mainly in Wytham Woods near Oxford and on the island of Skomer in West Wales. In addition there are laboratory facilities and aviary space for experimental work. The Institute houses the Alexander Library, one of the largest collections of 20th Century material on birds in the world and which is supported by the British Ornithologists Union which provides much of the material. It also houses the British Falconers Club library. The Library is open to members of the BOU and Oxford Ornithological Society; other bona fide ornithologists may use the library by prior arrangement.
Contact: Claire Harvey, PA to Professor Sheldon, The EGI, Department of Zoology, South Parks Road, Oxford OX1 3PS; +44(0)1865 271 275;
e-mail: claire.harvey@zoo.ox.ac.uk
www.zoo.ox.ac.uk/egi/

ENVIRONMENT AGENCY
A non-departmental body that aims to protect and improve the environment and to contribute towards the delivery of sustainable development through the integrated management of air, land and

water. Functions include pollution prevention and control, waste minimisation, management of water resources, flood defence, improvement of salmon and freshwater fisheries, conservation of aquatic species, navigation and use of inland and coastal waters for recreation. Sponsored by the Department of the Environment, Transport and the Regions, MAFF and the Welsh Office.

Contact: Environment Agency, National Customer Contact Centre, PO Box 544, Rotherham S60 1BY. General enquiries; 08708 506 506 (Mon-Fri, 8am - 6pm); pollution hotline 0800 807 060; floodline 0845 988 1188.

e-mail: enquiries@environment-agency.gov.uk
www.environment-agency.gov.uk

FARMING AND WILDLIFE ADVISORY GROUP (FWAG) (1969)

An independent UK-registered charity led by farmers and supported by government and leading countryside organisations. Its aim is to unite farming and forestry with wildlife and landscape conservation. Active in most UK counties. There are 120 Farm Conservation Advisers who give practical advice to farmers and landowners to help them integrate environmental objectives with commercial farming practices.

Contact: *English Head Office*, FWAG, National Agricultural Centre, Stoneleigh, Kenilworth, Warwickshire CV8 2RX. 02476 696 699;
e-mail: info@fwag.org.uk www.fwag.org.uk

Northern Ireland, FWAG, National Agricultural Centre, 46b Rainey Street, Magherafelt, Co. Derry BT45 5AH. 028 7930 0606;
e-mail: n.ireland@fwag.org.uk

Scottish Head Office, FWAG Scotland, 024 7669 6699;
e-mail: info@fwag.org.uk

Wales Head Office. FWAG Cymru, C/o Countryside Council For Wales, Eden House, Ithon Road, Llandrindod Wells, Powys LD1 6AS. 01341 421 456;
e-mail: helen.barnes@fwag.org.uk.

FIELD STUDIES COUNCIL (1943)

Manages Centres where students from schools, universities and colleges, as well as individuals of all ages, can stay to study various aspects of the environment under expert guidance. Courses include many for birdwatchers, providing opportunities to study birdlife on coasts, estuaries, mountains and islands. Others demonstrate bird ringing and others are for members of the BTO. Research workers and naturalists wishing to use the records and resources are welcome.

There are centres in England, Scotland, Wales and Northern Ireland, see website for contact details and courses available.

Contact: Field Studies Council, Preston Montford,

Montford Bridge, Shrewsbury SY4 1HW. 0845 345 4071; 01743 852 100; www.field-studies-council.orge-mail: enquiries@field-studies-council.org

FIELDFARE TRUST

A registered charity, Fieldfare works with people with disabilities and countryside managers to improve access to the countryside for everyone. It provides advice and training services to countryside management teams, supported by its research into national standards for accessibility under the BT Countryside for All Project. For members of the public it runs projects which can enable them to take action locally, provide information on accessible places to visit and run events like the Fieldfare Kielder Challenge which encourages young people to get active in the countryside.

Contact: Fieldfare Trust, Volunteer House, 69 Crossgate, Cupar, Fife KY15 5AS. 01334 657 708;
e-mail: info@fieldfare.org.uk www.fieldfare.org.uk

FORESTRY COMMISSION OF GREAT BRITAIN

The government department responsible for the protection and expansion of Britain's forests and woodlands, it runs from national offices in England, Wales and Scotland, working to targets set by Commissioners and Ministers in each of the three countries. Its objectives are to protect Britain's forests and resources, conserve and improve the biodiversity, landscape and cultural heritage of forests and woodlands, develop opportunities for woodland recreation and increase public understanding and community participation in forestry.

Contact: *Forestry Commission GB Functions*, 231 Corstorphine Road, Edinburgh EH12 7AT. 0131 334 0303; e-mail: enquiries@forestry.gsi.gov.uk
www.forestry.gov.uk

Forestry Commission England, England National Office, 620 Bristol Business Park, Coldharbour Lane, Bristol BS16 1EJ. 0117 906 6000;
e-mail: fcengland@forestry.gsi.gov.uk

Forestry Commission Scotland, 231 Corstorphine Road, Edinburgh EH12 7AT. 0131 334 0303, (Fax) 0131 314 6152; e-mail: fcscotland@forestry.gsi.gov.uk

Forestry Commission Wales, Welsh Assembly Government, Rhodfa Padarn, Llanbadarn Fawr, Aberystwyth, Ceredigion SY23 3UR. 0300 068 0300.e-mail: fcwenquiries@forestry.gsi.gov.uk

FRIENDS OF THE EARTH (1971; 100,000)

The largest international network of environmental groups in the world, represented in 68 countries. In the UK it has a unique network of campaigning local groups, working in 200 communities in England, Wales and Northern Ireland. It is largely funded by supporters with more than 90% of income coming from individual donations, the rest from special fundraising events, grants and trading.

Contact: Friends of the Earth, 26-28 Underwood Street, London, N1 7JQ. 020 7490 1555;
e-mail: info@foe.co.uk www.foe.co.uk

GAME CONSERVANCY TRUST (1933; 22,000)

A registered charity which researches the conservation of game and other wildlife in the British countryside. More than 60 scientists are engaged in detailed work on insects, pesticides, birds (30 species inc. raptors) mammals (inc. foxes), and habitats. The results are used to advise government, landowners, farmers and conservationists on practical management techniques which will benefit game species, their habitats, and wildlife. Each June the *Annual Review* lists about 50 papers published in the peer-reviewed scientific press.

Contact: Game Conservancy Trust, Burgate Manor, Fordingbridge, Hampshire, SP6 1EF. 01425 652 381; e-mail: info@gct.org.uk www.gct.org.uk

GAY BIRDERS CLUB (1994; 300+)

A voluntary society for lesbian, gay and bisexual birdwatchers, their friends and supporters, over the age of consent, in the UK and worldwide. The club has a network of regional contacts and organises day trips, weekends and longer events at notable birding locations in the UK and abroad; about 200+ events in a year. Members receive a quarterly newletter *Out Birding* with details of all events. There is a Grand Get-Together every 18 months. Membership £12 waged and £5 unwaged.

Contact: Gay Birders Club, GeeBeeCee, BCM-Mono, London WC1N 3XX. e-mail: contact@gbc-online.org.uk www.gbc-online.org.uk

GOLDEN ORIOLE GROUP (1987; 15)

Organises censuses of breeding Golden Orioles in parts of Cambridgeshire, Norfolk and Suffolk. Maintains contact with a network of individuals in other parts of the country where Orioles may or do breed. Studies breeding biology, habitat and food requirements of the species.

Contact: Golden Oriole Group, 5 Bury Lane, Haddenham, Ely, Cambs CB6 3PR. 01353 740 540; www.goldenoriolegroup.org.uk

HAWK AND OWL TRUST (1969)

Registered charity dedicated to the conservation and appreciation of wild birds of prey and their habitats. Publishes a newsletter *Peregrine* and educational materials for all ages.The Trust achieves its major aim of creating and enhancing nesting, roosting and feeding habitats for birds of prey through projects which involve practical research, creative conservation and education, both on its own reserves and in partnership with landowners, farmers and others. Members are invited to take part in fieldwork, population studies, surveys, etc. The Trust manages three main reserves: Sculthorpe Moor in Norfolk; Shapwick Moor on the Somerset Levels; and Fylingdales Moor conservation area in North Yorkshire. Its Sculthorpe reserve near Fakenham, Norfolk and National Conservation and Education

Centre at Chiltern Open Air Museum near Chalfont St Giles, Buckinghamshire, offer schools and other groups cross-curricular environmental activities

Contact: Hawk and Owl Trust, PO Box 100, Taunton TA4 2WX. Tel: 0844 984 2824; e-mail: enquiries@hawkandowl.org www.hawkandowl.org

INTERNATIONAL CENTRE FOR BIRDS OF PREY (1967)

The ICBP works for the conservation of birds of prey and their habitats through public education, captive breeding, treatment and rehabilitation of injured wild birds of prey. Conducts research for understanding health and the conservation of all birds of prey. The Centre is open to the general public for 10 months of the year. It also undertakes more in-depth education to specific groups and parties, from first schools to universities and offers off-site lectures and teaching. The Centre continues its captive breeding aims; to research species; breed from species not previously understood; provide teaching and written information for captive breeding programmes at home and abroad; maintain the Collection and provide birds for demonstrations, both in the UK and further afield. It undertakes and encourages non-invasive research with the Collection, working with colleges and universities to provide access to the birds for projects and papers. The Centre also works with the National Birds of Prey Trust and the National Aviary Pittsburgh, BNHS and many other groups and facilities to continue to support worldwide field research projects, undertakes international conservation programmes and accepts and treats and rehabilitates injured wild birds of prey. Open all year 10.30am-5.30pm (or dusk if earlier) Closed Christmas Day and Boxing Day.

Contact: International Birds of Prey Centre, Boulsdon House, Newent, Gloucestershire, GL18 1JJ. 01531 820 286 or 01531 821 581; e-mail: jpj@icbp.org www.nbpc.co.uk

IRISH RARE BIRDS COMMITTEE (1985)

Assesses records of species of rare occurrence in the Republic of Ireland. Details of records accepted and rejected are incorporated in the *Irish Bird Report*, published annually in *Irish Birds*. In the case of rarities trapped for ringing, ringers in the Republic of Ireland are required to send their schedules initially to the National Parks and Wildlife Service, 51 St Stephen's Green, Dublin 2. A copy is then taken before the schedules are sent to the British Trust for Ornithology.

Contact: Secretary: Kieran Fahy, Silveracre, Yoletown, Tacumshin, County Wexford. e-mail: secretary@irbc.ie www.irbc.ie

JOINT NATURE CONSERVATION COMMITTEE (1990)

A committee of the three country agencies (Natural England, Scottish Natural Heritage and the Countryside Council for Wales), together with independent members and representatives from Northern Ireland and the Countryside Agency. Supported by specialist staff, its statutory responsibilities include the establishment of common standards for monitoring, the analysis of information and research; advising Ministers on the development and implementation of policies for or affecting nature conservation; and the undertaking and commissioning of research relevant to these functions. JNCC additionally has the UK responsibility for relevant European and wider international matters. The Species Team, located at the HQ address, is responsible for terrestrial bird conservation.
Contact: Joint Nature Conservation Committee, Monkstone House, City Road, Peterborough PE1 1JY. 01733 562 626; e-mail: comment@jncc.gov.uk
www.jncc.gov.uk

LINNEAN SOCIETY OF LONDON (1788, 2,000)

Named after Carl Linnaeus, the 18th Century Swedish biologist who created the modern system of scientific biological nomenclature, the Society promotes all aspects of pure and applied biology. It houses Linnaeus' collection of plants, insects and fishes, library and correspondence. The Society has a major reference library of some 100,000 volumes. Publishes the *Biological, Botanical* and *Zoological Journals*, and the *Synopses of the British Fauna*.
Contact: Linnean Society of London, Burlington House, Piccadilly, London W1J 0BF. 020 7434 4479; e-mail: info@linnean.org
www.linnean.org

MAMMAL SOCIETY (1954; 2,500)

 The Mammal Society is the only organisation solely dedicated to the study and conservation of all British mammals. It seeks to raise awareness of mammal ecology and conservation needs, to survey British mammals and their habitats to identify the threats they face and to to promote mammal studies in the UK and overseas.
Contact: The Mammal Society, 3 The Carronades, New Road, Southampton SO14 0AA. 0238 0237 874; e-mail: enquiries@mammal.org.uk
www.mammal.org.uk

MARINE CONSERVATION SOCIETY (1983)

MCS is the UK charity that campaigns for clean seas and beaches around the British coastline, sustainable fisheries, and protection for all marine life. MCS is consulted on a wide range of marine issues and provides advice primarily to government. but also to industry, on topics ranging from offshore wind and oil and gas to marine strategies and fisheries reform. It provides advice to ensure that further action is taken to conserve our seas and reduce the effect of marine activities on marine habitats and species. It has an extensive programme for volunteers, ranging from fund-raising and an annual clean-up of UK beaches to surveys of species such as basking shark.
Contact: Marine Conservation Society, Unit 3 Wolf Business Park, Alton Road, Ross-on-Wye, Herefordshire HR9 5NB. 01989 566 017.
www.mcsuk.org

NATIONAL TRUST (1895; 3.5 million)

Charity that works for the preservation of places of historic interest or natural beauty in England, Wales and Northern Ireland. It relies on 3.5 million members, 49,000 volunteers, 500,000 schoolchildren and millions of visitors, donors and supporters. The Trust protects and opens to the public more than 300 historic houses and gardens, 49 industrial monuments and mills, plus more than 617,500 acres of land and 700 miles of coast. About 10% of SSSIs and ASSIs in England, Wales and Northern Ireland are wholly or partially owned by the Trust, as are 63 NNRs (e.g. Blakeney Point, Wicken Fen, Murlough and Dinefwr Estate), 33% of Ramsar sites include Trust land as do 45% of SPAs.
Contact: Central Office: Heelis, Kemble Drive, Swindon, Wiltshire SN2 2NA. Tel: 01793 817 400. Membership enquiries: National Trust, PO Box 39, Warrington, WA5 7WD. 0844 800 1895; e-mail: enquiries@thenationaltrust.org.uk
www.thenationaltrust.org.uk

NATIONAL TRUST FOR SCOTLAND (1931; 310,000)

The conservation charity that protects and promotes Scotland's natural and cultural heritage for present and future generations to enjoy. Its 128 properties open to the public are described in its annual *Scotland For You* guide.
Contact: National Trust for Scotland, Wemyss House, 28 Charlotte Square, Edinburgh, EH2 4ET. 0844 493 2100; e-mail: information@nts.org.uk
www.nts.org.uk

NATURAL ENGLAND

Natural England has been formed by bringing together English Nature, the landscape, access and recreation elements of the Countryside Agency and the environmental land management functions of the Rural Development Service. Natural England is working towards the delivery of four strategic outcomes:
• A healthy natural environment through conservation and enhancement.
• Encouraging more people to enjoy, understand and act to improve the natural environment, more often.
• Ensure the use and management of the natural environment is more sustainable.
• A secure environmental future.
Contact: Natural England, Northminster House, Peterborough, PE1 1UA. 0845 600 3078; e-mail: enquiries@naturalengland.org.uk
www.naturalengland.org.uk

NATURAL HISTORY MUSEUM AT TRING (1937)

Founded by Lionel Walter (later Lord) Rothschild, the Museum displays British and exotic birds (1,500 species) including many rarities and extinct species. Galleries open all year except 24-26 Dec. Adjacent to the Bird Group of the Natural History Museum — with over a million specimens and an extensive ornithological library, an internationally important centre for bird research.
Contact: The Natural History Museum at Tring, Akeman Street, Tring, Herts HP23 6AP. 020 7942 6171; e-mail: tring-enquiries@nhm.ac.uk www.nhm.ac.uk/tring

NATURE PHOTOGRAPHERS' PORTFOLIO (1944; 74)

A society for photographers of wildlife, especially birds. Circulates postal portfolios of prints and transparencies and an on-line folio.
Contact: A Winspear-Cundall, Hon Secretary, Nature Photographers' Portfolio, 8 Gig Bridge Lane, Pershore, Worcs WR10 1NH. 01386 552 103; e-mail: arthurcundall@hotmail.co.uk www.nature-photographers-portfolio.co.uk

NORTHERN IRELAND BIRDWATCHERS' ASSOCIATION (1991; 120)

The NIBA Records Committee, established in 1997, has full responsibility for the assessment of records in N Ireland. NIBA also publishes the *Northern Ireland Bird Report* and is responsible for Flightline, a local rate telephone hotline for rare bird sightings.
Contact: The Membership Secretary, Northern Ireland Birdwatchers' Assoc, 9 Ballymacash Rd, Lisburn, Co. Antrim, N Ireland BT28 3DX . 01247 467 408; e-mail: andrew.crory@gmail.com http://nibirds.blogspot.com

NORTHERN IRELAND ORNITHOLOGISTS' CLUB (1965; 150)

Formed to focus the interests of active birdwatchers in Northern Ireland, it operates Tree Sparrow and Barn Owl nestbox schemes and a winter feeding programme for Yellowhammers. Has a regular programme of lectures and field trips for members and organises a high quality annual photographic competition. Publishes *The Harrier* quarterly.
Contact: The Honorary Secretary, C Gillespie, Northern Ireland Ornithologists Club, 4 Demesne Gate, Saintfield, Co. Down, BT24 7BE. 02897 519 371; www.nioc.co.uk

NORTH SEA BIRD CLUB (1979; 200)

The stated aims of the Club are to: provide a recreational pursuit for people employed offshore; obtain, collate and analyse observations of all birds seen offshore; produce reports of observations, including an annual report; promote the collection of data on other wildlife offshore. Currently it holds in excess of 100,000 records of birds, cetaceans and insects reported since 1979.
Contact: The North Sea Bird Club, Ocean Laboratory

and Culterty Field Station, University of Aberdeen, Newburgh, Aberdeenshire AB41 6AA. 01224 274 428; e-mail: nsbc@abdn.ac.uk www.abdn.ac.uk/nsbc

PEOPLE'S DISPENSARY FOR SICK ANIMALS (1917)

Registered charity. Provides free veterinary treatment for sick and injured animals whose owners qualify for this charitable service.
Contact: PDSA, Whitechapel Way, Priorslee, Telford, Shropshire TF2 9PQ. 01952 290 999; e-mail: pr@pdsa.org.uk www.pdsa.org.uk

POND CONSERVATION

Pond Conservation is the national charity dedicated to creating and protecting ponds and the wildlife they support. It carries out research, surveys and practical conservation, working in partnership with others, and also works to protect the wildlife of other freshwaters. Key projects include: Million Ponds Project, an ambitious scheme to dig half a million new high-quality potential ponds in the UK that will be good for biodiversity; Garden ponds survey to find out what really lives in the UK's garden ponds; Pond Habitat Action Plan, in conjunction with the Environment Agency.
Contact: Pond Conservation, 01865 483 249; e-mail: info@pondconservation.org.uk www.pondconservation.org.uk

RAPTOR FOUNDATION (1989)

Involved in the care of wild disabled birds of prey, as well as raptors rescued from breeders. The foundation is involved in research into raptor ailments and assists veterinary schools with placement of student vets at the centre. A full 24 hour rescue service is available for injured raptors and owls and the centre assists in breed-and-release schemes to rebuild populations across Europe. Centre is open to the public (200 birds of 40 different species on display) 10am to 5pm each day apart from Jan 1 and Dec 25/26.
Contact: The Raptor Foundation, The Heath, St Ives Road, Woodhurst, Cambs PE28 3BT. 01487 741 140; e-mail: heleowl@aol.com www.raptorfoundation.org.uk

RAPTOR RESCUE (1978)

Since inauguration, Raptor Rescue has evolved into one of the UK's foremost organisations dedicated to ensuring all sick and injured birds of prey are cared for in heated hospital units by suitably qualified people, and wherever possible, released back into the wild. Facilities include secluded aviaries, rehabilitation aviaries/flights, foster birds for rearing young to avoid imprinting. Veterinary support. Reg charity.
Contact: Raptor Rescue, Bird of Prey Rehabilitation, 0870 241 0609; www.raptorrescue.org.uk e-mail: secretary@raptorrescue.org.uk

RARE BREEDING BIRDS PANEL (1973; 7)

An independent body funded by the JNCC and RSPB. Both bodies are represented on the panel, as are BTO and ACRE. It collects all information on rare

Rare Breeding Birds Panel

breeding birds in the United Kingdom, so that changes in status can be monitored as an aid to conservation and stored for posterity. Special forms are used (obtainable free from the secretary and the website) and records should be submitted via the county and regional recorders. Since 1996 the Panel also monitors breeding by scarcer non-native species and seeks records of these in the same way. Annual report is published in *British Birds*. For details of species covered by the Panel see Log Charts and the websites.
Contact: The Secretary, Rare Breeding Birds Panel, The Old Orchard, Grange Road, North Berwick, East Lothian EH39 4QT. 01620 894 037; e-mail: secretary@rbbp.org.uk www.rbbp.org.uk

ROYAL AIR FORCE ORNITHOLOGICAL SOCIETY (1965; 250)
RAFOS organises regular field meetings for members, carries out ornithological census work on MoD properties and mounts major expeditions annually to various UK and overseas locations. Publishes a Newsletter twice a year, a Journal annually, and reports on its expeditions and surveys.
Contact: General Secretary; www.rafos.org.uk
e-mail: rafos_secretary@hotmail.com

ROYAL NAVAL BIRDWATCHING SOCIETY (1946; 250 approx)
Covering all main ocean routes, the Society has a system for reporting the positions and identity of seabirds and landbirds at sea by means of standard sea report forms. Maintains an extensive worldwide seabird database. Members are encouraged to photograph birds and a library of images is maintained. Publishes a Bulletin and an annual report entitled *The Sea Swallow*. The Simpson Scholarship provides assistance to embryonic ornithologists for studies regarding seabirds and landbirds at sea.
Contact: General Secretary, CPO Steve Copsey (temporary position); by e-mail: copsey@tesco.net
www.rnbws.org.uk

ROYAL PIGEON RACING ASSOCIATION (1897; 39,000)
Exists to promote the sport of pigeon racing and controls pigeon racing within the Association. Organises liberation sites, issues rings, calculates distances between liberation sites and home lofts, and assists in the return of strays. May be able to assist in identifying owners of ringed birds caught or found.
Contact: Royal Pigeon Racing Association, The Reddings, Cheltenham, GL51 6RN. 01452 713 529;
www.rpra.org

ROYAL SOCIETY FOR THE PREVENTION OF CRUELTY TO ANIMALS (1824; 43,690)
In addition to its animal centres, the Society also runs a woodland study centre and nature reserve at Mallydams Wood in East Sussex and specialist wildlife rehabilitation centres at West Hatch, Taunton, Somerset TA3 5RT (0870 0101847), at Station Road, East Winch, King's Lynn, Norfolk PE32 1NR (0870

9061420), and London Road, Stapeley, Nantwich, Cheshire CW5 7JW (not open to the public). Inspectors are contacted through their National Communication Centre, which can be reached via the Society's 24-hour national cruelty and advice line: 08705 555 999.
Contact: RSPCA Headquarters, Willberforce Way, Horsham, West Sussex RH13 9RS. 0300 1234 555; 24-hour cruelty and advice line: 0300 1234 999.
www.rspca.org.uk

ROYAL SOCIETY FOR THE PROTECTION OF BIRDS (1899 1,000,000+)
UK Partner of BirdLife International, and Europe's largest voluntary wildlife conservation body. The RSPB, a registered charity, is governed by an elected body (see also RSPB Phoenix and RSPB Wildlife Explorers) Its work in the conservation of wild birds and habitats covers the acquisition and management of nature reserves; research and surveys; monitoring and responding to development proposals, land use practices and pollution which threaten wild birds and biodiversity; and the provision of an advisory service on wildlife law enforcement.

The RSPB currently manages 200 nature reserves in the UK, covering almost 130,00 hectares and home to 80% of Britain's rarest or most threatened bird species. The aim is to conserve a countrywide network of reserves with all examples of the main bird communities and with due regard to the conservation of plants and other animals.

Current national projects include extensive work on agriculture, and conservation and campaigning for the conservation of the marine environment and to halt the illegal persecution of birds of prey. Increasingly, there is involvement with broader environmental concerns such as climate change and transport.

The RSPB's International Dept works closely with Birdlife International and its partners in other countries and is involved with numerous projects overseas, especially in Europe and Asia.
Contact: RSPB, The Lodge, Sandy, Beds SG19 2DL. Membership enquiries: 01767 693 680. Wildlife enquiries: 01767 693 690; www.rspb.org.uk
e-mail: (firstname.name)@rspb.org.uk

Regional Offices:
ENGLAND
Eastern England, Stalham House, 65 Thorpe Road, Norwich NR1 1UD. 01603 661 662.
Covers: Beds, Cambs, Essex, Herts, Lincs, Norfolk, Suffolk.

London Office, RSPB London Office, 2nd Floor, 65 Petty France, London, SW1H 9EU. 0207 808 1240.

Midlands, 46 The Green, South Bar, Banbury, Oxfordshire, OX16 9AB. 01295 253 330.
Covers: Bucks, Derbys, Herefordshire, Leicestershire, Northants, Notts, Oxon, Rutland, Shropshire, Staffs, Warwickshire, West Midlands, Worcestershire.

Northern England, Denby Dale Office, Westleigh Mews, Wakefield Road, Denby Dale, Huddersfield,

HD8 8QD. 01484 861 148.
Covers: Cheshire, Cleveland, Cumbria, East Riding of Yorkshire, Greater Manchester, Lancashire, Merseyside, Middlesbrough, North, South and West Yorkshire, North East and North Lincolnshire, Northumberland, Tyne and Wear.

South East, 2nd Floor, 42 Frederick Place, Brighton, East Sussex, BN1 4EA. 01273 775 333.
Covers: East Sussex, Hampshire, Isle of Wight, Kent, Surrey, West Berkshire, West Sussex.

South West, Keble House, Southernhay Gardens, Exeter EX1 1NT. 01392 432 691.
Covers: Bristol, Cornwall, Devon, Dorset, Somerset, Gloucs, Wiltshire.

SCOTLAND
Scotland Headquarters, Dunedin House, 25 Ravelston Terrace, Edinburgh, EH4 3TP. 0131 311 6500.
e-mail: rspb.scotland@rspb.org.uk

East Scotland, 10 Albyn Terrace, Aberdeen, Aberdeenshire, AB10 1YP. 01224 624 824.
Covers: Aberdeen, Aberdeenshire, Angus, Moray, Perth and Kinross.

North Scotland, Etive House, Beechwood Park, Inverness, IV2 3BW. 01463 715 000;
e-mail: nsro@rspb.org.uk
Covers: Eilean Siar, Highland.

South and West Scotland, 10 Park Quadrant, Glasgow, G3 6BS. 0141 331 0993;
e-mail: glasgow@rspb.org.uk
Covers: Argyll and Bute, Clackmannanshire, Dumfries and Galloway, East Ayrshire, East Lothian, East Dunbartonshire, East Renfrewshire, Midlothian, North Ayrshire, North Lanarkshire, Renfrewshire, Scottish borders, South Ayrshire, South Lanarkshire, Stirling, West Dunbartonshire, West Lothian.

WALES
RSPB Wales, Sutherland House, Castlebridge, Cowbridge Road East, Cardiff CF11 9AB. 029 2035 3000.

NORTHERN IRELAND
Northern Ireland Headquarters, Belvoir Park Forest, Belfast, BT8 7QT. 028 9049 1547.
Covers: County Antrim,County Armagh, County Down, County Fermanagh, County Londonderry, County Tyrone.

RSPB WILDLIFE EXPLORERS and RSPB PHOENIX (formerly YOC) (1965; 168,000)
Junior section of the RSPB. There are more than 100 groups run by 300 volunteers. Activities include projects, holidays, roadshows, competitions, and local events for children, families and teenagers. Phoenix members (13 years and over) receive *BirdLife* magazine every two months, plus *Wingbeat* – the only environmental magazine written by teenagers for teenagers – four times a year.
Contact: The Youth Manager, RSPB Youth and Education Dept, The Lodge, Sandy, Beds SG19 2DL. 01767 680 551; e-mail: explorers@rspb.org.uk and phoenix@rspb.org.uk www.rspb.org.uk/youth

SAVE OUR SEABIRDS CHARITABLE TRUST (1988)
Founded following an oil spill which resulted in oiled birds being washed ashore in SE England, it now has two functions:1) to rescue and support the rescue of seabirds injured by pollution and 2) to raise awareness of the pollution that damages them. The Trust has built up a network of concerned people and carers along the South-East coast organised in five geographical areas: Medway to Folkestone; Rye to Bexhill; Pevensey Bay to Cuckmere; Newhaven to Hove; and Shoreham to Chichester. In practical terms, its members act to get injured seabirds to carers as quickly as possible; advise people who report casualties how best to help; keep carers in touch with each other and up-to date with the best methods of care for various injuries; and run money-raising events.
Contact: Save Our Seabirds Charitable Trust, 22 Pearl Court, Courtfield Terrace, Eastbourne, East Sussex BN21 4AA. e-mail: stanleysec@aol.com www.saveourseabirdscharitabletrust.org.uk

SCOTTISH BIRDS RECORDS COMMITTEE (1984; 7 members, plus secretary)
Set up by the Scottish Ornithologists' Club to ensure that records of species not deemed rare enough to be considered by the British Birds Rarities Committee, but which are rare in Scotland, are fully assessed; also maintains the official list of Scottish birds.
Contact: Angus Hogg, Secretary, Scottish Birds Records Committee, 11 Kirkmichael Road, Crosshill, Maybole, Ayrshire KA19 7RJ; www.the-soc.org.uk e-mail: dcgos@globalnet.co.uk

SCOTTISH ORNITHOLOGISTS' CLUB (1936; 2,250)
The Club has 14 branches (see County Directory), each with a programme of winter meetings and field trips throughout the year. The SOC organises an annual weekend conference in the autumn and a joint SOC/BTO one-day birdwatchers' conference in spring. In August 2009 it re-launched its magazine, *Scottish Birds*, which is now published quarterly and incorporates the *Scottish Bird News* and the scarce sightings journal *Birding Scotland*. The SOC is based in a large resource centre which offers panoramic views of Aberlady Bay and houses the George Waterston Library. Details can be found on the website.
Contact: The Scottish Birdwatching Resource Centre, The SOC, Waterston House, Aberlady, East Lothian EH32 0PY. 01875 871 330; (Fax) 01875 871 035; e-mail: mail@the-soc.org.uk www.the-soc.org.uk

SCOTTISH NATURAL HERITAGE (1991)
SNH is the Scottish Executive's statutory advisor in respect to the conservation, enhancement, enjoyment, understanding and sustainable use of the natural heritage.
Contact: Scottish Natural Heritage, Great Glen House, Leachkin Road, Inverness IV3 8NW. 01463 725 000; e-mail: enquiries@snh.gov.uk www.snh.org.uk

NATIONAL ORGANISATIONS

SCOTTISH SOCIETY FOR THE PREVENTION OF CRUELTY TO ANIMALS (1839; 45,000 supporters)

Represents animal welfare interests to Government, local authorities and others. Educates young people to realise their responsibilities. Maintains an inspectorate to patrol and investigate and to advise owners about the welfare of animals and birds in their care. Maintains welfare centres, two of which include oiled bird cleaning centres. Bird species, including birds of prey, are rehabilitated and where possible released back into the wild.
Contact: Scottish SPCA, Braehead Mains, 603 Queensferry Road, Edinburgh EH4 6EA. 03000 999 999; e-mail: enquiries@scottishspca.org www.scottishspca.org

SCOTTISH WILDLIFE TRUST (1964; 35,000)

The Trust aims to re-establish: a network of healthy and resilient ecosystems supporting expanding communities of native species across large areas of Scotland's land, water and seas. Its main activities focus on managing 123 wildlife reserves and undertaking practical conservation tasks; influencing and campaigning for better wildlife-related policy and action; and inspiring people to enjoy and find out more about wildlife. Member of The Wildlife Trusts partnership and organises Scottish Wildlife Week. Publishes *Scottish Wildlife* three times a year.
Contact: Scottish Wildlife Trust, Cramond House, Cramond Glebe Road, Edinburgh EH4 6NS. 0131 312 7765; e-mail: enquiries@swt.org.uk www.swt.org.uk

SEABIRD GROUP (1966; 350)

Concerned with conservation issues affecting seabirds. Co-ordinates census and monitoring work on breeding seabirds; has established and maintains the Seabird Colony Register in collaboration with the JNCC; organises triennial conferences on seabird biology and conservation topics. Small grants available to assist with research and survey work on seabirds. Publishes the *Seabird Group Newsletter* every four months and the journal *Atlantic Seabirds* quarterly, in association with the Dutch Seabird Group.
Contact: Linda Wilson, JNCC, Dunnet House, 7 Thistle Place, Aberdeen, AB10 1UZ; e-mail: linda.wilson@jncc.gov.uk www.seabirdgroup.org.uk

SOCIETY OF WILDLIFE ARTISTS (1964; 69 Members, 68 Associates)

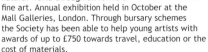

Registered charity that seeks to generate an appreciation of the natural world through all forms of fine art. Annual exhibition held in October at the Mall Galleries, London. Through bursary schemes the Society has been able to help young artists with awards of up to £750 towards travel, education or the cost of materials.
Contact: The Secretary, Society of Wildlife Artists, Federation of British Artists, 17 Carlton House Terrace, London SW1Y 5BD. 020 7930 6844; e-mail: info@mallgalleries.com www.swla.co.uk

SWAN SANCTUARY (2005)

Founded by Dorothy Beeson BEM. A registered charity which operates nationally. Has a fully equipped swan hospital with an operating theatre, X-ray facilities and a veterinary surgeon. New site has several nursing ponds and a four acre rehabilitation lake where around 4,000 swans and the same number of other forms of wildlife are treated. 24-hour service operated, with volunteer rescuers on hand to recover victims of oil spills, vandalism etc. Reg. charity number 1002582.
Contact: The Swan Sanctuary, Felix Lane, Shepperton, Middlesex TW17 8NN. Emergency number: 01932 240 790; e-mail: swans@swanuk.org.uk www.swanuk.org.uk

UK400 CLUB (1981)

Serves to monitor the nation's leading twitchers and their life lists, and to keep under review contentious species occurrences. Publishes a bi-monthly magazine *Rare Birds*. Membership open to all.
Contact: LGR Evans, UK400 Club, 8 Sandycroft Road, Little Chalfont, Amersham, Bucks HP6 6QL. 01494 763 010; e-mail: LGREUK400@aol.com www.uk400clubonline.co.uk

WADER STUDY GROUP (INTERNATIONAL) (1970; 500)

An association of wader enthusiasts, both amateur and professional, from all parts of the world. The Group aims to maintain contact between them, to help in the organisation of co-operative studies, and to provide a vehicle for the exchange of information. Publishes the *Wader Study Group Bulletin* three times a year and holds annual meetings throughout Europe.
Contact: The General Secretary, International Wader Study Group, The British Trust for Ornithology, The Nunnery, Thetford, Norfolk IP24 2PU. www.waderstudygroup.org

WELSH KITE TRUST (1996; 1,200)

A registered charity that undertakes the conservation and annual monitoring of Red Kites in Wales. It attempts to locate all the breeding birds, to compile data on population growth, productivity, range expansion etc. The Trust liaises with landowners, acts as consultant on planning issues and with regard to filming and photography, and represents Welsh interests on the UK Kite Steering Group. Provides a limited rescue service for injured kites and eggs or chicks at risk of desertion or starvation. Publishes a newsletter *Boda Wennol* twice a year, sent free to subscribing Friends of the Welsh Kite and to all landowners with nesting kites.
Contact: Tony Cross, Project Officer, Welsh Kite Trust, Samaria, Nantmel, Llandrindod Wells, Powys LD1 6EN. 01597 825 981; www.welshkitetrust.orge-mail: info@welshkitetrust.org

WELSH ORNITHOLOGICAL SOCIETY (1988; 250)

Promotes the study, conservation and enjoyment

of birds throughout Wales. Runs the Welsh Records Panel which adjudicates records of scarce species in Wales. Publishes the journal *Welsh Birds* twice a year, along with newsletters, and organises an annual conference.

Contact: Membership details from Welsh Ornithological Society, Alan Williams, Membership Secretary, 30 Fairfield, Penperlleni, Pontypool, NP4 0AQ; e-mail: mochdreboy@waitrose.com www.welshos.org.uk

WETLAND TRUST

Set up to encourage conservation of wetlands and develop study of migratory birds, and to foster international relations in these fields. Destinations for recent expeditions inc. Brazil, Senegal, The Gambia, Guinea-Bissau, Nigeria, Kuwait, Thailand, Greece and Jordan. Large numbers of birds are ringed each year in Sussex and applications are invited from individuals to train in bird ringing or extend their experience.

Contact: Phil Jones, Wetland Trust, Elms Farm, Pett Lane, Icklesham, Winchelsea, E Sussex TN36 4AH. 01797 226374; e-mail: phil@wetlandtrust.org

WILDFOWL & WETLANDS TRUST (1946; 130,000 members and 4,700 bird adopters)

Registered charity founded by the late Sir Peter Scott to conserve wetlands and their biodiversity. WWT has nine centres with reserves (see Arundel, Caerlaverock, Castle Espie, Llanelli, Martin Mere, Slimbridge, Washington, Welney, and The London Wetland Centre in Reserves and Observatories section). The centres are nationally or internationally important for wintering wildfowl. Programmes of walks and talks are available for visitors with varied interests – resources and programmes are provided for school groups. Research Department works on population dynamics, species management plans and wetland ecology. The Wetland Advisory Service (WAS) undertakes contracts, and Wetland Link International promotes the role of wetland centres for education and public awareness.

Contact: Wildfowl and Wetlands Trust, Slimbridge, Glos, GL2 7BT. 01453 891 900; www.wwt.org.uk e-mail: enquiries@wwt.org.uk

WILDLIFE SOUND RECORDING SOCIETY (1968; 327)

Works closely with the Wildlife Section of the National Sound Archive. Members carry out recording work for scientific purposes as well as for pleasure. A field weekend is held each spring, and members organise meetings locally. Four CD sound magazines of members' recordings are produced for members each year, and a journal, *Wildlife Sound*, is published twice a year.

Contact: Hon Membership Secretary, WSRS, Wildlife Sound Recording Society, www.wildlife-sound.org e-mail: enquiries@wildlife-sound.org

WILDLIFE TRUSTS (1995; 791,000)

Originally the Society of the Promotion of Nature Reserves, founded in 1912, now the largest UK charity exclusively dedicated to conserving all habitats and species, with a membership of more than 791,000 people including 108,000 junior members in 47 individual county trusts. Collectively, they manage more than 2,200 nature reserves spanning over 80,000 hectares. The Wildlife Trusts also lobby for better protection of the UK's natural heritage and are dedicated to protecting wildlife for the future. Members receive *Natural World* magazine three times a year. See also Wildlife Watch.

Contact: The Wildlife Trusts, The Kiln, Waterside, Mather Road, Newark NG24 1WT. 01636 677 711; e-mail: enquiry@wildlifetrusts.org www.wildlifetrusts.org

WILDLIFE WATCH (1977; 108.000)

The junior branch of The Wildlife Trusts (see previous entry) It supports 1,500 registered volunteer leaders running Watch groups across the UK. Publishes *Watchword* and *Wildlife Extra* for children and activity books for adults working with young people.

Contact: Wildlife Watch, The Wildlife Trusts, The Kiln, Waterside, Mather Road, Newark NG24 1WT. 01636 677 711; e-mail: watch@wildlifetrusts.org www.wildlifewatch.org.uk

WWF-UK (1961)

WWF is the world's largest independent conservation organisation, comprising 27 national organisations. It works to conserve and protect endangered species and address global threats to nature by seeking long-term solutions with people in government and industry, education and civil society. Publishes *WWF News* (quarterly magazine)

Contact: WWF-UK (World Wide Fund for Nature), Panda House, Weyside Park, Catteshall Lane, Godalming, Surrey GU7 1XR. 01483 426 444; www.wwf.org.uk

ZOOLOGICAL PHOTOGRAPHIC CLUB (1899)

Circulates black and white and colour prints of zoological interest via a series of postal portfolios.

Contact: Martin B Withers, Hon Secretary, Zoological Photographic Club, 93 Cross Lane, Mountsorrel, Loughborough, Leics LE12 7BX. 0116 229 6080.

ZOOLOGICAL SOCIETY OF LONDON (1826)

Carries out research, organises symposia and holds scientific meetings. Manages the Zoological Gardens in Regent's Park (first opened in 1828) and Whipsnade Wild Animal Park near Dunstable, Beds, each with extensive collections of birds. The Society's library has a large collection of ornithological books and journals. Publications include *the Journal of Zoology, Animal Conservation, Conservation Biology* book series, *The Symposia* and *The International Zoo Yearbook*.

Contact: Zoological Society of London, Regent's Park, London, NW1 4RY. 020 7722 3333; www.zsl.org

NATIONAL PROJECTS

National ornithological projects depend for their success on the active participation of amateur birdwatchers. In return they provide birdwatchers with an excellent opportunity to contribute in a positive and worthwhile way to the scientific study of birds and their habitats, which is the vital basis of all conservation programmes. The following entries provide a description of each particular project and a note of whom to contact for further information (full address details of project organisers are in the previous section).

BARN OWL MONITORING PROGRAMME
A BTO project
A survey dedicated to monitoring Barn Owls in their nests. Participants register known Barn Owl breeding sites and visit them each breeding season to record site occupancy and details of breeding attempts. Many registered sites are nest boxes that are erected and maintained by volunteers. Participants must be qualified bird ringers or nest recorders with a Schedule 1 licence for Barn Owl.
Contact: Carl Barimore,
e-mail: barnowls@bto.org

BIRD ATLAS 2007-11
BTO, run in partnership with BirdWatch Ireland and the Scottish Ornithologists' Club
Atlases have provided a periodic stock-take of the birds of Britain and Ireland, and this latest Atlas will do just that, only this time in both the breeding season and in winter. It will generate range and abundance maps for all species while giving the opportunity to contrast past and present distributions and assess changes, for better or worse. Fieldwork started in earnest in November 2007 and will run for 4 winters and 4 summers. Fieldwork will end July 2011. Observers can submit their records and see up-to-date results online. Mapping Britain and Ireland's birds is a major undertaking and the BTO needs your support.
Contact: e-mail: birdatlas@bto.org
www.birdatlas.net

BirdTrack
Organised by BTO on behalf of BTO, RSPB and BirdWatch Ireland.
BirdTrack is a free, online bird recording system for birdwatchers to store and manage bird records from anywhere in Britain and Ireland. The idea is simple — just make a note of the birds seen or heard at each site visited then enter the observations on an easy-to-use web page (www.birdtrack.net). Exciting real-time outputs are generated by BirdTrack, including species reporting rate graphs and animated maps of sightings, all freely-available online. The data collected are used by researchers to investigate migration movements and the distribution of scarce birds, and to support species conservation at local, national and international scales.
Contact: Nick Moran, BTO.
E-mail: birdtrack@bto.org

BREEDING BIRD SURVEY
Supported by the BTO, JNCC and the RSPB.
Begun in 1994, the BBS is designed to keep track of the changes in populations of our common breeding birds. It is dependent on volunteer birdwatchers throughout the country who can spare about five hours a year to cover a 1x1km survey square. There are just two morning visits to survey the breeding birds each year.

Survey squares are picked at random by computer to ensure that all habitats and regions are covered. Since its inception it has been a tremendous success, with more than 3,000 squares covered and more than 200 species recorded each year.
Contact: Kate Risely, e-mail: bbs@bto.org, or your local BTO Regional Representative (see County Directory).

CONSTANT EFFORT SITES (CES) SCHEME
The CES scheme, run since 1983, coordinates standardised summer ringing at 120 sites across Britain and Ireland. This allows the BTO to monitor trends in the numbers of adults at breeding sites, annual breeding productivity and survival rates of adults for 25 common songbirds. Information from CES complements demographic information from other surveys and feeds into the BTO's Integrated Population Monitoring, highlighting the causes of changes in bird populations.
The scheme is funded by a partnership between BTO, JNCC, The National Parks & Wildlife Service (Ireland) and ringers themselves.
Contact: Greg Conway, BTO

GARDEN BIRD FEEDING SURVEY
A BTO project.
The Garden Bird Feeding Survey is the longest-running study of garden birds in Britain. Each

309

year approximately 250 householders record the numbers and variety of birds using food supplements and water that they have provided in their garden. Observations are made on a weekly basis from October to March inclusive. Gardens are selected by region and type; from city flats, suburban semis, rural houses to outlying farms.
Contact: Tim Harrison, BTO.
E-mail: tim.harrison@bto.org

BTO GARDEN BIRDWATCH
A BTO project.
Started in January 1995, this project is a year-round survey that monitors the use that birds and other types of wildlife make of gardens. Approximately 15,000 participants from all over the UK and Ireland keep a weekly log of species using their gardens. The data collected are used to monitor regional, seasonal and year-to-year changes in the garden populations of our commoner birds, mammals, butterflies, reptiles and amphibians. To cover running costs there is an annual subscription of £15. Participants receive a quarterly colour magazine *The Bird Table* and all new joiners receive a full-colour, garden bird handbook. Results and more information are available online:
www.bto.org/gbw
Contact: Garden Ecology Team, BTO.
E-mail: gbw@bto.org

GOOSE CENSUSES
A WWT project
Britain and Ireland support internationally important goose populations. During the day, many of these feed away from wetlands and are not adequately censused by the Wetland Bird Survey. Additional surveys are therefore undertaken to provide estimates of population size. These primarily involve roost counts, supplemented by further counts of feeding birds.

Most populations are censused up to three times a year, typically during the autumn, midwinter, and spring. In addition, counts of the proportion of juveniles in goose flocks are undertaken to provide estimates of annual productivity. Further volunteers are always needed. In particular, counters in Scotland, Lancashire and Norfolk are sought. For more information
Contact: Richard Hearn, Programme Manager.
E-mail: richard.hearn@wwt.org.uk
T: +44 (0)1453 891 185;
e-mail: monitoring@wwt.org.uk

HERONRIES CENSUS
A BTO project.
This survey started in 1928 and has been carried out under the auspices of the BTO since 1934.

It represents the longest continuous series of population data for any European breeding bird (Grey Heron). Counts of apparently occupied nests are made at as many heronries as possible each year, throughout the UK, to provide an index of current population levels; data from Scotland and Northern Ireland are scant and more contributions from these countries would be especially welcomed. Herons may be hit hard during periods of severe weather and are vulnerable to pesticides and pollution. Currently, however, population levels are relatively high. Little Egret and other incoming species of colonial waterbird such as Cattle Egret are now fully included, whether nesting with Grey Herons or on their own; counts of Cormorant nests at heronries are also encouraged.
Contact: John Marchant, BTO

IRISH WETLAND BIRD SURVEY (I-WeBS)
A joint project of BirdWatch Ireland, the National Parks & Wildlife Service of the Dept of Arts, Culture & the Gaeltacht, and WWT, and supported by the Heritage Council and WWF-UK.
Established in 1994, I-WeBS aims to monitor the numbers and distribution of waterfowl populations wintering in Ireland in the long term, enabling the population size and spatial and temporal trends in numbers to be identified and described for each species.

Methods are compatible with existing schemes in the UK and Europe, and I-WeBS collaborates closely with the Wetland Bird Survey (WeBS) in the UK. Synchronised monthly counts are undertaken at wetland sites of all habitats during the winter.

Counts are straightforward and counters receive a newsletter and full report annually. Additional help is always welcome, especially during these initial years as the scheme continues to grow.
Contact: BirdWatch Ireland;
www.birdwatchireland.ie

NEST BOX CHALLENGE
A BTO project
A popular survey designed to monitor the breeding success of birds in Britain's green spaces. All you need to do is register one or more nest boxes in your garden or local green space and then observe what birds nest in them and how they get on. Since the project was launched in 2007, 20,000 nest boxes have been registered across the UK and participants have been recording whether or not these boxes are occupied, how many eggs have been laid in them and how many chicks have hatched and flown.

Since 2010, the survey has been extended to include open nests, so if you find a Blackbird nesting in your privet hedge or a Collared Dove in your cherry tree, you can register it and report on its progress too. This survey is 'paperless', so participants must be able to report their findings via the BTO website. For information on taking part, please visit www.bto.org/nbc
Contact: Carl Barimore, BTO
E-mail: nest.records@bto.org

NEST RECORD SCHEME
A BTO Project forming part of the BTO's Integrated Population Monitoring programme carried out under contract with the JNCC.
The NRS monitors changes in the nesting success and the timing of breeding of Britain's bird species by gathering information on nests found anywhere in the country, from a Blackbird in a garden to an Oystercatcher on a Scottish loch. Participants locate nests and then carefully monitor their progress over several visits, making counts of the number of eggs and/or chicks and recording whether they are successful. Over 30,000 such 'nest records' are submitted to the BTO each year by surveyors trained to visit nests safely and unobtrusively. Guidance on how to become a BTO nest recorder is available at www.bto.org/nrs and a free starter pack available on request.
Contact: Carl Barimore, BTO
E-mail: nrs@bto.org

RAPTOR AND OWL RESEARCH REGISTER
A BTO project
The Register has helped considerably over the past 30 years in encouraging and guiding research, and in the co-ordination of projects. There are currently almost 500 projects in the card index file through which the Register operates.

The owl species currently receiving most attention are Barn and Tawny. As to raptors, the most popular subjects are Kestrel, Buzzard, Sparrowhawk, Hobby and Peregrine, with researchers showing increasing interest in Red Kite, and fewer large in-depth studies of Goshawk, Osprey and harriers.

Contributing is a simple process and involves all raptor enthusiasts, whether it is to describe an amateur activity or professional study. The nature of research on record varies widely — from local pellet analyses to captive breeding and rehabilitation programmes to national surveys of Peregrine, Buzzard and Golden Eagle. Birdwatchers in both Britain and abroad are encouraged to write for photocopies of cards

relevant to the species or nature of their work. The effectiveness of the Register depends upon those running projects (however big or small) ensuring that their work is included.
Contact: David Glue, BTO.

RED KITE RE-INTRODUCTION PROJECT
An English Nature/SNH/RSPB project supported by Forest Enterprise, Yorkshire Water and authorities in Germany and Spain
The project involves the translocation of birds from Spain, Germany and the expanding Chilterns population for release at sites in England and Scotland.

Records of any wing-tagged Red Kites in England should be reported to Natural Engand, Northminster House, Peterborough, PEI IUA (tel 01733 455 281). Scottish records should be sent to the RSPB's North Scotland Regional Office, Etive House, Beechwood Park, Inverness, IV2 3BW (tel 01463 715 000).

Sightings are of particular value if the letter/number code (or colour) of wing tags can be seen or if the bird is seen flying low over (or into) woodland. Records should include an exact location, preferably with a six figure grid reference.

RETRAPPING ADULTS FOR SURVIVAL (RAS) SCHEME
Scheme is funded by a partnership between BTO, JNCC, The National Parks & Wildlife Service (Ireland) and ringers themselves.
The RAS scheme started in 1998 and gathers information on recaptures of adult birds. Projects are chosen and run by volunteer ringers and focus on species of conservation concern that are monitored relatively poorly by CES and general ringing activity. Collection of standardised capture/recapture data allows the BTO to monitor survival rates in adult birds. Detailed information about survival helps us to understand population changes as part of the BTO's Integrated Population Monitoring. Ringers themselves choose a target species and aim to catch all the breeding adults within that area on an annual basis.
Contact: Greg Conway, BTO

RINGING SCHEME
Scheme is funded by a partnership between BTO, JNCC, The National Parks & Wildlife Service (Ireland) and ringers themselves.
Marking birds with individually numbered metal rings allows us to study survival, productivity and movements of British and Irish birds. Nearly 2,500 trained and licensed ringers operate in Britain and Ireland, marking around 800,000 birds annually.

NATIONAL DIRECTORY

Training to ring, and use mist nets takes at least a year, but more often two or more years depending on the aptitude of the trainee and the amount of ringing they do. A restricted permit can usually be obtained more quickly. Anyone can contribute to the scheme by reporting any ringed or colour-ringed birds they see or find. Reports can be submitted online at www.ring.ac or direct to BTO HQ. Anyone finding a ringed bird should note the ring number, species, when and where found and, if possible, what happened to it. If the bird is dead, it may also be possible to remove the ring, which should be kept in case there is a query. Anyone reporting a ringed bird will be sent details of where and when the bird was originally ringed. More info: www.bto.org/ringing/ 'Demog Blog' for up to date news and stories: http://btoringing.blogspot.com/
Contact: Jacquie Clark, BTO

SWIFT CONSERVATION
Endorsed by the BTO and the RSPB,
Swift Conservation works to protect and restore the UK's fast-diminishing Swift population, a once-numerous species that because of changes in building technology and design is facing increasing difficulties in finding places to breed. Practical information on Swift conservation is provided to owners, architects, builders and others via a web site, by e-mail and in person. Swift Conservation also supports Swift populations through a network of "Swift Champions" who survey their localities for Swift colonies and work to preserve and enhance them. The help of interested bird watchers with this work is always welcome.

Swift Conservation runs a lectures, talks and training programme for bird clubs, local government and building professionals. Please contact them if you are interested in this or any aspect of their work.
Contacts: Edward Mayer: phone 020 7794 2098
e-mail: mail@swift-conservation.org
web site: www.swift-conservation.org/

TOOTH & CLAW
An independent project aimed at improving knowledge about Britain's predators and promoting discussion on the issues that surround them.

tooth&claw

Tooth & Claw explores some of the complex issues surrounding our relationship with wild predators and questions how we really feel and why.

Through the web site, Tooth & Claw provides

a meeting place between anecdotal input and scientific research and encourages constructive and imaginative dialogue on predator issues. A series of case studies led by powerful imagery will provide insightful interviews and personal accounts of our lives alongside the likes of eagles and foxes with a glimpse into the future and the return of creatures we have not known for centuries.
Contact: Peter Cairns, Northshots, Ballintean, Glenfeshie, Kingussie, Scotland, PH21 1NX. (44)(0)1540 651 352;
e-mail: peter@toothandclaw.org.uk
www.toothandclaw.org.uk

WATERWAYS BREEDING BIRD SURVEY
A BTO project, supported by the Environment Agency
WBBS uses transect methods like those of the Breeding Bird Survey to record bird populations along randomly chosen stretches of river and canal throughout the UK. Just two survey visits are needed during April-June. WBBS began in 1998 and has now taken over from the Waterways Bird Survey as the main monitoring scheme for birds in this habitat.
Contact: BTO Regional Representative (see County Directory) to enquire if any local stretches require coverage, otherwise John Marchant at BTO HQ.

WETLAND BIRD SURVEY (WeBs)
A joint scheme of BTO, WWT, RSPB & JNCC.
The Wetland Bird Survey (WeBS) is the monitoring scheme for non-breeding waterbirds in the UK.

The principal aims are:
1. to determine the population sizes of waterbirds
2. to determine trends in numbers and distribution
3. to identify important sites for waterbirds

WeBS data are used to designate important waterbird sites and protect them against adverse development, for research into the causes of declines, for establishing conservation priorities and strategies and to formulate management plans for wetland sites and waterbirds. Monthly, synchronised Core Counts are made at as many wetland sites as possible. Low Tide Counts are made on about 20 estuaries each winter to identify important feeding areas. Counts can take from a few minutes up to a few hours depending on the size of the site and are relatively straightforward. The 3,000 participants receive an annual newsletter and a comprehensive annual report. New counters are always welcome.
Contacts: General Webs Enquiries - Heidi Mellan - WeBS Office, BTO. E-mail webs@bto.org
www.bto.org/webs

INTERNATIONAL DIRECTORY

David Cromack

Egyptian Vultures are widely distributed in North Africa and the Mediterranean

BirdLife™
INTERNATIONAL

The BirdLife Partnership
BirdLife is a Partnership of non-governmental organisations (NGOs) with a special focus on conservation and birds. Each NGO Partner represents a unique geographic territory/country.

The BirdLife Network explained
Partners: Membership-based NGOs who represent BirdLife in their own territory. Vote holders and key implementing bodies for BirdLife's Strategy and Regional Programmes in their own territories.

Partners Designate: Membership-based NGOs who represent BirdLife in their own territory, in a transition stage to becoming full Partners. Non-vote holders.

Affiliates: Usually NGOs, but also individuals, foundations or governmental institutions when appropriate. Act as a BirdLife contact with the aim of developing into, or recruiting, a BirdLife Partner in their territory.

Secretariat: The co-ordinating and servicing body of BirdLife International.

SECRETARIAT ADDRESSES

BirdLife Global Office
BirdLife International
Wellbrook Court, Girton Road
Cambridge CB3 0NA
UNITED KINGDOM
Tel. +44 1 223 277 318
Fax +44 1 223 277 200
E-mail: birdlife@birdlife.org.uk
www.birdlife.org

Birdlife Africa Regional Office
c/o ICIPE Campus
Kasarani Road, off Thika Road
Nairobi KENYA
Postal Address
PO Box 3502
00100 GPO
Nairobi, KENYA
+254 20 862246
+254 20 862246
E-mail: birdlife@birdlife.or.ke
www.birdlife.org/regional/africa/
partnership

BirdLife Americas Regional Office
Birdlife International
Vicente Cárdenas 120 y Japon,
3rd Floor
Quito ECUADOR

Postal address
BirdLife International
Casilla 17-17-717
Quito ECUADOR
Tel. +593 2 453 645
Fax +593 2 459 627
E-mail: birdlife@birdlife.org.ec
www.birdlife.org/regional/americas/
partnership

BirdLife Asia Regional Office
Toyo-Shinjuku Building
2nd Floor, Shinjuku 1-12-15
Shinkuju-ku
Tokyo 160-0022, JAPAN
Tel.+3 3351 9981
Fax.+3 3351 9980
E-mail: info@birdlife-asia.org
www.birdlife.org/regional/asia/
partnership

BirdLife European Regional Office
Droevendaalsesteeg 3a PO Box 127,
NL- 6700 AC, Wageningen
THE NETHERLANDS
Tel. +31 317 478831
Fax +31 317 478844
E-mail: birdlife@birdlife.agro.nl

European Community Office (ECO)
BirdLife International
Avenue de la Toison d'Or 67
(2nd floor), B-1060 Brussels
BELGIUM
Tel. +32 2280 08 30
Fax +32 2230 38 02
E-mail: bleco@birdlifeeco.net
www.birdlife.org/regional/europe/
partnership

BirdLife Middle East Regional Office
BirdLife International - Amman
P. O. Box 2295
Amman 11953
JORDAN
Tel: +962 (6) 566-2945
Fax: +962 (6) 569-1838
E-mail: birdlife@nol.com.jo
www.birdlife.org/regional/
middle_east/partnership

AFRICA

PARTNERS
Burkina Faso
Fondation des Amis de la Nature (NATURAMA), 01 B.P. 6133, Ouagadougou 01; e-mail: naturama@fasonet.bf

Ethiopia
Ethiopian Wildlife and Natural History Society, PO Box 13303, Addis Ababa, Pub: *Agazen; Ethiopian Wildl.*

and Nat. Hist. News. (& Annual Report); Ethiopian Wildl. and Nat. Hist. Soc. Quarterly News (WATCH); Walia (WATCH) (Ethiopia);
e-mail: ewnhs@telecom.net.et
http://ewnhs.ble@telecom.net.et

Ghana
Ghana Wildlife Society, PO Box 13252, Accra, Pub: *Bongo News; NKO (The Parrots);* e-mail: wildsoc@ighmail.com

INTERNATIONAL ORGANISATIONS

Kenya
Nature Kenya, PO Box 44486, 00100 GPO. Nairobi.
Pub: *Bulletin of the EANHS; Journal of East African Natural; Kenya Birds;* e-mail: office@naturekenya.org
www.naturekenya.org

Nigeria
Nigerian Conservation Foundation, PO Box 74638, Victoria Island, Lagos. Pub: *NCF Matters/News/ Newsletter; Nigerian Conservation Foundation Annual Report;* e-mail: enquiries@ncf-nigeria.org
www.africanconservation.org/ncftemp/

Seychelles
Nature Seychelles, Roche Caiman, Box 1310, Victoria, Mahe, Seychelles. Pub: *Zwazo - a BirdLife Seychelles Newsletter;* e-mail: nature@seychelles.net
www.nature.org.sc

Sierra Leone
Conservation Society of Sierra Leone, PO BOX 1292, Freetown. Pub: *Rockfowl Link, The.*
e-mail: cssl@sierratel.sl

South Africa
BirdLife South Africa, PO Box 515, Randburg, Johannesburg 2125, South Africa, Pub: *Newsletter of BirdLife South Africa; Ostrich;*
e-mail: info@birdlife.org.za www.birdlife.org.za

Tanzania
Wildlife Conservation Society of Tanzania, PO Box 70919, Dar es Salaam, Pub: *Miombo.*
e-mail: wcst@africaonline.co.tz

Uganda
Nature Uganda, PO Box 27034, Kampala. Pub: *Naturalist - A Newsletter of the East Africa Nat. His. Soc;* e-mail: nature@natureuganda.org
www.natureuganda.org/

PARTNERS DESIGNATE

Tunisia
Association "Les Amis des Oiseaux", Avenue 18 Janvier 1952, Ariana Centre, App. C209, 2080 Ariana, Tunis. Pub: *Feuille de Liaison de l'AAO; Houbara, l'.*
e-mail: aao.bird@planet.tn

Zimbabwe
BirdLife Zimbabwe, P O Box RV 100, Runiville, Harare, Zimbabwe. Pub: *Babbler (WATCH) (Zimbabwe); Honeyguide;* e-mail: birds@zol.co.zw

AFFILIATES

Botswana
Birdlife Botswana, Private Bag 003 # Suite 348, Mogoditshane, Gaborone, Botswana
e-mail: blb@birdlifebotswana.org.bw
www.birdlifebotswana.org.bw

Burundi
Association Burundaise pour la Protection des Oiseaux, P O Box 7069, Bujumbura, Burundi;
e-mail: aboburundi@yahoo.fr

Cameroon
Cameroon Biodiversity Conservation Society (CBCS), PO Box 3055, Messa, Yaoundé;
e-mail: gdzikouk@yahoo.fr

Egypt
Sherif Baha El Din, 3 Abdala El Katib St, Dokki, Cairo.
e-mail: baha2@internetegypt.com

Rwanda
Association pour la Conservation de la Nature au Rwanda, P O Box 4290, Kigali,
e-mail: acnrwanda@yahoo.fr

Zambia
Zambian Ornithological Society, Box 33944, Lusaka 10101, Pub: *Zambian Ornithological Society Newsletter;* e-mail: zos@zamnet.zm
www.wattledcrane.com

AMERICAS

PARTNERS

Argentina
Aves Argentina / AOP, 25 de Mayo 749, 2 piso, oficina 6, 1002 Buenos Aires. Pub: *Hornero; Naturaleza & Conservacion; Nuestras Aves; Vuelo de Pajaro;*
e-mail: info@avesargentinas.org.ar
www.avesargentinas.org.ar

Belize
The Belize Audubon Society, 12 Fort Street, PO Box 1001, Belize City. Pub: *Belize Audubon Society Newsletter;* e-mail: base@btl.net
www.belizeaudubon.org

Bolivia
Asociacion Armonia, 400 Avenidad Lomas de Arena, Casilla 3566, Santa Cruz, Bolivia. Pub: *Aves en Bolivia;*
e-mail: armonia@scbbs-bo.com

Canada
Bird Studies Canada, PO Box/160, Port Rowan, Ontario N0E 1M0. Pub: *Bird Studies Canada - Annual Report; Birdwatch Canada;* e-mail: generalinfo@bsc-eoc.org
www.bsc-eoc.org

Canada
Nature Canada, 1 Nicholas Street, Suite 606, Ottawa, Ontario, K1N 7B7. Pub: *Grass 'n Roots; IBA News Canada; Nature Canada; Nature Matters; Nature Watch News (CNF);* e-mail: info@naturecanada.ca
www.naturecanada.ca

Ecuador
Fundación Ornitológica del Ecuador, La Tierra 203 y Av. de los Shyris, Casilla 17-17-906, Quito.
e-mail: cecia@uio.satnet.net www.cecia.org/

Jamaica
BirdLife Jamaica, 2 Starlight Avenue, Kingston 6, Pub: *Broadsheet: BirdLife Jamaica; Important Bird Areas Programme Newsletter;* e-mail: birdlifeja@yahoo.com
www.birdelifejamaica.com

Panama
Panama Audubon Society, Apartado 2026, Ancón, Balboa. Pub: *Toucan;*
e-mail: info@panamaaudubon.org
www.panamaaudubon.org

Venezuela
Sociedad Conservacionista Audubon de, Apartado 80.450, Caracas 1080-A, Venezuela. Pub: *Audubon*

(Venezuela) (formerly Boletin Audubon);
e-mail: audubon@cantv.net

PARTNERS DESIGNATE

Mexico
CIPAMEX, Apartado Postal 22-012, D.F. 14091, Mexico.
Pub: *AICA's; Cuauhtli Boletin de Cipa Mex.*
e-mail: cipamex@campus.iztacala.unam.mx
http://coro@servidor.unam.mx

Paraguay
Guyra Paraguay, Coronel Rafael Franco 381 c/ Leandro
Prieto, Casilla de Correo 1132, Asunción. Pub: *Boletin
Jara Kuera;* e-mail: guyra@guyra.org.py
or guyra@highway.com.py www.guyra.org.py/

United States
National Audubon Society, 700 Broadway, New
York, NY, 10003 -9562. Pub: *American Birds;
Audubon (USA); Audubon Field Notes; Audubon Bird
Conservation Newsletter;*
e-mail: audubonaction@audubon.org
www.audubon.org

Chile
Union de Ornitologis de Chile (UNORCH), Casilla
13.183, Santiago 21. Pub: *Boletin Chileno de
Ornitologia; Boletin Informativo (WATCH) (Chile).*
e-mail: unorch@entelchile.net
www.geocities.com/RainForest/4372

AFFILIATES

Bahamas
Bahamas National Trust, PO Box N-4105, Nassau. Pub:
Bahamas Naturalist; Currents; Grand Bahama Update.
e-mail: bnt@batelnet.bs
www.thebahamasnationaltrust.org/

Cuba
Centro Nacional de Áreas Protegidas (CNAP). Calle 18
a, No 1441, e/ 41 y 47, Playa, Ciudad Habana, Cuba.
e-mail: cnap@snap.cu www.snap.co.cu/

El Salvador
SalvaNATURA, 33 Avenida Sur #640, Colonia Flor
Blanca, San Salvador; e-mail: salvanatura@saltel.net
www.salvanatura.org

Falkland Islands
Falklands Conservation, PO Box 26, Stanley,. or
Falklands Conservation, 1 Princes Avenue, Finchley,
London N3 2DA, UK. Pub: *Falklands Conservation.*
e-mail: conservation@horizon.co.fk
www.falklandsconservation.com

Honduras
Sherry Thorne, c/o Cooperación Técnica, Apdo 30289
Toncontín, Tegucigalpa;
e-mail: pilar_birds@yahoo.com

Suriname
Foundation for Nature Preservation in Suriname,
Cornelis Jongbawstraat 14, PO BOX 12252,
Paramaribo
e-mail: research@stinasu.sr www.stinasu.sr

Uruguay
GUPECA, Casilla de Correo 6955, Correo Central,
Montevideo. Pub: *Achara.*
e-mail: info@avesuruguay.org.uy
www.avesuruguay.org.uy/

ASIA

PARTNERS

Japan
Wild Bird Society of Japan (WBSJ), 1/F Odakyu Nishi
Shinjuku Building, 1-47-1 Hatsudai Shibuya-ku, Tokyo
151-061, Japan. Pub: *Strix; Wild Birds; Wing.*
e-mail: int.center@wing-wbsj.or.jp
www.wing-wbsj.or.jp

Malaysia
Malaysian Nature Society, PO Box 10750, 50724 Kuala
Lumpur. Pub: *Enggang; Suara Enggang; Malayan
Nature Journal; Malaysian Naturalist.*
www.mns.org.my
e-mail: natsoc@po.jaring.my

Philippines
Haribon Foundation, Suites 401-404 Fil-Garcia Bldg,
140 Kalayaan Avenue cor. Mayaman St, Diliman,
Quezon CIty 1101. Pub: *Haribon Foundation Annual
Report; Haring Ibon; Philippine Biodiversity.*
e-mail: birdlife@haribon.org.ph
www.haribon.org.ph

Singapore
Nature Society (Singapore), 510 Geylang Road, #02-
05, The Sunflower, 398466. Pub: *Nature News; Nature
Watch (Singapore);* e-mail: nss@nss.org.sg
www.nss.org.sg

Taiwan
Wild Bird Federation Taiwan (WBFT), 1F, No. 3, Lane
36 Jing-Long St., 116 Taipei, Taiwan, R.O.C. Pub:
Yuhina Post; e-mail: wbft@bird.org.tw
www.bird.org.tw

Thailand
Bird Conservation Society of Thailand, 43 Soi Chok
Chai Ruam Mit 29, Vipahvadee-Rabgsit Road, Sansaen-
nok, Dindaeng, Bangkok 10320 Thailand. Pub: *Bird
Conservation Society of Thailand.*
e-mail: bcst@bcst.or.th www.bcst.or.th

PARTNER DESIGNATE

India
Bombay Natural History Society, Hornbill House,
Shaheed Bhagat Singh Road, Mumbai-400 023. Pub:
*Buceros; Hornbill; Journal of the Bombay Natural
History Society.*
e-mail: bnhs@bom4.vsnl.net.in www.bnhs.org

AFFILIATES

Hong Kong
The Hong Kong Birdwatching Society, Room 1612
Beverley Commercial Building, 87-105 Chatham Road
South, Tsim Sha Tsui, Kowloon, Hong Kong. Pub:
Hong Kong Bird Report; e-mail: hkbws@hkbws.org.uk
www.hkbws.org.hk

INTERNATIONAL ORGANISATIONS

Indonesia
BirdLife Indonesia (Perhimpunan Pelestari Burung dan Habitatnya), Jl. Dadali 32, Bogor 16161, PO. Box 310/ Boo, Bogor 16003, Indonesia; e-mail: birdlife@burung.org www.burung.org

Nepal
Bird Conservation Nepal, P.O.Box 12465, Lazimpat, Kathmandu, Nepal. Pub: *Bird Conservation Nepal (Danphe); Ibisbill;* e-mail: bcn@mail.com.np www.birdlifenepal.org

Pakistan
Ornithological Society of Pakistan, PO Box 73, 109D Dera Ghazi Khan, 32200. Pub: *Pakistan Journal of Ornithology;* e-mail: osp@mul.paknet.com.pk

Sri Lanka
Field Ornithology Group of Sri Lanka, Dept of Zoology, University of Colombo, Colombo 03. Pub: *Malkoha - Newsletter of the Field Ornithology Group of Sri Lanka.* e-mail: fogsl@slt.lk

EUROPE

PARTNERS

Austria
BirdLife Austria, Museumplatz 1/10/8, AT-1070 Wien. Pub: *Egretta; Vogelschutz in Osterreich.* e-mail: office@birdlife.at www.birdlife.at/

Belgium
BirdLife Belgium (BNVR-RNOB-BNVS), Natuurpunt, Kardinaal, Mercierplein 1, 2800 Mechelen, Belgium. e-mail: wim.vandenbossche@natuurpunt.be www.natuurreservaten.be

Bulgaria
Bulgarian Society for the Protection of Birds (BSPB), PO Box 50, Musagenitza Complex, Block 104, Entrance A, Floor 6, BG-1111, Sofia, Bulgaria. Pub: *Neophron (& UK);* e-mail: bspb_hq@bspb.org www.bspb.org

Czech Republic
Czech Society for Ornithology (CSO), Hornomecholupska 34, CZ-102 00 Praha 10. Pub: *Ptaci Svet; Sylvia; Zpravy Ceske Spolecnosti Ornitologicke.* e-mail: cso@birdlife.cz www.birdlife.cz

Denmark
Dansk Ornitologisk Forening (DOF), Vesterbrogade 138-140, DK-1620, Copenhagen V, Denmark. Pub: *DAFIF - Dafifs Nyhedsbrev; Dansk Ornitologisk Forenings Tidsskrift; Fugle og Natur;* e-mail: dof@dof.dk www.dof.dk

Estonia
Estonian Ornithological Society (EOU), PO Box 227, Vesti Str. 4, EE-50002 Tartu, Estonia. Pub: *Hirundo Eesti Ornitoogiauhing;* e-mail: eoy@eoy.ee www.eoy.ee

Finland
BirdLife SUOMI Finland, Annankatu 29 A, PO Box 1285, FI 00101, Helsinki. Pub: *Linnuston-Suojelu; Linnut; Tiira;* e-mail: office@birdlife.fi www.birdlife.fi

France
Ligue pour la Protection des Oiseaux (LPO), La Corderie Royale, B.P. 90263, 17305 ROCHEFORT CEDEX, France. Pub: *Lettre Internationale; Ligue Francaise Pour La Protection des Oiseaux; Oiseau, L' (LPO); Outarde infos.* e-mail: lpo@lpo.fr www.lpo.fr/

Germany
Naturschutzbund Deutschland, Herbert-Rabius-Str. 26, D-53225 Bonn, Germany. Pub: *Naturschutz Heute (NABU) Naturschutzbund Deutschland.* e-mail: nabu@nabu.de www.nabu.de

Gibraltar
Gibraltar Ornithological and Nat. History Society, Jew's Gate, Upper Rock Nature Reserve, PO Box 843, GI. Pub: *Alectoris; Gibraltar Nature News.* e-mail: gohns@gibnet.gi www.gibraltar.gi/gonhs

Greece
Hellenic Ornithological Society (HOS), Vas. Irakleiou 24, GR-10682 Athens, Greece. Pub: *HOS Newsletter.* e-mail: birdlife-gr@ath.forthnet.gr www.ornithologiki.gr

Hungary
Hungarian Orn. and Nature Cons. Society (MME), Kolto u. 21, Pf. 391, HU-1536, Budapest. Pub: *Madartani Tajekoztato; Madartavlat; Ornis Hungarica; Tuzok.* e-mail: mme@mme.hu www.mme.hu

Iceland
Icelandic Society for the Protection of Birds, Fuglaverndarfélag Islands, PO Box 5069, IS-125 Reykjavik, Iceland; e-mail: fuglavernd@fuglavernd.is www.fuglavernd.is

Ireland
BirdWatch Ireland, Rockingham House, Newcastle, Co. Wicklow, Eire. Pub: *Irish Birds; Wings (IWC Birdwatch Ireland);* e-mail: info@birdwatchireland.org www.birdwatchireland.ie

Israel
Society for the Protection of Nature in Israel, Hashsela 4, Tel-Aviv 66103. Pub: *SPNI News.* e-mail: ioc@netvision.net.il www.birds.org.il

Italy
Lega Italiana Protezione Uccelli (LIPU), Via Trento 49, IT-43100, Parma. Pub: *Ali Giovani; Ali Notizie.* e-mail: lipusede@box1.tin.it www.lipu.it

Latvia
Latvijas Ornitologijas Biedriba (LOB), Ak 1010, LV-1050 Riga, Latvia. Pub: *Putni Daba.* e-mail: putni@lob.lv www.lob.lv

Luxembourg
Letzebuerger Natur-a Vulleschutzliga (LNVL), Kraizhaff, rue de Luxembourg.L-1899 Kockelscheuer. Pub: *Regulus (WATCH); Regulus Info (& Annual Report) (WATCH); Regulus Wissenschaftliche Berichte (WATCH);* e-mail: secretary@luxnatur.lu
www.luxnatur.lu

Malta
BirdLife Malta, 57 Marina Court, Flat 28, Triq Abate Rigord, MT-Ta' Xbiex, MSD 12, MALTA. Pub: *Bird Talk (WATCH) (Malta); Bird's Eye View (WATCH) (Malta); Il-Merill;* e-mail: info@birdlifemalta.org
www.birdlifemalta.org

Netherlands
Vogelbescherming Nederland, PO Box 925, NL-3700 AX Zeist. Pub: *Vogelniews; Vogels.*
e-mail: info@vogelbescherming.nl
www.vogelbescherming.nl/

Norway
Norsk Ornitologisk Forening, Sandgata 30 B, N-7012 Trondheim, Norway. Pub: *Fuglearet; Fuglefauna; Var; Ringmerkaren;* e-mail: nof@birdlife.no
www.birdlife.no

Poland
Ogólnopolskie Towarzystwo Ochrony Ptaków (OTOP), Ul. Hallera 4/2, PL-80-401 Gdansk, Poland. Pub: *Ptaki; Ptasie Ostoje;* e-mail: office@otop.most.org.pl
www.otop.org.pl/

Portugal
Sociedade Portuguesa para o Estuda das, Aves (SPEA), Rua da Vitoria, 53-3° Esq, 1100-618, Lisboa. Pub: *Pardela;* e-mail: spea@spea.pt
www.spea.pt

Romania
Romanian Ornithological Society (SOR), Str. Gheorghe Dima 49/2, RO-3400 Cluj. Pub: *Alcedo; Buletin AIA; Buletin de Informare Societatea Ornitologica Romana; Milvus (Romania);* e-mail: office@sor.ro www.sor.ro/

Slovakia
Soc. for the Prot. of Birds in Slovakia (SOVS), PO Box 71, 093 01 Vranov nad Topl'ou. Pub: *Spravodaj SOVS; Vtacie Spravy;* e-mail: sovs@changenet.sk
www.sovs.miesto.sk

Slovenia
BirdLife Slovenia (DOPPS), Trzaska 2, PO Box 2990, SI-1000 Ljubljana, Slovenia. Pub: *Acrocephalus; Svet Ptic;* e-mail: dopps@dopps-drustvo.si
www.ptice.org

Spain
Sociedad Espanola de Ornitologia (SEO), C/Melquiades Biencinto 34, E-28053, Madrid. Pub: *Ardeola; Areas Importantes para las Aves.*
e-mail: seo@seo.org www.seo.org

Sweden
Sveriges Ornitologiska Forening (SOF), Ekhagsvagen 3, SE 104-05, Stockholm. Pub: *Fagelvarld; var; Ornis Svecica;* e-mail: birdlife@sofnet.org
www.sofnet.org

Switzerland
SVS/BirdLife Switzerland, Wiedingstrasse 78, PO Box, CH-8036, Zurich, Switzerland. Pub: *Oiwvos Ornis; Ornis Junior; Ornithologische Beobachter; Der Ornithos; Steinadler.*
e-mail: svs@birdlife.ch www.birdlife.ch

Turkey
Doga Dernegi, PK: 640 06445, Yenişehir, Ankarae, Turkey. Pub: *Kelaynak; Kuscu Bulteni.*
e-mail: doga@dogadernegi.org
www.dogadernegi.org/

United Kingdom
Royal Society for the Protection of Birds, The Lodge, Sandy, Bedfordshire, SG19 2DL;
e-mail: info@rspb.org.uk
www.rspb.org.uk

PARTNERS DESIGNATE

Belarus
BirdLife Belarus (APB), PO Box 306, Minsk, 220050 Belarus. Pub: *Subbuteo - The Belarusian Ornithological Bulletin.*
e-mail: apb@tut.by http://apb.iatp.by/

Lithuania
Lietuvos Ornitologu Draugija (LOD), Naugarduko St. 47-3, LT-2006, Vilnius, Lithuania. Pub: *Baltasis Gandras;* e-mail: lod@birdlife.lt
www.birdlife.lt

Russia
Russian Bird Conservation Union (RBCU), Building 1, Shosse Entuziastov 60, 111123, RU-Moscow. Pub: *Newsletter of the Russian Bird Conservation Union.*
e-mail: mail@rbcu.ru www.rbcu.ru/en/

Ukraine
Ukrainian Union for Bird Conservation (UTOP), PO Box 33, Kiev, 1103, UA. Pub: *Life of Birds.*
e-mail: utop@iptelecom.net.ua www.utop.org.ua/

AFFILIATES

Liechtenstein
Botanisch-Zoologische Gesellschaft, Im Bretscha 22, FL-9494 Schaan, Liechtenstein.
e-mail: broggi@pingnet.li or renat@pingnet.li

Andorra
Associacio per a la Defensa de la Natura, Apartado de Correus Espanyols No 96, Andora La Vella, Principat d'Andorra. Pub: *Aiguerola;* e-mail: and@andorra.ad
www.adn-andorra.org/

Croatia
Croatian Society for Bird and Nature Protection, Gunduliceva 24, HR-10000 Zagreb, Croatia. Pub: *Troglodytes;* e-mail: jasmina@hazu.hr

Cyprus
BirdLife Cyprus, PO Box 28076, 2090 Lefkosia, Cyprus.
e-mail: melis@cytanet.com.cy
www.birdlifecyprus.org

Faroe Islands (to Denmark)
Føroya Fuglafrødifelag (Faroese Orginithological
Society) (FOS), Postssmoga 1230, FR-110 Torshavn,
Faroe Islands; e-mail: doreteb@ngs.fo

Georgia
Georgian Centre for the Conservation of Wildlife, PO
Box 56, GE-Tbilisi 0160, Georgia;
e-mail: office@gccw.org
www.gccw.org/

MIDDLE EAST

PARTNERS

Jordan
Royal Society of the Conservation of Nature, PO Box
6354, Jubeiha-Abu-Nusseir Circle, Amman 11183. Pub:
Al Reem; e-mail: adminrscn@rscn.org.jo
www.rscn.org.jo

Lebanon
Society for the Protection of Nature in Lebanon, Awad
Bldg, 6th Floor, Abdel Aziz Street, P.O.Box: 11-5665,
Beirut, Lebanon; e-mail: spnlorg@cyberia.net.lb
www.spnlb.org

PARTNER DESIGNATE

Palestine
Palestine Wildlife Society (PWLS), Beit Sahour, PO Box
89. Pub: *Palestine Wildlife Society - Annual Report.*
www.wildlife-pal.org e-mail: wildlife@palnet.com

AFFILIATES

Bahrain
Dr Saeed A. Mohamed, PO Box 40266, Bahrain.
e-mail: sam53@batelco.com.bh

Iran, Islamic Republic of
Dr Jamshid Mansoori, Assistant Professor, College of
Natural Resources, Tehran University, Mojtame Sabz,
Golestan Shamali, Mahestan Ave, Shahrake Qarb,
Phase 1, P.O.Box 14657, Tehran, I.R. of Iran.
e-mail: birdlifeiran@yahoo.com

Kuwait
Kuwait Environment Protection Society, PO Box 1896,
Safat 13019, Kuwait; e-mail: rasamhory@hotmail.com
www.keps74.com

Saudi Arabia
National Commission for Wildlife Cons & Dev, NCWDC,
PO Box 61681, Riyadh 11575. Pub: *Phoenix; The.*
e-mail: ncwcd@zajil.net www.ncwcd.gov.sa/

Yemen
Yemen Society for the Protection of Wildlife (YSPW),
29 Alger Street, PO Box 19759, Sana'a, Yemen.
e-mail: wildlife.yemen@y.net.ye

PACIFIC

PARTNER

Australia
Birds Australia, 415 Riversdale Road, Hawthorn East,
VIC 3123, Australia. Pub: *Australia Garcilla; Birds
Australia Annual Report; Eclectus; Emu; Wingspan
(WATCH) (Australia); from* wingspan@birdsaustralia.
com.au; e-mail: mail@birdsaustralia.com.au
www.birdsaustralia.com.au

AFFILIATES

Cook Islands
Taporoporo'anga Ipukarea Society (TIS), PO Box 649,
Rarotonga, Cook Islands; e-mail: 2tis@oyster.net.ck

Fiji
Dr Dick Watling, c/o Environment Consultants Fiji, P O
Box 2041, Government Buildings, Suva, Fiji.
e-mail: watling@is.com.fj www.environmentfiji.com

French Polynesia
Société d'Ornithologie de Polynésie "Manu", B.P. 21
098, Papeete, Tahiti; e-mail: sop@manu.pf
www.manu.pf

Palau
Palau Conservation Society, PO BOX 1811, Koror,
PW96940. Pub: *Ngerel a Biib;*
e-mail: pcs@palaunet.com
www.palau-pcs.org/

Samoa
O le Si'osi'omaga Society Incorporated, O le
Si'osi'omaga Society Inc., P O Box 2282, Apia, Western
Samoa; e-mail: ngo_siosiomaga@samoa.ws

New Zealand
Royal Forest & Bird Protection Society of, PO Box 631,
Wellington. Pub: *Forest & Bird; Forest & Bird Annual
Report; Forest & Bird Conservation News.*
e-mail: office@forestandbird.org.nz
www.forestandbird.org.nz/

SPECIAL INTEREST ORGANISATIONS

AFRICAN BIRD CLUB.

c/o Birdlife International as below.
e-mail (general): contact@
africanbirdclub.org
e-mail (membership and sales):
membership@africanbirdclub.org
www.africanbirdclub.org
Pub: *Bulletin of the African Bird Club*.

BIRDLIFE INTERNATIONAL.
Wellbrook Court, Girton Road, Cambridge, CB3
ONA, +44 (0)1223 277 318; (Fax) +44 (0)1223
277 200; www.birdlife.org
e-mail: birdlife@birdlife.org
Pub:*World Birdwatch*.

**EAST AFRICA NATURAL HISTORY SOCIETY
see Kenya in preceding list.**

EURING (European Union for Bird Ringing).
Euring Data Bank, c/o BTO, The Nunnery,
Thetford, Norfolk IP24 2PU. 01842 750 050.
www.euring.org

FAUNA AND FLORA INTERNATIONAL.
Jupiter House, 4th Floor, Station Road, Cambridge,
CB1 2JD. Call on +44 (0)1223 571 000; (Fax) +44
(0)1223 461 481. www.fauna-flora.org
e-mail: info@fauna-flora.org
Pub: *Fauna & Flora News; Oryx*.

**LIPU-UK
(the Italian League for the Protection of
Birds).**
David Lingard, Fernwood,
Doddington Road, Whisby,
Lincs, LN6 9BX, +44
(0)1522 689 030,
e-mail: david@lipu-uk.org
www.lipu-uk.org
Pub:*The Hoopoe*,
annually, *Ali Notizie*, quarterley.

NEOTROPICAL BIRD CLUB.
(Central and South America and the Caribbean)
c/o The Lodge, Sandy,
Bedfordshire, SG19 2DL.
Pub:*Cotinga*.
email: secretary@
neotropicalbirdclub.org
www.neotropicalbirdclub.org

ORIENTAL BIRD CLUB.
P.O.Box 324, Bedford, MK42 0WG
Pub:*The Forktail; BirdingASIA.*
email: mail@orientalbirdclub.org
www.orientalbirdclub.org
**ORNITHOLOGICAL SOCIETY OF THE MIDDLE
EAST (OSME).**
c/o The Lodge, Sandy, Beds, SG19 2DL.
Pub:*Sandgrouse.*
www.osme.org

**TRAFFIC International (formerly Wildlife
Trade Monitoring Unit).**
219a Huntingdon Road, Cambridge, CB3 ODL,
+44 (0)1223 277 427; (Fax) +44 (0)1223 277 237.
Pub:*TRAFFIC Bulletin*.
e-mail: traffic@traffic.org
www.traffic.org

WEST AFRICAN ORNITHOLOGICAL SOCIETY.
R E Sharland, 1 Fisher's Heron, East Mills, Hants,
SP6 2JR. Pub: *Malimbus*.
e-mail bob@sharland2002.fsnet.co.uk
http://malimbus.free.fr

WETLANDS INTERNATIONAL.
PO Box 471, 6700 AL Wageningen, Netherlands,
+31 317 485 774; (Fax) +31 317 486 770,
Pub:*Wetlands*.
e-mail: post@wetlands.org
www.wetlands.org

WORLD OWL TRUST.
The World Owl Centre,
Muncaster Castle,
Ravenglass, Cumbria, CA18
1RQ, +44 (0)1229 717393;
(Fax) +44 (0)1229 717107,

**WORLD PHEASANT
ASSOCIATION.**
7-9 Shaftesbury St, Fordingbridge, Hants SP6 1JF.
01425 657 129; (Fax) 01425 658 053. Pub:*WPA
News*.
www.pheasant.org.uk

WORLD WIDE FUND FOR NATURE.
Panda House, Weyside Park, Godalming
United Kingdom. +44 1483 426 444;
(Fax) +44 1483 426 409,
e-mail: supporterrelations@wwf.org.uk
www.panda.org

QUICK REFERENCE SECTION

Oliver Smart

Little Ringed Plover is one of the species to enjoy protection under Schedule 1 of the Wildlife & Countryside Act 1981 (see page 332 for the complete list) – anyone found disturbing any of these birds at or near their nest sites is likely to end up in court.

TIDE TABLES: USEFUL INFORMATION

BRITISH SUMMER TIME

In 2011 BST applies from 01:00 on March 27 to 01:00 on October 30.
Note that all the times in the following tables are GMT.

During British Summer Time one hour should be added.

Shetland 42, 43
Orkney 44, 45

Predictions are given for the times of high water at Dover throughout the year.

The times of tides at the locations shown here may be obtained by adding or subtracting their 'tidal difference' as shown opposite (subtractions are indicated by a minus sign).

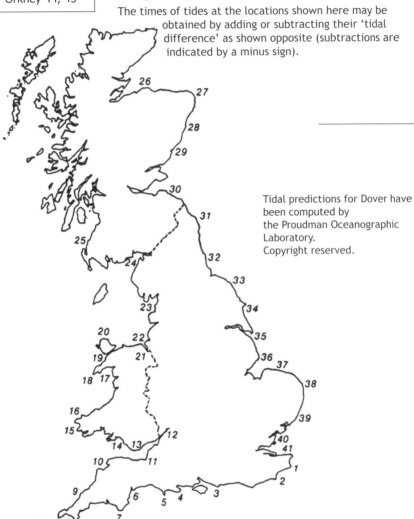

Tidal predictions for Dover have been computed by the Proudman Oceanographic Laboratory.
Copyright reserved.

Map showing locations for which tidal differences are given on facing page.

TIDE TABLES 2011

QUICK REFERENCE

Example 1
To calculate the time of first high water at Girvan on February 18
1. Look up the time at Dover (10 46)*
   = 10:46 am
2. Add the tidal difference for Girvan
   = 0.54
3. Therefore the time of high water at Girvan = 11.40 am

Example 2
To calculate the time of second high water at Blakeney on June 25
1. Look up the time at Dover (18 16)
   = 18:16 pm
2. Add 1 hour for British Summer Time (19 16) = 19:16 pm
3. Subtract the tidal difference for Blakeney = - 4.07
4. Therefore the time of high water at Blakeney = 16:16 pm

*All Dover times are shown on the 24-hour clock.
Following the time of each high water the height of the tide is given, in metres.

(Tables beyond April 2012 are not available at the time of going to press.)

TIDAL DIFFERENCES

1	Dover	See pp 338-341		23	Morecambe	0	20
2	Dungeness	-0	12	24	Silloth	0	51
3	Selsey Bill	0	09	25	Girvan	0	54
4	Swanage (Ist H.W.Springs)	-2	36	26	Lossiemouth	0	48
5	Portland	-4	23	27	Fraserburgh	1	20
6	Exmouth (Approaches)	-4	48	28	Aberdeen	2	30
7	Salcombe	-5	23	29	Montrose	3	30
8	Newlyn (Penzance)	5	59	30	Dunbar	3	42
9	Padstow	-5	47	31	Holy Island	3	58
10	Bideford	-5	17	32	Sunderland	4	38
11	Bridgwater	-4	23	33	Whitby	5	12
12	Sharpness Dock	-3	19	34	Bridlington	5	53
13	Cardiff (Penarth)	-4	16	35	Grimsby	-5	20
14	Swansea	-4	52	36	Skegness	-5	00
15	Skomer Island	-5	00	37	Blakeney	-4	07
16	Fishguard	-3	48	38	Gorleston	-2	08
17	Barmouth	-2	45	39	Aldeburgh	-0	13
18	Bardsey Island	-3	07	40	Bradwell Waterside	1	11
19	Caernarvon	-1	07	41	Herne Bay	1	28
20	Amlwch	-0	22	42	Sullom Voe	-1	34
21	Connahs Quay	0	20	43	Lerwick	0	01
22	Hilbre Island			44	Kirkwall	-0	26
	(Hoylake/West Kirby)	-0	05	45	Widewall Bay	-1	30

NB. Care should be taken when making calculations at the beginning and end of British Summer Time. See worked examples above.

323

TIDE TABLES 2011

Time Zone GMT
Units METRES

Tidal Predictions : HIGH WATERS 2011
Datum of Predictions = Chart Datum : 3.67 metres below Ordnance Datum (Newlyn)
British Summer Time : 27th March to 30th October

DOVER — January

Date	Day	Morning hr min	m	Afternoon hr min	m
1	Sa	08 11	6.0	20 52	5.9
2	Su	09 15	6.1	21 47	6.1
3	M	10 08	6.2	22 34	6.3
4	Tu	10 53	6.3	23 14	6.5
5	W	11 34	6.4	23 52	6.5
6	Th	** **		12 12	6.4
7	F	00 29	6.6	12 49	6.3
8	Sa	01 04	6.5	13 24	6.3
9	Su	01 39	6.5	13 59	6.1
10	M	02 14	6.3	14 33	5.9
11	Tu	02 49	6.1	15 11	5.6
12	W	03 27	5.8	15 56	5.4
13	Th	04 17	5.6	16 53	5.2
14	F	05 19	5.3	18 04	5.1
15	Sa	06 33	5.3	19 27	5.2
16	Su	07 45	5.4	20 27	5.5
17	M	08 44	5.7	21 20	5.9
18	Tu	09 34	6.0	22 07	6.2
19	W	10 19	6.4	22 50	6.5
20	Th	11 04	6.8	23 34	6.8
21	F	11 49	6.9	** **	
22	Sa	00 19	6.9	12 37	6.8
23	Su	01 04	7.0	13 24	6.8
24	M	01 49	6.9	14 10	6.6
25	Tu	02 33	6.8	14 56	6.4
26	W	03 19	6.5	15 47	6.1
27	Th	04 12	6.2	16 46	5.8
28	F	05 17	5.9	17 59	5.5
29	Sa	06 33	5.6	19 25	5.4
30	Su	08 02	5.6	20 41	5.6
31	M	09 11	5.8	21 37	5.9

DOVER — February

Date	Day	Morning hr min	m	Afternoon hr min	m
1	Tu	10 03	6.0	22 21	6.2
2	W	10 43	6.3	22 59	6.4
3	Th	11 20	6.3	23 34	6.5
4	F	11 54	6.4	** **	
5	Sa	00 08	6.6	12 27	6.4
6	Su	00 41	6.6	12 58	6.3
7	M	01 12	6.6	13 26	6.2
8	Tu	01 39	6.4	13 51	6.1
9	W	02 04	6.3	14 21	5.7
10	Th	02 35	6.0	14 56	5.4
11	F	03 16	5.8	15 47	5.4
12	Sa	04 14	5.4	16 57	5.1
13	Su	05 35	5.2	18 30	5.1
14	M	07 07	5.3	19 56	5.4
15	Tu	08 21	5.6	20 58	5.8
16	W	09 16	6.2	21 43	6.3
17	Th	10 03	6.4	22 31	6.6
18	F	10 46	6.7	23 16	6.9
19	Sa	11 31	6.9	23 58	7.1
20	Su	** **		12 16	6.9
21	M	00 41	7.2	13 03	6.9
22	Tu	01 25	7.1	13 46	6.7
23	W	02 07	6.9	14 30	6.5
24	Th	02 52	6.6	15 17	6.1
25	F	03 44	6.1	16 17	5.7
26	Sa	04 50	5.7	17 30	5.4
27	Su	06 18	5.3	19 05	5.3
28	M	07 53	5.4	20 26	5.5

DOVER — March

Date	Day	Morning hr min	m	Afternoon hr min	m
1	Tu	09 02	5.6	21 20	5.8
2	W	09 51	5.9	22 03	6.1
3	Th	10 28	6.1	22 38	6.3
4	F	11 00	6.3	23 11	6.6
5	Sa	11 31	6.4	23 44	6.6
6	Su	** **		12 02	6.4
7	M	00 15	6.6	12 30	6.4
8	Tu	00 41	6.5	12 54	6.3
9	W	01 03	6.4	13 17	6.2
10	Th	01 26	6.2	13 43	6.0
11	F	01 56	6.0	14 19	5.9
12	Sa	02 35	5.5	15 05	5.6
13	Su	03 32	5.5	16 17	5.3
14	M	04 59	5.2	17 55	5.2
15	Tu	06 40	5.4	19 28	5.4
16	W	07 57	5.6	20 33	5.9
17	Th	08 55	6.1	21 23	6.3
18	F	09 41	6.4	22 07	6.7
19	Sa	10 25	6.7	22 50	7.0
20	Su	11 09	6.9	23 34	7.1
21	M	11 54	7.0	** **	
22	Tu	00 18	7.2	12 39	6.9
23	W	01 01	7.0	13 24	6.7
24	Th	01 43	6.8	14 07	6.5
25	F	02 30	6.4	14 55	6.1
26	Sa	03 23	6.0	15 51	5.8
27	Su	04 29	5.5	17 03	5.4
28	M	05 59	5.2	18 36	5.2
29	Tu	07 38	5.5	19 56	5.5
30	W	08 38	5.5	20 51	5.8
31	Th	09 25	5.8	21 34	6.0

DOVER — April

Date	Day	Morning hr min	m	Afternoon hr min	m
1	F	10 03	6.0	22 11	6.3
2	Sa	10 35	6.3	22 45	6.4
3	Su	11 04	6.3	23 16	6.5
4	M	11 34	6.4	23 45	6.5
5	Tu	** **		12 01	6.4
6	W	00 09	6.4	12 25	6.3
7	Th	00 33	6.4	12 50	6.3
8	F	00 58	6.3	13 19	6.2
9	Sa	01 32	6.1	13 57	6.0
10	Su	02 14	5.9	14 48	5.8
11	M	03 15	5.6	16 01	5.5
12	Tu	04 42	5.4	17 31	5.4
13	W	06 16	5.6	18 56	5.6
14	Th	07 31	6.0	20 54	6.0
15	F	08 16	6.3	21 40	6.7
16	Sa	09 16	6.6	22 24	6.9
17	Su	10 01	6.7	23 09	7.0
18	M	10 46	6.8	23 55	6.9
19	Tu	11 33	6.9	** **	
20	W	** **		12 20	6.8
21	Th	00 41	6.9	13 05	6.7
22	F	01 26	6.6	13 49	6.4
23	Sa	02 13	6.3	14 37	6.1
24	Su	03 05	5.9	15 29	5.8
25	M	04 07	5.5	16 32	5.5
26	Tu	05 24	5.2	17 57	5.3
27	W	06 53	5.3	19 11	5.4
28	Th	07 56	5.7	20 10	5.7
29	F	08 47	5.7	20 58	5.9
30	Sa	09 27	5.9	21 37	6.1

TIDE TABLES 2011

Time Zone **GMT**

Tidal Predictions : **HIGH WATERS 2011**

Datum of Predictions = **Chart Datum : 3.67 metres below Ordnance Datum (Newlyn)**

British Summer Time : **27th March to 30th October**

Units **METRES**

DOVER — May

Date	Day	Morning hr min	m	Afternoon hr min	m
1	Su	10 03	6.1	22 12	6.2
2	M	10 35	6.2	22 45	6.3
3	Tu	11 04	6.3	23 14	6.3
4	W	11 34	6.3	23 42	6.3
5	Th	** **	**	12 04	6.3
6	F	00 12	6.3	12 36	6.3
7	Sa	00 46	6.2	13 12	6.2
8	Su	01 24	6.1	13 56	6.1
9	M	02 11	5.9	14 49	5.9
10	Tu	03 15	5.7	15 54	5.8
11	W	04 31	5.6	17 07	5.7
12	Th	05 48	5.6	18 20	5.8
13	F	06 58	5.8	19 26	6.1
14	Sa	07 57	6.0	20 23	6.3
15	Su	08 51	6.3	21 13	6.6
16	M	09 40	6.5	22 03	6.7
17	Tu	10 29	6.6	22 51	6.8
18	W	11 19	6.7	23 40	6.8
19	Th	** **	**	12 06	6.7
20	F	00 27	6.6	12 51	6.6
21	Sa	01 14	6.4	13 34	6.4
22	Su	01 57	6.2	14 17	6.2
23	M	02 45	5.9	15 05	5.9
24	Tu	03 39	5.6	15 58	5.6
25	W	04 43	5.4	17 03	5.5
26	Th	05 56	5.3	18 13	5.5
27	F	07 07	5.3	19 13	5.5
28	Sa	07 59	5.5	19 58	5.7
29	Su	08 47	5.7	20 59	5.8
30	M	09 27	5.9	21 39	6.0
31	Tu	10 04	6.0	22 14	6.1

DOVER — June

Date	Day	Morning hr min	m	Afternoon hr min	m
1	W	10 38	6.2	22 48	6.2
2	Th	11 11	6.3	23 21	6.3
3	F	11 49	6.3	23 59	6.3
4	Sa	** **	**	12 30	6.4
5	Su	00 41	6.3	13 12	6.4
6	M	01 26	6.3	13 59	6.3
7	Tu	02 16	6.1	14 48	6.1
8	W	03 12	6.0	15 41	6.0
9	Th	04 12	5.9	16 41	6.0
10	F	05 17	5.8	17 45	6.0
11	Sa	06 23	5.8	18 45	6.1
12	Su	07 28	5.9	19 53	6.2
13	M	08 28	6.1	20 52	6.3
14	Tu	09 26	6.2	21 49	6.3
15	W	10 19	6.4	22 41	6.5
16	Th	11 09	6.5	23 31	6.5
17	F	11 54	6.6	** **	**
18	Sa	00 16	6.6	12 34	6.6
19	Su	00 58	6.4	13 15	6.5
20	M	01 39	6.2	13 55	6.4
21	Tu	02 20	6.0	14 35	6.2
22	W	03 05	5.8	15 20	6.0
23	Th	03 56	5.6	16 11	5.8
24	F	04 53	5.4	17 06	5.6
25	Sa	05 58	5.4	18 16	5.5
26	Su	07 03	5.3	19 21	5.4
27	M	08 02	5.4	20 17	5.6
28	Tu	08 52	5.6	21 05	5.7
29	W	09 34	5.9	21 46	6.0
30	Th	10 14	6.1	22 25	6.1

DOVER — July

Date	Day	Morning hr min	m	Afternoon hr min	m
1	F	10 53	6.3	23 04	6.3
2	Sa	11 34	6.5	23 47	6.5
3	Su	** **	**	12 16	6.6
4	M	00 32	6.5	13 01	6.7
5	Tu	01 18	6.4	13 48	6.7
6	W	02 07	6.3	14 33	6.6
7	Th	02 56	6.1	15 20	6.4
8	F	03 47	5.9	16 12	6.4
9	Sa	04 45	5.9	17 11	6.3
10	Su	05 49	5.8	18 20	6.1
11	M	07 04	5.7	19 35	5.9
12	Tu	08 17	5.8	20 44	5.8
13	W	09 22	6.0	21 44	6.0
14	Th	10 27	6.2	22 35	6.2
15	F	10 57	6.4	23 20	6.4
16	Sa	11 37	**	23 59	6.4
17	Su	** **	**	12 16	6.6
18	M	00 37	6.4	12 53	6.6
19	Tu	01 14	6.3	13 28	6.5
20	W	01 50	6.1	14 04	6.4
21	Th	02 26	5.8	14 40	6.2
22	F	03 04	5.5	15 18	6.0
23	Sa	03 46	5.3	16 03	5.8
24	Su	04 39	5.1	17 03	5.4
25	M	05 49	5.1	18 18	5.2
26	Tu	07 10	5.2	19 34	5.3
27	W	08 16	5.5	20 34	5.6
28	Th	08 53	5.8	21 24	5.9
29	F	09 32	6.1	22 04	6.2
30	Sa	10 14	6.4	22 46	6.5
31	Su	11 14	6.7	23 28	6.7

DOVER — August

Date	Day	Morning hr min	m	Afternoon hr min	m
1	M	11 56	6.9	** **	**
2	Tu	00 12	6.8	12 40	7.0
3	W	00 58	6.7	13 25	6.9
4	Th	01 45	6.6	14 09	6.8
5	F	02 31	6.2	14 54	6.4
6	Sa	03 20	5.9	15 44	6.4
7	Su	04 15	5.9	16 45	6.0
8	M	05 23	5.6	17 59	5.7
9	Tu	06 49	5.5	19 28	5.6
10	W	08 13	5.7	20 45	5.8
11	Th	09 13	5.9	21 43	6.0
12	F	10 03	6.2	22 26	6.2
13	Sa	10 40	6.4	23 04	6.4
14	Su	11 17	6.6	23 38	6.4
15	M	11 52	6.7	** **	**
16	Tu	00 13	6.4	12 26	6.7
17	W	00 46	6.4	12 58	6.6
18	Th	01 17	6.3	13 28	6.5
19	F	01 43	6.0	13 55	6.3
20	Sa	02 15	6.0	14 24	6.1
21	Su	02 45	5.7	15 01	5.8
22	M	03 32	5.5	15 56	5.5
23	Tu	04 42	5.2	17 17	5.2
24	W	06 15	5.1	18 53	5.5
25	Th	07 41	5.4	20 06	5.5
26	F	08 41	5.8	20 59	6.0
27	Sa	09 27	6.2	21 43	6.3
28	Su	10 09	6.6	22 24	6.6
29	M	10 49	6.9	23 06	6.9
30	Tu	11 31	7.1	23 48	7.2
31	W	** **	**	12 13	7.2

TIDE TABLES 2011

Time Zone GMT

Tidal Predictions : HIGH WATERS 2011

Datum of Predictions = Chart Datum : 3.67 metres below Ordnance Datum (Newlyn)

British Summer Time : 27th March to 30th October

Units METRES

DOVER — September

Date	Day	Morning hr min	m	Afternoon hr min	m
1	Th	00 33	6.9	12 57	7.1
2	F	01 18	6.8	13 41	6.9
3	Sa	02 04	6.6	14 26	6.7
4	Su	02 54	6.3	15 19	6.3
5	M	03 50	5.9	15 58	5.8
6	Tu	05 05	5.6	17 47	5.5
7	W	06 34	5.4	19 28	5.5
8	Th	08 02	5.6	20 41	5.7
9	F	09 01	5.9	21 33	6.0
10	Sa	09 44	6.2	22 11	6.2
11	Su	10 19	6.5	22 43	6.4
12	M	10 53	6.6	23 14	6.5
13	Tu	11 26	6.7	23 45	6.5
14	W	11 58	6.7	** **	*
15	Th	00 15	6.5	12 27	6.6
16	F	00 41	6.4	12 51	6.5
17	Sa	01 05	6.3	13 14	6.4
18	Su	01 32	6.1	13 42	6.2
19	M	02 03	5.9	14 17	5.9
20	Tu	02 47	5.7	15 08	5.5
21	W	03 54	5.4	16 34	5.2
22	Th	05 30	5.4	18 16	5.2
23	F	07 04	5.4	19 36	5.6
24	Sa	08 10	5.8	20 33	6.0
25	Su	08 59	6.3	21 18	6.4
26	M	09 41	6.7	21 58	6.7
27	Tu	10 22	7.0	22 41	7.0
28	W	11 04	7.2	23 24	7.0
29	Th	11 47	7.2	** **	*
30	F	00 09	7.0	12 32	7.1

DOVER — October

Date	Day	Morning hr min	m	Afternoon hr min	m
1	Sa	00 54	6.9	13 17	6.9
2	Su	01 42	6.6	14 04	6.6
3	M	02 31	6.3	14 58	6.2
4	Tu	03 27	5.9	16 03	5.7
5	W	04 35	5.6	17 11	5.4
6	Th	06 06	5.4	19 11	5.4
7	F	07 34	5.6	20 20	5.7
8	Sa	08 33	5.9	21 08	5.9
9	Su	09 16	6.2	21 46	6.2
10	M	09 53	6.4	22 18	6.3
11	Tu	10 26	6.5	22 49	6.4
12	W	10 59	6.6	23 19	6.5
13	Th	11 30	6.6	23 47	6.5
14	F	11 56	6.5	** **	*
15	Sa	00 13	6.5	12 20	6.5
16	Su	00 39	6.4	12 46	6.3
17	M	01 07	6.3	13 15	6.2
18	Tu	01 41	6.1	13 53	6.0
19	W	02 24	5.8	14 45	5.7
20	Th	03 29	5.6	16 05	5.4
21	F	04 56	5.4	17 41	5.4
22	Sa	06 22	5.6	19 01	5.6
23	Su	07 32	5.9	20 00	6.0
24	M	08 26	6.3	20 49	6.4
25	Tu	09 12	6.7	21 33	6.7
26	W	09 56	7.1	22 15	6.9
27	Th	10 39	7.1	23 03	7.0
28	F	11 24	7.1	23 51	7.0
29	Sa	** **	*	12 12	7.0
30	Su	00 37	6.8	13 00	6.8
31	M	01 25	6.6	13 49	6.5

DOVER — November

Date	Day	Morning hr min	m	Afternoon hr min	m
1	Tu	02 13	6.4	14 41	6.1
2	W	03 05	6.1	15 40	5.7
3	Th	04 05	5.7	16 56	5.4
4	F	05 21	5.5	18 27	5.4
5	Sa	06 44	5.6	19 38	5.5
6	Su	07 49	5.8	20 30	5.8
7	M	08 40	6.0	21 12	6.0
8	Tu	09 22	6.2	21 49	6.2
9	W	09 58	6.3	22 22	6.3
10	Th	10 32	6.4	22 53	6.4
11	F	11 03	6.4	23 23	6.4
12	Sa	11 31	6.4	23 52	6.4
13	Su	11 59	6.4	** **	*
14	M	00 23	6.4	12 30	6.3
15	Tu	00 57	6.2	13 04	6.2
16	W	01 34	6.0	13 46	6.0
17	Th	02 16	5.9	14 37	5.6
18	F	03 16	5.8	15 44	5.6
19	Sa	04 24	5.9	17 03	5.9
20	Su	05 38	5.8	18 18	5.8
21	M	06 49	6.0	19 22	6.0
22	Tu	07 49	6.0	20 19	6.5
23	W	08 42	6.5	21 11	6.8
24	Th	09 33	6.8	22 01	6.8
25	F	10 22	6.9	22 50	6.9
26	Sa	11 11	6.9	23 40	6.9
27	Su	** **	*	12 01	7.0
28	M	00 26	6.8	12 49	6.8
29	Tu	01 11	6.7	13 35	6.7
30	W	01 55	6.5	14 21	6.5

DOVER — December

Date	Day	Morning hr min	m	Afternoon hr min	m
1	Th	02 41	6.3	15 12	5.8
2	F	03 32	6.0	16 12	5.5
3	Sa	04 32	5.7	17 24	5.4
4	Su	05 44	5.6	18 37	5.3
5	M	06 54	5.6	19 41	5.5
6	Tu	07 55	5.7	20 34	5.7
7	W	08 47	5.9	21 19	5.9
8	Th	09 29	6.0	21 57	6.1
9	F	10 07	6.2	22 31	6.2
10	Sa	10 39	6.2	23 03	6.3
11	Su	11 11	6.3	23 37	6.4
12	M	11 45	6.4	** **	*
13	Tu	00 12	6.5	12 22	6.4
14	W	00 50	6.5	13 00	6.3
15	Th	01 29	6.4	13 42	6.1
16	F	02 09	6.3	14 28	6.0
17	Sa	02 56	6.2	15 23	5.9
18	Su	03 56	6.1	16 26	5.8
19	M	04 57	6.0	17 34	5.8
20	Tu	06 06	6.0	18 44	5.8
21	W	07 15	6.1	19 53	6.0
22	Th	08 20	6.4	20 56	6.2
23	F	09 15	6.6	21 53	6.4
24	Sa	10 11	6.7	22 45	6.6
25	Su	11 06	6.7	23 31	6.7
26	M	11 52	6.7	** **	*
27	Tu	00 15	6.8	12 36	6.6
28	W	00 55	6.7	13 17	6.6
29	Th	01 34	6.6	13 57	6.2
30	F	02 14	6.5	14 40	6.0
31	Sa	02 58	6.2	15 27	5.8

TIDE TABLES 2012

Time Zone **GMT**

Tidal Predictions : **HIGH WATERS 2012**

Datum of Predictions = **Chart Datum : 3.67 metres below Ordnance Datum (Newlyn)**

British Summer Time : **25th March to 28th October**

Units **METRES**

DOVER — January

DATE	DAY	Morning hr min	m	Afternoon hr min	m
1	Su	03 44	6.0	16 21	5.5
2	M	04 41	5.6	17 27	5.3
3	Tu	05 49	5.4	18 40	5.3
4	W	07 03	5.3	19 49	5.3
5	Th	08 07	5.5	20 45	5.5
6	F	08 59	5.7	21 30	5.8
7	Sa	09 43	5.9	22 08	6.1
8	Su	10 18	6.1	22 43	6.3
9	M	10 53	6.3	23 19	6.5
10	Tu	11 30	6.5	23 56	6.6
11	W	** **	*	12 08	6.6
12	Th	00 36	6.7	12 49	6.5
13	F	01 17	6.7	13 31	6.5
14	Sa	01 56	6.7	14 13	6.4
15	Su	02 40	6.5	15 01	6.2
16	M	03 27	6.4	15 56	6.0
17	Tu	04 25	6.1	17 00	5.8
18	W	05 33	5.9	18 13	5.6
19	Th	06 50	5.8	19 36	5.7
20	F	08 09	5.9	20 51	5.9
21	Sa	09 19	6.1	21 50	6.2
22	Su	10 14	6.3	22 38	6.5
23	M	11 00	6.5	23 19	6.6
24	Tu	11 41	6.6	23 58	6.7
25	W	** **	*	12 19	6.6
26	Th	00 34	6.8	12 56	6.5
27	F	01 11	6.7	13 31	6.4
28	Sa	01 46	6.6	14 06	6.2
29	Su	02 21	6.4	14 42	6.0
30	M	02 58	6.1	15 23	5.7
31	Tu	03 40	5.7	16 12	5.3

DOVER — February

DATE	DAY	Morning hr min	m	Afternoon hr min	m
1	W	04 35	5.4	17 21	5.1
2	Th	05 49	5.1	18 50	5.0
3	F	07 21	5.1	20 04	5.2
4	Sa	08 27	5.4	20 59	5.6
5	Su	09 15	5.7	21 41	5.9
6	M	09 54	6.0	22 19	6.3
7	Tu	10 31	6.3	22 56	6.5
8	W	11 09	6.6	23 34	6.8
9	Th	11 48	6.7	** **	*
10	F	00 15	6.9	12 30	6.8
11	Sa	00 56	6.9	13 11	6.7
12	Su	01 35	6.9	13 55	6.6
13	M	02 17	6.7	14 40	6.4
14	Tu	03 04	6.5	15 32	6.1
15	W	04 01	6.1	16 35	5.8
16	Th	05 11	5.8	17 54	5.5
17	F	06 40	5.7	19 29	5.5
18	Sa	08 11	5.7	20 47	5.7
19	Su	09 19	5.9	21 41	6.1
20	M	10 08	6.2	22 24	6.4
21	Tu	10 49	6.4	23 03	6.6
22	W	11 28	6.5	23 37	6.7
23	Th	11 58	6.8	** **	*
24	F	00 12	6.7	12 32	6.5
25	Sa	00 44	6.7	13 04	6.4
26	Su	01 17	6.6	13 34	6.3
27	M	01 45	6.4	14 02	6.1
28	Tu	02 13	6.2	14 30	5.8
29	W	02 47	5.8	15 13	5.5

DOVER — March

DATE	DAY	Morning hr min	m	Afternoon hr min	m
1	Th	03 33	5.4	16 14	5.2
2	F	04 48	5.1	17 44	5.1
3	Sa	06 27	5.0	19 17	5.1
4	Su	07 48	5.2	20 23	5.5
5	M	08 42	5.6	21 11	5.9
6	Tu	09 26	6.0	21 51	6.3
7	W	10 04	6.4	22 29	6.6
8	Th	10 43	6.7	23 09	6.9
9	F	11 24	6.8	23 49	7.0
10	Sa	** **	*	12 06	6.9
11	Su	00 30	7.1	12 50	6.8
12	M	01 12	7.0	13 35	6.7
13	Tu	01 57	6.8	14 23	6.4
14	W	02 47	6.4	15 15	6.1
15	Th	03 46	6.0	16 18	5.7
16	F	04 59	5.6	17 40	5.4
17	Sa	06 36	5.4	19 17	5.5
18	Su	08 06	5.6	20 30	5.7
19	M	09 08	5.9	21 22	6.1
20	Tu	09 53	6.1	22 03	6.3
21	W	10 28	6.3	22 38	6.5
22	Th	11 02	6.5	23 13	6.6
23	F	11 34	6.6	23 47	6.5
24	Sa	** **	*	12 06	6.5
25	Su	00 19	6.6	12 37	6.4
26	M	00 47	6.5	13 04	6.3
27	Tu	01 11	6.3	13 28	6.2
28	W	01 36	6.1	13 57	5.9
29	Th	02 07	5.9	14 35	5.7
30	F	02 52	5.5	15 32	5.4
31	Sa	04 03	5.2	16 55	5.1

DOVER — April

DATE	DAY	Morning hr min	m	Afternoon hr min	m
1	Su	05 40	5.1	18 26	5.2
2	M	07 04	5.3	19 39	5.5
3	Tu	08 06	5.7	20 33	5.9
4	W	08 52	6.1	21 18	6.3
5	Th	09 34	6.4	21 58	6.7
6	F	10 17	6.7	22 39	6.9
7	Sa	10 59	6.9	23 23	7.1
8	Su	11 44	6.9	** **	*
9	M	00 08	7.1	12 32	6.9
10	Tu	00 54	6.9	13 21	6.7
11	W	01 43	6.7	14 10	6.5
12	Th	02 35	6.3	15 04	6.2
13	F	03 36	6.0	16 04	5.8
14	Sa	04 48	5.6	17 19	5.6
15	Su	06 20	5.4	18 47	5.5
16	M	07 40	5.6	19 57	5.7
17	Tu	08 40	5.8	20 51	6.0
18	W	09 23	6.1	21 33	6.2
19	Th	10 01	6.3	22 11	6.3
20	F	10 35	6.3	22 46	6.4
21	Sa	11 09	6.4	23 21	6.5
22	Su	11 42	6.4	23 54	6.4
23	M	** **	*	12 13	6.4
24	Tu	00 22	6.3	12 40	6.3
25	W	00 46	6.2	13 08	6.2
26	Th	01 14	6.1	13 38	6.0
27	F	01 48	5.9	14 17	5.9
28	Sa	02 33	5.7	15 11	5.6
29	Su	03 37	5.4	16 21	5.5
30	M	04 59	5.3	17 40	5.4

SUNRISE AND SUNSET TIMES
FOR 2011

Predictions are given for the times of sunrise and sunset on every Saturday throughout the year. For places on the same latitude as the following, add 4 minutes for each degree of longitude west (subtract if east).

These times are in GMT, except between 01:00 on Mar 27 and 01:00 on Oct 30, when the times are in BST (1 hour in advance of GMT).

		London		Manchester		Edinburgh	
		Rise	Set	Rise	Set	Rise	Set
January	1	08 06	16 02	08 25	16 00	08 44	15 49
	8	08 04	16 10	08 23	16 09	08 41	15 59
	15	08 00	16 20	08 17	16 20	08 34	16 11
	22	07 53	16 32	08 10	16 32	08 25	16 24
	29	07 44	16 44	08 00	16 45	08 14	16 39
February	5	07 33	16 57	07 48	16 59	08 00	16 54
	12	07 21	17 10	07 35	17 13	07 46	17 09
	19	07 08	17 22	07 20	17 27	07 30	17 25
	26	06 53	17 35	07 05	17 40	07 13	17 40
March	5	06 38	17 47	06 48	17 54	06 55	17 55
	12	06 23	17 59	06 32	18 07	06 37	18 09
	19	06 07	18 11	06 15	18 20	06 19	18 24
	26	05 51	18 23	05 58	18 33	06 00	18 38
April	2	06 35	19 35	06 41	19 45	06 42	19 52
	9	06 19	19 47	06 24	19 58	06 24	20 07
	16	06 04	19 58	06 08	20 11	06 06	20 21
	23	05 49	20 10	05 52	20 24	05 49	20 35
	30	05 35	20 22	05 37	20 36	04 38	21 44
May	7	05 23	20 33	05 23	20 49	05 17	21 03
	14	05 11	20 44	05 11	21 01	05 03	21 17
	21	05 01	20 54	05 00	21 12	05 51	21 29
	28	04 53	21 03	04 51	21 22	05 40	21 41
June	4	04 47	21 11	04 45	21 31	04 33	21 50
	11	04 44	21 17	04 41	21 37	04 28	21 58
	18	04 43	21 21	04 39	21 41	04 26	22 02
	25	04 44	21 22	04 41	21 42	04 28	22 03

SUNRISE AND SUNSET TIMES

		London		Manchester		Edinburgh	
		Rise	Set	Rise	Set	Rise	Set
July	2	04 48	21 21	04 45	21 41	04 32	22 01
	9	04 54	21 17	04 51	21 36	04 39	21 56
	16	04 02	21 11	05 00	21 30	04 49	21 48
	23	04 11	21 03	05 10	21 20	05 00	21 37
	30	04 21	21 53	05 21	21 09	05 13	21 25
August	6	05 31	20 41	05 32	20 57	05 26	21 11
	13	05 42	20 28	05 44	20 42	05 39	20 55
	20	05 53	20 14	05 56	20 27	05 53	20 38
	27	06 05	19 59	06 09	20 11	06 07	20 21
September	3	06 16	19 43	06 21	19 55	06 20	20 03
	10	06 27	19 28	06 33	19 38	06 34	19 45
	17	06 38	19 12	06 45	19 21	06 47	19 26
	24	06 49	18 55	06 57	19 04	07 01	19 08
October	1	07 01	18 39	07 10	18 47	07 15	18 49
	8	07 12	18 24	07 22	18 30	07 29	18 31
	15	07 24	18 08	07 35	18 14	07 43	18 13
	22	07 36	17 54	07 48	17 58	07 58	17 56
	29	07 48	17 40	08 02	17 43	08 12	17 40
November	5	07 01	16 27	07 15	16 29	07 27	16 25
	12	07 13	16 16	07 28	16 17	07 42	16 11
	19	07 25	16 07	07 41	16 07	07 56	15 59
	26	07 36	15 59	07 53	15 59	08 10	15 50
December	3	07 46	15 54	08 04	15 53	08 22	15 43
	10	07 55	15 52	08 13	15 50	08 32	15 39
	17	08 01	15 52	08 20	15 50	08 39	15 38
	24	08 05	15 55	08 24	15 53	08 43	15 41
	31	08 06	16 01	08 25	15 59	08 44	15 48

These tables are reproduced, with permission, from data supplied by HM Nautical Almanac Office, part of the UK Hydrographic Office, Crown Copyright. The UKHO does not accept any responsibility for loss or damage arising from the use of information contained in any of its reports or in any communication about its tests or investigations.

SEA AREAS

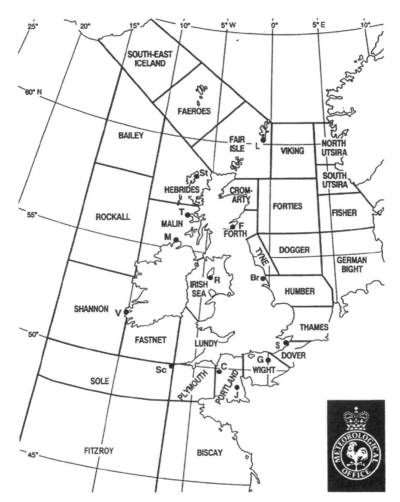

STATIONS WHOSE LATEST REPORTS ARE BROADCAST IN THE 5-MINUTE FORECASTS

Br Bridlington; C Channel Light-Vessel Automatic; F Fife Ness; G Greenwich Light-Vessel Automatic; J Jersey; L Lerwick; M Malin Head; R Ronaldsway; S Sandettie Light-Vessel Automatic; Sc Scilly Automatic; St Stornoway; T Tiree; V Valentia.

From information kindly supplied by the Meteorological Office

REVISION OF SEA AREAS

On 4 February 2002, the southern boundary of areas Plymouth and Sole, and the northern boundary of areas Biscay and Finisterre were realigned along the Metarea I/II boundary at 48°27′ North. At the same time, sea area Finisterre was renamed FitzRoy.

Did you know that the FitzRoy shipping area is named after the founder of the Met Office?

THE BIRDWATCHER'S CODE OF CONDUCT

Around three million adults go birdwatching every year in the UK. Following The birdwatchers' code is good practice, common sense and will help everybody to enjoy seeing birds.

This code puts the interests of birds first, and respects other people, whether or not they are interested in birds. It applies whenever you are watching birds in the UK or abroad. Please help everybody to enjoy birdwatching by following the code, leading by example and sensitively challenging the minority of birdwatchers who behave inappropriately.

1. The interests of the birds come first

Birds respond to people in many ways, depending on the species, location and time of year.

If birds are disturbed they may keep away from their nests, leaving chicks hungry or enabling predators to take their eggs or young. During cold weather, or when migrants have just made a long flight, repeatedly disturbing birds can mean they use up vital energy that they need for feeding.

Intentionally or recklessly disturbing some birds at or near their nest is illegal in Britain.

Whether you are particularly interested in photography, bird ringing, sound-recording or birdwatching, remember to always put the interests of the birds first.

- Avoid going too close to birds or disturbing their habitats – if a bird flies away or makes repeated alarm calls, you're too close. If it leaves, you won't get a good view of it anyway.
- Stay on roads and paths where they exist and avoid disturbing habitat used by birds.
- Think about your fieldcraft. You might disturb a bird even if you are not very close, eg a flock of wading birds on the foreshore can be disturbed from a mile away if you stand on the seawall.
- Repeatedly playing a recording of bird song or calls to encourage a bird to respond can divert a territorial bird from other important duties, such as feeding its young. Never use playback to attract a species during its breeding season.

2. Be an ambassador for birdwatching

Respond positively to questions from interested passers-by. They may not be birdwatchers yet, but good views of a bird or a helpful answer may ignite a spark of interest. Your enthusiasm could start lifetime's interest in birds and a greater appreciation of wildlife and its conservation.

Consider using local services, such as pubs, restaurants, petrol stations, and public transport. Raising awareness of the benefits to local communities of trade from visiting birdwatchers may, ultimately, help the birds themselves.

3. Know the Countryside Code, and follow it

Respect the wishes of local residents and landowners and don't enter private land without permission, unless it is open for public access on foot.

Follow the codes on access and the countryside for the place you're walking in. Irresponsible behaviour may cause a land manager to deny access to others (eg for important bird survey work). It may also disturb the bird or give birdwatching bad coverage in the media.

Access to the countryside

Legislation provides access for walkers to open country in Britain, and includes measures to protect wildlife. Note that the rules and codes are different in each part of Britain, so plan ahead and make sure you know what you can do legally.

4. The law

Laws protecting birds and their habitats are the result of hard campaigning by generations of birdwatchers. We must make sure that we don't allow them to fall into disrepute. In England, Scotland and Wales, it is a criminal offence to disturb, intentionally or recklessly, at or near the nest, a species listed on Schedule 1 of the Wildlife & Countryside Act 1981 (see www.rspb.org.uk/policy/wildbirdslaw for a full list). Disturbance could include playback of songs and calls. In Scotland, disturbing Capercaillie and Ruffs at leks is also an offence. It is a criminal offence to intentionally disturb a bird at or near the nest under the Wildlife (Northern Ireland) Order 1985.

The Government can, for particular reasons such as scientific study, issue licences to individuals that permit limited disturbance, including monitoring of nests and ringing. It is a criminal offence to destroy or damage, intentionally or recklessly, a special interest feature of a Site of Special Scientific Interest (SSSI) or to disturb the wildlife for which the site was notified.

If you witness anyone who you suspect may be illegally disturbing or destroying wildlife or habitat, phone the police immediately (ideally, with a six-figure map reference) and report it to the RSPB.

5. Rare birds

Mobile phones, telephone and pager services and the internet mean you can now share your sightings instantly. If you discover a rare bird, please bear the following in mind

- Consider the potential impact of spreading the news and make an effort to inform the landowner (or, on a nature reserve, the warden) first. Think about whether the site can cope with a large number of visitors and whether sensitive species might be at risk, such as breeding terns, flocks of wading birds or rare plants. The county bird recorder or another experienced birdwatcher can often give good advice.
- On private land, always talk to the landowner first. With a little planning, access can often be arranged.
- People coming to see a rare bird can raise money for a local reserve, other wildlife project or charity. Consider organising a voluntary collection at access points to the site.
- Rare breeding birds are at risk from egg-collectors and some birds of prey from persecution. If you discover a rare breeding species that you think is vulnerable, contact the RSPB; it has considerable experience in protecting rare breeding birds. Please also report your sighting to the county bird recorder or the Rare Breeding Birds Panel. (www.rbbp.org.uk). Also, consider telling the landowner – in most cases, this will ensure that the nest is not disturbed accidentally. If you have the opportunity to see a rare bird, enjoy it, but don't let your enthusiasm override common sense.

THE BIRDWATCHER'S CODE OF CONDUCT

In addition to the guidelines above:
- park sensibly, follow instructions and consider making a donation if requested
- don't get too close so that you can take a photograph – you'll incur the wrath of everyone else watching if you scare the bird away
- be patient if the viewing is limited, talk quietly and give others a chance to see the bird too
- do not enter private areas without permission
- not everyone likes to see an 'organised flush' and it should never be done in important wildlife habitats or where there are other nesting or roosting birds nearby. A flush should not be organised more frequently than every two hours and not within two hours of sunrise or sunset, so the bird has chance to feed and rest.

6. Make your sightings count
Add to tomorrow's knowledge of birds by sending your sightings to www.birdtrack.net This online recording scheme from the BTO, the RSPB and BirdWatch Ireland allows you to input and store all of your birdwatching records, which in turn helps to support species and site conservation. With one click, you can also have your records forwarded automatically to the relevant county recorder.

County recorders and local bird clubs are the mainstay of bird recording in the UK. Your records are important for local conservation and help to build the county's ornithological history. For a list of county bird recorders, look in the County Directory of *The Yearbook,* ask at your local library, or visit www.britishbirds.co.uk/countyrecorders

You can also get involved in a UK-wide bird monitoring scheme, such as the Breeding Bird Survey and the Wetland Bird Survey (see www.bto.org for details). If you've been birdwatching abroad, you can give your sightings to the BirdLife International Partner in that country by visiting www.worldbirds.org Your data could be vital in helping to protect sites and species in the country you've visited.

SCHEDULE 1 SPECIES

Under the provisions of the Wildlife and Countryside Act 1981 the following bird species (listed in Schedule 1 - Part I of the Act) are protected by special penalties at all times.

Avocet	Falcon, Gyr	Owl, Barn	Lark, Shore
Bee-eater	Fieldfare	Owl, Snowy	Shrike, Red-backed
Bittern	Firecrest	Peregrine	Spoonbill
Bittern, Little	Garganey	Petrel, Leach's	Stilt, Black-winged
Bluethroat	Godwit, Black-tailed	Pintail	Stint, Temminck's
Brambling	Goshawk	Phalarope, Red-necked	Swan, Bewick's
Bunting, Cirl	Grebe, Black-necked	Plover, Kentish	Swan, Whooper
Bunting, Lapland	Grebe, Slavonian	Plover, Little Ringed	Tern, Black
Bunting, Snow	Greenshank	Quail, Common	Tern, Little
Buzzard, Honey	Gull, Little	Redstart, Black	Tern, Roseate
Chough	Gull, Mediterranean	Redwing	Tit, Bearded
Crake, Corn	Harriers (all species)	Rosefinch, Scarlet	Tit, Crested
Crake, Spotted	Heron, Purple	Ruff	Treecreeper, Short-toed
Crossbills (all species)	Hobby	Sandpiper, Green	Warbler, Cetti's
Stone-curlew	Hoopoe	Sandpiper, Purple	Warbler, Dartford
Divers (all species)	Kingfisher	Sandpiper, Wood	Warbler, Marsh
Dotterel	Kite, Red	Scaup	Warbler, Savi's
Duck, Long-tailed	Merlin	Scoter, Common	Whimbrel
Eagle, Golden	Oriole, Golden	Scoter, Velvet	Lark, Wood
Eagle, White-tailed	Osprey	Serin	Wryneck

The following birds and their eggs (listed in Schedule 1 - Part II of the Act) are protected by special penalties during the close season, which is Feb 1 to Aug 31 (Feb 21 to Aug 31 below high water mark), but may be killed outside this period - Goldeneye, Greylag Goose (in Outer Hebrides, Caithness, Sutherland, and Wester Ross only), Pintail.

THE COUNTRYSIDE CODE

Launched on 12 July 2004, this Code for England has been produced through a partnership between the Countryside Agency and Countryside Council for Wales.

The Countryside Code has been revised and re-launched to reflect the introduction of new open access rights (Countryside & Rights of Way Act 2000) and changes in society over the last 20 years.

• Be safe – plan ahead
Follow any signs, even when going out locally, it's best to get the latest information about where and when you can go; for example, your rights to go onto some areas of open land may be restricted while work is carried out, for safety reasons or during breeding seasons. Follow advice and local signs, and be prepared for the unexpected.

• Leave gates and property as you find them
Please respect the working life of the countryside, as our actions can affect people's livelihoods, our heritage, and the safety and welfare of animals and ourselves.

• Protect plants and animals, and take your litter home
We have a responsibility to protect our countryside now and for future generations, so make sure you don't harm animals, birds, plants, or trees.

• Keep dogs under close control
The countryside is a great place to exercise dogs, but it's every owner's duty to make sure their dog is not a danger or nuisance to farm animals, wildlife or other people.

• Consider other people
Showing consideration and respect for other people makes the countryside a pleasant Environment for everyone – at home, at work and at leisure.

BIRDLINE NUMBERS - National and Regional

Birdline name	To obtain information	To report sightings (hotlines)
National		
Bird Information Service	09068 700 222	
www.birdingworld.co.uk		
Flightline (Northern Ireland)	028 9146 7408	
Regional		
Northern Ireland	028 9146 7408	
Scotland	09068 700 234	01292 611 994
Wales	09068 700 248	01492 544 588
East Anglia	09068 700 245	07941 333 970
Midlands	09068 700 247	01905 754 154
North East	09068 700 246	07974 358 988
North West	09068 700 249	01492 544 588
South East	09068 700 240	01845 570 444
www.southeastbirdnews.co.uk		or 08000 377 240
South West	09068 700 241	0845 4567 938

Charges
At the time of compilation, calls to premium line numbers cost 60p per minute.

INDEX TO RESERVES

INDEX TO RESERVES

INDEX TO RESERVES